THE BRITISH YEAR BOOK OF INTERNATIONAL LAW

THE BRITISH YEAR BOOK OF INTERNATIONAL LAW 1998

SIXTY-NINTH YEAR OF ISSUE

OXFORD
AT THE CLARENDON PRESS
1999

OXFORD
UNIVERSITY PRESS

Great Clarendon Street, Oxford, OX2 6DP

Oxford University Press is a department of the University of Oxford.
It furthers the University's objective of excellence in research, scholarship,
and education by publishing worldwide in

Oxford New York

Athens Auckland Bangkok Bogotá Buenos Aires Calcutta
Cape Town Chennai Dar es Salaam Delhi Florence Hong Kong Istanbul
Karachi Kuala Lumpur Madrid Melbourne Mexico City Mumbai
Nairobi Paris Sào Paulo Singapore Taipei Tokyo Toronto Warsaw

with associated companies in Berlin Ibadan

Published in the United States
by Oxford University Press Inc., New York

First published 1999

British Library Cataloguing in Publication Data
Data available

Library of Congress Cataloging in Publication Data
Data available

ISBN 0-19-826900-5

3 5 7 9 10 8 6 4 2

Printed in Great Britain
on acid-free paper by
Biddles Ltd., Guildford and King's Lynn

Editorial Communications should be addressed as follows:

Articles and Notes:
PROFESSOR IAN BROWNLIE
All Souls College, Oxford, OX1 4AL

Books for Review:
PROFESSOR J. G. MERRILLS
University of Sheffield Faculty of Law,
Crookesmoor Building, Conduit Road,
Sheffield, S10 1FL.

The British Year Book of International Law is indexed in *Current Law Index*, published by Information Access Company, and in *Legal Journals Index*, published by Legal Information Resources Limited.

CONTENTS

THE LAW AND PROCEDURE OF THE INTERNATIONAL COURT OF JUSTICE 1960–1989 (PART NINE)

By HUGH THIRLWAY — 1

STATE PRACTICE AND INTERNATIONAL LAW IN RELATION TO SUCESSION

By JAMES CRAWFORD — 85

SUSTAINABLE DEVELOPMENT AND THE EQUITABLE UTILIZATION OF INTERNATIONAL WATERCOURSES

By XIMENA FUENTES — 119

THE DAYTON AGREEMENT IN BOSNIA AND HERZEGOVINA: A STUDY OF IMPLEMENTATION STRATEGIES

By MARCUS COX — 201

NOTE:

The British Acquisition of the Nicobar Islands, 1869: A Possible Example of Abandonment of Territorial Sovereignty

By GEOFFREY MARSTON — 245

REVIEWS OF BOOKS:

Ager, Sheila L.: *Interstate Arbitrations in the Greek World* — 267

Alexandrov, Stanimir A.: *Self-Defense Against the Use of Force in International Law* — 268

Boisson de Chazournes,L., Desgagné, R., and Romano, C. (Editors): *Protection international de l'environnement* — 269

Cosnard, Michel: *La Soumission des États aux tribunaux internes face à la théorie des immunités des États* — 270

Council of Europe: *Yearbook of the European Convention for the Prevention of Torture and Inhuman or Degrading Treatment or Punishment*. Volume I, 1989–1992 — 272

Evans, Malcolm D.: *Religious Liberty and International Law in Europe* — 274

Francioni, Francesco, and Scovazzi, Tullio (Editors): *International Law for Antarctica* — 275

Geradin, Damien: *Trade and the Environment: A Comparative Study of EC and US Law* — 277

Henckaerts, Jean-Marie (Editor): *The International Status of Taiwan in the New World Order: Legal and Political Considerations* — 279

de Hoogh, André: *Obligations Erga Omnes and International Crimes* — 280

Hunt, Murray: *Using Human Rights Law in English Courts* — 282

Jia, Bing Bing: *The Regime of Straits in International Law* — 285

Kiss, A.C., and Shelton, D.: *Manual of European Environmental Law* (2nd edition) — 287

Knipping, F., von Mangoldt, H., and Rittberger, V. (Editors): *The United Nations System and its Predecessors* — 288

McCormack, T.L.H., and Simpson, G.J. (Editors): *The Law of War Crimes: National and International Approaches* 289

McGoldrick, Dominic:*International Relations Law of the European Union* 290

Merrills, J.G.: *Judge Sir Gerald Fitzmaurice and the Discipline of International Law. Opinions of the International Court of Justice, 1961–1973* 292

Muller, A.S. Raič, D., and Thurànszky, J.M. (Editors): *The International Court of Justice. Its Future Role after Fifty Years* 294

New Zealand Ministry of Foreign Affairs and Trade: *New Zealand Consolidated Treaty List as at 31 December 1996* 297

Peterson, M.J.: *Recognition of Governments: Legal Doctrine and State Practice, 1815–1995* 299

Treves, Tullio, and Pineschi, Laura (Editors): *The Law of the Sea: The European Union and its Member States* 300

Vandersanden, G., and Dony, M: *La Responsabilité des États membres en cas de violation du droit communautaire* 301

Various Authors: *Héctor Gros Espiell—Amicorum Liber* 302

de Yturriaga, José A.: *The International Regime of Fisheries. From UNCLOS 1982 to the Presential Sea* 302

DECISIONS OF BRITISH COURTS DURING 1998 INVOLVING QUESTIONS OF PUBLIC OR PRIVATE INTERNATIONAL LAW

A. *Public International Law. By* MICHAEL BYERS 305

B. *Private International Law. By* ADRIAN BRIGGS 332

DECISIONS ON THE EUROPEAN CONVENTION ON HUMAN RIGHTS DURING 1998

By LORNA WOODS 361

DECISIONS OF THE COURT OF JUSTICE OF THE EUROPEAN COMMUNITIES DURING 1998

By SARA MASTERS 411

UNITED KINGDOM MATERIALS ON INTERNATIONAL LAW 1998

Edited by GEOFFREY MARSTON 433

TABLE OF CASES 631

INDEX 637

THE LAW AND PROCEDURE OF THE INTERNATIONAL COURT OF JUSTICE 1960–1989*

PART NINE

By HUGH THIRLWAY‡

IV. QUESTIONS OF JURISDICTION AND COMPETENCE, 1954–1989

Introduction 2

CHAPTER I: JURISDICTION IN CONTENTIOUS CASES 4
1. Preliminary Observations: Terminology and Related Matters 4
 (1) Jurisdiction and competence 4
 (2) Seisin 10
 (3) Jurisdiction and the 'merits'. 13
 (4) Jurisdiction and the burden of proof 15
2. Preliminary, Incidental and Substantive Jurisdiction 17
 (1) The distinction in general 17
 (2) Jurisdiction and provisional measures 22
3. The Sources of Jurisdiction. 23
 (1) Is the enumeration of Article 36 exhaustive? 23
 (2) *Forum prorogatum* 27
 (3) Jurisdiction derived from treaty: effect of suspension or termination of treaty 30
4. Jurisdiction and the Propriety of Exercising it 34
 (1) The problem in general: the case law 34
  (a) The *Monetary Gold* case 37
  (b) The *Northern Cameroons* case. 39
  (c) The *Nuclear Tests* cases. 42
  (d) The *Military and Paramilitary Activities* case 47
  (e) The case of the *Land, Island and Maritime Frontier Dispute* 48

‡ Professor of International Law, Graduate Institute of International Studies, Geneva; formerly Principal Legal Secretary, International Court of Justice.

(f) The case concerning *Certain Phosphate Lands in Nauru* 48
(g) The *East Timor* case 50
(2) The Court and the Security Council 52
(a) The *United States Diplomatic and Consular Staff* case 54
(b) The *Military and Paramilitary Activities* case 56
5. Jurisdiction in relation to the Decisions of Other Tribunals .. 57
(1) The *Appeal Relating to the Jurisdiction of the ICAO Council* 58
(2) The case of the *Arbitral Award made by the King of Spain* 61
(3) The case of the *Arbitral Award of 31 July 1989* 63
6. Jurisdiction Inherited from the Permanent Court of International Justice 72
(1) The case of the *Aerial Incident of 27 July 1955* 74
(2) The case of the *Temple of Preah Vihear*. 76
(3) The *Barcelona Traction, Light and Power Co. Ltd.* Case .. 77
(4) The *Military and Paramilitary Activities* case. 80

[to be continued]

Boni judicis est ampliare jurisdictionem.

Ulpian

La juridiction ne se donne pas pour le juridiciant, mais pour le juridicié.

Blaise Pascal, *Pensées* (1670), 115 (202–879)

Introduction

If the articles in the present series, and those of Sir Gerald Fitzmaurice of which it is a continuation, have a value, it is, one may hope, more than historical. An indication of how the International Court of Justice has decided on the various issues which have come before it is generally regarded as giving at least some guidance as to how it would or will decide the same, similar or analogous issues in future cases. That in itself is the justification for the existence of the *ICJ Reports*; and for the analysis and commentary here presented, even if it is employed as no more than a glorified index to those *Reports*.[1]

At the outset of this article two recent texts may be noted of great interest on the question of the precedential value of the Court's decisions. The first is the set of Hersch Lauterpacht Memorial Lectures delivered in Cambridge by Judge Shahabuddeen, and published under the title

[1] A simple, unglorified but complete, index would be very valuable. The Registry has started to supply a more detailed annual index than was formerly the custom, and in time this will prove a very useful research tool; but the change of practice is of course only *ex nunc* and not *ex tunc*. (There were respectable reasons for the former practice, principally the reluctance of the Court to publish a form of gloss on its decisions which did not have its direct authority, but might be treated as though it did.)

Precedent in the World Court.[2] No more need be said of this than that it is, and will remain, the classic work on the subject. The second is the decision of the Court—given, alas, too late for Judge Shahabuddeen to have been able to comment on it in his lectures—on the preliminary objections in the case concerning the *Land and Maritime Boundary between Cameroon and Nigeria,* in which the Court defined its attitude to its earlier decisions. Nigeria had argued forcibly that the decision in the *Right of Passage* case as to the effect of an applicant State's Optional Clause declaration not yet notified to the respondent State should not be followed. The Court rejected Nigeria's arguments, observing that:

> It is true that, in accordance with Article 59 [of the Statute], the Court's judgments bind only the parties to and in respect of a particular case. There can be no question of holding Nigeria to decisions reached by the Court in previous cases. The real question is whether, in this case, there is cause not to follow the reasoning and conclusions of earlier cases,[3]

that is to say, to follow them on their own merits as a sound statement of the law.

The period covered by the present article is, for the reasons indicated in previous articles,[4] more extensive than the title of the series as a whole would indicate; and there is a lot of ground to be covered, as jurisdictional questions have been raised in a large proportion of the cases heard by the Court during that period. The same is perhaps even more true for the period 1990 to the present, and it has seemed appropriate to refer to some of these later decisions in any case where to neglect them, in the name of chronological consistency, might give a misleading picture of the development of the Court's thinking. For these reasons, it will be impossible to cover all questions of jurisdiction in a single article: in particular, the substantive case law on the operation of the Optional Clause and declarations under it, and the question of the jurisdiction to give advisory opinions, will have to be reserved for the following article.

It is jurisdiction as a general concept which will be studied; the precise grounds on which jurisdiction has been asserted in any particular case, and upheld or rejected by the Court, are not always of interest in the context of the general law relating to the Court's jurisdiction, but relate rather, for example, to the interpretation of treaties and comparable instruments, and questions of this kind will therefore not be dealt with here.

[2] Grotius Publications, Cambridge University Press, 1996; see also Jennings, 'The Judiciary, International and National, and the Development of International Law', *International and Comparative Law Quarterly*, 45 (1996), p. 1.

[3] *ICJ Reports*, 1998, para. 28 of the judgment.

[4] This *Year Book*, 60 (1989), p. 5; 62 (1991), pp. 2–3.

Chapter I

Jurisdiction in Contentious Cases

1. *Preliminary Observations: Terminology and Related Matters*

(1) *Jurisdiction and competence*

It is unfortunate that in both English and French, similar terms are used for the power of a tribunal to give a decision, and for the powers of a State deriving from its sovereignty in international law—powers which include those exercised through the judiciary. Thus in French, 'la compétence internationale de l'Etat' is 'le pouvoir juridique conféré ou reconnu par le droit international à un Etat de connaître d'une affaire, de prendre une décision, de régler un différend',[5] and State jurisdiction is defined in English as 'the capacity of a State under international law to prescribe or enforce a rule of law',[6] or as 'the State's right under international law to regulate conduct in matters not exclusively of domestic jurisdiction'.[7] An international tribunal too has 'jurisdiction' and 'compétence'. The psychological effect of this identity of terminology may be to vest an international tribunal, particularly a standing one such as the ICJ, with an implied or residual authority wider than it has been given; to assimilate it in effect to a court within a State enjoying the wide powers (often indeed residuary powers) conferred on it by the State. To do so is to lose sight of the basic truth that an international tribunal is no more than an instrument employed by States for dispute settlement, and can only address States in the imperative mood in so far as they have agreed in advance that it shall. It is a truism that international judicial jurisdiction is based on and derives from the consent of States, and this is well recognized in relation to the *scope* of jurisdiction; but it may sometimes be overlooked that it is also true in relation to the *type and effect* of jurisdiction. To say that the International Court was established as a court, as the 'principal judicial organ' of the United Nations, may sometimes permit conclusions to be drawn as to the authority it was intended to have; but this is a form of reasoning that has to be applied with more caution than has sometimes been employed.[8]

Sir Gerald Fitzmaurice insisted on the distinction between the two terms, jurisdiction and competence: 'although these terms are often used

[5] *Dictionnaire de la terminologie du droit international* (Sirey, 1960).

[6] American Law Institute, *Restatement of the Law, Second* (1965): *Foreign Relations Law of the United States*, ch. 1, s. 6, p. 20: quoted in Bowett, 'Jurisdiction: Changing Patterns of Authority over Activities and Resources', this *Year Book*, 53 (1982), p. 1.

[7] Mann, 'The Doctrine of Jurisdiction in International Law', *Recueil des cours*, 111 (1964–I), p. 9.

[8] Similarly, the concept of 'compulsory jurisdiction' must not be seen as corresponding to the idea of compulsory jurisdiction in municipal systems: cf. Oellers-Frahm, 'Probleme und Grenzen der obligatorischen internationalen Gerichtsbarkeit', *Archiv des Völkerrechts*, 27 (1989), p. 443.

interchangeably, they ought probably each to be confined to a particular aspect of the matter'. The usage which he proposed, but which has not been consistently adopted, is to distinguish between 'the question of the general class of case in respect of which a given tribunal has jurisdiction', and 'the question of its competence to hear and determine a particular individual case'.[9] Since jurisdiction and competence must exist *ratione materiae, rationae personae* and *ratione temporis*, Fitzmaurice distinguished six separate questions which might have to be resolved positively if a tribunal were to be entitled to proceed to examine the merits of a dispute.[10]

As a theoretical construct, this is impressive, if not alarming, but its usefulness may perhaps be doubted. In any given jurisdictional dispute, the question the Court has to answer is: did the parties agree that this dispute should be determined by the Court?—and this may frequently be equivalent to asking: is this dispute of a class which the parties agreed should be determined by the Court? For the Court to have to enquire whether it has competence to deal with this kind of dispute at all[11] is not a matter of enquiring into the existence or otherwise of the consent of the parties, but rather into the intentions of the drafters of the Statute—and for that reason Fitzmaurice is right to classify such an enquiry as something other than a question of jurisdiction/competence in the usual sense. But it is *a priori* unlikely that a State would ask the Court to do something the Statute gave it no power to do,[12] and this does not seem in fact to have occurred before the post-War Court.[13] In the case concerning the *Arbitral Award of 31 July 1989*, the Court indicated that it was not asked to act as a court of appeal from the award, with an apparent implication that it could not, as a matter of jurisdictional principle, so act, but other interpretations of its decision are possible.[14]

It may also be objected that the classification of jurisdictional questions involves more levels than the two identified by Fitzmaurice, of

[9] This *Year Book*, 34 (1958), p. 8; *Collected Edition*, II, p. 434.

[10] This *Year Book*, 34 (1958), p. 9; *Collected Edition*, II, p. 435.

[11] The fact that the dispute is essentially one of fact or of municipal law does not exclude it from treatment by the Court: cf. the *Serbian Loans* case, *PCIJ*, Series A, No. 20, and the *Guardianship of Infants* case, *ICJ Reports*, 1958, p. 55.

[12] The classic, if not the only, example, would seem to be the request made of the Permanent Court in the *Free Zones* case; but cf. the dissenting opinion of Judge Anzilotti in the *Memel* case, *PCIJ*, Series A/B, No. 49, pp. 349–50. See also *Request for an Examination of the Situation in accordance with Paragraph 63 of the Court's Judgment of 20 December 1974 in the* Nuclear Tests *Case*: *ICJ Reports*, 1995, p. 295, para. 23; p. 300, para. 40; pp. 303–4, paras. 52–4.

[13] The question arose out of some observations of the Albanian judge *ad hoc*, Judge Daxner, in the *Corfu Channel* case (*ICJ Reports*, 1947/1948, pp. 38 ff.). His distinction between two meanings of the term 'jurisdiction' in international law really referred to two stages of acceptance of jurisdiction: acceptance of the Court 'as an organ instituted for the purpose *jus dicere* and in order to acquire the ability to appear before it', as in the Protocol of Signature of the PCIJ Statute, and acceptance, for example by an Optional Clause declaration, 'to invest the Court with the right to [re]solve concrete cases' (loc. cit., at p. 39). The distinction drawn by Fitzmaurice is, it seems to the present writer, not the same.

[14] See section 5(3) below.

which the broader was to be called jurisdiction, and the more specific, competence. For example, if proceedings are brought before the Court on the basis of a bilateral treaty containing a compromissory clause, the following propositions underlie the decision on jurisdiction:

A. The Court has jurisdiction under Article 36, paragraph 1, over 'all matters specially provided for . . . in treaties and conventions in force'.

B. There is a treaty between applicant and respondent, and it is in force.

C. The treaty provides for certain matters to be referred to the Court unilaterally.

D. The subject of the dispute is one of those matters.

The Court's *competence* (to use Fitzmaurice's allocation of terms) may be challenged by questioning one or more of propositions B, C or D.[15] Is it useful to treat the issues higher up the table than that momentarily under examination as those of jurisdiction, and the issue selected for challenge as that of competence?

At all events, for the purposes of the present article, the distinction between jurisdiction and competence will not be pursued.[16] The view of Rosenne will be preferred: that 'the distinction sometimes encountered in national law between jurisdiction and competence, as independent concepts, is of little practical relevance to the working of the International Court'.[17]

On the other hand, some remarks seem necessary on the significance of a contention or a finding that the Court has jurisdiction in a particular case. This is a convenient way of expressing a factual/legal state of affairs, but it is nonetheless imprecise. When jurisdiction is referred to, it must always be asked, 'jurisdiction to do what?'. Jurisdiction or competence is not, in the sense in which those terms are used in relation to a dispute, a general property vested in the court or tribunal contemplated: it is the power, conferred by the consent of the parties, to make a determination on specified disputed issues which will be binding on the parties because that is what they have consented to.

The need for precision in this matter is highlighted by the effects of a change in procedure adopted by the Court in the 1970s in relation to challenges to its jurisdiction. When a preliminary objection is taken to the jurisdiction of the Court, and rejected, the Court is declaring no more than that that particular objection is not well-founded; if there are no

[15] Proposition A can hardly be seriously challenged, but a question of competence might arise at this level also if, for example, it was questioned whether the applicant was a party to the Statute: cf. *Application of the Convention on the Prevention and Punishment of the Crime of Genocide*, order of 8 April 1993 *(Provisional Measures), ICJ Reports*, 1993, pp. 12–14, paras. 15–19.

[16] A recent study of the distinction in relation to, in particular, the practice of the US/Iran Claims Tribunal does not, in the present writer's view, illuminate the question further: see Heiskanen, 'Jurisdiction v. Competence: Revisiting a Frequently Neglected Distinction', *Finnish Yearbook of International Law*, 5 (1994), p. 1.

[17] *The Law and Practice of the International Court, 1920–1996*, vol. 2, p. 535.

other objections which are sustained, the result is effectively to confirm the Court's jurisdiction in the case. Nevertheless, there will have been no general finding by the Court to that effect: and if it should subsequently appear that there is another defect or limitation in the jurisdiction of the Court, that can be judicially determined to be the case, and the consequences drawn, without inconsistency. However the Court, initially in the *Fisheries Jurisdiction* cases in 1972, adopted the procedure, where jurisdiction was known to be disputed by the respondent State (particularly, but not exclusively, in cases where that State was declining to appear in the proceedings[18]), of opening *proprio motu* a phase of the proceedings devoted to examination of the jurisdictional issues, which would be closed by a judgment declaring that the Court did or did not have jurisdiction in the case.[19]

That such a declaration might be over-broad appeared in fact in the *Fisheries Jurisdiction* case brought by the Federal Republic of Germany against Iceland; at the subsequent stage of examination of the merits, the Court found itself obliged to re-examine two questions of jurisdiction: whether it had jurisdiction to pronounce upon certain matters concerning conservation of fish stocks and the special dependence of Iceland on fisheries,[20] and whether it had jurisdiction to entertain a claim by Germany for compensation.[21] The Court's decision on each point was in the affirmative, though not unanimous; nevertheless this produced at the least an apparent contradiction with the general decision that the Court had jurisdiction in the case, which thus presumably signified jurisdiction over all issues raised in that application, including the first question (though that of compensation had not been specifically mentioned since the acts giving rise, in the contention of Germany, to the payment of compensation occurred after the proceedings had been instituted).

The effect of a decision finding that the Court has jurisdiction (or, *pro rata*, a decision rejecting preliminary objections to jurisdiction) is that the existence of jurisdiction becomes a matter of *res judicata*. (The same is of course true of a decision finding that there is no jurisdiction.) For the Court and its Members, this signifies that the matter cannot be re-opened (hence the awkwardness of the situation in the *Fisheries Jurisdiction* case, just mentioned); thus a judge who has voted against a finding of jurisdiction is bound by the decision of the majority, and must therefore proceed to examine the merits on the basis that jurisdiction

[18] Cf. the *Military and Paramilitary Activities* case, where the United States appeared in the phase of the proceedings devoted to jurisdictional issues, only to withdraw after the Court had upheld jurisdiction.

[19] On this procedure, see P. Lamberti Zanardi, 'Forme nuove di contestazione della competenza della Corte internazionale di giustizia e potere della Corte di aprire d'ufficio un procedimento sulla competenza', *Il processo internazionale, XIV Communicazioni i studi, Studi in onore di Gaetano Morelli* (Milan, 1975).

[20] *ICJ Reports*, 1974, p. 189, para. 34.

[21] *ICJ Reports*, 1974, p. 203, paras. 71–2.

does exist even though he does not believe in it. In the *Appeal relating to the Jurisdiction of the ICAO Council*, Judge Onyeama explained in his separate opinion why he did not consider that the Court had jurisdiction to consider the appeal; he then continued:

> The majority of the Court, however, has decided that the Court has jurisdiction to entertain the appeal, and this, in view of Article 36 (6) of the Statute, settles the matter. I am constrained, therefore to consider the substance of the appeal.[22]

In the final pages of his opinion he therefore expressed his views on the merits.

A more complex situation arose in the *Military and Paramilitary Activities* case. The Court decided in 1984 that 'it has jurisdiction to entertain the Application filed by the Republic of Nicaragua . . . on the basis of Article 36, paragraphs 2 and 5, of the Statute' and generally that 'it has jurisdiction to entertain the case'.[23] In the reasoning of the judgment however it had found that one particular argument against jurisdiction put forward by the United States (based on the so-called 'Vandenberg Reservation' to the United States' Optional Clause declaration) amounted to an objection which, in the terms of Article 79, paragraph 7, of the 1978 Rules of Court, 'does not possess, in the circumstances of the case, an exclusively preliminary character'. Accordingly, the Court found that that objection 'does not constitute an obstacle for the Court to entertain the proceedings',[24] hence the decision upholding jurisdiction. However, it was apparently thus open to the United States (which in fact took no further part in the case) to convince the Court at the merits stage that it did not have jurisdiction after all, in view of the reservation, thus contradicting the operative part of the 1984 decision. If the intention of the rule were otherwise, there would be no difference in effect between a finding that an objection does not possess an exclusively preliminary character and a rejection of the objection.

There was however some obscurity as to the Court's intentions when the relevant text was adopted in 1972. Judge Jiménez de Aréchaga, writing in 1973, expressed the view that the new provision was intended to discourage the filing of certain types of objection, those that 'cannot be decided without going into the merits', because the Court would be able to declare that the objection did not possess an exclusively preliminary character, 'thus *clearly rejecting* the objection of the objecting State'.[25] This view has now been repudiated by the Court.[25a]

[22] *ICJ Reports*, 1972, p. 90.

[23] *ICJ Reports*, 1984, p. 442, paras. 113 (1) (*a*) and (*c*).

[24] *ICJ Reports*, 1984, pp. 425–6, para. 76.

[25] 'The Amendments to the Rules of the International Court of Justice', *American Journal of International Law*, 67 (1973), p. 16.

[25a] *Land and Maritime Boundary between Cameroon and Nigeria, Preliminary Objections, ICJ Reports*, 1998, para. 116 of the judgment.

The Court in the *Nicaragua* case did however examine the effect of the Vandenberg Reservation at the merits stage, even though the United States was not present in the proceedings to ask it to do so, and may thus be taken to have disproved the interpretation advanced in 1973 by Judge Jiménez de Aréchaga. By examining the point, it was recognizing the possibility that it might come to the conclusion that the Reservation was a bar to jurisdiction, notwithstanding the terms of its 1984 decision.

This in fact was the conclusion arrived at by one Member of the Court—Judge Oda—after hearing argument on the merits. Having concluded that the Court had no jurisdiction, at least on the basis of Article 36, paragraph 2, of the Statute, Judge Oda regarded himself as entitled, if not bound, to vote against the Court's conclusions on the merits in so far as they were made on the basis of the jurisdiction which Judge Oda rejected, because he held, as he explained in his dissenting opinion, that the Court should not have pronounced on them, even though, as he made clear, he agreed with some of the Court's arguments.

Judge Oda was obviously faced with a dilemma: the Statute and Rules of Court do not permit a judge to abstain on the final votes on a case. Assume for the sake of argument that he agreed whole-heartedly, as a jurist, with a particular conclusion stated in the operative part of the judgment; nevertheless as a judge he considered that he, and his colleagues, should not announce this as a judicial finding. He was right, it is suggested, to vote against such a conclusion, since he could regard it as his judicial duty to do what he could to prevent the Court making a finding which it had no jurisdiction to make, even though he privately considered that the finding was correct in law. Yet in so doing he was apparently rejecting, and refusing to be bound by, the Court's sweeping finding of 1984, that it had jurisdiction under Article 36, paragraph 2.

The dilemma ought not to have arisen; the case shows how essential it is that questions of jurisdiction be settled, with binding force, before any decision is taken on the merits. This does not necessarily entail two distinct judgments; the 1986 judgment could have contained a further finding on jurisdiction in its operative part. In fact, all the Court did was to find formally that it was 'required to apply' the Vandenberg Reservation;[26] Judge Oda agreed that it was, but his interpretation of it was different from that adopted by his colleagues, so that for them it was no bar to jurisdiction while for him it was. If the Court had found some way of deciding, on a vote on the operative part, that its own interpretation of the reservation was the correct one, and that of Judge Oda legally mistaken, then Judge Oda, it is suggested, would have been bound by

[26] *ICJ Reports*, 1986, p. 146, para. 292 (1).

that finding as *res judicata*, and would have had to vote on the merits on the same jurisdictional basis as his colleagues.

The parties are similarly obliged to act on the basis that the Court has jurisdiction; assertions to the contrary, as have been made by States in this position—particularly those which have chosen not to appear—are therefore to be deprecated. A finding in favour of jurisdiction does not however impose on the State which had disputed it any new duty to appear in the proceedings: it will be obliged in due course to accept the decision on the merits as final and binding, in accordance with Article 59 of the Statute, and similarly the decision on jurisdiction is binding; but it is clear from the terms of Article 53 of the Statute, and the Court's practice, that the respondent State remains free to decline to appear in the case.[27]

(2) *Seisin*

In the light of the *Nottebohm* case, Fitzmaurice drew attention to the distinction between jurisdiction and the Court's seisin, the 'state of being seised of a dispute'. As he observed,

> if a tribunal has not been duly seised it is incompetent to hear the case. But it does not follow that because the tribunal is duly seised, and has therefore seisin of the case, it possesses on that account substantive jurisdiction and competence to hear and determine it on the merits. What seisin gives it is jurisdiction and competence to determine this very point[28]

and, one might add, the other types of preliminary jurisdiction which Fitzmaurice himself discerned (discussed below).[29]

Seisin is necessary for preliminary or incidental jurisdiction (for the meaning of these terms, see further below) to be exercised; but is it sufficient? Rosenne suggests that 'if it is obvious that the Court lacks all jurisdiction to deal with the case on the merits, then it automatically follows that it will lack all incidental jurisdiction whatever'.[30] The question raised by this suggestion is, 'obvious to whom?'. If a title of jurisdiction is asserted, then however weak or indeed specious it may appear, it has to be investigated and ruled upon; and pending a decision

[27] For a much fuller examination of this question, see the present writer's *Non-Appearance before the International Court of Justice* (Cambridge, 1985), *passim*, and in particular chapter 5, pp. 64 ff.

[28] This *Year Book*, 34 (1958), pp. 13–14; *Collected Edition*, II, pp. 440–1.

[29] 'La signification de la saisine réside ainsi dans le fait que, bien qu'elle soit impuissante en elle-même de doter la Cour de la compétence nécessaire pour connaître d'un litige au fond, elle lui fournit l'occasion – et parfois lui impose la nécessité – d'exercer la compétence extensive qui lui est attribuée par le Statut': H. Briggs, 'La compétence incidente de la Cour internationale de justice en tant que compétence obligatoire', *Revue générale de droit international public*, 64 (1960), p. 224.

[30] *The Law and Practice of the International Court, 1920–1996*, vol. 2, p. 599. Rosenne cites in support of this the non-joinder of the applications in the cases of *Treatment of US Aircraft and Crew in Hungary* (*ICJ Reports*, 1954, pp. 99, 103); but the fact that the cases were not joined before being removed from the list does not necessarily imply that they *could* not have been so joined – there would seem to have been little point in doing so.

disclaiming merits jurisdiction, the normal incidental jurisdiction may be exercised where appropriate.[31] Thus incidental jurisdiction results from mere seisin, with the possible exception of cases in which the applicant State admits that no merits jurisdiction exists.

This is the situation contemplated by a new provision introduced during the revision of the Rules of Court in 1978, as a result of which a procedural situation can arise in which, while the steps necessary under the Statute and Rules have been taken to seise it of a particular dispute, it is uncertain whether or not it has seisin. Article 38, paragraph 5, of the 1978 Rules provides that:

> When the applicant State proposes to found the jurisdiction of the Court upon a consent thereto yet to be given or manifested by the State against which such application is made, the application shall be transmitted to that State. It shall not however be entered in the General List, nor any action taken in the proceedings, unless and until the State against which such application is made consents to the Court's jurisdiction for the purposes of the case.

The purpose of the revision is clear: it was to exclude for the future what were known as the 'phoney cases', popular for a while in the 1950s: as a political gesture a State would bring proceedings against a State which, to the applicant State's knowledge, had not accepted and would not accept jurisdiction, so that, through the circulation by the Registrar of the application to all States entitled to appear before the Court, publicity would be gained for the applicant's support for international judicial settlement, and the respondent State's lack of such support.[32]

Effect has been given to the Article 38, paragraph 5, on two occasions: prior to the conclusion of the Special Agreement in the *Gabčíkovo/Nagymaros Project* case, Hungary endeavoured to bring the case by filing an application against Czechoslovakia, which declined to accept jurisdiction on that basis; but it was subsequently possible to seise the Court by agreement, and the previous application was allowed to drop into oblivion. Bosnia and Herzegovina followed up its institution of proceedings against Yugoslavia by filing an application instituting proceedings against the member States of NATO, alleging that their implementation of the Security Council's arms embargo was unlawful; no State accepted jurisdiction, and again the case simply vanished.

Normally, seisin without jurisdiction may be supplemented by acceptance of *forum prorogatum*, as is in fact contemplated by Article 38, paragraph 5. Seisin with an asserted title of jurisdiction, however

[31] In so far as it is discretionary (e.g., for the indication of provisional measures), the lack of likelihood of the existence of merits jurisdiction will be very material to the exercise of the discretion, but this is a different question.

[32] See, for example, *Treatment in Hungary of Aircraft and Crew of the United States of America, (United States* v. *Hungary)*, order of 12 July 1954, *ICJ Reports*, 1954, p. 99; idem *(United States v. USSR)*, ibid., p. 103; *Antarctica (United Kingdom* v. *Argentina)*, order of 16 March 1956, *ICJ Reports*, 1956, p. 12; idem *(United Kingdom* v. *Chile)*, ibid., p. 15; etc.

specious, still opens the way to a decision on jurisdiction, in exercise of the *compétence de la compétence*, and to the exercise of other preliminary competences.[33] When Article 38, paragraph 5, is applied, does the Court have seisin? If the respondent State accepts jurisdiction, no further action by the applicant is necessary for the proceedings to follow their normal course, so seisin has been effected at some stage; yet at the stage when the application is filed, none of the normal consequences of seisin are permitted to occur. Perhaps the situation may be viewed as a sort of seisin subject to a suspensory condition, fulfilled if and when jurisdiction is accepted.[34]

A totally unprecedented situation arose in 1995 as a result of the filing of a *Request for an Examination of the Situation in accordance with Paragraph 63 of the Court's Judgment of 20 December 1974 in the* Nuclear Tests (New Zealand *v.* France) *Case*. This request was presented by New Zealand in order to endeavour to re-open proceedings in the case; it appeared to fall into no clearly determined category under the Statute, and its handling clearly caused the Court considerable perplexity: was it seised of a case at all? In view of the unique circumstances of the case, and the fact that it falls outside the period covered by the present review, it seems appropriate here to do no more than call attention to the Court's handling of the matter.[35]

Also worthy of a brief mention is the contention of Rosenne, in the light of this case, that 'There is a possible pre-judicatory or threshold proceeding to determine whether the Court has been seised of a case at all', which he distingishes from cases of the *Nuclear Tests* or *Northern Cameroons* type, ' "moot" in the American sense',[36] where there is seisin, but the Court decides not to exercise jurisdiction. Whether the Court was 'seised' of anything in respect of the *Request for an Examination of the Situation* is debatable, and probably a 'moot' question in the British rather than the American sense. However, the other example given by Rosenne of this kind of 'pre-judicatory proceedings' is the first phase of the case of *Maritime Delimitation and Territorial Questions between Qatar and Bahrain*, which in the present writer's view is simply an exercise—though one conducted in a procedurally curious way—of the *compétence*

[33] See section 2, p. 17, below.

[34] It seems clear that the Court would never indicate provisional measures on the basis of an application to which Article 38, paragraph 5, applied, but this would be justified on the basis that measures will not be granted if there is no possibility of jurisdiction over the merits being found to exist (see below, section 2(2), and the present writer's comments in *Indication of Provisional Measures by International Courts*, Max-Planck-Institut, Heidelberg, 1994, p. 135). More difficult is the question whether, if measures were applied for on such a basis, the Court would have to go through the procedures laid down by Articles 73–8 of the Rules, even if the result were to be a foregone conclusion. If the Court has been effectively seised, it is arguable that this would have to be done; it has however now taken a contrary view: see ICJ Press Communiqué 99/4 (Eritrea/Ethiopia dispute).

[35] Order of 22 September 1995, *ICJ Reports*, 1995, p. 288.

[36] *The Law and Practice of the International Court, 1920–1996*, vol. 2, p. 905.

de la compétence, an examination of the title of jurisdiction asserted by the applicant, coupled with a rather curious invitation to the parties to supplement any defect in that title. It is suggested that the *Request for an Examination of the Situation* is the only case in which the Court has acted in circumstances in which it was at least arguable that it was without seisin.[37]

(3) *Jurisdiction and the 'merits'*

The distinction between matters of jurisdiction and matters relating to the merits of a case normally seems fairly straightforward; but as emerges from the discussion of that distinction in Fitzmaurice's 1958 article, the question is not always so simple. During the period under review, the case of the *Appeal relating to the Jurisdiction of the ICAO Council* highlighted some of the problems. Since the Court was asked to say whether or not a decision of the Council upholding its jurisdiction to deal with a particular application and complaint was well founded, the merits of the case before the Court were constituted by a question of jurisdiction; and the Court's own jurisdiction to entertain the case had also been challenged. In the course of its discussion, the Court however also found it necessary to refer to the merits of the application and complaint before the ICAO Council; it therefore found it necessary to add a terminological clarification, as follows:

> For the sake of clarity it should be mentioned at this point that when, in the present Judgment, reference is made to the 'merits' of the dispute or disagreement, what is meant is the merits of the case before the Council. When reference is intended to the substance of the purely jurisdictional issue now before the Court, the context will make this clear.[38]

The merits (in this sense) of the claim and the jurisdictional issue were however entangled in a more substantive way. It was the claim of India that the treaties on the basis of which the matter had been brought before the ICAO Council (the Chicago Convention and the related International Services Transit Agreement) were suspended between itself and Pakistan, and that therefore the Council was without competence. However, if (as the Council and the Court in fact found) the suspension, or purported suspension, of the treaties did not rob the Council of competence, the question would still remain whether the suspension was an answer to, or relevant to, Pakistan's claim on the merits before the Council. The point was adverted to by Judge Jiménez de Aréchaga in his separate opinion:

[37] This is not to say that no other circumstances are imaginable in which this might be so: if proceedings were brought by an entity which had dubious claims to be a sovereign State – though this would also involve the simpler question whether it was a party to the Statute. Attempts have been made by non-State entities to seise the Court, and have been met by an administrative decision that there was nothing for the Court to act on.

[38] *ICJ Reports*, 1972, p. 52, para. 12.

The Council of ICAO is competent to entertain this disagreement. This question has been settled.

If and when the Council of ICAO deals with the merits of the case, it will have to pronounce on Pakistan's submissions. But when doing so it will have to determine first what is the law applicable to the relations between the Parties . . .

Thus the ICAO Council, before pronouncing on Pakistan's submissions, would have to determine whether the Chicago Convention and the Transit Agreement apply or not in the relations between the Parties.

In such a way, it may again be faced, in a different context, with some of the arguments which were raised by India to oppose the Council's jurisdiction. Those arguments, while insufficient for the purpose of excluding that jurisdiction, would still remain available for India to invoke as defences on the merits, on the question of the substantive law to be applied.

But the jurisdictional question as such is closed by this decision. In other words, in the hypothesis that the Council should accept India's contentions as to suspension or special régime, this would not result, in my view, in the Council becoming incompetent or devoid of jurisdiction but would result in a rejection of Pakistan's submissions on the merits on the ground that the substantive law invoked in support of those claims would no longer be applicable (on that hypothesis) to the relations between the Parties.[39]

This view has to be seen in conjunction with the finding of the Court (with which Judge Jiménez de Aréchaga agreed) that a unilateral suspension of a treaty of this kind could not *per se* render its jurisdictional clause inoperative,[40] so that it was possible to uphold the jurisdiction of the Council without thereby ruling that the treaties had not been suspended. Cases are however not inconceivable in which the grounds of a jurisdictional decision might be more inextricably linked with arguments on the merits, so that the one question could not be decided without prejudging the other. It was for that reason that the Rules of Court provided, until 1978, for the possibility of joinder of preliminary objections to the merits, an option now replaced by that of deciding that an objection 'does not present, in the circumstances of the case, an exclusively preliminary character' (Article 79, para. 7 of the 1978 Rules).[41] This of course would not have afforded a solution in the special circumstances of the *ICAO Council* case, where the Court had to decide the jurisdictional question, but would not itself be deciding the merits (save in the event of a further appeal from the Council's decision on the merits).[42]

[39] *ICJ Reports*, 1972, pp. 155–6.

[40] See below, section 3 (3), and *ICJ Reports*, 1972, pp. 53–4, para. 16 (*b*).

[41] For a recent implementation of this provision, see the judgment of 11 June 1998 in *Land and Maritime Boundary between Cameroon and Nigeria* (pp. 8–9 and n. 25a, above).

[42] Article 79, paragraph 7, was applied in the *Military and Paramilitary Activities* case by analogy where the Court had itself opened a phase of the proceedings devoted to jurisdiction and admissibility; for the complications which arose in that context, see pp. 8 ff. above.

(4) *Jurisdiction and the burden of proof*

The two broad principles in the matter of proof which are applied by the Court are, first, that it is for the party making a claim or allegation to bear the burden of proving it; and second, that *jura novit curia*, that international law is deemed within the knowledge of the Court, so that there is no burden of proof involved—though, for obvious reasons, this does not deter parties to cases from arguing at length on what they consider the applicable law to prescribe. What then of jurisdictional questions? Is there a burden of proof on the applicant to establish that the Court has jurisdiction to hear and determine his claim?

The point was raised in the case concerning *Border and Transborder Armed Actions (Nicaragua* v. *Honduras)*,[43] where both parties cited the dictum in the *Military and Paramilitary Activities* case that 'it is the litigant seeking to establish a fact who bears the burden of proving it'.[44] The Court pointed out that

> The existence of jurisdiction of the Court in a given case is however not a question of fact, but a question of law to be resolved in the light of the relevant facts. The determination of the facts may raise questions of proof. However, the facts in the present case [relating to the jurisdictional question] . . . are not in dispute; the issue is, what are the legal effects to be attached to them?[45]

The question was rather one of degree of proof: if the Court was somewhat less than fully convinced of its jurisdiction, should it give the applicant the benefit of the doubt, or rule that jurisdiction had to be conclusively proved? As the Court put it, 'The question is whether in case of doubt the Court is to be deemed to have jurisdiction or not'. It then cited, and adopted for the purposes of the case before it, the dictum of the Permanent Court in the case of the *Factory at Chorzów (Jurisdiction)*:

> It has been argued repeatedly in the course of the present proceedings that in case of doubt the Court should decline jurisdiction. It is true that the Court's jurisdiction is always a limited one, existing only so far as States have accepted it; consequently, the Court will, in the event of an objection—or when it has automatically to consider the question—only affirm its jurisdiction provided that the force of the arguments militating in favour of it is preponderant. The fact that weighty arguments can be advanced to support the contention that it has no jurisdiction cannot of itself create a doubt calculated to upset its jurisdiction. When considering whether it has jurisdiction or not, the Court's aim is always

[43] This was a case in which the Court opened *proprio motu* a phase of the proceedings devoted to jurisdiction and admissibility, and called upon Honduras to file a memorial on these issues. Counsel for Honduras observed that normally Nicaragua would have had to file a memorial first asserting (*inter alia*) jurisdiction (CR 88/4), and therefore suggested that Nicaragua had the burden of proof of jurisdiction. If however Honduras had raised a preliminary objection to jurisdiction, would this still have been so?

[44] *ICJ Reports*, 1984, p. 437, para. 101, cited in *ICJ Reports*, 1988, pp. 75–6, para. 16.

[45] *ICJ Reports*, 1988, p. 76, para. 16.

to ascertain whether an intention on the part of the Parties exists to confer jurisdiction upon it.[46]

Both the Permanent Court and the present Court were thus strangely reluctant to state firmly that jurisdiction must be shown, beyond reasonable doubt, to exist. The point that jurisdiction is a matter of law is something of a red herring; as the Permanent Court observed, the essential element is the existence of an intention of the parties, and particularly of the Respondent; is this necessarily a matter of law? Where the interpretation of a compromissory clause, or of an Optional Clause declaration, is at stake, the Court may conclude that a particular form of words is, as a matter of law, to be interpreted as covering the dispute brought before the Court; yet the purpose of interpretation is to ascertain the intention of the parties, and that intention either existed, in relation to a possible set of circumstances, or it did not—is this a question of fact?

A question linked with that of the burden of proof (if not another form of the latter question) is whether instruments—particularly unilateral instruments—constitutive of jurisdiction are to be interpreted restrictively. Judge de Castro argued in the *Aegean Sea Continental Shelf* case that the principle that declarations conferring jurisdiction must be interpreted restrictively[47] was preferable to the Permanent Court's formula, quoted above, of the preponderance of arguments in favour of jurisdiction;[48] but it does not appear that in practice the one principle is much more helpful than the other.

In a recent decision (falling outside the period addressed by these articles) the Court in effect gave preference to a legal deduction of the existence of jurisdiction, over proof that, as a matter of fact, the intention to submit to jurisdiction was absent. In the case of *Maritime Delimitation and Territorial Questions between Qatar and Bahrain*, the Court was asked to find that Bahrain had accepted jurisdiction by signing the Minutes of consultations between the Foreign Ministers of Bahrain and Qatar (in the presence of the Foreign Minister of Saudi Arabia), and found that the Minutes amounted to an international agreement. Bahrain produced evidence that the Foreign Minister did not regard the Minutes he was signing as 'committing Bahrain to a legally binding agreement', and that under the Constitution of Bahrain he was not permitted to sign such an international agreement taking effect at the time of signature.[49] The Court however

> does not find it necessary to consider what might have been the intentions of the Foreign Minister of Bahrain or, for that matter, those of the Foreign Minister of

[46] *PCIJ*, Series A, No. 9, p. 32; quoted in *ICJ Reports*, 1988, p. 76, para. 16.
[47] Cf. *Anglo-Iranian Oil Co., ICJ Reports*, 1952, p. 105.
[48] Dissenting opinion, *ICJ Reports*, 1978, p. 71.
[49] *ICJ Reports*, 1994, p. 121, paras. 25, 26.

Qatar. The two Ministers signed a text recording commitments accepted by their Governments, some of which were to be given immediate application. Having signed such a text, the Foreign Minister of Bahrain is not in a position subsequently to say that he intended to subscribe only to a 'statement recording a political understanding', and not to an international agreement.[50]

The Court does not seem to have been troubled by doubts in this case, so that the original question remains intact: what is the proper course when the existence of jurisdiction is doubtful? A clue may be furnished by Article 53 of the Statute, dealing with cases in which one of the parties does not appear before the Court. Before deciding in favour of the other party's claim, the Court must, *inter alia*, 'satisfy itself . . . that it has jurisdiction in accordance with Articles 36 and 37'. The expression 'satisfy itself' must presumably mean, if not that the Court must be in no doubt about the matter, at least that there must be no doubt of a kind 'calculated to upset its jurisdiction', as the Permanent Court put it in the *Chorzów* case. If that is so, it can hardly be supposed that a lesser degree of satisfaction would be appropriate in a case in which the respondent has appeared and argued that there is no jurisdiction.[51] Accordingly, if the Court is not 'satisfied' that jurisdiction exists in the case before it, it must decline to act; and since it is in the interest of the applicant State, where jurisdiction is challenged, that jurisdiction be established, that State is therefore necessarily under a *de facto* obligation to do all in its power to establish it. Whether this is regarded *de jure* as a burden of proof will usually be an academic question.

2. *Preliminary, Incidental and Substantive Jurisdiction*

(1) *The distinction in general*

In his 1958 article in this *Year Book*, Fitzmaurice drew a distinction between 'preliminary issues of jurisdiction' and 'substantive issues of jurisdiction'. He was commenting on the *Ambatielos* case, and the examples he gave of the two jurisdictional categories were related to the problems arising in that case as to the obligation to establish an arbitral tribunal. They were the question, in relation to a dispute under a given treaty, whether the dispute is one that concerns the interpretation or application of the treaty, which is one of the substantive jurisdiction of the tribunal, and the question 'whether there is a dispute—or . . .

[50] *ICJ Reports*, 1994, p. 122, para. 27. The argument is of course circular: this was an agreement, therefore the Minister can't say afterwards that it was something less, therefore this is an agreement.

[51] Rosenne is apparently of a different view: 'Article 53 does not so much "reinforce" a general duty imposed on the Court as itself impose a special duty on the Court in a defined set of circumstances' (*The Law and Practice of the International Court, 1920–1996*, vol. 2, p. 892); but this remark is made in a different context.

whether the circumstances are sufficiently closely connected with the treaty to warrant setting up the treaty tribunal', a preliminary issue of jurisdiction.[52] He also pointed out, however, that

> For instance the question of a tribunal's competence to prescribe interim or provisional measures of protection or conservation . . . would afford an example of a 'preliminary' issue of jurisdiction in the sense that it tends to arise prior to, and quite independently of the issue of the substantive jurisdiction of the tribunal to hear and determine the claim.[53]

In the period covered by the present articles, the distinction has become more visible, and presented practical importance in relation not only to the indication of provisional measures, as observed by Fitzmaurice, but also as a wider problem which may be stated as follows: what does the Court have jurisdiction to do even before its jurisdiction to hear and determine the merits has been established? The principle of *la compétence de la compétence* empowers it to do all that is necessary to establish that jurisdiction; is that the limit of its powers at that stage, so that no other judicial act can be accomplished except in pursuance of, or ancillary to, the exercise of its merits jurisdiction once established? More specifically, has the Court jurisdiction to make findings in order to support a conclusion that it should refrain from exercising its merits jurisdiction at all? This is a problem which arose in the cases of *Monetary Gold Removed from Rome in 1943* (where however it was particularly not remarked on), *Northern Cameroons,* and most prominently *Nuclear Tests.*

In this sense, the distinction overlaps with that drawn between 'incidental jurisdiction' and jurisdiction to deal with the merits of the case (for which Rosenne has suggested the term 'mainline jurisdiction').[54] However, the essence of such incidental jurisdiction is that it is expressly conferred by the Statute whereas, as has become apparent, there may be preliminary issues as to the powers of the Court to take certain action in the absence of any express authorization in the Statute.

Jurisdiction derives from consent: in so far as it may require to be stated in a text, there are three different situations. The principle of *la compétence de la compétence* is regarded as universally applicable to international judicial bodies, but is also enshrined in Article 36, para-

[52] This *Year Book,* 34 (1958), p. 56; *Collected Edition,* II, p. 483. For a parallel problem when a third party is asked to exercise a power, conferred on him by a prior agreement, to appoint one or more arbitrators, cf. Muhammad Zafrulla Khan, 'The Appointment of Arbitrators by the President of the International Court of Justice', *Il proceso internazionale, XIV Communicazioni i studi, Studi in onore di Gaetano Morelli* (Milan, 1975), p. 1021.

[53] Ibid., footnote 2. That jurisdiction to indicate provisional measures is 'quite independent' of substantive jurisdiction to hear the merits has proved more controversial than might have appeared: see section (2) below.

[54] *The Law and Practice of the International Court, 1920–1996,* vol. 2, p. 596.

graph 6, of the Court's Statute: here the text is merely confirmatory of a power which exists independently of it.[55] The power (for example) to indicate provisional measures is provided for in Article 41 of the Statute of the Court, and is probably not exercisable by a tribunal in the absence of similar express authorization in its constituent instrument: hence the text (or more precisely, the agreement to accede to the text) is the source of the power. The power to examine the question whether the Court should refrain from exercising its substantive jurisdiction, and make findings for that purpose, is not conferred by any text, but has been declared by the Court to be an aspect of an inherent power. Another, less controversial, inherent power is that 'to interpret the submissions of the parties' in order to 'isolate the real issue in the case and to identify the object of the claim', asserted by the Court in the *Nuclear Tests* cases.[56]

In his judicial capacity, Fitzmaurice was able to develop his thinking in this field in his separate opinion in the *Northern Cameroons* case, in which the Court decided that 'even if, when seised of an Application, the Court finds that it has jurisdiction, it is not obliged to exercise it in all cases',[57] and declined to do so. Theoretically, the question whether the Court must in all cases exercise jurisdiction, and the question of what powers it possesses before substantive jurisdiction has been established, are quite separate; but by deciding that, in a proper case, the Court could or should decline to exercise jurisdiction it was implicitly deciding that it had jurisdiction to make that determination. It will therefore be more convenient to examine this question of 'inherent jurisdiction' not provided for in the Statute in the context of the Court's power (or duty) to refrain from exercising its jurisdiction where circumstances of 'propriety' so dictate (section 4 below).

Similarly, the relationship between the power conferred to indicate provisional measures in a particular case, and the jurisdiction over the merits in that case, will be examined under the heading of 'Jurisdiction and provisional measures' (section 2(2) below).

However, the question of the extent and source of the Court's preliminary jurisdiction also arises in the context of provisional measures in a different form, in relation to the problem whether such measures

[55] Thus in the case of the Tribunal which had rendered the *Arbitral Award of 31 July 1989*, the Court observed that 'Article 4, paragraph 2, of the Arbitral Agreement *confirmed* that the Tribunal had power to determine its own jurisdiction': *ICJ Reports*, 1991, p. 69, para. 46 (emphasis added). Unless such competence is a matter of *jus cogens* (for which there seems no warrant), presumably the agreement establishing a tribunal could exclude this power: cf. below, p. 69.

[56] *ICJ Reports*, 1974, p. 262, para. 29; p. 466, para. 30. Another such power is that to admit counter-claims, which are not referred to in the Court's Statute, but provided for in the Rules: see the recent cases of *Application of the Convention on the Prevention and Punishment of the Crime of Genocide*, order of 17 December 1997, *ICJ Reports*, 1997, p. 243, and *Oil Platforms*, order of 10 March 1998.

[57] *ICJ Reports*, 1963, p. 37.

have a binding and compulsory effect for the parties. The text of Article 41 of the Statute, and the *travaux préparatoires* of the 1920 Commission of Jurists, point to an intention that the measures indicated should rather be suggestions to the States concerned, to which indeed great respect should be paid, but the contravention of which would not in itself be an internationally wrongful act.[58] This is a point to be discussed further in a subsequent article on procedural questions; for present purposes, this interpretation of the Statute will be taken as starting-point.

It is however not a universally accepted interpretation. The strongest argument of those who consider that provisional measures indicated under Article 41 are binding on the parties to the case is that the power to indicate binding measures is an inherent power of an international tribunal, directed to ensuring that the ultimate decision of the tribunal is not frustrated. Fitzmaurice, with his usual fairness, puts this argument forcibly but recognizes at the same time that, for the proponents of this view, the text of Article 41 poses a problem.

> What can be asserted with some confidence is that the doubts as to the binding character of an indication of interim measures by the Court, are due wholly to the language of the above mentioned provisions [Articles 41 and 59 of the Statute, Article 94 of the Charter], and would not otherwise (or as a matter of principle) exist. The whole logic of the jurisdiction to indicate interim measures entails that, when indicated, they are binding,—for this jurisdiction is based on the absolute necessity, when the circumstances call for it, of being able to preserve, and to avoid prejudice to, the rights of the parties, as determined by the final judgment of the Court.[59]

The jurisdiction to indicate measures, binding or otherwise, is an instance of the 'preliminary jurisdiction' identified by Fitzmaurice in relation to the *Ambatielos* and *Northern Cameroons* cases, since it may have to be exercised (and in fact usually is) at a moment when merits jurisdiction has been challenged, and not yet established by the Court. For Fitzmaurice, the jurisdiction to indicate *binding* measures is an inherent jurisdiction; but he recognizes that it may yield to a contrary intention expressed in the constituent instrument of a tribunal, so that the terms of Article 41 of the Statute may cut down this inherent jurisdiction. A stronger view has however been taken by, for example, Vice-President Weeramantry, that the arguments based on the text of the Statute are overridden by the considerations of principle pointing to the

[58] Note the mildness of the Court's reaction to the non-compliance by the United States with the provisional measures indicated in the *Military and Paramilitary Activities* case, despite the fact that Nicaragua had asked for action to be taken: *ICJ Reports*, 1986, p. 144, paras. 287–9.

[59] This *Year Book*, 34 (1958), p. 121; *Collected Edition*, II, p. 548.

binding nature of measures.[60] If however a tribunal, simply because it is a tribunal, has, and indeed must have, power to indicate binding measures of protection, it is unclear why, for example, the Statute of the Court should have been drafted to confer a lesser power; and if (on the hypothesis as to the intentions of the Statute here employed) the lesser power was what was intended, to say that the principle overrules the intentions of the parties is to make the matter, in effect, one of *jus cogens*.

This, it is suggested, shows the dangers of attributing to an international tribunal such as the Court inherent powers traced on the basis of municipal analogies. It needs to be recalled once more that the essence of jurisdiction is consent: if the Statute expresses the consent of States to a limited power to indicate provisional measures, it is self-contradictory to argue that, by creating a *court*, they implicitly consented to a wider power. It needs also to be recalled that jurisdiction in the international sphere is no more than the power to determine, with binding effect for the parties, what their legal relations are, not to compel them to act in a certain way or abstain from certain behaviour; the weakness of Article 94 of the Charter is no more than a recognition of this. Thus the whole idea of frustration of the Court's eventual judgment is one which has to be handled with care; if an irrevocable step has been taken by the respondent (whether or not in defiance of an order indicating provisional measures), so that the applicant has to be content with such secondary reparation as may be appropriate, the Court has not failed in its mission, which was to resolve the legal dispute.

This is an uncomfortable truth, particularly in cases where provisional measures are sought to protect human life, as in the cases of *Trial of Pakistani Prisoners of War, United States Diplomatic and Consular Staff in Tehran,* and most recently and most acutely, *Vienna Convention on Consular Relations (Paraguay* v. *United States)*.[61]

The question of the indication of provisional measures, and their effect, will be dealt with further in a subsequent article; for the present,

[60] See the separate opinion of Judge Weeramantry annexed to the order of 13 September 1993 in the case concerning *Application of the Convention on the Prevention and Punishment of the Crime of Genocide (Bosnia and Herzegovina* v. *Yugoslavia), ICJ Reports*, 1993, pp. 374 ff.; particularly at p. 379, where it is argued that the objections based on the texts 'seem to be outweighed by the conceptual factors already outlined', i.e. the need in principle for measures to be binding. Judge Weeramantry however also argues that the texts can be read in the sense that measures were intended to be binding.

[61] See the Court's order of 9 April 1998 indicating measures directed to preventing or delaying the execution in the United States of a Paraguayan national. The United States argued convincingly that, while there had been a breach of the Convention, compliance with the Convention would have made no difference to the trial and conviction of the Paraguayan; there were therefore no rights of Paraguay to be protected. The Court was however virtually compelled to indicate measures, on pain of seeming indifferent to the fate of the condemned man, and neglecting a chance to save him. Judge Oda, who reluctantly voted in favour of the order, saw this clearly, and observed that the condemned man's fate 'however unreasonably' was in the hands of the Court: separate opinion attached to the order.

the matter is mentioned merely to highlight the difficulties of the concept of inherent preliminary jurisdiction.

(2) *Jurisdiction and provisional measures*

One of the most discussed issues in the field of jurisdiction during the period now under examination was the relationship between the power to indicate provisional measures conferred by Article 41 of the Statute, and the jurisdiction of the Court to hear and determine the merits in the case in which such measures are requested, assuming (as has almost always been the case) that at the time of the request for the measures, the jurisdictional title asserted has been challenged, and the Court has not yet had the opportunity to rule on the existence or otherwise of jurisdiction.

Two extreme views are clearly possible. One would be that the power conferred by Article 41 stands alone, and authorizes the indication of measures (if the Court sees fit) independently of the existence, or likelihood, of jurisdiction to hear and determine the merits. The other would be that measures may not be indicated until the Court is satisfied that it has jurisdiction over the merits. The latter view was advanced by two judges in the *Nuclear Tests* cases in 1973;[62] and one of those judges attributed to the Court in that case the former extreme view, though this was perhaps unjust.

The matter had already arisen in the *Anglo-Iranian Oil Co.* case, and was discussed by Fitzmaurice on that basis.[63] He dismissed the idea that the 'incidental' jurisdiction to indicate measures was incidental to the substantive jurisdiction, so as to be only exercisable if the latter jurisdiction was established. On the other hand, he read the *Anglo-Iranian* decision as clearly indicating that while the Court's jurisdiction to indicate measures 'existed so long, at any rate, as it was not *apparent* that no sufficient consent had been given by the party concerned to the exercise of jurisdiction by the Court in relation to the dispute as a whole', yet on the other hand 'if the absence of the necessary consent was *apparent, a priori*, then the Court would be unable to indicate interim measures'.[64]

As a result of the extensive jurisprudence of the Court on the question during the period under review, and subsequently, the issues have been clarified, and some aspects are free from doubt. In the first place, the jurisdiction to indicate provisional measures is an independent jurisdiction, deriving from consent to the application of the Statute effected by becoming a party thereto, and not by way of consequence or corollary to

[62] *Nuclear Tests (Australia* v. *France), Interim Protection*, order of 22 June 1973, dissenting opinion of Judge Forster, *ICJ Reports*, 1973, p. 111; dissenting opinion of Judge Gros, ibid., pp. 118–20; opinions of the same judges in the *New Zealand* v. *France* case, ibid., p. 148, pp. 155–7.

[63] This *Year Book*, 34 (1958), pp. 106–14; *Collected Edition*, II, pp. 533–45.

[64] This *Year Book*, 34 (1958), p. 110; *Collected Edition*, II, p. 537 (italics original).

the jurisdiction over the merits conferred by whatever consensual title may be relevant. The opposite view would mean that provisional measures could only be indicated once jurisdiction over the merits had been admitted or judicially established, and the consequence would be to rob the power to indicate measures of virtually the whole of its effectiveness. The view has been judicially expressed that 'A State either is or is not subject to a tribunal',[65] but it has become clear that this is an oversimplification.[66] If a State has consented to a tribunal exercising certain powers in relation to that State provided certain conditions (e.g. seisin of an alleged dispute to which it is a party) are fulfilled, the fact that certain other powers, and in particular the power to determine the dispute with binding effect, have not been conferred, or it has not yet been established that they have been conferred, is clearly irrelevant to the possibility of exercising the interim powers.

That is not however to say that the existence or otherwise of merits jurisdiction, or more precisely the degree to which it appears probable that merits jurisdiction will be established, is irrelevant to the appropriateness or propriety of exercising interim powers. The extreme view, already mentioned, that provisional measures may be indicated irrespective of the strength of the applicant's case on merits jurisdiction is clearly equally unacceptable, for reasons not of legal theory (since there is no link of dependency of the one jurisdiction on the other) but of practical effectiveness. To indicate measures in a case in which it is subsequently found that merits jurisdiction does not exist, as occurred in the *Anglo-Iranian Oil Co.* case, is legally irreproachable, but may be injudicious if it is the result of an incautious over-estimate of the chances of jurisdiction being established. The real problem which has faced the Court is whether, in each case in which measures have been requested, the likelihood of jurisdiction being established is high enough to justify the interference with the respondent State's affairs constituted by an indication of measures. Since this is not, strictly speaking, a jurisdictional question, and since it is linked with the controversial problem of the binding or non-binding effect of provisional measures, treatment of it will be reserved for a later section devoted to provisional measures.

3. *The Sources of Jurisdiction*

(1) *Is the enumeration of Article 36 exhaustive?*

The terms of Article 36 of the Court's Statute, defining the sources of its jurisdiction, are well known, and those sources are generally regarded

[65] Dissenting opinion of Judge Gros appended to the order of 22 June 1973 in the *Nuclear Tests* cases, *ICJ Reports*, 1973, p. 118.

[66] The present writer has dealt at greater length with the views of Judge Gros in the *Nuclear Tests* cases in *Non-Appearance before the International Court of Justice* (Cambridge, 1985), particularly at pp. 85 ff.

as exhaustively stated. They are 'all cases which the parties refer to it', i.e. cases brought by special agreement, and possibly *forum prorogatum*; 'all matters specially provided for in the Charter of the United Nations or in treaties or conventions in force', i.e. compromissory clauses in treaties, and dispute settlement treaties or protocols; and the so-called 'compulsory jurisdiction' under declarations made pursuant to the 'Optional Clause', paragraph 2 of Article 36. Can there be such a thing as an 'independent source of jurisdiction', not falling in any of these categories?

The point was raised at the jurisdictional stage of the *Military and Paramilitary Activities* case, and the Court's 1984 judgment, while ambiguous, does not entirely rule out such a possibility. The circumstances of the case were unusual, so much so that the Court regarded them as unique, or at least 'exceptional'[67] (though what legal conclusion, if any, follows from this is obscure). Nicaragua had made a declaration under the Optional Clause of the Statute of the Permanent Court, but had not ratified that Statute, which made the application of paragraph 5 of Article 36 (saving such declarations as were 'still in force', and transferring them to the new Court) problematical, at the least. Nicaragua had however been listed in the Court's *Yearbooks* as a State which had accepted the Optional Clause jurisdiction, though sometimes with a cautionary footnote; and neither Nicaragua itself, nor any other State, had ever objected or queried this statement. On this basis, Nicaragua contended that

> the validity of Nicaragua's recognition of the compulsory jurisdiction of the Court finds an independent basis in the conduct of the Parties. The argument is that Nicaragua's conduct over a period of 38 years unequivocally constitutes consent to be bound by the compulsory jurisdiction of the Court by way of a recognition of the application of Article 36, paragraph 5, of the Statute to the Nicaraguan Declaration of 1929. Likewise the conduct of the United States over a period of 38 years unequivocally constitutes its recognition of the essential validity of the Declaration of Nicaragua of 1929 as a result of the application of Article 36, paragraph 5, of the Statute.[68]

As the Court noted, the United States objected

> that this contention of Nicaragua is flatly inconsistent with the Statute of the Court, which provides only for consent to jurisdiction to be manifested in specified ways; an 'independent title of jurisdiction', as Nicaragua calls it, is an impossibility. The Statute provides the sole bases on which the Court can exercise jurisdiction, under Articles 36 and 37.[69]

[67] '. . . so far as the accomplishment of the formality of depositing an optional declaration is concerned, Nicaragua was placed in an exceptional position, since the international organs empowered to handle such declarations declared that the formality in question had been accomplished by Nicaragua': *ICJ Reports*, 1984, p. 412, para. 47.

[68] *ICJ Reports*, 1984, p. 411, para. 43.

[69] *ICJ Reports*, 1984, p. 411, para. 44.

The Court's conclusion, in the light of 'Nicaragua's particular circumstances' and 'exceptional position' was that

> having regard to the origin and generality of the statements to the effect that Nicaragua was bound by its 1929 Declaration, it is right to conclude that the constant acquiescence of that State in those affirmations constitutes a valid mode of manifestation of its intent to recognize the compulsory jurisdiction of the Court under Article 36, paragraph 2, of the Statute, and that accordingly Nicaragua is, vis-à-vis the United States, a State accepting 'the same obligation' under that Article.[70]

Judge Sir Robert Jennings, who dissented on the point, interpreted this passage, in his separate opinion, as a finding that the *Yearbooks* and other publications were 'a factor confirming its interpretation of the effect of Article 36, paragraph 5; if not an independent source of jurisdiction for the Court'.[71] It is suggested that the latter interpretation does not precisely correspond to the Court's finding: the source of jurisdiction identified by the Court is the Optional Clause, paragraph 2 of Article 36, but it regards conduct, in very special circumstances, as sufficient to replace the formal act of depositing a declaration with the Secretary-General. Judge Ago, in his separate opinion, defines the Court's argument, from which he is dissenting, as

> the very idea that the indisputable requirement of a formal act of acceptance could admissibly be replaced—and, what is more, in so special and delicate a field as acceptance of the obligation to submit one's international disputes to the jurisdiction of the Court—by mere evidence of conduct, even if the intention revealed by this conduct is not in doubt.[72]

Judge Ruda, in his separate opinion, also expresses his disagreement with the question of 'the conduct of States as a basis of the jurisdiction of the Court', but makes his thinking clearer further on:

> The conduct of a State is an important element in the interpretation of a convention, including the Statute, . . . but it is a totally different matter to regard this conduct as constituting acceptance of the international obligations set out in a treaty, without following the procedure laid down precisely for the entry into force of those obligations.[73]

Is the Court treating consent by conduct as 'an independent source of jurisdiction'? It is independent in the sense that the conduct replaces an act which was not performed, and ought normally to be performed as a necessary condition for the creation of jurisdiction; it is noticeable that the Court does not treat Nicaragua's conduct, in the passage here under discussion, as an acceptance of the application of the transitional

[70] *ICJ Reports*, 1984, p. 413, para. 47.

[71] *ICJ Reports*, 1984, p. 540.

[72] *ICJ Reports*, 1984, p. 527, para. 31; to similar effect, Judge Schwebel, ibid., p. 595, para. 54.

[73] *ICJ Reports*, 1984, p. 452, para. 1, and p. 458, para. 29.

provision of Article 36, paragraph 5, but as the equivalent of the deposit of a declaration under paragraph 2. But, it is suggested, the fears of certain dissenting judges that the Court was recognizing the existence of a separate means of creation of jurisdiction, *sui generis* and outside the scheme of Article 36 of the Statute, were not justified.

Rosenne[74] discusses the *Nicaragua* case under the heading of 'Consent by Conduct', which at first sight might imply the possibility of consent given in a form not contemplated by the Statute. In fact, however, his thesis is that 'If a State by its conduct induces in another the belief that it accepts the jurisdiction or will not contest it should a dispute arise between the two States, [then] should a dispute coming with[in] the title of jurisdiction later be brought before the Court, the Court will, subject to proper examination of the circumstances, not decline jurisdiction.'[74]

A distinction should perhaps be drawn between acquiescence by conduct in a particular interpretation of a compromissory clause in a treaty, or of a reservation attached to an Optional Clause declaration, where the interpretation (or indeed modification) of the text is a matter for the parties; and acquiescence in a particular provision of the Court's Statute.[75] No conduct expressing consent could get over the objection that a particular State seeking access to the Court was not a party to the Statute,[75a] because this is not a matter of consent. Similarly, if Article 36, paragraph 5, of the ICJ Statute and Article 36 of the PCIJ Statute, considered objectively (whatever that may mean), did not extend to a State in the exceptional situation of Nicaragua, could Nicaragua by acquiescence (or States generally by acquiescence) bring Nicaragua within the scope of those treaty texts?

The Court's finding in favour of jurisdiction in the *Nicaragua* case has also been interpreted as the creation of jurisdiction by estoppel.[76] The concept of estoppel is not however mentioned by the Court in this context in its judgment, though it was clearly aware of the theoretical possibility of appeal to it, since it considered and rejected an argument of the United States specifically based on estoppel;[77] and in fact the author referred to notes the absence, in the circumstances, of the necessary components of an estoppel.

Doubts may also be felt at certain reasoning used by the Court as a subsidiary argument in the jurisdictional phase of the *Barcelona Traction*

[74] *The Law and Practice of the International Court, 1920–1996*, vol. 2, pp. 583 ff.

[75] Cf. the question of exclusion by agreement of Article 60 of the Statute in *Continental Shelf (Tunisia/Libya), Request for Revision, ICJ Reports*, 1985, p. 216, para. 43.

[75a] Cf. *Application of the Convention on the Prevention and Punishment of the Crime of Genocide, Provisional Measures*, order of 8 April 1993, *ICJ Reports*, 1993.

[76] See Megan L. Warner, 'Jurisdiction by Estoppel in the International Court of Justice', *California Law Review*, 74 (1986), p. 1777.

[77] This was asserted on the basis of certain attitudes towards the existence of compulsory jurisdiction adopted by Nicaragua in 1955 in the context of the dispute with Honduras over the *Arbitral Award of the King of Spain*: see *ICJ Reports*, 1984, pp. 414–15, para. 51.

case. Belgium had asserted jurisdiction over its dispute with Spain on the basis of a 1927 Treaty coupled with Article 37 of the Statute, which, it claimed, operated between the parties to substitute the International Court of Justice for the Permanent Court, referred to in the Treaty. Initially Spain had not queried this particular assertion, but later it disputed that Article 37 was applicable. The Court observed that

> It [Spain] did not even broach the possibility that there might be a question as to the competence of the Court *qua* forum. If this attitude was based on the assumption that Article 37 of the Statute . . . conferred jurisdiction on the Court . . . , then the present finding of the Court, that this assumption was in fact correct, operates to restore the basis on which the Respondent itself appears originally to have recognized the same thing.[77a]

If the Statute is exhaustive as to the possible means of expressing consent to jurisdiction, then not merely will an alleged independent source be ineffective, but an interpretation of the Statute will not, merely because it is agreed to by the State concerned, necessarily operate to confer jurisdiction. If the interpretation of Article 37 advanced by Belgium was correct, there was no more to be said; nothing that Spain might have said or failed to say would make any difference.

(2) *Forum prorogatum*

There is clearly a link between the idea of a source of jurisdiction independent of Article 36 of the Statute, as discussed above, and that of *forum prorogatum*, conveniently defined by Rosenne: 'Where the agreement [giving rise to jurisdiction] is not express and not in writing, that is to say where it is reached in the course of the proceedings, the Court will become competent by what might be termed prorogated jurisdiction';[78] 'Its basic feature is that the Court's jurisdiction is established after the seisin'.[79] The distinction would seem to be, as Rosenne indicates, that *forum prorogatum* is created after the crystallization of a specific dispute,[80] and normally after that dispute has been brought before a tribunal, and by reaction to an invocation of an alleged existing title of jurisdiction, or an invitation to accept jurisdiction in a specific dispute in response to an *ad hoc* acceptance by the applicant State. *Forum prorogatum* only operates to provide the element of agreement constitutive of jurisdiction; thus it cannot make up for a jurisdictional or procedural defect which cannot be cured by the agreement of the parties—e.g. lack of status as a party to the Statute. For this reason, as was once observed by Judge de Castro, 'no *forum prorogatum* rule can apply to an advisory

[77a] *ICJ Reports*, 1964, p. 36.

[78] *The Law and Practice of the International Court, 1920–1996*, vol. 2, p. 575. The exclusion of written agreement would seem to exclude the *Corfu Channel* case (letter of 2 July 1947).

[79] Ibid., p. 695.

[80] Fitzmaurice in his 1958 article distinguished *forum prorogatum* from the situation of a State which indicates in advance that, if the other State desires to seise the Court, jurisdiction will be accepted: see this *Year Book*, 34 (1958), pp. 70–2; *Collected Edition*, II, p. 499.

opinion'.[81] No clear case of jurisdiction being found to exist on a basis of *forum prorogatum* has occurred since the *Corfu Channel* case, examined by Fitzmaurice in his 1952 and 1958 articles.[82] The question of such jurisdiction was however raised in the case of the *Appeal relating to the Jurisdiction of the ICAO Council* in 1972.

In that case, India had appealed to the Court, under the provisions of the 1944 Chicago Convention and related instruments, against a decision of the ICAO Council upholding the Council's jurisdiction to hear an application and a complaint by Pakistan against India. Before the Court, Pakistan had advanced certain objections to the jurisdiction of the Court itself to entertain the appeal, and India had contested Pakistan's right to do so, 'because the objections concerned were not put forward at an earlier stage of the proceedings before the Court as "preliminary" objections under Article 62 of the Court's Rules (1946 edition)'. The Court emphasized the desirability of objections to jurisdiction being put forward as preliminary objections, and the fact that it had always to be satisfied that it has jurisdiction 'and must if necessary go into that matter *proprio motu*'. It disposed of the *forum prorogatum* point as follows:

> The real issue raised by the present case was whether, in the event of a party's failure to put forward a jurisdictional objection as a preliminary one, that party might not thereby be held to have acquiesced in the jurisdiction of the Court. However, since the Court considers its jurisdiction to be established irrespective of any consent of Pakistan's on that basis, it will now proceed to consider Pakistan's objections.[83]

In short, it proceeded to 'consider' Pakistan's objections, having already announced that it was going to reject them—a somewhat unusual procedure. It is noteworthy that the Court put the matter in terms of 'acquiescence' and 'consent', which is surely right, even though the consent may in such circumstances be a deemed or fictitious one, the failure to present an objection at the proper time being an oversight or error rather than a deliberate choice. The scope of the jurisdiction conferred was the same in any event: if Pakistan failed to allege the invalidity or insufficiency of the titles of jurisdiction asserted by India, that did not create *de novo* a wide new jurisdiction; it simply meant that the Court could proceed as though Pakistan had expressly accepted their validity. This nevertheless leaves open the possibility that the applicant might rely on a title of jurisdiction to support a claim that went beyond such title, and the question would then arise whether the implied acceptance sufficed to create such extended jurisdiction as would be

[81] Dissenting opinion, *Application for Review of Judgment No. 158 of the United Nations Administrative Tribunal, ICJ Reports*, 1973, p. 274.

[82] This *Year Book*, 29 (1952), pp. 43–4; 34 (1958), pp. 81–6; *Collected Edition*, I, pp. 111–12; II, pp. 507–12. In the 1958 article Fitzmaurice suggested that the *Haya de la Torre* case also involved an element of *forum prorogatum*: op. cit., II, p. 507.

[83] *ICJ Reports*, 1972, p. 52, para. 13.

necessary for the Court to deal with the claim as submitted. This is possibly what the Court had in mind when it referred to its power to raise jurisdictional issues *proprio motu*.

On the basis that the extent of *forum prorogatum* jurisdiction created in these circumstances is the same as the jurisdiction asserted by the applicant, it might have seemed that judicial economy would have been served by investigating and if possible upholding the allegation of *forum prorogatum*. The fact that the Court chose to do otherwise suggests that it may not have been convinced, on the facts, of Pakistan's 'acquiescence', even though formally it left the point open.

There is no reason in principle why a respondent might not acquiesce in a wider jurisdiction than that asserted by the applicant. That this had occurred was suggested in the case (outside the period under review) of *Interpretation and Application of the Convention on the Prevention and Punishment of the Crime of Genocide*. In brief, Bosnia had sought the indication of provisional measures in reliance on a number of alleged titles of jurisdiction, but principally the Convention referred to in the case-title. The Court was only sufficiently satisfied of the likelihood of jurisdiction under that Convention to indicate provisional measures within its scope: the other titles it was unable to accept for the purposes of such measures. On a second request for the indication of measures, it was pointed out by Bosnia (in response to a question by a judge *ad hoc*) that at the stage of the first request, Yugoslavia had requested measures that might be regarded as going beyond the scope of the Genocide Convention, and suggested that this operated by way of *forum prorogatum* to justify, so far as the jurisdictional question was concerned, the indication of measures of the same nature on Bosnia's request.[84]

The Court's finding on this suggestion was as follows:

> whereas the question thus arises whether, by requesting such measures, the Respondent might have agreed that the Court should have a wider jurisdiction, in accordance with the doctrine known as that of *forum prorogatum*; whereas however the provisional measure requested by Yugoslavia in a subsequent request, dated 9 August 1993 . . . , was directed solely to protection of asserted rights under the Genocide Convention; whereas moreover the Respondent has constantly denied that the Court has jurisdiction to entertain the dispute, on the basis of that Convention or any other basis; whereas in the circumstances the communication from Yugoslavia cannot, even prima facie, be interpreted as 'an unequivocal indication' of a 'voluntary and indisputable' acceptance of the Court's jurisdiction (cf. *Rights of Minorities in Upper Silesia (Minority Schools), P.C.I.J., Series A, No. 15*, p. 24; *Corfu Channel, Preliminary Objection, Judgment, I.C.J. Reports 1947–1948*, p. 27).[85]

[84] Generally on the decision on the second request for measures, see Luigi Daniele, 'L'apport de la deuxième ordonnance de la CIJ sur les mesures conservatoires dans l'affaire Bosni-Herzegovine contre Yougoslavie (Serbie et Montenegro)', *Revue générale de droit international public*, 98 (1994), p. 931.

[85] *ICJ Reports*, 1993, pp. 341–2, para. 34.

In short the Court, while implicitly conceding that a wider jurisdiction *could* be created by *forum prorogatum* in such circumstances, regarded, reasonably enough, the Yugoslavian request as falling very far short of being sufficient indication of the clear and specific consent that would be required.[86]

(3) *Jurisdiction derived from treaty: effect of suspension or termination of treaty*

In his 1958 article Sir Gerald Fitzmaurice discussed the question of the effect of termination of a treaty on the obligation to refer to a tribunal contemplated by the treaty disputes about claims which had already arisen prior to the termination, but had not then been so referred.[87] This was in relation to the *Ambatielos* case, where the relevant tribunal had first to be constituted, and the main point examined was whether there may be an obligation to constitute the tribunal and permit it to hear the claim if the treaty has only been terminated after a request has been made for the matter to be referred to arbitration under the treaty.[88] On the basis of the *Nottebohm* decision, it would seem that the termination of the treaty after an *existing* judicial or arbitral body has already been seised should have no effect on the jurisdiction of that body.[89] Fitzmaurice considered that, just as it is not possible to refer a matter to the Court on the basis of an Optional Clause declaration which has been validly withdrawn,[90] so also no jurisdiction exists under a treaty which has been terminated even in respect of claims made (but of which the Court had not yet been seised) before termination of the treaty. While Fitzmaurice was of the opinion that there were 'equitable grounds' for holding that a request for arbitration would create or maintain in existence an obligation to create the arbitration tribunal and jurisdiction for that tribunal, even though the treaty had been terminated in the meantime, he clearly

[86] The question is discussed much more extensively in the separate opinion of Judge *ad hoc* Lauterpacht (*ICJ Reports*, 1993, pp. 416–21), who had provoked the raising of the matter by putting a somewhat leading question to the parties (reproduced at p. 418 of his opinion); Judge Lauterpacht found that there was *forum prorogatum*, for reasons essentially related to his interpretation of the various communications from Yugoslavia, which was not shared by the Court.

[87] This *Year Book*, 34 (1958), pp. 19–21; *Collected Edition*, II, pp. 445–7.

[88] For the problems raised in such a situation for the person or authority empowered to appoint the arbitrator or arbitrators, see Muhammad Zafrulla Khan, 'The appointment of arbitrators by the President of the International Court', *Il proceso internazionale, XIV Communicazioni i studi, Studi in onore di Gaetano Morelli* (Milan, 1975), p. 1021.

[89] 'When one party had already resorted to the organ provided for in the treaty, it would be difficult to accept, as a matter of principle, that the jurisdiction thus invoked might be ousted by the other party's allegation of a breach and claim that it constituted a ground for terminating the treaty or suspending its operation in whole or in part': separate opinion of Judge Jiménez de Aréchaga, *ICAO Appeal* case, *ICJ Reports*, 1972, p. 148, para. 22.

[90] Cf. the case of *Military and Paramilitary Activities in and against Nicaragua*, where the question was the validity of the withdrawal purportedly effected by the so-called 'Shultz letter'; it was accepted by Nicaragua that if that document had effected a valid withdrawal, the Court was without jurisdiction: *ICJ Reports*, 1984, p. 415, para. 52.

did not think that even in equity a belated reference to the International Court could similarly be saved.

However, the dispute may concern the very point whether the treaty has or has not been validly terminated or suspended, and this raises a more delicate problem. Some allusion to it has already been made in an earlier article in this series[91] in connection with the case of the *Appeal relating to the Jurisdiction of the ICAO Council*, and the reader is referred to that article for a brief indication of the relevant facts. The passage of the judgment in that case which is of particular interest in the present context is the following. The Court was dealing with Pakistan's contention that

> India is precluded from affirming the competence of the Court because she herself maintains (on the merits of the dispute) that the Treaties are not in force between the Parties, which contention, if correct, would entail that their jurisdictional clauses were inapplicable, and that the Treaties themselves did not fulfil the conditions contemplated by Article 36, paragraph 1, of the Court's Statute, in order that the Court should have jurisdiction in respect of disputes referred to it under those Treaties.[92]

This contention was rejected for a number of reasons, one of which was that:

> Nor in any case could a merely unilateral suspension *per se* render jurisdictional clauses inoperative, since one of their purposes might be, precisely, to enable the validity of the suspension to be tested. If a mere allegation, as yet unestablished, that a treaty was no longer operative could be used to defeat its jurisdictional clauses, all such clauses would become potentially a dead letter, even in cases like the present, where one of the very questions at issue on the merits, and as yet undecided, is whether or not the treaty is operative—i.e., whether it has been validly terminated or suspended. The result would be that means of defeating jurisdictional clauses would never be wanting.[93]

As a statement *de lege ferenda* as to why the contention of Pakistan ought not to prevail, this could hardly be bettered: but it is perhaps to be regretted that the Court did not tie the argument more closely to the essential element of judicial jurisdiction, namely consent. The point is surely that the parties to the Chicago Convention must be taken to have intended that a suspension of it between two parties should not escape the operation of the compromissory clause, so that the consent creative of jurisdiction existed for the validity of the suspension to be tested judicially.[94] The clause in question used the familiar wording 'any disagreement between two or more contracting States relating to the

[91] This *Year Book*, 63 (1992), pp. 35–8.

[92] *ICJ Reports*, 1972, p. 53, para. 16

[93] *ICJ Reports*, 1972, pp. 53–4, para. 16 (*b*).

[94] The matter was complicated by the fact that the merits were to be heard by the ICAO Council, the Court being merely an appeals body, and seised for the present only of an appeal against the Council's decision upholding its own jurisdiction.

interpretation and application of this Convention . . . '; but different wording (even perhaps the omission of the words 'and application') might have been taken to have a different effect. The Court indeed seemed to recognize this, when it observed that one of the purposes of a jurisdictional clause 'might be' to enable the validity of a suspension to be tested. Thus the matter is one of interpretation of the treaty in order to assess what was the extent of the consent creative of jurisdiction; and the way the Court expresses the point, as though it were a general principle of law independent of the form of words used, is misleading.

It is clear that the suspension—or even the termination—of a treaty containing a compromissory clause referring to a standing tribunal such as the ICJ[95] would not rob that tribunal of the *compétence de la compétence*; thus it could decide whether the termination of the treaty had or had not deprived it of any further competence on the substance. Whether the termination had this effect would however depend, as already noted, on the terms of the compromissory clause, and not on any general principle parallel to that of the *compétence de la compétence*. The complication in the *ICAO Council* case was that there were so many competences involved. The Council had, necessarily, the competence to decide if it had competence to hear India's complaint; it exercised that initial competence, and decided it did have competence on the merits. On the appeal to the Court, the latter had, necessarily, the competence confirmed by Article 36, paragraph 6, of the Statute, to decide whether it had competence to hear the appeal. If the Court had taken the view that the effect of suspension of the treaty was as Pakistan contended, to render the compromissory clause ineffective, the Court could hold, in exercise of the *compétence de la compétence*, that it was not competent to hear an appeal brought under a non-existent compromissory clause. However, since the appeal was brought against a decision rendered in exercise of the Council's *compétence de la compétence*, it could be argued that the Court's appeal jurisdiction, within that context, was unaffected by suspension of the treaty: and the Court would then hold that it had itself jurisdiction to decide that the Council, in exercise of the Council's *compétence de la compétence,* had reached the wrong decision, since the treaty clause conferring jurisdiction had ceased to be effective.

The problem has been discussed up to now on the basis that the suspension or termination of the treaty has taken place before the Court was seised of the case. Any subsequent alleged termination or suspension would, on the basis of the rule laid down in the *Nottebohm* case, have no effect on the existence of jurisdiction. Some slight doubt on this is however suggested by the *Northern Cameroons* case, in which the Republic of Cameroon filed an application on 30 May 1961 on the

[95] A reference to arbitration might involve practical difficulties of the kind that arose in the *Interpretation of Peace Treaties* case.

jurisdictional basis of a Trusteeship Agreement which was terminated with effect from 1 June 1961. The Court in fact declined to rule on the question of jurisdiction, preferring to dismiss the application on the grounds of 'mootness', finding that 'it cannot adjudicate upon the merits of the claim'. It also found, somewhat inconsistently with its decision to refrain from ruling on jurisdiction, that if the Trusteeship Agreement had conferred jurisdiction to entertain such a claim as was presented by Cameroon, the termination of that Agreement, while leaving the jurisdiction intact, deprived Cameroon of any material right to be protected through invocation of such jurisdiction. By filing its application,

> the Republic of Cameroon exercised a procedural right which appertained to it . . . But within two days after the filing of the Application the substantive interest which that procedural right would have protected, disappeared with the termination of the Trusteeship Agreement with respect to the Northern Cameroons . . .
>
> The Court cannot agree that under these circumstances the judicial protection claimed by the Applicant to have existed under the Trusteeship System, would alone have survived when all of the concomitant elements to which it was related had disappeared. Accordingly, the Republic of Cameroon would not have had a right after 1 June 1961, when the Trusteeship Agreement was terminated and the Trust itself came to an end, to ask the Court to adjudicate at this stage upon questions affecting the rights of the inhabitants of the former Trust Territory and the general interest in the successful functioning of the Trusteeship System.[96]

What is not clear in this argument is whether the obstacle that the Court sees as (hypothetically) blocking Cameroon's application is one of jurisdiction or admissibility. On the basis, as already observed, of the *Nottebohm* principle, Cameroon, having filed its application under a treaty in force, was invoking an existing jurisdiction which was unaffected by the lapse of the treaty. On the other hand, the substantive obligations of the treaty came to an end on 1 June 1961, and if the application had sought to enforce them after that date, the Court, in the exercise of its continuing jurisdiction, could and would have so declared. The Court appears to be saying that in those circumstances there was nothing positive the Court could do; and that an application asking the Court simply to declare as much would be inadmissible. Yet the language used comes very near (to say the least) to saying that the jurisdiction itself ceased to exist: it rejected the idea that the 'judicial protection claimed by the Applicant' would alone have survived—in other words, for the Court, *nothing* survived the termination of the Trusteeship Agreement. If this is

[96] *ICJ Reports*, 1963, p. 36.

what the Court meant, one hesitates to approve such a departure from the *Nottebohm* rule: it is, it is suggested, essential to keep questions of jurisdiction and of merits separate. It does not follow that, because it would be desirable that a matter be judicially determined, jurisdiction exists to determine it;[97] similarly, the fact that there are (apparently) no rights of the applicant left to be protected does not mean that the applicant no longer has the right to seise the Court, even if he is doomed to receive no more than a dusty answer.

4. *Jurisdiction and the Propriety of Exercising it*

(1) *The problem in general: the case law*

This question was referred to by Fitzmaurice in his 1958 article in this *Year Book*, but his comments are of tantalizing brevity. He stated the principle that 'The fact that an international tribunal has jurisdiction in a given case does not mean that it will necessarily be bound to, or will, exercise it'.[98] He referred to it as a matter which arises chiefly in connection with advisory opinions, but which can also arise in contentious cases, and indicated that it would 'be discussed in that connection in Chapter VIII below, when the point arose in the *Monetary Gold* case'.[99] However, Chapter VIII was apparently never completed, and it is therefore for the present writer to consider how the question arose in the *Monetary Gold* case, as well as the subsequent decision, in which Sir Gerald participated, in the *Northern Cameroons* case, classic examples of the Court's discretion to decline to exercise jurisdiction. Furthermore, the decisions in the cases of *Military and Paramilitary Activities, Nauru* and *East Timor* (the latter two given outside the period covered by the present articles) have added to the Court's jurisprudence on the subject.

The cases to be discussed establish two propositions, neither of which emerges from the text of the Statute: first, that in certain circumstances the Court may be validly seised of a case, and have (or appear to have) jurisdiction to entertain it, but be nevertheless debarred from exercising that jurisdiction; secondly, that the Court has, in certain circumstances, a discretion to decline to exercise jurisdiction in a contentious case, including the possibility of declining even to examine whether it has

[97] The 1984 judgment in the *Military and Paramilitary Activities* case is not free from suspicion in this respect.

[98] This *Year Book*, 34 (1958), p. 20: *Collected Edition*, II, p. 447.

[99] Ibid., p. 21; p. 448.

jurisdiction. No textual warrant for either proposition, in the Statute or elsewhere, has however been asserted by the Court.[100]

The relationship between these two propositions—indeed, the question whether they are independent propositions or two facets of the same principle—is not entirely clear. Is it sometimes the case that the Court *may* decline to exercise jurisdiction, and sometimes that it *must* do so? Or is the Court always obliged to decline jurisdiction if certain conditions are fulfilled, there merely being differences of a factual nature making it more or less of an automatic operation to establish that jurisdiction must be declined? In view of this doubt, the cases will be examined simply in chronological order, rather than according to an *a priori* categorization.

What can however be asserted is that the jurisprudence shows that where the interests of a third State would 'form the very subject-matter of the decision' asked for, there is no discretion involved: the Court has found that it *cannot* exercise jurisdiction in such circumstances. This point does not however seem to have troubled the Court in 1949 when, in the *Corfu Channel* case, it examined the allegation that the minefield had been laid by Yugoslavia with the connivance of Albania, only the latter State being before the Court as a party.[101] The Court rejected the allegation; but even to consider it involved examining claims that a State not before the Court had committed an internationally wrongful act.[102] In recent years, however, the question of the propriety of exercising jurisdiction where third States' interests were, to a greater or lesser

[100] Rosenne (*The Law and Practice of the International Court, 1920–1996*, vol. 2, p. 546) suggests that, to show the existence of a discretion, reliance can be placed on Article 36, paragraph 6, of the Statute, though he recognizes elsewhere (ibid., p. 552) that the Statute makes no specific reference to the Court's discretion. Where there is a dispute as to jurisdiction, 'the *matter* shall be settled by the decision of the Court' (emphasis added); for Rosenne, the use of this term 'suggests that more is involved than merely settling the dispute as to whether the Court has jurisdiction. It carries an implication, common in fact to all superior courts, that the Court possesses an element of discretion whether to entertain a case.' The present writer finds this unconvincing: there is no support for such an interpretation in the *travaux préparatoires*, and as Rosenne concedes, the French text contains nothing to correspond: and on its terms, the article only applies if jurisdiction is disputed, so that the Court would have no discretion to decline a case if jurisdiction were not disputed; and the natural place for including a discretion in the Statute, if that had been desired, would surely be Article 38 rather than Article 36.

[101] *ICJ Reports*, 1949, pp. 16–17. Yugoslavia did communicate with the Court, and submit certain documents which the Court considered (ibid., p. 17), but it was not a party.

[102] The decision is cited by Judge Schwebel in his dissenting opinion in the *Nauru* case (below), who considers that the Court would have been justified in finding against Albania on the basis that it had connived with an *unknown* third State – and the Court did in fact find that 'the authors of the minelaying remain unknown' (p. 17). It is difficult to see how a finding of connivance could be made without identifying the co-conspirator. Cf. Article 27 of the International Law Commission's draft articles on State Responsibility, according to which 'aid and assistance' by one State to another is unlawful 'if it is *established* that it is rendered for the commission of an internationally wrongful act *carried out by the latter*' (emphasis added); on complicity generally, see Quigley, 'Complicity in International Law: a New Direction in the Law of State Responsibility', this *Year Book*, 57 (1986), p. 77. However, the important point is that Yugoslavia *was* named, and the Court did not feel restrained from examining the allegations made against it.

extent, involved has arisen more and more frequently. The problem is linked with the role of intervention under Article 62 of the Statute.[103]

One further clarification seems appropriate: the postulate in all cases is that the Court does have jurisdiction as regards the actual dispute submitted to it, and in relation to the parties before it, or at least that that question has not yet been tested, and the Court is able to work on the hypothesis of the existence of jurisdiction. Other considerations, superficially similar, may come into play to justify a finding of no jurisdiction: for example, it is possible for the Court to find that there is in fact no dispute between the parties, and this may be a ground for a finding that there is no jurisdiction (particularly if the compromissory clause refers, for example, to 'disputes which it has not been possible to settle by negotiation'). But the fact that negotiations are continuing, which may lead to an amicable settlement of the dispute, is not in itself a reason for the Court *declining to exercise* jurisdiction.

This emerges clearly from the decision in the *Aegean Sea Continental Shelf* case:

> The jurisprudence of the Court provides various examples of cases in which negotiations and recourse to judicial settlement have been pursued *pari passu*. Several cases, the most recent being that concerning the *Trial of Pakistani Prisoners of War* (*I.C.J. Reports 1973*, p. 347) show that judicial proceedings may be discontinued when such negotiations result in the settlement of the dispute. Consequently, the fact that negotiations are being actively pursued during the present proceedings is not, legally, any obstacle to the exercise by the Court of its judicial function.[104]

The Court in that same judgment then dealt, as a separate issue, with whether the negotiations signified that no dispute existed between the parties (and rejected this contention also).

On the other hand, it is possible for the parties to a case to agree that proceedings before the Court should be 'frozen' pending negotiations or other procedures intended to lead to a peaceful settlement of the dispute. Whether the Court would be legally bound to respect such an agreement is not entirely clear: in the case of the *United States Diplomatic and Consular Staff in Tehran*, the Court found that there had not been any agreement of this kind to suspend proceedings pending the work of the Secretary-General's Commission (see below, section 4(2)(a)), and concluded on the basis of this and other considerations that there was no 'obstacle to the exercise of the Court's jurisdiction', which suggests that such an agreement would have constituted such an obstacle. The

[103] '1. Should a State consider that it has an interest of a legal nature which may be affected by the decision in the case, it may submit a request to the Court to be permitted to intervene . . . '

[104] *ICJ Reports*, 1978, p. 12, para. 29. This ruling was quoted and followed in the case of *Military and Paramilitary Activities, ICJ Reports*, 1984, p. 106.

question could really only arise if one party alleged the existence of such an agreement, and the other party denied it; if both parties come before the Court and ask for time to negotiate, the Court agrees,[105] and it is hardly conceivable that it would refuse.[106] In strict terms, an agreement between parties to suspend proceedings would be binding only upon them, not upon the Court, but the Court would presumably not allow a party to go back on such an agreement, and would therefore authorize a suspension of proceedings if satisfied that such an agreement had been made. This of course still does not amount to a legal fetter on the exercise of the Court's jurisdiction in such circumstances.

Similarly, the fact that another organ of the United Nations, e.g. the Security Council, is also active in the matter, does not oblige the Court to refrain from exercising jurisdiction; but this aspect will be dealt with separately, below.

(a) *The* Monetary Gold *case*

The case concerned a quantity of monetary gold removed from Rome by the Germans during the Occupation, which was claimed both by Albania and by Italy. Under the Washington Agreement between France, the United Kingdom and the United States, the three Governments submitted to an arbitrator the question whether the gold belonged to Albania or to Italy, or to neither. The arbitrator decided that it belonged to Albania. By a Statement annexed to the Agreement, the three Governments agreed further that if the arbitrator found that the gold belonged to Albania, it was to be transferred to the United Kingdom in settlement of the debt due from Albania for the unpaid damages awarded by the International Court in the *Corfu Channel* case, unless within a stated time-limit either Albania or Italy filed an application to the Court to determine the title to the gold. Italy filed such an application, but then raised the preliminary question whether the Court had or could exercise jurisdiction in the absence of Albania.

The Court took the view that it

> cannot decide such a dispute without the consent of Albania. But it is not contended by any Party that Albania has given her consent in this case either expressly or by implication. To adjudicate upon the international responsibility of Albania without her consent would run counter to a well-established principle

[105] For example, in the reparation phase of the *Military and Paramilitary Activities* case, order of 26 September 1991, *ICJ Reports*, 1991, p. 47, and in the case of the *Aerial Incident of 3 July 1988*, order of 22 February 1996, *ICJ Reports*, 1996, p. 10.

[106] Save perhaps in circumstances of extreme delay, for which the Court might incur the blame: see the comment on slowness of proceedings due to the demands of the parties in the *Barcelona Traction* case, *ICJ Reports*, 1970, pp. 30–1, para. 27, and the comments in the opinions of Judges Jessup and Fitzmaurice, ibid., p. 113 and p. 221.

of international law embodied in the Court's Statute, namely, that the Court can only exercise jurisdiction over a State with its consent.[107]

It referred to the possibility of intervention, of which Albania had not taken advantage, and explained that

In the present case, Albania's legal interests would not only be affected by a decision, but would form the very subject-matter of the decision. In such a case, the Statute cannot be regarded, by implication, as authorizing proceedings to be continued in the absence of Albania.[108]

It drew the conclusion that

although Italy and the three respondent States have conferred jurisdiction upon the Court, it cannot exercise this jurisdiction to adjudicate on the first claim submitted by Italy,[109]

and on that basis that it could not adjudicate on the second Italian claim either.

It is noteworthy that the Court does not find that it has no jurisdiction; nor does it express its decision in terms of any discretion. It is not that it is unable to act for lack of jurisdiction, nor that it chooses, for good and sufficient reason, to decline to exercise jurisdiction which has been conferred on it, but that it finds that it has, but *cannot* exercise, jurisdiction. This raises the question in what sense a tribunal can be said to have a particular jurisdiction, if that jurisdiction cannot lawfully be exercised: is there any distinction between this situation and the situation of not possessing the jurisdiction at all? Let us take a more extreme case: suppose that States A and B agree to ask the Court to decide whether some particular conduct of State C is or is not in accordance with international law; C does not give its consent, and, we may suppose, is not even invited to do so. Clearly the Court would not give a judgment on the question so submitted to it: but would this be because it had jurisdiction, but could not exercise it, or because it had no jurisdiction to determine the question submitted? Can States A and B confer jurisdiction—even a non-exercisable jurisdiction—to decide on the lawfulness of the conduct of C? One would suppose that the Court would, in any event, *have* no jurisdiction over C; yet in the *Monetary Gold* decision the principle is stated that 'the Court can only *exercise jurisdiction* over a State with its consent'.[110] This question will be examined further in

[107] *ICJ Reports*, 1954, p. 32. The arbitrator appointed under the Washington Agreement (Professor Sauser-Hall) took note of the failure of Albania to participate in the proceedings before him, and concluded that it had renounced its right to do so, but not its title to the gold; he did not however feel constrained to refrain from deciding the matter (and in fact decided in favour of Albania). See the award of 20 February 1953 in *Reports of International Arbitral Awards*, vol. 12, p. 35, and Rosenne, *The Law and Practice of the International Court, 1920–1996*, vol. 1, p. 245, footnote 78.

[108] *ICJ Reports*, 1954, p. 32.

[109] Ibid., p. 33.

[110] *ICJ Reports*, 1954, p. 32 (emphasis added).

connection with the case concerning *East Timor*, below, in which a situation close to that hypothesized was actually presented to the Court.

(b) *The* Northern Cameroons *case*

The *Monetary Gold* principle establishes that there may be cases in which the Court has jurisdiction, but may not lawfully exercise it: may there also be cases in which the Court has jurisdiction and may lawfully exercise it, but may (for good and sufficient reason) *choose* not to exercise it? This is the accepted reading of the case concerning the *Northern Cameroons*; however, the Court's dicta in the case do not necessarily support such an interpretation, but may be read as referring to another type of case in which the Court has jurisdiction but may not lawfully exercise it.

The Republic of Cameroon had brought proceedings against the United Kingdom as the Administering Authority under the United Nations Trusteeship Agreement for the Territory of the Northern Cameroons, alleging various breaches of its duties in that capacity; the case was brought before the Court on the jurisdictional basis of Article 19 of the Trusteeship Agreement, referring to 'any dispute whatever . . . between the Administering Authority and another Member of the United Nations relating to the interpretation or application of the provisions of this Agreement'. The Trusteeship Agreement was terminated, pursuant to a General Assembly resolution, two days after the filing by Cameroon of its application instituting proceedings.

The essential basis of the Court's disposal of the case was that, as a result of the termination of the Trusteeship Agreement, the Court could not 'render a judgment capable of effective application'.[111] At an early stage of its judgment the Court, referring to the distinction drawn in the *Nottebohm* case[112] between jurisdiction and seisin, stated that 'It is the act of the Applicant which seises the Court but even if the Court, when seised, finds that it has jurisdiction, the Court is not compelled in every case to exercise that jurisdiction'.[113] This suggests that the Court may choose not to exercise jurisdiction, as distinct from being required to refrain from exercising it. However the passage quoted continues: 'There are inherent limitations on the exercise of the judicial function which the Court, as a court of justice, can never ignore'; this points rather to a general rule that jurisdiction, if it exists, must be exercised, except in

[111] *ICJ Reports*, 1963, p. 33. For a criticism of this approach, with the suggestion that the Court could, and should, have decided the case on the basis that the *dispute* was moot rather than that the judgment would be, see Leo Gross, 'Limitations upon the judicial function', *American Journal of International Law*, 58 (1964), p. 415.

[112] *ICJ Reports*, 1953, p. 122.

[113] *ICJ Reports*, 1963, p. 29.

certain defined circumstances in which it not merely *need* not, but *may* not be exercised.

This was certainly the view of Fitzmaurice. In his separate opinion in the case, he stated that

> [I]t is in a general way evident that courts exist in order to go into and decide the cases they are both duly seised of, and have jurisdiction to entertain, without picking and choosing which they will pronounce upon, and which not.
>
> No doubt there is a duty in principle for an international tribunal to hear and determine the cases it is both seised of, and competent to go into; and therefore, equally to consider the question of its competence. But there must be limits to this duty.[114]

For Fitzmaurice, the question was one of propriety, and this raised

> a general issue of principle—that is to say, of how far and in what circumstances a court which has, or may have, jurisdiction to go into a case, can and should decline to exercise that jurisdiction (or even to consider the question of jurisdiction) on the ground that it would not be proper to do so in the circumstances.[115]

He suggested three sets of circumstances in which this might be so: first, where there was 'a plea that the Application did not disclose the existence, properly speaking, of any dispute between the parties'; secondly in face of 'the plea that the Application should not be entertained on the ground that, owing to events occurring since it was filed, it has manifestly lost all *raison d'être*—that it has become "moot"—so that a decision on the merits would be objectless'; and thirdly, the situation in the *Monetary Gold* case, where the Court, 'because of the absence of a necessary party, . . . could not examine the claim'.[116]

A point which did not escape Fitzmaurice, but which is not specifically adverted to in the judgment in the *Northern Cameroons* case, is that if the Court (or any tribunal) is to make any finding at all, even a finding that it should not exercise jurisdiction, it must have the jurisdiction to make that finding. Can it then make a finding that jurisdiction should not be exercised at a stage at which it is not yet established that it has jurisdiction at all? The well-established principle of *la compétence de la compétence* resolves the problem when it is the examination of the jurisdictional question itself which is to be embarked on; but does this extend to the question whether jurisdiction (if it exists) should be exercised?

Developing a line of argument already put forward in this *Year Book* in relation to the *Ambatielos* case,[117] Fitzmaurice outlined a division of questions of jurisdiction and admissibility into

[114] *ICJ Reports*, 1963, pp. 101–2 (footnote omitted).
[115] *ICJ Reports*, 1963, p. 101.
[116] *ICJ Reports*, 1963, p. 105.
[117] This *Year Book*, 34 (1958), pp. 56–60; *Collected Edition*, II, pp. 483–7.

(a) questions which, while remaining preliminary (in the sense of preliminary to the merits), are substantive in character, and *(b)* questions which are of a wholly antecedent or, as it were 'pre-preliminary' character. Considerations of propriety or suitability will certainly figure among the latter. Thus in the jurisdictional field, there is the substantive or basic jurisdiction of the Court (i.e. to hear and determine the ultimate merits) and there is the possibility of (preliminary) objections to the exercise of that jurisdiction. But also, there is the Court's *preliminary* or 'incidental' jurisdiction (e.g. to decree interim measures of protection, admit counter-claims or third-party interventions, etc.) which it can exercise even in advance of any determination of its basic jurisdiction as to the ultimate merits; even though the latter is challenged; and even though it may ultimately turn out that the Court lacks jurisdiction as to the ultimate merits. Although much (but not all) of this incidental jurisdiction is specifically provided for in the Court's Statute, or in Rules of Court which the Statute empowers the Court to make, it is really an inherent jurisdiction, the power to exercise which is a necessary condition of the Court—or any court of law—being able to function at all.

It clearly does not follow, however, from the fact that certain forms of incidental jurisdiction are provided for in the Court's Statute that these are examples of a wider inherent jurisdiction: the fact that they are so provided for could be used as a basis for the opposite argument. The true justification for an inherent jurisdiction must be, as stated by Fitzmaurice, that 'the power to exercise it . . . is a necessary condition of . . . any court of law . . . being able to function at all'. The *compétence de la compétence* fulfils this condition; but do the other powers referred to? If arbitral tribunals are to be supposed to have the same inherent jurisdictions, this would imply the existence of a power to admit third-party intervention, or to indicate provisional measures, even in the absence of stipulation in the *compromis*.[118] Yet such tribunals can and do function without such powers. Furthermore, the reason why an inherent jurisdiction is postulated is in order to render the power to exercise it independent of the existence or otherwise of jurisdiction to hear the merits, for reasons which are obvious at least in the case of the *compétence de la compétence*. But, it might be asked, is it necessary for the Court to decide at the outset that it should not exercise jurisdiction; could it not first settle the jurisdictional issue, and then, on the basis of that jurisdiction, decide that reasons of propriety militated against exercising it? This objection is however in effect answered in the judgment itself:

Whether or not at the moment the Application was filed there was jurisdiction in the Court to adjudicate upon the dispute submitted to it, circumstances that have since arisen render any adjudication devoid of purpose. Under these

[118] Or perhaps even to an extent, or in a form, going beyond what is *specifically* laid down in the *compromis*. Note that one of the arguments employed to support the view that provisional measures indicated under Article 41 of the ICJ Statute are binding is that the power to indicate measures having this quality is inherent in the quality of a tribunal, despite the fact that the text and *travaux préparatoires* of Article 41 point to the view that this was not intended.

conditions, for the Court to proceed further in the case would not, in its opinion, be a proper discharge of its duties.

The answer to the question whether the judicial function is engaged may, in certain cases where the issue is raised, need to wait upon an examination of the merits. In the present case, however, it is already evident that it cannot be engaged. No purpose accordingly would be served by undertaking an examination of the merits in the case for the purpose of reaching a decision which, in the light of the circumstances to which the Court has already drawn attention, ineluctably must be made.[119]

Fitzmaurice pursues his argument to a logical conclusion: if objection can be taken to the existence of merits jurisdiction, then similarly objection can be taken to preliminary jurisdiction:

Nevertheless [that is, despite the fact that the jurisdiction is inherent], there may in particular cases be objections (which would accordingly be of a pre-preliminary character) to the Court being entitled to exercise this power in relation to some specific part of its incidental jurisdiction. For example, a request for interim measures may be met either with a denial that, *on their merits*, these should be granted, or with a challenge to the *right* of the Court to grant them, or the propriety of its so doing in the given case—in effect a jurisdictional issue.[120]

This however introduces complication. As the word 'nevertheless' concedes, it is difficult to reconcile the idea of objections to a jurisdiction with the inherent character of that jurisdiction: an objection disputing the existence, at least in the hands of the Court, of the *compétence de la compétence* is hardly conceivable. But there is also the danger of entering a hall of mirrors, or descending spiral: if the Court's jurisdiction (say) to indicate provisional measures is challenged, whence comes the jurisdiction to adjudicate on the challenge? Must we postulate a further pre-preliminary jurisdiction for this purpose?

(c) *The* Nuclear Tests *cases*

The problem of inherent jurisdiction arose again in 1974 in the two *Nuclear Tests* cases, brought by Australia and New Zealand against France. One of the examples Fitzmaurice had given of a question of propriety was, as we have seen, a situation in which proceedings before the Court had, as a result of later developments, become 'objectless'. This was the basis on which the Court declined to rule on the claims by the applicants that the French atmospheric nuclear tests carried out at Mururoa atoll were contrary to international law. The French Government, which had disputed the jurisdiction of the Court, but declined to appear or take part in the proceedings, had made a number of public statements indicating that no further atmospheric tests would be carried

[119] *ICJ Reports*, 1963, p. 38.

[120] *ICJ Reports*, 1963, pp. 103–4, emphasis original, footnote omitted.

out. The Court ruled that, in the circumstances in which they were made, these statements were binding on France, and that thus 'the Court faces a situation in which the objective of the Applicant has in effect been accomplished, inasmuch as the Court finds that France has undertaken the obligation to hold no further nuclear tests in the atmosphere in the South Pacific';[121] 'The object of the claim having clearly disappeared, there is nothing on which to give judgment'.[122]

Whereas in the *Northern Cameroons* case, the facts and legal considerations on which it was able to base its conclusion were virtually all non-controverted, in the *Nuclear Tests* cases the finding that France had entered into a binding unilateral obligation was a bold one; and the conclusion that this circumstance sufficed to satisfy the applicants' claim came perhaps as a surprise to the applicants themselves (particularly New Zealand).[123] While this was a difference of degree rather than of kind, it did focus attention more directly on the problem of the Court's jurisdiction to make such findings when its jurisdiction on the merits had been challenged, and that challenge had not been determined. The judgment accordingly contained an explanatory paragraph on the point, which owes much to the foresight of Fitzmaurice eleven years earlier:

> [I]t should be emphasized that the Court possesses an inherent jurisdiction enabling it to take such action as may be required, on the one hand to ensure that the exercise of its jurisdiction over the merits, if and when established, shall not be frustrated, and on the other, to provide for the orderly settlement of all matters in dispute, to ensure the observance of the 'inherent limitations on the exercise of the judicial function' of the Court, and to 'maintain its judicial character' (*Northern Cameroons, Judgment, I.C.J. Reports 1963,* at p. 29). Such inherent jurisdiction, on the basis of which the Court is fully empowered to make whatever findings may be necessary for the purposes just indicated, derives from the mere existence of the Court as a judicial organ established by the consent of States, and is conferred upon it in order that its basic judicial functions may be safeguarded.[124]

An element additional to Fitzmaurice's definition is represented by the reference to the Court as 'a judicial organ established by the consent of States'; the implication appears to be that the inherent jurisdiction results from an implicit consent of States parties to the Statute. This in fact is the only source from which it could be derived; in the absence of established merits jurisdiction, and of any express provision in the Statute, it must be supposed that States, by becoming parties to the

[121] *ICJ Reports*, 1974, p. 270, p. 52 (Australia); p. 475, para. 55 (New Zealand).

[122] *ICJ Reports*, 1963, p. 272, para. 59 (Australia); p. 477, para. 62 (New Zealand).

[123] As was made clear when New Zealand returned to the Court in 1995 in an attempt to re-open the case; it was urged that New Zealand's original claim had gone beyond the mere cessation of *atmospheric* tests: see *Request for an Examination of the Situation in Accordance with Paragraph 63 of the Court's Judgment of 20 December 1974 in the* Nuclear Tests (New Zealand *v.* France) *case, ICJ Reports*, 1995, p. 288.

[124] *ICJ Reports*, 1974, pp. 259–60, para. 23 (Australia); p. 463, para. 23 (New Zealand).

Statute, gave the Court power 'to make whatever findings may be necessary' for the purpose of 'orderly settlement of all matters in dispute', observance of 'inherent limitations on the exercise of the judicial function' and the maintenance of the Court's 'judicial character'.

As a broad general statement, this is impressive; but in its application to the case, it begins to look rather too sweeping. The Court was probably right in thinking that the French Government had hoped, by its announcements of the cessation of atmospheric tests, to get rid of a politically awkward controversy and embarrassing litigation: it did not protest against the Court's handling of the matter in this respect.[125] But at the time of the Court's decision, it was perfectly possible that France, if the matter were put to it, would deny any intention to undertake a legally binding obligation. Thus the Court regarded its 'inherent jurisdiction' as sufficient for it to make so far-reaching a finding not merely in the absence of the State concerned—for France, it should be recalled, had declined to appear in the proceedings—but without notice to that State, since the Court's decision was not one that had been asked for by the applicants (and, as we have seen, may have come as a not entirely welcome surprise to them). The difference from the *Northern Cameroons* case is marked, since in that case all the relevant facts were uncontroverted, and the United Kingdom had invited the Court to throw out the case *in limine*.

Thus the exercise by the Court of its 'inherent jurisdiction' in the *Nuclear Tests* cases is, to say the least, open to criticism: but is the matter one simply of the *exercise* of the jurisdiction, or did the Court take too wide a view of what it possessed in the way of inherent jurisdiction? Let it be supposed that the Court had invited the parties to argue the point whether France's unilateral statements had created a legal obligation (thus meeting the criticism of the manner of exercise of the jurisdiction), and France had continued to decline to appear. Under Article 53 of the Statute, the absence of France from the proceedings obliged it to 'satisfy itself' that it had jurisdiction—jurisdiction to do whatever it was minded to do. Jurisdiction, once again, is based on consent; can it be said that France, by becoming a party to the Statute, gave its consent in advance to the Court making such a finding as it made in these cases, should the need arise?

We are here in the region of 'deemed' and artificial consents. Accepting the Court's own definition of the purposes for which States parties to the Statute confer preliminary jurisdiction upon it, which purpose was served by the *Nuclear Tests* decisions? The Court explained that

[125] It did protest at what it regarded as the 'leaking' of the decision on the requests for provisional measures to the Australian Government in advance of the delivery of the orders, an incident which caused the Court some embarrassment: see *ICJ Pleadings* in the case, vol. 2, at pp. 369 ff., and the separate opinion of Judge Gros (*ICJ Reports*, 1974, pp. 293–6).

provisions of the Statute and Rules . . . make it clear that the Court can exercise its jurisdiction in contentious proceedings only when a dispute genuinely exists between the parties. In refraining from further action in this case the Court is therefore merely acting in accordance with the proper interpretation of its judicial function,[126]

and, after referring to the *Northern Cameroons* precedent, continued:

It does not enter into the adjudicatory functions of the Court to deal with issues *in abstracto*, once it has reached the conclusion that the merits of the case no longer fall to be determined. The object of the claim having disappeared, there is nothing on which to give judgment.[127]

Thus the purpose referred to is that of ensuring observance of the inherent limitations on the exercise of the judicial function. The preliminary jurisdiction conferred for that purpose exists in order that the purpose may be achieved without the need first to establish the merits jurisdiction. Were the demands of respect for the limitations on the judicial function sufficiently pressing to justify the Court in exercising the preliminary jurisdiction? The Court thought so; and subject to one consideration, it is perhaps not necessary to differ from it on the point. In other words, though the manner of exercise of the jurisdiction was inappropriate (and the actual soundness of its determination of the intention of France to create a legal obligation at least arguable), the jurisdiction it invoked could be said to justify its action.

However, the choice to leave the question of merits jurisdiction unsettled posed one special problem. There is no doubt that the Court was anxious to avoid getting embroiled in the thorny question, noted in a previous article,[128] of the survival of the 1928 General Act for the Pacific Settlement of International Disputes, in view of its wider implications. But the dismissal of the case *in limine* prompted a doubt: if France were not to comply with the obligation which the Court found that it had accepted (and for this to happen, no lack of good faith needed to be imputed, since the Court might have been mistaken as to France's intentions), the applicants would be left without a remedy, France having in the meantime, *ex abundanti cautela*, denounced the General Act. The Court thus included a cryptic paragraph in its decision:

Once the Court has found that a State has entered into a commitment concerning its future conduct it is not the Court's function to contemplate that it will not comply with it. However, the Court observes that if the basis of this Judgment were to be affected, the Applicant could request an examination of the situation in accordance with the provisions of the Statute; the denunciation by France, by letter dated 2 January 1974, of the General Act for the Pacific

[126] *ICJ Reports*, 1974, p. 271, para. 57.
[127] *ICJ Reports*, 1974, pp. 271–2, para. 59.
[128] This *Year Book*, 63 (1992), pp. 94–6; cf. also *Aegean Sea Continental Shelf*, *ICJ Reports*, 1978, p. 17, para. 40, and the separate opinion of Vice-President Nagendra Singh, ibid., p. 46.

Settlement of International Disputes, which is relied on as a basis of jurisdiction in the present case, cannot by itself present an obstacle to the presentation of such a request.[129]

Unfortunately the contingency that the Court could not contemplate in time came to pass, at least in the opinion of the Government of New Zealand, which presented to the Court in 1995 a 'Request for an Examination of the Situation', citing this paragraph and claiming that underground nuclear testing by France in the region constituted a breach of its obligation assumed in 1974.

This request faced the Court with procedural and jurisdictional problems, some of which, in view of the chronological limitation of the decisions the subject of the present series, must be reserved for a later article. The Court in fact found that the 'basis of the Judgment' of 1974 had not been 'affected', and therefore dismissed the request; it did not comment on the source of its jurisdiction to do so. New Zealand argued in favour of the continuation of the 1974 proceedings: and since the merits jurisdiction in the original case had never been established, the Court's jurisdiction in 1995 must have been either the identical jurisdiction it exercised in 1974, or a fresh exercise of the preliminary, inherent jurisdiction. The only point to which attention is drawn here is that if the Court in 1974 had decided whether or not the 1928 General Act was a sufficient basis of jurisdiction, then either (if the answer was negative) it would have dismissed the case for want of jurisdiction, or (if the answer was positive) it could (and presumably would) still have dismissed it for lack of object, on the basis of France's unilaterally assumed obligation. In that case, the paragraph relied on by New Zealand in 1995 would have operated as it had been intended: the basis of jurisdiction would have been a continuing commitment under the General Act, declared to have survived the denunciation.[130]

The lesson of this case would seem to be that the 'mootness' relied on to justify the Court's declining to give judgment in a case ought to be a definitive or irrevocable mootness, and that if it depends on the will of one of the States concerned, greater hesitation should be felt in relying on it in view of the risk of subsequent injustice. It is impossible to say whether, if France had recommenced atmospheric nuclear tests, para. 63 of the judgment given in the New Zealand case would have provided a means of redress: but the procedural problems which arose when New Zealand sought to return to the Court are not encouraging in this respect.

[129] *ICJ Reports*, 1974, p. 272, para. 60 (Australia); ibid., p. 477, para. 63 (New Zealand).

[130] This of course is not without its problems: can the Court tie a State for an indefinite period to the obligations it had assumed under a treaty, but from which it has – perfectly lawfully – freed itself by denouncing the treaty? That however is also a question to be treated on another occasion.

(d) *The* Military and Paramilitary Activities *case*

The United States in this case endeavoured to convince the Court of a proposition going beyond the principle laid down in the *Monetary Gold* case, namely that because of the fundamental rule that the rights and obligations of States may not be determined judicially without their consent, 'a case cannot be allowed to go forward in the absence of "indispensable parties"', such parties being, in the United States contention, Honduras and to a lesser extent El Salvador, in view of the allegations made by Nicaragua against those States of complicity in the use of force against Nicaragua. The Court rejected this extension of the doctrine, in round terms:

> There is no doubt that in appropriate circumstances the Court will decline, as it did in the case concerning *Monetary Gold removed from Rome in 1943,* to exercise the jurisdiction conferred upon it where the legal interests of a State not party to the proceedings 'would not only be affected by the decision, but would form the very subject-matter of the decision' (*I.C.J. Reports 1954,* p. 32). Where however claims of a legal nature are made by an Applicant against a Respondent in proceedings before the Court, and made the subject of submissions, the Court has in principle merely to decide upon those submissions, with binding force for the parties only, and no other State, in accordance with Article 59 of the Statute. . . . [O]ther States which consider that they may be affected are free to institute separate proceedings or to employ the procedure of intervention. There is no trace, either in the Statute or in the practice of international tribunals, of an 'indispensable parties' rule of the kind argued for by the United States, which would only be conceivable in parallel to a power, which the Court does not possess, to direct that a third State be made a party to the proceedings. The circumstances of the *Monetary Gold* case probably represent the limit of the power of the Court to refuse to exercise its jurisdiction; and none of the States referred to can be regarded as in the same position as Albania in that case, so as to be truly indispensable to the pursuance of the proceedings.[131]

It is noticeable that the Court here speaks of the *Monetary Gold* case in terms of the Court 'declining' or 'refusing' to exercise jurisdiction, rather than in terms of the Court being *unable* to exercise the jurisdiction conferred on it. This supports the view that there is no sharp distinction between cases in which the Court is debarred from exercising jurisdiction, and cases in which it may with propriety decline to exercise it, but could, without infringing the principles governing its activity, have taken a different course. The distinction is rather between cases in which the impropriety of exercising jurisdiction is so clear (because the interests of another State would 'form the very subject-matter of the decision') that no discretion is needed or possible, and those in which the Court has to exercise discretion in the sense of weighing up the pros and cons of exercising jurisdiction in the case.

[131] *ICJ Reports,* 1984, p. 431, para. 88.

(e) *The case of the* Land, Island and Maritime Frontier Dispute

In these proceedings, instituted by special agreement between El Salvador and Honduras, Nicaragua sought to intervene under Article 62 of the Statute, and was in fact permitted to do so, subject to certain limitations;[132] in this context the question of the possible impact of the judgment on its rights or interests was of great importance. Analysis of the case in relation to Article 62 of the Statute must await a further article in this series; but the case was unusual in that Nicaragua claimed that not merely would its legal interests be 'affected', as contemplated by Article 62, but that those interests would 'form the very subject-matter of the decision', in the expression used in the *Monetary Gold* case, and that therefore if intervention was refused, the Chamber would have to decline to exercise jurisdiction, at least as regards those aspects of the case which affected Nicaragua's interests. The Chamber did not accept Nicaragua's contentions on this point, and therefore was able to decide freely whether or not Nicaragua should be permitted to intervene. The significance of its rejection of Nicaragua's arguments on the facts has been controversial;[133] the more general point is whether, if it had been shown that Nicaragua's interests would 'form the very subject-matter of the decision', the Chamber would have been compelled to admit the intervention, or would have been justified in rejecting it and then declining to exercise jurisdiction in so far as to do so would affect Nicaragua's interests.

(f) *The case concerning* Certain Phosphate Lands in Nauru

This case (which falls strictly outside the period here studied) raised the problem of what in English law would be called 'joint tortfeasors': it was alleged that unlawful injury had been caused by three States acting together, but proceedings were brought against only one.[134] In 1947 a United Nations trusteeship over Nauru was granted jointly to the United Kingdom, Australia and New Zealand; after independence Nauru claimed that the three States as administering authority had not complied with obligations as to rehabilitation of worked-out phosphate lands. Australia observed that the claim was not against Australia itself, but a claim against the administering authority, and the Court could not therefore pass upon the responsibility of Australia without adjudicating upon the responsibility of New Zealand and the United Kingdom. The question was also raised whether Australia would, in the event of

[132] See the 1990 judgment of the Chamber seised of the case, *ICJ Reports*, 1990, p. 92.

[133] See the dissenting opinion of Judge Schwebel in the *Nauru* case, in which he interprets the Chamber's decision as supporting his view in the latter case rather than that of the majority of the Court: *ICJ Reports*, 1992, pp. 335–7.

[134] As pointed out by Judge Ago in his separate opinion (*ICJ Reports*, 1992, pp. 326–8), why proceedings were brought only against Australia is unexplained: New Zealand had accepted jurisdiction, and the only obstacle to proceedings against the United Kingdom was the 'Commonwealth' reservation in its acceptance, which, in Ago's view, might well have been waived or regarded as obsolete.

judgment against it, be liable for the whole of the damage suffered, or for only a share of it along with the other two States, but this question was reserved by the Court for the merits of the case.[135]

On the question of propriety of exercising jurisdiction, the Court quoted at length from the *Monetary Gold* and *Nicaragua* decisions, and restated the fact that, unlike national courts, it had no 'power to order *proprio motu* the joinder of third parties who may be affected by the decision to be rendered', which would make it possible to 'settle a dispute in the presence of all the parties concerned'.[136] It referred to the possibility of intervention, but noted that the absence of a request for intervention in no way precluded the Court from adjudicating, provided the 'subject-matter of the decision' test is complied with.[137] So far as the case before it was concerned, the Court ruled that

> the interests of New Zealand and the United Kingdom do not constitute the very subject-matter of the judgment to be rendered on the merits of Nauru's Application and the situation is in that respect different from that with which the Court had to deal in the *Monetary Gold* case. In the present case, the determination of the responsibility of New Zealand or the United Kingdom is not a prerequisite for the determination of the responsibility of Australia, the only object of Nauru's claim.[138]

Nor would the Court accept Australia's contention that a *simultaneous* determination of the responsibility of all three States would be just as objectionable as a determination of the responsibility of other States as a *prerequisite* to the determination of Australia's responsibility.

> In the *Monetary Gold* case the link between, on the one hand, the necessary findings regarding Albania's alleged responsibility and, on the other, the decision requested of the Court regarding the allocation of the gold, was not purely temporal but also logical; as the Court explained,
>
> 'In order . . . to determine whether Italy is entitled to receive the gold, it is necessary to determine whether Albania has committed any international wrong against Italy, and whether she is under an obligation to pay compensation to her.' (*I.C.J. Reports 1954*, p. 32).
>
> In the present case, a finding by the Court regarding the existence or the content of the responsibility attributed to Australia by Nauru might well have implications for the legal situation of the other two States concerned, but no finding in respect of that legal situation will be needed as a basis for the Court's decision on Nauru's claims against Australia.[139]

The argument is thus that it is the logical link between the relevant findings which is determinative, not the temporal: if, as in the *Monetary Gold* case, a link in the chain of argument leading to the finding which the

[135] *ICJ Reports*, 1992, p. 258, para. 48.
[136] *ICJ Reports*, 1992, p. 260, para. 53.
[137] *ICJ Reports*, 1992, pp. 260–1, para. 54.
[138] *ICJ Reports*, 1992, p. 261, para. 55.
[139] *ICJ Reports*, 1992, pp. 261–2, para. 55.

Court is asked to make is a finding as to the rights or obligations of an absent State, then that State's interests form 'the very subject-matter of the decision', and the Court must decline to decide. It is however difficult on that basis to see the distinction between the two cases: a link in the necessary chain of argument in the *Nauru* case would seem to be that Australia, as a partner, and indeed the active partner, in the administering authority, had failed to comply with its obligations; this surely signified that the administering authority had so failed, *vis-à-vis* Nauru. While the authority was not a legal entity distinct from its members,[140] it is surely understating the case to say, as does the Court, that a finding as to the responsibility of Australia 'might well have implications for the legal situation' of the other two States concerned. Even on that basis, however, the 'implications for the legal situation' of an absent State are *logical* implications; the difference is merely that it is not necessary *first* to decide something as to the absent State's conduct or situation, and deduce from that the decision in the case; it is necessary, to decide the case, to make a finding which then, *secondarily*, amounts to a statement as to the conduct or situation of the absent State. The difference relied on by the Court is thus not a question of logic, but either a difference of degree (on the basis that 'implications' do not make the other State's interests 'the very subject-matter of the decision'), or temporal after all: on the basis of the Nauru decision, it may not decide *first* that a third State has committed a breach of its obligations, and *then* that the claim before it must be upheld; but it may decide that the claim before it is to be upheld even if it *thereby and simultaneously* rules on the behaviour of an absent State.[140a] Seen in this light, the distinction is unconvincing.

(g) *The* East Timor *case*

The most recent case in which the Court has asserted a discretion to decline to exercise jurisdiction is the *East Timor* case, between Portugal and Australia; again, this case falls outside the period referred to in the title of this series, but to omit any mention of it would be misleading. It will therefore be examined briefly.

Portugal, as the administering power of East Timor, which had been declared a 'non-self-governing territory' within the meaning of Chapter XI of the United Nations Charter, brought proceedings against Australia claiming that Australia had failed to observe the obligation to respect the duties and powers of Portugal as administering power, and the right of the people of East Timor to self-determination. In the background to the case was the Indonesian occupation of the territory, and its purported incorporation of it into Indonesia; Australia had recognized the incorporation *de facto*, and by opening negotiations with Indonesia for the

[140] *ICJ Reports*, 1992, p. 258, para. 47.

[140a] On this point, cf. the dissenting opinion of Judge Schwebel, *ICJ Reports*, 1992, at p. 331.

delimitation of the continental shelf between Australia and East Timor had recognized it *de jure* also. In December 1989 Australia concluded an agreement with Indonesia creating a zone of co-operation for the exploration of the continental shelf between Australia and East Timor.

Australia relied on the *Monetary Gold* case to argue that the Court should not decide the case because this would involve determining the rights and obligations of Indonesia. The Court recalled that 'one of the fundamental principles of its Statute is that it cannot decide a dispute between States without the consent of those States to its jurisdiction'.[141] It took the view that

> Australia's behaviour cannot be assessed without first entering into the question why it is that Indonesia could not lawfully have concluded the 1989 Treaty, while Portugal allegedly could have done so; the very subject-matter of the Court's decision would necessarily be a determination whether, having regard to the circumstances in which Indonesia entered and remained in East Timor, it could or could not have acquired the power to enter into treaties on behalf of East Timor relating to the resources of its continental shelf. The Court could not make such a determination in the absence of the consent of Indonesia.[142]

The conclusion at which the Court therefore arrived was wholly consistent with the *Monetary Gold* precedent: that it 'cannot in the present case exercise the jurisdiction conferred upon it by the declarations made by the Parties under Article 36, paragraph 2, of its Statute to adjudicate upon the dispute referred to it by the Application of the Portuguese Republic'.[143]

An additional element in the case was the argument of Portugal that the rights which Australia had breached were rights *erga omnes*, and that accordingly Portugal could require Australia, individually, to respect them regardless of whether or not another State had conducted itself in a similar unlawful manner.[144] The Court rejected this argument also, over the strong dissent of Judge Weeramantry; this part of the case is of considerable interest for the concept of rights and obligations *erga omnes*, but is not of direct relevance to the question at present under examination.

We may therefore here revert to the question raised above, in connection with the *Monetary Gold* case, of the distinction between absence of jurisdiction and inability of the Court to exercise jurisdiction which it possesses. In the *East Timor* case, as in the *Monetary Gold* case, the State or States which desired a decision of the Court were perfectly

[141] *ICJ Reports*, 1995, p. 101, para. 26. The expression 'fundamental principles of its Statute' is curious, as the Statute does not expressly state the principle. Also, 'the consent of those States to its jurisdiction' is insufficiently precise: the consent required is consent to the determination of the specific dispute or issue.

[142] *ICJ Reports*, 1995, p. 102, para. 28.

[143] *ICJ Reports*, 1995, p. 106, para. 38.

[144] *ICJ Reports*, 1995, p. 102, para. 29.

well aware that, under Article 59 of the Statute, the judgment sought would not be binding on the absent State: in both cases, the circumstances were such that it was not the absent State which was the direct 'target' of the recourse to a judicial finding. It was not sought to obtain a decision against that State which would be relied on or enforced against it; it could therefore be argued that the rights of Albania or Indonesia would not be infringed by a finding of the kind that the Court was asked to make, or certainly not in the same way, or to the same extent, as would be the case were it not protected by Article 50. It is therefore suggested that the *ratio* of the principle laid down is not, or not directly, the protection of the absent State, but rather the 'safeguarding of the judicial function', as the Court put it in the *Northern Cameroons* case. If proceedings had been brought directly against Albania or Indonesia, and the Court had decided that there was no jurisdictional basis, it could proceed no further, in direct application of the rule that there is no jurisdiction without consent. However, in the *Monetary Gold* case, there was jurisdiction between the parties under the Washington Agreement, and in the *East Timor* case there was jurisdiction to decide whether Australia had acted unlawfully; but the answer to the question put could not but involve the absent State. In the *East Timor* case, whether Australia had or had not acted unlawfully depended on the answer to a question the Court was not empowered to decide, namely whether Indonesia was in unlawful occupation of East Timor. Thus the only answer the Court could give would be that *if* Indonesia is in unlawful occupation, then Australia has acted wrongfully; if not, then not. This however would not be a proper decision for a judicial body. The same analysis is valid for the *Monetary Gold* case; one may conclude that the Court was right to express its decision in those cases in the form that it possessed jurisdiction, but could not lawfully exercise it.

(2) *The Court and the Security Council*

Two problems have arisen in recent cases before the Court concerning its relationship with the United Nations Security Council. The first results from the same question or matter being brought simultaneously, or in rapid succession, before the Court and the Security Council; in such circumstances, is there any duty on the Court to defer to the Council, in the sense of declining to give judgment where the Council has been seised, on the basis of a sort of litispendence?[145] The second problem is, or has been categorized as, that of the permissibility of judicial review of the decisions of United Nations organs, and in particular of the Security

[145] Cf. T.J.H. Elsen, *Litispendence between the International Court of Justice and the Security Council* (The Hague, T.M.C.Asser-Institut, 1986).

Council.[146] This latter problem arises if the Court, having been seised of a dispute between two States, and having jurisdiction to hear and determine it, finds that in order to decide the question in dispute it must first ascertain whether a particular decision of the Security Council is or is not valid, that validity forming a step in the legal chain of argument supporting the case of one or other of the parties.

Since this second question has only arisen as a practical problem after the end of the period now under examination, and the Court has yet to give a clear ruling on the point, it will not be discussed further here. What is of interest, in relation to the foregoing discussion, is the nature of the Court's decision to decline to examine the merits of a Security Council resolution. Such a decision might be motivated by an argument of substantive law, e.g. that under the Charter, decisions validly adopted by the Council on the formal level are unchallengeable on the level of legal justification. It might however also be motivated by an argument of procedure or judicial propriety, on the basis that it would be, as it were, unconstitutional for the Court to second-guess another principal organ. What then would be the consequence? If the substantive argument were relied on, the automatic legal conclusion on which the Court's decision would be based would be that the Security Council's decision was valid; if there were serious doubt on this point, the result could be embarrassing for a Court which is directed by its Statute to decide 'in accordance with international law'. The alternative might therefore conceivably be for the Court to decline to exercise its undoubted jurisdiction to determine the dispute on the grounds that this could not be done without calling in question a Security Council decision, rather as the question between Portugal and Australia in the *East Timor* case could not be decided without calling in question the legality of actions of Indonesia.

The question of litispendence, as it may be called for convenience, was first raised in the case concerning the *Aegean Sea Continental Shelf* between Greece and Turkey. Greece brought proceedings to restrain Turkey from carrying out seismic exploration of areas which Greece regarded as part of the continental shelf of Greece, and also requested the indication of provisional measures. Turkey did not appear in the proceedings. In its order declining to indicate provisional measures (for lack of demonstrated 'irreparable prejudice'), the Court referred to the question whether it had power to 'indicate interim measures of protection for the sole purpose of preventing the aggravation or extension of a

[146] See in particular *Questions of Interpretation and Application of the 1971 Montreal Convention arising from the Aerial Incident at Lockerbie (Libyan Arab Jamahirya* v. *United Kingdom)* and the parallel case brought against the United States; cf. Bowett, 'The Court's role in relation to international organizations', *Fifty Years of the International Court of Justice (Festschrift Jennings)* (1996), p. 181; Alvarez, 'Judging the Security Council', *American Journal of International Law*, 90 (1996), p. 1; Akande, 'The International Court of Justice and the Security Council: is there room for judicial control of the United Nations?', *International and Comparative Law Quarterly*, 46 (1997), p. 209.

dispute',[147] and in this connection stated that it 'has cognizance' of the fact that the Security Council had also been seised of the dispute and had adopted a resolution addressed to the two parties: since 'it is not to be presumed that either State will fail to heed its obligations under the Charter of the United Nations or fail to heed the recommendations of the Security Council addressed to them with respect to their present dispute', the matter could be left there.[148] This was thus not a case of the Court refraining from acting because of a litispendence with the Security Council; the action taken by the Security Council, on the facts of the case, made it unnecessary for the Court to deal with a particular issue.[149]

(a) *The case of the* United States Diplomatic and Consular Staff in Tehran

It will be recalled that Iran declined to appear in the proceedings in this case, and did not therefore raise any question of litispendence in relation to the Security Council. The Court, however,

> has also thought it right to examine, *ex officio*, whether its competence to decide the present case, or the admissibility of the present proceedings, might possibly have been affected by the setting up of the Commission announced by the Secretary-General of the United Nations.[150]

The Commission in question was set up on 20 February 1980 to undertake a fact-finding mission to Iran; it was, at the time of the Court's decision, the culmination of action in the United Nations Security Council, including Resolutions 457 and 461 of 1979, calling upon Iran to remedy the illegal situation in Tehran, and requesting the Secretary-General to use his good offices. The Court refers only to the setting-up of the Commission; but from the further discussion in the judgment, it is clear that it was concerned with the broader question of parallel action in the Security Council and before the Court.

The Court noted in this respect that the Security Council was fully aware of what was going on at The Hague when it took its own action.

> [T]he Security Council expressly took into account the Court's Order of 15

[147] A question answered in the affirmative by a Chamber of the Court in the *Frontier Dispute* between Burkina Faso and Mali (*ICJ Reports*, 1986, p. 3), a decision followed by the full Court in the case concerning the *Land and Maritime Boundary between Cameroon and Nigeria, ICJ Reports*, 1998, pp. 22–3, para. 41.

[148] *ICJ Reports*, 1976, pp. 12–13, paras. 37–43.

[149] Judge Tarazi, in a separate opinion, referred to the action of the Security Council, and urged the Court to take into consideration its position as 'an integral part of the United Nations', in terms which suggest that he was sympathetic to the idea that the Court should, as a matter of principle, not act when the Security Council is acting in the matter; but he does not go so far as to state as much.

[150] *ICJ Reports*, 1980, p. 20, para. 39. Apart from the reference to admissibility, it is noticeable that the Court contemplates the possibility of its 'competence' being 'affected', rather than there being a possible obstacle to the *exercise* of its competence; but too much attention should perhaps not be given to the choice of words in this purely introductory sentence.

December 1979 indicating provisional measures; and it does not seem to have occurred to any member of the Council that there was or could be anything irregular in the simultaneous exercise of their respective functions by the Court and the Security Council. Nor is there in this any cause for surprise.[151]

In itself, this argument amounts to no more than suggesting tolerance on the part of the Council, with the implication that the Court might be obliged to refrain from competing with the Security Council if the Council in a particular instance, where questions of the maintenance of international peace and security arose, considered that it should do so.

It has in fact been suggested that the Council might be authorized by the Charter to request the Court to suspend its proceedings pending the proceedings in the Council, or to order the parties to refrain from bringing their dispute to the Court.[152] Whether the Court would be obliged to comply with such a request must be, to say the least, doubtful. Elsen concedes that it would not be so bound, but that the same effect would be achieved through a directive to the parties; Klein pursues the same line of thought, arguing that if the Court must take account of *inter partes* reservations to jurisdiction, it must also respect limitations on its dealing with a case imposed from outside which are binding on the parties. This however confers a *jus cogens* character on such limitations, which may be a correct analysis in the context of the 'primary responsibility' of the Security Council for international peace and security, but cannot be taken as axiomatic.

However, in the *Tehran* case the Court went on to say that

Whereas Article 12 of the Charter expressly forbids the General Assembly to make any recommendation with regard to a dispute or situation while the Security Council is exercising its functions in respect of that dispute or situation, no such restriction is placed on the functioning of the Court by any provision of either the Charter or the Statute of the Court. The reasons are clear. It is for the Court, the principal judicial organ of the United Nations, to resolve any legal questions that may be in issue between the parties to the dispute; and the resolution of such legal questions by the Court may be an important, and sometimes decisive, factor in promoting the peaceful settlement of the dispute. This is indeed recognized by Article 36 of the Charter . . . .[153]

In the course of an examination in detail of the proceedings in New York and of the Secretary-General's Commission, the Court however indicated another possible reason why it might have been alleged that the exercise of its competence might be affected by these proceedings. It noted that in all the circumstances described,

[151] *ICJ Reports*, 1980, p. 21, para. 40.

[152] See Elsen, *Litispendence between the International Court of Justice and the Security Council* (T.M.C.Asser Institute, The Hague, 1986); Klein, 'Paralleles Tätigwerden von Sicherheitsrat und Internationalem Gerichtshof bei friedensbedrohenden Streitigkeiten', *Völkerrecht als Rechtsordnung Internationale Gerichtsbarkeit Menschenrechte, Festschrift für Hermann Mosler* (Berlin 1983), p. 481.

[153] *ICJ Reports*, 1980, p. 22, para. 40.

it can find no trace of any understanding on the part of either the United States or Iran that the establishment of the Commission might involve a postponement of all proceedings before the Court until the conclusion of the work of the Commission and of the Security Council's consideration of the matter.[154]

The word 'understanding' is ambiguous. It might mean that the two parties did not *suppose* that that would be the legal position, independently of their intentions or wishes; it might also mean that there was no trace of agreement between them that there should be a postponement. The French text[155] supports the first interpretation; but the second seems the more likely.

The Court's conclusion on the whole question of the relevance of the action in the Security Council and the Commission was that

neither the mandate given by the Security Council to the Secretary-General in resolutions 457 and 461 of 1979, nor the setting up of the Commission by the Secretary-General, can be considered as constituting any obstacle to the exercise of the Court's jurisdiction in the present case.[156]

(b) *The case of* Military and Paramilitary Activities

In the *Nicaragua* case, the allegations made against the United States included that of the unlawful use of force, and since the Charter confers primary responsibility on the Security Council for the maintenance of international peace and security (Article 24, paragraph 1, of the Charter), this provided an added dimension to the question whether the Court should disseise itself in favour of the Council, or refrain from exercising jurisdiction so long as the Council was dealing with the matter. Furthermore, since a draft resolution had been presented to the Council, which corresponded to the claim of Nicaragua before the Court, but had failed to achieve the requisite majority, Nicaragua's claim, the United States argued, amounted to an appeal to the Court from an adverse decision of the Council.

On the first question, the Court quoted and followed the decision in the *Tehran Hostages* case, observing that it was 'of the view that the fact that a matter is before the Security Council should not prevent it being dealt with by the Court and that both proceedings could be pursued *pari passu*'.[157] It slightly weakened the force of this finding by having recourse to an additional argument, peculiar to the facts of the specific case, namely that no notification had been made under Chapter VII of the Charter, and that thus Nicaragua's complaint 'is not about an ongoing

[154] *ICJ Reports*, 1980, p. 23, para. 42.

[155] '. . . la Cour ne découvre aucun élément faisant apparaître que les Etats-Unis ou l'Iran aient cru comprendre que la constitution de la Commission pourrait entraîner la suspension de toute procédure devant la Cour . . . '. The English text was the authoritative text, and the French the translation.

[156] *ICJ Reports*, 1980, pp. 23–4, para. 44.

[157] *ICJ Reports*, 1984, p. 433, para. 93.

armed conflict between it and the United States, but one requiring, and indeed demanding, the peaceful settlement of disputes between two States', and the Court concluded that 'Hence, it is properly brought before the principal judicial organ of the Organization for peaceful settlement'.[158] This however does not really answer the point that the circumstances might nevertheless be such that the judicial settlement of the dispute might appropriately wait upon the prior exercise by the Security Council of its special responsibilities.

5. *Jurisdiction in relation to the Decisions of Other Tribunals*

Sir Gerald Fitzmaurice observed in his 1962 article in this series that 'It is but seldom that an ordinary international tribunal will be called upon to determine any matter relating to the competence of another such tribunal'.[159] Yet during the period surveyed in his articles he was able to draw attention to three cases (and five 'phases' of cases in all) in which problems of this type had arisen.[160] In the period now under review, questions falling into this category have again arisen, but with one important difference. The cases studied by Fitzmaurice all concerned the period prior to the establishment of the other tribunal concerned in the matter, and consequently no question arose as to the validity or otherwise of any decision, jurisdictional or other, of that tribunal—indeed, in only one of the cases (*Ambatielos*) did the tribunal ever sit. More recently, the Court has been concerned with decisions already given by another judicial (or arbitral) body, and has been seised, either by way of appeal (*Appeal relating to the Jurisdiction of the ICAO Council*) or by way of *action en nullité* directed against the earlier decision (*Arbitral Award made by the King of Spain; Arbitral Award of 31 July 1989*). In addition, three applications were made to the Court for review by way of advisory opinion of judgments of the UN Administrative Tribunal under Article 11 of the Statute of that Tribunal.[161] These last present rather different features as regards jurisdiction, and will not be dealt with here (but see below, text and note 168).

Under the 1946 Rules of Court, the possibility of appeal to the Court 'against a decision given by some other tribunal' was expressly provided for in Article 67: but this provision disappeared without explanation in the course of the 1978 revision of the Rules of Court, to be replaced by

[158] *ICJ Reports*, 1984, p. 434, para. 94.

[159] 'Hersch Lauterpacht—The Scholar as Judge II', this *Year Book*, 38 (1962), p. 57: *Collected Edition*, II, p. 761.

[160] The two phases of the *Interpretation of Peace Treaties* case; the two phases of the *Ambatielos* case; and the *Interhandel* case.

[161] *Application for Review of Judgment No. 158 of the United Nations Administrative Tribunal [Fasla]*, *ICJ Reports*, 1973, p. 166: id., *Judgment No. 273 [Mortished]*, *ICJ Reports*, 1982, p. 325; id., *Judgment No. 333 [Yakimetz]*, *ICJ Reports*, 1987, p. 18.

a text headed rather obscurely 'Special Reference to the Court' (subsection 5, Article 87). This latter text contemplates a case in which 'in accordance with a treaty or convention in force a contentious case is brought before the Court concerning a matter which has been the subject of proceedings before some other international body',[162] and makes no more effective provision for such a case than by saying that 'the provisions of the Statute and of the Rules governing contentious cases shall apply'. Neither Article 67 of the 1946 Rules nor Article 87 of the 1978 Rules has ever been cited or referred to in a judgment of the Court.

(1) *The* Appeal Relating to the Jurisdiction of the ICAO Council

In this case, the appeal was brought, as the title of the case indicates, against a decision of that body; the governing texts were Article 84 of the Chicago Convention on Civil Aviation, and Section 2 of Article II of the related International Air Services Transit Agreement of 1944. Article 84 provided in terms that 'Any contracting State may . . . appeal from the decision of the Council to an *ad hoc* tribunal agreed upon with the other parties to the dispute or to the Permanent Court of International Justice';[163] the Transit Agreement referred disagreements over its interpretation and application to the provisions of the Chicago Convention for dispute settlement, including Article 84. As already noted, no reference to Article 67 of the Rules was made in the judgment; it might perhaps have been thought that the reference to 'a decision given by some other *tribunal*' was inappropriate to cover a decision of the ICAO Council, but, it is suggested, this would not be a sound view, since the Council, whatever its intrinsic nature and other functions, was clearly sitting as a judicial body when it took the decision attacked.[164] The Court seems to have taken for granted that it was qualified to carry out the appeal functions entrusted to it by the Chicago Convention; it would presumably however have endorsed the view stated in the separate opinion of Judge Onyeama, that

[162] The wording would seem to be wide enough to cover cases where parallel action is taken before the Court and the Security Council, provided there have been some 'proceedings' before the Security Council at the time that the Court is seised. On the implications of such parallel action, see section 4 (2) above.

[163] As between the parties (India and Pakistan) the effect of Article 37 of the ICJ Statute was to substitute the ICJ for the PCIJ in this provision. On the operation of Article 37, see section 6 below.

[164] For Judges Lachs and Jiménez de Aréchaga, the Council was performing 'quasi-judicial' functions (declaration of Judge Lachs appended to judgment, *ICJ Reports*, 1972, p. 74; separate opinion of Judge Jiménez, ibid., p. 153). One procedural problem which is connected with the categorization of the functions of the Council as judicial is that it was contended that, under the relevant constitutional provisions, the decision had to be adopted by a statutory majority of 14 votes. This could lead, as pointed out by Judge Dillard (*ICJ Reports*, 1972, p. 100), to paralysis of the decision-making powers, which may be acceptable in a political context (where if no decision is taken, things are presumably left as they were) but is unacceptable in a judicial body, where a yes-or-no answer has to be given.

The International Court of Justice is not, in the Charter of the United Nations of which the Statute of the Court is an integral part, designated a court of appeal, and its competence to hear an appeal from some other tribunal depends entirely on the terms of the agreement of the parties to refer a case to it by way of appeal from the decision of the tribunal concerned. Whether the Court can entertain a particular appeal is therefore a matter to be settled in the light of the intention of the parties as evidenced by the express terms of the agreement, and is not, in my view, based on considerations of principle or doctrine.[165]

One might carry this argument further: the term 'appeal' may not always carry precisely the same significance in all circumstances, and what powers exactly are conferred on the Court by a treaty requiring it to act on appeal must be determined by interpretation of the relevant instrument. On one issue the Court in the *ICAO Council* case was in fact divided as to what its role as an appeal tribunal entailed; India had contended not only that the decision of the ICAO Council upholding its jurisdiction was erroneous, but also that it was in any event 'vitiated by various procedural irregularities, and should accordingly, on that ground alone, be declared null and void'. India argued that 'but for these alleged irregularities, the result before the Council would or might have been different'.[166] The Court did not however even examine these contentions:

The Court however does not deem it necessary or even appropriate to go into this matter, particularly as the alleged irregularities do not prejudice in any fundamental way the requirements of a just procedure. The Court's task in the present proceedings is to give a ruling as to whether the Council has jurisdiction in the case. This is an objective question of law, the answer to which cannot depend on what occurred before the Council. Since the Court holds that the Council did and does have jurisdiction, then, if there were in fact procedural irregularities, the position would be that the Council would have reached the right conclusion in the wrong way. Nevertheless it would have reached the right conclusion. If, on the other hand, the Court had held that there was and is no jurisdiction, then, even in the absence of any irregularities, the Council's decision to assume it would have stood reversed.[167]

On the limited question of the relevance of procedural irregularities in the processes leading up to the seising of the Court, this approach may be contrasted with that adopted in 1982 in the *Mortished* case, where irregularities affecting both the United Nations Administrative Tribunal proceedings and the proceedings of the Committee on Applications for Review of UNAT Judgments (the body which had requested the opinion) were very carefully reviewed, even though the Court decided that it was seised of a valid request for opinion, and should give the

[165] *ICJ Reports*, 1972, p. 86.
[166] *ICJ Reports*, 1972, p. 69, para. 44.
[167] *ICJ Reports*, 1972, pp. 69–70, para. 45.

opinion requested.[168] Be that as it may, the most striking aspect of this passage is the idea that the Court is asked to rule on 'an objective question of law', rather than to say whether the decision of the Council was right or wrong. This would seem to imply that if, on the non-procedural aspects of the case, the Court had held the Council's own reasons for finding that it had jurisdiction to be unsound, but considered that, for different reasons, the Council had nevertheless possessed jurisdiction, the Court would have so ruled, rather than sending the matter back for re-hearing. This is not necessarily inconsistent with the role of a court of appeal; in terms of Article 84, the point is whether 'appeal from the decision' means 'ask the Court to rule whether the decision, on its own terms, was right or wrong' or 'ask the Court to decide *de novo* on the point which was the subject of the decision'. The former would seem to be the more appropriate reading of the term 'appeal', particularly in the light of the Court's own declaration that the appeal system under the Chicago Convention was directed to giving member States 'and through them the Council, the possibility of ensuring a certain measure of supervision by the Court over [the Council's] decisions'.[169]

But India's argument was that the Council's decision was null and void, that is to say that there was no decision of the Council, whether correct or incorrect. Assuming for the moment that India's claim to this effect was justified, was it open to the Court, acting by way of appeal, to settle the 'objective question of law' which, under Article 84 of the Convention, was to be determined in the first instance by the Council, when the Council had not settled it by any valid decision of its own? The Court indeed, in the passage quoted above, seems to have attempted to hedge its bets by including the sentence to the effect that 'the alleged irregularities do not prejudice in any fundamental way the requirements of a just procedure';[170] the implication seems to be that there was thus a decision to be appealed from even if perhaps voidable, or reached by unsatisfactory means. If an appeal were brought to the Court from a Council decision *solely* on the ground that the decision was void for procedural irregularities, it is difficult to see the Court simply substituting its own decision for that of the Council, on the ground that all that had to be determined was an 'objective question of law'. Does it make a difference that India was arguing simultaneously that there was no valid decision, and that (if there was) that decision was ill-founded?

One judge who expressed disagreement with the Court's handling of

[168] *Application for Review of UNAT Judgment No. 273*, advisory opinion, *ICJ Reports*, 1982, pp. 340–7. paras. 33–45.

[169] *ICJ Reports*, 1972, p. 60, para. 26.

[170] How it could determine that that was so without having 'gone into' the matter of the alleged irregularities is not at all clear; this objection was made very forcibly in the dissenting opinion of Judge Morozov (*ICJ Reports*, 1972, p. 158), who equated the Court's argument with the idea that 'the end justifies the means' (ibid., p. 159).

this question was Judge Jiménez de Aréchaga: in his separate opinion, he stated that he found the Court's view—that it was not necessary or appropriate to go into the matter of the procedural irregularities—'too limited' a view 'of the powers and duties of the Court when functioning as a court of appeal'.[171] He supported this by appealing, perfectly correctly, it is submitted, to the text under which the Court was seised:

> The right of appeal granted by Article 84 of the Chicago Convention comprises not only the right to obtain a pronouncement from the Court on whether the decision of first instance is correct from the point of view of substantive law but also on whether that decision was validly adopted in accordance with the essential principles of procedure which must govern the quasi-judicial function entrusted to the organ of first instance.[172]

An alternative reading of Article 84, whereby appeal would be limited to determining the substantive validity of Council decisions, would be perfectly sustainable: what is unfortunate is that the Court did not base itself on such an approach, or indeed on Article 84 at all, but on what looks like a sort of general principle of procedural economy the legal basis of which is undetermined.

That the Court can, in general, and in the context of contentious proceedings, entertain an appeal where there is an appropriate international treaty-instrument to support this is thus clearly established by the *ICAO Council* case; which makes it the more inexplicable that six years later the Court abolished Article 67 of the 1946 Rules. Appeal was not however the only way in which it might be asked to review the proceedings or decisions of other tribunals; in 1960 it had been seised by special agreement[173] of a dispute between Honduras and Nicaragua arising out of an arbitral award given by the King of Spain on 23 December 1906.

(2) *The case of the* Arbitral Award made by the King of Spain

In this case, Honduras asked for a declaration that Nicaragua was under an obligation to give effect to the 1906 award, while Nicaragua pleaded that the award 'does not possess the character of a binding arbitral award', and that it was 'in any case incapable of execution by reason of its omissions, contradictions and obscurities'.[174] The Court's

[171] *ICJ Reports*, 1972, p. 153, para. 37.

[172] *ICJ Reports*, 1972, p. 153, para. 37. He also pointed out the inconsistency, already mentioned, with the Court's analysis of the appeal procedure as directed to ensuring 'a certain measure of supervision by the Court' over the decisions of the Council, a point also raised by Judge Lachs (declaration, ibid., p. 75).

[173] This is somewhat of a simplification of what happened; further explanation will be reserved for a future article on procedural questions.

[174] *ICJ Reports*, 1960, pp. 204–5.

finding was that the award was valid and binding, and that Nicaragua was under an obligation to give effect to it.

Nicaragua's first arguments were that the King of Spain had never been invested with the powers of an arbitrator, because he was not designated arbitrator in conformity with the provisions of the relevant treaty between the parties (the Gámez-Bonilla Treaty of 7 October 1894), and secondly because that Treaty had lapsed before the King agreed to act as arbitrator. These are questions relating to the constitution of an arbitral body, akin to those that arose in the *Peace Treaties, Ambatielos,* and *Interhandel* cases: they do not concern us here. But Nicaragua went on to argue that the award made by the King was a nullity, being vitiated by (a) excess of jurisdiction; (b) essential error; and (c) lack or inadequacy of reasons in support of the conclusions arrived at by the Arbitrator; as already noted, Nicaragua also argued that the award was incapable of execution. The Court based its decision upholding the binding character of the award primarily on Nicaragua's recognition of it as valid; but it did also reject the arguments of nullity. When doing so, it clearly stated its view of its function in this respect:

> [T]he Court will observe that the Award is not subject to appeal and that the Court cannot approach the consideration of the objections raised by Nicaragua to the validity of the award as a Court of Appeal. The Court is not called upon to pronounce on whether the arbitrator's decision was right or wrong. These and cognate considerations have no relevance to the function that the Court is called upon to discharge in these proceedings, which is to decide whether the Award is proved to be a nullity having no effect.[175]

There may be a question whether the Court was here making any general statement of its powers, or merely had in view the jurisdiction specifically conferred on it, or was concerned with the proper interpretation of the Gámez-Bonilla Treaty which provided for the possibility of arbitration. Reserving that question, this statement could be read as no more than an expression of the principle *ne ultra petita*: if the Court was not asked to say whether the arbitrator's decision was right or wrong, then it would have been improper for it to do so, even assuming that it had the power to do so. What did Nicaragua ask it to do? It asked the Court to declare the award a nullity, for reasons most of which have nothing to do with whether the actual decision was right or wrong (failure to observe the powers conferred by the Treaty, etc.). It did however also contend that the award was a nullity by reason of 'essential error'. The Court had some difficulty establishing what this was, but concluded that it related 'to no more than evaluation of documents and of other evidence submitted to the arbitrator'; but 'The appraisal of the probative value of documents and evidence appertained to the discre-

[175] *ICJ Reports*, 1960, p. 214.

tionary power of the arbitrator and is not open to question'.[176] There is however in any event a clear distinction between asking for a declaration that an award is a nullity because of 'essential error'—which presumably means more than that the arbitrator got something wrong—and appealing against the decision, and asking for it either to be set aside or corrected on the basis simply that it is wrong. The decision in the *King of Spain* case does not, therefore, constitute a ruling that the Court cannot in principle act as a court of appeal from an arbitral award.

(3) *The case of the* Arbitral Award of 31 July 1989

In August 1989, Guinea-Bissau filed an application instituting proceedings[177] against Senegal in relation to an arbitral award delivered on 31 July 1989 by a three-member arbitral tribunal pursuant to an arbitration agreement between the two States dated 12 March 1985. Guinea-Bissau contended that the award was 'inexistent' [*frappé d'inexistence*] because one of the two arbitrators composing the majority had expressed a view, in an appended declaration, in contradiction with the one apparently adopted by the vote; and that it was 'absolutely null and void', for the following reason. The arbitration agreement had put two questions to the arbitrators:

1. Does the Agreement concluded by an exchange of letters on 26 April 1960, and which relates to the maritime boundary, have the force of law in the relations between the Republic of Guinea-Bissau and the Republic of Senegal?
2. *In the event of a negative answer to the first question*, what is the course of the line delimiting the maritime territories appertaining to the Republic of Guinea-Bissau and the Republic of Senegal respectively?[178]

The source of the trouble was the italicized words at the beginning of the second question. It had presumably been assumed, when the arbitration agreement was drafted, that the answer to the first question would be yes or no; but in fact, the answer given by the arbitral tribunal was 'yes, but only partly'. The problem faced by the tribunal was thus whether or not it should reply to the second question; and its conclusion was that 'it is not called upon to reply' to that question.[179] The President of the tribunal, in a declaration appended to its award, indicated that he would have preferred a slightly different wording of the reply to the first question, which, in his view, 'would have enabled the Tribunal to deal in

[176] *ICJ Reports*, 1960, pp. 215–16.

[177] The decision in this case falls strictly outside the period covered by these articles, but it is too important as a sequel to the other cases discussed to be reserved for later treatment.

[178] *ICJ Reports*, 1991, p. 58 (emphasis added).

[179] Para. 87 of the award, quoted in *ICJ Reports*, 1991, p. 60, para. 17.

its Award with the second question put by the Arbitration Agreement'.[180] It was on this basis that Guinea-Bissau contended that the award was 'inexistent' or 'null and void'.

The basis of jurisdiction of the Court invoked by Guinea-Bissau was the two Optional Clause declarations deposited by the parties; and the declaration of Senegal excluded 'Disputes in regard to which the parties have agreed to have recourse to some other method of settlement'. Senegal therefore observed that 'if Guinea-Bissau were to challenge the decision of the Arbitral Tribunal on the merits, it would be raising a question excluded from the Court's jurisdiction by the terms of Senegal's declaration', since the parties had agreed that the questions put to the arbitral tribunal should be settled by that tribunal. However, the parties were agreed that it was not the substantive dispute relating to maritime delimitation which was the subject of the proceedings before the Court, but a dispute relating to the award.

Guinea-Bissau also took the position, which Senegal accepted, that these proceedings are not intended by way of appeal from the Award or as an application for revision of it . . .

In this respect the Court would emphasize that, as the Parties were both agreed, these proceedings allege the inexistence and nullity of the Award rendered by the Arbitration Tribunal and are not by way of appeal from it or application for revision of it. As the Court had occasion to observe with respect to the contention of nullity advanced in the case of the *Arbitral Award Made by the King of Spain on 23 December 1906* . . . [181]

and the Court then set out the passage from its judgment in that case which has already been reproduced above.

Later in its judgment the Court reviewed a contention by Guinea-Bissau challenging the validity of the reasoning adopted by the tribunal on the issue whether it was required to answer the second question.

By its argument set out above, Guinea-Bissau is in fact criticizing the interpretation in the Award of the provisions of the Arbitration Agreement which determine the Tribunal's jurisdiction, and proposing another interpretation. However, the Court does not have to enquire whether or not the Arbitration Agreement could, with regard to the Tribunal's competence, be interpreted in a number of ways, and if so to consider which would have been preferable. By proceeding in that way the Court would be treating the request as an appeal and not as a *recours en nullité*. The Court could not act in that way in the present case. It has simply to ascertain whether by rendering the disputed Award the Tribunal acted in manifest breach of the competence conferred on it by the Arbitration Agreement, either by deciding in excess of, or by failing to exercise, its jurisdiction.

Such manifest breach might result from, for example, the failure of the

[180] Quoted in *ICJ Reports*, 1991, p. 60, para. 19.
[181] *ICJ Reports*, 1991, p. 62, paras. 24–5.

Tribunal properly to apply the relevant rules of interpretation to the provisions of the Arbitration Agreement which govern its competence.[182]

The Court examined Guinea-Bissau's arguments in this light, and concluded that the tribunal 'did not act in manifest breach of its competence', and that Guinea-Bissau's contentions had therefore to be rejected.

The Court was thus at pains to emphasize that it was not acting, and could not in this case act, as a court of appeal. Was this merely because of the existence of the reservation in Senegal's acceptance of jurisdiction, excluding matters as to which the parties had agreed some other means of settlement? The Court's emphatic statement of the position as recorded in its decision in the *King of Spain* case suggests more a position of principle. Also, while it was clear that Senegal's reservation excluded consideration of the merits of the dispute defined in the Arbitration Agreement, it was less clear that it excluded consideration of a problem of competence which the arbitrators had in fact had to consider, but which was not in terms referred to them by that Agreement. They were acting in exercise of the *compétence de la compétence*, which, despite its restatement in Article 36, paragraph 6, of the Statute, is generally recognized to exist independently of any agreement of the parties to an arbitral or judicial proceeding.[183] At least, one might have expected the point to be spelled out in the judgment. As it is, one has the impression that the Court was convinced either that it could not, as a matter of principle, act as a court of appeal (though this would be inconsistent with the *ICAO Council* decision), or that it could not do so on the jurisdictional basis of declarations—whatever their terms—under Article 36, paragraph 2, of the Statute.[184]

[182] *ICJ Reports*, 1991, p. 69, paras. 48–9.

[183] Thus the Court referred to Article 4, paragraph 2, of the Agreement establishing the Tribunal, not as conferring a power for the Tribunal to determine its own jurisdiction, but as *confirming* that it had that power: *ICJ Reports*, 1991, p. 69, para. 46; cf. above, pp. 18–19. Judge Shahabuddeen however, in his separate opinion in the case of the *Arbitral Award of 31 July 1989* reaches the opposite conclusion, that the power is based on 'the actual or presumed will of the parties' (*ICJ Reports*, 1991, p. 109). Fitzmaurice mentioned as one possible objection, with which he showed some sympathy, to the principle, that the *compétence de la compétence* 'is scarcely consistent with the fundamental principle that the jurisdiction of an international tribunal is derived from and depends on the will of the parties; for if the tribunal determines a jurisdictional issue itself, it will in most cases do so contrary to the expressed views and wishes of at least one, and possibly both, of the parties': this *Year Book*, 34 (1958), p. 27 (footnotes omitted); *Collected Edition*, II, p. 453. This does however seem to confuse the prior consent 'to Statute' with the immediate consent 'to seisin'.

[184] '[L]a Cour de La Haye ne peut avoir la qualité d'une instance d'appel, de cassation ou de révision, que si les Parties en cause lui ont expressément confié cette fonction': Guggenheim, 'La validité et la nullité des actes juridiques internationaux', *Recueil des cours*, 74 (1949–I), p. 217, referring to S. Rundstein, 'La Cour permanente de justice internationale comme instance de recours', *Recueil des cours*, 43 (1933–I), pp. 72 ff.

This latter view was indeed that of Judge Mbaye, who appeared to doubt whether even the more limited role the Court had adopted in the case was justifiable on that jurisdictional basis:

I fail to see why the International Court of Justice should automatically constitute itself a *cour de cassation* for all States having made declarations under Article 36, paragraph 2, of its Statute, with respect to all arbitral awards in cases to which those States are parties, even if the Court were each time to take care not to act as a court of appeal or as one revising the award. That the need to decide a 'question of international law' has been raised is surely not sufficient justification for such an inroad into another means of dispute settlement between States.[185]

Following up this approach, let us consider what would have been the position (independently of the reservation in the declaration of Senegal) if Guinea-Bissau had asked the Court, by way of appeal, to rejudge the question of the applicability of the 1960 exchange of letters. That would be a 'question of law'; but as between the parties, it would be a question already settled by a decision having the force of *res judicata*. Since the parties were bound by that decision, then, so long as they did not both agree to invite the Court to reopen it, the Court would also be bound by the decision; and the only decision it could give, on the basis of the jurisdiction conferred by the Optional Clause, would be that the position was determined by the award of the arbitral tribunal—even if the majority of the Members of the Court (or indeed the Court unanimously) were of the view that the decision of the tribunal had been mistaken. It should not be overlooked that, as the Permanent Court stated, and as was recalled in the *Frontier Dispute* case, a judicial decision 'is simply an alternative to the direct and friendly settlement' of the dispute between the parties, so that it 'merely substitutes for the solution stemming directly from their shared intention, the solution arrived at by a court under the mandate which they have given it'.[186] If Guinea-Bissau and Senegal had agreed as to the extent of the application of the 1960 exchange of letters, that agreement would define it as a matter of law between them, and could not be reopened by the Court in subsequent proceedings (unless they agreed so to reopen it[187]); similarly, the

[185] Declaration of Judge Mbaye, *ICJ Reports*, 1991, p. 80

[186] *Frontier Dispute, ICJ Reports*, 1986, p. 577, para. 46, quoting *PCIJ*, Series A, No. 22, p. 13.

[187] Cf. the 'voeu' proposed to the League Assembly in 1930 by the Committee set up to examine the question of recourse procedures against arbitral awards: 'dans les cas où . . . le Conseil constate que la validité de la sentence est contestée par l'une des Parties, il invite les Parties à *conclure un compromis* en vue de soumettre cette constatation à la Cour permanente de justice internationale . . .' (emphasis added). This correctly provides for the creation of new and specific jurisdiction to re-open the award.

decision, which they had agreed to accept, of the arbitral tribunal on the point could only be restated, not reopened.[188]

This analysis clarifies the distinction between the *ICAO Council* case, in which the Court acted as a court of appeal without the slightest self-questioning on the point, and the *King of Spain* and *Arbitral Award* cases, in which the Court was extraordinarily insistent that it was not acting as such a court. In the *ICAO Council* case, the force as *res judicata* of the decision of the Council was tempered by the express reservation in Article 84 of the Chicago Convention of the possibility of appeal to the Court, a reservation which presupposed that the Court would not be bound by the Council's decision, but would be entitled, and indeed expected, to re-examine the dispute on its merits. It does not however do away with all difficulties: in particular, how was the problem in the *Arbitral Award* case of the correctness or otherwise of the arbitral tribunal's view of its competence to be handled?

In the *ICAO Council* case, there was some division of views within the Court on the question whether Article 84 of the Convention authorized appeal on a preliminary decision as to the competence of the Council, or only appeal from the ultimate decision on the merits of the dispute. The views on either side on this question were however premised on the assumption that the question was solely one of the interpetation of Article 84. It was assumed, and, it is suggested, rightly, that if Article 84 had not provided for appeal, no appeal could have been brought; or perhaps, as suggested above, that any attempt to seise the Court, on whatever jurisdictional basis, of the question whether the Council had decided correctly, would be met by the plea (or indeed the finding) that whether academically correct or not, the Council's decision had the force of *res judicata*. This implies (though the point was probably not consciously appreciated) that the need for an express provision for appeal, by way of exception to the principle of *res judicata*, applied just as much to a decision on the Council's jurisdiction as to a decision on the merits of the dispute. Setting aside for a moment the jurisdictional question, it could be argued that the interpretation of Article 84 in this respect was immaterial since, as shown by the later *Arbitral Award* case, the Court can, without acting as a court of appeal, examine the findings

[188] It would presumably be possible for a State which had obtained an award of an arbitral body in its favour to bring proceedings before the Court against the other party, on the basis of a non-specific title of jurisdiction, to ask for a declaration that the award was binding (as was done by Senegal in the case of the *Arbitral Award of 31 July 1989*, but only in response to Guinea-Bissau's claim that it was void); the objective might be to obtain the benefit of Article 94 of the Charter. Cf. however the decision of the US-Iran Claims Tribunal in *Bendone-Derossi* v. *Iran*, *Iran-US Claims Tribunal Reports*, vol. 6, p. 130, rejecting a similar claim at the provisional measures stage; that decision was based on the grounds that the enforcement contemplated was on the municipal level, so that what was sought was a kind of *exequatur*, which the Tribunal could not give: it could not invest the awards of other tribunals 'with any validity or status under any system of national law that those awards do not already possess' (loc. cit., at p. 133). This ruling was followed in *Marks & Umman* v. *Iran*, *Iran-US Claims Tribunal Reports*, vol. 8, p. 296.

of another judicial body as to its own competence. However, in the first place, the extent of the Court's interference on this basis was, as we have seen, limited; and secondly, it must have a general basis of jurisdiction to act at all. It must therefore be concluded that the Court's handling of Article 84 in the *ICAO Council* case does not carry any implication as to the extent of its powers independently of a specific treaty provision contemplating appeal.

Is there any distinction between the force of *res judicata* attaching to the decision of a judicial body on the merits of a dispute submitted to it, and that attaching to any decision it may have to make on its own jurisdiction? In practical terms, the result of accepting Guinea-Bissau's arguments as to the *excès de pouvoir* committed by the tribunal would have been the nullity of the award, i.e. the disappearance of a decision having the force of *res judicata* on the merits.[189] It was because the Court's decision on jurisdiction and admissibility in the *Military and Paramilitary Activities in and against Nicaragua* case had the force of *res judicata* that the United States remained a party to the proceedings and was equally bound by the *res judicata* of the decision on the merits, notwithstanding its non-appearance in the second phase of the proceedings.[190] This however would imply that when States agree to refer a dispute to arbitration, they accept that the decision of the arbitrator or arbitration tribunal will be final and binding on them, not merely on the substantive case, but also on all questions of jurisdiction, or other interlocutory or ancillary matters.

This is not, however, the generally accepted interpretation. The idea that an arbitral award which would otherwise be final and binding may yet be void for reasons unrelated to its correctness in law on the merits, and specifically for *excès de pouvoir*, is one of the longest established rules in this field.[191] Had the Court accepted the opposite approach, that the arbitrator's decision is final even on jurisdictional and procedural questions, in the *Arbitral Award* case, it would not have been willing to go even so far as it did in reviewing the decision of the Tribunal as to its competence. The extent of the power which it regarded itself as possessing will be examined below; here the essential point is that, while the Court did not feel free simply to re-judge for itself whether or not the

[189] It is true that, as observed by Judge Oda, the nullity of the award would not alter the rights and interests of the parties relating to the disputed boundary (*ICJ Reports*, 1991, p. 88, para. 16), but that does not mean that those interests and rights were as defined by the award – or of course that they were not.

[190] On this, see the present writer's *Non-Appearance before the International Court of Justice*, chapter 4, pp. 46 ff.

[191] See, for example, the discussions of the Institut de droit international in 1874; de la Pradelle, 'L'excès de pouvoir de l'arbitre', *Revue de droit international*, 1928, p. 21; Castberg, 'L'excès de pouvoir dans la juridiction internationale', *Recueil des cours*, 35 (1931–I), p. 357; Borel, 'Les voies de recours contre les sentences arbitrales', *Recueil des cours*, 52 (1935–II), p. 5. The League Assembly studied the problem in 1929–31, but did not ultimately take any action: see Borel, loc. cit., pp. 42–55.

Tribunal's decision on the first question required the Tribunal also, as a matter of interpretation of the Arbitration Agreement, to answer the second, the Court did not treat the Tribunal's decision on that point as *res judicata*.

The matter is sometimes discussed as a conflict between, or a reconciliation of, two principles: that of *res judicata*, coupled with the principle of *la compétence de la compétence*, and that enshrined in the adage *extra compromissum arbiter nihil facere potest*.[192] This is however not to go to the root of the problem: the question is not whether the arbitrator has or has not exceeded his powers, but who is to decide whether or not he has done so.[193] The first maxim, in full, is that *res judicata pro veritate habetur*: if the arbitrator has ruled, with the force of *res judicata*, that the arbitration agreement gives him this or that power, his decision is deemed to be correct; on what basis then is any other body to rule that he is wrong?

The question is surely one of the intentions of the parties rather than of any general principle of procedural or arbitral law; if so, the first step should perhaps be to examine the terms of the arbitration agreement. If, for example, such an agreement provided that 'all decisions of the arbitrator, including those relating to his jurisdiction and powers, shall be final and binding on the parties', there would apparently be no room for any supervision by recourse to the Court or otherwise. The Arbitration Agreement between Guinea-Bissau and Senegal, interestingly, makes a distinction. Under Article 4, paragraph 2,

> The *decisions [décisions]* of the Tribunal relating to all questions of substance or procedure, including all questions relating to the jurisdiction of the Tribunal and the interpretation of the Agreement, shall be taken by a majority of its members.

Article 10, paragraph 2, however provides that

> The *Award [sentence]* shall be final and binding upon the two States which shall be under a duty to take all necessary steps for its implementation.[194]

On the basis of these texts, it would seem that the parties had not intended decisions on jurisdiction and interpretation of the Agreement to be non-appealable; this would however not resolve the difference of views between Judge Shahabuddeen and the majority as to the extent of

[192] In this sense, see the separate opinion of Judge Shahabuddeen in the *Arbitral Award* case, *ICJ Reports*, 1991, p. 108; Guggenheim, 'La validité et la nullité des actes juridiques internationaux', *Recueil des cours*, 74 (1949–I), p. 217.

[193] This too was a problem identified at an early date; it was proposed (by Mancini) to the Institut de droit international in 1874 that 'le compromis déterminera devant quelle personne ou faculté, ou Cour constituée, sera porté le recours en nullité, et dans quel délai' (quoted by Borel in *Recueil des cours*, 52 (1935–II), at p. 9). The Institut did not adopt this proposal.

[194] *ICJ Reports*, 1991, pp. 58–9, emphasis added.

the Court's powers. The Court however made no reference to the the text of the Agreement in this context.

Another way in which the will of the parties could play a role is in the definition of the task conferred on the Court in a case of the kind we are now examining: if the parties are agreed to ask the Court simply whether the arbitrator committed a 'manifest breach of his competence', rather than whether the arbitrator was, in the Court's view, competent—i.e. whether the arbitrator's decision on competence was correct—then prima facie it is for the Court to respect the wishes of the parties, and not to decide *ultra petita*. In paragraph 25 of its judgment, quoted above, the Court did 'emphasize that, *as the Parties were both agreed*, these proceedings allege the inexistence and nullity of the Award . . . and are not by way of appeal from it or application for revision of it'. This is however to say that the parties were instructing the Court to respect a recognized distinction, between *recours en nullité* and appeal, and that that distinction involved the limited role which the Court in fact played; in other words, one is forced back to the argument that there is an existing principle of judicial or procedural law which limits the powers of the reviewing body on a *recours en nullité,* and does so in a way which might prima facie seem to involve infringement of the basic principle of treaty interpretation.

This is, in the present writer's view, the major objection to the view of the majority of the Court, namely that it offends, not against any procedural principle, but against the law of treaties. For the Court it is not a question of deciding whether the arbitrator decided in breach of the competence conferred on him, but whether he acted 'in *manifest* breach' of the competence conferred. It does not have to enquire whether the *compromis* might be interpreted in a number of ways 'and if so consider which would have been preferable'. The concept of interpretation of a treaty involves endeavouring to ascertain what was the intention of the parties, on the fundamental assumption that there was a single such intention, and the consequence of this is that there is, as a matter of principle, only one correct interpretation, and (perhaps) any number of specious but incorrect ones. The Court argues on the basis that the Tribunal in the *Guinea-Bissau* case acted on an interpretation which was arguably correct, so that the Court does not have to look to see if it actually was correct. As Judge Shahabuddeen observes in his separate opinion,

> [T]o characterize the Tribunal's interpretation as being merely one which could be placed on the Arbitration Agreement 'without manifest breach of its competence' is to leave open the possibility that some other interpretation could also be placed on it 'without manifest breach of its competence'; . . . *All of such possible interpretations could not be right.*[195]

[195] *ICJ Reports*, 1991, pp. 107–8 (emphasis added).

Judge Shahabuddeen argues as follows:

> . . . when the parties invest an arbitrator, whether expressly or by implication of law, with competence to interpret the *compromis* [particularly on questions of jurisdiction], within what limits, if any, are they to be understood as thereby engaging to be bound by an exercise of the competence by the arbitrator which results in a misinterpretation by him of the *compromis* concerning his powers? In the present case, the question would be whether it was the will of the Parties that they should be bound by a misinterpretation—if there was any—of the *compromis* on the important and major issue as to whether the second question was required to be answered. Conceivably, in the larger interests of securing a resolution of their dispute, the Parties might be understood as having undertaken to be bound by decisions made within some tolerable margin of appreciation as to competence in minor matters even though erroneous. Should they be understood as having undertaken to be likewise bound by erroneous decisions as to the powers of the Tribunal going to the substance of its mission? Scarcely so.[196]

Judge Shahabuddeen thought that the Court should be able to investigate whether the arbitration tribunal's view as to its competence was or was not correct, rather than merely whether it corresponded to a possible interpretation of the Arbitration Agreement. He was however able to agree with the decision of the Court, by following a slightly different route:

> I agree with the view, underlying the Court's decision, that its authority to review the Tribunal's interpretation of the *compromis* is limited, but I differ as to the basis of the limitation. I regard the limitation not as one which in principle precludes the Court from pronouncing on the correctness of the Tribunal's interpretation, but as one which requires a certain measure of caution on the part of the Court when so pronouncing: I would link the limitation directly and firmly to considerations of stability of the arbitral process with respect to finality of awards, and to the consequential need for the Court to observe appropriate standards of cogency in determining whether its own interpretation of the *compromis* is so convincingly clear as to warrant displacement of the Tribunal's, should the two be different . . . I do not see the limitation as being linked to any idea that, as seems implied by paragraphs 47 and 60 of the Judgment of the Court, because these are not appeal proceedings, the Tribunal should be regarded by the Court as having an unreviewable freedom to select any of a number of possibly different interpretations of the *compromis* as to the substance of its mission, provided they are interpretations which could be made 'without manifest breach of its competence'.[197]

Whichever approach is adopted, the common idea is that some misinterpretations of its powers by an arbitral tribunal could be so gross

[196] *ICJ Reports*, 1991, p. 110. A weakness of this argument is that the parties had indubitably agreed to be bound by the decision of the arbitrators on the merits, even if it were, objectively (if that term means anything), erroneous. Thus one cannot say that errors on minor matters were acceptable, but not on major ones.

[197] *ICJ Reports*, 1991, p. 112.

that the Court should be entitled, in the exercise of a non-specific jurisdiction, as distinct from an agreed appeal, to set them aside or correct them. The matter does however need to be put in proportion: if both parties are agreed that the tribunal has gone off the rails, then they can set aside the award by agreement, and start the proceedings again, or adopt a different dispute settlement procedure. It is when only one party contends that the tribunal has departed from its mandate that any question of correction by the Court arises; which implies that the alleged departure is sufficiently defensible for the other party to regard it as no departure. This increases the likelihood that the Court, assuming it has either the powers it assumed in the *Arbitral Award* case, or those which Judge Shahabuddeen would attribute to it, would find that there was no 'manifest breach of competence'; and thus throws doubt on the justification for any interference by the Court with what the parties have agreed to accept as *res judicata*, whether on substance, jurisdiction or procedure.

It is however suggested that of the two approaches adopted, that of Judge Shahabudeen is to be preferred, as avoiding infringement of a fundamental concept of the interpretation of treaties.

6. *Jurisdiction Inherited from the Permanent Court of International Justice*

Articles 36, paragraph 5, and 37 of the Statute were inserted in 1946 in order so far as possible to preserve and transfer to the new Court the acceptances of jurisdiction, by treaty or by virtue of the Optional Clause, already given in favour of the Permanent Court of International Justice:

> *[Article 36, paragraph 5]* Declarations made under Article 36 of the Statute of the Permanent Court of International Justice and which are still in force shall be deemed, as between the parties to the present Statute, to be acceptances of the compulsory jurisdiction of the International Court of Justice for the period which they still have to run and in accordance with their terms.
> *[Article 37]* Whenever a treaty or convention in force provides for reference of a matter to a tribunal to have been instituted by the League of Nations, or to the Permanent Court of International Justice, the matter shall, as between the parties to the present Statute, be referred to the International Court of Justice.

At the time that Fitzmaurice was writing, these provisions had not given rise to any difficulties: Article 37 had been relied on in the 1950 advisory opinion in the *South West Africa* case to support the view that the jurisdictional clause in the Mandate for that territory would confer jurisdiction on the Court,[198] and was subsequently invoked by Liberia

[198] *ICJ Reports*, 1950, p. 138.

and Ethiopia in the contentious proceedings brought against South Africa; similarly, Article 37 was relied on by Greece in the *Ambatielos* case in relation to a treaty of 1926 referring to the Permanent Court.[199] However, Fitzmaurice noted in 1958 that Article 37 'is capable, potentially, of raising a considerable number of difficulties',[200] and this was to prove true not only for Article 37, but for its companion provision, Article 36, paragraph 5.

In relations between States who were original parties to the Charter and Statute, the two texts were unexceptionable. Each provides for operation 'as between the parties to the present Statute', and its effect is, fundamentally, that of modification by a multilateral treaty of a whole series of obligations contained in other conventional or quasi-conventional instruments previously entered into by the parties to the Statute. If the original parties to the Charter had included all States having entered into such obligations, the effect would have been clear and uncontroversial. However, a number of States which had, before 1946, entered into treaties conferring jurisdiction on the Permanent Court, or had deposited declarations accepting jurisdiction under the Optional Clause of that Court's Statute, did not become parties to the Charter (and thus to the ICJ Statute) until after the Permanent Court had ceased to exist. What was the status, during this interim period, of the jurisdictional obligations of this kind? As soon as their authors had become parties to the ICJ Statute, could these obligations be asserted against them on the basis of Articles 36, paragraph 5, and 37? Was any distinction to be made between the operation of the two articles, i.e. between treaty commitments and Optional Clause declarations? These problems were foreseeable: but in addition the Court found itself obliged to decide whether an Optional Clause declaration which had never come into effect before its author became an original party to the Statute could take effect subsequently by virtue of Article 36, paragraph 5; and whether a State party to the ICJ Statute which had purported to renew a declaration under the PCIJ Statute had or had not done anything legally effective.

It will be convenient to take the decisions of the Court on these various problems in chronological order. Since they have been examined in considerable detail in the literature; since, with the passage of time, the transition from the jurisdiction of the Permanent Court to that of the present Court is less and less likely to raise new controversies;[201] and since the cases lay down a clear, if at first sight inconsistent, approach,

[199] *ICJ Reports*, 1952, p. 39.

[200] This *Year Book*, 34 (1958), p. 138; *Collected Edition*, II, p. 563; referring to a discussion by Rosenne in the first (1957) edition of his *The International Court of Justice*, pp. 280–2.

[201] Though as late as 1984, the *Military and Paramilitary Activities* case raised a new and very specialized point: see section 6 (4) below.

the present analysis will not endeavour to cover or comment on every point in the decisions.

(1) *The case of the* Aerial Incident of 27 July 1955

The proceedings were brought by Israel against Bulgaria, on the jurisdictional basis of Israel's own acceptance of jurisdiction under Article 36, paragraph 2, of the Statute and the acceptance by Bulgaria in 1921 of the jurisdiction of the Permanent Court under the same article of that Court's Statute, coupled with Article 36, paragraph 5, of the ICJ Statute. Bulgaria was not an original member of the United Nations; it was admitted, and thus became a party to the ICJ Statute, by a General Assembly resolution taking effect on 14 December 1955. The majority of the Court found that it did not have jurisdiction under these instruments; four judges (including the Israeli judge *ad hoc*) took the opposite view, and a forceful dissenting opinion was filed by Judges Lauterpacht, Wellington Koo and Spender.

Before examining the arguments in support of each view, let us consider the position from the standpoint of the existence *vel non* of consent on the part of Bulgaria. Up to the date of dissolution of the Permanent Court (18 April 1946), Bulgaria had agreed that a certain class of disputes (those with other States having accepted 'the same obligation') could be referred unilaterally to the Permanent Court. Between 1946 and 1955, while there had been no explicit termination of this acceptance, it had become (at the least) ineffective for lack of an object—resembling, as it were, a bell rope with no bell on the other end. In 1945, Bulgaria agreed to become a party to the Statute of the post-war Court, a text which contained Article 36, paragraph 5. Did Bulgaria thereby agree, to continue the metaphor, to attach a new bell to its rope?

At first sight it seems strange that both the judgment and the joint dissenting opinion concentrate to such an extent on the interpretation of the Statute, and the intention of those who drafted it, rather than on the will and consent of Bulgaria. The explanation is that it was evident that Bulgaria had not expressly, or even by implication, accepted the substitution of the one court for the other; that this could be done *implicitly* was to be decided later by the Court, in the *Temple* case. The question was whether Bulgaria's consent to the substitution could be held to result from the simple acceptance of the ICJ Statute. Since the Statute is a *contrat d'adhésion*, this depended on the interpretation of the Statute: was it intended that acceptance of the Statute by a State in the position of Bulgaria should entail consent to the attachment of the post-war Court to the pre-war Optional Clause acceptance, despite the interim period of ineffectiveness?

The majority of the Court did not think it possible to interpret the Statute as having this effect; the dissenting judges took the opposite view. The question of interpretation of the text of the Statute, however, turned out to involve the question of the legal situation of Bulgaria's acceptance between 1946 and 1955. For the majority, that acceptance did not merely become ineffective, but lapsed; and in 1946 it could be foreseen that this was going to happen; but the draftsmen of the Statute either could not or did not provide in advance for a mechanism for revival.

Since this provision [paragraph 5] was originally subscribed to only by the signatory States, it was without legal force so far as non-signatory States were concerned: it could not preserve their declarations from the lapsing with which they were threatened by the impending dissolution of the Permanent Court. Since it could not maintain them in being, Article 36, paragraph 5, could not transfer their effect to the jurisdiction of the new Court as of the date when a State having made a declaration became a party to the Statute. Since these declarations had not been maintained in being, it would then have been necessary to reinstate lapsed declarations, then to transport their subject-matter to the jurisdiction of the International Court of Justice: nothing of this kind is provided for by Article 36, paragraph 5.[202]

The majority thus recognized that it would have been legally possible for the Statute to be so worded as to impose on any State becoming party to it the acceptance of the jurisdiction of the ICJ to the extent that that State had made an acceptance, which had not expired by lapse of time, of the jurisdiction of the PCIJ. They did not however think that the actual drafting of Article 36 could be read in that sense. In reaching that conclusion, however, they do seem to have been influenced by the idea of the 'lapse' of the declarations previously made under the PCIJ Statute, thus making necessary a 'reinstatement'.

The three dissenting judges took a different view on this point:

What is material in respect of the validity of a declaration in relation to the present Court is whether it fulfils the requirements of Article 36, paragraph 5. In other words, the dissolution of the Permanent Court was not intended to have any effect, and had none, upon the declarations of acceptance provided for in Article 36, paragraph 5, so far as the present Court is concerned . . .

In so far as its relation to the Permanent Court of International Justice and its Statute is concerned, the Bulgarian Declaration of 1921 ceased, both in fact and in the strict sense of the law, to be applicable when that Court was dissolved on April 18th, 1946.[203]

It is difficult to avoid tendentious language here: the undisputed fact is simply that the court on which jurisdiction had been conferred ceased to exist in 1946, but does that make acceptances of its jurisdiction 'lapsed' or merely not 'applicable', or 'ineffective'? Neither term means anything unless one argues back from a given interpretation of paragraph 5: if that paragraph could not, in conjunction with such an acceptance, constitute a jurisdictional title, then the declaration was dead, had lapsed; if it

[202] *ICJ Reports*, 1959, p. 138

[203] *ICJ Reports*, 1959, p. 166.

could, then the acceptance was merely in a state of suspended animation, was inapplicable.

(2) *The case of the* Temple of Preah Vihear

When Cambodia brought proceedings against Thailand in this case, it relied on Article 36 of the Statute and a declaration accepting jurisdiction made by Thailand on 20 May 1950. Thailand originally accepted the compulsory jurisdiction of the Permanent Court by a declaration dated 20 September 1929, renewed by a declaration dated 3 May 1940 which was due to expire on 6 May 1950. On 20 May 1950, Thailand made a declaration referring to the declaration of 20 September 1929 and its renewals, and stating that the Government of Thailand 'hereby renew the declaration above mentioned for a further period of ten years as from May 3, 1950, with the limits and subject to the same conditions and reservations as set forth in the first declaration of Sept. 20, 1929'.[204] Since the original declaration thus (apparently) renewed referred to the Permanent Court, Cambodia pointed to Article 36, paragraph 5, of the Statute, set out above. Thailand however relied on the Court's decision in the *Aerial Incident* case: like Bulgaria, Thailand did not become a party to the Statute, through admission to the United Nations, until after the Permanent Court had ceased to exist in 1946. Accordingly, Thailand contended that its 1940 declaration had lapsed with the disappearance of the Permanent Court, as did Bulgaria's, so that Article 36, paragraph 5, referring to declarations 'still in force' would not have applied to it. According to Thailand therefore,

> when Thailand made her Declaration of May 1950 purporting to renew for another 10 years her original Declaration of 1929, as itself renewed in 1940, all she would actually have achieved was a necessarily abortive and inoperative renewal of a declaration which never had any effect except as an acceptance of the compulsory jurisdiction of a tribunal that no longer existed.[205]

The Court was able to hold unanimously that it had jurisdiction under Article 36, paragraph 2, of its Statute, and to do so it did not need to reopen the question of the interpretation of Article 36, paragraph 5, with its reference to declarations 'still in force'. It held, for reasons to be examined in more detail in a later article, that the declaration of May 1950 had 'the character of an acceptance under paragraph 2' of Article 36 of the post-war Court, and that the references to the previous declarations under the PCIJ Statute 'must, as was clearly intended, be regarded simply as a convenient method of indicating, without stating them in terms, what were the conditions upon which acceptance was made'.[206]

However, two of the dissenters in the *Aerial Incident* case (Judges

[204] *ICJ Reports*, 1961, p. 24.
[205] *ICJ Reports*, 1961, p. 26.
[206] *ICJ Reports*, 1961, p. 34.

Wellington Koo and Spender) indicated that they had not changed their view as to the effect of Article 36, paragraph 5, of the Statute, and they were joined by three of the judges who had not sat in the previous case (Judges Alfaro, Tanaka and Fitzmaurice).[207] For them, this would have been an additional or alternative reason for upholding jurisdiction in the *Temple* case.

(3) *The* Barcelona Traction, Light and Power Co. Ltd. *case*

The basis of jurisdiction in the case brought by Belgium against Spain was Article 17 of a Hispano-Belgian Treaty of Conciliation, Judicial Settlement and Arbitration signed on 19 July 1927, and tacitly renewed at ten-year intervals, the latest in 1957. Subject to provisions for conciliation and possible arbitration, the Article provided for disputes between the parties 'involving a disagreement about their legal rights' to be brought by either party before the Permanent Court. Belgium relied on Article 37 of the Statute of the post-war Court, quoted above, to justify seising the Court on the basis of Article 17 of the Treaty. Spain however had not become a party to the Statute, by admission to the United Nations, until 1955; and therefore argued that

> the jurisdictional obligation represented by Article 17 (4) had necessarily lapsed, on the dissolution of the former Permanent Court on 18 April 1946, since this brought about the disappearance of the judicial organ to which Article 17 (4) referred; that no previous substitution of the present for the former Court had been effected by virtue of Article 37 before that date, Spain not being then a party to the Statute; and that, in consequence, the 1927 Treaty had ceased to contain any valid jurisdictional clause by the time Spain did become a party to the Statute upon admission to the United Nations in December 1955.[208]

As in the *Temple* case, this line of reasoning had been inspired by the Court's decision in the *Aerial Incident* case.

The Court began, rather surprisingly, by undermining its own previous stand in the latter case, emphasizing that it 'was in a certain sense *sui generis*', and that 'As some of the separate but concurring opinions show (and as is evident in other ways) it might have been decided—and still in favour of Bulgaria—on grounds which would not have involved the particular issue' of the effect of Article 36, paragraph 5.[209] For reasons indicated, which included the possible 'far-reaching effects' of the decision to be taken on the interpretation of Article 37, the Court indicated that it 'must decide the present case independently and without further reference to Article 36, paragraph 5, or to the previous cases

[207] See declarations of Vice-President Alfaro, Judge Wellington Koo and (jointly) Judges Fitzmaurice and Tanaka, *ICJ Reports*, 1961, pp. 35–8; separate opinion of Judge Spender, ibid., pp. 39 ff.

[208] *ICJ Reports*, 1964, pp. 27–8.

[209] *ICJ Reports*, 1964, p. 29.

which have, in one way or another, involved that provision or Article 37 of the Statute'.[210]

Now it is clear that Article 36, paragraph 5, had no direct application to the case of a treaty clause, as opposed to an Optional Clause declaration, but one would have thought that the two texts might throw light on each other, as each being devoted, one would suppose, to the achievement of the same object and purpose—the preservation, so far as possible, of the jurisdictional commitments undertaken by States in relation to the Permanent Court, and their transfer to the new Court. The purpose of Article 37 was explained by the Court as follows: at the time when the Statute was being drafted, the dissolution of the Permanent Court was essential and in fact inevitable:

> At the same time, there were then in existence a very large number of treaties, conventions and other instruments, bilateral and multilateral, containing jurisdictional clauses providing for recourse to that Court. If therefore nothing had been inserted in the new Statute to meet this situation, and to meet it automatically and in advance, the preservation of these clauses would have been left to the uncertain action of the individual parties to the various instruments concerned.[211]

This was of course equally true of the PCIJ Optional Clause declarations. It was clear that the intention of both Article 36, paragraph 5, and Article 37 of the Statute was, at the least, that in relations between original parties to the Statute, i.e. the original members of the United Nations, both jurisdictional clauses in treaties and Optional Clause declarations should be preserved and transferred in effect to the new Court. As regards States becoming parties to the Statute at a later date, the Court drew a distinction: jurisdictional clauses in bilateral and (presumably *a fortiori*) multilateral treaties were preserved in a state of suspended animation during the period between the dissolution of the Permanant Court and the moment when the relevant State became party to the Statute (*Barcelona Traction*), but Optional Clause declarations lapsed with the demise of the Permanent Court (*Aerial Incident*) (they could not be revived, but a purported renewal of such a declaration might be read as a new acceptance of the jurisdiction of the new Court: *Temple of Preah Vihear*). The most interesting aspect of the *Barcelona Traction* judgment is therefore its justification for this distinction.

The core of the argument is that Article 36, paragraph 5, was no more than a transitional provision: at the time of the adoption of the new Statute,

> the impending dissolution of the Permanent Court and, in consequence thereof, the lapsing of acceptances of its compulsory jurisdiction, were in contemplation. If nothing had been done there would have been a backward step in relation to

[210] *ICJ Reports*, 1964, p. 30.
[211] *ICJ Reports*, 1964, p. 31.

what had been achieved in the way of international jurisdiction. Rather than expecting that the States signatories of the new Statute would deposit new declarations of acceptance, it was sought to provide for this transitory situation by a transitional provision and that is the purpose of Article 36, paragraph 5. By its nature and purpose, that transitional provision is applicable only to the transitory situation it was intended to deal with, which involved the institution of a new Court just when the old Court was being dissolved. The situation is entirely different when, the old Court and the acceptance of its compulsory jurisdiction having long since disappeared, a State becomes party to the Statute of the new Court: there is then no transitory situation to be dealt with by Article 36, paragraph 5.[212]

With regard to Article 37, on the other hand,

It was this situation [the dissolution of the Permanent Court, and its impact on jurisdictional texts] that Article 37 was designed to meet, and the governing concept evidently was to preserve as many jurisdictional clauses as possible from becoming inoperative by reason of the prospective dissolution of the Permanent Court; and moreover, to do this by a process which would automatically substitute the new Court for the Permanent Court in the jurisdictional treaty relations between all Members of the United Nations and other parties to the Statute, thus avoiding the need for piecemeal action by special agreement between the parties to the various instruments.[213]

The arguments in the two judgments in combination in effect boil down to a finding that Article 36, paragraph 5, was merely a transitional provision, but that Article 37 was not, being intended 'to preserve as many jurisdictional clauses as possible'. Thus as regards treaties, and specifically in the case of the bilateral Hispano-Belgian Treaty,

the basic obligation to submit to compulsory adjudication was never extinguished by the disappearance of the Permanent Court, but was merely rendered functionally inoperative by the lack of a forum through which it could be implemented. What therefore happened in 1955, when this *lacuna* was made good by Spain's admission to the United Nations, was that the operation of the obligation revived, because the means of implementing it became available; but there was neither any new creation or revival of the basic obligation.[214]

Thus a treaty providing for reference to the Permanent Court is merely 'functionally inoperative';[215] it continues to float about in search of a fresh point of attachment, while an acceptance of jurisdiction under the PCIJ Optional Clause does not survive its detachment from the old

[212] *ICJ Reports*, 1959, p. 139.

[213] *ICJ Reports*, 1964, p. 31.

[214] *ICJ Reports*, 1964, p. 40; this passage in fact occurs in the Court's ruling on the 'Subsidiary Aspect' of Spain's preliminary objection, concerning the limitation *ratione temporis* of the obligation, but it expresses neatly the *ratio* of the principal decision.

[215] This is almost as difficult a concept to grasp as that coined eight years later, whereby saying that treaties are suspended 'is not the same thing as saying that they are not in force in the definitive sense': *Appeal Relating to the Jurisdiction of the ICAO Council, ICJ Reports*. 1972, p. 53, para. 16 (*a*); and see the comments in a previous article in this series, this *Year Book*, 63 (1992), p. 36.

Court. The distinction is not unconvincing; but it presupposes that the intention of the parties, either when the treaty was originally concluded, or when the Permanent Court ceased to exist, was that if a suitable forum came along, it should take the place of the old Court. It is possible to say that by acceding to the Statute containing Article 37, Spain was consenting to the jurisdiction of the new Court; but if it did so without there being any 'creation or revival' of the basic obligation, that obligation had to have continued to exist, as an obligation; and that was not possible unless it had been the parties' intention. In the *Aerial Incident* case, as noted above, the Court contemplated that it would have been possible so to word Article 36, paragraph 5, as to have the effect that any State becoming a party to it would be agreeing to the reinstatement, with reference to the new Court, of any declarations under the PCIJ Statute which had not expired at that date, but held that 'nothing of this kind is provided for by Article 36, paragraph 5'.[216] It is difficult to see how Article 37, for its part, provided for anything of the kind.

(4) *The* Military and Paramilitary Activities *case*

In 1994, when it might have been thought that the problems of the jurisdictional inheritance from the Permanent Court were exhausted as a result of lapse of time, a new question arose: what was the position of a State which had made an Optional Clause declaration under the Statute of the Permanent Court, but one which had never entered into force, that State being an original party to the Statute, but having taken no other action in relation to Article 36? Paragraph 5 of that Article, it will be recalled, applies to declarations which 'are still in force'.

As already noted above, the Court referred to the exceptional situation of Nicaragua in relation to the Statute of the two Courts; and since no other State was, or could now be, in that exceptional situation, the case is a *unicum* which is only of interest as illustrating the continued variations in the Court's assessment of the *raison d'être* and effect of Articles 36, paragraph 5, and 37 of the Statute, and will be examined only from that standpoint. Similarly, while the history of Nicaragua's pre-war declaration under Article 36 of the Statute of the Permanent Court was somewhat curious,[217] the details need not concern us, since it was accepted for the purposes of the decision that at the time that the new

[216] *ICJ Reports*, 1959, p. 138; see above, text and note 202.

[217] Briefly: Nicaragua, as a Member of the League of Nations, signed the Protocol of Signature of the Statute of the Permanent Court on 24 September 1929, and made a declaration the same day accepting the compulsory jurisdiction of that Court. However, the Protocol provided that it was subject to ratification, so that until Nicaragua filed an instrument of ratification, its declaration would not have any legal effect. In 1934–35 the Nicaraguan parliament decided to ratify the Protocol; on 29 November 1929 a telegram was sent to the Secretary-General of the League by the Nicaraguan Foreign Ministry announcing that the Statute and Protocol had been ratified, and that the instrument of ratification would be sent 'in due course'. No trace of the instrument having been received in Geneva could be found, nor was there any evidence that it had ever been sent from Nicaragua.

Statute entered into force, and at the time when the Permanent Court ceased to exist, that declaration had never entered into force. There is however one way in which the exceptional nature of Nicaragua's position is material to the discussion of the effect of Article 36 of the Statute; in the absence of evidence that such an exceptional case was foreseen and provided for, one cannot interpret general words in the text as having been aimed at the special case. If the special case does not fall within the general aim and ambit of the treaty provision, one must assume that it was a *casus omissus,* and the fact that, had they thought of it, the authors of the text would have done better not to omit it, or might have not wished to omit it, does not affect the question.

The Court's finding was that the declaration was at that time 'certainly valid', since it complied with the conditions laid down by the PCIJ Statute,[218] even though it 'had not acquired binding force prior to such effect as Article 36, paragraph 5, of the Statute of the International Court of Justice might produce'.[219] Nevertheless, in the Court's view,

> while the declaration had not acquired binding force, it is not disputed that it could have done so, for example at the beginning of 1945, if Nicaragua had ratified the Protocol of Signature of the Statute of the Permanent Court . . . It follows that such a declaration as that made by Nicaragua had a certain potential effect which could be maintained indefinitely . . . . In sum, Nicaragua's 1929 Declaration was valid at the moment when Nicaragua became a party to the Statute of the new Court . . .

If the word 'valid' is read as meaning no more than that the Nicaraguan declaration was not, in 1945, a complete nullity, this is correct; but as the Court recognized, its legal effect was purely in the realm of the potential or hypothetical: it had no impact on the legal position of Nicaragua or any other State. The word 'valid' thus points forward to the view that the declaration was 'in force' for the purposes of Article 36, paragraph 5, of the Statute, a finding at which the Court duly arrived.

Before deciding on the correct interpretation of Article 36, paragraph 5, the Court announced its intention of examining 'to what extent the general considerations governing the transfer of the powers of the former Court to the new one, and thus serving to define the object and purpose of the provisions adopted, throw light upon the correct interpretation'.[220] In the *travaux préparatoires* (the records of the San Francisco Conference), the Court found support for the view that

> If, for a number of circumstantial reasons, it seemed necessary to abolish the former Court and to put the new one in its place, at least the delegates to the San Francisco Conference were determined to see that this operation should not

[218] *ICJ Reports*, 1984, p. 403, para. 25.
[219] Ibid., p. 404, para. 26.
[220] *ICJ Reports*, 1984, p. 407, para. 32.

result in a step backwards in relation to the progress accomplished towards adopting a system of compulsory jurisdiction.[221]

This is strikingly reminiscent of what the Court said in the *Barcelona Traction* case, not in relation to Article 36, paragraph 5, which it had put aside as (apparently) immaterial, because transitional, but in relation to Article 37; in the *Aerial Incident* case, on the other hand, the Court had emphasized the purely transitional nature of Article 36, paragraph 5, and found that the delegates were unconcerned by the 'step backwards' involved in the lapse of those declarations which had been made by States other than the original parties to the new Statute.

The Court in fact 'distinguished' (as a common lawyer would say) the *Aerial Incident* case, observing that it featured quite a different issue—'whether the effect of a declaration that had unquestionably become binding at the time of the Permanent Court could be transposed to the International Court of Justice when the declaration in question had been made by a State which had not been represented at the San Francisco Conference and had not become a party to the Statute of the present Court until long after the extinction of the Permanent Court. In view of this difference in the issues, the Court does not consider that its decision in the *Aerial Incident* case, whatever may be its relevance in other respects, provides any pointers to precise conclusions on the limited point now in issue.'[222] Perhaps the provision of such pointers was hardly to be expected: yet some guidance on the general intentions underlying the two Articles of the Statute might, it is suggested, have been gained. The Court continued with a sort of *argumentum ad hominem* (or perhaps *ad civitatem*) referring to the fact that in the *Aerial Incident* case the United States had taken 'a particularly broad view of the separability of an Optional-Clause declaration and its institutional foundation', and that the present case also involved a problem of separability.[223] The weakness of relying on the arguments adduced by a party in a different case in support of a particular view of the law has been commented on in an earlier article in this series.[224]

The reconciliation of the cases, in such a way as to produce a coherent approach to the preservation of PCIJ jurisdiction by the post-war Statute, is not easy. It is fair to say that the one case in which the Court declined to found jurisdiction on the transfer (not to say 'transitional') provisions of the Statute, the *Aerial Incident* case, was that in which, as a matter of common-sense expectations, it was least reasonable to suppose that the State concerned (Bulgaria) had become a party to the

[221] *ICJ Reports*, 1984, p. 407, para. 33.

[222] *ICJ Reports*, 1984, p. 405, para. 29.

[223] But is this a significant comparison? As Fluellen might have said, 'the situations, look you, is both alike', just as there is a river both in Macedon and Monmouth: see Shakespeare, *King Henry V*, Act IV, scene 7.

[224] This *Year Book*, 60 (1989), pp. 40–1.

Statute with the intention of reviving jurisdiction, or at least in awareness that that was the unavoidable effect of its action. The essential element in the interpretation and application of Article 36, paragraph 5, and Article 37 of the Statute is consent; but both consent and lack of consent have to be defined in legal terms. For the Court to have jurisdiction, there had to be the consent of the States concerned; one link in the chain of consent would be a pre-war acceptance of the Optional Clause, or a treaty referring to the Permanent Court; another would be the two articles mentioned; but did these links interlock? What was it to which States were consenting in becoming parties to a Statute which contained Articles 36, paragraph 5, and 37? This in turn depends on the intentions of the authors of the Statute: were they concerned to preserve as much of the existing PCIJ jurisdiction as possible, or merely to make transitional provision for conservation of jurisdictional titles in the short term? To what extent did they intend the transfer provisions to remain indefinitely alive so as to attach to States acceding to the Statute years later?

Reading the cases, in particular the *Military and Paramilitary Activities* decision, one has the impression that an interpretation of the relevant articles was adopted which was teleological—less in the sense of looking to the purposes of the Statute than that of looking to the result (jurisdiction or no jurisdiction) in the case under consideration. It is a sustainable view that in the course of the history of the Court, it has moved from a restrictive to a more extensive view of its jurisdiction: having at the outset shown a reluctance to uphold jurisdiction, and thus entertain claims against a State, unless thoroughly satisfied of the existence of the necessary consent, it shows now a tendency to lean somewhat towards a positive finding of jurisdiction, possibly influenced by the consideration that it would be desirable that the dispute be heard and resolved judicially. To demonstrate this would however involve consideration of a number of decisions that fall outside the period presently under review.

STATE PRACTICE AND INTERNATIONAL LAW IN RELATION TO SECESSION*

By JAMES CRAWFORD[1]

1. Introduction

Secession is the process by which a particular group seeks to separate itself from the State to which it belongs, and to create a new State. It is

[1] Whewell Professor of International Law, University of Cambridge. The author would like to thank Mr Roger O'Keefe, of Magdalene College, Cambridge, for his assistance. This article is closely based on an independent expert report commissioned by the Canadian Department of Justice, and annexed to the Factum of the Government of Canada in the Reference concerning certain questions relating to the secession of Quebec from Canada, 27 February 1997. For the terms of the Reference, see Order in Council PC 1996–1947, 30 September 1996. Three questions were asked of the Court in that Reference. Question 1 concerned the legality of the unilateral secession of Quebec under the Canadian Constitution. Question 2 concerned the legality of the unilateral secession of Quebec under international law. The question was as follows:

> 'Does international law give the National Assembly, legislature or government of Quebec the right to effect the secession of Quebec from Canada unilaterally? In this regard, is there a right to self determination under international law that would give the National Assembly, legislature or government of Quebec the right to effect the secession of Quebec from Canada unilaterally?'

Question 3 asked which of the two, i.e. 'domestic and international law', would take precedence in Canada in the event of a conflict between them on the issue of unilateral secession. On 20 August 1998 the Court, in a unanimous opinion, summarized its answer in Question 2 in the following terms:

> 'We have also considered whether a positive legal entitlement to secession exists under international law in the factual circumstances contemplated by Question 1, i.e., a clear democratic expression of support on a clear question for Quebec secession. Some of those who supported an affirmative answer to this question did so on the basis of the recognized right to self-determination that belongs to all "peoples". Although much of the Quebec population certainly shares many of the characteristics of a people, it is not necessary to decide the "people" issue because, whatever may be the correct determination of this issue in the context of Quebec, a right to secession only arises under the principle of self-determination of peoples at international law where "a people" is governed as part of a colonial empire; where "a people" is subject to alien subjugation, domination or exploitation; and possibly where "a people" is denied any meaningful exercise of its right to self-determination within the state of which it forms a part. In other circumstances, peoples are expected to achieve self-determination within the framework of their existing state. A state whose government represents the whole of the people or peoples resident within its territory, on a basis of equality and without discrimination, and respects the principles of self-determination in its internal arrangements, is entitled to maintain its territorial integrity under international law and to have that territorial integrity recognized by other states. Quebec does not meet the threshold of a colonial people or an oppressed people, nor can it be suggested that Quebecers have been denied meaningful access to government to pursue their political, economic, cultural and social development. In the circumstances, the National Assembly, the legislature or the government of Quebec do not enjoy a right at international law to effect the secession of Quebec from Canada unilaterally.'

Reference re Secession of Quebec, 1998 SCJ No. 61, para. 154. But the Court added, in relation both to Questions 1 and 2, the following rider:

to be distinguished from a consensual process by which a State confers independence on a particular territory and people by legislative or other means, a process which may be referred to as *devolution* or the *grant of independence*.[2] The key difference between secession and devolution is that the former is essentially a unilateral process, whereas the latter is bilateral and consensual.

The usual way in which secession begins is by a 'unilateral declaration of independence' (or UDI). This is a term commonly used to refer to the unilateral act by which a group declares that it is seceding and forming a new State. Although usually declaratory in form, a unilateral declaration of independence is not a self-executing act. The independence of a State is established by the process of the extension of effective control over territory and its recognition by other States, especially the State on whose territory the secession is occurring. As will be seen, many attempts at unilateral secession fail, and even those that succeed take time. Thus a declaration of independence is a necessary, but not a sufficient, condition for unilateral secession.[3]

It is often said that a group or people has a legal right to secede from the State to which they belong, by virtue of their right of self-determination. Conversely, it may be asserted that secession is actually unlawful under international law because it breaches the territorial integrity of the predecessor State. It has, however, always been possible for a group to separate from a State and to achieve independence by achieving exclusive control over its territory—if necessary, by winning a war of independence. The Spanish American colonies did so in the early nineteenth century, and the Confederacy attempted to do so in the American Civil War. Secession of this kind was a process, which could take years and which might or might not lead to a successful outcome. From the perspective of different participants it might be seen either as an expression of an inherent right to be free from oppression or as an act of treason. But, however described by the participants, unilateral secession did not involve the exercise of any right conferred by international law.

> 'Although there is no right, under the Constitution or at international law, to unilateral secession . . . this does not rule out the possibility of an unconstitutional declaration of secession leading to a de facto secession. The ultimate success of such a secession would be dependent on recognition by the international community, which is likely to consider the legality and legitimacy of secession having regard to, amongst other facts, the conduct of Quebec and Canada, in determining whether to grant or withhold recognition. Such recognition, even if granted, would not, however, provide any retroactive justification for the act of secession, either under the Constitution of Canada or at international law.'

Ibid., para. 155. For commentary on the opinion, see D.P. Haljan, 'A Constitutional Duty to Negotiate Amendments: *Reference re Secession of Quebec*', *International and Comparative Law Quarterly*, 48 (1999), p. 447.

[2] See J. Crawford, *The Creation of States in International Law* (Oxford: Clarendon Press, 1979), pp. 215, 247, for an explanation of the distinction.

[3] An entity which does not claim to be a State in international law will not be recognized as such. This has hitherto been a justification for the non-recognition of a separate State of Taiwan. See Crawford, op. cit. above (n. 2), p. 119.

International law has always favoured the territorial integrity of States, and correspondingly, the government of a State was entitled to oppose the unilateral secession of part of the State by all lawful means. Third States were expected to remain neutral during such a conflict, in the sense that assistance to a group which had not succeeded in establishing its independence could be treated as intervention in the internal affairs of the State in question, or as a violation of neutrality—as in the *Alabama* arbitration.[4]

But on the other hand international law has been prepared to acknowledge political realities once the independence of a seceding entity was firmly established and in relation to the territory effectively controlled by it.[5] This had, and has, nothing to do with any pre-existing right in international law on the part of any group or territory to secede. In international law before 1945, there was no such right. The only arguable basis in modern international law by which a right to secession might exist would be by virtue of the principle of self-determination, which has developed since 1945 on the basis of certain provisions of the Charter of the United Nations and related State practice. In examining this practice, it is necessary to discuss first the question of secession as a form of decolonization.

II. Secession and Self-determination of Colonial Territories

Chapters XI and XII of the United Nations Charter made specific provision for territories of colonial type, i.e. dependent territories geographically distinct from the metropolitan territory of the State, as referred to in Article 74. None of the Articles of Chapters XI and XII actually use the phrase 'right to self-determination'. But their concern was evidently the progress to self-government of the peoples of dependent territories. The territories concerned fell into two classes.

One was the class of trust territories, covered by Chapter XII of the Charter. This included the territories formerly covered by the system of Mandates under the League of Nations, as provided for in Article 22 of the Covenant of the League. Mandated territories were territories taken from Germany and the Ottoman Empire (Turkey) at the end of the First World War and whose administration was conferred on one or other of the victorious States on terms agreed by the Council of the League of Nations. Those mandated territories which had not achieved independence were to be brought under the international trusteeship system by

[4] Moore, *International Arbitrations*, vol. 1 (1872), p. 495.

[5] See Crawford, op. cit. above (n. 2), pp. 247–66, for an analysis of international law rules relating to secession in the nineteenth and twentieth centuries.

separate agreements pursuant to Article 77 of the Charter.[6] Although Article 77 envisaged that certain additional territories might be brought under the trusteeship system by agreement, in fact this only happened in one case, that of Somalia (Italian Somaliland).[7]

Under Article 22 of the Covenant, mandates fell into three classes.[8] With one exception, the 'A Class' mandates (formerly parts of the Ottoman Empire) had become or shortly after 1945 became independent (Iraq, Jordan, Syria, Lebanon). The exception was Palestine, a British 'A class' mandate. Israel became independent after a short war of independence against neighbouring Arab States following the British withdrawal from Palestine in 1948. The remaining parts of Palestine were not brought under trusteeship, but the future of the Palestinian people was then and remained a matter of concern to the United Nations, and is covered by the rubric of self-determination.[9]

Of the 'B Class' and 'C Class' mandates, only one was not brought under the Trusteeship system under Chapter XII of the Charter, viz. South West Africa (Namibia). The International Court however repeatedly reaffirmed that the United Nations had responsibility for the self-government of the people of South West Africa. The territory became independent as Namibia on 31 March 1990, after the United Nations had conducted multi-party elections.[10]

The second class of colonial territories covered by the United Nations Charter was non-self-governing territories. These were dealt with in Chapter XI of the Charter. In the words of Article 73 of the Charter, they were 'territories whose peoples have not yet attained a full measure of self-government'. Initially these territories were identified by a voluntary listing process on the part of the States responsible for their administration—Australia, Belgium, France, Netherlands, New Zealand, United Kingdom and United States. Problems however arose when Portugal and Spain, which only became United Nations members in 1955, refused to bring any of their colonial territories within the reporting system of Chapter XI. In response to this refusal, the General Assembly moved to specify criteria for non-self-governing territories,

[6] The International Court held that there was no automatic transfer of mandated territories to the trusteeship system: *International Status of South West Africa* advisory opinion, *ICJ Reports*, 1950, p. 128.

[7] See Crawford, op. cit. above (n. 2), p. 428.

[8] A list of the three classes of mandates and the territories covered is in Crawford, op. cit. above (n. 2), Appendix 2, pp. 426–8.

[9] Ibid, pp. 337, 426. See, e.g., General Assembly Resolution 48/94, 20 December 1993, paras. 3, 5, 6.

[10] See Security Council Resolution 682, 17 April 1990; General Assembly Resolution S–18/1, 23 April 1990. See further Crawford, op. cit. above (n. 2), pp. 340–1, 355–6, 427–8; R. Goy, 'L'indépendance de la Namibie', *Annuaire français de droit international,* 37 (1991), p. 387; M. Kamto, 'L'accession de la Namibie à l'indépendance', *Revue générale de droit international public,* 94 (1990), p. 577; G. Abi-Saab, 'Namibia and International Law', *African Yearbook of International Law,* 1 (1993), p. 3.

which it did in Resolution 1541 (XV). In accordance with those criteria it has made several determinations that particular territories fell within Chapter XI. These concerned certain overseas territories of Spain and Portugal and, subsequently, Southern Rhodesia and certain French territories of which the most recent was New Caledonia.[11]

All the territories covered by the international trusteeship system have now proceeded to 'self-government or independence' in terms of Article 76 (*b*) of the United Nations Charter. So have almost all of the non-self-governing territories covered by Chapter XI, with the exception of a number of small island territories, and certain larger territories whose status or future are disputed—in particular, East Timor and Western Sahara. The position was succinctly summarized by the International Court of Justice in the *Namibia* opinion in 1971.[12]

It should be noted that the principle of self-determination which, in the Court's words, was 'made . . . applicable' to all non-self-governing territories, did not involve an automatic right of unilateral secession for the people of those territories. In the vast majority of cases, the progress to self-government or independence was consensual. It occurred with the agreement of the State responsible for the administration of the territory, in accordance with law and pursuant to arrangements between the government of that State and local leaders. These arrangements dealt with the modalities of transfer of power and, in many cases, made provision for succession with respect to treaties, property and debt. The United Nations General Assembly urged that rapid decisions be made as to the self-government or independence of those territories, especially after the adoption of the Declaration on the Granting of Independence to Colonial Countries and Peoples in 1960. But it did not advocate or support unilateral rights of secession for non-self-governing territories, except where self-determination was opposed by the colonial power. This was the case for example in the Portuguese African territories (Angola, Mozambique, Guinea-Bissau). In the vast majority of cases, self-government or independence was achieved peacefully and by agreement with the administering authority.

Independence for a colonial territory was the most common outcome of this process, but it was not the only one. As Principle VI of Resolution 1541 recognized, self-determination could lead to a number of different outcomes, including 'integration with an independent State', whether the metropolitan State or a third State. The point was reaffirmed by the

[11] See General Assembly Resolution 1542 (XV), 15 December 1960, para. 1 (Portuguese territories); para. 5 (Spanish territories); General Assembly Resolution 1747 (XVI), 28 June 1962 (Southern Rhodesia); General Assembly Resolution 2069 (XX), 16 December 1965 (Condominium of New Hebrides); General Assembly Resolution 2228 (XXI), 20 December 1966 (French Somaliland); General Assembly Resolution 3161 (XXVIII), 14 December 1973 (Comoros); General Assembly Resolution 41/41A, 2 December 1986 (New Caledonia).

[12] *ICJ Reports*, 1971, p. 6 at p. 31 (para. 52).

International Court in the *Western Sahara* opinion.[13] Integration with the former metropolitan State or a third State occurred in a number of cases. For example, the electorate in the northern part of the British trust territory of the Cameroons preferred to be integrated with Nigeria, while in the southern part the preference was for integration with the Republic of Cameroon.[14]

Nearly 100 territories designated as colonial under Chapters XI and XII have become independent and have been admitted to the United Nations.[15] A few colonial territories, by contrast, have opted for a formal association arrangement with the former colonial power, under which they achieved a form of separate status falling short of independence; they did not become United Nations members in their own right. This applied to Puerto Rico (United States), the West Indies Associated States (United Kingdom), Cook Islands and Niue (New Zealand). More recently similar arrangements were made with different parts of the United States strategic trust territory of the Pacific Islands, but the territories concerned have been regarded as independent and have been admitted to the United Nations. They are the Federated States of Micronesia, Marshall Islands and Palau.

Other former colonial territories have been integrated in a State following an act of self-determination: these include Cocos (Keeling) Islands (Australia); Greenland (Denmark); Northern Cameroons (Nigeria); Northern Mariana Islands (United States); Southern Cameroons (Cameroun). (West Irian (Indonesia) is a disputed example of integration.) The people of other territories have voted to remain dependent and continue to fall within Chapter XI of the Charter: this is true, for example, of Bermuda.

Although in exceptional cases, such as the British trust territory of Cameroons, a particular territory was divided for the purposes of the exercise of self-determination, the General Assembly has usually insisted on maintaining the unity of territories identified as colonial under Chapters XI and XII, and has resisted attempts to fragment them, even

[13] *ICJ Reports*, 1975, p. 12 at pp. 32–3 (paras. 57–8).

[14] See *Northern Cameroons* case, *ICJ Reports*, 1963, p. 15.

[15] They are: Algeria; Angola; Antigua and Barbuda; Bahamas; Bahrain; Barbados; Belize; Benin; Botswana; Brunei; Burkina Faso; Burma (Myanmar); Burundi; Cambodia; Cameroon; Cape Verde; Central African Republic; Chad; Comoros; Congo (Brazzaville); Côte d'Ivoire; Cyprus; Djibouti; Dominica; Equatorial Guinea; Federated States of Micronesia; Fiji; Gabon; Gambia; Ghana; Grenada; Guinea; Guinea-Bissau; Guyana; India; Indonesia; Jamaica; Jordan; Kenya; Kiribati; Kuwait; Laos; Lesotho; Liberia; Libya; Madagascar; Malaysia; Malawi; Maldives; Mali; Malta; Marshall Islands; Mauritania; Mauritius; Morocco; Mozambique; Namibia; Nauru; Niger; Nigeria; Oman; Pakistan; Palau; Papua New Guinea; Philippines; Qatar; Rwanda; St Christopher and Nevis; St Vincent and the Grenadines; Sao Tome and Principe; Seychelles; Sierra Leone; Solomon Islands; Somalia; Sri Lanka; Sudan; Surinam; Swaziland; Syria; Tanzania (formed by the union of Tanganyika and Zanzibar); Togo; Tonga; Trinidad and Tobago; Tunisia; Tuvalu; Uganda; United Arab Emirates; Vanuatu; Vietnam (formerly North & South Vietnam); Western Samoa; Yemen (formed by union of North and South Yemen); Zaire (formerly Congo (Kinshasa)); Zambia; Zimbabwe (94).

if sub-groups within such territories have sought to separate. An example is the island of Mayotte, which was part of the Comoros Archipelago, a Chapter XI territory which became independent in 1975. The expressed wishes of the inhabitants of Mayotte to remain under French administration have been opposed by the General Assembly on the basis of the territorial integrity and declared wishes of the people of the Comoros as a whole.[16] This illustrates a broader point, viz., that the principle of self-determination in the colonial context has been applied by reference to existing colonial boundaries. The identification of sub-groups within a given territory as separate 'peoples' has been discouraged, and colonial territories have acceded to independence—or to other forms of self-government—as a whole.[17]

Even in the period before achieving self-government or independence, colonial territories are regarded as having a special status in international law. In particular, colonial territory is distinct from the metropolitan territory of the administering State. The distinction is implicit in Article 74 of the Charter, which contrasts metropolitan and non-self-governing territory. It is further elaborated in the so-called 'Friendly Relations Declaration', in its influential restatement of the Charter principle of 'equal rights and self-determination of peoples'.[18] The Declaration provides, in part, as follows:

> The territory of a colony or other non-self-governing territory has, under the Charter, a status separate and distinct from the territory of the State administering it; and such separate and distinct status under the Charter shall exist until the people of the colony or non-self-governing territory have exercised their right of self-determination in accordance with the Charter, and particularly its purposes and principles.

Underlying the special status accorded to colonial territories is the idea that by achieving self-government or independence a formerly colonized people achieves equality of rights with all other peoples. If it accedes to

[16] General Assembly Resolution 3161 (XXVIII), 14 December 1973, and for a recent repetition of its position, General Assembly Resolution 49/18, 28 November 1994. For the dispute, see Ahmed W. Mahamoud, *Mayotte: le contentieux entre la France et les Comores* (Paris: L'Harmattan, 1992); Malyn Newitt, *The Comoro Islands. Struggle against Dependency in the Indian Ocean* (Boulder: Westview Press, 1984), pp. 48–70. Conversely, in the case of Southern Rhodesia the international community opposed secession of a territory by a settler minority regime, in circumstances where the majority of the territory had no say in the process: see Crawford, op. cit. above (n. 2), pp. 103–6, 123–4; John Dugard, *Recognition and the United Nations* (Cambridge: Grotius, 1987), pp. 90–8; Jericho Nkala, *The United Nations, International Law and the Rhodesian Independence Crisis* (Oxford: Clarendon Press, 1985).

[17] Cf. case concerning the *Frontier Dispute (Burkina Faso/Mali), ICJ Reports*, 1986, p. 554, at pp. 565–7 (paras. 22, 25)

[18] General Assembly Resolution 2625 (XXV), Declaration on Principles of International Law concerning Friendly Relations and Co-operation among States in accordance with the Charter of the United Nations, 24 October 1970. The Declaration was adopted without a vote after lengthy preparation, and is widely regarded as an authoritative interpretation of the principles dealt with: see, e.g., *Military and Paramilitary Activities in and against Nicaragua (Merits), ICJ Reports*, 1986, p. 14, at p. 101.

independence, the continued right of self-determination is reflected in control over the State, and is legally protected by the principles of territorial integrity and non-intervention. If it is integrated in an independent State, it thereafter shares on a basis of equality in the exercise of self-determination on the part of the people of that State as a whole. These propositions may be illustrated by a review of practice with respect to self-determination outside the colonial context.

III. Secession and Self-determination of Non-colonial Territories

By comparison with the acceptance of self-determination leading to the independence of colonial territories covered by Chapters XI and XII of the Charter (so-called 'external self-determination'), the practice regarding unilateral secession of non-colonial territories is very different. Since 1945 the international community has been extremely reluctant to accept unilateral secession of parts of independent States in situations where the secession is opposed by the government of that State. In such cases the principle of territorial integrity has been a significant limitation. There is only one clear example of successful unilateral secession during this period, viz. Bangladesh. Since 1945 no State which has been created by unilateral secession has been admitted to the United Nations against the declared wishes of the government of the predecessor State.[19] By contrast there are many examples of failed attempts at unilateral secession, including cases where the seceding entity maintained *de facto* independence for some time.

It is necessary to distinguish unilateral secession of part of a State and the outright dissolution of the predecessor State as a whole. In the latter case there is, by definition, no predecessor State continuing in existence whose consent to any new arrangements can be sought. But the distinction between dissolution of a State and unilateral secession of part of a State may be difficult to draw in particular cases. The dissolution of a State may be initially triggered by the secession or attempted secession of one part of that State. If the process goes beyond that and involves a general withdrawal of all or most of the territories concerned, and no substantial central or federal component remains behind, it may be evident that the predecessor State as a whole has ceased to exist. As will be seen, this was the position taken by the international community in the cases of Yugoslavia and Czechoslovakia.[20] None the less, even a successful unilateral secession of one part of a State will not normally

[19] Bangladesh, although it applied for UN admission in 1972 (S/10759), was not admitted until 1974, subsequent to its recognition by Pakistan. See below, pp. 95–6.

[20] See below, pp. 98–106.

produce that result.[21] There is a strong presumption in favour of the continuity of States, and the normal situation is that the predecessor State will continue in existence and be recognized as such.

Thus the distinction between unilateral secession and dissolution is clear in principle. It is adopted, for example, in the two Vienna Conventions on State Succession. The main difference is that in cases of dissolution, no one party is allowed to veto the process. By contrast where the government of the predecessor State maintains its status as such, its assent to secession is necessary, at least unless and until the seceding entity has firmly established control beyond hope of recall. Bangladesh is the only clear case in international practice since 1945. The position stated by the Commission of Jurists appointed by the League of Nations to examine the *Aaland Islands* situation remains true, notwithstanding subsequent developments in the principle of self-determination:

> Positive international law does not recognise the right of national groups, as such, to separate themselves from the State of which they form a part by the simple expression of a wish.[22]

Post–1945 practice in respect of unilateral secession and dissolution

Since 1945, the only new States, emerging from situations which were not formally recognized as colonial and covered by Chapters XI and XII of the Charter, have been:

— Senegal (1960);
— Singapore (1965);
— Bangladesh (1971);
— the three Baltic States, Latvia, Lithuania, Estonia (all 1991);[23]
— the eleven successor States of the former Soviet Union: Armenia; Azerbaijan; Belarus; Georgia; Kazakhstan; Kirgizstan; Moldova; Tajikistan; Turkmenistan; Ukraine; Uzbekistan (all 1991);[24]
— the five successor States of the former Yugoslavia: Slovenia, Macedonia, Croatia, Bosnia-Herzegovina, Federal Republic of Yugoslavia (Serbia and Montenegro) (1991–2);
— Czech Republic and Slovakia (1993), and
— Eritrea (1993).

[21] e.g., Pakistan after the secession of Bangladesh, when Pakistan retained its legal existence and UN membership notwithstanding the loss of over 50% of its population.

[22] *League of Nations Official Journal*, Special Supplement 3 (1920), at p. 5.

[23] As explained below, the Baltic States were strictly not 'new' but re-emerged after their illegal annexation in 1940.

[24] As explained below, the Russian Federation was recognized as continuing the legal personality of the former Soviet Union and was therefore not a 'new' State.

The list excludes the so-called divided States formed in the aftermath of the Second World War (North Korea, South Korea and East Germany), which are subject to special considerations.[25]

Senegal emerged from the dissolution of the Mali Federation, a federal arrangement formed between it and Soudan. Under the French Constitution of 1958, the former colonies of Senegal and Soudan became 'autonomous States' within the French Community. Subsequently, it was agreed that the Mali Federation would be established, and Senegal and Soudan agreed to join it. Under the Constitution of the Mali Federation of 17 January 1959, its constituent units were regarded as 'sovereign', as was the Federation itself. Shortly after the Federation was inaugurated, serious difficulties arose between Senegal and Soudan and on 20 August 1960 Senegal purported to withdraw. This was initially opposed by Soudan, but was accepted on 22 September 1960, when Soudan asserted its independence outside the French Community under the name of Mali. The situation was described in different terms by different members of the Security Council when it considered the applications for United Nations membership by Senegal and Mali on 28 September 1960. But it was common ground that the two entities had resolved their differences, that each had achieved separate independence, and that the Federation of Mali had thereby ceased to exist.[26]

Singapore was another former colony which became independent after a short-lived attempt at federation. This was done pursuant to a Separation Agreement which recited that:

> it has been agreed by the parties hereto that fresh arrangements should be made for the order and good government of the territories comprised in Malaysia by the separation of Singapore from Malaysia upon which Singapore shall become an independent and sovereign state and nation separate from and independent of Malaysia and so recognized by the Government of Malaysia.[27]

Pursuant to this agreement, Singapore separated from Malaysia, which

[25] Korea was a Japanese colony which was, like Germany, subject to divided military government by the Allies after the end of World War II. Separate States were established by the military occupants, and were eventually recognized as *faits accomplis*. Vietnam was divided as a result of a ceasefire in a colonial war of independence. On the 'divided States', see Crawford, op. cit. above (n. 2), pp. 271–87.

[26] For the Security Council debate see *Security Council Official Records*, 907th meeting, 28 September 1960. Generally, see F. Borella, 'L'Évolution de la Communauté en 1960: de la Communauté Constitutionnelle à la Communauté Conventionnelle', *Annuaire français de droit international*, 6 (1960), p. 925, at p. 945; R. Cohen, 'Legal Problems arising from the Dissolution of the Mali Federation', this *Year Book*, 36 (1960), p. 375; A. Gandolfi, 'Naissance et mort sur le plan international d'un état ephémère: la Fédération du Mali', *Annuaire français de droit international*, 6 (1960), p. 881.

[27] See Government of Malaysia–Government of Singapore, Independence of Singapore Agreement, 7 August 1965.

retained its international identity and United Nations membership. Singapore was forthwith admitted unopposed to the United Nations.[28]

Bangladesh is a very different case. East Pakistan (otherwise known as East Bengal) was a geographically separate part of the State of Pakistan, which had been created when British India became fully independent in 1947. Its population accounted for rather more than half the population of Pakistan (estimate: East Pakistan, 62 million; West Pakistan, 56.5 million). In 1970 national elections were held with universal suffrage, and were won by the Awami League, a party based in East Pakistan, which obtained 167 out of 313 seats in the National Assembly. In March 1971, the military leadership of Pakistan refused to accept the result of the elections, and the leader of the Awami League thereupon (26 March 1971) proclaimed the independence of East Pakistan. The military government of Pakistan responded with bombing of cities and a civil war broke out. Some 9.5 million refugees fled to India, and there was widespread repression in East Bengal. On 4 December 1971 India declared war on Pakistan and attacked its forces in East Bengal and the Punjab. On 6 December 1971 India recognized the independence of Bangladesh. The General Assembly on 7 December 1971 called for withdrawal of Indian forces, while 'recognizing the need to deal appropriately *at a subsequent stage*, within the framework of the Charter of the United Nations, with the issues which have given rise to the hostilities' (emphasis added). That resolution, which referred to 'India-Pakistan borders' and to the return of 'East Pakistan refugees', was adopted by 104–11 with 10 abstentions.[29] The Soviet Union vetoed a similar resolution proposed in the Security Council. On 16 December 1971 Pakistani forces in East Bengal surrendered, and the Awami League came to have full *de facto* control over the territory of East Bengal. But despite the military defeat of Pakistan, Bangladesh was not admitted to the United Nations until 1974. This was shortly after its recognition by Pakistan, which occurred on 2 February 1974, although it had before then been individually recognized by many States.[30]

Commentators have disagreed on whether in the circumstances of 1970–1, the people of East Bengal had a right of self-determination, whether this was a case of what may be called 'remedial secession', or whether the acceptance of its secession following the withdrawal of the Pakistan Army after the ceasefire of 16 December 1971 merely produced a *fait accompli* which in the circumstances the international community had no alternative but to accept. It has been pointed out that under the

[28] See Security Council Resolution 213 (1965), 20 September 1965; General Assembly Resolution 2010 (XX), 1 September 1965.

[29] General Assembly Resolution 2793 (XXVI), 7 December 1971.

[30] See Security Council Resolution 351, 10 June 1974; General Assembly Resolution 3203 (XXIX), 17 September 1974.

criteria enunciated in General Assembly Resolution 1541 (XV),[31] East Bengal clearly qualified as a non-self-governing territory in 1971, after the election result had been cancelled and the territory placed under a repressive military rule from Islamabad.[32] But the fact is that it was not designated as such a territory at the time, nor treated as one by the General Assembly. On the other hand, despite the violence of the military response to UDI, the large numbers of dead and displaced persons, and the sympathy for the position of East Bengal thereby generated, no State other than India was prepared to recognize Bangladesh prior to the retreat of the Pakistan forces from East Bengal in December 1971. General Assembly Resolution 2793 (XXVI) made no mention of the right of self-determination, and the Security Council took no action at all until after 16 December 1971, when it called for the withdrawal of 'all armed forces to their respective territories', with emphasis on the 'western theatre'.[33] By that stage the 'eastern theatre', that is, East Bengal, had finally fallen outside the control of Pakistan.

The Baltic States were separate States during the inter-war period and were members of the League of Nations. They were, however, occupied and illegally annexed by the Soviet Union in 1940 in circumstances involving the use of force and duress. There was little express recognition on the part of third States of the extinction of the Baltic States, and this was a relevant factor when those States sought to regain their independence in the changed circumstances of the Soviet Union after 1990.

— Lithuania declared its independence on 11 March 1990. In January 1991 it resisted a half-hearted attempt on the part of Soviet Interior Ministry troops to force it to withdraw its UDI. In an ensuing referendum in February 1991, 90.47% of valid votes cast favoured independence from the Soviet Union.

[31] See above, p. 89.

[32] Crawford, op. cit. above (n. 2), p. 116.

[33] See Security Council Resolution 307 (1971), 21 December 1971; India–Pakistan Agreement on Bilateral Relations, Simla, 3 July 1972: *International Legal Materials*, 11 (1972), p. 954. On Bangladesh, see further Crawford, op. cit. above (n. 2), pp. 115–17; Dugard, op. cit. above (n. 16), pp. 75–6; V.P. Nanda, 'Self-Determination in International Law. The Tragic Tale of Two Cities – Islamabad (West Pakistan) and Dacca (East Pakistan)', *American Journal of International Law*, 66 (1972), p. 321; T.M. Franck and N.S. Rodley, 'The Law, the United Nations and Bangla Desh', *Israel Yearbook on Human Rights*, 2 (1972), p. 142; T.M. Franck and N.S. Rodley, 'After Bangladesh: the Law of Humanitarian Intervention by Military Force', *American Journal of International Law*, 67 (1973) p. 275; International Commission of Jurists, 'East Pakistan Staff Study', *ICJ Review*, No. 8 (June 1972), p. 23; J.J.A. Salmon, 'Naissance et reconnaissance du Bangladesh', *Multitudo legum, lex unum. Mélanges en honneur de Wilhelm Wengler* (Berlin, 1973), vol. 1, p. 467; J. Salzberg, 'UN Prevention of Human Rights Violations: The Bangladesh Case', *International Organisation*, 27 (1973), p. 115.

— In Estonia, after several transitional measures and a March 1991 referendum in which 77.83% of valid votes cast supported independence, the Supreme Soviet declared independence on 20 August 1991. By this stage it had become clear that the hardline coup attempt in Moscow had failed.
— In Latvia, a referendum in March 1991 showed 73.68% of valid votes cast in favour of independence. The Latvian Supreme Soviet declared independence on 21 August 1991.

On 6 September 1991, the State Council of the Soviet Union voted unanimously to recognize the independence of the Baltic States. On 12 September 1991, the Security Council without dissent recommended their admission to the United Nations. Speaking after the adoption of the resolution, the President of the Security Council stated:

> The independence of the [Baltic States] was restored peacefully, by means of dialogue, with the consent of the parties concerned, and in accordance with the wishes and aspirations of the three peoples. We can only welcome this development, which obviously represents progress in respecting the principles of the Charter of the United Nations and in attaining its objectives.[34]

The twin emphasis on restoration of independence and on the 'consent of the parties concerned' was clearly significant. It may be noted that the Security Council did not consider the applications for recognition made by the Baltic States until 12 September 1991, six days after the Soviet Union had agreed to recognize them. Thus the position of the Soviet authorities was treated as highly significant even in a case of suppressed independence. Individual member States emphasized that, since the independence of the Baltic States had been unlawfully suppressed, they had the right of self-determination. This was articulated not as a right of unilateral secession, but as a right 'to resolve their future status through free negotiation with the Soviet authorities in a way which takes proper account of the legitimate rights and interests of the parties concerned'.[35]

[34] SCOR, S/PV/3007, 12 September 1991 (Mr Merimée (France)). See Security Council Resolutions 709–11, 12 September 1991; Committee on Admission of New Members, *Report*, S/23021, 11 September 1991. On the Baltic States, see R. Yakemtchouk, 'Les républiques baltes en droit international. Échec d'une annexion opérée en violation du droit des gens', *Annuaire français de droit international*, 37 (1991), p. 259; Cassese, *Self-Determination of Peoples* (Cambridge: CUP, 1995), pp. 258–64; R. Pullat, 'The Restoration of the Independence of Estonia', *Finnish Yearbook of International Law*, 2 (1991), p. 512; R. Rich, 'Recognition of States: The Collapse of Yugoslavia and the Soviet Union', *European Journal of International Law*, 4 (1993), p. 36.

[35] HL Debates, vol.525 (written answers), col. 9 (23 January 1991), in this *Year Book*, 62 (1991), p. 573 (Minister of State, Foreign and Commonwealth Office). See also 'Pratique française du droit international', *Annuaire français de droit international*, 37 (1991), pp. 976–9.

The eleven successor States of the former Soviet Union achieved independence by a form of break-away from the Soviet Union, a process which soon acquired the support of all the constituent republics, including the Russian Federation. The position of the Russian Federation was crucial, since, despite initial uncertainty and some discontinuity of government personnel with the former Soviet Union, it was rapidly recognized as continuing the latter's legal personality, both by the other constituent republics[36] and by the United Nations.[37] At the same time the Russian Federation accepted the emergence to independence of the other republics and supported their applications for United Nations membership. Moldova, Kazakhstan, Kirgizstan, Tajikistan, Turkmenistan and Uzbekistan were admitted to the United Nations on 2 March 1992, as were Armenia and Azerbaijan (despite the fact that they were then at war over Nagorny-Kharabakh). Ukraine and Belarus were original members of the United Nations, a position they retained after independence. On 31 July, Georgia became the last of the former Soviet republics to be admitted to the United Nations, having also been the last to apply (on 6 May 1992). In all cases, admission to the United Nations was unopposed.

The successor States of the former Yugoslavia came into existence through a complex and violent process, beginning in late 1990 and reaching a certain, by no means complete, conclusion at the time of the

[36] On 8 December 1991, the heads of State of Belarus, the Russian Federation and Ukraine signed an Agreement establishing the Commonwealth of Independent States, declaring in the preamble that 'the Union of Soviet Socialist Republics as a subject of international law and as a geopolitical reality no longer exists': *International Legal Materials*, 31 (1992), p. 143. This Agreement was modified by a Protocol of Alma Ata of 21 December 1991, signed by 11 of the Republics (but not by Georgia): ibid., p. 147. An accompanying 'Decision' by the Council of the CIS (ibid., p. 151) recorded the agreement of the CIS to 'support Russia's continuance of the membership of the Union of Soviet Socialist Republics in the United Nations, including permanent membership of the Security Council, and other international organizations'. By letter of 24 December 1991, President Yeltsin informed the UN Secretary-General of the view of Russia and the other republics: ibid., p. 138. The implications of Russia's position as continuing the legal personality of the USSR have since been accepted for non-UN purposes as well (e.g., ownership of extraterritorial property, residual responsibility for the external debt of the USSR, etc.). On the dissolution of the Soviet Union, see R. Rich, 'Recognition of States: The Collapse of Yugoslavia and the Soviet Union', *European Journal of International Law*, 4 (1993), p. 36; R. Mullerson, 'The Continuity and Succession of States, by reference to the former USSR and Yugoslavia', *International and Comparative Law Quarterly*, 42 (1993), p. 473; M. Bothe, 'Sur quelques questions de succession posées par la dissolution de l'URSS et celle de la Yougoslavie', *Revue générale de droit international public*, 96 (1992), p. 811; W. Czaplinski, 'La Continuité, l'identité et la succession d'états – évaluation de cas recents', *Revue belge de droit international*, 26 (1993), p. 374; M. Scharf, 'Musical Chairs: The Dissolution of States and Membership of the United Nations', *Cornell International Law Journal*, 28 (1995), p. 29; P. Juviler, 'Contested Ground: Rights to Self-Determination and the Experience of the Former Soviet Union', *Transnational Law and Contemporary Problems*, 3 (1993), p. 71.

[37] No resolution was necessary; the USSR seat was simply taken up without objection by the Russian Federation following President Yeltsin's letter of 24 December 1991: see Sharf, loc. cit. above (n. 36), pp. 46–7.

Dayton-Paris Peace Agreement of 14 December 1995.[38] For present purposes it is sufficient to note that a breakdown in the constitutional arrangements occurred in May 1991, when the normal rotation arrangements for the federal presidency were rejected by the Government of Serbia. On 25 June 1991, following earlier plebiscites, Slovenia and Croatia declared their independence and civil war broke out; by this stage the Yugoslav National Army was effectively in Serb hands. By an agreement signed at Brioni on 7 July 1991, the two constituent republics suspended their declarations of independence for three months. In the absence of any agreement on the restructuring of the federation, those declarations were, however, renewed on 8 October 1991, and further armed conflict occurred in Croatia and Bosnia (which declared its 'sovereignty' on 15 October 1991). Macedonia adopted a new constitution proclaiming its independence, following a referendum, on 17 November 1991. Through seizing control of the Yugoslav National Army and by other means, Serbia and Montenegro sought to maintain the territorial integrity of Yugoslavia, and they claimed legal continuity with the former Yugoslavia. In their view, the other four constituent Republics were in secession from Yugoslavia.

The international response to the Yugoslav crisis was largely articulated through the Conference on Yugoslavia established on 27 August 1991 by the European Communities. The Conference on Yugoslavia established an Arbitration Commission presided over by M. Robert Badinter, President of the French Constitutional Court, to advise it on

[38] On the Yugoslav crisis, see, e.g., R. Bieber, 'European Community Recognition of Eastern European States: A New Perspective for International Law?', *Proceedings of the American Society of International Law*, 86 (1992), p. 374; Y. Blum, 'UN Membership of the New Yougoslavia—Continuity or Break?', *American Journal of International Law*, 86 (1992), p. 830; M. Bothe, 'Sur quelques questions de succession posées par la dissolution de l'URSS et celle de la Yougoslavie', *Revue générale de droit international public*, 96 (1992), p. 811; Geneviève Burdeau and Brigitte Stern (eds.), *Dissolution, continuation et succession en Europe de l'est* (Paris: Montchrestien, 1994); J. Charpentier, 'La Déclaration des Douze sur la reconnaissance des nouveaux états', *Revue générale de droit international public*, 96 (1992), p. 343; M.C.R. Craven, 'What's in a Name? The Former Yugoslav Republic of Macedonia and Issues of Statehood', *Australian Yearbook of International Law*, 15 (1995), p. 1; id., 'The European Community Arbitration Commission on Yugoslavia', this *Year Book*, 66 (1995), p. 333; W. Czaplinski, 'La Continuité, l'identité et la succession d'états—évaluation de cas récents', *Revue belge de droit international*, 26 (1993), p. 374; L.S. Eastwood, 'Secession: State Practice and International Law after the Dissolution of the Soviet Union and Yugoslavia', *Duke Journal of Comparative and International Law*, 3 (1993), p. 299; C. Gray, 'Bosnia and Herzegovina: Civil War or Inter-State Conflict? Characterization and Consequences', this *Year Book*, 67 (1996), p. 155; R. Mullerson, 'The Continuity and Succession of States, by reference to the Former USSR and Yugoslavia', *International and Comparative Law Quarterly*, 42 (1993), p. 473; Alain Pellet, 'L'Activité de la Commission d'Arbitrage de la Conférence Européenne pour la Paix en Yougoslavie', *Annuaire français de droit international*, 38 (1992), p. 220; R. Rich, 'Recognition of States: The Collapse of Yugoslavia and the Soviet Union', *European Journal of International Law*, 4 (1993), p. 36; M. Scharf, 'Musical Chairs: The Dissolution of States and Membership of the United Nations', *Cornell International Law Journal*, 28 (1995), p. 29; B. Stern (ed.), *Le Statut des états issus de l'ex-Yougoslavie à l'ONU. Documents* (Paris: Montchrestien, 1996); Marc Weller, 'The International Response to the Dissolution of the Socialist Federal Republic of Yugoslavia', *American Journal of International Law*, 86 (1992), p. 596.

legal issues in relation to the crisis. That Commission gave a series of opinions, of which Numbers 1, 2, 3 and 8 are particularly relevant.

In its Opinion No. 1, dated 29 November 1991, the Commission expressed the view that the situation in Yugoslavia was one involving the dissolution of the Federal Republic and the consequent emergence of its constituent republics as independent States, although that process was not yet complete.[39] The underlying rationale of Opinion No. 1 was that, in the absence of a reconstituted federal government which represented the population of Yugoslavia as a whole, there was no government which had the authority to seek to prevent the separation of the constituent republics, and that such separation would lead inevitably to the disappearance of the Socialist Federal Republic itself. It should be noted that the Commission did not use the phrase 'self-determination'. Rather its focus was on the breakdown of the federal arrangements for power sharing, arrangements which involved the representation of the constituent republics as such, and in a context where the breakdown of the federal system was accompanied by widespread ethnically-motivated violence and displacement of persons ('ethnic cleansing').

Following Opinion No. 1, the European Community issued Guidelines on Recognition of New States in Eastern Europe and the Soviet Union, and an associated Declaration on Yugoslavia, both dated 16 December 1991. The Guidelines on Recognition referred to 'the principles of the Helsinki Act and the Charter of Paris, in particular the principle of self-determination', as well as to 'the normal standards of international practice [on recognition of new States] and the political realities in each case'. They laid down various preconditions for recognition of new States in Eastern Europe and the Soviet Union, including respect for minority rights and maintenance of existing boundaries. The Declaration on Yugoslavia invited the constituent republics to apply for recognition on the basis laid down in the Guidelines, and all except Serbia-Montenegro did so. On 11 January 1992, the Arbitration Commission gave opinions considering each of these four applications.

The case of Slovenia was the least problematic. There had been no military outbreaks on the territory for many months, and the Government of Slovenia securely controlled its territory. The Arbitration Commission found that Slovenia fully satisfied the criteria for recognition. The member States of the European Union extended recognition on 15 January 1992.[40]

As for Croatia, conflict continued on its territory with elements of the Yugoslav National Army (JNA) and local Serb militias. The Arbitration Commission was concerned that a constitutional amendment of

[39] Conference on Yugoslavia, Arbitration Commission, Opinion No. 1, 29 November 1991: 92 ILR 162 at pp. 164–6.

[40] See Conference on Yugoslavia, Arbitration Commission, Opinion No. 7, 11 January 1992: 92 ILR 188.

4 December 1991 did not fully reflect the necessary guarantees with respect to the protection of minorities. Following an undertaking by the Croatian President, the member States recognized Croatia on 15 January 1991, although the Croatian Government did not control a significant part of its territory at that time. On 8 May 1992, the Constitution was further amended, and in observations dated 4 July 1992, the Arbitration Commission concluded that:

even if the Constitutional Law in question does sometimes fall short of the obligations assumed by Croatia when it accepted the Draft Convention of 4 November 1991, it nonetheless satisfies the requirements of general international law regarding the protection of minorities. Article 6(e) in particular is consistent with the fundamental principle of international law whereby all human beings are entitled to recognition, in the national context, of their membership of the ethnic, religious or language group of their choice.[41]

Macedonia, like Slovenia, substantially controlled its territory by December 1991, and the Arbitration Commission held that it satisfied each of the requirements in the Guidelines. Macedonia had adopted a constitutional amendment providing that it 'has no territorial claim on neighbouring States', and the Commission held that:

the Republic of Macedonia has, moreover, renounced all territorial claims of any kind in unambiguous statements binding in international law; that the use of the name 'Macedonia' cannot therefore imply any territorial claim against another State.[42]

Greece was, however, not prepared to agree to the recognition of Macedonia under that title, and recognition by members of the European Union did not occur until 16 December 1993, well after Macedonia had been admitted to the United Nations under the title 'The Former Yugoslav Republic of Macedonia'.

Bosnia-Herzegovina was a still more difficult case, given the large Serbian minority and its strong military opposition to separation. At no stage did the Bosnian federal authorities control more than a fraction of the territory of the republic. None the less 'sovereignty' was proclaimed on 15 October 1991. On 11 January 1992 the Arbitration Commission noted the disagreement between the various ethnic groups in the republic as to its future and concluded 'that the will of the peoples of Bosnia-Hercegovina to constitute the SRBH as a sovereign and independent State cannot be held to have been fully established'. On 29 February–1 March 1992 a referendum was held, which was boycotted by the Bosnian Serb population but which resulted in a 63% vote of the total electorate

[41] See Conference on Yugoslavia, Arbitration Commission, Opinion No. 5, 11 January 1992: 92 ILR 188; Conference on Yugoslavia, Arbitration Commission, Observations on Croatian Constitutional Law, 4 July 1992: 92 ILR 209 at p. 211.

[42] Conference on Yugoslavia, Arbitration Commission, Opinion No. 6, 11 January 1992: 92 ILR 182 at p. 187.

in favour of independence, which was declared on 3 March 1992. The members of the European Community recognized the independence of Bosnia-Herzegovina on 6 April 1992.[43]

Serbia and Montenegro, under the name of the Federal Republic of Yugoslavia, adopted a new constitution on 27 April 1992, which maintained its claim to continuity with the Socialist Federal Republic but at the same time excluded from its scope the other four Republics. At the same time it announced that it was:

disposée à respecter pleinement les droits et les intérêts des républiques yougoslaves qui ont déclaré leur indépendance. La reconnaissance des Etats nouvellement constitués interviendra une fois qu'auront été réglées les questions en suspens actuellement en cours de négociation dans le cadre de la Conférence sur la Yougoslavie.[44]

In the case of Bosnia-Herzegovina, recognition by the Federal Republic of Yugoslavia did not occur until the signature of the Peace Agreement in December 1995.

It should be noted that none of the constituent republics was admitted to the United Nations prior to the adoption by Serbia-Montenegro of its new Constitution, which clearly implied renunciation of any territorial claim to the territory of the other republics, and to its declaration of 27 April 1992, which has already been quoted. Slovenia, Croatia and Bosnia-Herzegovina were admitted to the United Nations on 22 May 1992. Macedonia was admitted, under an assumed name, on 8 April 1993. The United Nations has so far taken the view that Serbia-Montenegro is not entitled to participate as a United Nations member on the basis of continuity with the membership of the former Yugoslavia. In other words, like the EC Arbitration Commission, it has proceeded on the basis that the former Yugoslavia has been dismembered.[45]

The Arbitration Commission repeated this view in its Opinion No 8 of 4 July 1992. In that Opinion it said, *inter alia*:

2. The dissolution of a State means that it no longer has legal personality, something which has major repercussions in international law. It therefore calls for the greatest caution.

The Commission finds that the existence of a federal State, which is made up of a number of separate entities, is seriously compromised when a majority of these entities, embracing a greater part of the territory and population, constitute themselves as sovereign States with the result that federal authority may no longer be effectively exercised.

By the same token, while recognition of a State by other States has only

[43] See Conference on Yugoslavia, Arbitration Commission, Opinion No. 4, 11 January 1992: 92 ILR 173 at p. 178.

[44] UN Doc. A/46/915, 7 May 1992, reprinted in B. Stern (ed.), *Le Statut des états issus de l'ex-Yougoslavie à l'ONU. Documents* (Paris: Montchrestien, 1996), p. 58.

[45] Security Council Resolution 757 (1992), 30 May 1992; Security Council Resolution 777 (1992), 19 September 1992.

declarative value, such recognition, along with membership of international organizations, bears witness to these States' conviction that the political entity so recognized is a reality and confers on it certain rights and obligations under international law.

After a review of developments, including the Constitution adopted by Serbia-Montenegro on 27 April 1992 and the admission of three of the other former Republics to the United Nations, it concluded that the process of dissolution of the Socialist Federal Republic of Yugoslavia 'is now complete and that the SFRY no longer exists'.[46]

A General Framework Agreement for Peace in Bosnia and Herzegovina was initialled at Dayton, Ohio on 21 November 1995, and came into force upon its signature by the parties in Paris on 14 December 1995. It established a new federal constitution for Bosnia and Herzegovina, and sought to guarantee the territorial integrity of Bosnia and Herzegovina, both as against the Federal Republic of Yugoslavia and in relation to the two constituent entities of Bosnia and Herzegovina (the Federation of Bosnia and Herzegovina and Republika Srpska).[47]

It should be stressed that the questions of international status in relation to Yugoslavia since 1991 have focused on the constituent republics, which were treated from an early stage not as entities seceding from a functioning State but as the product of the dissolution of a State the majority of whose territories and people, faced with violent attempts to hold the State together by one of its ethnic groups, wished to separate. This emphasis on the constituent republics as such, at a time when the State was in a process of dissolution, had a series of important consequences.

In particular, it has meant that international recognition has been limited to the four republics. There has been no correlative acceptance that any groups within the constituent republics have any right to secede. Nor has such a right been recognized to any other territorial entities within the former Yugoslavia, including for example the autonomous area of Kosovo.

The Arbitration Commission was in fact specifically asked whether the Serbian population in Croatia and Bosnia-Herzegovina had the right of self-determination. The answer given, in Opinion No. 2 on 11 January 1992, is revealing. It said, *inter alia*:

1. The Commission considers that international law as it currently stands does not spell out all the implications of the right to self-determination. However, it is well established that, whatever the circumstances, the right to self-determination must not involve changes to existing frontiers at the time of independence (*uti possidetis juris*) except where the States concerned agree otherwise.

[46] See Conference on Yugoslavia, Arbitration Commission, Opinion No. 8, 4 July 1992: 92 ILR 199 at pp. 201, 202.

[47] General Framework Agreement for Peace in Bosnia and Herzegovina, Paris, 14 December 1995, *International Legal Materials*, 35 (1996), p. 75.

> 2. Where there are one or more groups within a State constituting one or more ethnic, religious or language communities, they have the right to recognition of their identity under international law. As the Commission emphasized in its *Opinion No. 1* of 29 November 1991, published on 7 December, the—now peremptory—norms of international law require States to ensure respect for the rights of minorities. This requirement applies to all the Republics vis-à-vis the minorities on their territory. The Serbian population in Bosnia-Hercegovina and Croatia must therefore be afforded every right accorded to minorities under international conventions as well as national and international guarantees consistent with the principles of international law and the provisions of Chapter II of the Draft Convention of 4 November 1991, which has been accepted by these Republics.
>
> 3. Article 1 of the two 1966 International Covenants on Human Rights establishes that the principles of the right to self-determination serves to safeguard human rights. By virtue of that right every individual may choose to belong to whatever ethnic, religious or language community he or she wishes. In the Commission's view one possible consequence of this principle might be for the members of the Serbian population in Bosnia-Hercegovina and Croatia to be recognized under agreements between the Republics as having the nationality of their choice, with all the rights and obligations which that entails with respect to the States concerned.[48]

It should be noted that by January 1992 the Serbian population in Bosnia-Herzegovina (which constituted about 35% of the population of the Republic) had constituted their own parliament, conducted a plebiscite, and, on 9 January 1992, had proclaimed their own republic (Republika Srpska). Opinion No. 2, however, treated them as a 'minority' and, implicitly, denied that they had any right to form an independent State. On the other hand, it did not deny the right of self-determination at the internal level, with the consequence, first, that 'every individual may choose to belong to whatever ethnic, religious or language community he or she wishes', and, secondly, that they might possibly have the right to adopt the nationality of their choice, under agreements to be concluded between the various republics.

In the result, external self-determination was denied to Republika Srpska, notwithstanding the latter's proclamation of independence on 4 July 1992. So too was it denied to the lesser territorial units within former Yugoslavia, and in particular the autonomous region of Kosovo. Kosovo (like Vojvodina) was an autonomous region within the Republic of Serbia; it had nearly two million inhabitants, nearly 90% ethnic Albanians. Its substantial autonomy was unilaterally terminated by the Serbian Government in 1990, and there has since been a substantial measure of repression. More than one-sixth of the population has fled abroad. The Albanian leadership of Kosovo declared its independence in October 1991, but this has been recognized only by Albania.

[48] Conference on Yugoslavia, Arbitration Commission, Opinion No. 2, 11 January 1992: 92 ILR 167 at pp. 168–9.

The appropriateness of the international response to the Yugoslav crisis continues to be debated. In particular the early recognition of Croatia and Bosnia-Herzegovina by member States of the European Union continues to be controversial—as too does the unduly delayed recognition of Macedonia, contrary to the advice of the Arbitration Commission and out of deference to Greek sensitivities. The Arbitration Commission, for its part, has been criticized for advocating, *inter alia*, notions about protection of minorities which go well beyond current international law, and for failing to take into account standard criteria for independence based on effective control of territory.[49]

In assessing the relevance or otherwise of the Yugoslav case to whether there is a right of unilateral secession, a number of points must be borne in mind.

First, the Arbitration Commission, which provided the underlying legal rationale for the positions taken by the members of the European Community and eventually by most members of the United Nations, proceeded on the basis that the 'process of breaking up' of the Yugoslav Federation was a matter of fact, and that the emergence to independence of the constituent republics was a *consequence* of that fact.

Secondly, it did not articulate any prior right to independence on the part of the constituent republics (although the Yugoslav Constitution of 1974 did purport to guarantee such a right to the six 'nations' it treated as indigenous to Yugoslavia). In particular the Commission did not rely on any right of self-determination of the constituent republics, as distinct from the continued proper functioning of federal organs in which those republics were intended to be directly represented.[50]

Thirdly, the situation was strongly affected by the following facts: (1) four of the six republics, containing a substantial majority of the population, were attempting to break away; (2) the constitutional order, under which the constituent republics themselves 'participate[d] in the exercise of political power within the framework of institutions common to the Federation',[51] had completely broken down, and (3) Yugoslavia was undergoing large-scale and unrelenting ethnic conflict which threatened to lead and did in fact lead to war crimes and crimes against humanity.

In each of these respects, the way in which the Yugoslavian situation was handled provides no precedent for the extension of any international legal right to secede in the case of the constituent units of federal States. To paraphrase the Commission of Jurists in the *Aaland Islands* case,

[49] M.C.R. Craven, 'The European Community Arbitration Commission on Yugoslavia', this *Year Book*, 66 (1995), p. 333, at p. 335. But see Alain Pellet, 'L'Activité de la Commission d'Arbitrage de la Conférence Européenne pour la Paix en Yougoslavie', *Annuaire français de droit international*, 38 (1992), p. 220.

[50] Craven, loc. cit. above (n. 49), at pp. 389–90.

[51] Conference on Yugoslavia, Arbitration Commission, Opinion No. 1, 29 November 1991: 92 ILR 162, at p. 163.

international law does not recognize the right of the constituent units of federal States, as such, 'to separate themselves from the State of which they form a part by the simple expression of a wish'.[52] Instead, early recognition of the successor States was based on the conclusion that as a matter of political fact the former Yugoslavia was dissolving, that this process was irreversible, and that the so-called 'federal authorities' were nothing but an emanation of Serbia-Montenegro and had no title to represent the former Yugoslavia as a whole. Even then, the successor States were not admitted to the United Nations until after Yugoslavia (Serbia-Montenegro) had reconstituted itself as a new entity under a constitution which excluded the other four former republics, and had announced its preparedness in principle to recognize them.[53]

By comparison with the complex and tragic story of the former Yugoslavia, the separation of the Czech Republic and Slovakia was a straightforwardly consensual process at the level of the governments and parliaments concerned. The two constituent republics became separate States after an agreement between them dissolving the Czechoslovak Federation. Dissolution was achieved by parliamentary action under a Constitutional Act of 1992, rather than by a secession referendum as provided for in a Constitutional Act of 1991. By the time agreed upon as the date for independence (1 January 1993), most of the arrangements for the dissolution of the Federation had been worked out by agreement between the two governments and ratified by the Federal Assembly, although certain other changes (including minor exchanges of territory) were subsequently agreed to. On 31 December 1992, the State of Czechoslovakia ceased to exist. The two new States were subsequently admitted unopposed to the United Nations.[54]

Eritrea was formerly a separate Italian, then British, colonial territory.

[52] See p. 93, above

[53] This is not to say that the principle of self-determination was without consequences internally, for example in terms of the recognition of the identity of ethnic, religious and linguistic communities within the State, and of the right of individuals to associate themselves with these communities: see Conference on Yugoslavia, Arbitration Commission, Opinion No. 2, 11 January 1992: 92 ILR 167, at pp. 168–9; ibid., Observations on Croatian Constitutional Law, 4 July 1992: 92 ILR 209, at p. 211. On the issue of internal self-determination, see further below, p. 114. Generally on the issue of external self-determination in the former Yugoslavia, see further Marc Weller, 'The International Response to the Dissolution of the Socialist Federal Republic of Yugoslavia', *American Journal of International Law*, 86 (1992), p. 596; R. Bieber, 'European Community Recognition of Eastern European States: A New Perspective for International Law?', *Proceedings of the American Society of International Law*, 86 (1992), p. 374; J. Charpentier, 'La déclaration des Douze sur la reconnaissance des nouveaux états', *Revue générale de droit international public*, 96 (1992), p. 343; Geneviève Burdeau and Brigitte Stern (eds.), *Dissolution, continuation et succession en Europe de l'est* (Paris: Montchrestien, 1994).

[54] See Czech and Slovak Federal Republic, Constitutional Act No. 541/1992 on the Division of Property, 13 November 1992; Czech and Slovak Federal Republic, Constitutional Act No. 542/1992 on the Extinction of the Czech and Slovak Federal Republic, 25 November 1992. See further J. Malenovsky, 'Problèmes juridiques liés à la partition de la Tchécoslovaquie', *Annuaire français de droit international*, 39 (1993), p. 305. For an account of the political background see Robert A. Young, *The Breakup of Czechoslovakia* (Kingston: Institute of Intergovernmental Relations, 1994).

It was federated with Ethiopia under UN auspices in 1952. In 1962 the federal arrangement was abolished unilaterally by Ethiopia, without any reaction from the United Nations. The Eritrean Peoples Liberation Front (EPLF) fought for many years to gain independence without achieving any international recognition. In 1991 that movement assisted an Ethiopian movement (EPRDF) in defeating the forces of the military regime under Menghistu Haile Mariam, who later fled to Zimbabwe. The Transitional Government of Ethiopia, which emerged after this military victory, accepted that the people of Eritrea had a right of self-determination. A plebiscite was held under UN auspices, resulting in a 99.8% vote for independence. General Assembly Resolution 47/114 established an observer mission for that purpose, on the basis that 'the authorities directly concerned have registered their commitment to respect the results of the referendum in Eritrea'. Eritrea was admitted to the United Nations with the support of the Transitional Government of Ethiopia, and without any opposition.[55] None of the United Nations resolutions concerning Eritrea since 1952 referred to self-determination, despite the agreement between the Transitional Government and the EPLF that this was a case of self-determination.[56]

Post–1945 practice in respect of attempted unilateral secession

Before summarizing the modern practice, it is useful to mention some of the many cases of attempted or threatened unilateral secession of non-colonial territories. It is precisely because of the threat represented by unilateral secession to many States and the potential for instability that this creates that States are so insistent on the principle of territorial integrity.

Since 1945 there have been numerous attempts unilaterally to secede by groups or territories within independent States. The cases include, for example:

— Tibet (China);
— Katanga (Congo);
— Biafra (Nigeria);
— Kashmir (India);
— East Punjab (India);
— The Karen and Shan States (Burma);

[55] Security Council Resolution 828, 26 May 1993; General Assembly Resolution 47/230, 28 May 1993.

[56] See further E. Gayim, *The Eritrean Question. The Conflict between the Right of Self Determination and the Interests of States* (Uppsala: Iustus Förlag, 1993); R. Goy, 'L'indépendance de l'Erythrée', *Annuaire français de droit international*, 39 (1993), p. 337; M. Haile, 'Legality of Secessions: The Case of Eritrea', *International Law Review*, 8 (1994), p. 479; R. Iyob, *The Eritrean Struggle for Independence* (Cambridge: Cambridge University Press, 1995); O. Yohannes, 'The Eritrean Question: A Colonial Case?', *Journal of Modern African Studies*, 25 (1987), p. 643.

— Turkish Federated State of Cyprus (Cyprus);
— Tamil Elam (Sri Lanka);
— South Sudan (Sudan);
— Somaliland (Somalia);
— Bougainville (Papua New Guinea);
— Kurdistan (Iraq/Turkey);
— Republika Srpska (Bosnia-Herzegovina);
— Chechnya (Russian Federation);
— Kosovo (Serbia-Montenegro);
— Abkhazia (Georgia);
— South Ossetia (Georgia);
— Nagorny-Kharabakh (Azerbaijan);
— Democratic Republic of Yemen (Yemen)

In many other cases, support for unilateral secession has existed in a territory, but has not risen to the level of a unilateral declaration of independence or some other formal attempt at unilateral secession with substantial popular support. In Europe alone such cases include, for example:

— Corsica (France);
— the Basques (Spain);
— South Tyrol (Italy);
— the Bretons (France);
— the Alsatians (France);
— Catalonia (Spain);
— Faroes (Denmark);
— Scotland (United Kingdom);
— the Flemish (Belgium);
— Padania (Italy).

In all these cases one common feature can be observed. Where the government of the State in question has maintained its opposition to the secession, such attempts have gained virtually no international support or recognition, and this has been true even when other humanitarian aspects of the situations have triggered widespread concern and action. For example, the situation of the Kurds in Northern Iraq has been a matter of international concern, triggering action by the Security Council under Chapter VII of the Charter and by individual States by way of humanitarian intervention, both military and civil. But the operations in Northern Iraq, including the 'no-fly' zones policed by some western States, have been explicitly carried out on the basis of the territorial integrity of Iraq, and this despite continued Iraqi repression of the

Kurds and the stringent United Nations response to most other aspects of Iraqi policy.[57]

It is sufficient to refer only to a few of the cases referred to above.

The Faroes are a Danish territory under Home Rule. Unlike Greenland, they were never treated as a colonial territory after 1945.[58] But in a referendum on 14 September 1946 the electorate by a very narrow majority of valid votes cast favoured secession over autonomy, and this was followed by a parliamentary vote on 18 September 1946 in favour of secession. The Danish Government rejected unilateralism, and on 24 September 1946 the King, acting on the advice of the Danish Government, intervened, dissolving the Parliament and calling a general election (which was won by the Home Rule party). Following negotiations, a new arrangement for Home Rule was ratified by the Danish Parliament and took effect on 1 April 1948. The Home Rule arrangements have evolved since but have remained stable. There was at no stage any international recognition of the Faroes as independent, nor any international reaction to the unprecedented intervention by the King on 24 September 1946. The matter was throughout treated as internal to Denmark.[59]

No international acceptance or recognition has been forthcoming for various seceding entities within the constituent republics of the former Yugoslavia. For example, by January 1992 the Serbian population in Bosnia-Herzegovina (which constituted about 35% of the population of the Republic) had constituted their own parliament, conducted a plebiscite, and, on 9 January 1992, proclaimed their own republic—Republika Srpska. Opinion No. 2 of the EC's Arbitration Commission specifically addressed the right to self-determination of the Serbs within Bosnia-Herzegovina. The Commission treated them as a 'minority' and denied that they had any right to form an independent State. On the other hand, it did not deny the right of self-determination at the internal level, with the consequence, first, that 'every individual may choose to belong to whatever ethnic, religious or language community he or she wishes', and, secondly, that they might possibly have the right to adopt the nationality of their choice, under agreements to be concluded between the various republics.[60] In the result, external self-determination was denied to

[57] See Security Council Resolutions 686 (1991), 2 March 1991; 687 (1991), 3 April 1991; 688 (1991), 5 April 1991; 949 (1994), 15 October 1994. Each of these resolutions explicitly affirms Iraq's territorial integrity.

[58] See Isi Foighel, 'A Framework for Local Autonomy: The Greenland Case', in Yoram Dinstein (ed.), *Models of Autonomy* (New Brunswick: Transaction Books, 1981), p. 31.

[59] See A. Olafsson, 'International Status of the Faroe Islands', *Nordic Journal of International Law*, 51 (1982), p. 29; E. Patursson, 'Some Critical Observations on the Political Development of the Faroe Islands and their Present Political Situation', ibid., 54 (1985), p. 52; F. Harhoff, 'Faroe Islands', in R. Bernhardt (ed.), *Encylopedia of Public International Law*, vol. 2 (1995), p. 357.

[60] Conference on Yugoslavia, Arbitration Commission, Opinion No. 2, 11 January 1992: 92 ILR 167 at pp. 168–9.

Republika Srpska, notwithstanding the latter's proclamation of independence on 4 July 1992. That position was expressly confirmed in the Dayton-Paris Peace Agreement.[61]

So too was external self-determination denied to the lesser territorial units within former Yugolsavia, and in particular the autonomous region of Kosovo. Kosovo (like Vojvodina) was an autonomous region within the Republic of Serbia; it had nearly two million inhabitants, of whom nearly 90% were ethnic Albanians. Its substantial autonomy was unilaterally terminated by the Serbian Government in 1990, and there has since been a considerable measure of repression. More than one-sixth of the population has fled abroad. The Albanian leadership of Kosovo declared its independence in October 1991, but this has been recognized only by Albania.

The situation in Chechnya is also of interest. Under the USSR, the Chechen and Ingush peoples were united in the autonomous republic of Chechen-Ingushetia, a constituent republic of the Russian Federative Soviet Socialist Republic. On 2 November 1991, Chechnya declared its independence from the Russian Federation, the USSR and also Ingushetia, the other region constituting the former autonomous republic of Chechen-Ingushetia.[62] After a brief skirmish with Russian troops, Chechnya was largely left to its own devices; its government maintained effective control over the republic, even requiring that citizens of the neighbouring republics obtain special Chechnyan visas.[63] In December 1994 the Russian Army made a large-scale attempt to suppress the separatist movement. However, a ceasefire was agreed between the Russian Federation and the Chechen Republic, and was followed by a Joint Declaration of 31 August 1996, which referred *inter alia* to 'the commonly recognized right of peoples to self-determination' and provided for an agreement on mutual relations 'in accordance with commonly recognized principles and the norms of international law' to be achieved by 31 December 2001.[64] Despite the Russian military defeat and subsequent withdrawal, there has so far been no international recognition of the independence of Chechnya. Many governments have

[61] Bosnia and Herzegovina–Croatia–Yugoslavia, General Framework Agreement for Peace in Bosnia and Herzegovina with Annexes, Paris, 14 December 1995: *International Legal Materials*, 35 (1996), p. 75. The Agreement and its Annexes seek to guarantee the territorial integrity of Bosnia and Herzegovina against any form of secession or dismemberment.

[62] This occurred on 2 November 1991 under the leadership of retired Air Force General Djokar Dudayev. It was not put to a referendum. On 6 June 1992, activists also declared Ingushetia a sovereign republic. This was unceremoniously crushed by troops of the Russian Interior Ministry in November and Ingushetia was placed under direct rule from Moscow. On 10 December 1992, Ingushetia was made a republic of the Russian Federation. See R. Yakemtchouk, 'Les conflits de territoire et de frontière dans les états de l'ex-URSS', *Annuaire français de droit international*, 39 (1993), p. 393, at pp. 424–6.

[63] Ibid., at p. 426.

[64] Joint Declaration, and Principles for Determining the Basics for Mutual Relations between the Russian Federation and the Chechen Republic, 31 August 1996.

criticized the conduct of Russian forces in Chechnya on grounds of the use of disproportionate force, violations of international humanitarian law and breach of arms control agreements.[65] But it has also been accepted that the conflict with Chechnya is an internal armed conflict, and that the principle of territorial integrity applies. For example, the French Foreign Minister said on 9 January 1995:

> La Tchétchénie fait partie de la Fédération de Russie. Le respect du principe de souveraineté et d'intégrité territoriale est une des règles de base de la vie internationale. Mais les Etats membres de la OSCE ont pris des engagements et sont reconnus un droit de regard mutuel sur ce qui se passe à l'intérieur de leurs propres territoires nationaux.[66]

The British Government stated that:

> the exercise of the right [of self-determination] must also take into account questions such as what constitutes a separate people and respect for the principle [of] territorial integrity of the unitary State. In the case of Chechnya no country has recognized President Dudayev's unilateral declaration of independence, but we have repeatedly called on the Russians to work for a political solution which would allow the Chechen people to express their identity within the framework of the Russian Federation.[67]

The United States Government said that:

> We support the sovereignty and territorial integrity of the Russian Federation . . . We oppose attempts to alter international boundaries by force, whether in the form of aggression by one State against another or in the form of armed secessionist movements such as the one led by Dzhokhar Dudayev. That is why we have said that we regard Chechnya as a matter which the Russian Government and the people of Chechnya will have to resolve together peacefully by political means . . . [A]lthough Chechnya is an integral part of the Russian Federation, Moscow should limit any use of force to a minimum, and respect human rights . . . [68]

The point is that, even though other governments qualified the Chechens as a 'people', and even though this people was subject to violations of human rights and humanitarian law on a large scale, the principle of territorial integrity was respected. The relations between the Russian Federation and Chechnya were, and remain, a matter for negotiation between them. They were not resolved by the latter's unilateral declaration of independence—or even, for that matter, its subsequent military successes.

[65] In particular the Treaty on Conventional Armed Forces in Europe, Paris, 19 November 1990, Art. V, *International Legal Materials*, 30 (1991), p. 1, at p. 5.

[66] 'Pratique française du droit international', *Annuaire français de droit international*, 41 (1995), at p. 911.

[67] HL Debates, vol. 563, col. 476, 18 April 1995; in this *Year Book*, 66 (1995), p.621.

[68] Deputy Secretary of State S. Talbott, 'Supporting Democracy and Economic Reform in the New Independent States', *US Department of State Dispatch*, 6 (1995), p. 119, at p. 120.

A final example, illustrating the unwillingness of some constitutional systems to use the term 'people' for distinctive linguistic and historic groups, is Corsica. Article 2 of the Constitution of the French Republic of 1958 declares that France is an 'indivisible Republic'. On the basis of Article 2, the French Government denies that there are even linguistic or cultural minorities within its metropolitan territory.[69] But Corsica, acquired by purchase from Genoa in 1768, has its own language and culture. On 13 October 1988 the Corsican Assembly affirmed 'the existence of a living historical and cultural community comprising native-born Corsicans and Corsicans by adoption: the Corsican people'. Partly in response, the French Parliament in 1991 enacted a law 'portant statut de la collectivité territoriale de Corse', Article 1 of which provided:

> La République française garantit à la communauté historique et culturelle vivante que constitue le peuple corse, composante du peuple français, les droits à la préservation de son identité culturelle à la défense de ses intérêts économiques et sociaux spécifiques. Ces droits, liés à l'insularité, s'exercent dans le respect de l'unité nationale, dans le cadre de la Constitution, des lois de la République et du présent statut.

In a decision of 9 May 1991, the Constitutional Court held Article 1 invalid, although other aspects of the law were upheld. It said, *inter alia*:

> Considérant que la France est, ainsi que se proclame l'article 2 de la Constitution de 1958, une République indivisible, laïque, démocratique et sociale qui assure l'égalité devant la loi de tous les citoyens quelle que soit leur origine; que dès lors la mention faite par le législateur du 'peuple corse, composante du peuple français' est contraire à la Constitution, laquelle ne connaît que le peuple français, composé de tous les citoyens français sans distinction d'origine, de race ou de religion . . . [70]

On the other hand the Court upheld provisions allowing the territorial assembly to promote the teaching of Corsican language and culture.[71]

[69] When France ratified the International Covenant on Civil and Political Rights in 1980, it made the following reservation: 'In the light of Article 2 of the Constitution of the French Republic, the French Government declares that Article 27 [minority rights] is not applicable so far as the Republic is concerned': United Nations, *Multilateral Treaties Deposited with the Secretary-General. Status as at 31 December 1995* (ST/LEG/SER.E/14, 1996), p. 124. The position of French overseas departments and territories is different under French constitutional law and practice, as the Constitutional Court recognized in its decisions of 30 December 1975 concerning Mayotte, and of 2 June 1987 concerning New Caledonia.

[70] Cour Constitutionnel, Décision 91–290 DC, 9 May 1991: *Revue du droit public*, 1991, p. 969, at p. 971.

[71] Ibid., at pp. 975–6. For commentary, see François Luchaire, 'Le Statut de la Collectivité de Corse', ibid., p. 943. It should be noted that the separatist movement in Corsica has little popular support (ca. 10%).

Summary of post-1945 practice

To summarize, outside the colonial context, the principle of self-determination is not recognized in practice as giving rise to unilateral rights of secession by parts of independent States. Self-determination outside the colonial context is primarily a process by which the peoples of the various States determine their future through constitutional processes without external interference. Faced with an expressed desire of part of its people to secede, it is for the government of the State to decide how to respond, for example by insisting that any change be carried out in accordance with constitutional processes. In fact, no new State formed since 1945 outside the colonial context has been admitted to the United Nations over the opposition of the predecessor State.

The unwillingness of the international community to accept unilateral secession from an independent State can be illustrated by reference to the so-called 'safeguard' clause to the Friendly Relations Declaration, which, in elaborating the Charter principle of self-determination, specifies that:

> Nothing in the foregoing paragraphs shall be construed as authorizing or encouraging any action which would dismember or impair, totally or in part, the territorial integrity or political unity of sovereign and independent States conducting themselves in compliance with the principle of equal rights and self-determination of peoples as described above *and thus possessed of a government representing the whole people belonging to the territory without distinction as to race, creed or colour.*[72]

The 'safeguard clause' was reaffirmed in slightly different language by the United Nations World Conference on Human Rights held in Vienna in 1993. The Vienna Declaration provides, in relevant part:

> In accordance with the Declaration on Principles of International Law concerning Friendly Relations and Co-operation Among States in accordance with the Charter of the United Nations, this [*sc.* the right of self-determination] shall not be construed as authorizing or encouraging any action which would dismember or impair, totally or in part, the territorial integrity or political unity of sovereign and independent States conducting themselves in compliance with the principle of equal rights and self-determination of peoples and thus possessed of a Government representing the whole people belonging to the territory *without distinction of any kind.*[73]

According to this formula, a State whose government represents the whole people of its territory without distinction of any kind, that is to

[72] Declaration on Principles of International Law concerning Friendly Relations and Co-operation among States in accordance with the Charter of the United Nations, General Assembly Resolution 2625 (XXV), 24 October 1970, 'The principle of equal rights and self-determination of peoples', para. 7 (emphasis added).

[73] United Nations World Conference on Human Rights, Vienna Declaration and Programme of Action, 25 June 1993, *International Legal Materials*, 32 (1993), p. 1661, at p. 1665 (emphasis added).

say, on a basis of equality, and in particular without discrimination on grounds of race, creed or colour, complies with the principle of self-determination in respect of all of its people and is entitled to the protection of its territorial integrity. To put it another way, the people of such a State exercise the right of self-determination through their participation in the government of the State on a basis of equality.[74]

There is a distinct issue of internal self-determination, in the sense of the recognition of cultural identity and internal self-government for different groups or peoples within the State. Traditionally international law treated such issues as essentially matters of domestic jurisdiction, as reflected in the very reserved formulation in the minority rights clause, Article 27, of the International Covenant on Civil and Political Rights.[75] Developments in respect of the idea of internal self-determination and self-government are, however, occurring, and they are accompanied by an extension of minority rights, including the rights of national minorities,[76] and an increased recognition of the rights of indigenous peoples.[77] Consistently with these developments, the term 'peoples' is coming to be seen as more inclusive, and is not limited to the people of the State as a whole. But these developments are still tentative (*de lege ferenda*), and they do not affect the established rules and practices with respect to self-determination and the territorial integrity of States.

IV. Conclusion

As this review demonstrates, State practice since 1945 shows very clearly the extreme reluctance of States to recognize or accept unilateral secession outside the colonial context. That practice has not changed since 1989, despite the emergence during that period of 22 new States. On the contrary, the practice has been powerfully reinforced.

Of the new States which have emerged since 1945 outside the context of decolonization, only one case can be classified as a successful unilateral secession in the sense described above, that is, Bangladesh—and its

[74] See Cassese, op. cit. above (n. 34), pp. 109–25, for a full discussion of the 'safeguard clause'.

[75] This provides: 'In those States in which ethnic, religious or linguistic minorities exist, persons belonging to such minorities shall not be denied the right, in community with the other members of their group, to enjoy their own culture, to profess and practise their own religion, or to use their own language'.

[76] See, e.g., General Assembly Resolution 47/135, 18 December 1992, Declaration on the Rights of Persons belonging to National or Ethnic, Religious or Linguistic Minorities; at the regional level, Council of Europe, Framework Convention for the Protection of National Minorities, 1 February 1995, *International Legal Materials*, 34 (1995), p. 351.

[77] ILO Convention No. 169 concerning Indigenous and Tribal Peoples in Independent Countries, 27 June 1989: *International Legal Materials*, 28 (1989), p. 1382; UN Commission on Human Rights, Draft Declaration on the Rights of Indigenous Peoples, E/CN.4/SUB.2/1994/2/Add.1 (1994), *International Legal Materials*, 34 (1995), p. 535.

emergence was hardly 'unilateral'.[78] In truth the indications are that the United Nations did not treat the emergence of Bangladesh as a case of self-determination, despite good grounds for doing so—but rather as a *fait accompli* achieved as a result of foreign military assistance in special circumstances. The violence and repression engaged in by the Pakistan military regime made reunification unthinkable, and in effect legitimized the creation of the new State. In all other cases which might otherwise be classified as unilateral secession (Senegal, Singapore, the Baltic States and Eritrea), the consent of the relevant parties was given before independence was externally recognised as accomplished, and the process was accordingly not unilateral.[79] The key feature in the cases of Senegal, Singapore and Eritrea was that separation was expressly agreed to by the parties directly concerned. With the Baltic States, the essential rationale was the recovery of independence forcibly suppressed.[80] Even so, considerable importance was attached to the indication of consent given by the State Council of the Soviet Union.

A second group of cases involved States in Eastern and Central Europe immediately after the collapse of communism (Soviet Union, Yugoslavia, Czechoslovakia).[81] With the exception of Yugoslavia, the emergence of the constituent units of these States took place on a basis of agreement by those concerned, and international recognition followed upon that agreement. The position of Yugoslavia was different, but the articulated basis for the European and international response to the outbreak of violence and armed conflict in Yugoslavia was that this was inevitably producing the dissolution of Yugoslavia as a matter of fact. Neither the European Union nor the United Nations proclaimed that the peoples of Yugoslavia had a prior right to secede by virtue of the principle of self-determination. On the contrary, the emergence of the constituent republics was treated as a consequence of the dissolution of Yugoslavia, and early international recognition was seen (rightly or wrongly) as a way of containing the violence and limiting the issues to be resolved.

By contrast, many attempts at unilateral secession have occurred, and continue to occur. Where the government of the State in question has maintained its opposition to the unilateral secession, such attempts have

[78] By the time Bangladesh was admitted to the United Nations in 1974, it had been recognized by Pakistan.

[79] It may be noted that in each of these cases the territory concerned had been either an independent State or a separate colonial territory to which the principle of self-determination had expressly applied. In each case the exercise of self-determination had either misfired (Senegal, Singapore) or been suppressed (Baltic States, Eritrea).

[80] This is the only case since 1989 in which the rationale for admission to the United Nations was expressly spelled out by the Security Council at the time it recommended admission to the United Nations. In all other cases the recommendation for admission, however controversial, was made in purely formal terms, suggesting an awareness of a need for an articulated justification in the case of the Baltic States.

[81] Cf. Luzius Wildhaber, 'Territorial Modifications and Breakups in Federal States', *Canadian Yearbook of International Law*, 33 (1995), p. 1, at pp. 12–13.

gained virtually no international support or recognition, and this has been true even when other humanitarian aspects of the situation have triggered widespread concern and action.

Thus there is a common pattern of international responses to unilateral secession and threats of such secession in the non-colonial context, a pattern which has normative significance. This may be summarized as follows:

(*a*) There is strong international reluctance to support unilateral secession or separation, and there is no recognition of a unilateral right to secede based merely on a majority vote of the population of a given subdivision or territory. In principle, self-determination for peoples or groups within the State is to be achieved by participation in its constitutional system, and on the basis of respect for its territorial integrity.

(*b*) In most cases, referenda conducted in territories wishing to secede have returned very substantial majorities in favour (in the range of 65–99%). But even in cases where there is a strong and continued call for independence, it is a matter for the government of the State concerned to consider how to respond.[82]

(*c*) Even in the context of separate colonial territories, unilateral secession was the exception. Self-determination was in the first instance a matter for the colonial authority to implement; only if it was blocked by the colonial authority did the United Nations support unilateral secession. Outside the colonial context, the United Nations is extremely reluctant to admit a seceding entity to membership against the wishes of the government of the State from which it has purported to secede. In fact, there is no case since 1945 where it has done so. Where the parent State agrees to allow a territory to separate and become independent, the terms on which separation is agreed between the parties concerned will be respected, whether it involves continued association with that State (e.g., Faroes) or emergence to independence (e.g., Eritrea). If independence is achieved under such an agreement, rapid admission to the United Nations will follow. But where the government of the State concerned has maintained its opposition to an attempted unilateral secession, such secession has in modern practice attracted virtually no international support or recognition.

[82] In such cases the State must comply with its obligations under international human rights and international humanitarian law. The latter are contained *inter alia* in Protocol II additional to the Geneva Conventions of 12 August 1949, and relating to the Protection of Victims of Non-International Armed Conflicts, Geneva, 12 December 1977, *International Legal Materials*, 16 (1977), p. 1442. It should be noted that certain 'internal' conflicts are specifically included in Additional Protocol I relating to the Protection of Victims of International Armed Conflicts, ibid., p. 1391, specifically 'armed conflicts in which peoples are fighting against colonial domination and alien occupation and against racist regimes in the exercise of their right of self-determination, as enshrined in the Charter of the United Nations and the Declaration on Principles of International Law concerning Friendly Relations and Co-operation among States in accordance with the Charter of the United Nations': see Protocol I, Art. 1 (4).

(*d*) This pattern is reflected in the so-called 'safeguard' clause to the Friendly Relations Declaration of 1970, as restated by the 1993 Declaration of the Vienna World Conference on Human Rights. In accordance with this formula, a State whose government represents the whole people of its territory on a basis of equality complies with the principle of self-determination in respect of all of its people and is entitled to the protection of its territorial integrity. The people of such a State exercise the right of self-determination through their participation in the governmental system of the State on a basis of equality.

(*e*) But the inhibitions on international recognition of unilateral secession movements go further, and are even stronger than the 'safeguard clause' in the 1970 and 1993 Declarations imply. If the 1970/1993 proviso is taken to mean that unilateral secession is permissible where the government is constituted on a discriminatory basis, it is doubtful whether the proviso reflects international practice. But however this may be, a State which *is* governed democratically and respects the human rights of all its people is entitled to respect for its territorial integrity.

(*f*) Propositions (*a*)–(*d*) above apply to secession movements within independent States, even in cases where the State itself may be in the process of dissolution. However, there is a distinction between cases of unilateral secession and dissolution. If it becomes clear that the process of dissolution of the State as a whole is irreversible, the consent of the government of the predecessor State may cease to be required for the separation of its constituent parts. In such a case that government will itself be in the process of dissolution, and may have ceased to represent the former State. But there is a strong presumption against dissolution, and the only case of successful separation under these circumstances is that of the constituent republics of the former Yugoslavia.

(*g*) There is a distinct issue of internal self-determination, in the sense of the recognition of cultural identity and internal self-government for different groups or peoples within the State. But these developments do not affect the established rules and practices with respect to self-determination and the territorial integrity of States. They lend no support to the view that peoples within independent States have a unilateral right to secede.

SUSTAINABLE DEVELOPMENT AND THE EQUITABLE UTILIZATION OF INTERNATIONAL WATERCOURSES*

By XIMENA FUENTES‡

Introduction

Sustainable development is a concept that attempts to reconcile economic development and the protection of the environment. This concept was propounded by the World Commission on Environment and Development (WCED)[1] which defined it as 'development that meets the needs of the present without compromising the ability of future generations to meet their own needs'.[2] Sustainable development, therefore, imposes constraints upon the right of States to choose and apply their own developmental policies and is based on the idea that due regard ought to be paid to the protection of the environment, but it also involves the idea that development cannot be completely conditioned by environmental protection. This integration of environmental and developmental concerns requires a process which combines already existing principles of international law with principles which do not have the status of *lex lata*. It is in this context that this study examines the relationship between sustainable development and the principle of equitable utilization of international watercourses.

The utilization of international watercourses is governed by the well-established principle of equitable and reasonable utilization, which requires that in determining the rights of the watercourse States upon their international watercourses, account is to be taken of all factors and circumstances relevant to the particular case. This principle is embodied in the UN Convention on the Law of the Non-Navigational Uses of International Watercourses which was adopted by the General Assembly of the United Nations on 21 May 1997.[3] Article 5 of the Convention provides that:

‡ Bachelor of Social and Legal Sciences (University of Chile); D.Phil. (Oxon.). Lawyer. This article is based on the author's research as a D. Phil. student at the University of Oxford.

[1] Also known as the Brundtland Commission, it was established in 1983 by the General Assembly of the United Nations.

[2] WCED, *Our Common Future* (Oxford, 1987), p. 43.

[3] The recorded vote was as follows: 103 States in favour, 3 against and 27 abstentions. However, Belgium stated later that, though its vote was recorded as an abstention, it had been its intention to vote in favour. Fiji and Nigeria, the vote of which was not recorded, also expressed that their

1. Watercourse States shall in their respective territories utilize an international watercourse in an equitable and reasonable manner. In particular, an international watercourse shall be used and developed by watercourse States with a view to attaining optimal and sustainable utilization thereof and benefits therefrom, taking into account the interests of the watercourse States concerned, consistent with adequate protection of the watercourse.
2. Watercourse States shall participate in the use, development and protection of an international watercourse in an equitable and reasonable manner. Such participation includes both the right to utilize the watercourse and the duty to co-operate in the protection and development thereof, as provided in the present Convention.

The meaning of equitable and reasonable utilization is further developed in Article 6, which stipulates that:

1. Utilization of an international watercourse in an equitable and reasonable manner within the meaning of Article 5 requires taking into account all relevant factors and circumstances, including:
   (*a*) Geographic, hydrographic, hydrological, climatic, ecological and other factors of a natural character;
   (*b*) The social and economic needs of the watercourse States concerned;
   (*c*) The population dependent on the watercourse in each watercourse State;
   (*d*) The effects of the use or uses of the watercourse in one watercourse State on other watercourse States;
   (*e*) Existing and potential uses of the watercourse;
   (*f*) Conservation, protection, development and economy of use of the water resources of the watercourse and the costs of measures taken to that effect;
   (*g*) The availability of alternatives, of corresponding value, to a particular planned or existing use.
2. In the application of Article 5 or paragraph 1 of this Article, watercourse States concerned shall, when the need arises, enter into consultations in a spirit of co-operation.
3. The weight to be given to each factor is to be determined by its importance in comparison with that of other relevant factors. In determining what is a reasonable and equitable use, all relevant factors are to be considered together and a conclusion reached on the basis of the whole.[4]

Thus, sustainable development as such has not been included as a relevant criterion to be taken into account in the establishment of an equitable regime for the utilization of international watercourses. The 1994 Draft Articles on the Law of the Non-Navigational Uses of International Watercourses adopted by the International Law Commission did not contain any reference to the principle of sustainable

intention was to vote in favour. Text of the Convention in *International Legal Materials*, 36 (1997), pp. 700 ff.

[4] The relevance of the prospective equitable factors has been analysed in Fuentes, 'The Criteria for the Equitable Utilization of International Rivers', this *Year Book*, 67 (1996), pp.337 ff.

development, apart from its inclusion in Article 24 regarding the management of international watercourses. The text of Article 24, which has been maintained in the 1997 UN Convention, reads as follows:

Management

1. Watercourse States shall, at the request of any of them, enter into consultations concerning the management of an international watercourse, which may include the establishment of a joint management mechanism.

2. For the purposes of this article, 'management' refers, in particular, to:

(*a*) planning the sustainable development of an international watercourse and providing for the implementation of any plans adopted; and,

(*b*) otherwise promoting rational and optimal utilization, protection and control of the watercourse.

The commentary which the ILC attached to this provision explained that watercourse States are not required to 'manage' the watercourse in question and that the use of the terms 'sustainable development' and 'rational and optimal utilization' are to be understood as relevant to the process of management. The commentary emphasized that Article 24 in no way affected the application of Articles 5 and 7.[5]

The omission of sustainable development was criticized by various States. In this connection, Finland observed that: 'the principle of sustainable development, which has become widely quoted and accepted since the Rio Conference, has not been adequately reflected in the draft articles'.[6] Therefore, Finland proposed that the term sustainable development be introduced in Article 5 (principle of equitable and reasonable utilization) or in Article 6 (equitable factors). In Finland's view, sustainable development would in any case have to be taken into consideration in the search for balance between the factors relevant to equitable and reasonable utilization.

During the debate in the United Nations, the inclusion of sustainable development was proposed by Finland and the Netherlands. Finland's proposal referred to the inclusion of sustainable development in the chapeau of Article 6.1.[7] For its part, the Netherlands proposed to include a reference to sustainable development in Article 5.[8]

Other countries proposed to include references to the term 'sustainable utilization'. In this regard, Egypt proposed to include sustainable utilization as one of the objectives of water utilization.[9] Canada, Germany, Italy, Romania and the United States proposed to include a reference to the notion of sustainable utilization in Article 5 and to add

[5] ILC, *Report of the International Law Commission to the General Assembly on the Work of its Forty-Sixth Session* (hereinafter, 1994 *ILC Report*), Doc. A/49/10 (1994), p.301.

[6] *Comments and Observations Received from States*, Doc. A/51/275, 6 August 1996. See also the observations of Portugal, Colombia, Hungary and Turkey.

[7] Doc. A/C.6/51/NUW/WG/CRP.18.

[8] Doc. A/C.6/51/NUW/WG/CRP.11.

[9] Doc. A/C.6/51/NUW/WG/CRP.93.

'the importance of managing the watercourse in a sustainable manner for present and future generations' to the text of Article 6.[10] For its part, Jordan proposed to include the concept of 'sustainability' in Article 7.[11] The debate in the Drafting Committee and in the Working Group shows that only two States opposed the inclusion of 'sustainable utilization': India and the Czech Republic.[12]

The result of this discussion was that a reference to sustainable utilization was incorporated into Article 5.1 and this notion was also included in the Preamble of the Convention. The pertinent paragraph of the Preamble states that the Parties express their conviction that:

> . . . a framework convention will ensure the utilization, development, conservation, management and protection of international watercourses and the promotion of the optimal and sustainable utilization thereof for present and future generations.

Article 5.1 reads:

> Watercourse States shall in their respective territories utilize an international watercourse in an equitable and reasonable manner. In particular, an international watercourse shall be used and developed by watercourse States with a view to attaining optimal and sustainable utilization thereof and benefits therefrom, taking into account the interests of the watercourse States concerned, consistent with adequate protection of the watercourse.

Therefore sustainable development is only mentioned in Article 24, while the Preamble of the Convention and Article 5 speak of sustainable utilization. Nevertheless, and given the fact that sustainable development is a concept which 'refers to processes, principles and objectives, as well as to a large body of international agreements on environment, economics and civil and political rights',[13] the incorporation of all or some of these elements into the process of the establishment of an equitable regime for international watercourses cannot be discarded. Apart from the question concerning the role of sustainable development in the application of the principle of equitable utilization, it is also necessary to examine what would be the role of equitable utilization in the process of the attainment of sustainable development.

[10] Doc. A/C.6/51/NUW/WG/CRP.35.

[11] Jordan's proposal for Article 7.1 reads as follows: '1. Watercourse States shall take appropriate measures to utilize an international watercourse in such a way as not to introduce to the watercourse changes that jeopardize the sustainability of existing or potential uses of the watercourse by other States': Doc. A/C.6/51/NUW/DC/CRP.8.

[12] Docs. A/C.6/51/SR.61 and A/C.6/51/SR.62.Add.1.

[13] Sands, 'International Law in the Field of Sustainable Development', this *Year Book*, 65 (1994), p. 379.

I. The Two Essential Elements Embodied in the Notion of Sustainable Development

As was pointed out before, the Brundtland Commission defined sustainable development as 'development that meets the needs of the present without compromising the ability of future generations to meet their own needs'.[14] The concept, therefore, involves the idea of a balance between socio-economic development and the protection of the environment which can be traced back to the 1972 Stockholm Declaration on the Human Environment. While establishing an obligation to protect the environment, the Stockholm Declaration also recognized that a priority for developing countries was development.[15] Principle 2 of the Stockholm Declaration states that:

> The natural resources of the earth including the air, water, land, flora and fauna and especially representative samples of natural ecosystems must be safeguarded for the benefit of present and future generations through careful planning or management, as appropriate.

However, Principle 11 makes clear that the aim of protecting the environment should not affect the possibilities of economic development in developing countries. Principle 11 reads as follows:

> The environmental policies of all states should enhance and not adversely affect the present or future development potential of developing countries, nor should they hamper the attainment of better living conditions for all, and appropriate steps should be taken by States and international organizations with a view to reaching agreement on meeting the possible national and international economic consequences resulting from the application of environmental measures.

For its part, Principle 23 states that:

> Without prejudice to such criteria as may be agreed upon by the international community, or to standards which will have to be determined nationally, it will be essential in all cases to consider the systems of values prevailing in each country and the extent of the applicability of standards which are valid for the most advanced countries but which may be inappropriate and of unwarranted social cost for the developing countries.

The 1992 Rio Declaration on Development and Environment also underscores the interrelationship between economic development and the duty to protect the environment.[16] It speaks of a right to development (Principle 3) and it asserts that environmental protection cannot be

[14] WCED, op.cit. above (n. 2), p. 43.

[15] Declaration of the United Nations Conference on the Human Environment, A/CONF.48/14: *International Legal Materials,* 11 (1972), p. 1416. See the Preamble and Principles 8,11, 13, 14 and 23.

[16] *International Legal Materials,* 31 (1992), pp. 874 ff.

considered in isolation from the development process (Principles 4 and 25). Principle 3 reads as follows:

The right to development must be fulfilled so as to equitably meet developmental and environmental needs of present and future generations.

Principle 4 states that:

In order to achieve sustainable development, environmental protection shall constitute an integral part of the development process and cannot be considered in isolation from it.

The International Court of Justice has also understood sustainable development as a notion that reconciles the need for environmental protection with the developmental concerns of States. In its recent decision in the *Gabčíkovo/Nagymaros* case it held that:

Throughout the ages, mankind has, for economic and other reasons, constantly interfered with nature. In the past, this was often done without consideration of the effects upon the environment. Owing to new scientific insights and to a growing awareness of the risks for mankind—for present and future generations—of pursuit of such interventions at an unconsidered and unabated pace, new norms and standards have been developed, set forth in a great number of instruments during the last two decades. Such new norms have to be taken into consideration, and such new standards given proper weight, not only when States contemplate new activities but also when continuing with activities begun in the past. This need to reconcile economic development with protection of the environment is aptly expressed in the concept of sustainable development.[17]

As for the recognition of the legitimate pursuit of development, mention should be made of the Declaration on Social Progress and Development proclaimed by the General Assembly of the United Nations on 11 December 1969.[18] Article 1 of this Declaration states that:

All peoples and all human beings without distinction as to race, colour, sex, language, religion, nationality, ethnic origin, family or social status, or political or other conviction shall have the right to live in dignity and freedom and to enjoy the fruits of social progress and should, on their part, contribute to it.

Article 8 states that:

Each Government has the primary role and ultimate responsibility of ensuring the social progress and well-being of its people, of planning social development measures as part of comprehensive development plans, of encouraging and co-ordinating or integrating all national changes in the social structure.

In this field it is also important to mention the Charter of Economic

[17] *ICJ Reports*, 1997, para. 140, p. 67.

[18] Text in UNITAR, *A New International Economic Order. Selected Documents, 1945–1975*, vol. 2, pp. 850 ff.

Rights and Duties adopted by the General Assembly on 12 December 1974,[19] of which Article 7 provides that:

Every State has the primary responsibility to promote the economic, social and cultural development of its people. To this end, each State has the right and the responsibility to choose its means and goals of development, fully to mobilize and use its resources, to implement progressive economic and social reforms and to ensure the full participation of its people in the process and benefits of development. All States have the duty, individually or collectively, to co-operate in order to eliminate obstacles that hinder such mobilization and use.

The Declaration on the Right to Development adopted by the General Assembly on 4 December 1986 is significant in this respect.[20] It provides in Article 2.3 that:

States have the right and the duty to formulate appropriate national development policies that aim at the constant improvement of the well-being of the entire population and of all individuals, on the basis of their active, free and meaningful participation in development and in the fair distribution of the benefits resulting therefrom.

Finally, the Arbitral Tribunal in the *Guinea—Guinea-Bissau* arbitration concerning maritime delimitation, while stating that the economic inequalities between the parties could not justify a modification of the delimitation line, also held that it could not

completely lose sight of the legitimate claims by virtue of which economic circumstances are invoked, nor contest the right of the peoples concerned to a level of economic and social development which fully preserves their dignity.[21]

II. The Criteria for the Attainment of Sustainable Development and the Nature of the Balancing Process

In a substantial article published in the 1994 issue of this *Year Book*, Philippe Sands attempted to ascertain the meaning of the notion of sustainable development, asserting that sustainable development is

a legal term which refers to processes, principles and objectives, as well as to a large body of international agreements on environment, economics and civil and political rights.[22]

He added that 'international law in the field of sustainable development' endorses an approach requiring existing principles, rules and institutional arrangements to be treated in an integrated manner.[23] Therefore,

[19] Text in *International Legal Materials*, 14 (1975), pp.251 ff.

[20] This Declaration was annexed to General Assembly Resolution 41/128. The vote was as follows: 146 votes in favour and only one vote against.

[21] *Guinea—Guinea-Bissau* arbitration (1983), 77 ILR 636, para. 123.

[22] Sands, loc.cit. above (n. 13), p. 379.

[23] Ibid.

the attainment of sustainable development requires the balancing up of various factors, principles and rules of international law with a view to achieving the reconciliation of the legitimate interest of States in pursuing their economic development and the protection of the environment.[24] It has national and international implications and, rather than providing a set of rules for the solution of international disputes concerning specific rights and obligations of States, it endorses a set of objectives and principles that should influence national and international policy-making.

There have been some efforts to identify the relevant criteria, principles and rules of international law which are relevant to the attainment of sustainable development. In this connection, the United Nations Commission on Sustainable Development appointed a group of experts to identify the principles of international law for sustainable development. In its 1995 Report,[25] the Expert Group identified nineteen relevant principles and concepts. The legal status of these principles varies. Some of them are part of general international law and some others 'are only in the process of gaining relevance in international law'.[26] The principles and concepts identified by the Expert Group are:

A. The fundamental principle of interrelationship and integration;
B. Principles and concepts related to the environment and development:
   1. right to development;
   2. right to a healthy environment;
   3. eradication of poverty;
   4. equity, including equitable use of natural resources and inter-generational equity;
   5. sovereignty over natural resources and responsibility not to cause damage to the environment of other States or to areas beyond national jurisdiction;
   6. sustainable use of natural resources;
   7. prevention of environmental harm;
   8. precautionary principle;
C. Principles related to international co-operation:
   1. duty to co-operate in the spirit of global partnership:
      (*a*) common concern of humankind;
      (*b*) common but differentiated responsibilities; and,
      (*c*) special treatment of developing countries, including

[24] The idea of a balancing process is also shared by Birnie and Boyle, *International Law and the Environment* (Oxford, 1992), p. 4.

[25] *Report of the Expert Group Meeting on Identification of Principles of International Law for SustainableDevelopment*, Geneva, Switzerland, 26–28 September 1995. Text in: gopher://gopher.un.org/00/esc/cn17/1996/backgrnd/law.txt.

[26] Ibid. See also Sands, 'International Law in the Field of Sustainable Development,' in Lang (ed.), *Sustainable Development and International Law* (London/Dordrecht/Boston, 1995), p. 54.

small island developing States and countries with economies in transition;

2. common heritage of mankind;
3. co-operation in a transboundary context:
   (*a*) equitable and reasonable use of transboundary natural resources;
   (*b*) notification to and consultations with neighbouring and potentially affected States;
   (*c*) environmental impact assessment in a transboundary context;
   (*d*) prior informed consent as an emerging principle in specific contexts;
   (*e*) co-operation to discourage or prevent the relocation and transfer of activities and substances that cause severe environmental degradation or are harmful to human health;

D. Principles related to participation, decision-making and transparency:
   1. public participation;
   2. access to information;
   3. environmental impact assessment and informed decision-making;

E. Principles related to dispute avoidance, resolution procedures, monitoring and compliance:
   1. peaceful settlement of disputes in the fields of environment and sustainable development;
   2. equal, expanded and effective access to judicial and administrative proceedings;
   3. national implementation of international commitments; and,
   4. monitoring of compliance with international commitments.

Sands also elaborated a list of relevant principles on the basis of the instruments adopted by the 1992 United Nations Conference on Environment and Development.[27] These principles are inherent in the notion of sustainable development and they place limits on the use of natural resources:

1. integration of environment and development;
2. application of equity between States;
3. consideration of the needs of future generations; and

[27] At the 1992 United Nations Conference on Environment and Development the following instruments were adopted: (1) The Rio Declaration on Environment and Development, (2) Agenda 21, (3) a Statement of Forest Principles, (4) The Convention on Biological Diversity, and (5) the Convention on Climate Change.

4. non-exhaustion of renewable natural resources.

Sands also includes a second category of principles that derive from other areas of international law and that provide assistance in achieving sustainable development:

1. that States have sovereignty over natural resources and the responsibility not to cause environmental damage;
2. good neighbourliness and international co-operation;
3. common but differentiated responsibility;
4. precaution; and
5. polluter-pays principle.

The long list of criteria that can be included in the notion of sustainable development makes it evident that, at present, sustainable development can be described as an all-embracing concept which may include almost any aspect of the international relations between States. The fundamental problem is that sustainable development appears to be a process that would combine already existing obligations with principles and concepts which do not have the status of *lex lata*. In order to make sense of the inclusion of principles *de lege ferenda*, it has to be admitted that the result of this combination could be the modification of and even derogation from existing principles of international law.

In so far as the concept of sustainable development involves the consideration of notions which do not form part of the body of existing principles of international law, the achievement of sustainable development necessarily relies on the will of States because it would be necessary for States to give their consent to the modification of or derogation from existing principles. How far States will be prepared to go depends on a number of factors. For example, developing States might accept the imposition of more stringent environmental obligations on condition of receiving significant technical and financial assistance. Therefore, the viability of the whole process of balancing existing rules and emerging principles relies on the implementation of the principle of co-operation, which, though it has been characterized as an auxiliary principle,[28] is absolutely essential for the achievement of sustainable development.

In this context, sustainable development has been envisaged more as a principle to influence legislation than as a principle to be applied in the judicial solution of disputes between States. It is in relation to this point that the difference between the principle of equitable utilization and the concept of sustainable development becomes evident. Equitable utilization is narrower in scope: its aim is the solution of international disputes concerning the allocation and utilization of the waters of international watercourses. As an existing principle of general international law, it can be applied in the context of the judicial settlement of disputes. There-

[28] Sands, loc.cit. above (n. 13), p. 338.

fore, equitable utilization, while not negating the benefits of co-operation, does not depend on it for its operation.

Given the difference in the legal status of sustainable development and the principle of equitable utilization, it becomes clear that it is not necessary to include sustainable development as such in the process of the establishment of an equitable regime for the utilization of international watercourses. The correct approach to the problem of the relationship between equitable utilization and sustainable development should be to examine whether any of the criteria for sustainable development might also be relevant in the application of the principle of equitable utilization. In this regard, it must be borne in mind that equitable utilization is a very flexible principle in which no factor should be discarded as a possible relevant criterion. Sustainable development might, therefore, contribute some relevant factors to the process of the establishment of equitable regimes for the utilization of international watercourses. However, the scope for incorporation of new criteria is not unlimited. There would be a point at which the notion of sustainable development would modify the normal effects of the principle of equitable utilization.

Before proceeding with the examination of the relevant criteria for sustainable development and their possible inclusion into the process of the establishment of an equitable regime for the utilization of international watercourses, it is important to specify the legal nature of the principle of equitable utilization.

III. Equitable Utilization as the Basis of Entitlement to Undertake Certain Activities on International Watercourses or Entitlement to Certain Volumes of Water Therefrom

The principle of equitable utilization has often been said to share a common legal nature with other principles of international law such as good neighbourliness, the principle that rights should be exercised in good faith or the prohibition of abuse of rights. However, equitable utilization differs substantially from these other principles. Though in its origins the principle of equitable utilization might have been closely related to these principles, it has evolved into a separate principle of international law with a legal nature of its own. In particular, equitable utilization differs from good neighbourliness, good faith and the prohibition of abuse of rights in that its function is not interpretative but constitutive of the right to use an international watercourse. The distinction between these two functions is central to a correct understanding of the principle of equitable utilization and its implications.

When applied to the resolution of disputes concerning the utilization of international watercourses, the principles of good neighbourliness, good faith and the prohibition of abuse of rights presuppose that the rights of usage which they attempt to reconcile exist independently from the outcome of the accommodation process. In other words, these principles attempt to interpret rights of water usage which have been established by other rules or principles of international law. The principle of equitable utilization, on the other hand, does not presuppose any specific rights to the utilization of international watercourses before its operation. Prior to the establishment of an equitable regime for the utilization of international watercourses there is only a generic right to participate in the sharing of the watercourse, but it is equitable utilization which constitutes the basis of the specific right to certain volumes of water or the right to undertake certain activities on the watercourse.

The resolution of inter-State water disputes on the basis of principles such as good neighbourliness, good faith and the prohibition of abuse of rights only, without reference to the principle of equitable utilization, relates to the no longer defensible position according to which rights of usage over international watercourses have to be established with reference to sovereignty over the territory. Territorial sovereignty, however, merely provides that States have the right to the use of international watercourses that flow through their respective territories. For these reasons, the early principles which attempted to solve the disputes between co-riparians, namely the principles of absolute territorial sovereignty and territorial integrity, were based on territorial sovereignty. According to the absolute territorial sovereignty thesis, riparian States have the right to dispose freely of the waters flowing through their respective territories. On the basis of the absolute territorial integrity thesis, lower riparians have demanded the continuation of the natural flow of the waters coming from upstream.

The United States resorted to the absolute territorial sovereignty thesis in its dispute with Mexico concerning the waters of the Rio Grande. In 1895, the US Attorney-General, Mr Harmon, stated that: '. . . the rules, principles and precedents of international law impose no liability or obligation upon the United States'.[29] However, the 1906 Convention between the United States and Mexico concerning the equitable distribution of the waters of the Rio Grande for irrigation[30] did not implement this theory, but granted a certain volume of water to Mexico. According to Johnston, the United States 'negotiated from the outset on the assumption that a fair division of the waters was the proper

[29] Moore, *Digest of International Law* (Washington, 1906), vol. 1, p. 654.

[30] Text in *United Nations Legislative Texts and Treaty Provisions*, ST/LEG/SER.B/12, pp. 232 ff.

solution'.[31] Some years later, the absolute territorial sovereignty argument was completely abandoned in the negotiation of the 1944 Treaty relating to the Utilization of the Waters of the Colorado and Tijuana Rivers and of the Rio Grande between these two countries.[32]

The absolute territorial integrity doctrine is often invoked by downstream States,[33] which consider that the *Lake Lanoux* arbitration may support their position. This dispute concerned the legality of the French utilization of the waters of the Lake Lanoux water system. Spain claimed that the French project required Spanish consent. The Arbitral Tribunal rejected this argument on the basis that there was no international practice which supported the Spanish claim.[34] Nevertheless, the Tribunal was of the opinion that France was under an obligation to take Spanish interests into account and to seek to give them every satisfaction compatible with the pursuit of its own interests.[35] Therefore, the Tribunal had to adjudicate on the question of safeguarding the interests of the two States. In this context Spain had to show which interests were affected by the French project. In fact, the Tribunal found that the French project had not impaired the volume of water in the system and, therefore, that it had not caused effects detrimental to Spanish interests. To illustrate which interests could have been affected, however, the Tribunal maintained that Spain could have claimed that:

> by their technical character, the works envisaged by the French project could not in effect ensure the restitution of a volume of water corresponding to the natural contribution of the Lanoux to the Carol, either because of defects in measuring instruments or in mechanical devices to be used in making the restitution.[36]

The advocates of the territorial integrity doctrine read this paragraph as implying that the Tribunal was of the opinion that any diversion of international waters without restitution was contrary to international

[31] Johnston, 'The Columbia River Basin', in Garretson, Hayton and Olmstead (eds.), *The Law of International Drainage Basins* (New York, 1967), p. 185.

[32] *United Nations Treaty Series*, vol.3, pp. 314 ff. For a more detailed account of the negotiation of the 1906 and of the 1944 Treaties, see Lammers, *Pollution of International Watercourses* (The Hague, 1984), pp. 267–70.

[33] Dellapena, 'Treaties as Instruments for Managing Internationally-Shared Water Resources: Restricted Sovereignty vs. Community of Property', *Case Western Reserve Journal of International Law*, 26 (1994), p. 35; Naff and Matson, *Water in the Middle East, Conflict or Cooperation?* (London, 1984), pp. 164–5.

[34] In this connection, the Tribunal held that: '. . . international practice does not so far permit more than the following conclusion: the rule that States may utilize the hydraulic power of international watercourses only on condition of a *prior* agreement between the interested States cannot be established as a custom, even less as a general principle of law'. And in another passage it asserted that: 'Customary international law, like the traditional Law of the Pyrenees, does not supply evidence of a kind to orient the interpretation of the Treaty and of the Additional Act of 1866 in the direction of favouring the necessity of prior agreement; even less does it permit us to conclude that there exists a general principle of law or a custom to this effect': 24 ILR 130 (1957).

[35] Ibid., p. 139.

[36] Ibid., p. 123.

law. However, the Tribunal was far from saying that. The Tribunal referred to this hypothetical argument—which was not made by Spain—only to make it clear that Spain failed to claim and to demonstrate a real injury to her interests. It was not, thus, the intention of the Tribunal to convey the idea that any diversion without restitution constituted a breach of international obligations. In fact, in another passage of the award, the Tribunal asserted that: 'The state of modern technology leads to more and more frequent justifications of the fact that waters used for the production of electric energy should not be returned to their natural course'.[37]

Therefore, the principles of absolute territorial sovereignty and territorial integrity have found little support in international practice. Apart from these extreme doctrines, the concept of territorial sovereignty is not very helpful in the resolution of inter-State water disputes. Professor Andrassy claimed that a solution to disputes between watercourse States was to be found in the principle of good neighbourliness, which acknowledges the legitimate claims of States based on territorial sovereignty and attempts to reconcile them in a manner similar to that in which private law has dealt with interference between the owners of neighbouring lands.[38] However, with regard to international watercourses the problem is that there is no ownership of the waters of international watercourses and, therefore, water disputes do not involve a question of reconciling conflicting rights only, but the more basic question of establishing the right. While acknowledging that States have a sovereign right over the waters of international watercourses, equitable utilization proposes the application of a method by which to establish the precise object of that sovereign right. In doing so, equitable utilization goes beyond the simple proposition that in using their international watercourses States should take into account the interests of the other States concerned.

The novelty is that equitable utilization purports to become the principal basis of entitlement to the use of international watercourses. This assertion rests upon a basic assumption that, unless there is resort to the principle of equitable utilization, international watercourses cannot be characterized as the property of any particular watercourse State and the activities that might be undertaken on the watercourse cannot be said to derive from any other right. Therefore, claims to a portion of the waters of an international watercourse or to undertake a particular activity cannot be separated from the question of equitable utilization. This fact has been recognized in India by the special tribunals that have resolved inter-State water disputes. The practice of these municipal courts is relevant for this study because they have had recourse

[37] Ibid., p. 125.

[38] Andrassy, 'Le Droit international de voisinage', *Recueil des cours*, 79 (1951–II), pp. 102–9.

to the principle of equitable utilization as a principle of international law applicable to the resolution of inter-State or inter-provincial water disputes. The Krishna Tribunal, which was appointed for the resolution of a dispute between the States of Mysore, Maharashtra and Andra Pradesh, stated that in the application of the principle of equitable apportionment, 'the decisions of courts and tribunals and opinion of jurists on international law may be consulted'.[39] Having said this, the Krishna Tribunal felt free to invoke the 1966 Helsinki Rules on the Use of International Rivers adopted by the International Law Association. For its part, the Narmada Tribunal, which was appointed for the resolution of a dispute between the States of Madhya Pradesh, Gujarat, Rajasthan and Maharashtra, applied the principle of equitable use and observed that: 'The doctrine [*sic*] of Equitable Apportionment is derived from the basic concepts of international law'.[40]

In relation to the question of property rights over inter-State waters, the Krishna Tribunal stated that:

> No State has a proprietary interest in a particular volume of water of an inter-State river on the basis of its contribution or irrigable area. Rules of law based on the analogy of private proprietary interests in water do not afford a satisfactory basis for settling inter-state water disputes.[41]

For its part, the Narmada Tribunal maintained that:

> As a matter of law, no State has a proprietary right in a particular volume of water of an inter-State river on the basis of its contribution to the available flow or drainage area. It is well-established that the waters of a natural stream or other natural body of water are not susceptible of absolute ownership as specific intangible property.[42]

Similarly, another Indian special tribunal, the Ravi-Beas Waters Tribunal, in examining the State of Punjab's claim that the waters of the Ravi and Beas rivers belonged entirely to it to the exclusion of Haryana and Rajasthan, held that:

> There is nothing in the law for any one including the State to claim absolute proprietary rights in river waters. Running water has, therefore, rightly been called 'a negative community' as it belongs to no one and is not susceptible to absolute ownership rights. The only right which a State can legitimately claim in river waters flowing within its territory is the right to make use thereof provided that such use does not affect adversely the right which another State has to make use of the said waters.[43]

[39] Government of India, *Report of the Krishna Water Disputes Tribunal* (New Delhi, 1973), vol. 1, p. 95.

[40] Government of India, *Report of the Narmada Water Disputes Tribunal* (New Delhi, 1978), vol. 1, p. 115.

[41] *Report of the Krishna Water Disputes Tribunal*, vol. 1, p. 94.

[42] *Report of the Narmada Water Disputes Tribunal*, vol. 1, p. 114.

[43] Government of India, *Report of the Ravi and Beas Waters Tribunal* (New Delhi, 1987), p. 94.

Seen in this light, as a principle which solves the question of entitlement to the utilization of the waters of international watercourses, the principle of equitable utilization can be separated from other principles of entitlement, such as territorial sovereignty or the principle of acquired rights. It can also be distinguished from the principles that are invoked to interpret principles of entitlement, such as the principles of good neighbourliness, good faith and the prohibition of abuse of rights. It follows that equitable utilization should also be separated from other principles the purpose of which is to protect rights which have been established by other rules.

IV. The Role of Environmental Protection in the Process of the Establishment of an Equitable Regime for the Utilization of International Watercourses

As stated previously, the basic idea embodied in the notion of sustainable development is the integration of developmental and environmental concerns. Does the principle of equitable utilization adopt this integrated approach? The answer to this question depends on the role that the environmental protection of water resources has to play in the process of the establishment of an equitable regime for the utilization of international watercourses. In this connection, two positions can be taken. On the one hand, it could be argued that there is an obligation to protect the environment of international watercourses which is not subject to equitable balancing. On the other hand, it could be said that the adequate protection of international watercourses is one more factor to take into consideration in the application of the principle of equitable utilization.

One thing must be clarified from the outset. Equitable utilization calls for the consideration of all relevant factors and circumstances without any factor having a pre-established priority over the others. That is to say that, in principle, environmental impact is one more criterion to be taken into account in the process of the establishment of an equitable regime for the utilization of international watercourses. However, this does not mean that equitable utilization should be the ultimate test of legality of the activities that might be undertaken on international watercourses. Therefore, if a rule of international law were to prohibit the pollution of international watercourses, pollution would fall outside the scope of equitable utilization. This rule can be established in a treaty or it can derive from customary international law. However, in the absence of such a rule, the pollution of international watercourses is an element that the principle of equitable utilization should take into consideration.

It is contended here that, as a matter of customary international law, the environmental impact of the use of international watercourses is a relevant factor that has to be included in the process of the establishment of an equitable regime for the utilization of international watercourses. This is so because, as regards international watercourses, there is no principle of general international law which prohibits the infliction of significant environmental damage upon other watercourse States in all cases. Many writers disagree with this view because they think not only that a so-called 'no significant harm' principle exists in general international law, but also that this principle would prevail over the application of the principle of equitable utilization. The next section will demonstrate that such a view is the result of a confusion between principles of international law which perform different but complementary functions.

A. The False Conflict between the Principle of Equitable Utilization and the Obligation not to Cause Significant Harm

Traditionally, the question of the place of environmental impact in the process of determining what is an equitable utilization of an international watercourse has been approached from the perspective of a conflict between the principle of equitable utilization and the obligation not to cause significant harm. The discussion, therefore, has focused on which of the two must prevail.[44] However, this discussion has been affected by a serious problem of terminology, which will be examined first.

(1) *Questions of terminology*

The terminology employed by commentators has not always been clear. The reference to Principle 21 of the 1972 Stockholm Declaration made by those who claim that a 'no significant harm principle' exists in general international law permits the conclusion that these authors understand harm as denoting damage. Principle 21 reads as follows:

> States have, in accordance with the Charter of the United Nations and the principles of international law, the sovereign right to exploit their own resources pursuant to their own environmental policies, and the responsibility to ensure that activities within their jurisdiction or control do not cause damage to the environment of other States or areas beyond the limits of national jurisdiction.[45]

[44] This has been the approach adopted by the International Law Commission. Among the authors that adopt this view, see Utton, 'Which Rule Should Prevail in International Water Disputes: That of Reasonableness or That of No Harm?', *Natural Resources Journal*, 36 (1996), pp. 635–41; Wouters, 'An Assessment of Recent Developments in International Watercourse Law through the Prism of the Substantive Rules Governing Use Allocation', ibid., pp. 419 ff.; Berrisch, 'The Danube Dam Dispute under International Law', *Austrian Journal of International Law*, 1994, p. 261; Nollkaemper, *The Legal Regime for Transboundary Water Pollution: Between Discretion and Constraint* (Dordrecht, 1993), p. 68.

[45] *International Legal Materials*, 11 (1972), p. 1416.

However, a problem of terminology arises when, in support of the customary law status of Principle 21, these authors quote the decisions of the International Court of Justice in the *Corfu Channel* case and of the Arbitral Tribunal in the *Trail Smelter* arbitration. The International Court in the *Corfu Channel* case stated that a State is under the obligation 'not to allow knowingly its territory to be used for acts contrary to the rights of other States'.[46] The Arbitral Tribunal in the *Trail Smelter* arbitration held that:

> no State has the right to use or permit the use of its territory in such a manner as to cause injury by fumes in or to the territory of another or the properties or persons therein, when the case is of serious consequences and the injury is established by clear and convincing evidence.[47]

In the *Corfu Channel* case the unlawful behaviour consisted of the fact that Albania 'neither notified the existence of the minefield, nor warned the British warships of the danger they were approaching'. In this context, the obligation 'not to allow knowingly its territory to be used for acts contrary to the rights of other States'[48] did not exist in a vacuum, but depended on the finding by the International Court that the United Kingdom was entitled to the protection of two rights: (*a*) its right of innocent passage through an international highway through which passage could not be prohibited by a coastal State in time of peace,[49] and (*b*) its right to receive from another State a treatment according to elementary considerations of humanity.[50]

For its part, the Arbitral Tribunal in the *Trail Smelter* arbitration recognized that with regard to the duty that a State ought to protect other States against injurious acts from within its jurisdiction, the real difficulty consisted in the determination of 'what, *pro subjecta materia,* is deemed to constitute an injurious act'.[51] In this context, the duty was described as 'relative'.[52] The injurious act, in the opinion of the arbitrators, was an act of encroachment on the territory of the neighbouring State which prejudiced the latter's natural use of its territory. This view is explained by the fact that the parties and the Tribunal adopted a territorial approach for the resolution of this dispute. In this context, the environmental interference caused by a Canadian smelter on the territory of the United States was defined in terms of territorial integrity. It must be borne in mind that in 1941 the concept of equitable utilization had not yet emerged. Therefore, the Tribunal applied the principle that no State may cause legal injury to the territory of another, and in so doing it

[46] *ICJ Reports*, 1949, p. 22.
[47] *United Nations Reports of International Arbitral Awards*, vol. 3, p. 1965.
[48] *ICJ Reports*, 1949, p. 22.
[49] Ibid., pp. 29–30.
[50] Ibid., p.22.
[51] *United Nations Reports of International Arbitral Awards*, vol. 3, p. 1963.
[52] Ibid.

understood that the US had the right to exclude encroachment which could prejudice the natural use of its territory.[53] Therefore, neither the *Corfu Channel* case nor the *Trail Smelter* arbitration applied the so-called no harm (damage) principle, but rather the long-established principle that States must refrain from acting illegally.

The use of the notions of harm, damage and injury has important consequences for the determination of the extent of the freedom of States to use their territory and it is essential, therefore, to be precise about their meaning. In his First Report on State Responsibility, the Special Rapporteur, Professor Crawford, states that:

> As to the basic distinction between 'injury' and 'damage', it is clear that the concept of 'injury' in the term 'injured State' involves the concept of a 'legal injury' or *injuria*, whereas the term 'damage' refers to material or other loss suffered by the injured State.[54]

The use of the notion of harm, therefore, requires further interpretation on a case-by-case basis to specify whether it refers to 'factual harm' (damage) or to 'legal harm' (legal injury). Because it has been directly associated with Principle 21 of the 1972 Stockholm Declaration, the notion of harm embodied in the so-called 'no significant harm principle' has to be understood as denoting damage.

Two other concepts require some commentary: environmental damage and significant damage. In relation to the first, the relevant question relates to whether or not environmental damage is a special category of damage. If damage is understood as material or other loss and the 'environment' is understood as comprising the various components of the earth, including natural and man-made elements, then it is difficult to see any difference between environmental damage and damage in general. For this reason no distinction will be made between these two notions. As regards significant damage, it must be pointed out that this notion denotes the threshold of seriousness at which damage becomes legally relevant. The purpose, therefore, is to leave aside minor interference.

(2) *The principle of equitable utilization and the obligation not to inflict legal injury upon other States*

If harm is understood as denoting legal injury, then the alleged conflict between the principle of equitable utilization and the no-harm principle does not exist. This is so because the obligation not to inflict legal injury upon other States and the principle of equitable utilization of international watercourses perform very different functions in the system of

[53] Ibid.

[54] ILC, 'First Report on State Responsibility by Mr James Crawford', Doc. A/CN.4/490/Add.4, 26 May 1998, para. 105, p. 3.

international law. Indeed, on the one hand, equitable utilization establishes entitlement to the use of volumes of water or entitlement to undertake certain activities on an international watercourse; on the other, the obligation not to inflict legal injury does not allocate entitlements, but its function is to protect entitlements which have been established by other rules and principles of international law.[55]

In the field of international watercourses the principle of entitlement is equitable utilization, but with reference to other natural resources the principle of entitlement might be territorial sovereignty. Such would be the case with water resources occurring entirely within the territory of one State. The same may be said of the land areas which form the territory of States and of gas and oil deposits and other mineral resources, all of which are not subject to the principle of equitable use. With regard to fisheries that are found in the EEZs of coastal States, entitlement to these resources does not depend on equitable utilization either, but on a principle of functional jurisdiction established by the 1982 UN Convention on the Law of the Sea. The obligation not to cause legal injury to the territory of other States, therefore, has different implications depending on the particular natural resource in question. To illustrate this point one might consider the situation in which the discharge by State A of certain dangerous substances into the sea would destroy the fisheries occurring in the EEZ of coastal State B. As there is no principle of equitable utilization of the fishery resources occurring in the EEZ of State B applicable between States A and B, the obligation not to cause injury to the rights of State B results in the prohibition of causing damage to the fishery resources occurring in the EEZ of State B. In this context, therefore, legal injury consists of significant damage to the fisheries in question. However, in the field of international watercourses, because the allocation of rights depends on the principle of equitable utilization rather than on the principle of territorial sovereignty, damage is only relevant in so far as it coincides with an interference with the right of equitable use of another State. Therefore, the obligation not to cause injury to other States cannot be construed as protecting the 'integrity' of the watercourse as such, but as protecting each State's share of the benefits of the watercourse.

(3) *The principle of equitable utilization and the no significant damage rule*

What would be the implications of the existence of a rule prohibiting the infliction of significant damage on international watercourses? If such

[55] In this approach to the problem of the relationship between the principle of equitable utilization of international watercourses and the so-called no significant harm principle, the author follows Guido Calabresi and A. Douglas Melamed's framework for the analysis of property and torts: 'Property Rules, Liability Rules, and Inalienability: One View of the Cathedral', *Harvard Law Review*, 85 (1972), pp.1089 ff.

a rule were to exist, the principle of equitable utilization would still be the basis of entitlement to the use of international watercourses, but the no significant damage rule would constitute the basis of another entitlement: entitlement to keep international watercourses free from significant transboundary damage. The conflict between these two entitlements would be resolved by application of the maxim that *lex specialis derogat lege generali*. Therefore, the legality of the activities undertaken on international watercourses would be subject to the principle of equitable utilization and to the rule of no significant damage. This would have major consequences for the utilization of international watercourses. Indeed, it is difficult to conceive of economic activities with no significant impact on the environment of international watercourses.

At this point it could be objected that a principle prohibiting the causing of transboundary environmental damage to international watercourses is already in place and, therefore, that environmental damage should not be included in the balancing process called for by the principle of equitable utilization. A brief account of State practice concerning the environmental degradation of international watercourses will show that at present there is no rule of general international law prohibiting the infliction of significant damage on international watercourses. However, before proceeding with the examination of this State practice, it is interesting to note that in the context of environmental interference in general there is also no rule of no significant damage.

B. The Role of the Obligation to Protect the Environment in the System of International Law

In their textbook on *International Law and the Environment*, Birnie and Boyle maintain that:

> It is beyond serious argument that states are required by international law to take adequate steps to control and regulate sources of serious global environmental pollution or transboundary harm within their territory or subject to their jurisdiction.[56]

This statement has to be read carefully. In the first place, it does not say that general international law puts States under an obligation to prevent and abate pollution or transboundary environmental damage. Instead, these authors speak of an obligation to control and regulate sources of serious environmental pollution or transboundary harm. In this regard, it must be acknowledged that control and regulation of polluting sources are not the same thing as prevention and abatement of pollution. Secondly, the obligation to control and regulate sources of pollution and

[56] Birnie and Boyle, op.cit. above (n. 24), p. 89.

transboundary environmental harm is qualified by the expression 'adequate steps'.

If leading writers in the field of international environmental law are so cautious in their description of the environmental duties of States, can it still be said that in general international law there exists an obligation to prevent and abate significant environmental damage? Some other authors find no difficulty in asserting that indeed such an obligation forms part of the body of existing principles of general international law.[57] These writers quote Principle 21 of the 1972 Stockholm Declaration on the Human Environment in support of their claim.[58] However, State practice seems to invalidate the conclusion that this provision establishes an obligation (not even one of due diligence) to prevent and abate transboundary environmental damage in respect of each and every component element of the environment.

With regard to environmental damage which might be the result of the accumulative effect of emissions of pollutants in various States and where it is difficult to identify the source of the damage, the tendency that States have followed is to agree on the gradual reduction of emissions. This is the case with the 1985 Vienna Convention for the Protection of the Ozone Layer[59] and the 1987 Montreal Protocol on Substances that Deplete the Ozone Layer[60] which set up a regime for the protection of the ozone layer from human activities which modify or are likely to modify it. In particular, this regime is intended to reduce the world-wide emission of substances that can significantly deplete and otherwise modify the ozone layer. There is scientific evidence that the release of chlorofluorocarbons (CFCs), halons and other chlorine-based substances contributes to the depletion of the ozone layer.[61] In view of the fact that today it is not possible to establish with scientific certainty the link between particular emissions and damage caused to the ozone layer, States have adopted a regime in which, instead of determining individual responsibility for the depletion of the ozone layer, they have agreed on the equitable control of substances that contribute to this depletion. The important thing to note is that while the 1985 Vienna Convention recalls

[57] In this connection, Sands maintains that: 'the responsibility not to cause damage to the environment of other states or of areas beyond national jurisdiction has been accepted as an obligation by all states'. Furthermore, he states that: 'it is generally accepted that customary international law establishes an obligation to prevent significant damage to the environment of other states or to areas beyond national jurisdiction': *Principles of International Environmental Law* (Manchester and New York, 1995), vol. 1, pp. 190 and 632. See also Lefeber, *Transboundary Environmental Interference and the Origin of State Liability* (The Hague, London, Boston, 1996), pp. 19 ff.

[58] *International Legal Materials,* 11 (1972), p. 1416. The same principle is contained in Article 2 of the Rio Declaration on Environment and Development: ibid., 31 (1992), p. 876. See also GA Resolution 2995 (XXVII), of 15 December 1972.

[59] Text in *International Legal Materials,* 26 (1987), pp. 1529 ff.

[60] Text: ibid., pp. 1550 ff.

[61] Birnie and Boyle, op.cit. above (n. 24), p. 388; Sands, op.cit.above (n. 57), p. 261.

in its Preamble 'the pertinent provisions of the Declaration of the United Nations Conference on the Human Environment, and in particular principle 21', the 1987 Montreal Protocol states in its Preamble that the parties are 'determined to protect the ozone layer by taking precautionary measures to *control equitably* total emissions of substances that deplete it . . . taking into account technical and economic considerations and bearing in mind the developmental needs of developing countries'.[62] Thus, instead of taking precautionary measures to prevent damage to the ozone layer and thus implement Principle 21, by introducing an element of 'equitable control' it is clear that what the parties to the Montreal Protocol understand to be the meaning of Principle 21 of the Stockholm Declaration does not correspond to an obligation not to damage the environment.

In other fields of international law concerned with the protection of the environment, the obligation not to cause damage to the environment has also been adapted to the particular situation. In this regard, the 1979 Convention on Long-range Transboundary Air Pollution[63] also refers in its Preamble to Principle 21 of the Stockholm Declaration:

> Considering the pertinent provisions of the Declaration of the United Nations Conference on the Human Environment, and in particular Principle 21, which expresses the common conviction that States have, in accordance with the Charter of the United Nations and the principles of international law, the sovereign right to exploit their own resources pursuant to their own environmental policies, and the responsibility to ensure that activities within their jurisdiction or control do not cause damage to the environment of other States or of areas beyond the limits of national jurisdiction . . .

Article 1 defines air pollution and long-range transboundary air pollution in the following terms:

> (*a*) 'air pollution' means the introduction by man, directly or indirectly, of substances or energy into the air resulting in deleterious effects of such a nature as to endanger human health, harm living resources and ecosystems and material property and impair or interfere with amenities and other legitimate uses of the environment, and 'air pollutants' shall be construed accordingly;
> (*b*) 'Long-range transboundary air pollution' means air pollution whose physical origin is situated wholly or in part within the area under the national jurisdiction of one State and which has adverse effects in the area under the jurisdiction of another State at such a distance that it is not generally possible to distinguish the contribution of individual emission sources or groups of sources.

The Convention acknowledges the fact that it is not generally possible to distinguish the contribution of individual emissions sources or groups of sources to air pollution. For this reason States have preferred to set up a regime for the gradual reduction and prevention of air pollution in which

[62] Emphasis added.

[63] Text in Birnie and Boyle, *Basic Documents on International Law and the Environment* (Oxford, 1995), pp. 277 ff.

the parties have agreed to develop policies and strategies which will serve as a means of combating the discharge of air pollutants, but where the issue of liability has been omitted. Therefore, to interpret the reference to Principle 21 of the Stockholm Declaration in the Preamble of the Convention in accordance with the articles of the Convention, one must read Principle 21 as providing for a reconciliation between sovereignty and the protection of the environment of other States. This is corroborated by the 1994 Protocol on Further Reduction of Sulphur Emissions,[64] which recognizes 'the need for a cost-effective regional approach to combating air pollution that takes account of the variations in effects and abatement costs between countries' and acknowledges 'that any sulphur control policy, however cost-effective it may be at the regional level, will result in a relatively heavy economic burden on countries with economies that are in transition to a market economy'.

It could be objected that this version of Principle 21, in which there is an attempt to reconcile equitably the right to the use of the territory and the protection of the environment in other States, is only applicable to these special cases where it is difficult to establish the causal link between one country's activities and the harmful effects on areas outside its jurisdiction. However, the relativization of the so-called no significant damage principle contained in Principle 21 of the Stockholm Declaration is also evidenced in the field of the protection of the marine environment, where the causal link between certain activities and their harmful consequences does not pose, generally speaking, the same problems discussed in relation to the protection of the ozone layer and long-range transboundary air pollution.

Principle 21 of the Stockholm Declaration is incorporated into Article 193 of the 1982 UN Convention on the Law of the Sea, which provides that: 'States have the sovereign right to exploit their natural resources pursuant to their environmental policies and in accordance with their duty to protect and preserve the marine environment'. As regards the prevention, reduction and control of pollution of the marine environment from land-based sources, Article 207 of the 1982 UN Convention provides that:

1. States shall adopt laws and regulations to prevent, reduce and control pollution of the marine environment from land-based sources, including rivers, estuaries, pipelines and outfall structures, taking into account internationally agreed rules, standards and recommended practices and procedures.
2. States shall take other measures as may be necessary to prevent, reduce and control such pollution.
3. States shall endeavour to harmonize their policies in this connection at the appropriate regional level.
4. States, acting especially through competent international organizations or

[64] Text: ibid., pp. 285 ff.

diplomatic conference, shall endeavour to establish global and regional rules, standards and recommended practices and procedures to prevent, reduce and control pollution of the marine environment from land-based sources, taking into account characteristic regional features, *the economic capacity of developing States* and *their need for economic development*. Such rules, standards and recommended practices and procedures shall be re-examined from time to time as necessary.

5. Laws, regulations, measures, rules, standards and recommended practices and procedures referred to in paragraphs 1, 2 and 4 shall include those designated to minimize, *to the fullest extent possible*, the release of toxic, harmful and noxious substances, especially those which are persistent, into the marine environment.[65]

As Birnie and Boyle maintain, the reason for this weak provision is that States have opted for maintaining the possibility of balancing environmental protection measures against their economic needs.[66]

Therefore, in particular contexts, States have interpreted Principle 21 of the 1972 Stockholm Declaration as permitting the accommodation of the need for environmental protection, on the one hand, and economic and developmental concerns, on the other. Hence, Principle 21 is a flexible principle which can be adapted to different situations. Accordingly, it does not contain a simple prohibition of the infliction of transboundary damage, but it also allows the content of the obligation to be influenced by economic factors. What this article will demonstrate is that in the context of the environmental protection of international watercourses, Principle 21 has also been implemented in this qualified form, allowing for the consideration of the economic needs of the States concerned.

The International Court of Justice in its recent advisory opinion on the *Legality of the Threat or Use of Nuclear Weapons* acknowledges that a general obligation of States to protect the environment exists in international law. However, the advisory opinion does not invalidate the conclusion that the application of Principle 21 may involve weighing up the need to protect the environment with other interests of the States concerned. In this regard, the Court stated that:

The existence of the general obligation of States to ensure that activities within their jurisdiction or control respect the environment of other States or of areas beyond national control is now part of the corpus of international law relating to the environment.[67]

Nevertheless, the Court found that in times of military conflict it was necessary to balance this obligation with the right of self-defence. In this connection the Court said that:

[65] Emphasis added.

[66] Birnie and Boyle, op.cit. above (n. 24), p. 307.

[67] Para. 29. Text in *International Legal Materials*, 35 (1996), pp. 809 ff. Also in www.law.cornell.edu/icj/icj1/unan5afin.htm.

> . . . the Court is of the view that the issue is not whether the treaties relating to the protection of the environment are or are not applicable during an armed conflict, but rather whether the obligations stemming from these treaties were intended to be obligations of total restraint during military conflict.
>
> The Court does not consider that the treaties in question could have intended to deprive a State of the exercise of its right of self-defence under international law because of its obligation to protect the environment. Nonetheless, States must take environmental considerations into account when assessing what is necessary and proportionate in the pursuit of legitimate military objectives. Respect for the environment is one of the elements that go to assessing whether an action is in conformity with the principles of necessity and proportionality.[68]

The advisory opinion shows that the obligation to protect the environment is not an unqualified obligation. Of course, it could be said that the intention of the Court was only to convey the idea that in times of military conflict the obligation to protect the environment must be weighed against the right of self-defence. However, there is nothing in the advisory opinion that would prevent the application of the same reasoning to explain the relationship between the right to exploit natural resources occurring in one State's territory or the right to the equitable utilization of international watercourses and the obligation to protect the environment. The Court spoke of the need to take environmental considerations into account when assessing what is necessary and proportionate in the pursuit of legitimate military objectives. In this connection, the relationship between the pursuit of other legitimate objectives, such as the exploitation of natural resources, and the obligation to protect the environment could also be said to consist of a balancing of interests.[69]

Therefore, it would be consonant with the present state of customary international law to say that the achievement of a balance between the right to use international watercourses, on the one hand, and the obligation to protect the environment, on the other, would require that respect for the environment be considered as one element when determining whether an activity conforms with the principle of equitable utilization.

It is also worth noting that the International Court did not speak of an obligation not to cause significant environmental damage to other States. The language it used was more ambiguous. The obligation was said to consist of 'respect' for the environment of other States. Indeed, the term 'respect' permits a number of interpretations. For example, 'respect' could be understood as 'due regard'. Accordingly, it would be possible to

[68] Para. 30: ibid.

[69] In this connection see Koskenniemi, 'International Pollution in the System of International Law', *Eripainos. Oikustiede-Jurisprudentia*, 17 (1984), pp. 121–2.

respect an interest by giving it due consideration in a process of balancing up all relevant interests. This balancing process might result in a certain degree of damage to that interest.

An examination of State practice concerning the protection of international watercourses will demonstrate that there is no rule of general international law prohibiting the infliction of significant damage to international watercourses. But before proceeding with this examination of State practice it is useful to clarify the meaning of certain concepts. As regards the definition of pollution, the OECD has stated that it is

> . . . the introduction by man, directly or indirectly, of substances or energy into the environment resulting in deleterious effects of such a nature as to endanger human health, harm living resources and ecosystems, and impair or interfere with amenities and other legitimate uses of the environment.[70]

For its part, Article 21.1 of the 1997 UN Convention states that:

> 'pollution of an international watercourse' means any detrimental alteration in the composition or quality of the waters of an international watercourse which results directly or indirectly from human conduct.

Environmental impact is much broader than pollution. It was defined by the World Commission on Environment and Development (WCED) as:

> any impairment of human health, living resources, ecosystems, material property, amenities or other legitimate uses of a natural resource or the environment caused, directly or indirectly, by man through polluting substances, ionizing radiation, noise, explosions, vibration or other forms of energy, plants, animals, diseases, flooding, sand-drift or other similar means.[71]

The examination of the relevant State practice will show that in the field of the protection of international watercourses States have assumed a range of different obligations, the effects of which have not always been the complete protection of international watercourses. It is true that in certain agreements, States appear to have effectively prohibited causing transboundary environmental damage to international watercourses. However, this State practice is not sufficiently well-established to infer the emergence of a general customary principle that States should always refrain from causing transboundary damage on the sections of international watercourses located in other States.

C. State Practice concerned with the Protection of International Watercourses

(1) *The prohibition of pollution in the context of frontier agreements*

Some treaties prohibit pollution of international watercourses in the context of a more general prohibition of any activities likely to change the

[70] 1974 OECD Recommendation on Principles concerning Transfrontier Pollution: *International Legal Materials,* 14 (1975), p. 234.

[71] WCED, op.cit. above (n. 2), p. 38.

regime of a watercourse constituting the frontier between the States concerned. In this connection, Article 17 of the 1950 Treaty between the Government of the Soviet Socialist Republics and the Government of the Hungarian People's Republic concerning the Regime of the Soviet-Hungarian State Frontier provides that:

The competent authorities of the Contracting Parties shall take steps to maintain the frontier waters in such due state of cleanliness as to prevent the waters from being poisoned or polluted by acids or refuse from factories or industrial establishments, or from being fouled by any other means.[72]

This type of treaty has been concluded for the purpose of avoiding potential difficulties in frontier waters. Beside this, the provisions concerning pollution have to be read in the context of the other obligations assumed by the parties. In this regard, it must be noticed that, in general, the parties have agreed to restrict their right to use the waters of frontier watercourses to an extent that goes beyond the general requirements of international law. For example, in the 1949 Agreement between Norway and the USSR, besides the prohibition of pollution, the parties also agreed that 'questions relating to the construction or management of any works or building on the Pasvikelve (Patso-joki) or Jakobselv (Voriema) Rivers and their tributaries capable of affecting the level and volume of those rivers shall be settled by agreement between the

[72] *United Nations Legislative Texts and Treaty Provisions concerning the Utilization of International Rivers for Other Purposes than Navigation*, p. 824. See also Article 3 of the 1934 Agreement between the Belgian Government and the Government of the United Kingdom of Great Britain and Northern Ireland regarding Water Rights on the Boundary between Tanganyika and Ruanda-Urundi: ibid., pp. 97–8; Article 17 of the 1948 Agreement between the Government of the Polish Republic and the Government of the Union of Soviet Socialist Republics concerning the Regime on the Soviet-Polish State Frontier: ibid., p. 890; Article 14(1) of the 1949 Agreement between Norway and the Union of Soviet Socialist Republics concerning the Regime of the Norwegian-Soviet Frontier and Procedure for the Settlement of Frontier Disputes and Incidents: ibid., p. 880; Article 13 of the 1958 Treaty between the Government of the Union of Soviet Socialist Republics and the Royal Government of Afghanistan concerning the Regime of the Soviet-Afghan State Frontier: ibid., p.278; Article 15 of the 1960 Agreement between Finland and the Soviet Union concerning the Regime of the Finnish-Soviet State Frontier and the Procedure for the Settlement of Frontier Incidents: ibid., p.656; Article 13 of the 1948 Agreement between the Government of the Union of Soviet Socialist Republics and the Government of the Republic of Finland concerning the Regime of the Soviet-Finnish Frontier: *United Nations Treaty Series*, vol. 217, p. 135; Article 14 of the 1956 Agreement between the Union of Soviet Socialist Republics and the Czechoslovak Republic concerning the Regime of the Soviet-Czechoslovak Frontier and the Procedure for the Settlement of Frontier Incidents: ibid, vol. 266, p. 302; Article 2(7) of the 1956 Treaty between Austria and Hungary concerning the Regulation of Water Economy Questions in the Frontier Region: ibid., vol. 428, p. 123; Article 10(1) of the 1957 Treaty between the Union of Soviet Socialist Republics and Iran concerning the Regime of the Soviet-Iranian Frontier and the Procedure for the Settlement of Frontier Disputes and Incidents: ibid., vol. 357, p. 161; Article 11 of the 1964 Agreement between Poland and the Union of Soviet Socialist Republics concerning the Use of Water Resources in Frontier Waters: ibid., vol. 552, p.175; Article 3(4) of the 1967 Treaty between Austria and Czechoslovakia concerning the Regulation of Water Management Questions relating to Frontier Waters: ibid., vol. 728, p.313.

Contracting Parties' (Article 14.2).[73] In the same vein, Article 19 of the 1958 Treaty between the USSR and Afghanistan concerning the Regime of the Soviet-Afghan State Frontier[74] provides that: '2. Bridges, dams and other similar structures likely to hinder navigation or influence the flow of water shall not be erected on frontier watercourses except by agreement between the two Parties'. And paragraph 4 of the same article states that: 'Should the need arise for reconstruction or demolition of any installation on frontier rivers that might change the water level of those rivers, the necessary work may not be undertaken without the consent of the other Party'. In the context of these treaties, then, activities which can usually be undertaken by the riparians, such as irrigation, require the consent of the other party. Therefore, care should be taken when attempting to infer general obligations from the provisions of this type of treaty. This does not imply that boundary waters agreements are not capable of incorporating environmental values. However, in assessing the contribution of these treaties to the formation of a general principle prohibiting the pollution of international watercourses, the provisions concerning pollution cannot be separated from the context in which they have been adopted. In this connection, it must be noted that in frontier agreements in which the regime for water utilization has not been as strict as in the case of the above-mentioned treaties, pollution has not been entirely prohibited. To illustrate this point, one might consider the 1960 Frontier Treaty concluded between the Federal Republic of Germany and the Netherlands,[75] Article 57 of which provides that:

> The Contracting Parties agree to conduct regular consultations on all questions relating to the use and management of water resources in so far as they affect the boundary waters within the territory of the neighbouring State, with a view to solving such questions in a manner satisfactory to both Contracting Parties. Such consultations shall be held in the Permanent Boundary Waters Commission and its sub-commissions referred to in article 64.

For its part Article 58(1) provides that 'the Contracting Parties undertake to give due regard . . . to the neighbouring State's interest in the boundary waters'. With regard to pollution, Article 58(2)(*e*) states that the parties shall take all measures required 'to prevent such excessive pollution of the boundary waters as may substantially impair customary use of the waters by the neighbouring State'.

Finally, another agreement concerning a contiguous watercourse in relation to which it might be said that pollution is forbidden is the 1973 Rio de la Plata Treaty concluded between Argentina and Uruguay, Article 5 of which states that:

[73] *United Nations Legislative Texts and Treaty Provisions concerning the Utilization of International Rivers for Other Purposes than Navigation*, p. 882.

[74] Ibid., p. 276.

[75] Ibid., p. 757.

Each Party shall be liable to the other for detriment suffered as a consequence of pollution caused by their operations, or by those of physical or corporate persons domiciled on their soil.[76]

However, care should be taken when attempting to invoke this provision for the purpose of demonstrating the existence of a customary rule forbidding transboundary pollution. In particular, it must be borne in mind that this provision was not concluded to tackle a problem of existing pollution. It has been reported that at present, owing to increasing industrial activity in the area, the De la Plata River shows signs of chemical pollution.[77] However, this pollution has motivated no dispute between the parties.[78]

(2) *The absolute prohibition of pollution in successive rivers*

There are other international agreements that prohibit transboundary pollution of successive watercourses. For example, in the 1971 Declaration on Water Resources signed by Argentina and Uruguay, these two States agreed on the following basic principles to govern the regime for the utilization of international rivers and their tributaries:

1. The river waters shall be utilized in fair and reasonable manner.
2. States shall refrain from polluting international rivers and tributaries in any manner and shall conserve the ecological resources in the areas within their respective jurisdictions.[79]

In the same vein, the Act of Santiago (1971) signed by Argentina and Chile, states that:

1. The waters of rivers and lakes shall always be utilized in a fair and reasonable manner.
2. The Parties shall avoid polluting their river and lake systems in any manner and shall conserve the ecological resources of their common river basins in the areas within their respective jurisdictions.[80]

Neither of the above-mentioned treaties have been concluded to tackle an existing problem of pollution. Argentina and Uruguay's main interest in their international watercourses is navigation and the production of hydroelectric energy. These uses do not normally result in serious water

[76] *International Legal Materials*, 13 (1974), p. 260. This provision might be read as forbidding all pollution. However, it is interesting to note that the parties have not been explicit and have rather preferred to make the polluter liable to pay compensation for the detriment suffered by the victim State. The meaning of the term 'detriment' is open to interpretation and it might well be that it should be understood as comprising damage that is financially quantifiable, thus excluding non-financially quantifiable damage to the environment.

[77] Nolon, 'The State of the Argentine Environment: An Overview', *Pace Environmental Law Review*, 13 (1996), p. 617.

[78] In this regard, del Castillo states that: 'So far no incident involving pollution has "triggered" this rule': 'The Legal Regime of the Rio de la Plata', *Natural Resources Journal*, 36 (1996), p. 292.

[79] Text in *ILC Yearbook*, 1974, vol. 2, part 2, p. 324.

[80] Ibid.

pollution. The same should be said of the Act of Santiago. Again, the main use that Chile and Argentina could make of their shared water resources is the production of hydroelectric power. For this reason, it has not been difficult for these countries to agree on provisions which prohibit the pollution of international watercourses. The real significance of these provisions is, therefore, unclear. Is the lack of pollution the result of the treaty or of the innocuous character of the activities actually engaged in? Further, if pollution were to be reported, would the parties apply these treaties or would they find another solution?

(3) *Treaties that prohibit pollution but with reference to the impairment of specific uses of the watercourse*

Article 17 of the 1952 Agreement between the Government of the Polish Republic and the Government of the German Democratic Republic concerning Navigation in Frontier Waters and the Use and Maintenance of Frontier Waters prescribes that:

in order to maintain the frontier waters in proper condition, each contracting party undertakes . . .

(4) To prevent, by appropriate means and installations, any waters entering the frontier sector of the rivers Oder and Nysa Luzycka and any effluents from towns, settlements or industrial plant from introducing into the said rivers physical, chemical or bacteriological impurities of such nature and in such quantities as:
  (*a*) To affect adversely the use of the water of the said rivers for domestic requirements, water supply, industry and agriculture;
  (*b*) To cause bridges, dams, other water engineering works and installations, and vessels to become corroded and overgrown with slime and aquatic flora and fauna;
  (*c*) To cause the executive accumulation of slime on the bed and banks;
  (*d*) To affect adversely the normal development of the typical aquatic flora and fauna of the said rivers.[81]

Other treaties concluded for the specific purpose of regulating fishing and protecting fish often include provisions prohibiting pollution that may affect fisheries. In this connection, the 1960 Agreement between the Kingdom of Norway and the Republic of Finland regarding New Fishing Regulations for the Fishing Area of the Tana River provides that: 'Any pollution of, or discharge of waste or sewage into the waters in the fishing area shall be prohibited unless duly authorized'.[82]

[81] *United Nations Legislative Texts and Treaty Provisions concerning the Utilization of International Rivers for Other Purposes than Navigation*, p. 769.

[82] See Article 18 of the Fishing Regulations: ibid., p. 620. See also Article 17 of the 1904 Convention between France and Switzerland for the Regulation of Fishing in their Frontier Waters: ibid., p. 706; Article 6 of the 1980 Agreement between France and Switzerland concerning Fishing in the Leman Lake: FAO, *Treaties concerning the Non-Navigational Uses of International Watercourses—Europe* (Rome, 1993), Legislative Study 50, p. 354.

(4) *Treaties that prohibit pollution in so far as it damages specific interests mentioned by the treaty*

Article IV of the 1909 Treaty between the United States and Great Britain relating to Boundary Waters and Questions Arising between the Unites States and Canada[83] provides that:

> . . . It is further agreed that the waters herein defined as boundary waters and waters flowing across the boundary shall not be polluted on either side to the injury of health or property on the other.

The International Joint Commission between the United States and Canada has had occasion to interpret this provision in relation to various international watercourses. This binational organization was established by the 1909 Treaty for the purpose of issuing orders of approval in response to applications for the use, obstruction or diversion of the waters that flow along, and in certain cases across, the international boundary if such uses affect the natural water levels or flows on the other side.[84] In addition, the IJC may also investigate specific issues if so requested by the Governments of the two States.[85] In a number of cases the Commission has been requested to investigate issues relating to pollution. In this regard, the following cases are worthy of mention:

(a) *The Rainy River and the Lake of the Woods*. In 1959 the Governments of Canada and the United States requested the International Joint Commission to inquire into the pollution of the Rainy River and the Lake of the Woods and the extent to which this pollution was causing injury to health and property on the other side of the boundary.[86] The Commission delivered its report on 24 February 1965. It concluded that, indeed, the waters of the Rainy River and the Lake of the Woods were polluted and that pollution was resulting in injury to health and property on both sides of the boundary. Potential injury to health derived from the pollution of waters that were used for domestic and recreational bathing purposes. Injury to property involved the increase in the cost of water supply for municipalities and a decrease in the attractiveness of bathing beaches and waterfront areas which could result in the lower valuation of resorts and other properties. The Commission also found that there was a potential economic loss for certain industries from the inability to secure a satisfactory water supply. In particular, the Commission found that the recreational industry had already suffered losses because the pollution was such that the waters were unsafe for bathing, unsuitable for fishing, detrimental for fish propagation and aesthetically offensive.[87]

[83] Text in *British and Foreign State Papers*, vol. 102, pp. 137 ff.

[84] Articles III and IV.

[85] Article IX.

[86] International Joint Commission, *Report on the Pollution of Rainy River and Lake of the Woods* (Washington D.C. and Ottawa, 1965), p. 29.

[87] Ibid., pp. 61–2.

(b) *Lake Erie, Lake Ontario and the international section of the St Lawrence River.* In 1964 Canada and the United States referred the following question to the International Joint Commission: 'Are the waters of Lake Erie, Lake Ontario, and the International Section of the St Lawrence River being polluted on either side of the boundary to an extent which is causing or is likely to cause injury to health or property on the other side of the boundary?'[88] The Commission found that the waters in question were being seriously polluted on both sides of the boundary to the detriment of both countries and to an extent which was causing injury to health and property on the other side of the boundary.[89] According to the Commission, future industrial and urban development would be adversely affected and postponed unless the necessary remedial measures to correct the pollution problem were implemented.[90] Certain polluting substances were found to be present in the waters and the Commission concluded that these substances had had a detrimental effect on the fisheries and, as a consequence, commercial fishermen, processors and distributors, as well as the tourist and sport fishing industry, were suffering economic loss.[91] Furthermore, the Commission observed that the adverse effects of pollutants on wildlife provided an early warning of the presence of contaminants which could become health problems.[92]

(c) *The Garrison Diversion Unit.* In October 1975, the Governments of Canada and the United States of America requested the International Joint Commission to examine and report on the transboundary implications of the proposed completion and operation of the Garrison Diversion Unit in the State of North Dakota, and to make recommendations as to such measures, including modifications, alterations or adjustments to the Garrison Diversion Unit, as might be taken to assist governments in ensuring the fulfilment of the obligation contained in Article IV of the Boundary Waters Treaty.[93]

The Governments of Canada and Manitoba objected to the Garrison Diversion Unit (GDU) project on the basis that the return flows would increase the amount and frequency of flooding on the Souris, Assiniboine and Red Rivers. They also claimed that the project could adversely affect the water quality of these rivers and of Lakes Winnipeg and Manitoba. Detrimental effects on water quality could also affect fish and wildlife resources in Manitoba by transferring foreign biota from the Manitoba

[88] International Joint Commission, *Pollution of Lake Erie, Lake Ontario and the International Section of the St Lawrence River* (1970), p. 161.

[89] Ibid., p. 136.

[90] Ibid., p. 34.

[91] Ibid., p. 95.

[92] Ibid., p. 105.

[93] International Joint Commission, *Transboundary Implications of the Garrison Diversion Unit* (1977), p. 131.

River into the Hudson Bay Drainage. With the introduction of alien fish, fish diseases and fish parasites, the commercial and recreational fisheries on Lake Winnipeg and Lake Manitoba could be seriously affected. Finally they claimed that the introduction of other biota could interfere with the existing aquatic systems or cause diseases in animals or humans using the water.[94]

The Commission concluded that, in fact, the construction and operation of the Garrison Diversion Unit as envisaged by the United States would cause injury to health and property in Canada as a result of adverse impacts on the water quality and on the biological resources of Manitoba.[95] With regard to water quality the IJC maintained that:

> A high concentration of almost any chemical constituent of water can by itself, or in combination with others, interfere with established water uses. If concentrations are excessive, they could cause health problems. Municipal and industrial uses can usually be protected by additional treatment. However, water for agricultural purposes cannot be economically treated.[96]

The uses which could be detrimentally affected by the GDU included domestic, industrial and agricultural uses in the Province of Manitoba.[97] The Commission also found that there would be adverse effects on the fisheries as a result of the introduction of foreign species. As a result, the IJC calculated that the commercial fishing industry would suffer a loss of approximately six million Canadian dollars. It added that 'under such conditions the commercial fishing industry could be eliminated with all the attendant consequences'.[98] With regard to wildlife, the Commission predicted that the GDU would result in an annual loss of 35,000 ducks in Manitoba.[99] The Commission recognized that this last issue exceeded the terms of Article IV of the Boundary Waters Treaty. In fact, the detrimental effects on the waterfowl in Manitoba did not amount to a breach of Article IV. However, the Commission was authorized to investigate and report upon this issue because the terms of the Reference concluded by the parties required the IJC to examine into and to report upon the general transboundary implications of the proposed completion and operation of the GDU.[100]

The final conclusion of the Commission's report was that the GDU would cause adverse impacts in Canada and that, although most of the impacts could be mitigated, those from the possible biota transfers were so serious that the only acceptable solution was to delay the construction

[94] Ibid., p. 5.
[95] Ibid., p. 3.
[96] Ibid., p. 42.
[97] Ibid., p. 59.
[98] Ibid., pp. 59–60.
[99] Ibid., p. 60.
[100] Ibid., pp. 112 and 131.

of those features of the GDU which could result in such transfers.[101] The adverse impact on the waterfowl population was also a factor which the Commission took into account in recommending a delay of construction of the GDU. It must be pointed out, though, that the Commission did not say that the GDU should not have any adverse impact on the waterfowl, and it only suggested that these adverse effects and the provisions of the International Migratory Birds Convention of 1916 should be taken into consideration.[102] Indeed, the Commission concluded that these detrimental effects 'would be largely offset by the implementation of the wetland habitat restoration concept', but it was prepared to accept that even with the implementation of such a concept some damage would be caused to the waterfowl population.[103]

(d) *The Poplar River*. In August 1977 the Governments of Canada and the United States agreed to request the International Joint Commission to examine and report upon the water quality of the Poplar River. The pertinent passage of the Reference reads as follows:

> . . . the Governments of Canada and the United States have agreed, pursuant to Article IX of the Boundary Waters Treaty of 1909, to request the International Joint Commission to examine into and report upon the water quality of the Poplar River, including the transboundary water quality of the Poplar River, including the transboundary water quality implications of the thermal power station of the Saskatchewan Power Corporation and its ancillary facilities, including coal-mining, at a site near Coronach, Saskatchewan, and to make recommendations which would assist Governments in ensuring that the provisions of Article IV of the said Treaty are honoured.[104]

The IJC found that water quantity reductions resulting from the apportionment of the waters of the Poplar River and the operation of the thermal power station would not pollute the waters of the river to a degree which would affect health or property on the other side of the boundary. Therefore, the apportionment of water already effected by the Commission and the future operation of the thermal power station would not violate Article IV of the Boundary Waters Treaty. However, the Commission found that the reduction in the amount of water crossing the boundary was expected to affect adversely the maintenance of the existing biological community in the East Fork of the Poplar River. This detrimental effect did not involve the pollution of the river and, therefore, it did not amount to a violation of Article IV of the 1909 Treaty. For this reason the Commission did not propose measures to ensure compliance with Article IV. Nevertheless, it suggested that this detrimental effect, though not considered by the Commission in its

[101] Ibid., p. 114.
[102] Ibid., p.112.
[103] Ibid., p.113.
[104] International Joint Commission, *Water Quality in the Poplar River Basin* (1981), p. 210.

recommendation concerning the apportionment of the waters of the Poplar River, should be taken into account by the Governments.[105]

Apart from clarifying that the detrimental environmental effects resulting from changes in water quantity did not amount to pollution, the IJC considered it important to remark that Article IV does not say that there shall be no transboundary pollution, but rather it requires that injury does not result from such pollution. In this connection the Commission stated:

Thus, the Commission concludes that Article IV does not require non-degradation per se. In some cases the upstream country could degrade the water quality of a transboundary stream without causing injury to health or property in the downstream country; in other cases, any degradation of water quality could cause such injury. There is no general rule to define the degree of 'pollution' that constitutes a violation of Article IV of the Treaty. As a consequence, each situation must be examined on a case-by-case basis and the course of action that is selected will reflect the particular circumstances of the case.[106]

(e) *The Flathead River*. By letters of December 1984 and February 1985, the IJC was requested to investigate and report on the water quality and quantity of the Flathead River, with respect to the trans-boundary water quality and quantity implications of the proposed coal mine on Cabin Creek, a tributary of the Flathead River.[107] According to the text of the Reference:

. . . the Governments of Canada and the United States have agreed, pursuant to Article IX of the Boundary Waters Treaty of 1909, to request the International Joint Commission to examine into and report upon the water quality and quantity implications of the proposed coal mine development on Cabin Creek in British Columbia near its confluence with the Flathead River, and to make recommendations which would assist Governments in ensuring that the provisions of Article IV of the said treaty are honoured.

The Commission found that the coal mine would pollute the waters of the Flathead River and that this pollution would have a serious impact on the fisheries of the Flathead River. This finding was enough for the Commission to conclude that the effects of the proposed coal mine would constitute a breach of Article IV of the 1909 Treaty.[108] In explaining its conclusion, the IJC stated that:

This conclusion is not based on the dollar losses calculated by the Water Uses Committee, although the Commission is satisfied that there will be demonstrable and sustained economic loss to a number of interests, dependent on this

[105] Ibid., pp. xiii and 197.

[106] Ibid., pp. 190–1.

[107] International Joint Commission, *Impacts of a Proposed Coal Mine in the Flathead River Basin* (1988), p. 3.

[108] Ibid., pp. 8–9.

fishery. Far more important, the Commission feels, and conclusive in this regard, is the integrity of the fishery itself. While the fishery is in the public domain, that fact does not render it any less a property. A reduction of the fish population to the extent and of the duration involved here would undoubtedly be an injury of most serious consequence to the integrity of the fishery itself, and thus to that property interest in the public domain on the other side of the border.

Conclusions regarding the practice of the International Joint Commission. The experience of the International Joint Commission between the United States and Canada shows that the Commission has been careful in characterizing the detrimental effects of pollution as injury to health and property. The Commission has attempted to stick to the terms of Article IV of the Boundary Waters Treaty. It is important to note that the Commission, though sometimes requested to investigate and to report on the general transboundary environmental impact of certain projects, has made no mention of the existence of an obligation not to cause significant environmental harm (damage) to the territory of other States. In this regard, the IJC has reported on certain environmental interferences which exceed the strict terms of Article IV of the 1909 Treaty and, instead of suggesting that these interferences might be unlawful under general international law, it has only suggested that the Governments of the United States and Canada take these matters into consideration.

(5) *Treaties that do not prohibit pollution in absolute terms but regulate it by setting emission standards*

The purpose of the 1978 Agreement between the United States of America and Canada on the Great Lakes Water Quality[109] was to eliminate or reduce, to the maximum extent practicable, the discharge of pollutants into the Great Lakes System. The parties agreed on the general objective of restoring the quality of the waters of the Great Lakes Basin to a minimum level of water quality, but they also agreed that there should be limited zones for discharging municipal and industrial waste. The Treaty prescribes that waste treatment facilities shall be implemented and that measures for the abatement of pollution from polluting activities shall be taken. The annexes attached to the Agreement specify the maximum quantities of polluting substances that can be discharged into the waters of the Great Lakes System.

The 1976 Convention concerning the Protection of the Rhine against Chemical Pollution regulates the discharge of certain substances with the intention of improving the quality of the waters of the Rhine so that these waters may still be used by the riparian States. The purpose of the Convention is to eliminate the pollution of the surface waters of the

[109] *United States Treaties and Other International Agreements*, vol. 30, p. 1384.

Rhine basin caused by the discharge of the dangerous substances mentioned in Annex I and to reduce the pollution caused by the dangerous substances mentioned in Annex II.[110] The Convention shows that the riparian States were not prepared to eliminate all pollution from the Rhine. Rather, the Convention establishes emissions standards which the respective Governments shall follow in granting permission for discharging certain substances into the surface waters of the Rhine basin, but these emission standards are fixed by the Convention only in relation to the toxic substances mentioned in Annex I. The substances mentioned in Annex II are subject only to the emission standards fixed by each Government.

The 1976 Convention on the Pollution of the Rhine by Chlorides[111] does not provide for the full protection of the Rhine against pollution by chlorides either. In fact, as Lammers states, 'fully implemented it could have reduced the salinity by less than 20 per cent of the total chloride load'.[112] It is also worth mentioning that the cost of the reduction of the French discharges of chlorides into the Rhine is to be met not only by France but also by Germany, Switzerland and the Netherlands. It should also be stressed that the Netherlands does not contribute to the salinity of the Rhine but is a victim State.

In relation to these obligations, Nollkaemper rightly concludes that:

> The regime [for transboundary water pollution] shows several examples of incoherencies. One example is that the no-appreciable harm principle . . . is poorly reflected in the specific obligations. Many specific obligations . . . do not adequately address transboundary harm. Although their aim to reduce pollution can, as a side-effect, lead to prevention of transboundary harm, they do not aim to guarantee that result. The movement at the level of principles to specify in greater detail the obligations of states concerning transboundary pollution, is paralleled by the development of specific obligations that leave essentially unanswered the question of the permissibility of transboundary pollution.[113]

(6) *Treaties that prohibit environmental damage in order to enforce the allocation of international waters agreed by the States concerned*

Article 4 of the 1960 Indus Water Treaty concluded between India and Pakistan provides that:

> (10) Each Party declares its intention to prevent, as far as practicable, undue pollution of the waters of the Rivers which might affect adversely uses similar in nature to those to which the waters were put on the Effective Date, and agrees to take all reasonable measures to ensure that, before any sewage or industrial waste is allowed to flow into the Rivers, it will be treated, where necessary, in such manner as not materially to affect those uses: Provided that the criterion of

[110] See Art.1 of the Convention. Text in *International Legal Materials,* 16 (1977), p. 242.
[111] Text: ibid., p. 265.
[112] Lammers, op.cit. above (n. 32), p. 183.
[113] Nollkaemper, op.cit. above (n. 44), pp. 308–9.

reasonableness shall be the customary practice in similar situations on the Rivers.[114]

The object of the Indus Water Treaty was to apportion the water resources of the Indus basin between India and Pakistan, whose economies are largely based on the use of water for irrigation. For this reason it was important to prevent undue pollution that could interfere with the agreed allocation. In this connection, it is important to note that the obligation not to pollute does not refer to any pollution but to that which affects adversely uses similar to those to which the waters were put on the effective date, and that this obligation is further qualified by the expression 'as far as practicable'.

The 1972 Agreement on the Permanent and Definitive Solution to the International Problem of the Salinity of the Colorado River between Mexico and the United States[115] was concluded precisely because it was necessary to enforce the agreement on the apportionment of the waters of the Colorado River. According to the 1944 Treaty relating to the Utilization of the Waters of the Colorado and Tijuana Rivers and of the Rio Grande, Mexico was allocated 1,500,000 acre-feet of the waters of the Colorado River to be delivered by the United States. In 1961 Mexico protested because the water delivered by the United States was unusable for irrigation. In December 1972 the parties agreed to a permanent solution to the salinity problem whereby the United States assumed the obligation of improving the quality of the water delivered to Mexico. To have accepted that the United States was entitled to pollute the river and to deliver to Mexico an amount of unusable water would have been to admit that the apportionment effected by the 1944 Treaty was a dead letter.

The 1994 Treaty of Peace between the State of Israel and the Hashemite Kingdom of Jordan provides in its Annex II that:

1. Israel and Jordan undertake to protect, within their own jurisdiction, the shared waters of the Jordan and the Yarmouk Rivers and Arava/Araba groundwater, against any pollution, contamination, harm or unauthorized withdrawals of each other's allocations.

. . .

3. Israel and Jordan will each prohibit the disposal of municipal and industrial wastewater into the courses of the Yarmouk and the Jordan Rivers before they are treated to standards allowing their unrestricted agricultural use. Implementation of this prohibition shall be completed within three years from the entry into force of the Treaty.[116]

[114] *United Nations Legislative Texts and Treaty Provisions concerning the Utilization of International Rivers for Other Purposes than Navigation*, p. 305.

[115] *International Legal Materials*, 12 (1973), p. 1105.

[116] *International Legal Materials*, 34 (1995), p. 59.

It is clear that for Israel and Jordan water is essential for domestic uses and agriculture. For this reason water has to be of such a quality that these uses are not impaired. The parties agreed on a division of the volume of water of the rivers Jordan and Yarmouk and, though the parties did not make it explicit, it would be logical to interpret the rule prohibiting pollution as a necessary rule to protect the agreed apportionment.

(7) *Treaties that take into consideration the economic and technical capability of the parties to abate pollution*

In this regard, Article 3(4) of the 1958 Agreement between Czechoslovakia and Poland concerning the Use of Water Resources in Frontier Waters[117] states that:

> The Contracting Parties have agreed to abate the pollution of frontier waters and to keep them clean to such extent as is specifically determined in each particular case in accordance with the economic and technical possibilities and requirements of the Contracting Parties.

(8) *Treaties that prohibit the causing of transboundary environmental impact*

In August 1991 Argentina and Chile signed a Treaty concerning the environment, to which a Protocol on Shared Water Resources was annexed. Article 1 of the Protocol states that:

> The Parties agree that the actions and programmes regarding the utilization of shared water resources shall be undertaken according to the concept of integrated management of drainage basins.
>
> The utilization of the water resources in the territory of one of the parties shall not cause injury to the shared water resources, to the common basin or to the environment.[118]

Article 5 provides that:

> The actions and programmes aimed at the utilization of the shared water resources shall be undertaken in a coordinated or joined manner through general plans of utilization.

Though the causing of detrimental environmental impact is prohibited by the Protocol, it is important to realize that the implementation of this prohibition is a matter for the parties to discuss during the negotiation of the general plans for the utilization of their international watercourses.

[117] *United Nations Treaty Series*, vol. 538, p. 89.

[118] Author's translation. Text in *Diario Oficial de la República de Chile,* Nr. 34,540, 14 April 1993, p. 3.

(9) *Treaties that establish mechanisms of co-operation to deal with the problem of the environmental degradation of international watercourses*

The 1994 Agreements on the Protection of the rivers Meuse and Scheldt[119] state that it is the aim of the parties to co-operate regarding the protection of these rivers. For the purposes of this international co-operation, the parties established an International Commission.[120] Among the principles of co-operation, Article 3 provides that '[t]he Contracting Parties shall protect and, *as far as possible,* improve, by management measures and by the way in which the environment is used, the quality of the Meuse's aquatic ecosystem'.[121] And Article 4.2 prescribes that 'the Parties shall limit, *as far as possible*, the dumping and discharge of dredged material, as well as its movement downstream'.[122] In the same vein, the 1994 Convention on Co-operation for the Protection and Sustainable Use of the Danube River[123] establishes mechanisms of co-operation in order to 'at least maintain and improve the current environmental and water quality conditions of the Danube River and of the waters in its catchment area and to prevent and reduce *as far as possible* adverse impacts and changes occurring or likely to be caused'.[124] The forms of co-operation specified include consultations, joint activities in the framework of the International Commission established by the Treaty and the exchange of information.[125] In addition, the parties agree to take certain measures to avoid transboundary impacts, such as the establishment of emission limits applicable to individual industrial sectors, the prevention of the release of hazardous substances and the definition of water quality objectives where appropriate (Article 7).

The 1995 Agreement between the Government of the People's Republic of China and the Government of Mongolia on the Protection and Utilization of Transboundary Waters[126] also provides that the parties should co-operate in the protection of transboundary waters. In this regard, Article 4.1 prescribes that:

1. The Two Contracting Parties should jointly protect the ecological system of the transboundary waters and develop and utilize transboundary waters in a way that should not be detrimental to the other side. Any development and utilization of transboundary waters should follow the principle of fairness and equability [sic]without impeding any reasonable use of transboundary waters.

[119] Concluded between France, the Netherlands and some regions of Belgium. Text in *International Legal Materials,* 34 (1995), pp. 851 ff. and pp. 859 ff.

[120] Article 2.2.

[121] Emphasis added.

[122] Emphasis added.

[123] Text on diskette accompanying *Yearbook of International Environmental Law* (1994), doc. 16. The Convention was concluded between Austria, Bulgaria, Croatia, Germany, Hungary, the Republic of Moldova, Romania, Slovenia and Ukraine on 29 June 1994.

[124] Article 2.2.

[125] Article 4.

[126] Text on file with the author.

Again, none of these agreements establish an obligation not to cause environmental damage to the other watercourse States.

(10) *Treaties that only establish the obligation to consult in relation to activities likely to cause pollution of international watercourses*

In this regard, Article 12 of the 1964 Agreement concerning the River Niger Commission and Navigation and Transport on the River Niger provides that the riparian States:

> . . . undertake further to abstain from carrying out on the portion of the River, its tributaries and sub-tributaries subject to their jurisdiction any works likely to pollute the waters, or any modification likely to affect biological characteristics of its fauna and flora, without adequate notice to, and prior consultation with, the Commission.[127]

(11) *Treaties that refer to the principles of equitable utilization and no significant environmental damage as if they were simultaneously applicable*

The 1992 Helsinki Convention on the Protection and Use of Transboundary Watercourses and Lakes provides in Article 2 that:

> 1. The Parties shall take all appropriate measures to prevent, control and reduce any transboundary impact.
> 2. The Parties shall, in particular, take all appropriate measures:
> (*a*) To prevent, control and reduce pollution of waters causing or likely to cause transboundary impact;
> (*b*) To ensure that transboundary waters are used with the aim of ecologically sound and rational water management, conservation of water resources and environmental protection;
> (*c*) To ensure that transboundary waters are used in a reasonable and equitable way, taking into particular account their transboundary character, in the case of activities which cause or are likely to cause transboundary impact;
> (*d*) To ensure conservation and, where necessary, restoration of ecosystems.[128]

Transboundary impact is defined as:

> any significant adverse effect on the environment resulting from a change in the conditions of transboundary waters caused by a human activity, the physical origin of which is situated wholly or in part within an area under the jurisdiction of a Party, within an area under the jurisdiction of another Party. Such effects on the environment include effects on human health and safety, flora, fauna, soil, air, water, climate, landscape and historical monuments or other physical structures or the interaction among these factors; they also include effects on the cultural heritage or socio-economic conditions resulting from alterations to those factors.

[127] Text in Hohmann (ed.), *Basic Documents on International Environmental Law* (London, Dordrecht and Boston, 1992), vol. 1, p. 1263.

[128] Text in Birnie and Boyle, op.cit. above (n. 63), p. 347.

This Convention has been interpreted by some authors as giving priority to the prohibition of transboundary environmental impact over the equitable utilization of transboundary watercourses.[129] However, the Convention only sets up a very general objective in relation to the prevention, control and reduction of transboundary impact. This objective has to be attained by the parties through the conclusion of bilateral and multilateral agreements to define their mutual relations and conduct in this regard (Article 9). Therefore, it is yet to be seen whether in implementing this Convention the parties will actually give priority to the prohibition of transboundary environmental impact over equitable utilization. In relation to this point it is interesting to note that the 1994 Convention on Co-operation for the Protection and Sustainable Use of the Danube River,[130] which is an attempt to implement the 1992 Helsinki Convention,[131] mentions equitable and sustainable water management as its purposes and the obligation of the parties to prevent and reduce adverse environmental impact is qualified by the expression *as far as possible* (Article 2.2).

Another treaty in which the obligation to prevent environmental damage and the principle of equitable utilization appear to be simultaneously applicable is the 1995 Protocol on Shared Watercourse Systems in the Southern African Development Community (SADC) Region, of which Article 2 provides that:[132]

> . . .
>
> 2. Member States undertake to respect and apply the existing rules of general or customary international law relating to the utilisation and management of the resources of shared watercourse systems and, in particular, to respect and abide by the principles of community of interests in the equitable utilisation of those systems and related resources.
>
> 3. Member States lying within the basin of a shared watercourse system shall maintain a proper balance between resource development for a higher standard of living for their peoples and conservation and enhancement of the environment to promote sustainable development.
>
> . . .
>
> 6. Member States shall utilise a shared watercourse system in an equitable manner. In particular, a shared watercourse system shall be used and developed by member States with a view to attaining optimum utilisation thereof and

[129] See Nollkaemper, op.cit. above (n. 44), p. 68. The reasons he gives in support of his conclusion that the prohibition of pollution has priority over the principle of equitable utilization are that the latter was included primarily with a view to water quantity issues and that there is broad support for the 'no-appreciable harm principle'. Neither of these arguments is convincing. In particular, Nollkaemper does not give evidence in support of his assertion that equitable use was included only to deal with disputes concerning quantity.

[130] Text on diskette accompanying *Yearbook of International Environmental Law* (1994), doc. 16. The Danube River Protection Convention was concluded between Austria, Bulgaria, Croatia, Germany, Hungary, the Republic of Moldova, Romania, Slovenia and Ukraine on 29 June 1994.

[131] See the Preamble.

[132] Text on file with the author.

obtaining benefits therefrom consistent with adequate protection of the watercourse system.

. . .

12. Member States shall maintain and protect shared watercourse systems and related installations, facilities and other works in order to prevent pollution or environmental degradation.

Though the Protocol speaks of the obligation to prevent pollution and environmental degradation, it also provides that the parties shall maintain a *proper balance* between resource development for a higher standard of living for their peoples, on the one hand, and conservation and enhancement of the environment to promote sustainable development, on the other.

Finally, another instance in which the obligation to prevent pollution and environmental degradation and the obligation to use international watercourses in an equitable and reasonable manner appear as two different obligations which are simultaneously applicable is the 1997 UN Convention on the Law of the Non-Navigational Uses of International Watercourses. While Article 5.1 prescribes that watercourse States shall utilize their international watercourses in an equitable and reasonable manner consistent with the adequate protection of the watercourse, and Article 7 states that watercourse States shall take appropriate measures to prevent the causing of significant harm to other watercourse States, Articles 20 and 21 establish the obligation to protect and preserve the ecosystems of international watercourses and to prevent, reduce and control pollution. The interpretation of these provisions is examined in section E, where it is demonstrated that, as a matter of general international law, the obligation not to cause significant environmental harm has to be applied within the framework of the principle of equitable utilization.

(12) *Conclusion*

The examination of international agreements which deal with the protection of the environment of international watercourses leads to the conclusion that, in the context of the utilization of international watercourses, it is not possible to assert that apart from the principle of equitable utilization there is a separate obligation to refrain from causing environmental damage to the portions of the watercourse located in the territory of other States. In most cases where the parties have agreed on the prohibition or regulation of transboundary environmental damage, this prohibition or regulation performs a particular function: the avoidance of potential disputes in frontier waters, the protection of specific uses or interests of the parties, the mitigation of the polluted condition of certain watercourses or the enforcement of an agreed water apportionment. Apart from this, practice under the agreements in which the purpose of protecting international watercourses has been more clearly established is limited and certainly not sufficient to establish the existence of a principle of general international law prohibiting significant damage to the environment of international watercourses.

D. The Position of the International Law Association

The International Law Association has made a significant contribution to the development of the principle of equitable utilization. In particular, its 1966 Helsinki Rules on the Use of International Rivers were the first attempt to identify the factors relevant for establishment of an equitable regime for water utilization. With regard to pollution, Article X of the Helsinki Rules provides that:

> 1. Consistent with the principle of equitable utilization of the waters of an international drainage basin, a State (a) must prevent any new form of water pollution or any increase in the degree of existing water pollution in an international drainage basin which would cause substantial injury in the territory of a co-basin State, and (b) should take all reasonable measures to abate existing water pollution in an international drainage basin to such an extent that no substantial damage is caused in the territory of a co-basin State.

When commenting on this provision the International Law Association observed that:

> The optimum goal of international drainage basin development is to accommodate the multiple and diverse uses of the co-basin States. The concept of equitable utilization of the waters of an international drainage basin has the purpose of promoting such an accommodation. Thus, uses of the waters by a basin State that cause pollution resulting in injury in a co-basin State must be considered from the overall perspective of what constitutes an equitable utilization.
>
> Any use of water by a basin State, whether upper or lower, that denies an equitable sharing of uses by a co-basin State conflicts with the community of interests of all basin States in obtaining maximum benefit from the common resource. Certainly a diversion of water that denies a co-basin State of an equitable share is in violation of international law. A use that causes pollution to the extent of depriving a co-basin State of an equitable share stands on the same basis. By parallel reasoning, a State that engages in a use or uses causing pollution is not required to take measures with respect to such pollution that would deprive it of equitable utilization.[133]

Immediately after the adoption of the Helsinki Rules, the Committee on Water Resources commenced studies for the elaboration of more precise provisions on pollution. The Rapporteur, Professor Charles Bourne, submitted his Report to the Sixtieth Conference of the Association held in 1982 in Montreal. In this Report Bourne stated that:

[133] ILA, *Report of the Fifty-Second Conference* (Helsinki, 1966), p. 499.

. . . those who would codify and develop this branch of the law still do not find it possible to do more than state a few general principles of law. The negotiation of an agreement by the states concerned remains the best and often the only means of dealing with pollution of the waters of an international drainage.[134]

Those few general principles of law concerning the pollution of international drainage basins were presented in the form of Draft Articles on Water Pollution in an International Drainage Basin, Article 1 of which stipulated that:

Consistent with the Helsinki Rules on the equitable utilization of the waters of an international drainage basin, states shall ensure that activities conducted within their territory or under their control conform with the principles set forth in these Articles concerning water pollution in an international drainage basin. In particular states shall:

(*a*) prevent new or increased water pollution that would cause substantial injury in the territory of another state;

(*b*) take all reasonable measures to abate existing water pollution to such an extent that no substantial injury is caused in the territory of another state; and

(*c*) attempt to further reduce any such water pollution to the lowest level that is practicable and reasonable under the circumstances.[135]

Therefore, the obligation to prevent, reduce and control water pollution was not established as a parallel principle but its content was subject to the principle of equitable utilization. This is clear from the text of Article 1, and the commentary attached to this provision dispels any doubts in this respect. In fact, in explaining the implications of Article 1, Professor Bourne stated that:

4. The principle of equitable utilization remains dominant in the law governing water resources shared by two or more states and, therefore, the formula used in Article X is properly repeated in this restatement of the law. It is a sound principle to build on, for its essence is that international water resources must be exploited rationally and equitably. It recognizes that the activity that produces water pollution is itself a utilization of the water resource, and that this utilization may be reasonable and equitable in the particular circumstances. It provides a desirable flexibility in the disposition of disputes concerning the complex questions raised in cases of water pollution.

5. Questions of liability and compensation for injury caused by pollution of water, therefore, must be approached in the light of the overriding principle of equitable utilization. In view of the difference in the circumstances of each drainage basin, the implementation of the principle will often require the application of different methods and solutions. A wide range of factors are relevant in reaching wise decisions . . . It is difficult, then, to devise rules of universal application. The rule of reasonableness requires flexibility.[136]

[134] ILA, *Report of the Sixtieth Conference* (Montreal, 1982), p. 535.

[135] Ibid. (emphasis added).

[136] Ibid., p. 536.

The subsequent work of the International Law Association in the field of water resources shows that up to now this approach has not changed. In 1996, the Association adopted supplemental rules on pollution.[137] These rules read as follows:

Article 1. In using the waters of an international drainage basin, States shall, consistent with the Helsinki Rules and the rules on international water resources subsequently adopted by the International Law Association, individually or jointly take all reasonable measures to prevent or minimize significant transboundary pollution of another environmental medium.
Article 2. Consistent with applicable international rules and standards, States shall, insofar as technically and economically feasible, ensure that waste, pollutants, and hazardous substances are handled, treated, and disposed of in the manner that produces the least transboundary environmental harm.
Article 3. In using the waters of an international drainage basin, States individually or jointly as appropriate shall ensure prior assessment of the impact of programmes or projects that may have a significant transboundary effect on the environment or on the sustainable use of the waters.
Article 4. States shall use their best efforts to achieve integrated management of the water resources of their international drainage basins.

Article 1 is concerned with cross-media pollution and it is not its purpose to modify the already existing rules adopted with regard to pollution of the drainage basins. Article 2 applies to environmental impact in general; however, this provision does not negate that the infliction of transboundary damage on international watercourses is subject to the principle of equitable utilization. The same should be said of Articles 3 and 4, which do not invalidate the provisions of the 1966 Helsinki Rules or the 1982 Montreal Rules.

E. The 1997 UN Convention on the Law of the Non-Navigational Uses of International Watercourses

Having explained the different functions that the principle of equitable utilization and the obligation not to cause injury to other States perform in the system of international law, and having examined the practice of States and the work of the International Law Association, it is now necessary to examine the 1997 UN Convention on the Law of the Non-Navigational Uses of International Watercourses with a view to reconciling provisions which appear to conflict with each other. In this analysis the work of the International Law Commission and the debate held at the Sixth Committee of the United Nations are taken into account.

[137] ILA, *Report of the Sixty-Seventh Conference* (Helsinki, 1996).

It will be recalled that Article 5.1 of the 1997 UN Convention provides that watercourse States shall use international watercourses in an equitable manner and it adds that this utilization should be consistent with the adequate protection of the watercourse:

Watercourse States shall in their respective territories utilize an international watercourse in an equitable and reasonable manner. In particular, an international watercourse shall be used and developed by watercourse States with a view to attaining optimal and sustainable utilization thereof and benefits therefrom, taking into account the interests of the watercourse States concerned, consistent with adequate protection of the watercourse.

For its part, Article 6.1(*d*) mentions the effects of the use or uses of the watercourse in one State on other watercourse States as a relevant factor to take into account when deciding what is a reasonable and equitable utilization.

The so-called no significant harm principle is established in Article 7, which prescribes that:

1. Watercourse States shall, in utilizing an international watercourse in their territories, take all appropriate measures to prevent the causing of significant harm to other watercourse States.
2. Where significant harm nevertheless is caused to another watercourse State, the States whose use causes such harm shall, in the absence of agreement to such use, take all appropriate measures, having due regard for the provisions of Articles 5 and 6, in consultation with the affected State, to eliminate or mitigate such harm and, where appropriate, to discuss the question of compensation.

Finally, Articles 20 and 21 provide that States shall protect the ecosystems of international watercourses and prevent, reduce and control pollution:

Article 20
Protection and preservation of ecosystems
Watercourse States shall, individually and, where appropriate, jointly, protect and preserve the ecosystems of international watercourses.
Article 21
Prevention, reduction and control of pollution
1. For the purpose of this article, pollution of an international watercourse means any detrimental alteration in the composition or quality of the waters of an international watercourse which results directly or indirectly from human conduct.
2. Watercourse States shall, individually and, where appropriate, jointly, prevent, reduce and control the pollution of an international watercourse that may cause significant harm to other watercourse States or to their environment, including harm to human health or safety, to the use of the waters for any beneficial purpose or to the living resources of the watercourse. Watercourse States shall take steps to harmonize their policies in this connection.
3. Watercourse States shall, at the request of any of them, consult with a view to

arriving at mutually agreeable measures and methods to prevent, reduce and control pollution of an international watercourse, such as:

(*a*) Setting joint water quality objectives and criteria;

(*b*) Establishing techniques and practices to address pollution from point and non-point sources.

(*c*) Establishing lists of substances the introduction of which into the waters of an international watercourse is to be prohibited, limited, investigated or monitored.

The relationship between these articles has been the object of much discussion. The controversial point has been the reconciliation of the apparent contradictions between the principle of equitable utilization and the obligation not to cause significant harm. The debate that preceded the adoption of the 1997 Convention on the Law of the Non-Navigational Uses of International Watercourses by the General Assembly illustrates the essence of the controversy. Of the three States which voted against the adoption of the Convention, one of them, Turkey,[138] manifested that one of the reasons for its negative vote was that, in its view, the Convention should have established the primacy of the principle of equitable utilization over the obligation not to cause significant harm.[139] In the same vein, the representative of Ethiopia, which abstained, explained that:

> With regard to articles 5, 6 and 7, my delegation would have liked to see the primacy of article 5 clearly established, as was proposed by the International Law Commission in its draft. However, this proposal has been tampered with by the Working Group of the Whole. It is the view of my delegation that the well-established right of equitable utilization in the Convention was the only reason and incentive for any upper riparian country in the position of Ethiopia to accept the Convention. In the absence of this clearly defined right, the Convention will mean very little to these countries. [140]

A similar opinion was advanced by the representative of Spain, who observed that:

> In our view, article 7, relating to the obligation not to cause significant harm in utilizing international watercourses, is among the most important in the Convention. It has always been our understanding, however, that this obligation cannot be dissociated from the cardinal principle of equitable and reasonable utilization as set out in articles 5 and 6. If a watercourse is utilized in conformity with this principle, it is unfair to oblige a watercourse State to eliminate or mitigate significant harm and or even less to discuss the question of compensation with affected States.
>
> This, in our view, is one of the most significant consequences of articles 5 and 6; to our mind, such consequences should have been addressed clearly and decisively in article 7. The wording of article 7—'having due regard for the

[138] The other two States that voted against were Burundi and China.

[139] GA, *Verbatim Record, 99th Plenary Meeting*, Doc. A/51/PV.99 (1997), p. 5.

[140] Ibid., p. 11.

provisions of articles 5 and 6'—is not sufficiently explicit, and could give rise to friction and disputes when the Convention is implemented.

Given the key role of that article, my delegation was obliged to abstain in the vote.[141]

For its part, Egypt, which voted in favour of the Convention, pointed out that in its opinion the principle of equitable utilization was necessarily linked to the obligation not to cause significant harm. It explained that the latter was a principle of customary international law which could not be replaced or superseded by the factors mentioned in Article 6 of the Convention.[142]

When reading these opinions, the idea that harm might have had different meanings for the various delegations comes to mind. It is true that Article 7 establishes an obligation to prevent harm. However, it is not clear whether Article 7 takes harm as denoting damage or 'legal injury'. If harm denotes damage, a problem arises in relation to the impairment of existing uses, which could be one of the normal effects of the principle of equitable utilization.[143] If harm denotes 'legal injury', which is an encroachment on another State's equitable share of the benefits of an international watercourse, it would be an inconsistency to speak, as Article 7 does, of legal injury in the case of an agreement authorizing the injurious activity. It would also be pointless to provide that in eliminating or mitigating legal injury States must have due regard to the provisions of Articles 5 and 6. These articles contain the criteria of equitable utilization, the application of which specifies what amounts to legal injury. In this context, the phrase 'having due regard for the provisions of Articles 5 and 6' can only make sense if harm is understood as damage. It is necessary, therefore, to provide a meaningful definition for the concept of harm which will allow a coherent interpretation of Article 7.

In the draft Articles on the Law of the Non-Navigational Uses of International Watercourses adopted by the International Law Commission (1994), draft Article 7 seems to have employed the notion of harm for denoting damage. Draft Article 7 provided that:

1. Watercourse States shall exercise due diligence to utilize an international watercourse in such a way as not to cause significant harm to other watercourse States.

2. Where, despite the exercise of due diligence, significant harm is caused to another watercourse State, the State whose use causes the harm shall, in the absence of agreement to such use, consult with the State suffering such harm over:

[141] Ibid., p. 13. See also the opinions of the representatives of Israel, of the Czech Republic and of Slovakia: ibid., pp. 6, 7 and 12.

[142] Ibid., pp. 11–12.

[143] This point is further developed in Fuentes, loc. cit. above (n. 4), pp. 356–73.

(*a*) the extent to which such use is equitable and reasonable taking into account the factors listed in Article 6.

(*b*) the question of ad hoc adjustment to its utilization, designed to eliminate or mitigate any such harm caused and, where appropriate, the question of compensation.

In its commentary to draft Article 7, the ILC stated that:

. . . the fact that an activity involves significant harm, would not of itself necessarily constitute a basis for barring it. In certain circumstances 'equitable and reasonable utilization' of an international watercourse may still involve significant harm to another watercourse State. Generally, in such instances, the principle of equitable and reasonable utilization remains the guiding criterion in balancing the interests at stake.[144]

In the course of the debate in the Sixth Committee of the General Assembly, the Drafting Committee found it difficult to adopt a final text for Article 7 which would have satisfied the competing interests of the various States.[145] Consultations on this provision were held by the Working Group on the Elaboration of the Convention and it became evident that the final text of Article 7 would have to consist of a balanced compromise between the various opposing views.[146] Reading the final text of Article 7, it can be realized that a compromise solution was adopted at the cost of the clarity of the text. In fact, the ambiguity concerning the relationship between the principle of equitable utilization and the obligation not to cause significant harm to the territory of the other watercourse States is evident. In particular, it is not clear whether Article 7 establishes an obligation not to cause damage to other watercourse States which would exist independently of the application of the principle of equitable utilization, or whether environmental damage inflicted upon the watercourse should be included as one more relevant factor in the balancing process contemplated by Articles 5 and 6. The interpretation of the notion of harm in Article 7, therefore, is central to the application of the principle of equitable utilization.

Some commentators, instead of focusing on the interpretation of the notion of harm, have taken for granted that an obligation not to cause damage to other watercourse States exists in general international law and have claimed that the conflict between this obligation and the principle of equitable utilization can be easily solved by reference to the standard of due diligence. In their view, significant damage resulting from failure to exercise due diligence would violate the principle of equitable utilization, and 'where significant harm [damage] is caused

144 1994 *ILC Report*, p. 236.

145 See *Summary Record of the 52nd Meeting of the Sixth Committee, Report of the Chairman of the Drafting Committee,* Doc. A/C.6/51/SR.53.

146 See *Summary Record of the 57th Meeting of the Sixth Committee*, Doc. A/C.6/51/SR.57.

despite the exercise of due diligence it will be *prima facie* inequitable'.[147] The problem with this argument is that the standard of due diligence can only assist in the determination of the manner in which certain activities must be undertaken but it is of no assistance in the determination of which activities should be allowed to be undertaken.[148]

To illustrate the importance of the distinction between damage and legal injury, it would be helpful to consider the following situation: on the basis of the principle of equitable utilization, State A plans to construct a hydroelectric plant, the consequences of which will be the causing of serious damage to the fish population of the watercourse to such extent that the population of State B would be unable to fish in those waters. In this case, recourse to the standard of due diligence does not resolve the question of whether or not the construction of the hydroelectric plant is lawful. In fact, in so far as State A has relied on the rule of equitable use when planning the construction of the hydroelectric plant, it has intentionally decided to cause certain harmful effects to the territory of a neighbouring State. State B could object that the conduct of State A is unlawful because it contradicts paragraph 1 of Article 7 of the UN Convention on the Law of the Non-Navigational Uses of International Watercourses. State A claims that this argument should be rejected because damage is a factor which, according to Article 6(*d*) of the Convention, should be included in the balancing process. If the dispute were to be submitted to the decision of an international tribunal, one possibility would be for the tribunal to conclude that the conduct of State A is unlawful because it contradicts the terms of Article 7 but that to reconcile this provision with Article 6 of the Convention it is necessary to conclude that the operation of the principle of equitable utilization precludes wrongfulness. However, the 1996 draft Articles on State Responsibility show that equitable utilization is not among the circumstances precluding wrongfulness.[149] A more consistent interpretation of the provisions of the 1997 UN Convention would be that damage plays a role in the process of the establishment of an equitable regime for the utilization of the watercourse in question, as one more relevant factor that has to be taken into account. This means that the prevention of legal injury, as a general obligation of international law, does not operate in the application of the principle of equitable use. The obligation not to cause injury becomes operative afterwards, when there is a need for safeguarding the allocation of rights which has been effected in accordance with the principle of equitable utilization. Therefore, despite the fact that the notion of harm employed in Article 7 of the 1997 UN Convention has

[147] Brunnée and Toope, 'Environmental Security and Freshwater Resources: A Case for International Ecosystem Law', *Yearbook of International Environmental Law*, 5 (1994), p. 64.

[148] This view is shared by Wouters, loc.cit. above (n. 44), p. 437.

[149] See the 1996 draft Articles on State Responsibility adopted by the ILC at first reading: *International Legal Materials*, 37 (1998), pp. 450 ff.

to be understood as denoting damage, it is not possible to conclude that paragraph 1 establishes a separate obligation not to cause damage. Article 7.1, therefore, compels watercourse States to prevent damage, but in the context of an equitable utilization of international watercourses. In other words, the actual prevention of damage depends on equitable factors.

The objection could be raised that the conclusion that environmental damage is one more factor to take into account in the establishment of an equitable regime for the utilization of international watercourses contradicts the terms of Articles 20 and 21 of the 1997 UN Convention. Articles 20 and 21 seem to protect territorial integrity instead of the right to the equitable utilization of international watercourses. In this connection, Article 20 introduces the notion of 'ecosystems of international watercourses' and Article 21 attempts to prevent significant harm to the 'environment' of watercourse States. However, and notwithstanding that they are drafted in very rigid terms, it can hardly be said that Articles 20 and 21 codify customary international law. In fact, when the International Law Commission included these provisions in its draft Articles, it cited precedents that gave only 'evidence of recognition by States of the necessity of protecting essential ecological processes'[150] and of 'a long-standing concern of States with the problem of pollution on international watercourses'.[151] None of these instances of State practice was conclusive as to the existence of a rule of general international law that international watercourses must always be kept free from significant damage. In section C it has been shown that the protection of international watercourses adopts various forms, none of which permits the conclusion that in general international law the environment of international watercourses must always be kept free from significant transboundary damage.

The conclusion, therefore, should be that the environmental impact of the use of an international watercourse is one factor that should be taken into account, among others, in the establishment of an equitable regime for the utilization of international watercourses. Could it be argued that this factor should be accorded priority over other relevant criteria? In the process of weighing up the various relevant factors for the establishment of an equitable regime for the utilization of international watercourses, no factor has inherent priority over the others.[152] However, Article 10 of the 1997 UN Convention acknowledges that special regard should be given to the requirements of vital human needs. Article 10 provides that:

> 1. In the absence of agreement or custom to the contrary, no use of an international watercourse enjoys inherent priority over other uses.

[150] 1994 *ILC Report*, p. 287.
[151] Ibid., p. 296.
[152] Ibid., p. 232.

2. In the event of a conflict between uses of an international watercourse, it shall be resolved with reference to articles 5 to 7, with special regard being given to the requirements of vital human needs.

Therefore, by saying that the requirements of vital human needs deserve a special regard, paragraph 2 gives a certain inherent priority to these requirements. When drafting this provision, the International Law Commission indicated that special attention should be paid to providing sufficient water to sustain human life, including both drinking water and water required for the production of food in order to prevent starvation.[153] This argument should be read with caution. Most uses of water could be linked to the maintenance of human life. As regards the environmental protection of international watercourses, a link between the need for this protection and the provision of sufficient water to sustain human life is not difficult to establish. However, if the Commission's intention was to stress that certain uses could be considered more important than others, it is clear that its commentary cannot be interpreted as covering all the activities that can be undertaken in international watercourses. Therefore, the special relationship between water and the maintenance of human life, for the purposes of the establishment of an inherent priority between uses, has to be understood as referring to certain circumstances in which the denial of water to a certain community may imply catastrophic consequences. Therefore, to accord priority to environmental considerations is not simply a matter of establishing a link between the environment and human life. It would be necessary, therefore, to connect the need for the protection of the environment with the prevention of catastrophic consequences on human life.

In 1993 the Special Rapporteur, Mr Rosenstock, proposed a redraft of Article 7 concerning the obligation of watercourse States not to cause significant harm to other watercourse States. His intention was to ascribe a special role to pollution, while equitable and reasonable utilization would have remained the decisive criterion in determining generally which other harmful uses of a watercourse were to be allowed. In this regard, the proposed version of Article 7 read as follows:

Watercourse States shall exercise due diligence to utilize an international watercourse in such a way as not to cause significant harm to other watercourse States, absent their agreement, except as may be allowable under an equitable and reasonable use of the watercourse. A use which causes significant harm in the form of pollution shall be presumed to be an inequitable and unreasonable use unless there is:

(*a*) a clear showing of special circumstances indicating a compelling need for ad hoc adjustment; and
(*b*) the absence of any imminent threat to human health and safety.[154]

[153] Ibid., p. 257.

[154] See Rosenstock, First Report on the Law of the Non-Navigational Uses of International Watercourses, 1993, Doc. A/CN.4/451, p. 10.

In this proposal, there is a presumption that pollution may constitute an imminent threat to human health and safety. The International Law Commission did not adopt Rosenstock's proposal. However, the special protection he granted to human health and safety was acknowledged by the Commission, which in the commentary attached to draft Article 7 maintained that: 'a use which causes significant harm to human health and safety is understood to be inherently inequitable and unreasonable'.[155] Therefore, the Commission appears as adopting the view that harm to human health and safety is a factor which should always be ascribed priority over other factors. This view is not consistent with Article 10 which, for the purposes of establishing an inherent priority with respect to a certain use, requires a connection between harm to human health and safety, and catastrophic consequences for human life.

Needless to say, this link between a threat to human health and safety and catastrophic consequences for human life is usually non-existent. Indeed, a threat to human health and safety does not necessarily affect the possibilities of sustaining human life. Moreover, it must be realized that it is false to say that harm to human health and safety transforms *ipso facto* what was an equitable use into an inequitable one. Watercourses are sometimes used for the discharge of wastes which could cause serious damage to human health if the water were drunk. One example might be the 1978 Agreement between the United States and Canada on the Great Lakes Water Quality, in which the parties established specific zones for discharging municipal and industrial waste.[156] If, in fact, someone were to drink that water, the relevant question for the purposes of establishing responsibility would be whether the States fulfilled the terms of the 1978 Agreement and employed due diligence when carrying out this activity. With regard to human safety, one might think of the huge dams which pose a threat to the communities that live nearby. If something went wrong and harm were caused by the dam, the first question to address is whether in the operation of the dam the State incurred responsibility. It might be the case that harm to human health and safety is the result of the failure of the State to exercise due diligence, in which case there would be no question about the equitableness of an activity which has already been qualified as equitable. If harm to human health and safety results in spite of the employment of due diligence it would be necessary to reconsider the equitableness of the activity. In doing so, and because the relation between harm to human health and safety and catastrophic effects over human life usually does not exist, this kind of damage would be one factor, among others, which should be taken into account. Of course, the result of the balancing process could be that a use which

[155] 1994 *ILC Report*, p. 242.

[156] *United States Treaties and Other International Agreements*, vol. 30, p. 1384.

resulted in harm to human health and safety should be discontinued. However, the point which is worth noting is that harm to human health and safety does not necessarily have an inherent priority over other factors.

F. Should Environmental Impact Remain an Equitable Criterion?: A view into the Future

The inclusion of environmental impact as a relevant factor which has to be considered alongside other equitable criteria might result in significant and detrimental environmental effects on other watercourse States. In this context, the principle of equitable utilization might fail to promote a more effective environmental protection of international watercourses.[157] This does not necessarily contradict the requirements of sustainable development. In this regard, it has already been explained that the concept of sustainable development does not put environmental interests above developmental concerns, but that it adopts an integrated approach. This approach is also adopted by the principle of equitable utilization. In fact, the latter requires that the social and economic needs of the States concerned be taken into consideration as well as adequate protection of the watercourse.

However, there is an important difference between the notion of sustainable development and the principle of equitable utilization. While the latter simply admits the possibility of the causing of significant environmental harm to other watercourse States, sustainable development permits the adoption of more stringent obligations with regard to the protection of the environment without abandoning the integrated approach. This is so because, as Brunnée and Toope have pointed out, 'the focus of the equitable use principle is on the balancing of different use interests in the resources and not on the protection of ecological interests'.[158]

In order to attain a more effective protection of international watercourses, Brunnée and Toope propose that there should be a synthesis between international water law and international environmental law.[159] The assumption that these are two separate systems of applicable law is not correct. The utilization of international watercourses is regulated by public international law, and it would be false to say that States look for the rules that regulate the use of their freshwater resources in two different systems of law. However, if what these authors want to say is simply that a more effective protection of international watercourses requires that environmental protection should play a more important

[157] This claim has been advanced by Brunnée and Toope, loc.cit above (n. 147), pp. 42 and 53–4.

[158] Ibid., p.54.

[159] Brunnée and Toope, 'Environmental Security and Freshwater Resources: Ecosystem Regime Building', *American Journal of International Law,* 91 (1997), p.49.

role in the regulation of international watercourses utilization, then it is interesting to examine their proposal. According to their view, it is necessary to adopt an 'ecosystem approach' to the utilization of international watercourses. They state that the ecosystem orientation must be both substantive and procedural. The substantive aspect would be represented by the development of principles such as sustainable development, intergenerational equity, the precautionary principle, the common concern of mankind and the drainage basin focus, and the procedural aspect would consist of processes to promote the identification of common interests and the involvement of all relevant players.[160] They add that:

> The framework-protocol model already adopted in a few environmental contexts is best suited to achieving this procedural ecosystem orientation and to ensuring the necessary interplay between substantive and procedural elements in the context of shared freshwater resources.[161]

At this point one might ask whether this 'ecosystem approach' is appropriate for dealing with the various problems linked with the utilization of international watercourses. It must be borne in mind that not every dispute concerning international watercourses is related to the environmental protection of watercourses. Ethiopia's claim to a greater portion of the water of the River Nile might require a legal solution which the ecosystem approach cannot provide. In fact, the framework-protocol model proposed by Brunnée and Toope and which has been adopted in the field of the protection of the Ozone Layer, in the Convention on Climate Change and in the Convention on Biological Diversity, involves the adoption of what they call a 'soft approach to obligations'. This approach, they say, would 'facilitate the confidence building necessary for the creation of a regime, as well as encourage broader participation by states'.[162] However, this soft approach to obligations would be inadequate to resolve disputes concerning the apportionment of water between watercourse States or the accommodation between competing uses. What would be Mexico's reaction if the obligation assumed by the United States to deliver 1,500,000 acre-feet of water from the Colorado were to be characterized as 'soft'?

For these reasons, it would not be adequate to adopt the 'ecosystem approach' to water utilization. Given the fact that equitable utilization is not the ultimate test of legality of the activities which might be undertaken on international watercourses, the development of rules for the protection of international watercourses may follow a separate path which might lead to the adoption of rules especially devised for that purpose. If such rules were to be adopted, environmental damage would

[160] Ibid., p. 59.
[161] Ibid.
[162] Ibid., p. 57.

cease to play a role in the balancing process called for by the principle of equitable utilization.

V. Other Criteria for the Attainment of Sustainable Development and their Compatibility with the Principle of Equitable Utilization

A. Other Environmental Concerns

The principle of equitable utilization has been devised as a norm to regulate the relations between watercourse States. Hence the establishment of an equitable regime for the utilization of international watercourses does not require, in principle, the consideration of the interests of non-watercourse States. In this regard, Article 6.1(*d*) of the 1997 UN Convention mentions only the effects of the use or uses of the watercourse in one watercourse State on other watercourse States as a relevant factor to be taken into account. In its turn, paragraph 1(*f*) prescribes that account should be taken of the conservation and protection of the water resources of the watercourse. Thus, the environmental concerns of non-watercourse States and the protection of natural resources other than freshwater have not been explicitly included in Article 6. However, it must be borne in mind that Article 6 contains a non-exhaustive list of prospective criteria. In this connection, the notion of sustainable development may contribute to enlargement of the environmental interests that could be taken into account by the principle of equitable utilization. By having recourse to the concept of sustainable development, the interests of non-watercourse States and the protection of other natural resources occurring in the watercourse and of areas beyond the watercourse itself might well be included as relevant factors.

An example of an environmental concern that relates to non-watercourse States is the pollution of the marine environment due to polluted rivers.[163] The 1994 draft Articles adopted by the International Law Commission were criticized for not adequately taking into account the pollution of the sea due to polluted rivers. In this connection, Alan Boyle pointed out that the following features of the law regulating the use of international watercourses demonstrated its inadequacy for the prevention of the pollution of the sea from land-based sources: the law of international watercourses is not concerned with national rivers, it only applies to the geographical area of the watercourse, and it is not concerned with the rights of non-riparian coastal States nor with the

[163] For a criticism of the ILC's draft Articles for not adequately taking into account the pollution of the sea, see Boyle, 'The Law of the Sea and International Watercourses', *Marine Policy*, 14 (1990), p. 155.

interests of the international community.[164] It is true that the principle of equitable utilization might not solve the problem of the pollution of the sea from land-based sources. This does not mean, however, that the pollution of the sea due to polluted rivers could not be an equitable factor to be taken into account in the process of the establishment of an equitable regime for the utilization of international watercourses. Indeed, the inclusion of the environmental impact of the utilization of an international watercourse in areas beyond the territory of the watercourse States is a factor which would contribute to the equitableness of water utilization. Of course, if watercourse States succeed in concluding specific rules for the prevention of land-based pollution of the sea, and in so far as these rules eliminate the element of an equitable balance, these rules will prevail over the principle of equitable utilization of international watercourses. In the meantime, while these rules await further development, it would be correct to include this factor in the process of the establishment of equitable regimes for water utilization. The 1997 UN Convention on the Law of the Non-Navigational Uses of International Watercourses promotes the inclusion of this factor in the balancing process, proclaiming in Article 23 that:

> Watercourse States shall, individually or jointly, take all measures with respect to an international watercourse that are necessary to protect and preserve the marine environment, including estuaries, taking into account generally accepted international rules and standards.

Recourse to the notion of sustainable development might also result in the inclusion of the national environmental effects of the utilization of international watercourses as a relevant factor to consider in the application of the principle of equitable utilization.

B. Equity

The Expert Group Meeting on the Identification of Principles of International Law for Sustainable Development pointed out that equity includes both intergenerational equity (relating to the rights of future generations and our obligations to them) and intragenerational equity (relating to members of generations existing today).[165] Without doubt the rule of equitable utilization is concerned with the achievement of intra-generational equity, at least, as between the populations of different States. But sustainable development, apart from intragenerational equity, also aims at the achievement of intergenerational equity, which

[164] Ibid.

[165] *Report of the Expert Group Meeting on Identification of Principles of International Law for Sustainable Development* (1995) (above, n. 25).

means that the needs of future generations should be taken into account.

The implications of the consideration of these needs are difficult to determine. The idea of intergenerational equity states that 'every generation is in a position of equality to other generations in its relationship with the natural system'.[166] The consequence of this notion is to impose restrictions on the manner in which the present generation manages its natural resources. Nevertheless, the concept recognizes that the imposition of limitations on the behaviour of the present generation has to take into consideration the existence of intragenerational inequities, as the following quotation shows:

> Thus, to implement intergenerational equity, countries need to help poor communities to use the natural environment on a sustainable basis, to assist them in gaining equitable access to the economic benefit from our planet, such as potable water, and to help protect them from degraded environmental quality.[167]

In this regard, intergenerational equity depends on the achievement of intragenerational equity. This last commitment seems very difficult to achieve at the present time. In fact, 'the economic development of states continues to be fiercely unequal'.[168] In this context, the notion of intergenerational equity is another way of stating the original question addressed by sustainable development: how to reconcile the developmental needs of States with the global concern for the protection of the environment? As Elder has said, this problem cannot be solved by simply postulating a global collective sacrifice which in all likelihood will result in increasing the already existing economic inequalities between States.[169]

Another difficulty with the notion of intergenerational equity refers to the possibility or impossibility of quantifying the needs of future generations.[170] Of course each State might project the scope of its needs into the future, and these projections might well be included as a relevant factor for the apportionment of waters from an international watercourse. The resulting apportionment could remain equitable in the future. However, owing to the uncertainties that may surround any projection of the future water-related needs of the States concerned, it might be advisable to apportion the waters of international watercourses

[166] Weiss, 'Intergenerational Equity and Rights of Future Generations', in Trindade (ed.), *Human Rights, Sustainable Development and the Environment* (Brasilia, 1992), p. 72.

[167] Weiss, 'Our Rights and Obligations to Future Generations for the Environment', *American Journal of International Law,* 84 (1990), p. 201. See also, Weiss, loc.cit. above (n.166), p. 75.

[168] Gündling, 'Our Responsibility to Future Generations', *American Journal of International Law,* 84 (1990), p. 211.

[169] Elder, 'Sustainability', *McGill Law Journal*, 1991, p. 838.

[170] See Birnie and Boyle, op. cit. above (n. 24), p. 211.

on the basis of the present needs, providing for periodical revision of the allocation in order to take into account future needs.

In conclusion, as a workable notion, intergenerational equity should be understood as referring to the conservation of natural resources, which is examined below. This notwithstanding, certain categories of uses would certainly go against the interests of future generations. This would be the case, for example, in the irreversible pollution of an international river of such a magnitude that use by the neighbouring States would be rendered impossible now and for the future.

C. Sustainable Use (Conservation)

Sustainable use of water resources means that they should be utilized in such a manner and to such an extent that the benefits from those resources will be made available indefinitely.[171] The promotion of sustainable utilization is mentioned in the Preamble of the 1997 UN Convention and Article 6.1(*f*) includes, as one relevant criterion to take into account in the establishment of the equitable utilization of international watercourses, the conservation of the water resources of the watercourse. For its part, Article 5.1 stipulates that States should use international watercourses with a view to attaining sustainable utilization.

In examining the role that conservation may play in the establishment of an equitable regime for the utilization of international watercourses, it would be useful to consider the following claim advanced by a State in the context of a water dispute with its neighbours: 'The apportionment of the waters of an international watercourse should foster the sustainable utilization of international water resources'. This claim could have different implications. First, it could be interpreted as a claim to the waters of an international watercourse on the basis of conservation. In this sense, conservation would be a direct basis for the allocation of international waters. Alternatively, it might imply that conservation should work as a relevant criterion in determining the real water requirements of the States concerned. In this second role, conservation would be an indirect basis for the apportionment of water. While conservation as a direct basis of allocation implies that the additional volumes of water which are made available by the application of sustainable methods of water utilization should be allocated to the State which has applied those sustainable methods, conservation as an indirect basis of water apportionment does not dispense with the requirement that the allocation of the water resources of international watercourses

[171] Singh, 'Foreword' in Munro and Lammers (eds.), *Environmental Protection and Sustainable Development* (London/Dordrecht/Boston, 1987), p. xii.

should be the result of a balancing process in which all relevant factors are taken into account.

Conservation should not be used as a direct basis for the apportionment of the water resources of international watercourses. The application of better conservation practices by State A may increase the total volume of water available for apportionment. Would it be consonant with the principle of equitable utilization to allocate the surplus automatically to State A? Should the surplus be divided between the watercourse States? It is claimed here that the conservation practices applied by one State do not give it a better right over the surplus waters.

To use conservation as a direct basis for the division of the waters of international watercourses would negate the relevance of the socio-economic needs of the watercourse States. In fact, if the apportionment of the water resources of an international watercourse is based on a comparison between the level of conservation achieved by the respective watercourse States, the danger is that the water-related needs of one State might be sacrificed for the sake of rewarding the conservation practices of the neighbouring States. From another perspective, the apportionment of water on the basis of conservation might punish a population for the failure of its government to advance sustainability. It must also be considered that if the additional volumes of water are allocated to a State by reason of its conservation practices alone, those waters might be used for the satisfaction of superfluous needs.

To illustrate the irrelevance of conservation as a direct basis for the apportionment of international watercourses one might consider the lengthy dispute concerning the Indus river and its tributaries, which originated before the 1947 partition of British India. In 1938, the Province of Punjab contemplated the construction of a storage reservoir on the Sutlej river, a tributary of the Indus river. This reservoir, located upstream, would have interfered with the old system of irrigation of the Province of Sind, namely, a system based on inundation canals. Irrigation by means of inundation canals consists in 'shallow cuts [that] are made through the river banks into which the excess water flows when the level of the water in the river rises higher in the floods which occur during the rainy seasons'.[172]

A Commission (the Rau Commission) was appointed to give a report on the basis of which the parties could solve their dispute. The Commission rendered its report in 1942, observing that, in the absence of agreement between the parties, the applicable rule was equitable apportionment.[173] The Rau Commission observed that 'the most important factor calling for notice [was] the large quantity of water that [was] running waste to the sea',[174] and it found that 'undoubtedly inundation

[172] Srinivason, *Irrigation and Water Supply* (Madras, 1991), p. 176.

[173] *Report of the Indus (Rau) Commission*, vol. 1, para. 14, p. 10.

[174] Ibid., p. 27.

canals [were] a wasteful anachronism'.[175] But it also took notice that a considerable number of people were dependent for their livelihood on this anachronistic and wasteful system of irrigation. And, what was more important, the Commission found that the explanation for the existence of this system of irrigation was the economic poverty of the Province of Sind, the government of which could not afford to install a weir-controlled method of irrigation.[176] In view of the paramount importance of irrigation for the survival of the population of Sind, the Commission adopted a preventive approach, concluding that it was reasonable to ask the Province of Punjab to contribute in part to the cost of the replacing of the inundation canals.

The Indus river and its tributaries remained a source of disputes after the 1947 partition of British India. The partition line between India and the newly formed State of Pakistan left the principal irrigation canals in the territory of India,[177] the prospective water uses of which constituted a threat to the existing uses of Pakistan. The dispute was finally settled in 1960 when both parties concluded the Indus Waters Treaty thanks to the good offices of the World Bank.[178] The Indus Waters Treaty provides for the continuation of Pakistan's existing uses. This was a key element during the negotiations and the parties were able to agree on this point because it was materially possible to increase the availability of water in the basin. In fact, Pakistan's water storage capacity was increased, otherwise there would have been no water available to satisfy Pakistan's existing uses and the needs of the Indian population. In this context, the 1960 Indus Waters Treaty did not address the question of dividing a fixed available water supply. Instead, it provided for an increase in the quantity of usable water in order to allocate water that prior to 1960 was running waste to the sea. A more sustainable use of the waters of the Indus basin was made possible by the construction of dams and new irrigation canals, particularly in the territory of Pakistan, the cost of which was met by India and Pakistan, with financial aid from several other countries.[179] Pakistan also received money on loan from the United States and the World Bank.

Undoubtedly, sustainable use of the water resources of the watercourse has a part to play in the process of the establishment of an equitable regime for the utilization of the Indus river system. A more sustainable system of management made it possible to increase the water available for allocation between the parties. However, sustainable utilization was not taken into account when determining the parties' share in

[175] Ibid., p. 52.

[176] Ibid.

[177] Caponera, 'International Water Resources Law in the Indus Basin', in Radosevich and Khan (eds.), *Water Resources Policy for Asia* (The Netherlands, 1987), p. 511.

[178] Text in *United Nations Legislative Texts and Treaty Provisions*, pp. 300 ff.

[179] Baxter, 'The Indus Basin', in Garretson, Hayton and Olmstead (eds.), *The Law of International Drainage Basins* (Dobbs Ferry, 1967), p. 468.

the augmented waters of the Indus river system. The Rau Commission in 1942 and the parties in 1960 had to resort to a more sustainable use of the waters of the basin as a way to solve the dispute, but they did not take this element into account as a direct basis for the apportionment of the said waters.

At this point, it should be recalled that in the *Gulf of Maine* case concerning the delimitation of the continental shelf and fishery zone between the United States and Canada, conservation was rejected as a criterion of delimitation. The United States put forward the argument that the delimitation should take into account the principle that the delimitation should facilitate the conservation and the management of the natural resources of the area.[180] Accordingly, the United States argued that the delimitation should give exclusive jurisdiction over the Georges Bank to a single State as this would facilitate the conservation and the management of the fisheries of that area.[181] Canada rejected the monopolistic claim of the United States, pointing out that efficiency in the conservation and management of the resources of the area was not a principle of delimitation in so far as it ruled out the equitable division of those resources.[182] In its counter-memorial Canada argued that:

> Since the solution proposed by the United States would be inequitable in this case, the question whether 'single-State management' is more efficient or expedient than co-operative management must be irrelevant.

In Canada's view, the element of efficiency in the conservation and management of the resources of the area, in the particular form it assumed in the United States memorial, could not be invoked as a principle applicable to the delimitation in so far as it contradicted the rule of equitable delimitation. Canada contended that:

> It is beyond question that the proper conservation and management of the resources of the sea and the avoidance of international disputes are valid objectives and important rules of behaviour. But their distortion into false principles of delimitation that rule out equitable division of the resources of the relevant area is almost perverse. The United States has misapplied two perfectly reasonable concepts to justify the most unreasonable results. For its theory of 'single-State management' would deny to Canada—and to other coastal States similarly placed—the sovereign rights and jurisdiction flowing from the distance principle enshrined in the 1982 Convention on the Law of the Sea and in customary international law.[183]

The Chamber of the International Court dismissed the American argument based upon single State management. It devoted only one paragraph to rejecting the argument. The Chamber did not explicitly say

[180] *ICJ Pleadings* (1984), *Gulf of Maine* case, US memorial, p. 63.
[181] Ibid., p. 74.
[182] Ibid., Canadian counter-memorial, paras. 230 and 497, pp. 84 and 186.
[183] Ibid., para. 497, p. 186.

that efficiency in the conservation and management of the resources of the area was irrelevant as a criterion for maritime delimitation. Instead, it preferred to subsume the claim based on efficiency in conservation and management of the resources of the area under the United States claim that the delimitation should avoid disputes between the parties. Accordingly, the Chamber asserted that 'it [was] unable to discern any inevitable source of insurmountable disputes in the fact that its decision [did] not endorse the single management of this Bank's fisheries, and the assignment to one country of the task of conserving them, which the United States would have preferred to see instituted'.[184] Therefore, for the Chamber, the achievement of sustainable use of the resources of the area was more an issue for the parties to solve than for it to judge upon.

The judgment in the *Gulf of Maine* case demonstrates that conservation is not a criterion of delimitation because it does not qualify as a criterion of entitlement to maritime zones. Regarding international watercourses, the irrelevance of conservation can also be explained by the fact that this factor does not qualify as a criterion of entitlement. Entitlement with regard to the allocation of the waters of international watercourses is related to two main groups of considerations: those related to the social and economic needs of the States concerned and, to a lesser extent, geographical and hydrological factors, such as the extent of the watercourse or of the drainage area lying in the territory of the watercourse States and the extent of their contribution to the flow of the watercourse.[185]

However, as an indirect basis for the apportionment of the water resources of international watercourses, conservation may be a very relevant criterion. Indeed, conservation can play a very important role in the determination of the real water requirements of the parties. Accordingly, the water requirements of the States concerned may be established *inter alia* in accordance with a certain degree of sustainability which should be achieved by the respective States. This degree of sustainability should be commensurate with the financial resources of the States concerned. In this respect, the International Law Association stated that:

> A 'beneficial use' need not be *the* most productive use to which the water may be put, nor need it utilize the most efficient methods known in order to avoid waste and ensure maximum utilization. As to the former, to provide otherwise would dislocate numerous productive and, indeed, essential portions of national economies; the latter, while a patently imperfect solution, reflects the financial limitations of many States in its application, the present rule is not designed to foster waste but to hold States to a duty of efficiency which is commensurate with their financial resources. Of course, the ability of a State to obtain international financing will be considered in this context. Thus, State A, an

[184] *ICJ Reports*, 1984, para. 240, p. 344.

[185] These criteria are examined in detail in Fuentes, loc.cit. above (n. 4), pp. 394–408.

economically advanced and prosperous State which utilizes the inundation method of irrigation, might be required to develop a more efficient and less wasteful system forthwith, while State B, an underdeveloped State using the same method might be permitted additional time to obtain the means to make the required improvements.[186]

It follows that in order to play a role in the achievement of equitable utilization, conservation necessarily must be coupled with the criterion of need. In this context, when a State has the means to use its water resources in a sustainable manner, then its water requirements should be calculated on the basis of the degree of sustainability which that State is capable of achieving. Intentional or negligent wastefulness evidences the absence of real need for the water.

In *Wyoming* v. *Colorado* (1931)[187] and in *Colorado* v. *New Mexico* (1982)[188] conservation served as an indirect basis for water apportionment,[189] that is to say, as a factor relevant to the determination of the water requirements of the parties. *Wyoming* v. *Colorado* (1931) concerned Wyoming's claim to prevent a proposed diversion by Colorado of part of the waters of the Laramie river. The US Supreme Court concluded that uses in Wyoming were senior to the ones in Colorado and, by applying the principle of prior appropriation, it concluded that these uses had to be safeguarded. However, the Court did not accept Wyoming's calculation of the water required to supply its uses. In this regard the Court stated that:

The evidence shows that the Wyoming appropriations having priorities senior to the one in Colorado . . . cover 181,500 acres of land, and that the amount of water appropriated and reasonably required for the irrigation of these lands is 272,500 acre-feet. A much larger amount is claimed, but our finding restricts the amount to what the evidence shows is reasonably required . . .

In *Colorado* v. *New Mexico* (1982), the former State sued the latter to obtain an equitable apportionment of the waters of the Vermejo river. The US Supreme Court has this to say in relation to conservation:

Our prior cases clearly establish that equitable apportionment will protect only those rights to water that are 'reasonably required and applied' . . . Thus wasteful or inefficient uses will not be protected.

Accordingly, the Court stated that it was appropriate to examine New

[186] ILA, *Report of the Fifty-Second Conference* (Helsinki, 1966), p. 487.

[187] 259 US 419.

[188] 459 US 178.

[189] The case law of the United States Supreme Court is pertinent for the purposes of this study because the Supreme Court has applied equitable apportionment as a principle of international law applicable to the resolution of inter-State water disputes. In *Kansas* v. *Colorado* (1906) the Supreme Court applied for the first time the principle of equitable apportionment and in doing so it asserted that: 'International law is no alien in this tribunal': 106 US 46.

Mexico's uses and Colorado's proposed utilization in the light of a duty of efficiency and conservation:

We have invoked the principle of equitable apportionment not only to require the reasonably efficient use of water, but also to impose on States an affirmative duty to take reasonable steps to conserve and augment the water supply of an interstate stream. In *Wyoming* v. *Colorado*, Wyoming brought suit to prevent a proposed diversion by Colorado from the Laramie River. This Court calculated the dependable supply available to both States, subtracted the senior Wyoming uses, and permitted Colorado to divert an amount not exceeding the balance. In calculating the dependable supply we placed on each State the duty to employ 'financially and physically feasible' measures 'adopted to conserving and equalizing the natural flow' . . .

We conclude that it is entirely appropriate to consider the extent to which reasonable conservation measures by New Mexico might offset the proposed Colorado diversion and thereby minimize any injury to New Mexico users. Similarly, it is appropriate to consider whether Colorado has undertaken reasonable steps to minimize the amount of diversion that will be required.

Apart from its role in the determination of the real water requirements of the watercourse States, conservation may be a relevant factor in the determination of the volumes of water available for apportionment between the States concerned. Therefore, sustainability may require that only part of the waters of an international watercourse should be divided between the parties. However, this consideration should be weighed against the socio-economic interests of the population. In this connection, the social and economic interests of the population might be more important than sustainability. In other words,

. . . just because an activity is sustainable does not necessarily mean we have to undertake it; impact analyses may show that activities , although sustainable, will have negative social effects and should be rejected.[190]

Therefore, recourse to sustainability is not a *conditio sine qua non* of the equitable division of the water resources of international watercourses.

D. Common but Differentiated Responsibility

This principle seeks 'to balance the objective of developing principles and standards of universal application whilst taking account of the different needs and responsibilities of States'.[191] It is not a principle to mitigate the international responsibility of States which have breached their international obligations concerning the environment. In fact, it must be borne in mind that, in general, States have to apply due diligence with regard to their environmental obligations and due diligence does not

[190] Elder, 'Sustainability', *McGill Law Journal*, 1991, p. 838.

[191] Sands, loc.cit. above (n. 13), p. 344.

incorporate distinctions regarding the state of economic development of the States concerned. For this reason, common but differentiated responsibility has to be understood as a principle which purports to influence international legislation. As such, its application exceeds the scope of the principle of equitable utilization of international watercourses. Only if common but differentiated responsibility is incorporated into particular international agreements regarding international watercourses can equitable utilization take into account the different responsibilities assumed by States in those international agreements.

E. The Precautionary Principle

Foreseeable and significant transboundary damage to international watercourses is a relevant factor in the establishment of an equitable regime for the utilization of international watercourses. The precautionary principle, in so far as it might be considered part of general international law,[192] could have implications for the implementation of the principle of equitable utilization. In particular, the element of foreseeability could experience change. This means that not only foreseeable damage but also the risk of damage, however low, might be a relevant factor to be taken into account in the process of the establishment of an equitable regime for water utilization. Therefore, a State that wishes to stop a certain activity which may interfere with its share of the benefits of an international watercourse would not need to prove that legal injury will in all likelihood be inflicted but it would be sufficient to establish that there is a risk of injury.

The precautionary principle results in a shift of the burden of proof, because a State which claims that a risk of injury exists needs to prove only the existence of the risk, while it will be for the other party to prove that injury will not be inflicted. In its strongest version, the precautionary principle might shift the burden of proof completely by prescribing that when planning activities which might have detrimental effects, States have to prove the innocuous character of their activities. In this second form, the precautionary principle can hardly be said to be customary international law.

There are strong practical objections to the application of the precautionary principle. In 1990 the Bergen Ministerial Declaration on Sustainable Development stated that 'lack of full scientific certainty should not be used as a reason for postponing measures to prevent environ-

[192] In support of the argument that the precautionary principle has the status of a norm of customary international law: McIntyre and Mosedale, 'The Precautionary Principle as a Norm of Customary International Law', *Journal of Environmental Law*, 9 (1997), pp. 223–35; Cameron and Abouchar, 'The Status of the Precautionary Principle in International Law', in Freestone and Hey (eds.), *The Precautionary Principle and International Law* (Dordrecht, 1996), p. 30.

mental degradation'.[193] However, it is clear that not every situation of risk warrants the implementation of precautionary measures. The problem relates, therefore, to the assessment of the risk. How much risk would it be necessary to show in order to require precautionary measures to be taken?

Risk assessment is relevant at two different levels. First, risk assessment may serve as the basis for environmental policy. On the basis of an assessment of risks and according to a decision concerning the management of that risk, States may take into account the precautionary principle in the formulation of environmental legislation and in the conclusion of international agreements concerned with the protection of the environment. Secondly, risk assessment also serves as the basis for a State individual decision whether and in what manner to undertake certain activities. In the absence of norms detailing the relation which should exist between measures and level of risk, it is difficult to establish whether a State has or has not complied with the requirements of the precautionary principle. Therefore, the operation of the precautionary principle requires the following points to be clarified:

1. Is the precautionary principle a principle of general application or does it only become operative where the possible damage is beyond a certain threshold of seriousness?;
2. What level of risk would warrant the implementation of precautionary measures?; and,
3. What should be the relationship between the precautionary measures and the magnitude of the risk?

In relation to the first point, Principle 15 of the Rio Declaration on Environment and Development[194] provides that:

> In order to protect the environment, the precautionary approach shall be widely applied by States according to their capabilities. Where there are threats of serious or irreversible damage, lack of full scientific certainty shall not be used as a reason for postponing cost-effective measures to prevent environmental degradation.

The 1992 Climate Change Convention[195] includes the precautionary principle in Article 3.3, which states that:

> The Parties should take precautionary measures to anticipate, prevent and minimize the causes of climate change and mitigate its adverse effects. Where there are threats of serious or irreversible damage, lack of full scientific certainty should not be used as a reason for postponing such measures . . .

[193] Text in *Environmental Policy and Law*, 20 (1990), p. 100.
[194] Text in *International Legal Materials*, 31 (1992), pp. 874 ff.
[195] Text in Birnie and Boyle, op. cit. above (n. 63), pp. 252 ff.

Some other instruments do not limit the scope of precautionary measures to situations in which there is a threat of serious or irreversible damage, but require the adoption of these measures in relation to particular activities such as the release of hazardous substances. In this connection, Article 2.5(*a*) of the 1992 Helsinki Convention on the Protection and Use of Transboundary Watercourses and Lakes[196] provides for

The precautionary principle, by virtue of which action to avoid the potential transboundary impact of the release of hazardous substances shall not be postponed on the ground that scientific research has not fully proved a causal link between those substances, on the one hand, and the potential transboundary impact, on the other hand.

Some other treaties provide for the application of the precautionary principle in a more general way. In this connection, Article 6.1 of the 1995 Agreement relating to the Conservation and Management of Straddling Fish Stocks and Highly Migratory Fish Stocks[197] provides that:

States shall apply the precautionary approach widely to conservation, management and exploitation of straddling fish stocks and highly migratory fish stocks in order to protect the living marine resources and preserve the marine environment.

With regard to the level of risk which warrants the adoption of precautionary measures, it is necessary to clarify whether there should be a distinction between risks which do not justify the adoption of measures and risks which do so. This point needs to be associated with the question of the relationship between precautionary measures and the magnitude of the risk. This last point is a key issue in the interpretation of the precautionary principle. Without a certain degree of proportionality between the magnitude of the risk and the required degree of caution, the precautionary principle might require States to adopt an unreasonable behaviour towards risk. The magnitude of the damage would also be relevant to the question of proportionality, because it might be right to prefer a high risk of moderate damage to a small risk of very serious and irreversible damage.[198]

The *Beef Hormones* case[199] illustrates how the uncertainties surrounding the implications of the precautionary principle make its judicial application difficult. In 1996 Canada and the United States filed separate complaints against the European Communities, claiming that the EC import ban on meat and meat products from animals treated with certain hormones for growth promotion purposes was in violation of the

[196] Text in ibid., pp. 345 ff.

[197] Text in *International Legal Materials*, 34 (1995), pp. 1542 ff. See Article 6.

[198] Bodansky, 'Remarks on New Developments in International Environmental Law', *Proceedings of the American Society of International Law*, 1991, p. 415.

[199] WT/DS26/R/USA, WT/DS48/R/CAN and WT/DS26/AB/R.

provisions of the World Trade Organization Agreement on the Application of Sanitary and Phytosanitary Measures (SPS Agreement). In particular, the SPS Agreement prescribes that either sanitary measures are based on existing international standards, in which case they are presumed to be lawful, or they are supported by a scientific justification. The EC claimed *inter alia* that, in accordance with the precautionary principle, it was justified in imposing the measure. Because the EC import ban on meat and meat products from animals treated with certain hormones for growth promotion purposes was not based on international standards, the Panel of the World Trade Organization went on to examine the scientific justification of the measure. It concluded that a scientific justification required an objective risk assessment, and stated that 'an assessment of risks is, at least for risks to human life or health, a scientific examination of data and factual studies; it is not a policy exercise involving social value judgments made by political bodies'.[200] In explaining what should be understood by a risk assessment, the Panel specified that:

> we consider that, in this dispute, a risk assessment carried out in accordance with the SPS Agreement should (i) identify the adverse effects on human health (if any) arising from the presence of the hormones at issue when used as growth promoters in meat or meat products, and (ii) if any such adverse effects exist, evaluate the potential or probability of occurrence of these effects.[201]

And it added that:

> We finally note that the parties agree that, for the purposes of the EC measures in dispute, a risk assessment in accordance with Article 5 is a scientific process aimed at establishing the scientific basis for the sanitary measure a Member intends to take.[202]

Accordingly, the Panel evaluated the scientific evidence which could lead to the conclusion that the use of certain hormones for growth promotion purposes in cattle posed an 'identifiable risk' for human health, concluding that:

> the European Community has not demonstrated that the scientific evidence it referred to, which generally addresses the safety of some or all of the hormones in dispute, would indicate that an identifiable risk arises for human health from the use of these hormones for growth promotion purposes if good practice is followed. In this respect we recall that all scientific experts advising the Panel confirmed this conclusion and stated that, as of today, no scientific evidence is available which concludes that an identifiable risk arises from the use of any of the hormones at issue for growth promotion purposes in accordance with good practice.[203]

[200] WT/DS48/CAN, para. 8.97, p. 228.
[201] Ibid., para. 8.101, p. 229.
[202] Ibid., para. 8.110, p. 231.
[203] Ibid., para. 8.137, p. 238.

Therefore, though the Panel's finding that a sanitary measure needed to be based on a risk assessment does not by itself preclude the application of the precautionary principle, the Panel adopted a different view. The Panel required that a minimum risk ('identifiable risk') was necessary to justify the adoption of sanitary and phytosanitary measures, implying therefore that below that minimum risk States were not allowed to impose precautionary measures. Accordingly, the Panel concluded that the precautionary principle was relevant only with regard to the adoption of temporary measures adopted in accordance with Article 5.7 of the SPS Agreement. This provision reads as follows:

> In cases where relevant scientific evidence is insufficient, a Member may provisionally adopt sanitary or phytosanitary measures on the basis of available pertinent information, including that from the relevant international organizations as well as from sanitary or phytosanitary measures applied by other Members. In such circumstances, Members shall seek to obtain the additional information necessary for a more objective assessment of risk and review the sanitary or phytosanitary measure accordingly within a reasonable period of time.

The decisions of the Panel were reviewed by the Appellate Body, which found that the requirement of a minimum risk was at odds with the SPS Agreement, which only requires that sanitary and phytosanitary measures be based on a risk assessment without setting a certain magnitude or threshold level of risk to be demonstrated. However, this finding was not sufficient to persuade the Appellate Body of the applicability of the precautionary principle. While acknowledging that the implementation of sanitary and phytosanitary measures could relate to different magnitudes of risk, the Appellate Body interpreted the SPS Agreement as requiring a 'rational relationship between the measure and the risk assessment'. The way in which the Appellate Body applied this requirement resulted once more in the rejection of the applicability of the precautionary principle. In this connection, the Appellate Body stated that:

> . . . the Panel appeared to be using the term 'scientifically identified risk' to prescribe implicitly that a certain magnitude or threshold level of risk be demonstrated in a risk assessment if an SPS measure based thereon is to be regarded as consistent with Article 5.1. To the extent that the Panel purported to require a risk assessment to establish a minimum magnitude of risk, we must note that imposition of such a quantitative requirement finds no basis in the SPS Agreement. A panel is authorized only to determine whether a given SPS measure is 'based on' a risk assessment . . . this means that a panel has to determine whether an SPS measure is sufficiently supported or reasonably warranted by the risk assessment.[204]

And it added that:

[204] Appellate Body Decision, WT/DS26/AB/R, para. 185, p. 51.

The requirement that an SPS measure be 'based on' a risk assessment is a substantive requirement that there be a rational relationship between the measure and the risk assessment.[205]

The Appellate Body failed to realize that the requirement of a rational relationship between the measure and the risk assessment does not necessarily imply the dismissal of the precautionary principle, which does not call for the adoption of irrational measures. The way in which the Appellate Body explained its conclusion that the precautionary principle was not relevant to the decision of the case is not persuasive. In this connection it stated that:

The status of the precautionary principle in international law continues to be the subject of debate among academics, law practitioners, regulators and judges. The precautionary principle is regarded by some as having crystallized into a general principle of customary international environmental law. Whether it has been widely accepted by Members as a principle of general or customary international law appears less than clear. We consider, however, that it is unnecessary, and probably imprudent, for the Appellate Body in this appeal to take a position on this important, but abstract, question. We note that the Panel itself did not make any definitive finding with regard to the status of the precautionary principle in international law and that the precautionary principle, at least outside the field of international environmental law, still awaits authoritative formulation.

It appears to us important, nevertheless, to note some aspects of the relationship of the precautionary principle to the SPS Agreement. First, the principle has not been written into the SPS Agreement as a ground for justifying SPS measures that are otherwise inconsistent with the obligations of Members set out in particular provisions of that Agreement. Secondly, the precautionary principle indeed finds reflection in Article 5.7 of the SPS Agreement. We agree, at the same time, with the European Communities, that there is no need to assume that Article 5.7 exhausts the relevance of a precautionary principle. It is reflected also in the sixth paragraph of the preamble and in Article 3.3. These explicitly recognized the right of Members to establish their own appropriate level of sanitary protection, which level may be higher (i.e. more cautious) than that implied in existing international standards, guidelines and recommendations. Thirdly, a panel charged with determining, for instance, whether 'sufficient scientific evidence' exists to warrant the maintenance by a Member of a particular SPS measure may, of course, and should, bear in mind that responsible, representative governments commonly act from perspectives of prudence and precaution where risks of irreversible, e.g. life-terminating, damage to human health are concerned. Lastly, however, the precautionary principle does not, by itself, and without a clear textual directive to that effect, relieve a panel from the duty of applying the normal (i.e. customary international law) principles of treaty interpretation in reading the provisions of the SPS Agreement.[206]

[205] Ibid., para. 193, p. 54.
[206] Ibid., paras. 123–4, pp. 33–4.

By negating the relevance of the precautionary principle, the requirement of a rational relationship between the risk assessment and the measure can only be understood as a requirement for a certain level of scientific certainty which would justify the adoption of a particular preventive measure but which would not warrant the adoption of a precautionary measure.

F. The Eradication of Poverty

Principle 5 of the Rio Declaration (1992)[207] proclaims that:

> All States and all peoples shall co-operate in the essential task of eradicating poverty as an indispensable requirement for sustainable development, in order to decrease the disparities in standards of living and better meet the needs of the majority of the people of the world.

Various other agreements recognize that the eradication of poverty should be a prominent goal to be achieved in developing countries. In this regard, the Framework Convention on Climate Change (1992)[208] recognizes in its Preamble that:

> . . . responses to climate change should be coordinated with social and economic development in an integrated manner with a view to avoiding adverse impacts on the latter, taking into full account the legitimate priority needs of developing countries for the achievement of sustained economic growth and the eradication of poverty.

In the same vein, the Preamble of the United Nations Convention on Biological Diversity (1992)[209] recognizes that:

> . . . economic and social development and poverty eradication are the first and overriding priorities of developing countries.

The Convention to Combat Desertification in those Countries Experiencing Drought and/or Desertification, Particularly in Africa (1994),[210] also states in its Preamble that:

> . . . sustainable economic growth, social development and poverty eradication are priorities of affected developing countries, particularly in Africa, and are essential to meeting sustainability objectives.

The principle of equitable utilization may contribute to the eradication of poverty in so far as the equitable regime for the use of international watercourses takes into account and attempts to give as much satisfaction as possible to the water-related needs of the States concerned. The fact

207 Text in Birnie and Boyle, op.cit. above (n. 63), p. 11.
208 Ibid., pp. 252 ff. The Convention entered into force on 21 March 1994.
209 Ibid., pp. 390 ff. The Convention entered into force on 29 December 1993.
210 Ibid., pp. 513 ff.

that a particular use of the waters of international watercourses could contribute to alleviating the poverty in which certain communities live is certainly a factor that should be taken into account. However, the principle of equitable utilization cannot be used as an instrument to overcome the inequalities between countries, and for this reason it should be said that the eradication of poverty exceeds the scope of the principle of equitable utilization. It must be borne in mind that equitable utilization is a principle that can be applied in the judicial settlement of disputes concerning the waters of international watercourses, and it would not be appropriate to require from judicial bodies political decisions which should be taken by States.

G. *Special Treatment of Developing Countries*

Principle 6 of the Rio Declaration (1992)[211] proclaims that:

> The special situation and needs of developing countries, particularly the least developed and those most environmentally vulnerable, shall be given special priority. International actions in the field of environment and development should also address the interests and needs of all countries.

To take into account the special situation and needs of developing countries means that these countries should not be required to apply the same environmental policies as developed countries (common but differentiated responsibilities) and that they should receive financial aid and the transfer of technology in order to assist them in the strengthening of their endogenous capacity-building for sustainable development.

Various conventions have acknowledged that developing countries deserve a special treatment. Among these, the Framework Convention on Climate Change (1992), the Convention on Biological Diversity (1992) and the Convention to Combat Desertification (1994) acknowledge that economic and social development are the first and overriding priorities of developing countries and recognize that social provision is required to meet the needs of developing countries, including the provision of new and additional financial resources and appropriate access to relevant technologies.

In the field of the equitable utilization of international watercourses, the 1997 UN Convention on the Law of the Non-Navigational Uses of International Watercourses states in its Preamble that the parties are 'aware of the special situation and needs of developing countries'. However, this cannot be understood as implying that the water-related needs of developing countries should be preferred to those of developed countries.

[211] Text in Birnie and Boyle, op.cit. above (n. 63), p. 11.

Before the adoption of the 1997 UN Convention, the then Special Rapporteur, Stephen Schwebel, included the stage of economic development of the riparian States as a relevant criterion in the determination of the reasonableness and equitableness of the utilization of an international watercourse.[212] This criterion was also included in the First Report of Jens Evensen, who succeeded Schwebel as Special Rapporteur.[213] But one of the members of the ILC was right to point out that the reference to the stage of economic development of the States concerned 'did not make it clear whether preference should be given to developing or to developed countries'.[214] The stage of economic development was not mentioned as a relevant criterion in any of the subsequent revised versions of the list of relevant factors, and it was not included in the final wording of Article 6 of the ILC's 1994 draft Articles on the Law of the Non-Navigational Uses of International Watercourses nor in the final text of the list of relevant criteria included in the 1997 UN Convention.

The principle of equitable utilization cannot not be construed as an instrument to overcome the economic disparities between States. This of course does not imply that in view of factors such as the vital needs of the population, the degree of economic dependence on the watercourse or the non-existence of alternatives of comparative value, the needs of developing countries could not be preferred to the needs of developed States. However, what is clear is that to accord special treatment to developing countries would exceed the scope of the principle of equitable utilization.

VI. The Relationship between Sustainable Development and Equitable Utilization in State Practice

The incorporation of sustainable development into international agreements concerning international watercourses is a relatively recent occurrence. An examination of international agreements which refer to both sustainable development and equitable utilization shows that European treaties have emphasized the environmental aspects of sustainable development. This tendency has not been followed in non-European treaties.

[212] Schwebel, 'Third Report on the Law of the Non-Navigational Uses of International Watercourses', Doc. A/CN.4/348: *ILC Yearbook*, 1982, vol. 2, part 1, p. 90.

[213] *ILC Yearbook*, 1983, vol. 2, part 1, p. 171, Doc. A/CN.4/367.

[214] See remarks by Flitan, ibid., vol. 1, p. 213.

(1) *The 1992 Helsinki Convention on the Protection and Use of Transboundary Watercourses and Lakes*[215]

This Convention refers to the sustainable management and use of transboundary watercourses in two paragraphs of its Preamble, which state that the parties to the Convention commend 'the efforts already undertaken by the ECE Governments to strengthen co-operation, on bilateral and multilateral levels, for the prevention, control and reduction of transboundary pollution, sustainable water management, conservation of water resources and environmental protection', and are '[c]onscious of the role of the United Nations Economic Commission for Europe in promoting international co-operation for the prevention, control and reduction of transboundary water pollution and sustainable use of transboundary waters . . . '.

In its turn, Article 2, paragraphs 1 and 2, provides that:

> 1. The Parties shall take all appropriate measures to prevent, control and reduce any transboundary impact.
> 2. The Parties shall, in particular, take all appropriate measures:
> (*a*) To prevent, control and reduce pollution of waters causing or likely to cause transboundary impact;
> (*b*) To ensure that transboundary waters are used with the aim of ecologically sound and rational water management, conservation of water resources and environmental protection;
> (*c*) To ensure that transboundary waters are used in a reasonable and equitable way, taking into particular account their transboundary character, in the case of activities which cause or are likely to cause transboundary impact;
> (*d*) to ensure conservation and, where necessary, restoration of ecosystems.

Article 2.5 prescribes that in taking these measures the parties shall be guided by the precautionary principle, the polluter-pays principle and intergenerational equity.

This Convention represents a European effort to strengthen co-operation for the achievement of sustainable development. The text of the Convention shows that sustainable development has been understood as a concept that emphasizes the environmental aspect rather than the developmental one. Therefore, the Convention require the parties to take all appropriate measures to prevent, control and reduce any significant adverse effect on the environment resulting from a change in the conditions of transboundary waters caused by human activity.[216] It seems, therefore, that the parties have preferred to separate the issues of environmental protection and equitable utilization. However, the Convention still leaves room for a balance between environmental protection

[215] *International Legal Materials*, 31 (1992), pp. 1312 ff. This treaty was negotiated under the auspices of the United Nations Economic Commission for Europe. Also in Birnie and Boyle, op. cit. above (n. 63), pp. 345 ff.

[216] See Article 1.2 which defines 'transboundary impact'.

and other interests of the parties. According to Article 9, the general objective of preventing, controlling and reducing transboundary impact has to be implemented by bilateral and multilateral agreements in which the parties will define their mutual relations and conduct.

(2) *The 1994 Convention on Co-operation for the Protection and Sustainable Use of the Danube River*[217]

This Convention emphasizes the duty to prevent, control and reduce significant adverse transboundary impact from the release of hazardous substances, and it represents an effort to implement the 1992 Convention on Transboundary Watercourses and Lakes. Indeed, the Preamble of the Danube Convention states that the parties refer 'in particular to the Convention on the Protection and Use of Transboundary Watercourses and Lakes of 17 March 1992'.

The final paragraph of the Preamble adds that it has been the intention of the parties to strive for 'a lasting improvement of the Danube River and of the waters within its catchment area in particular in the transboundary context and at sustainable water management taking duly into account the interests of the Danubian States in the field of water use . . . '.

Article 2.1 specifies that the aim of the Convention is the achievement of sustainable and equitable water management, including the conservation, improvement and rational use of the waters of the Danube River basin. The main obligation of the parties is to co-operate in the achievement of these objectives, and for this purpose they establish an International Commission (Article 18). Like the Helsinki Convention, it emphasizes the achievement of sustainable use of the water resources of the Danube basin and the avoidance of detrimental transboundary impact. Even though it is not possible to say that this Convention gives priority to environmental protection over the attainment of equitable utilization, it must be realized that the Convention is not particularly concerned with the implementation of the equitable use of the Danube basin. In fact, throughout the articles and annexes of the Convention the expression 'equitable' is mentioned only twice.

(3) *The 1994 Agreements on the Protection of the River Meuse*[218] *and the River Scheldt*[219]

France, the Netherlands, the Walloon Region, the Flemish Region and the Brussels-Capital Region of Belgium concluded these Agreements for the purpose of co-operating in the preservation and improvement of the quality of the Meuse and the Scheldt rivers (Article 2). Article 3 refers to

[217] Text on diskette accompanying *Yearbook of International Environmental Law*, 1994, Doc.16.

[218] *International Legal Materials*, 34 (1995), pp. 852 ff.

[219] Ibid., pp. 859 ff.

the 'principles of co-operation', including: the precautionary principle, the principle of preventive action, the principle of containment of pollution, the polluter-pays principle, integrated management and sustainable development. An International Commission was created for the purpose of assisting the parties in fulfilling their duty of co-operation.

These Agreements are not concerned with the equitable utilization of the Meuse or the Scheldt and their sole objective is the abatement of pollution.

(4) *The 1995 Agreement on Co-operation for the Sustainable Development of the Mekong River Basin*

This Agreement was concluded between the governments of Cambodia, Laos, Thailand and Vietnam[220] with the aim of co-operating in all fields of the sustainable development, utilization, management and conservation of the water and related resources of the Mekong River Basin.[221] The pertinent part of the Preamble states that the parties are determined

> to continue to co-operate and promote in a constructive and mutually beneficial manner in the sustainable development, utilization, conservation and management of the Mekong River Basin water and related resources for navigational and non-navigational purposes, for social and economic development and the well-being of all riparian States, consistent with the needs to protect, preserve, enhance and manage the environmental and aquatic conditions and maintenance of the ecological balance exceptional to this river basin

For the achievement of sustainable development, the parties agreed:

> *Article 3*. To protect the environment, natural resources, aquatic life and conditions, and ecological balance of the Mekong River Basin from pollution or other harmful effects resulting from any development plans and uses of water and related resources in the basin;
> *Article 4*. To co-operate on the basis of sovereign equality and territorial integrity in the utilization and protection of the water resources of the Mekong River Basin;
> *Article 5*. To utilize the waters of the Mekong River system in a reasonable and equitable manner in their respective territories, pursuant to all relevant factors and circumstances, . . .
> . . .
> *Article 7*. To make every effort to avoid, minimize and mitigate harmful effects that might occur to the environment, especially the water quantity and quality, the aquatic (eco-system) conditions, and ecological balance of the river system, from the development and use of the Mekong River Basin water resources or discharge of wastes and return flows . . . .

[220] Ibid., pp. 866 ff.
[221] See Preamble and Article 1.

The Mekong Agreement is an agreement for co-operation. In the context of this co-operation, equitable utilization is one more relevant factor to take into account. It is worth noting that diversion of the waters of the Mekong River is subject to prior notification to the Joint Committee of the Mekong River Commission or prior authorization by the Joint Committee, depending on whether the diversion refers to intra- or inter-basin transfers of water (Article 5). The parties also agreed to maintain a minimum flow of water in the mainstream during the dry season, and the Joint Committee has the power to adopt guidelines for the locations and levels of the flows (Article 6). Article 26 empowers the Joint Committee with the authority to prepare and propose, for the approval of the Council of the Commission, rules for water utilization and inter-basin diversions, including but not limited to: (1) establishing the time frame for the wet and dry seasons; (2) establishing the location of hydrological stations and determining the flow level requirements at each station; (3) setting out criteria for determining surplus quantities of water during the dry season on the mainstream; (4) improving upon the mechanism to monitor intra-basin use; and (5) setting up a mechanism to monitor inter-basin diversions from the mainstream.

In view of these provisions and the authority conferred upon it, the Commission could modify the normal effects of the principle of equitable use in order to attain the sustainable development of the water resources of the Mekong Basin.

(5) *1995 Protocol on Shared Watercourse Systems in the Southern African Development Community*

Article 2.2 of this Agreement states that member States undertake to respect and apply the existing rules of general or customary international law relating to the utilization and management of the resources of shared watercourse systems and, in particular, to respect and abide by the principles of community of interests in the equitable utilization of those systems and related resources. This provision has to be read in connection with Article 2.6, which is almost an exact transcription of Article 5.1 of the 1997 UN Convention on the Law of the Non-Navigational Uses of International Watercourses:

> Member States shall utilise a shared watercourse system in an equitable manner. In particular, a shared watercourse system shall be used and developed by member States with a view to attaining optimum utilisation thereof and obtaining benefits therefrom consistent with adequate protection of the watercourse system.

Article 2.3 speaks of sustainable development, stating that:

> Member States lying within the basin of a shared watercourse system shall maintain a proper balance between resource development for a higher standard

of living for their peoples and conservation and enhancement of the environment to promote sustainable development.

It is interesting to note that the Protocol does not mention sustainable development among the factors that ought to be taken into account for the establishment of equitable utilization (Article 2.7). It is also important to note that the parties have referred to sustainable development as a goal that has to be attained nationally (Article 2.3).

This Protocol, like the Mekong Agreement, differs from the European conventions examined above in that it does not refer to sustainable development as giving priority to the protection of the environment, but it refers to the maintenance of a proper balance between resource development for a higher standard of living of the population and the conservation and enhancement of the environment. It must also be pointed out that while the parties assume an obligation to promote sustainable development in the national sphere (Article 2.3), as regards the relations between States, they assume the obligation to respect and apply the rule of equitable utilization (Article 2.2).

VII. Conclusions

Factors which are relevant to the establishment of an equitable regime for the utilization of international watercourses might also be relevant to the attainment of sustainable development. Such would be the case of conservation (sustainable use) of the water resources of international watercourses. Despite this, equitable utilization and sustainable development differ in that the first is an existing principle of general international law while the second is a goal to be achieved at the national and international levels, and which aims at the harmonization of existing and emerging principles of international law. This means that, in the context of sustainable development, equitable utilization is one of the principles that have to be taken into consideration. The inclusion of equitable utilization in the process of attaining sustainable development might entail the modification of the equitable result arrived at on the basis of equitable criteria. Given the flexibility which characterizes the establishment of equitable regimes for the utilization of international watercourses, the modification of the equitable result might not change the essential nature of the principle of equitable use. In this regard, certain criteria which are relevant to the attainment of sustainable development, but which are not necessarily relevant to the establishment of an equitable regime for water utilization, might also be taken into account by the principle of equitable utilization. This is the case with certain environmental interests. However, there are other sets of criteria which, though relevant for the attainment of sustainable development, exceed the scope of the principle of equitable utilization. In particular this applies to the factors related to the promotion of development. This does not imply that the principle of equitable utilization might not contribute to the alleviation of poverty in developing States, but what is important to emphasize is that equitable utilization has not been devised as an instrument to end the differences between developed and developing countries. In this context, the attainment of sustainable development might require, for example, that account should be taken of the degree of economic development in the apportionment of waters from international watercourses, implying, therefore, the modification of the normal effects of the principle of equitable utilization.

With regard to the inclusion of certain environmental interests, it is necessary to take account of the fact that the principle of equitable utilization has been designed for the resolution of disputes between watercourse States. For this reason, the environmental impact of water utilization on non-watercourse States or on areas which are not subject to national jurisdiction is not necessarily a relevant factor. The notion of sustainable development may help to improve this situation by enlarging the range of environmental interests which could play a role in the operation of the principle of equitable utilization.

For some authors this contribution of sustainable development to the operation of the principle of equitable utilization might seem too modest. They would rather see that environmental concerns play a more important role in the establishment of regimes for the equitable utilization of international watercourses. However, the concept of sustainable development does not put environmental interests above developmental concerns, but requires the adoption of an integrated approach. This approach is also required by the principle of equitable utilization. In fact, the latter calls for the consideration of the social and economic needs of the States concerned as well as of the adequate protection of the watercourse.

It follows that sustainable development and equitable utilization imply the view that environmental protection might sometimes be sacrificed for the sake of development. However, while the principle of equitable utilization simply admits that the causing of certain significant environmental harm might be a normal effect of the utilization of international watercourses, the notion of sustainable development can be used for the promotion of a more effective environmental protection. In this connection, the protection of the environment of international watercourses might be more effectively achieved in the context of a regime in which States agree gradually to improve the quality of the waters of international watercourses and to prevent significant environmental harm on condition of receiving financial and technical assistance for that purpose. This notwithstanding, the principle of equitable utilization would remain the basic principle governing all other aspects of the utilization of international watercourses.

THE DAYTON AGREEMENT IN BOSNIA AND HERZEGOVINA: A STUDY OF IMPLEMENTATION STRATEGIES*

By MARCUS COX‡

PART I: THE CHALLENGE OF INTERNATIONAL INTERVENTION IN BOSNIA AND HERZEGOVINA

1. *Introduction*

This article explores the strategies and methods of international intervention in post-war Bosnia and Herzegovina. From the design of the peace agreement to the establishment of a major civilian and military implementation mechanism, the intervention to build a State of Bosnia and Herzegovina and restore a society torn apart by ethnic conflict is the most ambitious of its kind in the post-Cold War era. The complexity and range of problems involved, and the number of different actors engaged in the search for solutions, makes the operation a major experiment in the reconstruction of war-torn societies. While there have been important successes, progress in most areas of the intervention has been consistently disappointing. The return of refugees and displaced persons has progressed slowly, the effectiveness of the new constitutional structures is limited, and Bosnian society is still overwhelmingly divided along ethnic lines. While international intervention has prevented the resumption of armed conflict, it is not yet clear if or when the international military and civilian presence could be withdrawn without risk of renewed armed conflict and State collapse.

The article takes as its theme the centrality of ethnic identity and conflict in the formation of the new State of Bosnia and Herzegovina. Although the international community[1] is as heavily engaged in other

‡ An earlier version of this article was commissioned by the Centre for Applied Studies in International Negotiations, a non-profit, Geneva-based foundation, as a contribution to the Third International Security Forum of the NATO Partnership for Peace programme, held in Zurich on 19–21 October 1998. The author is a former legal adviser to the Commission for Real Property Claims of Displaced Persons and Refugees in Sarajevo. The views expressed are solely those of the author.

[1] In this article, the term 'international community' is used as shorthand for the collection of external actors engaged in the intervention in Bosnia. Empirically, there is no such single actor, and the international interest is often poorly represented through the conflicting mandates, policies and programmes of the different States and agencies. However, the concept of the 'international community' as a collective entity has become extremely important in Bosnian political discourse, and is imputed with an opinion or policy on almost any political or social issue. As a result, the positions

aspects of the reconstruction of Bosnian society—the physical repair of war damage, for instance, or the transition of the former communist system into a market economy—it is the sharp divisions among the ethnic groups which provide the frame for all international programmes. The first Part of the article provides an introduction to the issue, with a brief history of international involvement in the dissolution of the former Yugoslavia, and the complex role of ethnic identity in post-war society. Within the theme of ethnic identity and conflict, the remainder of the article addresses the two areas of the international intervention in Bosnia which present the most acute strategic dilemmas. First, the article addresses the role of the international community in establishing the State of Bosnia and Herzegovina. The Dayton Agreement used the foundation of an uncertain ceasefire to establish a sophisticated constitutional structure. This represents one of the most ambitious experiments ever undertaken in the constitutional engineering of ethnic conflict, and offers many interesting lessons. The formal structures of the State have so far performed extremely poorly, drawing the international community into an increasingly interventionist role. The article examines the strategies of the international community in assisting, supervising and even overruling the national political institutions in order to keep the peace process intact. It examines both the practicality and the legitimacy of current experiments with forms of international trusteeship.

Second, the article addresses international strategies for dealing with the results of ethnic cleansing. Intervention into an environment of ethnic separatism raises a series of difficult moral and strategic questions. The international community has made its principal goal the reversal of ethnic cleansing through the return of refugees and displaced persons[2] to their pre-war homes. The last two and a half years of minority return programmes, however, have produced limited results, and there is no sign of a sustained movement towards ethnic reintegration. The article examines the different strategies which have been used to force ethnic reintegration in the face of widespread obstruction from local authorities, and the reasons for their failure. It analyses the relationship between ethnic reintegration and reconciliation, and suggests that international policy should focus on promoting the conditions required for grass-roots reconciliation over a longer period of time. The relationship between economic development patterns and ethnic reconciliation is considered,

that are ascribed to the international community are cumulative and often unintended effects of a range of competing agendas.

[2] The term 'refugee' is used in this article to describe any citizen of Bosnia and Herzegovina displaced by the conflict across State borders, irrespective of status under the 1951 Convention. The term 'displaced person' refers to any person displaced from his home, but remaining on the territory of Bosnia and Herzegovina. The term 'minority return' is used to describe the return of an individual to a pre-war home which is located in an area now under the control of another ethnic group, whatever the ethnic distribution in the area prior to the war.

together with an introduction to the complex problems of property rights.

The factual material in this article is gathered from the author's own field research, including interviews with a large number of key informants in international and non-governmental organizations operating in Bosnia and Herzegovina, and a survey of field reports on various aspects of the intervention. It also draws upon an extensive survey of attitudes among displaced persons and refugees.[3]

2. *The Strategic Background to the Intervention*

International involvement in the Bosnian war was characterized by the lack of clear aims or strategies, and the reluctance of the key actors to become involved. Western nations were concerned by the security implications of the collapse of the Yugoslav federation, and determined to resist any further fragmentation below the level of the former Republics. They feared the spread of ethnic separatism through the Balkan Peninsula, and the creation of a potentially militant Islamic State within Europe. Over the course of the conflict, however, it became clear that the fighting, and even the flow of refugees, could be contained within the borders of the former Yugoslavia. Without an immediate security threat, the complexity and localized nature of the conflict was a major disincentive for close international engagement. Over the same period, the worsening humanitarian situation led to a pattern of gradually increasing international involvement, through successive unsuccessful peace plans and the use of international forces to protect humanitarian aid deliveries. Tension between the United States and Europe, and the failure of the common European foreign and security policy, made consensus very difficult to obtain, while the cumbersome United Nations-NATO 'dual key' command over international forces hampered strategic planning. Ultimately, the United States may have been forced into action almost inadvertently, through its commitment to provide US forces in support of any UNPROFOR evacuation.[4] Faced with that difficult and dangerous prospect, taking over diplomatic and military leadership of international operations in Bosnia was the more palatable alternative, particularly following the public attention given to the fall of Srebrenica and the market-place shelling in Sarajevo. This uncertainty which marked the early intervention has continued in the post-war period.

[3] The survey results are set out in full in CRPC and UNHCR, 'Return, Relocation and Property Rights: A Discussion Paper' (unpublished paper, December 1997).

[4] Warren Bass, 'The Triage of Dayton', *Foreign Affairs*, 1998, pp. 99–101.

The US initiatives, first in creating an alliance between the Croat and Muslim parties,[5] and then in negotiating an overall ceasefire at Dayton, were a considerable achievement in all the circumstances, and have successfully maintained order in the region against the odds. What appears less convincing is the attempt to use the fragile consensus at Dayton to create an entire constitutional structure for the new State. It is now clear that the Bosnian war was not so much concluded as suppressed, with the underlying issues left unresolved. At Dayton, the same nationalist leaders who were responsible for the war negotiated over the peace treaty. Their involvement ensured that the Dayton Agreement[6] took the form of a territorial bargain: the division of Bosnia through the trading of territorial shares, borders and areas of strategic or economic importance. The condition of retaining a single State of Bosnia and Herzegovina within the old Republican borders was the creation of a loose federation with a weak central government, leaving each ethnic group substantially autonomous within its own territory. While this formula may have been essential to achieving a ceasefire, it has proved to be a weak foundation for a peace process. The three wartime regimes remain intact, and the ideology of ethnic separatism remains the dominant political force. The parties have consistently obstructed the creation of the State institutions, preferring to preserve their own autonomy and extra-constitutional power structures. The impetus for State-building has therefore come almost solely from the international community, through a sustained military and civilian implementation operation. In this environment, it is proving difficult to initiate a self-sustaining peace process, or to engineer political and social changes which will outlast the period of international involvement.

The most difficult challenge for the international community in Bosnia is dealing with the results of ethnic cleansing. The military and political campaigns of nationalist leaders were effective in separating the populations into the three principal ethnic groups, and Bosnian society remains overwhelmingly divided along ethnic lines. International revulsion towards the goals and methods of the war has given the intervention in Bosnia a prominent moral element, with the international community determined to reverse ethnic cleansing through the return of refugees and displaced persons to their original homes. Progress in doing so, however, has been very limited, and there is currently no sustained movement towards ethnic reintegration. The goal of reversing ethnic cleansing is proving difficult to reconcile with the basic structure of the

[5] See the Washington Agreement on the Establishment of the Federation of Bosnia and Herzegovina: *International Legal Materials*, 33 (1994), p. 743.

[6] The General Framework Agreement for Peace in Bosnia and Herzegovina, which was initialled at Dayton on 21 November 1995, and signed in Paris on 14 December 1995 (hereafter 'the Dayton Agreement'): *International Legal Materials*, 35 (1996), p. 75. For an account of the negotiations leading to the agreement, see Richard Holbrooke, *To End a War* (New York, 1998).

Dayton Agreement, with its pragmatic acceptance of ethnic separation. Many of the local authorities now under pressure to accept the return of minorities are the same wartime leaders responsible for ethnic cleansing, now strengthened and legitimated through internationally sponsored elections. International programmes to promote minority return have been consistently obstructed throughout the country. The lack of progress poses the international community with an ethical and strategic dilemma of considerable difficulty: should ethnic separatism be opposed at all cost, or is it necessary to tolerate existing levels of ethnic separation for the time being in order to achieve a self-sustaining peace process? For the time being, there is no consensus among the international community on this question.

Differences in interest among the different international actors during the Bosnian war have been reflected in a cumbersome institutional structure in the post-war phase. Early proposals for an international presence powerful enough to take control over reconstruction and institution building came to nothing. Mistrust between American and European policy-makers made it impossible to bring the intervention within a single institutional structure. Troop-contributing countries would not accept a single chain of command over the military, nor place their forces under civilian control.[7] IFOR and SFOR[8] have operated as separate national contingents, rather than an integrated force, each with their own methods and force protection rules. The High Representative, appointed by the London Peace Implementation Conference[9] and mandated by Annex 10 of the Dayton Agreement, has an ambiguous role. He is responsible for co-ordinating civilian aspects of the peace process, but lacks the direct authority or the institutional resources to co-ordinate other international agencies effectively.[10] He has been unable to achieve policy coherence in the provision of international aid, where the major actors—the World Bank, the European Commission, UNHCR as lead

[7] The Dayton Agreement provides: 'The High Representative . . . shall remain in close contact with the IFOR Commander or his designated representatives and establish appropriate liaison arrangements with the IFOR Commander to facilitate the discharge of their respective responsibilities . . . . The High Representative shall have no authority over the IFOR and shall not in any way interfere in the conduct of military operations or the IFOR chain of command': Annex 10, Article II(5) and II(8).

[8] The Implementation Force (IFOR), mandated under Annex 1A of the Dayton Agreement, was renamed the Stabilization Force (SFOR) following the extension of its mandate in 1997.

[9] A Peace Implementation Conference was held in London on 8–9 December 1995, and created a Peace Implementation Council (PIC) to be a successor body to the International Conference on the Former Yugoslavia, to oversee the Dayton peace process. The PIC works through a Steering Board, composed of representatives of Canada, France, Germany, Italy, Japan, Russia, United Kingdom, United States, the Presidency of the European Union, the European Commission and the Organization of the Islamic Conference, under the chair of the High Representative: Conclusions of the Peace Implementation Conference held at Lancaster House, *International Legal Materials*, 35 (1996), p. 223.

[10] 'The High Representative shall respect their autonomy within their spheres of operation while as necessary giving general guidance to them about the impact of their activities on the implementation of the peace settlement': Annex 10, Article II(1)(c).

agency on humanitarian assistance, and the major bilateral donors—have their own interests and responsibilities. It is also unclear what powers the High Representative has as against the national authorities. He has binding powers of interpretation of the Dayton Agreement, and in December 1997 received additional powers from the Peace Implementation Council (PIC) to issue interim laws when the national authorities are unable to reach agreement. These powers are sufficient to make him a central player within the national political process, but it is unclear to what extent he can or should supplement or overrule the legitimate constitutional structures.

3. *Ethnic Identity and Bosnian Society*

There has never been a modern State of Bosnia and Herzegovina, nor a national identity associated with its territory, nor a single economic space within its borders. When the international community recognized the independence of Bosnia in the midst of political and social breakdown, it created something profoundly new. The former Yugoslavia was a complex structure—a federation built along both geographical and ethnic lines, with each of the principal ethnic groups holding the status of 'constituent nation' under the 1974 Constitution. Its precarious inter-ethnic structure was balanced by an official ideology of State socialism, the personality cult of Josip Tito, and a unique geo-political position between East and West. When Yugoslavia dissolved, it took with it the political structures that supported the ethnic balance within Bosnia. With no common experience except war and atrocity, and little genuine support for the project of nation-building, there is not yet a Bosnian identity to counteract the centrifugal forces of ethnic separatism. National ties across the borders with Croatia and Serbia are far stronger than civil identity within Bosnia. The most basic challenge of the peace process is to create a single society out of three sharply defined ethnic groups.

All international strategies in Bosnia are based on assumptions as to the extent of these ethnic divisions, and whether they are a permanent or transient feature of the social environment. Every international programme has an ethnic dimension to it, whether the programme expressly promotes ethnic reconciliation or merely meets with obstacles presented by ethnic conflict. International strategic planning can be analysed along a spectrum from ethnic reintegration on the one side, which assumes that ethnic identity can ultimately be removed from the political process, to ethnic accommodation on the other, whereby ethnicity is assumed to be a quasi-permanent feature of the region, to be controlled or contained within political structures. Literature on the dissolution of Yugoslavia and the war in Bosnia contains three different accounts of the origins and nature of ethnic conflict, which are presented briefly here. The purpose is not to make a case for any one of the alternatives, but to show the multi-dimensional nature of ethnic conflict.

The first account is sometimes called **'primordialism'**: the idea that ethnic hatred is embedded deeply within the history and culture of the Balkans.[11] According to this view, extreme ethnic consciousness is a function of the religious fault-line between Catholicism, Orthodox Christianity and Islam which runs through the region, and of a long history of repression and manipulation of identity by the Ottoman and Austro-Hungarian empires. The ancient hatreds which are endemic to Yugoslavia were suppressed during the communist regime by the personality cult and considerable political skills of Tito, but exploded following the collapse of communism. Recent wars are a continuation of ethnic conflict which was unresolved at the end of the Second World War, and which has continued in a more or less unbroken chain since the Battle of Kosovo Polje in 1389. This account has clear ideological overtones, echoing the rhetoric used by nationalist politicians to mobilize the population along ethnic lines. However, this perspective appeared frequently during the Bosnian war in statements of Western leaders, who used it as an argument for the futility of engaging directly with the conflict.

The second position ascribes the rapid descent into ethnic conflict to **'elite manipulation'**.[12] Ethnic mobilization was a political strategy used by former communist leaders, especially Slobodan Milosevic, to sustain their power following the collapse of communism. It was imposed from the top down, and is essentially an artificial creation. The techniques by which political elites were able to foment ethnic hatred are well documented, and included the manipulation of emotionally charged historical material, and massive media propaganda to convince each ethnic group that its survival was threatened by coexistence with the others.[13] This position is favoured by those who attribute responsibility for the conflict to a small number of unscrupulous individuals. One should add to this perspective the phenomenon that ethnic extremism, once it takes hold,

[11] This view is often associated with Robert Kaplan's book *Balkan Ghosts: A Journey Through History* (New York, 1993).

[12] Misha Glenny, *The Fall of Yugoslavia* (Penguin, 1992); Susan Woodward, *Balkan Tragedy: Chaos and Dissolution after the Cold War* (Washington, 1995); Christopher Bennett, *Yugoslavia's Bloody Collapse: Causes, Course and Consequences* (London, 1995).

[13] Keith Doubt, 'On the Latent Function of Ethnic Cleansing in Bosnia' (unpublished paper, 1995); Roy Gutman, *A Witness to Genocide* (New York, 1993); Mark Thompson, *Forging War: The Media in Serbia, Croatia and Bosnia-Herzegovina* (London, 1994); Françoise Hampson, *Incitement and the Media: Responsibility of and for the Media in the Conflicts in the Former Yugoslavia* (Essex, 1992); Robert Hayden, 'Recounting the Dead: The Rediscovery and Redefinition of Wartime Massacres in Late and Post-communist Yugoslavia', in Rubie Watson, (ed.), *Memory and Opposition Under State Socialism* (Santa Fe, 1993); Michael Ignatieff, *Blood and Belonging: Journeys into the New Nationalism* (London, 1993); Drazen Petrovic, 'Ethnic Cleansing – An Attempt at Methodology', *European Journal of International Law*, 5 (1994), p. 342; Gojko Vuckovic, *Ethnic Cleavages and Conflict: The Sources of National Cohesion and Disintegration* (Ashgate, 1997).

may be impossible to reverse. However artificial the heightened ethnic identity which fed the conflict, ordinary people in Bosnia now have very real memories of recent atrocities to sustain their hostility.

The third approach focuses on the **political economy** of the region,[14] and accounts for the conflict in terms of competition for economic and political capital during the declining years of the communist regime in Yugoslavia. It describes the dynamics of an unwieldy federation, where poor management of national resources through centralized investment decisions caused a crisis of legitimacy and control in the federal structure. Over a period of some fifteen years, increasing decentralization to republican level with no corresponding democratisation presented regional elites with incentives to compete to secure a greater share of dwindling national resources, in a struggle that became increasingly nationalistic in tone. Once communism collapsed as the official State ideology, ethnic nationalism was the only ideology capable of mobilizing support for regional elites, and last minute attempts at free elections, before any democratic alternatives were able to organize, left the nationalist parties able to dominate the political scene. Ascribing the conflict to structural features and incentive patterns is an important analysis, but does not easily explain the rapid escalation of violence. Some combination of the second and third explanations seems necessary, whereby elite manipulation is a 'tipping phenomenon' that turns structural competition into violence.[15]

International strategic thinking has oscillated among these alternatives. At times, ethnic identity is treated as an artificial phenomenon which can be countered through education and democratization, and which will ultimately disappear through the exercise of free choice in the ballot box by ordinary citizens. At other times, it is treated as a lasting structural feature, which can at best be channelled into non-destructive competition through constitutional engineering. The Dayton Agreement itself is ambivalent on the point. It demands ethnic reintegration through the return of refugees and displaced persons to their original homes, but at the same time creates constitutional structures which assume continuing ethnic separation. Both the State and the Federation Constitutions describe the different ethnic groups as 'constituent peoples'. Both provide for highly decentralized distribution of functions, giving ethnic groups the greatest possible autonomy. Both make ethnicity the explicit criteria for representation in parliament and in executive posts. Both give ethnic groups broad powers of veto over legislative or executive measures

[14] Vesna Bojicic and Mary Kaldor, 'The Political Economy of the War in Bosnia-Herzegovina', in Mary Kaldor and Basker Vashee (eds.), *Restructuring the Global Military Sector: Volume I: New Wars* (London, 1997), p. 137; Sabrina Ramet and Ljubisa Adamovich (eds.), *Beyond Yugoslavia: Politics, Economics, and Culture in a Shattered Community* (Boulder, 1995); Branka Magas, *The Destruction of Yugoslavia* (Verso, 1993).

[15] Russel Hardin, *One for All: The Logic of Group Conflict* (Princeton, 1995), p. 151.

which they consider destructive of their vital interests. These structures would become obsolete if Bosnia were to achieve a significant degree of ethnic reintegration. For example, in the House of Peoples of Bosnia and Herzegovina, each ethnic group is entitled to elect five members. The Constitution provides that all five members elected from Republika Srpska must be Serbs,[16] even though before the war Serbs were only 53% of the population in that area. If significant levels of minority return to Republika Srpska took place, these provisions would amount to discrimination under international human rights law.[17]

The lack of a coherent approach to managing ethnic conflict is the greatest weakness of the intervention. To date, the chief political actors among the international community have advocated solely for ethnic reintegration through minority return, fearing that any weakening of the international position would close off all possibility of further returns. There is a tendency to equate ethnic reintegration (return of refugees and displaced persons into ethnically mixed living areas) with the longer-term goal of ethnic reconciliation. Attempts to force reintegration through international pressure have been counter-productive, tending to increase insecurity among the displaced population and strengthen the position of nationalist leaders. A more appropriate role for the international community may be to work at creating the environment in which reconciliation can occur autonomously, in the meantime using international forces to prevent fresh outbreaks of open conflict. In a more stable and secure environment, the passage of time, physical reconstruction and economic development, demographic pressures, public education and democratization may gradually reduce the power of nationalist ideology, allowing alternative political and social movements to emerge. This process can be supported by the international community, but cannot be imposed from the outside.

Part II: Building the State of Bosnia and Herzegovina

1. *Modelling Ethnic Conflict*

Constitutional modelling of ethnic conflict has become an important field of international expertise in the post-Cold War era, offering a system of techniques that can be applied across a range of practical cases. Conflict resolution in the Balkans, the Caucasus, Africa and Northern Ireland is being approached through the use of constitutional models to create a stable environment in which grass-roots reconciliation can take

[16] Constitution of Bosnia and Herzegovina (Annex 4 of the Dayton Agreement), Article IV, para.1.

[17] See the analysis in Ronald Slye, 'The Dayton Peace Agreement: Constitutionalism and Ethnicity', *Yale Journal of International Law*, 21 (1996), p. 459.

hold. There are various models in use, based on certain common principles. They offer constitutional protection to the vital interests of each group, in order to decrease the risks of co-operation. Usually based on a federal system, they aim to create incentives for ethnic elites to co-operate within a State structure, breaking down the monolithic nature of ethnic group behaviour. In theory, they work by establishing a framework in which ordinary political, economic and social activity will create social bonds and divisions which are not exclusively ethnic in nature. As the complexity of social life increases over time, the risk that ethnic divisions will lead to open conflict gradually diminishes.

The peace process in Bosnia offers important lessons in this field. The Dayton Constitution contains a number of techniques for dealing with ethnic conflict, including a highly decentralized federation, a structure of representation in parliament, the executive and the judiciary based on ethnic quotas, mutual veto over legislative and executive measures, and minority rights protection mechanisms. However the Bosnian experience suggests that the fundamental obstacle in constitutional modelling lies in implementing the model. At both State and Federation levels, the Constitutions were annexed to peace treaties under heavy international pressure, were drafted in English by international lawyers, and were adopted by wartime leaders with no constitutional mandate.[18] As the handiwork of external actors, the constitutional structures are weakly legitimated. So long as they lack popular support, they are easily obstructed or manipulated by nationalist leaders, diluting or nullifying their contribution to ethnic reconciliation.

Considerable international efforts have been devoted to making the new institutions operational, but there is little sign of their becoming self-sustaining. They remain subordinate to wartime power structures, and have not become a genuine forum for decision-making or policy formulation. Because of the poor progress of the institutions, and their regular obstruction of international policy goals, the international community has been drawn into an increasingly interventionist role in national politics. It has taken on the responsibility, not merely of supporting the institutions with technical advice and resources, but also of convening them, supervising their operation and, in many cases, controlling their output. One of the most difficult strategic dilemmas facing the international community in Bosnia is the extent to which it should seek to supplement and even overrule the national institutions. The current trend towards a more robust role appears to be a response to the pressures of the moment, rather than a long term strategic plan. It carries with it the risk that the international community may become so

[18] The Constitution of Bosnia and Herzegovina has never been adopted by any formal process within the country, and no official translation exists in the local languages. For a description of the events surrounding the execution of the Dayton Agreement, see Richard Holbrooke, *To End a War* (New York, 1998).

deeply embroiled in national politics that it inhibits the development of genuine democratic institutions.

2. *Establishing the Constitutional Structures*

The State of Bosnia and Herzegovina is a federation of two Entities: the Republika Srpska and the Federation of Bosnia and Herzegovina, the latter being itself a federation of Bosniac[19] and Croat areas. Under the State Constitution, the institutions of Bosnia and Herzegovina have responsibility for a very limited number of matters (foreign affairs and trade, customs and monetary policy, immigration, inter-Entity criminal law enforcement, communications, transport and air traffic control).[20] There are three political organs of the State—the Presidency, the Parliament and the Council of Ministers. The Presidency is a committee of three members representing each of the constituent peoples, with the Chair rotating periodically. In the Presidency and the Parliament, each ethnic group has power of veto over measures which it considers destructive of its vital interests.[21] Three Ministries have been established—Foreign Affairs; Trade and Economic Affairs; and Civil Affairs and Communications—with ministerial posts shared among the ethnic groups. The High Representative is mandated to oversee the establishment of these institutions.[22]

In the two and a half years since the Dayton Agreement, disputes over venues, agendas and other formalities have frequently prevented the institutions even from meeting, let alone undertaking responsible governance. As the High Representative searches for ways to make them functional, attention often becomes focused on their formal aspects—the appointment of officials, the time and place of meetings, agendas, symbols and so on—as the criteria for assessing the compliance of local politicians with their obligations to co-operate. These formalities become an arena for political gamesmanship. When national politicians wish to appear co-operative, they may simply feed back to the international community its own rhetoric, without using the institutions to perform any substantive work on behalf of Bosnian society. The nationalist parties have followed a pattern of general obstruction balanced by occasional concessions to the international community. In the process, the international community itself becomes the central pillar of the new institutions, unable to extricate itself from close management of even their most superficial aspects.

19 The term 'Bosniac' was adopted by Bosnian Muslims during the war as a secular label for their ethnic group, and is used in the Constitutions of Bosnia and Herzegovina and the Federation.

20 Article III, para.1.

21 Article IV, para.3, and Article V, para.2(*d*).

22 Annex 10 of the Dayton Agreement.

Of the three political institutions at the State level, the Council of Ministers is the principal forum, preparing legislative drafts for presentation to the Parliament. Despite encouragement from the Office of the High Representative (OHR), the Parliament itself has not taken a proactive role in preparing or debating legislative measures. The Council of Ministers has met irregularly, and often refuses to pass measures essential for the functioning of the State. It required two years for an agreement on the basic legal framework for State institutions, and this is not yet fully implemented. The legal and institutional framework for the State budget is not yet in place, so no legitimate disbursements of State funds have been made. The three Ministries consist of personnel carried over from the wartime Republic of Bosnia and Herzegovina. The number of people employed and the source of their salaries is not known, but they are clearly under the control of the main Bosniac party, the SDA. The High Representative and the PIC have repeatedly condemned the continuation of these 'illegal parallel structures'.

At the Entity level, the fragile nature of the Bosniac-Croat alliance creates similar problems. The Federation was created by the Washington Agreement of March 1994 as an alliance against the Serbs, and was later incorporated into the State of Bosnia and Herzegovina at Dayton. The alliance altered the military balance, and was an essential ingredient in the ultimate settlement at Dayton. However, in many respects the alliance was more formal than real, and did not conclusively end the conflict between Bosniacs and Croats. During the course of the war, Bosniac and Croat regions were governed by two separate administrations: the former calling itself the Republic of Bosnia and Herzegovina, nominally the State government; and the latter the Republic of Herzeg-Bosna, with its capital in Mostar. As the Constitution of the Federation had not been implemented at all by the end of the war, the Bosniac and Croat parties entered into a further agreement at Dayton to dissolve the institutions of Herzeg-Bosna, and to transfer the domestic functions of the Republic to the Federation.[23]

The Federation consists of ten Cantons, with powers allocated across three levels of government: Federation, Cantons and Municipalities. It is an extremely decentralized and complex creation. The Federation level has exclusive responsibility for defence, economic policy, trade, finance, communications and energy, but shares responsibility with the Cantons for health, infrastructure, social welfare, immigration and natural resources. Cantons have exclusive responsibility for police, education, housing, local business and media, as well as any other matter not expressly reserved to the Federation.[24] However, if any Municipality has a majority ethnic population different from that of the Canton as a whole,

[23] Dayton Agreement on Implementing the Federation of Bosnia and Herzegovina, 10 November 1995.

[24] Constitution of the Federation of Bosnia and Herzegovina, Chapter III, Articles 1–4.

the Cantonal government is obliged to delegate to that Municipality all functions concerning education, culture, local business and media.[25] Ethnic vetoes apply in the Federation Parliament, and in the Central Bosnia and Herzegovina-Neretva Cantons.[26] Such is the complexity of the Federation Constitution that it can be extremely difficult to determine where functions lie, and all three levels are able to obstruct measures such as minority return. Ironically, it is only the domination of the Federation by the two nationalist parties which enables the system to function at all.

In certain respects, the Federation institutions are more effective than those at State level. Hostility between Croats and Bosniacs is still present, but does not act as a barrier to co-operation in areas which are genuinely within the common interest, particularly where dealings with the international community are involved. Compromises are successfully negotiated within the Federation Parliament, and the ruling Bosniac and Croat nationalist parties maintain close contacts. However, the Federation has not achieved any degree of mixed governance at a lower level. International efforts to establish multi-ethnic administrations at Cantonal and Municipal levels have not been successful, with real power either extremely localized or else held by illegal wartime authorities. Parallel structures operate extensively in breach of the Federation Constitution. The institutions of Herzeg-Bosna administer Croat areas, while the organs of the former Republic of Bosnia and Herzegovina perform a mixture of State- and Federation-level functions. Each area has important features of an independent State, maintaining its own currency, taxation, citizenship and armed forces. Croat areas are well integrated into Croatia in respect of telecommunications, transport and trade, and enjoy considerable economic benefits from this relationship. Many Bosnian Croats have Croatian passports, many Croat public officials and military officers are paid from Zagreb, and the Croatian army is still present in Herzegovina.

The core obstacle to the proper functioning of all of these structures is the low level of loyalty to the State of Bosnia and Herzegovina, and the lack of incentive for nationalist politicians to participate in good faith in the Dayton scheme. The ruling powers co-operate only so far as necessary to prevent an extreme reaction by the international community. The main Bosniac party, the SDA, exhibits the greatest loyalty to the common institutions, because Bosniacs have a strategic interest in securing a dominant position within a multi-ethnic Bosnian State. The Serb and Croat nationalist parties, on the other hand, have strong ties with Serbia and Croatia, and little interest in strengthening the State. Both obstruct the joint institutions regularly and systematically, to

[25] Chapter V, Article 2(2).

[26] Chapter V, Article 5, added by subsequent agreement on 11 May 1994: *International Legal Materials*, 33 (1994), p. 771.

prevent limitations of their own autonomy. The September 1998 election results confirmed that these basic dynamics remain unchanged since the end of the conflict. Croat and Serb politicians appear to be pursuing a strategy which preserves the option of withdrawal from the State of Bosnia and Herzegovina at some point in the future. Senior politicians, including those in Zagreb and Belgrade, have frequently called for a redrafting of the Dayton Agreement, for the creation of a third Croat Entity, or for closer ties across the borders to Croatia and Serbia. This leads some international observers to believe that the nationalist leaders are 'waiting out' the period of international involvement, after which the Dayton structures may collapse or be altered radically.

3. *The Trend Towards International Trusteeship*

Frustration with the slow progress of the joint institutions has caused the international community to take an increasingly interventionist role in political life. Whenever a key international policy goal is blocked within one of the institutions, pressure is brought to bear on the offending parties. Interventions usually take the form of letters, visits and public condemnations from high international officials. They may involve economic incentives, or threats of punitive measures in connection with international aid programmes. The conduct of elections by the OSCE has offered opportunities for pressure, with nationalist politicians struck from lists of candidates for breach of the Dayton Agreement or the electoral rules. The High Representative has been the leading actor in these interventions, under the authority of the PIC. In mid-1997, the OHR prepared a number of essential State laws which became known as 'the Quick Start Package', which were passed following threats of suspension of economic aid by the PIC. The High Representative forced through passport legislation by asking Western States to impose travel restrictions on five leading Serb politicians, including former Serb member of the Presidency Momcilo Krajisnik. In December 1997, the PIC increased the power of the High Representative by authorizing him to take interim decisions which would be binding on the parties until replaced by laws or executive measures consistent with the Dayton Agreement.[27] He was also authorized to dismiss any public official, elected or otherwise, who obstructs the peace process. The legal basis of these additional powers is unclear, perhaps resting on an extremely broad interpretation of the High Representative's powers of interpretation under Annex 10. In practice, the 'Bonn powers', as they have become known, amount to a significant revision of the Dayton Agreement, made without the consent of the Bosnian signatories.

[27] Conclusions of the Peace Implementation Conference, Bonn, 8 December 1997, Arts. XI–2, II–1A and XI.

Since then, the High Representative's interventions have become increasingly robust. He has imposed a number of major, substantive laws, on subjects including foreign investment, vehicle licensing, privatization, media, telecommunications and property rights. Most of these measures consisted of imposing a draft law which had already been debated in either the Council of Ministers or the State Parliament, but whose passage had been obstructed by one of the nationalist parties. In some cases, the laws had previously been rejected by the State Parliament. The foreign investment law is the only one of these measures to have been subsequently ratified by the Parliament. He has also imposed measures on important symbolic matters, such as the design of the national flag, the design of the currency, and the selection of the national anthem.

The measures taken by the High Representative have all been in key areas, removing obstacles to the peace process and the successful functioning of the State. For example, the creation of a uniform vehicle licensing regime has greatly facilitated freedom of movement across the Inter-Entity Boundary Line, the telecommunications law will for the first time integrate the three telephone networks, and the media law creates the first institutional framework capable of promoting independent media. However, there are growing signs that nationalist parties on all sides have begun to welcome these interventions. By arbitrating on ethnic conflicts, the High Representative allows national politicians to avoid compromise and political risk. They are able to present a hard-line stance to their own people, while at the same time enjoying the benefits brought by reasonable laws. In short, the elected leaders and delegates are being relieved of the responsibilities of governance by the High Representative's actions. If this is the case, then a more aggressive international role in national politics may in fact inhibit the development of the functioning local institutions.

This poses a difficult dilemma for the High Representative. Without a method of clearing deadlocks, the reconstruction and development of Bosnia can be held hostage by a small number of extremist politicians. Most of the important progress in the peace process to date can be attributed to the High Representative's interventions. As a result, each time an important issue is blocked by one of the parties, there is considerable pressure on him to take decisive action to remove the obstruction. The more resistance there is to international policy goals, the more he is drawn into this trusteeship role. It is not clear how long he will continue to act in this way, or how he will ultimately withdraw from close management of the common institutions. He also risks becoming involved beyond his current institutional capacity. The High Representative may be able to intervene effectively to resolve disputes that are purely formal in nature, or where one party is clearly withholding consent to a reasonable measure for unacceptable motives.

However, many inter-ethnic disputes are genuine, substantive disagreements on complex matters concerning the development of post-war and post-communist society, beyond the expertise or resources of the OHR. There is also real concern as to the legitimacy of an international official overruling the constitutional organs. No matter how poorly the elected parliaments are functioning, disregarding their decisions is unlikely to strengthen democratic processes.

4. *Controlling Local Politics*

Throughout the country, the political and social environment is highly localized. Conditions vary significantly from one village to the next, influenced by ethnic profile, war history, the number of displaced persons and so on. Many of the most significant obstructions to the peace process occur at a local level: human rights abuses by local police, evictions from property, discrimination in public services, obstruction of minority return. A large number of local leaders remain in power since the war, many of them military leaders, and some effectively warlords ruling in a lawless environment. One of the essential goals of the international community in Bosnia is to break down the climate of impunity in which local leaders operate, making them accountable for their actions. The experience of the past two years shows how difficult it is for the international community to control local politics. This section outlines some strategies which have been tried over the past two years.

4.1. *Economic conditionality*

Economic conditionality is often cited as the main source of international influence over domestic politics, but has proved in practice to be an unwieldy tool. Threats of suspension of aid, and conditions attached to particular aid projects, are used to send messages to local leaders as to what conduct is acceptable to the international community, and to create a pattern of incentives for compliance with the peace process. In practice, local politicians in Bosnia are very experienced at avoiding the effects of conditionality, playing donors off against each other to gain the maximum aid for the minimum concessions. Because the High Representative has no direct control over other international organizations, and limited influence on bilateral donors, he is unable to co-ordinate the application of the aid budget according to a consistent set of policy goals. As a result, there is a market place in international aid, where local leaders facing the suspension of a project are often able to find another donor to replace the lost funds. The process through which international aid commitments are made is not conducive to sensitive political judgements about the behaviour of local authorities. Most donors are not sufficiently attuned to the political process to distinguish between regions or political factions in a meaningful way. Those aid administrators who are close enough to the field to make political assessments are usually preoccupied with securing funds for their area of responsibility, and are reluctant to suspend or cancel projects for fear of losing their budgetary allocation. Funds are often pledged a year or more in advance of the commencement of a project, and cannot easily be altered in response to changes in local conditions. Suspension of projects involves major bureaucratic and financial waste. When formal sanctions are imposed against a particular municipality, donors often insist on granting exemptions to ongoing or supporting projects, and projects denoted as humanitarian, with the result that the municipality may not notice any real reduction in support.

Various classification schemes have been developed over the past two years to assist donors with distinguishing among municipalities or regions. These include UNHCR 'black-listed' municipalities, UNHCR target areas, RRTF priority areas[28] and the UNHCR Open Cities scheme. Each of these involved some form of assessment of the behaviour of local officials, although in some cases they also incorporated investment criteria and absorption capacity for return. In June 1998, the PIC requested the High Representative to establish a more formal municipal evaluation scheme to determine compliance and co-operation in the fields of refugee return, implementation of election results, police integration and prosecution of war criminals. Donors are called upon to take these evaluations into account when allocating funding. In none of these schemes has it proved possible to apply the assessment criteria in a meaningful way. Municipal authorities have obstructed the Dayton Agreement so consistently that no behaviour has stood out as particularly worthy of reward. Because of the poor record on compliance, the international community often recognizes 'good behaviour' which is purely formal in nature. In respect of minority return, for example, municipalities may be given a favourable status in reward for public declarations of willingness to accept minority return, the preparation of regional return plans, or the creation of municipal return offices which employ members of the returning minority. It has been easy for those municipalities which seek international support to meet these secondary criteria without making any substantive contribution to the peace process.

Perhaps most fundamentally, economic conditionality can send the wrong message to ordinary people. The poverty of the local population, particularly displaced persons living in vulnerable circumstances, is one of the factors which promote ethnic extremism. When the international community suspends aid to these people, it increases their insecurity,

[28] The Reconstruction and Return Task Force is an inter-agency body under the joint chair of OHR and UNHCR, responsible for the co-ordination of international reconstruction aid.

making them more dependent on funding sources controlled by the nationalist parties, and therefore more easily mobilized in opposition to the peace process. If, as many observers have commented, ethnic separatism is best addressed through employment creation and economic development over an extended period of time, then punitive action may be counterproductive.

4.2. *Dismissing local officials*

During 1998, a new strategy for controlling local politics was developed, where responsibility was attributed to specific officials. In December 1997, the PIC gave the High Representative authority to dismiss any official, elected or otherwise, who obstructs the peace process.[29] The High Representative has since dismissed a number of municipal and local police officials, most notably in Stolac and Drvar following violence against minority returnees. Dismissing individual officials seems to be more a gesture of frustration with the slow progress of the peace process than a coherent strategy. There is no sign that dismissing a single official changes the political environment in strategic locations. Nationalist parties retain the power to appoint replacements or select new candidates for election. Where political conditions are conducive to extremism, it is likely that another extremist will be chosen to take the place of any individual dismissed by the High Representative. The dismissed official may continue to be influential, as his or her party position may be more powerful than the official post. There can also be a problem with filling the vacated position. In a number of instances, the nationalist parties have refused to appoint a successor to the post, creating a vacancy which becomes a further pretext for avoiding compliance with the Dayton Agreement.

One exception to this pattern may be international operations to arrest war criminals. Despite prohibitions on indicted war criminals holding public office, they continue to be influential in many locations, where wartime military or criminal power structures remain intact. The few SFOR operations to arrest war criminals have had a marked, though temporary, effect on repressing the influence of these illegal networks. The arrests obviously help to reduce the climate of impunity in which local leaders operate, and more operations would be a very positive contribution.

4.3. *Governance by international officials*

Another recent strategy to counter local obstruction is the appointment of Special Envoys of the High Representative to specific localities, sometimes with power to overrule local authorities. Local trusteeships

[29] Decision of the Ministerial Meeting of the Steering Board of the PIC, Luxembourg, 9 June 1998, Article 74.

have been tried on a substantial scale with the European Union Administrator in Mostar and the International Supervisor under the Brcko arbitration award.[30] Each of these officials had power to issue orders or decisions with the status of binding local laws. The EU Administrator operated in a divided city in extremely difficult circumstances, and was unsuccessful in establishing a joint city administration or a return mechanism. Although the Bosniac and Croat parties formally agreed to his powers, he was able to exercise little or no influence over local politics. The International Supervisor in Brcko has had more success, conducting a minority return programme to empty villages around Brcko and greatly improving freedom of movement across the Inter-Entity Boundary Line. However there have been no lasting changes to the political environment in Brcko, and the June 1998 PIC Declaration described the new multi-ethnic administration as 'shallowly-rooted'.[31]

Despite the poor record to date, the June 1998 PIC Declaration foreshadows the appointment of Special Envoys of the High Representative to a number of localities.[32] The High Representative appointed a Special Envoy to Drvar, and the OSCE and the High Representative appointed an international chair of an Interim Executive Board in the Municipality of Srebrenica, following failure to implement the local election results.[33] The exact function of the Special Envoys is not clear. They have no authority vested directly in them, in respect of either the local authorities or other international organizations operating in the same area. A Special Envoy will certainly bring the international community closer to the local level, improving monitoring and knowledge of local personalities. He or she may have better access to local officials, providing opportunities for advocacy. However at the end of the day the local leaders know that they will still be in power long after the Special Envoy is withdrawn. They can simply maintain an appearance of co-operation, and wait for international attention to be directed elsewhere.

This has been a sceptical account of the international community's capacity to control local politics. Uncritical confidence in the power of the international community leads to poor strategic thinking. There is no value in the international community purporting to manage a situation when it has no real capacity to do so. Gestures such as sacking officials or appointing Special Envoys are essentially bluffs which diminish in effectiveness the more they are used. Local leaders are skilled at reading the degree of commitment of the international community, and are very

[30] Award of the Brcko Arbitral Tribunal for Dispute over the Inter-Entity Boundary in Brcko Area, 14 February 1997.

[31] Above, n.29, Article 93.

[32] Ibid., Article 74.

[33] Arbitration award on the Implementation of the Municipal Election Results in Srebrenica, 12 March 1998.

difficult to control. The lessons of the last two years teach that the international community should avoid becoming too closely involved in local politics. Where local leaders develop entrenched positions over issues they perceive as affecting their vital strategic interests, heavy pressure from the international community at best produces temporary results, and at worst increases inter-ethnic fear and suspicion. At such times, the only option available to the international community is to withdraw temporarily and concentrate its resources into more promising areas.

5. *Elections, Democracy and Democratization*

The first priority of the intervention in Bosnia was the conduct of elections, which were pushed through in the shortest possible time.[34] Enormous resources were invested in the design of the electoral system and the conduct and monitoring of the elections. The goal was to create a stable and legitimate government, giving the international community elected officials with whom it could deal in implementing the peace process. There was clearly a hope that elections would secure regimes changes around the country, giving the citizens of Bosnia and Herzegovina the opportunity to 'vote for peace' by supporting non-nationalist candidates. In successive rounds of elections, this has not occurred. Wartime leaders have been returned to power across the country. The new electoral system has not produced responsible or accountable government, but merely reinforced the power of the nationalist parties. The Bosnian experience shows that internationally sponsored elections do not of themselves create a genuine democratic system, and that the path to democratization in a severely divided society is extremely difficult.

Four rounds of elections conducted in the two and a half years following the Dayton Agreement returned nationalist leaders to power in all three ethnic groups, legitimated and strengthened by their new constitutional mandate. In the 1996 elections, conducted under controversial circumstances, the nationalist parties won strong majorities in each round of the election, including the State Presidency and Parliament, the Parliaments of both Entities, and the Cantonal Parliaments in

[34] Annex 3, Article II, para.4 of the Dayton Agreement provides: 'Elections shall take place on a date . . . six months after entry into force of this Agreement or, if the OSCE determines a delay necessary, no later than nine months after entry into force'. This attempt to limit the discretion of the OSCE in setting the election date came from the mistaken belief that the election would mark the end of international military involvement in Bosnia. This period of time was unrealistic, not merely because of the difficulty of establishing conditions for free and fair elections, as required by Annex 3, but also because the OSCE was required to undertake the registration of voters in extremely difficult circumstances. As it transpired, State and Entity level elections were held in September 1997, at the latest possible date, but irregularities in voter registration obliged OSCE to delay Municipal elections until September 1998, notwithstanding the requirements of Annex 3.

the Federation. The strongest performance of non-nationalist parties was in Sarajevo Canton, with 35% of the vote. In 1997, elections were held for 4,789 council seats in 135 municipalities. The principal nationalist parties took 80% of seats in the Federation, and a large majority in Republika Srpska. Parties running on multi-ethnic platforms took just 6% of the council seats, winning power only in Tuzla. Independent candidates performed very poorly, winning only 13 seats throughout the country. Candidates representing displaced persons performed better than expected, with absolute majorities in five municipalities, and more than 20% of the vote in a further 42 municipalities. The September 1998 State and Entity election results showed a resurgence of extreme nationalist leaders in the Republika Srpska, and despite some gains by moderate parties, the nationalist parties retained their commanding position across the board.[35]

Although the elections themselves have been conducted in a largely free and fair manner, the results continue to reflect the strong ethnic divisions across the country. With the population dividing overwhelmingly into ethnic voting blocks, the elections function more as a census of ethnic groups than a forum for selecting among alternative governments or policies. Most individuals are aware that the greatest threat to their security and livelihood is the risk of living under local authorities of a different ethnic group. As a result, very few people vote for representatives of another ethnicity, and multi-ethnic coalitions perform very poorly. Nationalist politicians know they have no prospect of winning votes from other ethnic groups, and therefore have no incentive to serve the interests of other groups while in power. An important control mechanism in a democratic system—the fear of losing subsequent elections—is largely absent from Bosnian politics.

Attempts by the international community to influence voting patterns away from support for nationalist parties have had little or no effect. The most substantial attempt took place in Republika Srpska. In November 1997, a contest for power within Republika Srpska led to the creation of a new regime under the control of President Biljana Plavsic and Prime Minister Milorad Dodik. Plavsic appears to have sensed a political opportunity in the extremely low standards of living in Republika Srpska, and launched an attack on the Pale regime for its corruption and its association with war criminals. A constitutional crisis between the President and the Parliament ensued, each purporting to dismiss the other, until new Parliamentary elections were organized by OSCE in November 1997. Dodik, whose party won only two seats in that election, was appointed Prime Minister by a majority of one with the support of Bosniac and Croat members. His appointment took place during a boycott of the Parliament by the main Serb parties, and was heavily

[35] These figures are summaries of results supplied by OSCE in Sarajevo.

engineered by the international community. During 1998, leading up to the September elections, the international community extended prominent support to Plavsic and Dodik, lifting the aid embargo on Republika Srpska and communicating to Serb voters that continued international aid was conditional upon their supporting the two moderates. In the September 1998 elections, Plavsic lost the Presidency to an extremist opponent, Nikola Poplasen, who has pledged to prevent the return of minorities to the Republika Srpska, and to pursue the goal of a Greater Serbia through political and democratic means. It is not known at the time of writing whether Dodik will be able to form a majority in the Parliament and retain the Prime Ministership. These results have sent a clear message that international support does not dictate voting patterns.

5.1. *International control over the electoral process*

The Dayton Agreement gives the Organization for Security and Co-operation in Europe (OSCE) important powers over the design, planning and conduct of the elections. In advance of the 1996 election, it was responsible for certifying that the conditions existed for free and fair elections, a highly controversial decision when freedom of movement was limited, voter intimidation and fraud were widespread, and the dominant political parties were exercising tight control over the media. Although aware of these shortcomings, OSCE proceeded with the election, apparently taking the view that an elected government of some form would be an advance over the unconstitutional regimes in power at the time. The Head of the OSCE Mission controls the Provisional Electoral Commission (PEC), a mixed international and local body created to regulate the conduct of elections.[36] The PEC established rules for the registration of political parties, eligibility of candidates and voters, the conduct of the campaign, and the determination, publication and certification of election results. These rules were by no means merely technical in nature, but involved many significant political choices as to the shape and direction of the political process. The OSCE also established an Election Appeals Sub-Commission (EASC) to adjudicate complaints about the electoral process.[37] It has the power to impose penalties for violations of the electoral rules, including disqualification of candidates and de-certification of parties. The power to exclude nationalist leaders from the electoral process has been one of the more important forms of influence held by the international community. In 1996, OSCE nego-

[36] Annex 3, Article II, para.3.
[37] PEC Rules and Regulations, Chapter 4.

tiated the resignation of indicted war-criminal Radovan Karadzic from the chairmanship of the principal Serb party, the SDS.[38]

Annex 3 of the Dayton Agreement, which governs elections, provides that citizens of Bosnia and Herzegovina should in general vote in the municipality in which they lived before the war, but may also apply to cast their vote elsewhere.[39] This has allowed displaced persons to be represented on municipal councils in their pre-war place of origin, even if they are now unable to live in or even to visit that municipality. It is hoped that multi-ethnic administrations will gain enough control over local police and administrative bodies to force them to allow returns to take place. However there have been enormous difficulties in implementing the local election results, producing some anomalous situations. In the five municipalities where displaced minorities won control of the council,[40] and others where they achieved substantial representation, strong international pressure has been required even to bring the elected delegates together. OSCE has the responsibility to certify that the new council has been properly installed, and may decertify any municipality for breach of the rules up to six months after certification. Under the PEC rules, the obligations of the council are to convene its first session with all sides participating, to elect or appoint officers and committees with a fair representation of minority parties, and to adopt rules of procedure. Certification may be rejected by OSCE if councillors are denied access to the municipality or the council itself, if there is harassment of officials, if councillors are prevented from living in the municipality, or if council proceedings are not secular.[41]

The certification process has inevitably been highly superficial, with many councils not meeting again after their first session. Illegal parallel administrations are still widespread. The OSCE and UNHCR are conducting a priority return programme for elected officials, but it is clear that many of the officials, particularly Bosniacs from Republika Srpska, do not in fact want to live in the municipality which they represent. In Srebrenica, which the original Bosniac residents cannot yet visit, failure of the new council to meet the certification requirements led to the OSCE Head of Mission and the High Representative arbitrating on the distribution of council posts among the ethnic groups. When the arbitration award itself was not implemented, they created an Interim

[38] However, when the EASC tried to decertify the SDS in certain municipalities during the 1997 elections for displaying election posters with pictures of Radovan Karadzic, in open defiance of the election rules, the OSCE Chief of Mission overruled it, prompting widespread criticism. OSCE was probably motivated by fear of prompting a boycott of the election by Serb nationalist parties, which would have made the results impossible to implement.

[39] Annex 3, Article IV.

[40] Bosniacs took Srebrenica from the Serbs and Zepce from the Croats, while Serbs took Bosanski Petrovac from the Bosniacs and Bosanski Grahovo and Drvar from the Croats.

[41] PEC Rules and Regulations, Chapter 15. A number of municipalities have subsequently been decertified by decision of the PEC, or subject to a compulsory arbitration order issued jointly by the High Representative and the OSCE.

Executive Board with power to decide on 'disputed issues', with an international official appointed as Acting Chair. Not surprisingly, the Interim Executive Board has also been unable to function, and there are plans to post a Special Envoy to Srebrenica early in 1999. Although Srebrenica is the most extreme example, the future of multi-ethnic councils in most parts of the country is not promising. This poses a dilemma for the international community, which cannot force the multi-ethnic councils to become effective, but also cannot afford to let the issue drop.

Unless the mandate of the OSCE is extended, the September 1998 elections may be the last round controlled by the international community, beyond a continuing monitoring role. A joint international and local body is now preparing a permanent electoral law, bringing the authority of the PEC to an end. This may be the last opportunity for the international community to effect changes to the basic design of the system. Various observers have suggested that a different electoral system might produce radically different results. One proposal calls for the division of the country into three separate ethnic voting rolls, and a system where candidates would be elected by all three ethnic groups.[42] This would eliminate ethnic block-voting, and create an incentive for the nationalist parties to field moderate candidates with electoral appeal across ethnic boundaries. This proposal seeks to engineer a gradual evolution of the nationalist parties into more moderate institutions. To date, solutions such as this have not been feasible, both because of the difficulty of amending the Constitution, and because of the risk that such an election would produce results that are impossible to implement. Ultimately, substantial electoral reform will be necessary if the current ethnic divisions are not to be solidified and endlessly repeated in the electoral process. However it is doubtful that the international community will be able to impose such a solution against the will of the nationalist parties.

5.2. *Democratization, civil society and ethnic reconciliation*

The development of political alternatives to the nationalist parties has been very limited. While the international community regards as 'moderate' any party offering lip-service to the Dayton Agreement and a friendly rhetorical stance in this respect, there are in fact very few real differences among the parties. Of approximately eighty parties participating in the recent elections, most are small-scale, single-issue parties offering no policy alternatives to the nationalist parties. Many are formed by displaced persons wishing to return to a specific area, representing only a single ethnic group and by no means necessarily committed to

[42] International Crisis Group, 'Changing the Logic of Bosnian Politics: Discussion Paper on Electoral Reform' (unpublished paper, March 1998).

multi-ethnic policies. There are a handful of multi-ethnic parties or coalitions, but these are poorly organized and tend to have no political platform beyond opposition to the nationalist parties. The PEC rules required all candidates in the September elections to express their views on refugee return, minority rights, economic reform, reconstruction and social services, to try to broaden political debate.[43] OSCE has a programme to support those opposition parties it sees as most promising. For the September elections, it established fifteen public resource centres where approved parties were able to use printing and other facilities to assist with campaigning. While recognizing that these parties have limited prospects in the short term, OSCE's strategy is to identify potential transitional parties which could contribute to broadening the political environment, and allowing more grass-roots alternatives to emerge.

Explanations for the slow emergence of moderate leaders are not difficult to find. The political dynamics of ethnic conflict count against moderate political forces. Extremists are always able to outbid any moderate opposition by feeding the fears of ordinary people.[44] Individuals who oppose the leaders of their own ethnic group on substantive issues, or try to form networks with other ethnic groups, are easily branded as traitors and isolated from the centre of power. Because of the difficulty of establishing formal political opposition, some observers see civil society movements as the first step on the path to democratization. Civil society is the sphere of association of individuals and private organizations independent of the formal State, including local NGOs, trade unions, religious groups, academic institutions and cultural organizations. According to liberal political theory, civil society is the site for the formation of the values which make democracy possible. A healthy civil society will help to promote a plural democracy based on popular participation and genuine policy platforms.[45] However, for the time being Bosnia does not have a strong network of civil society organizations, even compared to those found in Croatia and the Federal Republic of Yugoslavia. This is partly a result of the social disruption of the war, with many communities dispersed and much of the educated middle class abroad as refugees. International efforts to promote the growth of local NGOs can easily distort their development. According to one report, many international agencies used or created local organizations to

[43] PEC Rules and Regulations, Article 7.40.

[44] 'Ethnic extremists . . . are nearly always present, and they can be expected to become prominent whenever at least one of the strategic dilemmas above is initiated. Analytically, ethnic activists and political entrepreneurs are as much a product as a producer of ethnic fears and are dependent for their "success" upon the underlying strategic dilemmas': Lake and Rothchild, 'Containing Fear: The Origins and Management of Ethnic Conflict', *International Security*, 21 (1996), p. 41, at p. 55.

[45] Cohen and Arato, *Civil Society and Political Theory* (Massachusetts, 1992); A. Hadenius and F. Uggla, 'Making Civil Society Work', *World Development*, 24 (1996), p. 1621.

continue their humanitarian programmes at the end of the war.[46] The aim was to secure a continuation of service delivery at a minimal cost, rather than to strengthen civil society. Local NGOs were given funding for projects beyond their organizational capacity, and expanded in an unsustainable manner. Training and capacity-building often consist of teaching staff of local NGOs how to write project proposals and reports for international donors, creating a market where organizations spend most of their energies competing for international funds. As a result, the NGO sector in Bosnia is effective in certain areas of service delivery, but weaker at advocacy and community development, and makes little contribution to democratization.

Although there is clearly a value in a strong civil society network, it is less clear what should be the nature of international involvement. There is no consensus as to how to promote authentic, grass-roots social and political movements without distorting their development. In an environment of ethnic conflict, overt international advocacy on behalf of local organizations may politicize their role, attracting hostility from local authorities and limiting their impact. There may be little that the international community can do beyond contributing funding and other resources, and resource constraints are not the main limiting factor. Spontaneous movements arising out of genuine sectional interests are far more effective than institutions created by the international community. Over time, these sectional interests may come to cut across ethnic lines, strengthening democracy by diversifying the interests represented in public life.

Part III: Return, Reintegration and Reconciliation

1. *The Return Dilemma*

Ethnic cleansing in the wars which accompanied the dissolution of Yugoslavia was one of the most disturbing phenomena of the post-Cold War era. The greater part of the violence in Bosnia was directed at driving civilians from their homes for the express purpose of creating ethnically pure areas. Four years of systematic atrocities against civilians were ruthlessly effective in separating the ethnic groups. For reasons which are well documented elsewhere, the international community failed to respond effectively to ethnic cleansing during the course of the war. Its humanitarian assistance efforts tended if anything to facilitate

[46] Ian Smillie, 'Service Delivery or Civil Society? Non-governmental Organizations in Bosnia and Herzegovina'(unpublished paper, 1996).

the movement of population.[47] The complex and unstable pattern of ethnic enclaves which resulted from the war, and the pace and volume of population displacement, defeated successive international peace plans. The Dayton formula became feasible only once the process of ethnic separation was close to completion, with the Muslim-Croat alliance providing a framework for dealing with the remaining mixed areas in Central Bosnia. None the less, the Dayton map (49% of territory to the Republika Srpska, 51% to the Federation) required further substantial movements of population in order to match the situation on the ground, and the process of ethnic separation was completed in the months following the ceasefire.

Strong opposition to the ideology, methods and results of ethnic cleansing has given the international intervention in Bosnia and Herzegovina a prominent moral dimension. The international community has made its principal goal the reversal of ethnic cleansing through the return of refugees and displaced persons to their homes of origin. All attempts by the national authorities to cement the results of ethnic cleansing, by erecting legal and institutional barriers to return, or by facilitating the relocation of population into property abandoned by minorities, have been strongly opposed. However, to date the international community has not been successful in beginning a movement towards ethnic reintegration. Despite the application of sustained international pressure and very substantial resources, minority return programmes have achieved only marginal results. It is becoming increasingly apparent that the Dayton peace formula itself poses an obstacle to ethnic reintegration, by allowing each ethnic regime virtual autonomy within its own territory. As a result, the strategic interests of all parties lead them to be implacably opposed to ethnic reintegration.

The poor progress of return is widely recognized,[48] and the figures need only be summarized here. Of more than 1.2 million refugees, only 250,000 have returned to Bosnia since Dayton, and over 500,000 have resettled permanently abroad. Of just over a million internally displaced persons, more than 800,000 remain displaced, most occupying the houses of other people. More than 40% of the population is therefore still

[47] One UNHCR publication in 1995 noted: 'As the parties to the conflict quickly realized, if UNHCR could be induced to organize the evacuation of threatened populations, the process of ethnic cleansing could be completed under humanitarian auspices. Despite UNHCR's unwillingness to be exploited in this manner, the organization was ultimately obliged to concede that evacuation was in some cases the lesser of two evils. As UNHCR's senior official in the region observed, "we chose to have more displaced persons and refugees, rather than more dead bodies" ': UNHCR, *The State of the World's Refugees 1995* (New York, 1996).

[48] These figures are a compilation of data contained in UNHCR, 'Progress and Prospects for Sustainable Return and Solutions in the Former Yugoslavia' (unpublished paper, November 1998); OHR, 'Report on the Implementation of the Peace Agreement for Bosnia and Herzegovina' (unpublished paper, September 1998); UNHCR, 'Repatriation Operation 1998' (unpublished paper, 1997); CRPC and UNHCR, op. cit. above (n.3); International Crisis Group, 'Minority Return or Mass Relocation?' (unpublished paper, 1998).

displaced. Most of the returns so far have been cases of majority return, occurring early in the peace process. The outstanding caseload is the difficult component: return of individuals whose homes are in areas now controlled by another ethnic group. Despite enormous international efforts, only 50,000 minority returns have been achieved,[49] concentrated in a small number of locations. Because of the barriers to minority return, only 42,700 refugees returned to Bosnia and Herzegovina in the first half of 1998, and almost all of these were obliged to relocate among their own ethnic group. No promising strategy for addressing the problem has been developed, and each year the international community finds itself in the position of repeating resource-intensive strategies which have proved a consistent failure.

The major reason for the failure of minority return is opposition from nationalist leaders. Authorities at all levels and in all parts of the country have consistently obstructed international return programmes. The difficulty of forcing local leaders to co-operate against their own perceived interests has already been described.[50] It is also clear that there are complex psychological and social barriers to return among the general population. International actors in Bosnia often assume that obstruction to minority return comes from a relatively small number of nationalist leaders with a personal interest in maintaining ethnic separatism. If that obstruction could be removed, by overruling local leaders or offering them incentives to moderate their opposition, then ordinary people would welcome a return to pre-war levels of ethnic integration. That assumption may be misleading. In focus groups and surveys carried out among Bosnian citizens, most state that they wish to return to their homes of origin, and would be happy to live with their pre-war neighbours, whatever their ethnicity.[51] However, they also see the prospect of living under the control of authorities of another ethnic group as the greatest threat to their physical and economic security. In post-war Bosnia, after years of territorial exchanges and the manipulation of election results through the movement of people, ethnic distribution has become inextricably linked with territorial control. Large-scale minority return is opposed on all sides because it raises the possibility of losing control of territory gained or successfully defended during the war. It particularly threatens displaced persons of the majority ethnic group in the return area, who fear being displaced again by the return of others. Minority return may be tolerated to empty villages without economic or strategic significance, or in small numbers into large urban centres, but

[49] Only some 2,000 of these minority returns have been to the Republika Srpska. Of the 220,000 refugees still in Germany, almost all are Bosniacs from Republika Srpska.

[50] A UNHCR strategy paper reveals an awareness of the problem, ascribing the deadlock in the return process to a whole series of factors beyond the control of UNHCR, particularly the ongoing influence of wartime leaders: UNHCR, 'A Regional Strategy for Sustainable Return of Those Displaced by Conflict in the Former Yugoslavia' (unpublished paper, June 1998).

[51] CRPC and UNHCR, op. cit. above (n.3).

outside those marginal situations it is consistently opposed. By the same token, the determination of displaced persons to return to their homes often represents a desire to take back control of their place of origin from another ethnic group. Experience shows that people are less interested in returning into a minority living situation, with the substantial personal risk which that entails. So long as these strategic and psychological factors are widespread among the population, local leaders will inevitably obstruct minority return.

The Dayton Agreement itself takes an ambiguous position on ethnic reintegration, and does not dictate a definite policy. It does make the right of refugees and displaced persons to return to their homes of origin an essential principle of the peace process, written into the Constitution and Annex 7 and binding upon authorities at all levels. The right is reinforced by an array of legal and human rights principles, and protected by various international and local institutional mechanisms. However, the right to return in Annex 7 is weakened by being coupled with the possibility of compensation for lost property, as though the authorities might legitimately choose between allowing return or providing money in lieu of return. The right to compensation, and to choose a return destination or place of residence,[52] is frequently cited by Serb leaders as equal in status to the right to return, with some textual justification. The structure of the constitutional system, dividing the country into largely autonomous regions with a weak central government and providing an ethnic formula for Parliamentary representation, is not consistent with widespread minority return. The Dayton Agreement, and the Constitutions of the State and both Entities, are clearly premised on continuing separation of the ethnic groups.

This presents an acute ethical and strategic dilemma. Weakening the strong political pressure for ethnic reintegration might be interpreted by nationalist politicians as *carte blanche* to consolidate the results of ethnic cleansing, by establishing impassable barriers to return. This would render ineffective important elements of the Dayton Agreement concerning return and human rights, with great personal cost to those victims of ethnic cleansing still determined to return. Displaced persons and returning refugees would be permanently relocated into housing abandoned by the displacement of others, eliminating the possibility for the original inhabitants to return to those homes. Any international involvement in this process, through reconstruction aid or other forms of assistance, might implicate international agencies and their donors in the process of ethnic cleansing.

However, the consistent failure of minority return programmes throughout the country suggests that a fundamental change of strategy

[52] Annex 7, Chapter One, Article 1, paras. 1 and 4.

must take place. The reality of Bosnia and Herzegovina for the foreseeable future is a high degree of ethnic separation. A large proportion of the internally displaced are living in dire circumstances. Their physical and economic insecurity is an important contributing factor to political extremism, making them easily radicalized in support of nationalist causes. If no solution can be found for them, they will remain a destabilizing factor indefinitely. Clearly, return to home of origin is the ideal solution to the displacement problem. However for many people, returning to their homes would involve entering into a situation of physical insecurity and discrimination, with limited access to employment or basic social services. To date, international policy has focused on removing these obstacles to return, but with limited success. Where return proves impossible, or where the displaced persons themselves choose not to return, should the international community be involved in the search for alternative solutions? UNHCR now considers that population relocation will be an essential component of the search for durable solutions for refugees and displaced persons, and that it may be supported so long as it is voluntary and does not diminish the prospects for return.[53] From an operational perspective, it is clear that minority return programmes of such intensity cannot be sustained indefinitely in the face of minimal success rates. However for the time being, international agencies are unwilling to undertake programmes to assist displaced persons and returning refugees to integrate successfully among their own ethnic group.

It is suggested that the only way to resolve the return dilemma is to make a realistic assessment of the international community's capacity to influence post-war demographic patterns in Bosnia and Herzegovina. The experience of return programmes over the last two years makes it clear that the international community is not in control of the movement of population. Although the moral and legal arguments in favour of minority return are indisputable, an exclusive focus on that solution has not proved an effective strategy. One of the lessons of Bosnia is that following such a bitter conflict, physical reintegration of the population may not be the first step on the path to ethnic reconciliation. On the contrary, using international influence to 'enforce' minority return tends to harden the strategic positions of the ethnic groups, strengthening the hand of nationalist forces and making it more difficult to achieve grassroots reconciliation. This article therefore argues that the focus of international strategy should shift to promoting reconciliation in the political, social and economic fields.

[53] UNHCR, op. cit. above (n.50).

2. *A Review of Strategies Used to Date*

There has been no shortage of innovative return programmes attempted over the past two and a half years. Although most agencies are working in an environment of funding shortfalls, the failure of the programmes cannot be attributed primarily to resource shortages. Rather, the problem lies in generating a self-sustaining return process, which mobilizes local resources and goodwill behind the goal of improving the return environment. So long as this is absent, direct international pressure results in very limited numbers of returns. This section provides a brief overview of the main strategies used to date.

2.1. *Reconstruction-driven return*

Reconstruction-driven return is the typical case of a current minority return project. There is no effective legal framework for removing displaced persons from houses which they are occupying illegally. Nor is it generally desirable to achieve return at the expense of further displacement of others. International programmes have therefore focused on homes which are empty because of war-damage, making housing reconstruction the key element of most minority return programmes. Considerable care is needed to identify appropriate areas, houses and beneficiaries for participation in a programme. To minimize political opposition and avoid threatening the majority population, the return area is usually an empty, isolated village of no economic or strategic significance. Local authorities are persuaded to accept a specified number of returns through political pressure or economic inducements. Equivalent sums are spent on the majority population in the surrounding areas to avoid popular resentment against returnees. Houses which are appropriate for reconstruction are identified, and must be clustered together for the security and well-being of returnees, and to minimize the cost of reconnecting the infrastructure. Beneficiaries must be identified who are genuinely committed to returning, rather than merely accepting the benefit of the reconstruction work and then selling their properties. To make the return sustainable, some form of community development must be undertaken, so that the returnees have access to health care, education and other basic services. Some programmes also include temporary employment creation programmes, to provide the returnees with some income during the resettlement phase.

The complexity of programmes of this type makes them extremely resource intensive. The number of factors which must be co-ordinated in a successful programme means that this modality of return has a limited sphere of operation. It does not offer any means of returning people to occupied housing. It is dependent on the supply of damaged housing suitable for reconstruction, which will diminish over time. Experience shows that it is very difficult to recreate a viable rural community in this way, or to offer returnees any economic security. Overall, the occupancy rate of property which has been reconstructed has been around 60%.[54] Many of those who have returned in this way are elderly people in rural areas, who exhibit the greatest attachment to their land. Returnees usually remain dependent on family elsewhere to support them, and return to the nearest population centre of their own ethnic group to obtain necessary goods and services. If there is no economic activity in the immediate area, young people and families do not remain for long in their properties, relocating as soon as possible in search of employment.

Perhaps the most unfortunate aspect of these programmes is that the entire return process must be managed and funded by an international agency. The resources of the local community are not mobilized at all. In fact, the majority population of the return area also absorbs international resources through economic conditionality and other demands. Investments of this type are only appropriate if they generate a sustained cycle of return, giving other pre-war residents from the area the confidence to return and rebuild their own properties. There is little sign that this is occurring. As a result, it is unlikely that reconstruction-driven return programmes will continue on any scale beyond 1999.

2.2. *Incentive-driven return*

A second strategy has been to create incentives for local authorities by linking willingness to accept minority returns with reconstruction and development projects. Various general problems with using economic conditionality in Bosnia were outlined in the previous Part. Of several different schemes which have been attempted, the best articulated and publicized has been the UNHCR Open Cities initiative. Under this scheme, local authorities are given the opportunity to declare themselves publicly to be open to minority return, and therefore become candidates for increased levels of reconstruction aid. Although this concept was initially greeted enthusiastically by the international community, its results have been disappointing. One recent study found no general linkage between Open City status and either levels of donor funding or levels of return.[55] Several Open Cities have seen declining rates of minority return, or international funding, or both, since the confirmation of their status. Declarations of openness do not necessarily translate into positive actions, and displaced persons and refugees are extremely sceptical of promises from local authorities.

Perhaps the most fundamental problem is that economic conditionality does not give rise to any general, lasting pattern of incentives which could lead to self-sustaining returns. On the contrary, the danger is that local

[54] UNHCR estimates provided to the author.
[55] ICG, op. cit. above (n.48).

authorities come to expect a *quid pro quo* from the international community for all returns. Five of the Open Cities—Gorazde, Konjic, Vogosca, Bihac and Busovaca—received altogether in excess of US$50 million in aid in 1996 and 1997, while their total minority returns for the same period were approximately 1,600 individuals.[56] The danger is clear: the international community may establish a 'going rate' for returns on a case by case basis which is far in excess of what it can or should pay.

2.3. *Managed return*

Managed return initiatives are those where the international community identifies certain specific individuals who wish to return to their homes, and puts pressure on local authorities to allow those returns. In the first months after Dayton, UNHCR commenced a number of pilot projects for minority return in strategic areas, working closely with local authorities and monitoring success on an individual basis. In many cases the returns were met with obstruction and violence. Some observers have been concerned that individuals were encouraged to return into dangerous situations, believing that their security would be guaranteed internationally.[57]

The International Supervisor appointed under the Brcko arbitration award has also undertaken a managed return project. Using his powers under the award, the Supervisor created a Return Commission to approve return cases, and successfully returned several hundred displaced persons from the Federation to empty properties on the Republika Srpska side of the Zone of Separation, but has not achieved any returns into Brcko town itself, nor returned any Serbs from Brcko to their homes in the Federation. Perhaps the most ambitious managed return programme has been undertaken in Sarajevo, following an international conference in February 1998 at which senior international politicians demanded 20,000 minority returns in 1998, the removal of legal and administrative obstacles to return, and an improvement in living conditions for minorities.[58] The conference identified the misallocation of housing stocks as the most substantial obstacle to minority returns. In Sarajevo and all other major cities, many thousands of the original inhabitants took possession of more than one housing unit during the war, and now refuse to return possession of the properties to those who fled the conflict.[59] A Sarajevo Housing Committee, under an

[56] Ibid.

[57] All international agencies are extremely careful not to offer security guarantees to returnees. However, where returnees meet in advance with committees comprised of OHR, UNHCR, International Police Task Force and SFOR representatives, they will inevitably be given the impression that they will be supported by these agencies after they return.

[58] The Sarajevo Declaration, 3 February 1998.

[59] One report calculates that at least 13,000 former residents of Sarajevo have illegal possession of more than one home: International Crisis Group, 'Too Little Too Late: Implementation of the Sarajevo Declaration' (unpublished paper, September 1998).

international chair but with the involvement of local authorities, was created to oversee the management of housing. The Committee finds itself increasingly called upon to manage a situation over which it has little influence. It demanded that the city authorities produce a list of 2,000 apartments which were held by double occupants, which would be targeted for evictions. To date, only twenty-three evictions have resulted from this initiative. In total, only 1,200 minorities have returned to Sarajevo since the international conference. The main donors participating in the return conference suspended projects to the value of US$20 million from the Sarajevo aid budget, because of the failure to make satisfactory progress on minority return.

The process of managed return encounters all the problems of managing the local political process outlined in the previous Part. The experience of the Sarajevo Housing Committee shows that even maintaining an effective monitoring system over the local authorities is extremely difficult, and that when they have no interest in compliance, there is little that can be done to compel them. When their motivation comes purely from international pressure, the best that can be hoped for is that local authorities will offer the minimum possible compliance. When a specific number of return cases are demanded of them, they will perceive that as the limit of their obligation. Overall, it is a strategic error for the international community to purport to take over the management of a complex situation, which it has no capacity to control. Its limitations will quickly become apparent to local leaders, and its influence will decline.

2.4. *Return through administrative process*

Another approach has been to focus on the procedural side of return, creating institutional mechanisms that process return claims on an individual basis and make rulings on the right to return. The strategy is to confront local authorities with evidence of the property rights of individual families. One mechanism was created in the Dayton Agreement—the Commission for Real Property Claims of Displaced Persons and Refugees established under Annex 7 ('the Property Commission')—which has final authority to rule on property rights, and the power to disregard laws which are obstructive of return. In 1997, special International Housing Commissions were created to process applications to return to the Zone of Separation. In 1998, following pressure from the Peace Implementation Council, the Federation Refugee Ministry issued an instruction to all municipalities to establish Municipal Return Offices to receive applications for return, and establish a database of properties. In April 1998, after heavy international pressure, the Federation Parliament adopted new laws on abandoned property which provide for another administrative mechanism at municipal level to process return claims. These laws oblige municipal authorities to evict temporary occupants and allow original inhabitants to return within specified time limits.

These administrative mechanisms have made little contribution to the return process. Where the international community has control over decision-making, as in the case of the Property Commission, the problem becomes one of enforcement. Because the obstacle to return is not, in reality, a dispute over property title, a binding decision on property rights is of little immediate help. The local authorities responsible for enforcement are frequently the same individuals responsible for ethnic cleansing in the first place, and have a strong interest in preventing return. A Property Commission decision is more likely to be useful for proving title for the purpose of disposing of property, particularly where property records have been destroyed or tampered with. Where the decision-making process is left to local authorities, as with the Municipal Return Offices or the claims procedures under the Federation laws, there is ample scope for the process to be obstructed. In September 1998, the High Representative used his Bonn powers to impose an extension to the time period for claiming apartments, because fewer than half of the potential claimants had been able to register their claims. Forms of obstruction included harassment and intimidation, prohibitive filing fees, refusal to accept claims lodged through personal representatives, and requiring claimants to submit documentation that was not accessible to them. Because of the intense political pressures on local officials not to allow returns, both from their own constituencies and from the nationalist parties, it is difficult to imagine enforcement of return decisions taking place in significant numbers. There is a danger that these administrative mechanisms can become a smoke-screen, focusing international attention on bureaucratic mechanisms rather than substantive progress.

3. *The Relationship between Reintegration and Reconciliation*

This overview of return strategies shows that there have been substantial and sustained attempts by the international community to achieve ethnic reintegration. The political consensus behind the need for minority return has been firm. Some US$5 billion has been pledged for housing and infrastructure reconstruction, currently representing the biggest development programme per head of population in any country of the world. Many innovative programmes have been tried, both to achieve return directly and to create procedural mechanisms to facilitate return. It is of course always possible to point to missed opportunities. More arrests of war criminals, better co-ordination of economic conditionality, a slower rate of refugee return from Western Europe or more focused political pressure may all have helped the return process. However, the missed opportunities are not the key to the problem. International efforts have been strong, consistent and even innovative, but have not succeeded in creating a sustained movement towards minority return. The lessons of the last two years of efforts are that the international community is not in control of the post-war demographics of Bosnia and Herzegovina, and cannot enforce ethnic reintegration. Ethnic separatism is not simply a matter of the misbehaviour of local nationalist leaders. There are deep-rooted social and political forces which resist integrated governance and living conditions. No matter what resources the international community channels into the intervention, it cannot replace the local political system with direct governance, nor achieve enough control over local elites to make them act contrary to the way in which they perceive their strategic interests.

All the evidence suggests that *ethnic reintegration* through the return of minorities may not be an effective strategy of achieving *ethnic reconciliation*. To resolve the current impasse, what is needed is a vision of ethnic reconciliation which is broader than reversing the immediate effects of ethnic cleansing. International tactics should shift away from demanding the implementation of international policies by nationalist leaders, towards developing the conditions that would give ethnic elites a genuine interest in governing on behalf of all the ethnic groups. The Dayton agreement provides a constitutional model in which ethnic elites can undertake joint governance despite their strategic differences. However, the immediate post-war environment is characterized by tight control over political expression, inflexible assertion of group interests, and general intransigence towards inter-group dialogue. For the constitutional model to become operative in these conditions, the elites must have incentives to co-operate constructively with each other. Annexing a written constitution to a peace treaty establishes the legal basis for the system, but does not set it in motion. Nor can the international community intervene directly to supply the incentives for co-operation. The social forces which make the system operative must emerge autonomously and from the ground up, perhaps over a considerable period of time.

The path to genuine reconciliation must begin with the normalization of living conditions, easing the insecurity of ordinary people. Alleviating the fear of persecution, loss of housing and economic hardship among the population would have an immediate effect in weakening the platform of political extremists. As more people return to a stable living environment and ordinary life expectations, there will be an easing of pressure in the political and social environment, allowing it to become more diverse. Interests which are not articulated purely in terms of ethnicity will begin to find expression. There will be gradual development of social strata and divisions which are not solely ethnic in nature, based on class, regional, educational or other differences. Over time, this will result in a gradual moderation and broadening of the political sphere. People will look to their leaders to provide prosperity, rather than immediate protection.

The dominant nationalist parties may respond to this change in environment by becoming more conciliatory towards other ethnic groups, and developing genuine policy platforms.

Economic forces will play an important part in this process. The first step on the path to reconciliation is an increase in economic contacts across ethnic lines, which can be driven by individual financial interest, even without developed institutional support. Economic contacts among the ethnic groups occurred to a remarkable degree even during the war, and trade has no necessary connection with peace-building. However, increased commercial activity has already restored freedom of movement throughout the Federation, and is gradually making the Inter-Entity Boundary Line more permeable. Trade increases the volume of personal contacts between the ethnic groups, building relationships of trust and the possibilities for joint activity. This gradually decreases the security dilemmas between the groups, undermining the political rhetoric of extremists. It is probably inevitable that nationalist parties will continue to dominate politics for a long period of time, while a democratic political culture gradually emerges. The path to democratization is long and slow, and it will be a long time before non-nationalist parties are in a position to offer a credible alternative government. However, in the meantime, economic development will give rise to common interests among the elites in the existing nationalist parties. The more the ethnic groups become economically interdependent, the greater the cost to nationalist leaders of reverting to open conflict.

The physical reintegration of the population into ethnically mixed living areas may be the last step along this path, some years into the future. The psychological effects of civil war and genocide are not easily overcome. For the time being, it is difficult to convince the victims of atrocities that their security is not threatened by the return of members of the responsible ethnic group. Similarly, returnees may fear retribution from other ethnic groups for crimes committed during the war which are attributed to their ethnic group as a whole. Of course this pattern varies in different locations. In some areas, war fatigue and the desire to resume ordinary lives are stronger than ethnic tensions, and a degree of ethnic reintegration is feasible immediately. However in general, the psychological obstacles to reintegration are enduring. If so, it is more productive to promote contacts among the groups in public spaces and neutral zones. International reconciliation initiatives that develop neutral places such as markets have been quite successful. Mixed residential areas have not yet been successful.

One important contribution which the international community can make to the reconciliation process is the arrest and prosecution of war criminals. War crimes trials also have an important symbolic function. The sense of injustice which follows unpunished atrocities reinforces and exaggerates group divisions, because victims blame their suffering not only on the specific perpetrators of the crimes, but on the other ethnic group as a whole. War crimes trials direct blame and resentment back to the responsible individuals, provide an outlet for resentment, and give public recognition of suffering, all of which are essential for a process of healing to begin. The process is equally important for the ethnic group to which the war criminals belong. It acts as a symbolic rejection of the crimes, opening up the possibility for reconciliation.

4. *The Problem of Property Rights*

The movement of population, whether refugee return or population relocation, is complicated by the current breakdown in the rule of law concerning property. The loss of property is the most lasting humanitarian consequence of the war, and the most widespread source of human rights abuses. Displaced persons throughout the country are living in abandoned properties, either illegally or with temporary occupancy rights allocated by local authorities, and their lack of permanent accommodation makes them extremely vulnerable to manipulation by nationalist extremists. The scale of the displacement means that there are very few properties that are both habitable and vacant. During and since the war, all three ethnic groups used property rights to cement the results of ethnic cleansing, erecting legal and administrative barriers in the way of return. The result is a highly complex and unsatisfactory property legal system, with elements of the old laws, wartime regulations and the Dayton Agreement all vying for precedence, the property record system substantially broken down, and the courts functioning poorly.

With so much of the population now illegally occupying property, re-establishing the rule of law will be one of the most difficult challenges of the coming years. As the prospects of large-scale minority return fade, the need to address illegal occupancy and the denial of property rights becomes more apparent. One solution favoured by the Serb authorities and many local people is compensation for lost property. Annex 7 of the Dayton Agreement contains a mechanism for compensation to be determined and awarded by the Property Commission, which becomes the successor in title to any individual who is compensated. It may take the form of a monetary award or bond, drawn against a Refugees and Displaced Persons Property Fund, and may be funded through grants or by the activities of the Property Commission trading with the properties it receives pursuant to compensation awards.[60] The system has never become operative, because no funds are available for compensation, and

[60] Annex 7, Chapter Two, Article XII, para.5

the Property Commission has no means of gaining possession of abandoned properties. While there is unlikely ever to be cash compensation funded from international sources, the Property Fund mechanism may nonetheless have a role. If compensation took the form of the right to purchase other properties from the Property Fund, then the system would become a form of clearing house for property exchanges.

A simpler solution may be to improve the property market to the point where ordinary transactions accomplish the recognition or redistribution of property title. Although sales and exchanges are taking place, the legal system is not currently providing sufficient protection for a property market to operate fairly or efficiently. Improving the regulatory framework is one contribution the international community might be able to make, as well as initiatives such as public education to protect individuals from fraud or exploitation. Transactions are presently inhibited by the difficulty of proving title, because of numerous political and practical problems with the property registration system. A mechanism such as the Property Commission claims process may be useful here, providing individuals with definitive proof of title. A certificate of title would also give individuals the security to delay any decision on their property until the political situation and the property market have stabilized further. It might also be used to promote lease agreements, which allow for recognition of property rights without accomplishing a permanent redistribution of title. An essential element of property reform, although too complex a topic to consider here, is the process of privatizing socially owned housing. Close international involvement will be needed to prevent corrupt distribution of housing.

For the time being, proposals such as these are politically unacceptable because of a widespread fear that allowing population relocation to take place on a permanent basis would eliminate further prospects of minority return. There is certainly a real risk that any such mechanism would be exploited by nationalist authorities, who would make sure that minorities had no genuine choice in the exercise of their property rights. However, in practice there is no clear 'either-or' relationship between minority return and reallocation of property rights. Assisting displaced persons to acquire permanent housing among their own ethnic group may have the effect of making the property they currently inhabit available for minority return. For most displaced persons, their original home represents their entire store of wealth. If they were able to receive either alternative permanent housing or a reasonable sale price for their pre-war property, they would be given the means to solve their own displacement. As they return into acceptable living conditions with ordinary life expectations, their opposition to the return of minorities will decrease. Returning displaced persons into normal living conditions is an essential first step in the political evolution of all three ethnic areas.

Part IV: The Path Ahead

The final part of this article draws together the conclusions made so far as to the obstacles encountered in the intervention to date, and tries to define a constructive role for the international community in Bosnia and Herzegovina in the future. It offers policy directions in the two main areas considered in the article: first, the appropriate level of involvement for the international community in the formal institutions and the national political sphere, and second, the role of the international community in ethnic reconciliation.

1. *The International Community and Bosnian Political Life*

In the first area, it is clear that the international community has become too deeply engaged in the national political dynamic. Its efforts have been well intentioned, directed at putting in place the Dayton constitutional model with its various techniques for containing ethnic conflict. The model has proved difficult to implement, owing to the low level of loyalty to the State of Bosnia and Herzegovina on the part of ethnic elites. Lacking any real incentive to co-operate, the nationalist parties have participated only because of constant international pressure. This has forced the international community to become the central pillar of the Dayton structure, unable to withdraw without risking State collapse. Frustration with the slow progress has led the international community to take an increasingly interventionist role, using the powers of the High Representative to remove obstructions to the peace process. As a result, the international community finds itself undertaking the responsibilities of governance on behalf of the institutions, with little prospect of making them independent.

To develop an effective strategy for creating a self-sustaining State, the international community must take a longer-term perspective. Planning has for too long been dominated by the imminent withdrawal of international military forces. Once it becomes clear that the international military and civilian presence will remain for a sustained period, more effective strategic planning becomes possible. There is a need for a public commitment to maintain some form of military and civilian presence over at least a ten-year period.

Current experiments with trusteeship should be abandoned in favour of smaller numbers of higher quality interventions. An example of an appropriate measure might be the High Representative's decision to create a uniform license-plate system, which had an immediate effect on improving freedom of movement throughout the country. In that case, the decision offered long-term benefits for ethnic reconciliation which warranted the irregular procedure for its adoption. By contrast, the High Representative should avoid taking decisions on complex regulatory fields, where responsibility for implementing the legislation will be thrust back upon the international community. In such cases, the international role should be limited to facilitating agreement among the ethnic groups, and providing technical support and advice wherever it is needed. The international community should avoid being drawn into local politics. It has little or no capacity to control local events, and should not attempt to do so. The international community should define a more limited role for itself in the national institutions, and then discipline itself to keep to that role, whatever the provocation of the day.

The international military and civilian presence should gradually decrease in intensity over a ten-year period. During this period, the military presence can evolve considerably, becoming more focused on crowd control and security functions, along the lines of the Multi-National Specialized Units deployed since August 1998. Heavy combat capacity can be moved elsewhere, on the understanding that it will return to Bosnia rapidly if the need arises. Throughout this period, the international community must remain ready to act decisively to remove major threats to the peace process. Secession attempts within Bosnia and Herzegovina could rapidly reverse the gains of the peace process. Interference in Bosnian internal affairs from the Federal Republic of Yugoslavia and Croatia could undermine the State. High-level political, economic and military pressure should be reserved for responding to major threats of this nature. In general, however, international civilian involvement in the functioning of the State should become less intrusive in form, concentrating on technical assistance and institutional support. Assistance should be oriented towards economic and social development, in common with the support offered to other transition economies. Direct links with other governments of the region can offer a stabilizing influence, as well as building the capacity of government institutions. As the work of the special institutions created for the Bosnian intervention comes to a close, European institutions should take over their remaining functions, ensuring that the international commitment to Bosnia does not come to a complete halt. Membership of institutions such as the Council of Europe, and perhaps ultimately the European Union itself, can be used not only as an incentive for moderate politics, but as a tool for improving the quality of governance. Lasting European engagement with the development of Bosnia is essential for progress on issues such as minority rights, judicial and policing institutions, social policy, and the development of a modern economic regulatory framework.

2. *The International Community and Ethnic Reconciliation*

The second area in which conclusions are offered is the international role in promoting ethnic reconciliation, and the search for permanent solutions for refugees and displaced persons. The two years of efforts devoted to minority return were a necessary moral response to ethnic cleansing. However, despite consuming enormous resources, minority return programmes have not been successful in generating any sustained movement towards ethnic reintegration. There are deep-rooted strategic and psychological obstacles to return, which are beyond the capacity of the international community to control. When the international community tries to force reintegration, it increases fear and tension among the ethnic groups, hardening the resistance to international goals. The impasse between the moral necessity of opposing ethnic cleansing on the one hand, and the practical impossibility of achieving ethnic reintegration on the other, has left the international community in a period of strategic limbo, repeating resource-intensive programmes that have proved a consistent failure.

The international community should focus on the longer-term goal of ethnic reconciliation, rather than the immediate goal of ethnic reintegration. Reconciliation is a process that occurs from the ground up, in response to social and economic development. A reconciliation strategy involves a shift of emphasis away from controlling the conduct of national politics, towards developing the post-war social environment. International involvement in ethnic reconciliation can only be indirect in nature and gradual in effect. Continuing military presence is important, to provide a secure environment for social and economic activity. Restoring the rule of law and repairing judicial and police institutions is an essential step. Independence of the media is crucial, and the prosecution of war criminals would have a positive effect. The development of a healthy network of civil society institutions helps to promote alternatives to ethnic extremism. Economic forces play a key role in reconciliation, providing incentives for increased interaction among the ethnic groups. All forms of economic development assistance are therefore important, including reconstruction of housing and infrastructure. A comprehensive list of these areas is neither possible nor necessary, as all forms of social and economic development assistance make an indirect contribution over time to ethnic reconciliation.

Strategy on refugees and displaced persons should focus on normalizing living conditions for the greatest number of people as soon as possible. Large numbers of displaced persons living in poverty and insecurity are a major destabilizing factor, contributing to the power of extremist politicians and retarding the process of ethnic reintegration. It is essential to find permanent solutions for their displacement. Return to home of origin should remain the preferred solution, but is not likely to solve the bulk of the displacement problem. The international community should support return wherever it is occurring, but be wary of trying to force return in the face of local opposition. Direct confrontation with extreme nationalist leaders should be avoided, because of the risk of contributing to the environment of fear and insecurity which sustains their power. The international community should recognize that in many instances, reintegration of the population will be the last step along the path to reconciliation. Much of the displacement problem will have to be solved by resettlement, principally to majority areas offering employment opportunities. The international community should become involved in facilitating this process, minimizing humanitarian and human rights problems along the way. New housing will be needed to house refugees in Western Europe who cannot return to Eastern Republika Srpska. As far as possible, local resources should be mobilized to assist with the resettlement process. The most effective way of doing this is to assist displaced persons to recover the value of their lost property through sale or exchange. This is essential to restoring the rule of law in property, and in most cases represents the only possible remedy for the most enduring human rights and humanitarian consequence of displacement.

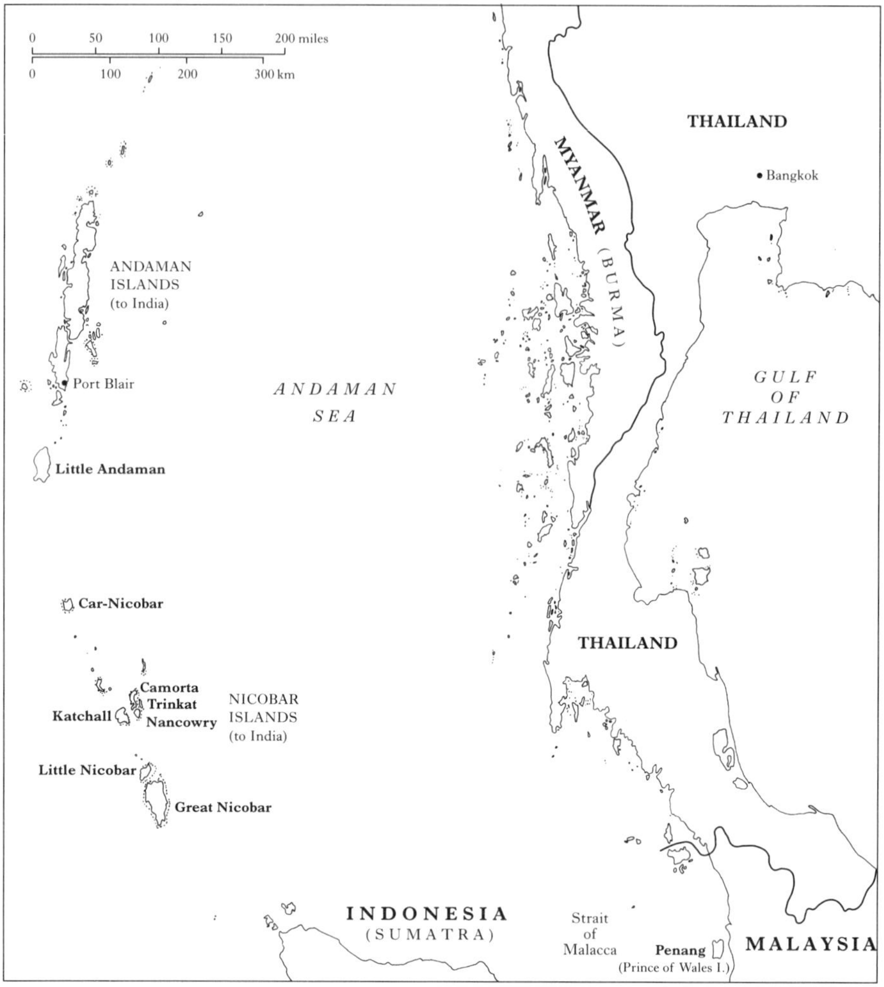

Sketch-map showing the location of the Nicobar Islands

THE BRITISH ACQUISITION OF THE NICOBAR ISLANDS, 1869: A POSSIBLE EXAMPLE OF ABANDONMENT OF TERRITORIAL SOVEREIGNTY*

By GEOFFREY MARSTON[1]

I. Introduction

In the Indian Ocean north-west of the Indonesian island of Sumatra lies a chain of islands called the Nicobars, which are part of the Andaman and Nicobar Islands, a Territory of the Union of India. The Nicobars extend over nearly 200 miles from north-west to south-east and comprise three parts: in the north is the isolated island of Car-Nicobar; south-east of Car-Nicobar is a central group whose principal components are Katchall, Camorta, Trinkat, Nancowry, Teressa and Tillanchong; and further to the south-east lie Great Nicobar and Little Nicobar. It is proposed in this paper to recount how the Nicobar Islands were brought under British sovereignty in 1869 and in so doing to bring to light a possible, though controversial, example of an abandonment of territorial sovereignty.

II. The Period to 1841

A map shows the strategic importance of the Nicobars as a whole: potentially the chain controls the route in and out of the north end of the Strait of Malacca. The likelihood that vessels sailing between Europe or the Indian mainland and the Straits Settlements would pass near to the Nicobars was probably the reason why they received more attention from European Powers than their size and natural assets warranted.[2]

[1] LL M, Ph.D. (Lond.), Lecturer in Law, University of Cambridge; Fellow of Sidney Sussex College, Cambridge. The Crown Copyright documents cited are located in two archives: the Public Record Office, London (PRO) and the India Office Records in the British Library, London (IOR). In order to improve clarity, some abbreviations and contractions used in the originals have been expanded.

[2] On the other hand, missionary activity rather than commercial or strategic considerations could have been the main reason for the settlement. One writer has stated: 'The history of the Nicobars since the eighteenth century till the occupation of the islands by the British in 1869 is a long record of unsuccessful attempts of Christian missionaries to colonise and convert the islanders' (L. P. Mathur, *Kala Pani: History of Andaman and Nicobar Islands* (1985), p. 226).

Conflicting claims to sovereignty were made. On 5 June 1775, a Dutchman, William Bolts, was granted by the Empress of the Holy Roman Empire, Maria Theresa, a charter to found a commercial company and 'to take possession in the name of the Empress and her successors of all territories, settlements and grounds which he might acquire from Indian Princes in favor of all subjects of the Empress disposed to carry on trade with India'. Furthermore, Bolts was authorized 'to enter into such negotiations and conclude such agreements with the princes and rulers of India, as might seem calculated to promote the interests of Her Majesty's subjects engaged in commerce in those distant regions; further, to take possession of all territories, lands and settlements which he might be in a position to acquire in this way . . . '. In September 1776, Bolts set sail from Trieste in the Imperial ship *Joseph und Theresia*, formerly the East Indiaman *Earl of Lincoln*. After a voyage around the Cape of Good Hope to Madagascar, the captain of the vessel, Bennet, founded a factory on the Nicobars between April and September 1778 and 'with the consent of the natives' took possession of the Islands of Nancoveri (Nancowry), Souri (either Chowry or Car-Nicobar), Tricutta (Trinkat), and Catchiout (Katchall) in the name of His Majesty the Emperor Joseph II.[3]

The Austrian factory seems to have been short-lived.[4] However, another European Power, Denmark, established an earlier and less transitory settlement on the Nicobars. According to Danish accounts,[5] the Nicobars were taken into possession in 1756 by the Danish East India Company operating from the Danish settlement at Tranquebar south of Madras, having been ceded by a formal act of the native chiefs. Although the history remains obscure, and there is a report of the Danish

[3] The account of the Austrian expedition and annexation is taken from *Selections from the Records of the Government of India, Home Department*: No. LXXVII, *Papers relating to the Nicobar Islands*, Calcutta, 1870, pp. 197–8 (IOR: fiche 130). This contains extracts (in English translation) from *Journal of the Voyage of the Imperial Ship Joseph und Theresia to the new Austrian Colonies in Asia and Africa*, addressed by Nicholaus Fontana, late Ship's Surgeon, to Herr Brambilla, Surgeon to the Emperor, Protochyrurgus of the Army, etc.; translated from the Italian manuscript into German by Joseph Eyerle, 1787, Leipzig, 'in der Buchhandlung der Gelehrten'. For an account of the expedition based on Austrian archival sources, see Franz von Pollack-Parnau, *Eine österreichisch-ostindische Handelscompagnie 1775–1785: ein Beitrag zur österreichischen Wirtschaftsgeschichte unter Maria Theresia und Joseph II* (1927).

[4] But it was not forgotten. In 1858, the Austrian frigate *Novara* visited the Nicobars. The official account of the voyage, having considered local claims to fly the English flag over the islands to be unfounded, declared: 'Thus, as far as the climate or the claims of other Governments are concerned, there appears to exist no reason why the flag of Austria should not again float, and that permanently, on these shores, where it was once unfurled 85 years ago' (*Selections from the Records of the Government of India, Home Department*: No. LXXVII, *Papers relating to the Nicobar Islands*, Calcutta, 1878, p. 206 (IOR: fiche 130)).

[5] See, for example, letter from the Danish Governor of Serampore to the Government of Bengal, 15 February 1841 (PRO: FO 22/139, ff. 237r–8r).

settlement on the Nicobars having been abandoned in 1768,[6] there is evidence that it continued to exist in an attenuated fashion, consisting mainly of missionaries and provisioned from Tranquebar, until war between Denmark and Britain occurred. British forces occupied the Danish possessions on the mainland of India from 1801 to 1802 and again from 1808 to 1814. In early 1809 British forces removed to Madras the small Danish garrison on the Nicobars. When peace was re-established, the Danish possessions on the mainland of India were restored. Their Governor then applied for the restoration of the Nicobars. The question arose whether the Nicobars had ever been properly under Danish control. By a letter dated 26 September 1816, the Government of the Presidency of Madras notified the Court of Directors of the East India Company that they had told the Danish Governor of Tranquebar 'that the British Government had not held any possession on those Islands, and that it rested with His Excellency to renew the Danish Establishments there or not, as he thought proper'.[7]

III. The Events of the 1840s

Denmark did not hurry to re-assert its position in the Nicobars. It was not until the arrival of a letter dated 15 February 1841 sent by the Governor of the Danish settlement of Serampore, P. Hanson, to the Government of the Presidency of Bengal that the British authorities in India were officially advised of what had happened in the period since the Napoleonic wars. Hanson sought details of 'summary justice' meted out to inhabitants of the island of Camorta by the captain of Her Majesty's sloop *Cruizer* for an alleged murderous and piratical attack on a London whaler. Hanson, who considered that the Nicobarese were 'generally inoffensive', continued:[8]

> The Nicobar Islands were taken possession of by the Danish Government on the lst of January 1756, and have been ceded by a formal act of the Native Chiefs at Great Nicobar and on the Islands adjacent the Nancowry Harbour. Several establishments have been formed first at Sambalong or Great Nicobar and afterwards at Camorta and Nancowry. A small Military Guard was kept up at the latter Island until the war in 1808, and the occupation of the Danish Colonies broke off the communication. In 1816 the Government of Madras informed the Danish Government of Tranquebar that the Islands had not been occupied by the British during the war. In the year 1831 a new Settlement was formed at Camorta but withdrawn in 1838 on account of the insalubrity of the climate.

[6] Mentioned in the précis prepared by the Government of India in 1856 (IOR: P/188/56 [Home Department, Public Proceedings of 6 August 1858, No. 81] (see n. 26, below). See also E. Thornton, *A Gazetteer of the Territories under the Government of the East India Company and of the Native States on the Continent of India* (1857), p. 702.

[7] IOR: L/P & S/6/262, p. 316; also in FO 22/139, f. 236r.

[8] Ibid.

The Danish Government have however not given up their claims to the sovereignty of the Islands which had been acknowledged by the natives at several periods, and some of the Chiefs at the Islands of Camorta and Nancowry do as far as I am informed hoist the Danish colors.

The Governor of Bengal, Lord Auckland, writing from Fort William, now Calcutta, enclosed Hanson's letter in a communication dated 3 March 1841 to the Court of Directors of the East India Company in which he also enclosed copies of the correspondence of 1816. Lord Auckland pointed out that the Nicobars lay 'directly in the track of vessels bound to the Straits from this Port' and concluded:[9]

Whether any formal restoration of the flag took place is not at present known. It would seem from the present Letter of the Governor of Serampore that several years ago after that restoration, a new Danish Settlement was formed on one of the islands of the Nicobars, but subsequently withdrawn.

The Court of Directors sent the correspondence to the Board of Commissioners for the Affairs of India (commonly known as the Board of Control or the India Board) in London which in turn sent it to the Foreign Office on 6 July 1841.[10] Within the Foreign Office the India Board's letter was endorsed in pencil: 'To await application from Danish Government'.[11] As no such application seems to have been made, the matter fell dormant.

By an agreement[12] made in Calcutta on 22 February 1845 between the Governor General of India and the Governor of the Danish possessions in India, Denmark agreed to transfer 'the Danish Settlements on the Continent of India' to the British East India Company for a sum of rupees. The transfer comprised Tranquebar, Serampore (also called Frederiksnagore), and a small area at Balasore. The Nicobars were not mentioned in the agreement.

The question of the sovereignty over the Nicobars was agitated, however, a few months later when the Secretary to the British Legation in Copenhagen, Peter Browne, in a despatch dated 23 June 1845, advised the Foreign Office that a Danish corvette, the *Galatea*, had left the city on a two-year scientific journey round the world under the command of Captain Steen Billé. He wrote:[13] 'My own opinion is that the principal object of the expedition is to ascertain the *value of the Nicobar Islands* and in what way they might be made available to Denmark, especially if they can be employed as a Station for Steamers, (to take in provisions and coals,) which in the event of the trade to China being extended, may eventually be of some moment.'

On 23 July 1845, Browne sent a longer despatch in which he advised

[9] PRO: FO 22/139, f. 234r–v.
[10] Ibid., f. 230.
[11] Ibid., f. 231v.
[12] *Consolidated Treaty Series*, vol. 98, p. 69.
[13] Browne to Foreign Office, No. 6 of 1845 (PRO: FO 22/149, f. 147r–v (original emphasis)).

the Foreign Office that he had well-grounded reasons for believing that Billé had been commissioned and empowered 'to treat as to the sale of these Islands before his return, and at all events to take the usual steps to establish the claims of his Country to them'.[14] Browne considered that '[u]ndoubtedly according to the received opinions of the most reputed Writers on international law and rights, Denmark has long since ceased to possess any title to them, having administered to these Islands in none of the usual ways, on the contrary, having for a series of years completely abandoned them'. Browne added that had his Mission been consulted by the British Government while the negotiations for the transfer of the Danish mainland possessions were pending 'it would have been suggested to include the Nicobar Islands in the sum to be paid for Tranquebar, a requirement which it would have been unreasonable to refuse, as had the Danish Government at all valued this Possession, they would not have treated it with such utter neglect'. He considered that the Nicobars might be suitable as a steamboat station between Hindustan and China and he was persuaded that 'even now Denmark will dispose of her title to them on very reasonable conditions' without the risk of much competition for them. Recounting that a few years ago a Danish merchant captain had entered into 'a sort of understanding' with the chief of the island of Bali, Browne concluded:[15]

I know not how your Lordship may like to see this principle extended, of Nations wandering over the oceans, not in search of new lands which they appropriate by the Right of Priority of Discovery, but to take under their Protection and assume authority over lands already well known, from the ignorance of the Natives of which they extract compacts for a small consideration, afterwards to be disposed of, at an advanced Price.

Denmark can have no direct or natural advantage from thus getting into her Possession scattered spots of land so very distant from her own shores; what her object therefore can be in taking such a step (if I have been rightly informed as to her intentions) it is difficult with certainty to assert, but of this I am certain, that if England cannot prevent the establishment of such a system, it will not be long before she feels its inconvenience.

No action on Browne's two despatches seems to have been taken by the Foreign Office.

Meanwhile, the ship *L'Espiègle* under a British captain, H. Lewis, visited the Nicobars with a Danish surveying expedition. The expedition leader, H. Busch, having mentioned in his journal that no trace of the earlier Danish settlement was found on Little Nicobar, recorded that the Danish flag was hoisted on the islands of Pulo Caudul, Little Nicobar and Great Nicobar and that the Danish ensign was left in charge of the headman of Pulo Caudul with the following certificate dated 5 May 1845 and signed by Busch and Lewis:[16]

[14] Browne to Foreign Office, No. 13 of 1845 (ibid., ff. 172–7).

[15] Ibid., ff. 175v–176v.

[16] *Selections from the Records of the Government of India, Home Department*: No. LXXVII, *Papers relating to the Nicobar Islands*, Calcutta, 1870, p. 27 (IOR: fiche 128). Mathur (op. cit. above (n. 2), p. 232) describes *L'Espiègle* as 'English'.

To all persons who may visit the Islands of Pulo Caudul and Great Nicobar, we do hereby certify that, having this day hoisted the Danish Ensign on these two islands, we have resumed possession thereof in the name of His Danish Majesty, King Christian VIII; we have entrusted the flag to the headman of Pulo Caudul, by name Tomorra, in order that he may guard the same until further measures can be taken for the contemplated occupation and colonization of the said island.

Although it was stated in a summary of events compiled by the Government of India in 1856[17] that the expedition had been organized 'with the concurrence of the Danish Government' by the Danish Consul in Calcutta, D.C. Mackey, it is not certain on the evidence found that Busch had Danish governmental authority to resume possession as he did.

After the *Galatea* had returned to Copenhagen in September 1847, the British Minister there, Sir H. W. Wynn, reported on 29 December 1847 that the Danish King, on the advice of his Admiralty, had approved the final abandonment of the Nicobars and that a corvette was to be sent in a few days to bring off those of Billé's crew left on the islands.[18] Wynn considered that this intelligence about abandonment was important 'as Her Majesty's Government may think it advisable to take some measures to prevent their becoming a refuge for Pirates'. Within the Foreign Office, Wynn's despatch was endorsed with the pencilled question, written probably by the Parliamentary Under-Secretary of State, Edward Stanley: 'Where are they?', to which question an official appended the reply on 7 January 1848: 'The Nicobar Islands are situated in a line between the Northwestern point of Sumatra and the mouths of the Ganges'.[19]

By a note dated 9 November 1848, Count Bielke, the Danish *chargé d'affaires* in London, reminded the Foreign Office of 'the intention of His Majesty the King of Denmark to alienate the Nicobar Islands' and of the disenchantment of the India Board with an informal overture made by the Danish Minister in London. Bielke went on to state that the Danish Government had received 'communications' with the object of acquiring possession of the Nicobars but were unwilling to enter upon negotiations before giving Great Britain the opportunity to secure them. He continued:[20]

The undersigned has therefore been instructed to make the above communication to [the Secretary of State for Foreign Affairs], and has the honor to add that the sum of £st 50,000 has been suggested as a fair equivalent for the transfer of the Rights of the Danish Crown, in consideration of the expenses incurred by the Danish Government in clearing the Islands.

The Foreign Office referred the matter to the India Board, observing

[17] IOR: P/188/56 [Home Department, Public Proceedings of 6 August 1858, No. 81].
[18] Wynn to Foreign Office, No. 40 of 1847 (PRO: FO 22/157, f. 130).
[19] Ibid., f. 132r.
[20] PRO: FO 22/166, f. 310v.

at the same time 'that the question for consideration seems to be not merely what would be the value of these Islands as an acquisition to the East India Company, but what might be the inconvenience which might result to British Interests if these Islands were to pass into the possession of any other European Power'.[21] The India Board, through its Secret Committee, replied on 19 December 1848 that it was not in a position to judge the validity of Danish title to the Nicobars or the Danish Government's right to sell them. But it did not perceive 'any cause to apprehend danger, or inconvenience, should the Danish Government transfer its alleged title to these islands to any Foreign Power'.[22] The Board's view was that the islands were ineligible for settlement by Europeans and that it would be inexpedient to incur any expense in acquiring them. Consequently, on 31 December 1848, the Foreign Office advised the Danish Minister that Her Majesty's Government considered the islands ineligible for European settlement and 'must therefore decline to incur any expense in order to obtain possession of them'.[23]

IV. The Events of the 1850s

No further official consideration of the status of the Nicobars seems to have been taken in London or India for some years, although there were a number of reported atrocities carried out by the indigenous people against crews and passengers of ships stranded in the Andamans and Nicobars or which had gone there for shelter or water. In February 1856, official attention was aroused when it was suggested to the Bengal Government that a British settlement should be established on the Andamans for the protection of British subjects so situated and that the Nicobars should be put under British authority as well.[24] In a letter dated 1 October 1856 addressed to the Governor General of India and which dealt substantially with the possible annexation of the Andamans, the Court of Directors of the East India Company also asked for information about the Nicobars 'calculated to enable us to form an opinion respecting the expediency or inexpediency of taking final possession of the islands'.[25]

In response, the Court of Directors was sent a précis, compiled in the Foreign Department of the Government of India by W.H. Hoff, which briefly reviewed the history of European settlement in the Nicobars from

[21] PRO: FO 22/168, f. 284r–v.

[22] Ibid., f. 298r–v.

[23] PRO: FO 22/166, f. 340.

[24] Letter of 8 February 1856 from Captain Henry Hopkinson, Commissioner of Arrican, who wrote: 'Those islands have acquired a horrid notoriety of late years for the murderous piracies committed by their inhabitants' (IOR: P/188/56 [Home Department, Proceedings of 6 August 1858, No. 78]).

[25] Ibid., No. 81.

the first Danish activity in 1756 to the determination to abandon them taken after the return of Captain Steen Billé in 1847.[26]

Action to take formal possession of the Andamans began on 15 January 1858 when the Government of India instructed the Executive Engineer and Superintendent of Convicts at Moulmein, Captain H. Man, as follows:[27]

> ... I am directed to request that on your arrival at Port Blair, you will hoist the British Flag and take formal possession of the group of islands called the Andaman Islands, consisting of the Great and Little Andamans and all the islands adjacent thereto, in the name of Her Majesty the Queen and the East India Company.
> 2. Although it is certain that formal possession of these islands was taken by the British Government in 1789, and that the sovereignty of them is legally vested in the East India Company in trust for the British Crown, yet as they were deserted in 1796, and have been only nominally in possession of the Government ever since, it is desirable, as a measure of precaution, and to avoid the possibility of future doubt, that the right should be again asserted and recorded.

Man hoisted the flag on the Andamans on 22 January 1858.

V. The Prelude to Annexation

Once again an official silence fell over the Nicobars, during which period an Act of Parliament transferred responsibility for the government of India from the East India Company and India Board to a Secretary of State advised by officials of the new India Office in London.[28] The silence was broken in October 1866 when it was announced in Prince of Wales Island (Penang) that twenty-one of those on board the British brig *Futteh Islam* of Penang, bound for Rangoon from Penang, had been murdered by natives off Trinkat Island in the Nicobars.[29] Three survived to bring the ship back to Penang. In a letter dated 23 January 1867 addressed to the Government of India, the Government of the Straits Settlements wrote:[30]

> ... it would be in the power of the Supreme Government to come to a decision as to the propriety of adopting one of the three following plans
> *First* To take possession of the Island [Trinkat] and establish on it a military post for the protection of trade.
> *Second* To organize a small expedition for the purpose of penetrating into the interior and inflicting severe punishment upon the murderers by the destruction of their villages.
> *Third* To simply destroy such villages along the coast as might be reached by the fire of the cruisers or by small boat parties.
> In any case it would certainly be advisable to make arrangements so as to ensure a visit

[26] Ibid.
[27] IOR: P/188/49 [Home Department, Proceedings of 15 January 1858, p. 53].
[28] Government of India Act 1858 (21 & 22 Vict. c. 106).
[29] IOR: L/P & S/6/551 [Political Department, No. 134 of 1867].
[30] Ibid.

to the island on the part of a man-of-war at least twice every year, so that the natives would not fail to understand that due retaliation would be required [*sic*] for any wrong inflicted upon a British subject.

In June 1867, HMS *Wasp* under the command of Captain Norman Bedingfield was sent from Penang to the Nicobars on the orders of the Commodore, East India Station, with the task of investigating the circumstances of the massacre and in particular a report by a survivor that a white woman had been seen in captivity on the islands.[31] The Governor of the Straits Settlements thought it certain that not only had ships' crews been murdered by the inhabitants but 'any women on board reserved by them for a fate literally far worse than instant death'.[32] Bedingfield, who reported that the massacre had taken place off Great Nicobar Island, not Trinkat, found no such female captives but brought back to Penang and thence to Singapore four Nicobarese, three male and one female, suspected of having been implicated in the killing, together with a Eurasian child. He also heard reports that four European females and a boy were in captivity in the islands.[33]

HMS *Wasp* and HMS *Satellite* were then ordered to visit the islands, carrying a detachment of fifty native infantry from Penang and the Chief of Police of the Straits Settlements, with the objectives of procuring the release of the Europeans believed to be in captivity and of punishing those responsible for the massacre. The visit took place in July and August 1867. Huts and canoes were burned and livestock killed in the villages of the suspects but no European captives were found.[34] The Government of India then determined to mount a major expedition to the Nicobars with two or three companies of native troops 'to recover the whole of the white captives and to punish the chief offenders'. In authorising the Commodore, East India Station, Bombay, to mount the expedition, the Government of India, in a document dated 17 August 1867, added the following to the list of measures to be taken:[35]

The appointment of Colonel Man, lately a Resident Councillor in the Straits Settlements, as Civil and Political Officer, should he be able and willing to undertake the duty, to enquire into and report on all that has occurred, and to advise the Government of India as to the measures to be taken in future for the effectual suppression of the piratical and plundering tendencies of these people, especially as to the expediency of holding the Island[s] or not, and, if so, whether it should be by annexing them to the Government of the Straits or of India.

That such action would only be a short-term solution, like a blockade of the islands favoured by the Admiralty, was recognized by British

[31] Ibid.; also in PRO: CO 273/15, f. 535.

[32] Ord to Bedingfield, 11 July 1867 (PRO: CO 273/15, f. 540v).

[33] Bedingfield's report, dated in Penang on 28 June 1867, is printed in PRO: CO 273/15, ff. 537–8.

[34] The report of Captain Edge of the *Satellite* is in PRO: CO 273/14, ff. 71–88.

[35] Military Department, No. 253 of 1867 (PRO: CO 273/15, ff. 541v–2).

officials in London and in the East. What should be done in the long-term, however, was unclear. Annexation with a local agent put in charge was one of the solutions advanced by the Governor of the Straits Settlements, Colonel Ord, in a despatch to the Colonial Office, dated 20 August 1867, which gave a lengthy account of the two expeditions to the Nicobars and enclosed photographs of the persons brought back by the *Wasp* in June 1867.[36] Colonel Man himself, in a letter dated 23 September 1867 to the Government of India, wrote: 'I am clearly of opinion that India should have the charge, when it might be attached to the Andaman Command to which it would seem to be intended by nature as a dependency'.[37]

Within the Colonial Office, however, the option of outright annexation raised problems. Sir Frederic Rogers, the Permanent Under-Secretary, wrote a minute dated 2 October 1867 in which he stated of this option:[38]

> . . . it seems to me there are considerable objections:
>
> It seems to me much easier to deal with wild beasts of this kind when they are not British subjects than when they are. Captain Bedingfield's proceedings as operations of war are beyond dispute. If, besides burning the villages he had hanged a few of the people on flagrant suspicion ... he would have been only responsible to his official superiors. It would have been a different matter if they were British subjects.
>
> Again Colonel Ord says we have nothing to do but to pay a few dollars a year to a half caste in order to keep these people in order. This is easily said—but will it be so?
>
> Again if they, being our Subjects plunder foreign vessels and murder the crews, we become responsible for their proceedings. Are we prepared to adopt this responsibility?
>
> Again what English authority is to govern them? I suppose the Governor of the Straits Settlements. But he has plenty to do at home, and cannot deal with these people nearly so effectively or visit them so frequently in person or by some trustworthy representative as the naval commander on the Station.
>
> Lastly, I do not like the first step in annexation. If we agree to take the Nicobars in 1867 we shall be asked to take something else (perhaps in the mainland) in 1868 and land in a position where it will be very difficult to avoid annexation. I should like to check the very notion at once.

As already mentioned, annexation was also the solution advanced by the Government of India in their instructions of 17 August 1867 as the means to prevent the occurrence of further atrocities. By a letter of 4 December 1867,[39] the India Office forwarded this correspondence to the Colonial Office where Rogers modified his earlier position. He minuted on 14 December 1867:[40]

> . . . my objections to annexation do not apply or apply with decreased force to an annexation by the Indian Government—which has at its command vessels of war and a

[36] Ord to Colonial Office, No. 78 of 1867 (PRO: CO 273/11, ff. 233–53).
[37] IOR: L/P & S/6/554 [Political No. 17 of 1868].
[38] PRO: CO 273/11, ff. 255r–6r.
[39] PRO: CO 273/15, f. 529.
[40] Ibid., f. 530r.

Revenue on which it can unhesitatingly charge any expenses necessary for keeping these natives in order. To keep the seas clear of piracy is a task which it is utterly impossible for a Colonial Government to undertake with any chance of success. And the Government of the Straits is quite sufficiently scattered as it is.

Nevertheless, the reply from the Colonial Office to the India Office, dated 13 January 1868, made no reference to a possible attachment to India and was uncompromisingly hostile to attachment to the Straits Settlements. It then added:[41]

In his Grace's opinion the best way to keep these People in order and prevent Piracy would be frequent visits by Vessels of War, and full measure of punishment for any crimes committed. And this it appears to his Grace can be much better done while these People are not British Subjects than if the Islands were annexed to any British Territory and the People be thus endowed with the privileges of British Subjects.

In a letter to the India Office dated 13 February 1868, the Government of India 'inclined to the view' that the best arrangement would be to make over the Nicobars to the Indian Government, there being 'no political difficulty' and 'no objection to the British flag being hoisted'.[42] Enclosed with the letter was a copy of a letter sent to the Chief Commissioner of British Burma by Captain H. Lewis who, it will be recalled, had been master of *L'Espiègle* on the Danish survey expedition to the Nicobars in 1845 and who was now Master Attendant in Rangoon. Lewis, who had seen a newspaper article about the Nicobars, wrote that 'since this group of islands had been formally ceded to the British Government by the King of Denmark, no steps have been taken to assure ourselves of the possession of them'. He continued:[43]

I am not sufficiently versed in the Law of Nations to know if it be essentially necessary to a title of possession that the nation claiming this title should have hoisted its flag on one or more of the principal islands of the group, at the same time proclaiming her title of possession.

Such, however, was the course pursued by the Danish Government when I was in command of their surveying expedition, and I have thought it advisable to call the attention of the Chief Commissioner of British Burmah to this subject, so that, should he deem it necessary, he may remind the Governor General of India that as yet the British flag has not been hoisted, nor formal possession taken of the Nicobar Islands.

In a letter to the India Office dated 3 April 1868,[44] the Government of India stated that they had considered the anti-annexation view of the Colonial Office expressed in its letter of 13 January 1868, '[b]ut after due deliberation we are unable to come to any other conclusion than that the time has come for taking these islands under the control of the British power' and 'the only plan was to occupy with a proper degree of

[41] PRO: CO 273/15, f. 532r–v.

[42] IOR: P/438/1 [Foreign Department, Proceedings of February 1868, pp. 263–4]; also in PRO: FO 22/355 (unfoliated).

[43] Ibid., p. 263.

[44] IOR: P/438/1 [Foreign Department, Proceedings of April 1868, pp. 10–11].

permanency one of the islands, and from that vantage-ground to endeavour to reform and civilize the inhabitants'.

After stressing the urgency to punish and prevent outrages against ships and crews, the letter concluded:

Another consideration which we have not overlooked is the possibility of the occupation of the islands by a Foreign power. It is needless to dwell on the inconvenience which would be felt from the existence of a Foreign naval station in the immediate neighbourhood of our settlements in the Indian seas.

The India Office passed the above correspondence to the Foreign Office under cover of a letter dated 22 May 1868 asking whether there was any objection to the placing of the Nicobars under the British flag.[45] The Secretary of State for Foreign Affairs, Lord Stanley (a different person from the Under-Secretary of State for the Colonies of that name in 1848), did not accept as necessarily correct Lewis's assertion that Denmark had 'formally ceded' the Nicobars to Britain, since he minuted on the back of the India Office letter:[46]

This requires a little consideration. In the first place are we sure that no other nation claims them? Have we anything on the subject? And ought this to be done without reference to the Cabinet?

But first let me have information as to the chance of other claims.

The doubt in the mind of the Foreign Secretary was reflected in the reply sent by the Foreign Office to the India Office on 28 May 1868:[47]

. . . before taking any steps for the annexation of the Nicobar Islands, the Indian Government should satisfy themselves that Denmark has unquestionably and definitively abandoned her claim to the possession of those islands. There is no question that they previously belonged to that Power, and they have apparently been spoken of as appurtenances of the Danish Crown in works published at a recent date in Copenhagen. If this question of priority of possession is satisfactorily disposed of, Lord Stanley sees no objection to the acquisition of the islands by the Government of India, but His Lordship is clearly of opinion that no doubt must be allowed to exist in that point, and if [the India Office] wishes it, would be prepared to take such steps as might be in his power to obtain information on the subject.

The India Office did so wish and information was produced in the form of a memorandum dated 11 June 1868 written by Alfred Green, a sub-librarian in the Foreign Office, which set out a brief history of Danish activity in the Nicobars together with a summary of the correspondence with the British Mission in Copenhagen in the 1840s. Green concluded 'that it would appear that although Denmark has for some years withdrawn all emblem of Sovereignty over these Islands she does not appear to have formally surrendered her rights of possession either to Great Britain or any other Foreign Power'.[48]

[45] Ibid.
[46] PRO: FO 22/355 (unfoliated).
[47] Ibid.
[48] Ibid.

Lord Stanley, in a note on the file, questioned whether action could be taken without consulting the Danish Government.[49] An official, probably the Permanent Under-Secretary, Edmund Hammond, replied on 16 June 1868:[50]

I think there can be no doubt as to our obligation not to occupy the Islands, without the assent of the Danish Government. They may ask us to buy them as formerly: that of course we should not do: but if they would be satisfied with a pepper corn rent, we might pay that. They might be told that if they retain the Islands, they are bound to suppress piracy on the part of their subjects, or make compensation for piratical outrages.

Lord Stanley agreed. On his instructions, and after obtaining the concurrence of the India Office, the Foreign Office sent a letter dated 27 June 1868 to the British Minister in Copenhagen, Sir C. Wyke, enclosing a copy of Green's memorandum and stating that the Government of India considered that 'in the interests of civilization, it might be advisable that the islands should be brought under the British Crown'.[51] The letter continued: 'It is obvious that no steps can be taken in this direction by Great Britain without its being clearly ascertained that Denmark has definitively and absolutely abandoned her claim. I wish you therefore to ascertain this point from the Danish Government.'

After stressing that under no circumstance would a pecuniary consideration be paid, the letter went on: 'If Denmark is disposed to cede any claim to them which she may possess, Great Britain is prepared to undertake the duties of their government, but she would do so solely in the interests of civilization and for the protection of commerce.' In conclusion, the Foreign Office stated:

. . . it seems to be clearly established that the present state of the islands is so unsatisfactory that the Power assuming the protectorate over them incurs no inconsiderable responsibility, and that if Denmark claims them and insists in retaining them, it is not improbable that she may be called upon to keep her subjects in order, or, if she fails [to] do so, to compensate sufferers for injuries suffered by them from the violence of savages controlled by no authority.

Having taken up the matter with the Danish Foreign Minister, Count Frijs, through a note to him dated 24 July 1868,[52] Wyke reported to the Foreign Office in a despatch on that date that Frijs had told him in a conversation that a company of French speculators had endeavoured to obtain the islands but that the Danish Government had refused to sanction their possession by 'a set of private individuals'.[53] In a further despatch, dated 10 September 1868, Wyke reported that in 1861 the

[49] Ibid.

[50] Ibid.

[51] Foreign Office to Wyke, No. 4 of 1868 (PRO: FO 211/127 (unfoliated) contains the original as sent).

[52] Copy enclosed in Wyke to Foreign Office, No. 13 of 1868 (PRO: FO 22/349 (unfoliated)).

[53] Wyke to Foreign Office, No. 13 of 1868 (ibid.).

French had opened negotiations, inconclusive but not entirely abandoned, and consequently the Danish Government did not like to cede the Islands to any other State until they were aware that France did not want them.[54] It is not clear whether the latter intelligence referred to the earlier incident involving French speculators or to a new overture by the French Government.

On 19 October 1868, Frijs wrote to Wyke.[55] He first set out the point at issue as follows: 'Vous m'avez demandé dans votre note du 24 Juillet dernier si le Danemark se considère encore comme ayant des droits à exercer sur les îles en question ou s'il en a fait un abandon définitif et absolu'. He then pointed out that in 1848 the garrison had been withdrawn, external signs of Danish sovereignty removed and the Danish station closed down. He explained away the subsequent Danish diplomatic conduct in respect of the islands as follows:

L'abandon des Iles de Nicobar a donc eu lieu en 1848, et si le Danemark néanmoins depuis cette époque s'est trouvé engagé, à plusieurs reprises, dans des pourparlers avec d'autres Etats au sujet de ces îles, la raison en est qu'aussi longtemps qu'elles n'avaient pas encore été occupées par quelque autre puissance, l'ancien propriétaire devait tout naturellement se considérer comme celui qui était particulièrement en mesure d'en disposer.

Frijs concluded with the opinion that the Danish Crown could have no objection to Great Britain or any other State taking necessary measures to prevent piracies in or around the Nicobars.

In his covering despatch to the Foreign Office enclosing Frijs's note, Wyke suggested that if the Indian authorities had any idea of settling the islands, it might be as well to obtain from the Danish Government a formal act of cession to avoid the possibility of future doubt over the nature and origin of British tenure.[56] The Foreign Office referred the correspondence to the India Office which replied on 19 November 1868 that 'the Government of India has had no desire to occupy these islands except in the general interests of humanity, for the suppression of Piracy', but if Denmark declined to offer protection to shipping the Government of India would undertake to police the waters on condition that British sovereignty was assumed, such acquisition being made only by a 'free cession'.[57]

The Foreign Office replied to Wyke on 23 November 1868 as follows:[58]

I have to instruct you to inform the Danish Government that if Denmark is prepared to make a free cession of the Nicobar Islands to the British Crown, instructions will be sent for the hoisting of the British Flag, and every possible effort will be made to put a stop

[54] Wyke to Foreign Office, No. 22 of 1868 (ibid.).

[55] Copy enclosed in Wyke to Foreign Office, No. 32 of 1868 (PRO: FO 22/349 (unfoliated)).

[56] Wyke to Foreign Office, No. 32 of 1868 (ibid.).

[57] PRO: FO 22/355 (unfoliated).

[58] Foreign Office to Wyke, No. 17 of 1868 (PRO: FO 211/127 (unfoliated)).

to those Acts of Piracy which have hitherto occurred in the neighbourhood of those Islands.

The India Office, to which the Foreign Office had sent the above correspondence, replied on 4 December 1868 that if the Nicobars were to be brought under the British flag 'it is strongly urged by the Government of India that they should be annexed to the Indian Empire, in preference to the Colony of the Straits Settlements'.[59]

Meanwhile, in a despatch to the Foreign Office dated 30 November 1868, Wyke reported that on that day Frijs had told him that a formal act of cession could only be given with the sanction of the Danish legislature, a step which might occasion difficulty and delay.[60] Wyke enclosed with his despatch a copy of a note which he had sent to Frijs on that same day. In this, as instructed, he informed the Danish Government that if Denmark was prepared to make 'a free cession' of the Nicobars to the British Crown, the British flag would be hoisted there and every effort made to put an end to the piracies. Wyke also reported that he had informed Frijs of his personal view that the British Government would never incur the expense which this would entail without some more solid grounds for doing so than were contained in Frijs's earlier note.

Frijs replied to Wyke in a note dated 2 December 1868 which began:[61]

Par ma note du 17 du mois passé [*sc.* 19 October] j'ai eu l'honneur de vous communiquer que le Gouvernement du Roi ayant déjà en 1848 virtuellement fait abandon des Iles de Nicobar, celles-ci, à partir de cette époque, ne peuvent être considérées que comme 'res derelicta', sujet à devenir par un acte d'occupation la Propriété de toute puissance étrangère qui voudrait en prendre possession.

He continued:

Afin d'écarter tout doute sur la vraie portée de ma première déclaration je m'empresse, Monsieur le chevalier, de vous déclarer que si malgré l'abandon susmentionné le Gouvernement Britannique nous regarde encore comme ayant des droits relativement aux Iles de Nicobar, le Gouvernement du Roi cède volontiers par la présente ces droits à celui de Sa Majesté Britannique. Je crois pourtant devoir ajouter que, dans le cas qu'une autre puissance se serait emparée des Iles de Nicobar avant que l'Angleterre y ait arboré son pavillon, le Gouvernement du Roi ne saurait en vertu de la présente cession être rendu responsable d'un tel fait, qui selon lui n'est qu'une conséquence naturelle de la position qu'il a prise vis-à-vis de ces îles, en faisant disparaître les signes extérieurs de la souveraineté que le Danemark a antérieurement exercé sur elles.

In communicating Frijs's note with a despatch of 5 December 1868, Wyke advised the Foreign Office that he thought that the views of the Indian Government could now safely be carried out.[62] The Foreign

[59] PRO: FO 22/355 (unfoliated). On the other hand, the Admiralty had advised the Foreign Office in a letter dated 2 November 1868 that the Nicobars should be attached to the Straits Settlements (ibid.).

[60] Wyke to Foreign Office, No. 38 of 1868 (PRO: FO 22/349 (unfoliated)).

[61] Copy enclosed in Wyke to Foreign Office, No. 39 of 1868 (ibid.).

[62] Wyke to Foreign Office, No. 39 of 1868 (ibid.).

Office in reply told Wyke that his actions were fully approved and that it seemed clear from Frijs's note of 2 December 1868 'that whenever the Government of India thinks fit to annex the islands, no opposition may be expected to be raised on the part of the Danish Government'.[63] Accordingly, by a letter of 8 December 1868 transmitting the correspondence, the Foreign Office told the India Office that 'it is clear that no difficulty will be raised by the Danish Government to the annexation of the islands whenever it may seem fit to the Government of India to take that step'.[64] On 20 January 1869, the Secretary of State for India, the Duke of Argyll, gave authority to the Governor General of India, Earl Mayo, as follows:[65]

As it is clear from this correspondence that no difficulty will be raised by the Danish Government, Your Excellency is authorized to take such steps as you may think fit to bring the islands under the British flag, and to provide for their future administration under the supervision of the Superintendant of the Andaman Islands.

VI. Annexation

The Government of India did not waste time in implementing the above authority. By orders dated 25 February 1869 the Commander of the East India Station, Commodore Heath, was directed to take immediate possession of the Nicobars by one of Her Majesty's ships.[66] The orders continued:

3. The measures should be carried out as quietly as possible, and without any public intimation being given of the intentions of Government, but it is most essential that the formalities should be observed which are proper in such occasions, that the British flag should be hoisted on the principal island or islands; and that a Proclamation be read out to the effect that these territories are occupied by British officers acting under authority, and that they will be henceforth regarded as part of the dominions of the Sovereign of Great Britain. A royal salute of 21 guns should be fired on the occasion of hoisting the flag on the main island.
4. It is also necessary and in accordance with international law, that to render the occupation of these islands effective, it should be continuous; and the vessel which takes possession must therefore remain at the Nicobars until such time as the islands can be regularly handed over to the Military or Civil administration.

In a letter of 4 March 1869, Heath reported to the Governor General and Viceroy that he had ordered Commander Morrell of HMS *Spiteful* at Trincomalee to proceed to Nancowry with a proclamation and to fire

[63] Foreign Office to Wyke, No. 21 of 1868 (PRO: FO 211/127 (unfoliated)).
[64] PRO: FO 22/355 (unfoliated).
[65] *Selections from the Records of the Government of India, Home Department*: No. LXXVII, *Papers relating to the Nicobar Islands*, Calcutta, 1870, p. 316 (IOR: fiche 131).
[66] FO 22/362 (unfoliated).

a royal salute upon hoisting the English flag.[67] The proclamation which was to be used read:[68]

PROCLAMATION

I, Arthur Morrell, a Commander in Her Britannic Majesty's Naval Service, and now commanding Her Majesty's Ship-of-War *Spiteful*, having received instructions thereto from Commander Sir Leopold Heath, K.C.B., Commanding Her Majesty's Naval Forces in the Indian Seas, acting on the requisition of the Earl Mayo, Viceroy and Governor General of India, do now on this the—day of—AD 1869, in the name and on behalf of Her Most Gracious Majesty Victoria, Queen of Great Britain and Ireland, take possession of this Island of Nangcowrie, together with all others commonly known as the Nicobar Islands, that is to say, the Islands of Car-Nicobar and Great Nicobar, with those lying between them including Tillanchong and in token thereof, I now hoist the flag of Great Britain proclaiming to all concerned the supremacy of Her Most Gracious Majesty, and calling upon the inhabitants of the said Islands to submit themselves to Her Majesty's laws.

Writing to the Commodore from Trincomalee on his return, Morrell reported that he had erected a flag-staff on Nancowry Island at a place which he named Mayo Point after the Governor General and Viceroy, Earl Mayo. He described the ceremony as follows:[69]

On the 27th, at 8 am, I, with a party of officers, seamen and mariners, landed and hoisted the British flag in the presence of about 50 natives; made the proclamation forwarded by you, also its translation in Malay, which was read by the interpreter, and took possession of all the Nicobar Islands on behalf of Her Majesty, at the same time dressing ship and firing a royal salute.

What Morrell had not known at that time was that on 24 March 1869 the Government of India had despatched to him a revised version of the proclamation, instructing him to go through the ceremonies again with the revised proclamation, should he have used the original proclamation before the revised version arrived. The reason for the revision was explained as follows:[70]

You will have perceived that the effect of the latter document [i.e. the earlier version] would be to place the Nicobars entirely under the control of Her Majesty the Queen, and subject them to the legislative action of the British Parliament alone. The possession of the islands in question was, however, determined upon with the express intention of attaching them to Her Majesty's dominions in India, and bringing them under the jurisdiction of the Indian Government. For these reasons His Excellency the Governor General in Council considers it necessary to adopt the revised proclamation herein enclosed.

After the same recitals as those in the earlier version, the revised proclamation continued:[71]

[67] *Selections from the Records of the Government of India, Home Department*: No. LXXVII, *Papers relating to the Nicobar Islands*, Calcutta, 1870, p. 316 (IOR: fiche 131); also in IOR: P/434/16 [Home Department, Proceedings of 6 March 1869, No. 26].

[68] Ibid.

[69] Morrell to Heath, 24 April 1869 (ibid.).

[70] Ibid.

[71] Ibid.

> . . . do now . . . in the name and on behalf of the Indian Government of Her Majesty the Queen of Great Britain and Ireland, take possession of this island of Nangcowry, together with all others commonly known as the Nicobar Islands, that is to say, the island of Car-Nicobar and Great Nicobar with those lying between them including Tillanchong, and in token thereof I now hoist the flag of Great Britain, proclaiming to all concerned the supremacy of Her Most Gracious Majesty, declaring the said islands to be subject to Her Majesty's Indian Government, and calling upon the inhabitants of the said islands to submit themselves to Her Majesty's laws as administered by the Government of India.

The revised proclamation arrived in the Nicobars on 15 April 1868 with the Bengal Marine Steamer *Aracan*. On board was Colonel Man, who had been entrusted by the Governor General with the administration of the new territory. In his message to Commodore Heath, dated in Trincomalee on 24 April 1869, Morrell described what happened next:[72]

> I received from him [i.e. Man] an amended proclamation which the Governor General desired me to make, the latter one placing the Islands under the control of the Indian instead of the Imperial Government, as was the case with the first.
>
> This was made, and the customary ceremony again gone through on the 16th; and my services being no longer required by Colonel Man, I left on the following day, 17th, for the place, where I have to report my arrival this day.

Thus were the Nicobars annexed twice over.

VII. Conclusion

In British constitutional law, the acquisition of the Nicobars is significant as an example of the prerogative annexation of new territory by an entity other than the central Imperial authority. In international law, it is significant with regard to the concept of abandonment of territorial sovereignty. The principal aspects of the latter will now briefly be discussed.

Abandonment, or dereliction, is a well recognized method of losing territorial sovereignty although actual examples of it are scarce. Two requirements, the counterparts to those needed for a valid acquisition of territory, are usually given, namely physical withdrawal and the intention to abandon (*animus derelinquendi*).[73] Of these, the latter is the essential one, since physical withdrawal could take place without any intention to abandon and in such a situation sovereignty is not necessarily lost. As *Oppenheim* observes:[74] 'Actual abandonment alone does not

[72] Ibid. Man's account of the events, dated 12 May 1869, is in IOR: L/P & S/6/569 [No. 4 of 1870].

[73] See, for example, *Oppenheim's International Law*, vol. 1 (9th edn. by R. Y. Jennings and A. D. Watts, 1992), p. 717; C. Rousseau, *Droit international public*, vol. 3 (1977), p. 158; A. Verdross and B. Simma, *Universelles Völkerrecht: Theorie und Praxis* (3rd edn., 1984), pp. 754–5. See also *Clipperton Island* arbitration (1931), *Reports of International Arbitral Awards*, vol. 2, p. 1110.

[74] *Oppenheim*, op. cit. above (n. 73), p. 717; see also D.P. O'Connell, *International Law*, vol. 1 (2nd edn., 1970), pp. 444–5.

involve dereliction as long as it must be presumed that the owner has the will and ability to retake possession of the territory'.

The general concept of abandonment of territorial sovereignty may be narrowed in two ways. First, it can be distinguished from the abandonment of a mere claim. Again *Oppenheim* remarks:[75] 'The forfeiture of an inchoate title is not the same as the dereliction of territory which has been definitely acquired, whether by occupation or otherwise'. British practice in respect of Bouvet Island and of Spratly Island, described in an earlier volume of this *Year Book*,[76] would fall into this category, since in each of those situations Britain had only a claim to title, the title itself remaining in doubt throughout. Secondly, it can be distinguished from the situation whereby a State, under the guise of abandonment, really cedes or transfers its rights to another State without the territory in question having become in the interim period a *res nullius*. Brownlie writes that '[i]n principle the term "abandonment" could be reserved for the rare situation in which a state *intends* to abandon and expressly and formally renounces title (without this involving a procedure by which the territory falls under another sovereignty)'.[77] The question is now posed: was the case of the Nicobars one of Danish abandonment in the above narrow sense?

The first issue is whether at any period Denmark possessed territorial sovereignty over the Nicobars or whether it had only an unsubstantiated claim to them. If the latter, then the British annexation of 1869 was that of a *terra nullius*. Applying the usual two tests—an intention to acquire sovereignty followed by effective occupation—the evidence is strong that Denmark manifested such an intention from 1756 at least up to the 1840s. The requirement of effective occupation, however, is more difficult to satisfy. Danish occupation was at best tenuous and spasmodic and, furthermore, there is no evidence that Denmark occupied the whole chain of the Nicobars as opposed to particular parts of particular islands. However, at the time of the first Danish activity in the mid-eighteenth century, very little in the way of effective occupation was needed.[78] Furthermore, Denmark's claim was not overtly contested by other powers.

If Denmark is given the benefit of the considerable doubt on whether it held sovereignty at any period, the second issue is whether immediately before the British annexation of 1869 Denmark continued to hold sovereignty so as to be able to cede the Nicobars, or whether on the other

[75] *Oppenheim*, op. cit. above (n. 73), p. 716, second footnote 2.

[76] G. Marston, 'Abandonment of Territorial Claims: the Cases of Bouvet and Spratly Islands', this *Year Book*, 57 (1986), pp. 337–56.

[77] I. Brownlie, *Principles of Public International Law* (5th edn., 1998), p. 143, note 28 (original emphasis).

[78] *Oppenheim*, op. cit. above (n. 73), p. 689.

hand the islands were then already *res derelictae* and so no longer capable of being ceded by Denmark or any other State.

Physical abandonment of the Nicobars took place in 1848, as stated expressly by the Danish Foreign Minister in his note to the British Minister of 19 October 1868 in the following words:[79]

> . . . déjà en 1848 par ordre du Roi un vaisseau de la Marine Royale a été envoyé aux îles de Nicobar pour repatrier la garnison et faire disparaître les signes extérieurs de la souveraineté du Danemark. Après avoir executé ses ordres le Capitaine a donné avis au Gouverneur Général Britannique dans les Indes orientales que la station danoise qui jusque là avait été établie aux îles, venait d'être supprimée.

It does not appear, however, that the Danish Government necessarily intended thereby to renounce sovereignty. First, their proposal in December 1848 to sell 'the Rights of the Danish Crown' to Britain for £50,000—made after the physical abandonment had taken place—was an express demonstration of their continuing intention to retain sovereignty. Secondly, the fact that in 1861 the Danish Government were prepared to enter into negotiations with French interests over the Nicobars indicated that the position had not changed over the intervening thirteen years. Thirdly, the explanation by the Danish Foreign Minister in his note to the British Minister of 19 October 1868 of the basis on which the Danish Government had continued to treat over the Nicobars was consistent only with an intention to retain at least some vestiges of sovereignty after the physical abandonment in 1848.

Against the above evidence should be placed the Danish Foreign Minister's note of 2 December 1868 to the British Minister, the opening words of which, quoted earlier, indicated that an abandonment had been intended in 1848. On the other hand in the second part of this note, also quoted earlier, the Danish Foreign Minister, anxious not to disturb Britain's view that Denmark still retained sovereignty, agreed to an informal 'cession' of Danish rights with the warning that it was not responsible to Britain if a third State annexed the islands before the British flag was raised. This might be regarded as evidence of a retention of title, but the relevant passage—'si malgré l'abandon susmentionnée le Gouvernement Britannique nous regarde . . . '—took the form of a subsidiary alternative to Denmark's primary position that the islands were *res derelictae*. That the Foreign Office interpreted the passage in this way is clear from its letter of 6 December 1868 to the India Office in which, with reference to Frijs's letter of 2 December 1868, it wrote: ' . . . he has formally stated in a note to Her Majesty's Minister that he considers the islands, since their abandonment by Denmark, to be "derelict"; and in case the Government of India should not be satisfied with this, he states further that his Government voluntarily cedes its

[79] PRO: FO 22/349 (unfoliated).

rights over them to that of Her Britannic Majesty, on the understanding that no other Power shall have already taken possession of them'.[80]

In conclusion, the evidence suggests that in international law the story of the Nicobars was one of abandonment of territorial sovereignty in the strict sense; by December 1868 Denmark had not only physically abandoned the islands but had fulfilled its intention to relinquish sovereignty over them and had made this known to Britain through diplomatic channels. The informal 'cession' was a cosmetic camouflage so contrived as not to appear to challenge Britain's opinion—not shared by the Danish Government—that sovereignty still lay with Denmark.

[80] PRO: FO 22/355 (unfoliated).

REVIEWS OF BOOKS

Interstate Arbitrations in the Greek World. By SHEILA L. AGER. Berkeley: University of California Press, 1996. 579 pp. $70.

Although the author is a classical scholar rather than a lawyer, she has provided a superb work of reference on the early history of international law. The book is essentially a digest of 171 cases of third-party dispute settlement in the Hellenistic world. It continues on from earlier work by the Italian scholar Luigi Piccirilli, whose *Gli arbitrati interstatali greci* (1973) covered cases ending in 338 BC. (Unfortunately, Piccirilli's book remains untranslated into English.) Professor Ager picks up where Piccirilli left off and continues to the admittedly somewhat arbitrary date of 90 BC.

The title of the book is slightly misleading, since it covers third-party dispute settlement in general and is not confined to arbitration in the modern sense of that term. (The author is well aware of this point.) Many of the cases were mediations. Some were, in effect, dictated settlements by Rome, which was looming steadily larger as a presence throughout the period. The author has chosen to err somewhat on the side of over-inclusion, as some of the cases concern unsuccessful attempts at settlement. The focus is on inter-State disputes, although some of the cases also involve settlements of private claims ancillary to the principal controversy.

By far the most common type of dispute concerned boundaries or title to territory. (The character of the sources sometimes makes these difficult to distinguish.) A surprising number entail settlements of armed conflicts. And an intriguing miscellany of other matters arises — including title to moveable property, sacrilege, indebtedness, embezzlement, abduction of persons from foreign territory, refusals to comply with prior awards, attacks on nationals abroad. There is, in short, much that is depressingly familiar.

The sources for the cases are of two types. (Only rarely does a given case have evidence of both kinds.) One is the historians. Polybios is naturally the most prominent, given the time period covered, with Livy in second place. The other main source is epigraphic, i.e., inscriptions from various ancient sites. This epigraphic evidence — accounting for nearly two-thirds of the cases — is of course primary source material in the strictest sense. It consists of such matters as the texts of awards, narratives of the cases and sometimes the actual first-hand testimony of witnesses. This evidence from inscriptions is particularly welcome, since it would otherwise be virtually inaccessible to general readers.

The book commences with an excellent introductory essay on the salient features of third-party dispute settlement in the Greek world. It then sets out the cases, in chronological order. For each one, the author quotes the ancient source in full, in the original Greek or Latin (although without translation). She then gives a clear and succinct narrative account, including the larger context in which the dispute occurred. She carefully identifies any particularly striking features of the case. Any previous account by another scholar is also carefully noted (although over half the cases have not been covered in previous secondary writing). Where there are scholarly disagreements over aspects of a case, these are clearly and fairly identified.

In the aggregate, the cases convey a strong sense of how third-party dispute settlement actually functioned in the Greek world. We receive a particularly good picture of the procedural aspects of the process — from the *compromissum* and the selection of the arbitrators to the gathering of evidence and the rendering of the awards (although we do not have the whole of this in detail for any single case).

Those interested in the substance of international law in the period will suffer some disappointment, because the sources usually do not present the substantive issues in the detail that modern lawyers would wish. Very occasionally, however, they do. One of the best examples is a dispute between Mytilene and Pitane (with Pergamene arbitrators), involving the question of conquest as a root of title to territory. Sometimes, at the other extreme, the evidence is so fragmentary that we do not even know the nature of the dispute, and sometimes not even the identities of the litigant States.

The principal value of this work is as a reference. But seldom has a reference work been so excellently put together or so readable. It is very well organised and easy to use. There are no fewer than five separate indexes: of the classical literary sources (alphabetically by author); of the epigraphic sources (alphabetically by the journal in which they have been published); of persons and places mentioned in the cases and text; of subject-matters of the disputes (this will be the most valuable for legal historians); and of key Greek and Latin terms. There is also a bibliography.

The scholarly community of international law is remarkably fortunate to have so fine a work conferred upon it from, as it were, the outside. We would be even more honoured if the author would put us yet further in her debt by continuing her invaluable work beyond the terminal date of this volume.

STEPHEN C. NEFF

Self-Defense Against the Use of Force in International Law. By STANIMIR A. ALEXANDROV. The Hague: Kluwer Law International, 1996. 352 pp. £81.

Dr Alexandrov's book chronicles the efforts of lawyers and diplomats since the end of the First World War to outlaw the use of force, against what might be seen as an obdurate concern of States which wish to see the option of force remain as at least an ultimate means of settling disputes. This last ditch gesture, the inherent right to defend oneself against armed attack, survives cloaked not only in vestments of necessity and proportionality, but in a myriad of other shades based on the interpretative claims of the users of force. The book is based on its author's doctoral research and is well grounded in history and extraordinarily competently documented with sources. Professor Louis B. Sohn, Dr Alexandrov's former supervisor, in a Foreword to the book points out, correctly, its wide-ranging scope and thorough historical analysis.

The first four chapters centre on the articulation in international instruments of the right of States to use force to defend themselves. A brief but fascinating account of early claims to use force, either as all-out war or as a means of self-help, self-preservation or self-defence, is followed by detailed and equally absorbing review of the debates and negotiations leading to the Covenant of the League of Nations, the Pact of Paris and the United Nations Charter. In many ways the attitude of States towards the use of force is well epitomized in the negotiations leading to the Pact of Paris which the author outlines in some detail. States were not happy to renounce any use of force which interfered with their right to defend themselves, and yet were equally worried by the self-judging character which the proposals contained. Some of these self-judging issues were, of course, addressed by the United Nations Charter, particularly in its approach to Regional Organizations whose activities were made subject to the overriding competence of the Security Council. The author argues that the failure of the Security Council to operate as was intended, and the inability of the Organization to carry out in full the requirements of Chapter VII of the Charter, have had an important impact on the use of force and the development of the concept of collective self-defence.

The final and major part of the work explores individual and collective use of force by States. In each section examples illustrating the development of the aspect being considered are related and a final analytical discussion closes the chapter. Force may be used not only as a proportionate response to an armed attack; it may be an anticipatory action or be pre-emptive of attack. Similarly, force has been used to protect nationals abroad or as an instrument of human rights protection through humanitarian intervention or support of self-determination. The author shows through case-by-case studies that States are aware of the dangers of widening the definition of self-defence and that many such claims have met with little support in the United Nations. He suggests at this point that States should not be seen to have been arguing to expand the right of self-defence as laid down in Article 51, but rather to broaden the interpretation of the term 'armed attack'. Nevertheless, he reminds us, these arguments have received little support within United Nations practice. This does not mean that States, although more and more unwilling to use force, have not been prepared to use forceful measures where they judge the sympathy or support of the international community will approve or turn a blind eye. The use of self-defence measures, however, must cease upon action being taken by the Security Council, and it is in the area of collective self-defence that the author sees the greatest development. The use of Article 48 merges enforcement measures with collective defence, a useful and successful device which overcomes the failure of the Organization to comply with all the requirements of Chapter VII of the Charter, and also removes the self-judging aspect of individual self-defence.

To posit, as some may, that within the dynamics of international relations the parameters of the use of force cannot be drawn by the international lawyer, and that international fora for debate will avoid genuine legal discussion wherever possible, would be to underline the apparent weakness of law as a determinant force in the pursuit of order. On the other hand, failure to analyse behaviour in legal terms is to do a disservice to the development of law. The case-by-case discussion of the major examples of the use of force since the founding of the United Nations is likely to be one of the most useful and rewarding aspects of this work. One of the difficulties of a historical approach, of course, particularly in dealing with events in recent history, is to get a feel for the time-scale involved in disputes and to discover any real information on the knowledge available to the protagonists and on which they based their actions.

RALPH BEDDARD

Protection international de l'environnement. Edited by L. BOISSON DE CHAZOURNES, R. DESGAGNÉ and C. ROMANO. Paris: Éditions Pedone, 1998. 1117 pp. French francs 560.

Professor Boisson de Chazournes and her two colleagues have produced a most authoritative collection of international instruments—in their French language versions—relating to the protection of the environment. It comprises some 68 instruments, the majority of which are treaties. The other instruments include the non-binding declarations one might expect to see (for example, the 1972 Stockholm Declaration and the 1992 Rio Declaration); acts of inter-governmental organizations (for example, a Security Council resolution and OECD recommendations); and EC regulations. The instruments go back to 1902 (the Convention for the Protection of Birds Useful to Agriculture), the most recent being the 1997 UN Convention on Non-Navigational Uses of International Watercourses. The collection is arranged into thirteen chapters (Principles; Institutional Aspects; Nature Conservation; Marine Environment; Antarctic and Arctic; Atmosphere; Hazardous Activities; International Trade; Financial Mechanisms; Armed Conflicts; Human Rights; Responsibility; Settlement of Disputes). Each chapter is introduced with a helpful note—also in French—setting out, in general terms, the historical background and the current state of the law, with references to some recent case law. Each chapter has a select bibliography, and for each instrument there is an indication as to its place and date of adoption, entry into force, source, and the number of parties (if applicable). The collection concludes with a select bibliography (collections of documents and reports, monographs and collected works), a chronological index of the instruments set out in the collection, and (most helpfully) an analytical index.

The collection thus benefits from numerous useful features and will be most helpful for English speakers requiring ready access to French texts (even if only to obtain instant translations of such current—but often impenetrable—terms such as 'sustainable development' ('développement durable')). The instruments are clearly and logically presented. They are up to date: amendments have been incorporated or are otherwise referenced in footnotes. The advantages of this are apparent with the single text presented of the Montreal Protocol on Substances that Deplete the Ozone Layer, incorporating the amendments and adjustments introduced in 1990, 1992 and 1995. For the advanced user, however, the approach raises the difficulty that it is unclear which amendments have been introduced by which instrument, and accordingly which States are or are not bound by the change. Nevertheless, given the page limitations, this is probably a sensible way of proceeding. In conclusion, one can only agree with Professor Condorelli in his Preface: the editors have made available for the interested public 'an excellent tool for teaching, research and, more generally, understanding concerning the domain which is at the centre of publications of a constantly growing number of actors and observers' (p. 7, translated). The publication also confirms the vibrancy and richness of the francophone world of international law, both directly and by indicating references to the relevant French literature—a world which is most certainly not yet 'une éspèce menacée d'extinction'.

PHILIPPE SANDS

La Soumission des États aux tribunaux internes face à la théorie des immunités des États. By MICHEL COSNARD. Paris: Éditions Pedone, 1996. 478 pp. French francs 320.

In a letter to the *American Journal of International Law* in 1988, Anthony D'Amato claimed that American international lawyers no longer cite their French counterparts because there is 'not . . . very much that is new or challenging in French scholarship at the present moment'.[1] However, important books about international law are still written in the French language. This detailed examination of the law of State immunity, written by Michel Cosnard of the University of Bourgogne, is one of them.

Cosnard advances a simple but devastating thesis: that the shift from absolute to restrictive State immunity which has occurred over the course of the twentieth century has resulted in the importation of concepts of private international law into the law of State immunity. This, in turn, has corrupted and diminished State immunity to the point where it has virtually disappeared, with the continued use of the term being little more than a linguistic residue.

In accordance with the best French tradition, Cosnard divides his book into two parts. He begins by examining, in a highly useful but relatively uncritical way, the institution of State immunity as that institution is currently seen to exist by most international lawyers. Only then, having described the institution in some detail, does he reveal that most of what is understood to be the modern law of State immunity has almost nothing to do with immunity at all.

The first part of the book is of enormous value in itself, as a detailed analysis of the law, theory and practice of State immunity. Cosnard canvasses most of the many difficult issues involved, and in the course of doing so cites a staggering number of cases (1003) and an equally impressive range of books and articles in many languages. Moreover, he expresses thoughtful—if often debatable—views of his own on virtually every issue. In these respects, the first part of this book is comparable to the work of the International

[1] *American Journal of International Law*, 82 (1988), p. 564.

Law Commission leading up to its 1991 Draft Articles on State immunity, and to the work of the Australian Law Reform Commission set out in its well-known 'Report No. 24' of 1984.

The second part of the book is even more thought-provoking. Here Cosnard reveals how the public international law of State immunity has almost completely been replaced by a multitude of rules of national law, and particularly rules of private international law, applied in a variety of different ways within different national legal systems. The sheer diversity of these rules and the ways in which they are applied make it unlikely, he argues, that much customary international law could still exist in this area. Instead, the application of private international law rules has resulted in the introduction of an absence of jurisdiction, in place of the non-exercise of jurisdiction that has been characteristic of State immunity. Similarly, in respect of immunity from execution, the non-exercise of jurisdiction has been replaced by the non-seizability of the property concerned.

According to Cosnard, the development of restrictive immunity has led to a focus on questions of State responsibility, and of liability in national law, rather than on immunity *per se*. Questions of State responsibility arise here whenever an individual or non-State entity is claimed to have acted on behalf of a State and thus to benefit from State immunity. This is because the State in question may, under international law, then be legally responsible for the consequences of those acts. That said, it remains the case that questions of responsibility arise in the initiation of claims *against* States, whereas claims of immunity are made *by* States in response to other claims.

Similarly, questions of liability in national law arise when, for example, it is necessary to determine whether the property of one State-owned 'separate entity' may be seized in order to meet the debts of another separate entity owned by the same State. As Cosnard points out, the International Law Commission and others have incorrectly regarded this latter question as one which concerns State immunity from execution. They have been wrong to do so for the simple reason that the determining factor in such cases will be one of private rather than public international law, namely which national legal system applies to the relevant questions of corporate organization and liability.

Diplomatic protection was traditionally considered to be an adequate substitute for the inability to have recourse to national courts that resulted from State immunity. However, in most cases concerning commercial activities, for instance, such as breaches of contract, there will be no violation of international law giving rise to State responsibility, and thus no question of whether international law rather than national law should apply. The traditional rationale for State immunity has been rendered largely obsolete by the involvement of States in an increasingly broad and complex range of activities, by the development of the concept of restrictive State immunity, and by increased recognition that the rights of individuals should not be compromised by inter-State political considerations.

Cosnard explains that national courts now exercise jurisdiction over certain kinds of activities by imputing an 'objective submission' on the part of any State that engages in them. To the degree that the jurisdiction of national courts is limited, this is accomplished by rules of private international law, or by rules such as the 'act of State' doctrine which are similar in character and effect to rules of private international law. Other examples of such rules include the direct effect test contained in the commercial activities exception of the United States Foreign Sovereign Immunities Act, and the territorial limitation set out in the non-commercial tort exceptions of all national State immunity statutes. The basis of the law of State immunity, that jurisdiction exists and underlies any immunity, has been replaced by questions concerning whether the court has competence, i.e. whether it has jurisdiction at all.

According to Cosnard, a public international law of State immunity can still be said to exist only in situations, such as those involving non-commercial torts abroad, where the international law of diplomatic protection properly applies. Here the law of State immunity itself acts as a 'choice of law' rule between public international law and national law. That said, Cosnard does give some credence to the argument that national courts should not accord immunity in certain of those situations that would normally be reserved to public international law, such as cases concerning serious violations of human rights abroad. He does so on the basis that such an approach would expand the category of persons able to make claims beyond those able to benefit from diplomatic protection, in a manner consistent with recent developments in international law. Nevertheless, he qualifies this view with the—somewhat questionable—assessment that most authors and the practice of national courts still support the opposite position, namely that *all* violations of public international law are reserved to the traditional mechanism of inter-State claims.

Cosnard's rigorous analysis convincingly demonstrates that the ongoing development of restrictive State immunity does not involve an increase in the number and scope of the exceptions to immunity, but rather an increase in affirmations of competence by national courts and legislatures. Although the two kinds of development are not necessarily incompatible, this subtle but important distinction enables him to conclude that '[l]'étude de ce qui a été un privilège des États se révèle la chronique d'une mort annoncée'. Fortunately for us, the same cannot be said of French language scholarship in international law.

MICHAEL BYERS

Yearbook of the European Convention for the Prevention of Torture and Inhuman or Degrading Treatment or Punishment. Volume I, 1989–1992. COUNCIL OF EUROPE. Nottingham: Human Rights Law Centre, University of Nottingham, 1997. 445 pp. £90.

The European Convention for the Prevention of Torture (ECPT) came into force in February 1989 and the Committee for the Prevention of Torture established under the Convention was appointed in September 1989. The purpose of the Convention is preventive: to make less likely that which is prohibited by Article 3 of the European Convention of Human Rights. The function of the Committee (CPT) is to make visits of inspection to places of detention in States party and thereby formulate recommendations which will better safeguard those persons detained on the authority of State agencies from being subjected to torture or inhuman or degrading treatment or punishment. Now, nine years later, the CPT, whose reports may only be published if authorization is forthcoming from the governments to which they are addressed, is well established. The number of States party has grown from 15 in 1989 to 35 and will shortly reach 40. The Committee, whose membership comprises independent persons elected by the Committee of Ministers on the basis of their 'competence in the field of human rights' or their 'professional experience in the areas covered by the Convention' (Article 4(2))—one member for each State party—has correspondingly grown and the programme of visits has expanded. By the end of 1997, 44 country visits had been made and, contrary to early expectations, the vast majority of the resultant reports, together with one or more government responses, have seen the light of day, albeit sometimes after a considerable delay. All this means that there is now a considerable body of CPT 'jurisprudence', even though the CPT is a non-judicial body, does not define its key terms (except by way of example), and is not bound by the jurisprudence of the Commission or Court, but, as the Explanatory Report to the Convention (paras. 26–7) makes clear, draws on that case law, and other international instruments, as a 'source of guidance'. By the beginning of 1998 there were almost 100 CPT reports and government responses available for analysis. The University of Nottingham Human Rights Law Centre, in collaboration with the CPT Secretariat in Strasbourg, has performed the valuable service of placing between hard covers the first batch of this otherwise easily lost or, if much used, soon decayed material.

The first volume covers the period 1989–1992, years during which the Committee was finding its feet and few reports (five CPT reports and three government responses) were authorized for publication. Subsequent volumes will be published for each successive year.

This first volume incorporates all the essential materials a student of the subject might require. In addition to the published country reports and CPT annual General Reports, there is the text of the Convention and Explanatory Report; signatures, ratifications and declarations; the Committee Rules Procedure; the composition of the Committee (names and brief biographical details) and Secretariat as at December 1992; the dates of plenary meetings; and lists of countries and institutions visited. The only routine documents omitted are the Council of Europe press releases issued shortly after each country visit has taken place or announcing ratifications, election of members, and so on. Where reports are available in both French and English, both versions are given, and all the general material is usefully presented in both languages on facing pages. There is also a valuable bibliography of material on the ECPT to 1992. The editors have, however, eschewed practically all commentary and offer no analysis. The editorial introduction, one-third of which describes what this and subsequent volumes will contain, comprises only two pages. This is a pity. It suggests that in the absence of an analysis by the CPT Secretariat itself of the Committee's operations (the size of the CPT budget, the number of days spent undertaking visits each year, the use of *ad hoc* experts to assist the Committee, the changing pattern in the type of visits made, and so on) and standards (what cumulative position has been taken by the Committee regarding detention procedures, accountability frameworks, custodial facilities and regimes, and so on)—something which Secretariat resources seem as yet not to have made possible—the CPT student is to be provided with no more than the raw materials, usefully standardized, but cleaned and packaged like rather expensive supermarket vegetables. No incisive editorial flavour or grit is to be added to the whole. Nor does it appear that readers will be informed, for example, of relevant Commission and Court judgments. For this students will have to turn to commentaries contained in other books or articles.

Given this policy of editorial abstinence, the principal decision confronting the compilers of this and subsequent volumes was whether to publish CPT reports and government responses consecutively in the same volume or separately in the years in which they originally appeared. They have decided on the latter course and in truth they had little choice. Though this means that analysts will simultaneously have to have open several volumes in order to chart the dialogue between the CPT and a State party, it would not have been possible, even with the advantages of editorial hindsight, always to place documents consecutively. For example, the first volume contains the CPT report of the visit to Denmark in December 1990 published in October 1991. The Danish Government responses to this report are absent. Owing to Danish oversight (the relevant ministry was unaware, until informed by myself, that authorization for publication had never been transmitted to Strasbourg) the Danish responses were not published until March 1996 and will therefore be contained in Volume Six. They could have been included in Volume One. However, the CPT report on the visit to Turkey of September 1990, and the government response to the CPT visit to Malta of July 1990 (the report of which is contained in this volume), are also absent. Neither document has been authorized for publication, and though we can reasonably presume that after this long delay they never will be, we cannot be certain. The CPT report of the visit to Spain of April 1991 was not authorized for publication until March 1996, after the fall of the Socialist Government. It remains conceivable that the Turkish authorities will yet have a change of heart and be more open about the several CPT reports that have concluded that torture is widespread in Turkey. We know this because the CPT has twice used its only real sanction—that of issuing a Public Statement where ill-treatment has been found and the State party fails to co-operate or refuses to improve the situation (Article 10(2)).

The first occasion was in December 1992 and the Statement on Turkey is contained in this first volume.

ROD MORGAN

Religious Liberty and International Law in Europe. by MALCOLM D. EVANS. Cambridge: Cambridge University Press, 1997. xxxi +394 pp. £45.

Few rights are so many-faceted as religious liberty. At various times it has been asserted to encompass such matters as: the right of individuals to adhere to a religion of their choice without undue pressure or discrimination; the duty on the part of the State to protect religions from attack by hostile private parties; the freedom of religious organizations to operate with a certain degree of autonomy from State supervision; the right of persons to claim exemptions from normal legal or civic duties (such as military service) on religious grounds; the right of persons to act without penalty on their religious convictions; or even the fully blown separation of church and State.

It is hardly surprising that the international legal community has had immense difficulty in dealing with the subject. Fortunately, there is now an excellent book which will do much to assist. This treatise impressively combines a historical summary of experience in this area with an analysis of contemporary practice, particularly under the European Convention on Human Rights. The result is the leading treatment of this topic.

The first portion of the book will be of more interest to historians than to practising lawyers. A sweeping historical survey traces the impact of just-war thought on religious freedom. There is also an account of the way in which religious-freedom issues were dealt with in State practice from the seventeenth century to the First World War (chiefly in the context of the decline of the Ottoman Empire).

After World War I, the protection of religious freedom was one of the foremost concerns of the minority-treaty system which the international community devised. The book gives a very clear description of the welter of different arrangements that were instituted, explaining the reasons for them and the experience with them in practice. There is also an account of the attempt to include a general principle of religious freedom in the League of Nations Covenant and an explanation of why this attempt failed.

For the UN period, the author provides an informative discussion of the *travaux préparatoires* of the religious-freedom provision of the Covenant on Civil and Political Rights, together with an analysis of the practice of the Human Rights Committee in implementing it. Similarly, there is an analysis of the drafting of the 1981 UN General Assembly declaration on religious freedom. On the prospects for a binding UN convention, however, the author is firmly pessimistic.

Only in the final portion, devoted to the European Convention on Human Rights, is the focus specifically on European law. (There is no attempt to cover, even in passing, American constitutional practice.) This section, comprising between a third and a quarter of the book, will be the most useful part for practising lawyers. Two articles in the European Convention are particularly relevant. The first is Article 9, on the basic right to 'freedom of thought, conscience and religion', together with, crucially, the right to 'manifest' one's 'religion or beliefs'. The other key provision is Article 2 of the First Protocol, which requires States parties to 'respect' the 'religious or philosophical convictions' of parents regarding their children's education.

The author very clearly identifies the key legal issues to which these articles give rise. Regarding Article 9, the freedom to 'manifest' applies to 'religion or beliefs' but not to general freedom of thought and conscience. As a result, the Strasbourg organs are compelled to distinguish between these categories. In addition, it is necessary to determine what the right of manifestation actually entails—and, in particular, how the manifestation of a religion or belief differs from action which is merely inspired or motivated by religious concerns. Regarding the First Protocol, the Strasbourg organs have the task of distinguishing the 'religious and philosophical convictions' of parents from their mere personal preferences, since the one category is entitled to 'respect' and the other not. Then there is the problem of what the States' duty of respect actually entails.

On all of these questions, the author gives a clear and thorough account of the case-law from Strasbourg. The account is far from being merely descriptive. The decisions are subjected to a searching critique which makes it clear that there is considerable room for improvement. At the same time, the author is scrupulously fair-minded and non-polemical.

The book is produced to the highest standard. It is very clearly written. The index is extremely thorough, and there are tables of treaties and cases, together with a fine bibliography. Historians, legal scholars and practitioners alike owe a great debt to the author for this thorough, up-to-date and immensely informative book.

STEPHEN C. NEFF

International Law for Antarctica. Edited by FRANCESCO FRANCIONI and TULLIO SCOVAZZI. 2nd edition. The Hague/London/Boston: Kluwer Law International, 1997. xvii + 681 pp. £152.

The ever-increasing complexity and sophistication of international law has led inevitably, as it has in other disciplines, to a proliferation of sub-divisions of its subject-matter. Each of these novel fields of study has tended to generate its own specialist literature, which has in turn served to fuel the further development of the particular sub-discipline to which it relates. In recent years this process has been accompanied, and perhaps to an extent accelerated, by the emergence throughout the British higher educational system of correspondingly specialized programmes of postgraduate study within the general area of international law. Thus, it is currently possible to pursue a taught postgraduate degree in such highly-focused areas as the international law of human rights or of the environment. Of all the available modes of presentation of the scholarly analysis which enables these sub-disciplines to develop and flourish, the collection of essays undoubtedly represents one of the most valuable, since it permits the exploration of a series of key themes by those with special interest and expertise, both in the particular aspects of the sub-discipline selected for consideration and in those cognate areas of law which set them in context and shape the path of their evolution.

Admittedly, such collections are prone to attract criticism from reviewers, commonly on the grounds that they contain excessive repetition or exhibit insufficient cohesion, but observations of this kind mistake the primary function of such works and all too often betray the fact that the reviewer's own real need may be for a brief, introductory textbook. Few textbook writers, however, can match the collective knowledge and insight which can be brought to bear by a team of contributors, each offering his or her specialist perspective on the subject, and it is this feature which renders the collection of essays potentially an ideal medium for advanced-level, seminar-based postgraduate study. Indeed, given that the perusal of an essay collection for the purposes of review may well represent the only occasion upon which such a work will be read in its entirety, questions of repetition and cohesion are of rather limited relevance. In reality, by far the most important aspect of the editorial role concerns the selection of topics and contributors, though a useful function can undoubtedly be served by an element of judicious cross-referencing and, where appropriate, by the drawing together of fundamental themes and principles in a chapter of reflections or conclusions. Ultimately, however, the true value of the work is determined primarily by the quality of the analysis presented by the contributors, and also, perhaps, by the extent to which they take the opportunity to interact and seek the benefit of each other's wisdom.

International Law for Antarctica is relatively unusual within the genre in that it represents the second edition of a collection first published by Giuffre in 1987, and updated as part of an ongoing collaborative project between the Universities of Siena, Genoa and Milan. One sobering feature is that while the original 532-page volume was marketed at £26.50, its 681-page successor is offered by Kluwer at £152.00, and purchasers may therefore feel justified in expecting a substantial value-added element in the new edition. Certainly there has been no shortage of developments in the decade preceding its appearance, and these are duly reflected in both the structure and detailed content of the work. As to the latter, two contributions, those of van der Essen on the origins of the Antarctic system and of Brunner on Article 10 of the Antarctic Treaty, have been reproduced in unamended form, while half a dozen or so of the other original topics have been substantially revised and updated. The remainder have been completely replaced by novel offerings, under the hand either of new contributors or of participants in the original project who have sought to refocus their interest. There are twenty-one chapters in total, grouped as before under a number of generic headings. These have, however, also been modified to reflect contemporary concerns, with the conservation of resources and the protection of the Antarctic environment now featuring particularly prominently. Other themes which have been given added emphasis include dispute settlement, the implementation of Antarctic Treaty System instruments and the question of liability for harm.

Unlike the first edition, all contributions are now presented in English, which, as the editors readily admit, presented considerable practical problems, given that this was not the first language of the majority of participants. The process of translation has undeniably resulted in a smattering of eccentricities in terms of spelling, grammar and style, though it could not be claimed that these represent a serious impediment to the intelligibility of the work. It is nevertheless unfortunate that more of them were not eliminated at some stage of the editorial process.

A number of the individual contributions are of high quality and continued interest, of which conspicuous examples include those by Charney on the ATS and customary international law, Maffei on the protection of whales, Trombetta-Panigadi on the exploitation of icebergs and de Cesari on scientific research. As regards the new topics, the editors themselves provide worthwhile offerings on liability for environmental damage and selected aspects of the law of the sea respectively, while Bou contributes a thorough analysis of waste management and disposal.

Some chapters seem less impressive, however. Vignes' 'cursory synthesis' (his own description) of CCAMLR indeed seems sketchy and superficial, and is perhaps best regarded as a mere addendum to the more substantial analysis by Orrego Vicuña. At the other extreme, only limited benefit can be derived from Focarelli's mammoth chapter on acts adopted under Article 9 of the Antarctic Treaty and their implementation in Italy. It is noteworthy that no fewer than 32 pages are devoted by the author to a meticulously catalogued but ultimately tiresome and unenlightening list of expressions employed in these measures with a view to determining whether they have mandatory or merely hortatory effect. To take but one example to demonstrate the limitations of such an exercise, it is rather troubling to find the verb 'to consult' specified as one of those which 'cannot in any way be object of a precise obligation' when duties of consultation number amongst the most fundamental and widely-recognized obligations of international environmental law. One would have thought, as the author himself seems in passing to concede, that the context in which words appear was of no little significance, and it is noteworthy that the expression 'consult the other governments' is included in the list of terms judged to carry mandatory effect! Although Focarelli explains this apparent contradiction by declaring the latter usage to be exceptional, it may be doubted whether the value of his analysis is fully commensurate with the 70 or so pages which it is accorded. Its likely impact upon the price of the work alone may rather serve to confirm the earlier observation of another contributor that 'every human activity provokes the existence of waste'.

One or two contributions are primarily factual and descriptive in character, and thus essentially of background interest to the international lawyer, though this may none the less be considerable, as in the case of Casarini's historical review of activities in Antarctica prior to the conclusion of the 1959 Treaty. On the other hand, one might have hoped for a livelier account of the inspections conducted under the Antarctic Treaty than is provided by Giuliani. Barnes and Webb's treatment of State practice and the role of NGOs in the implementation of the Protocol on Environmental Protection combines two topics which might preferably have been kept distinct and each pursued in greater depth.

Viewed as a whole, this volume undoubtedly represents a substantial and welcome addition to the literature on international law as it impacts upon Antarctica, and seems certain to fulfil its avowed aspiration of contributing to the dialogue regarding the development of an appropriate legal regime to apply to that region at the dawn of a new century. At the same time, some minor reservations must be expressed. As regards the editorial function, while Francioni's introduction is helpful in highlighting general themes and setting the other chapters in context, there was perhaps scope for a more active approach in relation to the cross-referencing of the treatment of similar issues by different contributors, particularly where the views expressed are not entirely concordant.

Furthermore, the book is not entirely free of certain problems posed by the process of fragmentation of international law referred to at the beginning of this review. One of these concerns the virtual impossibility for any specialist to keep abreast of developments in areas outside his or her own specialism. Where a team of contributors is assembled to produce a collection such as this, however, there should surely be scope for some of these difficulties to be overcome through the exchange and cross-fertilization of ideas, but it is unclear to what extent such a process occurred in this case. Gautier's chapter on institutional developments in the ATS, for example, would surely have benefited from a consideration of the wide variety of institutional arrangements and formal implementation instruments which have been adopted under the battery of environmental treaties concluded over the last couple of decades. Instead, he feels constrained to draw comparisons with such institutions as the UN, OSCE and GATT, which, as he himself recognizes, are scarcely close relatives of the Antarctic Treaty System.

Finally, one should not overlook the inevitable risk that the growth of sub-disciplinary specialisms will lead to a progressive lessening of interest, or even of familiarity, with the established *general* principles of international law, such as those concerning jurisdiction, dispute settlement and the law of treaties. Happily, there are no major problems of this kind here, though several chapters offer observations on aspects of treaty law which are certainly open to question. Elsewhere, highly pertinent and interesting points are raised, but not always pursued in sufficient detail, such as Scovazzi's observations on successive treaties or Treves' argument regarding the interpretation of Article 20(2) of the Environmental Protocol. Nevertheless, these are relatively minor blemishes and the abiding overall impression is of a work which has much to offer.

M. J. Bowman

Trade and the Environment: A Comparative Study of EC and US Law. By Damien Geradin. Cambridge: Cambridge University Press, 1997. xxiv + 231pp. £40.

This book offers readers a thorough comparative study of European Court of Justice (ECJ) and US Supreme Court decisions on environmental issues within the framework of each system's provisions for free trade between the States. While the author refrains from the international debate, the study will be of interest to international trade and environment watchers as well as federal law practitioners.

In Part I, the author compares ECJ and Supreme Court decisions that limit a State's ability to restrict trade, dividing the decisions into categories of waste, product standards and process standards. While the Commerce Clause of the US Constitution confers a general grant of power to Congress to regulate trade between the States, the EC Treaty regulates a member State's power to hinder intra-Community trade. Despite these two different approaches, Geradin finds that the jurisprudence has nevertheless developed along parallel lines, with both courts exhibiting 'a strong antagonism to state measures discriminating on their face or in their effects against interstate trade'.

Closer analysis reveals dissimilarities. Supreme Court decisions on the import of waste, for example, have taken a stricter line than those of the ECJ. The Supreme Court reviewed a Michigan statute barring waste generated in another county, State or country unless it was explicitly authorized in the receiving county's plan, and found the measure discriminatory. The Court held such discrimination against inter-State commerce to be unconstitutional unless justified by a valid factor unrelated to economic protectionism. By contrast, the ECJ held that a Belgian regional law barring imported waste was not discriminatory given the differences between wastes produced in different areas, and their connection with the place they were produced. For the ECJ, origin was a valid justification for discrimination.

Geradin found relatively greater compatibility between the two systems in the product standards category. While product standards rarely discriminate against inter-State trade, they may nevertheless affect it. When confronted with this issue, both the Supreme Court and the ECJ employ balance tests that weigh the relative importance of the environmental and trade interests at stake. Geradin finds that the balance test is widely accepted in the United States, while its recent use in the Danish bottle case is a departure from the ECJ's general deference to environmental concerns. The author counsels against wider adoption of such a standard in the EU, arguing that it is not the role of the courts to decide whether the level of environment protection chosen by a State is 'unreasonable' or 'disproportionate'.

Geradin culminates his comparison of the 'negative harmonization' cases by proposing that harmonization of State environmental standards is preferable to the selective invalidation of State environmental measures restricting trade. He claims joint legislative and judicial harmonization would address the current incentive for each State to lower its environmental standards in an effort to compete, and carries the advantage of offering proactive legislative action over comparatively reactive judiciary action.

Part II concerns positive harmonization, and here Geradin explores several issues: the possibility for a legal or constitutional basis for environmental action in the EC Treaty and the US Constitution; the principles of subsidiarity and proportionality; how each system has attempted to balance trade and the environment; and finally the issue of pre-emption, meaning the degree of autonomy left to a State once the EU or the federal government has legislated.

In searching for the legal basis for environmental legislation, Geradin finds a link between the two systems in the notion of attributive powers. Geradin discusses the ways in which the SEA and TEU amended the EC Treaty to specifically allow Community action in the environmental field, and provides a very useful breakdown of the four categories of legislative procedure for environmental measures provided by Article 100A and Article 130s(1–3). The parallel discussion of the US Constitution is more straightforward, as the Supreme Court has authorized federal action in the environmental field based on a broad interpretation of the Constitution's Commerce Clause.

In the EU, Geradin finds the subsidiarity principle to be justiciable but limited to procedural grounds. But he predicts that the principle of proportionality will increasingly serve as a guidelines in favour of less regulatory density in Community legislation and the adoption of non-uniform rather than uniform solutions. While the US Constitution does not contain a strict corollary to these principles, the author concludes that Supreme Court decisions support the view that 'it is the political process rather than judicially enforceable limits that should structure the allocation of powers between the federal government and the states' (p.150).

Geradin provides a good discussion of EC and US directives governing car emissions standards. The use of Article 100A, which employs the co-decision procedure and needs only a qualified majority vote in the Council, permitted the adoption of stricter emission limits and in general 'strongly favours the adoption of stricter environmental legislation'. The EC measures are uniform, while on the US side the 1970 Clean Air Act allows a two-tier approach that gives States the ability to adopt stricter measures than the federal emission limits.

This book's meticulously reasoned and comprehensive treatment of the topic is of great benefit to the reader. Practitioners of either EU or US law will find the perspective gained from a comparative study refreshing. International lawyers will benefit from the author's current examination of the legal principles each system uses to balance trade and environmental concerns. The considerations each judiciary employs have parallels in the GATT, and the two systems are those most likely to influence international trade and environmental law issues in coming years.

BEATRICE CHAYTOR

The International Status of Taiwan in the New World Order: Legal and Political Considerations. Edited by JEAN-MARIE HENCKAERTS. London, The Hague, Boston: Kluwer Law International, 1996. xvii + 337 pp. including (appendices) 45 pp., (bibliography) 10 pp., (index) 16 pp. £60.

In the summer of 1995, a one-day conference was held in Brussels to study the 'oddity' of the lack of representation of Taiwan at the United Nations. This collection of essays has its origins in that conference, although the original papers have been expanded and fortified and new material has been added. Plainly, this work is not meant to be simply a record of conference proceedings. It is an attempt to analyse the legal and political problems associated with the status of Taiwan in international law, particularly (but not exclusively) its relationship, or possible future relationship, with the United Nations. Importantly, there is no attempt to minimize or disguise the obvious political overtones which must accompany any discussion of an enhanced role for Taiwan. The express acknowledgement of this critical fact endows the work with a realism and authority which a strictly rule-based analysis would not produce.

Although one may have (probably idiosyncratic) reservations about the title of the book — what, after all, is the 'New World Order'? — this is a work of solid scholarship and considerable interest. The essays are divided into five parts, Part V being concluding observations by the editor and containing a single essay on self-determination in action for the people in Taiwan. This is not meant to be, and is not, an analysis of the application of the legal right of self-determination in the Taiwanese context, but is instead a glance through the proposals mooted in the previous essays. It is good place to start for an overview of the choices that lie ahead for Taiwan and the international community in which it undoubtedly operates. Part I, entitled 'The International Legal Status of Taiwan', has three essays tackling some basic questions. Chiu's 'The International Legal Status of China' is short and pointed and good for historical facts, whereas Kuijper's conclusion in 'Is Taiwan a Part of China?' that 'China is China and Taiwan is Taiwan' (p. 17) offers the positivist's answer based on the realities of separation. As a lawyer, the reviewer would like to join him in whispering defiance of a world that 'bawl[s] that Taiwan is a part of China' (p. 18), but in Michael Davis' excellent essay 'Toward Modern

Concepts of Sovereignty and Statehood' we see why the lawyer cannot have it all his own way and must re-define, or perhaps refine, his approach in a world where legal notions of sovereignty have grown up since the simplicity of the Montevideo Convention on the Rights and Duties of States of 1933.

The remaining parts of the book cover 'Responses to Diplomatic Isolation: Informal Diplomacy' (Part II); 'Responses to International Isolation: Participation in International Organizations' (Part III); and 'Relations Across the Taiwan Strait' (Part IV), These are supplemented by five Appendices reprinting official UN, Chinese or Taiwanese position documents or resolutions. Of the parts, the essays on Taiwan's participation in international organizations give the most informative account of Taiwan's present role and the difficulties it faces. There is a healthy dose of politics here but only rarely does the bias in favour of Taiwan feel too heavy. No doubt the conference organizers were never so naive as to hope for participation or essays from scholars from mainland China, but such a contribution is missed. Even so, these are eight thoughtful essays for the political scientist and the international lawyer. Although it is not intended to damn the rest by exclusion, Lord's essay on 'Taiwan's Right to be Heard Before the Security Council' and Sohn's 'Taiwan's Option of Becoming a Permanent Observer' are fully and convincingly argued and the best of this good group. Parts II and IV, with two essays each, are less substantial, both in terms of the range of issues considered and their treatment. Nevertheless, even if they add little to the weight of this work, they detract nothing.

The collection is, assuredly, one of the most comprehensive treatments of Taiwan's position currently available. It is not the last word — that lies with the governments and authorities involved — and it offers no quick medicine and no 'ideal' solution. It does, however, inform and challenge the reader. If one's interest lies here specifically, or if one's work raises such conundrums of sovereignty, independence and status as those swirling around Taiwan, this is a book to read.

MARTIN DIXON

Obligations Erga Omnes and International Crimes. By ANDRÉ DE HOOGH. The Hague: Kluwer, 1996. xii + 465 pp. (including appendix, bibliography and index). £124.

Over the past thirty years or so we have seen the emergence of a number of concepts of international law whose content is unclear or controversial and whose interrelation is in certain respects obscure. These include rules of *jus cogens*, fundamental principles of international law, obligations *erga omnes*, international crimes and, recently, 'intransgressible principles of customary international law'.[1] The present work started off as a doctoral thesis on obligations *erga omnes* but, its author tells us, he decided that the subject was not viable except in relation to international crimes (of States), so he shifted his focus. In this and other respects the book, which is the thesis itself with very little alteration, is the worse for the failure of the author to omit any of the research which he did to earn his doctorate. The reader is forced to follow Dr de Hoogh up a number of what, by his own admission, turn out to be blind alleys. There is a mass of detail which might conceivably be appropriate to a doctoral thesis (though your reviewer has strong reservations even in that regard), but is unnecessary in a book. Moreover, the author at times seems himself overwhelmed by its density, so that he—and consequently his reader—loses sight of the forest for the trees.

These problems are exacerbated by a convoluted style of writing and a less-than-perfect command of English. The following is an egregious, but by no means isolated,

[1] Advisory opinion on the *Legality of the Use of Nuclear Weapons, ICJ Reports*, 1996, p. 226, at p. 257, para. 79.

example, taken from a discussion of the criteria for determining which States have a legal interest in the performance of international legal obligations. In considering whether the criterion is to be found in 'the performance [*sic*] of obligations towards certain, or all, States subjected to the rule', and in repudiating Riphagen's and Sachariew's view that obligations are normally bilateral, the author says (p. 29):

> It is submitted that such a conception is doubtful. For either the obligation is performed by a certain State, in which case it is obviously being performed towards all the States obligated by the rule. If one takes as example the rule prohibiting the threat or use of force against States, clearly a State refraining from such a threat or use of force performs its obligation towards all the States bound by the rule. If it breaches its obligation, it will incur responsibility. It could be asserted that such responsibility is entailed objectively, and towards all States bound by the rule. It would follow that responsibility will be incurred upon the breach of an obligation irrespective of the exercise by another State of its right to demand performance of that obligation.

It is most unfortunate that no one was prepared to wield a sharp editorial scalpel.

Another unsatisfactory aspect of this book is its methodology. Its subtitle is 'A *Theoretical* Inquiry into the Implementation and Enforcement of the International Responsibility of States',[2] and the author stresses that he is concerned with theory, not with State practice. This is in itself questionable. For example, he concludes on 'theoretical' grounds that humanitarian intervention is impermissible, without any examination of the State practice on this matter. This seems a little like *Hamlet* without the Prince. Perhaps an even more serious methodological defect is the use of the International Law Commission's work on State responsibility and on international crimes as his theoretical and normative framework. Some aspects of the Commission's work in these areas are open to serious doubt on theoretical, as well as policy, grounds; but the author, although occasionally quibbling with the drafting, does not seriously question the premisses.

All States have a political and moral interest in international crimes not being committed, but the author rightly emphasizes that this does not automatically mean that they have a *legal* interest. He therefore sets out to discover who has such an interest and stresses the importance of establishing the correlatives: who, precisely, has what rights in relation to what conduct? It is surprising that he has not taken into account the important contributions to the theory of correlative rights and duties by such writers as Hohfeld and Hart. Some of his opinions in this regard are also questionable. In its well-known *obiter dictum* in the *Barcelona Traction* case, the International Court of Justice spoke of 'obligations of a State towards the international community as a whole'.[3] But it does *not* follow that the United Nations is the personification of the international community, nor that it has a legal interest in the narrow sense, analogous to that of States, in the performance of such obligations or in the redress of their breach. The author exercises some caution here; but he does seem to think that, at any rate in relation to crimes concerning which the Security Council has powers under the Charter (notably aggression), the UN does have a legal interest. It seems wrong to analyse the role of the Council in this way. It is not a party in interest, a claimant: it is more like the policeman whose job it is to restore the peace. In jurisprudential terms, there appears to be a failure here to distinguish between rights and powers.

The heart of the enterprise is an attempt to discover exactly what legal difference it makes if a State's wrongful act is labelled an international crime, rather than just a tort.[4] Specifically, what additional legal *consequences* flow from something being a crime? In the

[2] Emphasis added.

[3] Apparently interchangeably with 'obligations *erga omnes*', which seems clearly to connote every State having a several right against the wrongdoer.

[4] The more usual term 'delict' is actually unhelpful here, as it is apt to cover both torts and crimes.

course of this examination, Dr de Hoogh discusses what he considers to be the legal interest of the generality of States and of the United Nations in preventing international crimes and securing reparation for them and guarantees against their repetition (e.g. in the case of Iraq); and in that connection to resort to both non-military countermeasures and the use of force against the wrongdoer, and institute or intervene in proceedings before the International Court of Justice. He comes to the conclusion that there are distinctive legal consequences which flow from crimes. In investigating these matters, the author offers some useful insights. This is by no means to say that all of his reasoning can be accepted, however. For instance, his arguments for saying that any State can invoke a breach of a *jus cogens* norm are unconvincing. In particular, just because such a norm must (by his definition) be one of universal customary international law, it does not automatically follow that every State has the standing to invoke the offending treaty's nullity: universal customary law *binds* all States, but this does not necessarily mean that every State has a right to rely on its breach, even when it was not a party to the offending treaty nor a victim of the breach. (Neither, of course, is the category of rules of *jus cogens* coterminous with that of rules of universal customary law.)

The book addresses an important subject and offers much food for thought; it is a shame that it was not presented in a more appetizing or digestible form.

M. H. MENDELSON

Using Human Rights Law in English Courts. By MURRAY HUNT. Oxford: Hart Publishing, 1997. xxxvi + 431 pp. including appendices and index.

The central thesis of Murray Hunt's insightful book (written prior to the recent incorporation of the European Convention on Human Rights into English law) is that the traditional account of the United Kingdom's constitutional framework fails to offer 'a satisfactory foundation for the domestic status of international human rights law' (p. 2). Prior to the incorporation of the ECHR, the strict dualism of the traditional account was the difficulty; post-incorporation, the doctrine of parliamentary sovereignty and its concomitants remain as a hindrance. In place of 'the black and white language of incorporation' (p. 42), Hunt favours a 'more nuanced vocabulary of [degrees of] reception' (ibid.); and, in place of unqualified parliamentary sovereignty, he argues for judicial recognition of what he terms the 'interpretive obligation', namely 'an obligation to construe domestic law so as to conform with international human rights norms' (p. 44).

In the opening chapter, Hunt advances an elegant critique of 'sovereigntism'. According to this account, the United Kingdom's international obligations, until incorporated, are not 'a part of' domestic English law (meaning, at its most unyielding, that unincorporated international law is entirely irrelevant to domestic law). Once incorporated, international law, like all domestic law, remains subject to the doctrine of parliamentary sovereignty and is, thus, open to repeal or revision. Against this account, Hunt argues that strict dualism does not fit modern English judicial practice—witness, for example, a willingness to treat *customary* international law as part of domestic law and the strengthening of the presumption that legislation is not intended to run counter to international commitments—and, equally, that the doctrine of parliamentary sovereignty is out of line with the growing interdependence of nation States, exemplified in the case of the United Kingdom by its membership of the European Community. Even more tellingly, in so far as the rationale of the traditional account is the protection of the interest of citizens against abuse of executive power, the refusal to treat human rights commitments as obligatory within domestic law is counter-productive.

Hunt gives considerable substance to his critique by examining the implications for the traditional account of the United Kingdom's accession to, and membership of, the

European Community. First, in chapter 2, Hunt considers whether the pre-accession doctrines of supremacy of Community law (as *per Costa* v. *ENEL*) and direct effect (as *per Van Gend en Loos*) can be squared with the sovereigntist view; and then, in chapter 3, the same question is posed in relation to the post-accession doctrine of indirect effect (as *per von Colson*). To some extent, the traditional account can accommodate such developments by relying on the will of Parliament as expressed in the key sections of the European Communities Act 1972. However, the author's thesis is that even the most creative forms of traditional accounting are found wanting, especially in the light of the evolving judicial willingness to submit to the jurisprudence of the ECJ. Reflecting on such judicial compliance, Hunt suggests that, after a number of false dawns, the House of Lords' approach in *Webb* v. *EMO Air Cargo (UK) Ltd.* can 'justifiably be said to mark the point of departure from the earlier reconciliation of the interpretive obligation with traditional sovereignty theory' (p. 121).

A number of commentators, contemplating domestic entrenchment of human rights, have sought to draw lessons from the United Kingdom's membership of the EC—and, of course, some have argued that, in the sphere of Community law, the principles of the ECHR have been indirectly incorporated for some time via the ECJ's jurisprudence (a matter considered in some detail in chapter 7). For Hunt, however, the most significant lesson lies in the way that the courts have begun to elaborate a novel jurisprudence setting out 'the basis on which [they] may legitimately have regard to legal norms emanating from sources other than the domestic Parliament' (p. 125). Crucially, a revised account, fitting with the obligation to construe domestic law so as to conform with EC norms, offers a more general model for such an obligation in relation to international human rights norms.

In chapters 4 and 5, Hunt returns to his principal subject-matter, the *de facto* domestic recognition of international human rights obligations. The received wisdom—that unincorporated international human rights instruments, although not strictly speaking part of domestic law, nevertheless may be relied on to resolve uncertainties or ambiguities in domestic law—is dismissed as simplistic, 'obscur[ing] far more than it reveals' (p. 128). In order to draw out the complexity of judicial practice in relation to use of the ECHR in domestic litigation, Hunt tracks the key cases through three phases. In the first phase (the mid-1970s), a judicial vanguard (headed by Lords Reid and Scarman) seemed willing to accept the interpretive obligation (without ambiguity or uncertainty first having to justify a reference to human rights sources). In the second phase, such a willingness persisted in some areas of law but, in the field of administrative law, the interpretive obligation was strenuously resisted. Such resistance was epitomized in *Brind*, where the House of Lords took the line *inter alia* that if the ECHR had not been incorporated through the legitimate legislative front door then the Courts had no warrant to incorporate it through the back door. More generally, Hunt remarks, 'the concern seemed to be primarily one of administrative efficiency, a fear that if the courts imposed a requirement that the Convention be taken into account whenever discretion is exercised, the administration would be brought to a grinding halt' (p. 152). As we move into the third phase (the 1990s), a common law human rights jurisdiction, having across-the-board application, begins to take shape. This jurisdiction—manifested, for example, in the 'anxious scrutiny' refinement to *Wednesbury* judicial review where fundamental rights are at issue (as *per* Lord Bridge in *Bugdaycay*), in the exercise of judicial discretion, and generally in the tendency to assert an identity between ECHR and common law principles—attests to the way in which ECHR provisions are feeding back into domestic law. According to Hunt, the logical end point of this third phase would be 'unqualified judicial recognition of a full interpretive obligation, [that is] an acceptance by courts of a constitutional requirement that they must conscientiously strive to interpret all domestic law (common law and statute alike, and in all contexts) so as to achieve consistency with international human rights law' (p. 164).

The development of the interpretive obligation in the context of administrative law provides the focus for a wide-ranging discussion in chapter 6. On the one hand, Hunt detects an unstated application of a human rights-style proportionality test where a reviewing court, employing an 'anxious scrutiny' approach, 'must carry out an exercise which involves assessing the importance of the right, the seriousness of the interference and the weight of the competing public interest before it can reach a sensible view as to the sufficiency of the justification offered' (p. 218). Similarly, proportionality is immanent in the presumption that legislation is not intended to interfere *unnecessarily* with fundamental rights. On the other hand, the reluctance of judges openly to embrace proportionality betokens a concern not to 'collapse the crucial distinction between a supervisory and an appellate jurisdiction, on which the legitimacy of judicial review is presumed to depend' (p. 212). Such a concern supports a culture of judicial restraint that pays more attention to matters of manner, procedure, process, and approach than to the merits raised by substantive human rights issues. Thus: 'So long as courts are satisfied with bare assertions that the ECHR has been taken into account, and hold back from requiring that the decision-maker's reasoning process be set out so as to demonstrate to the court's satisfaction that a conscientious effort has been made to decide whether any infringement is justified, English courts cannot be said to be truly exercising a human rights jurisdiction' (p. 260).

In the penultimate chapter, the argument loops back to the UK's membership of the European Community. Within the traditional framework, it is arguable that the effect of the European Communities Act 1972, in conjunction with the jurisprudence of the ECJ as it evolved from the mid-1970s, has been to incorporate the principles of the ECHR in some areas of domestic law. Famously, Lords Browne-Wilkinson and Bingham, for example, have said as much. However, Hunt reminds readers that, rather than relying on a version of sovereigntism, he prefers to view the ECHR principles as part of an emerging European constitutional backcloth to which a common law human rights jurisdiction is sensitive. In other words, acceptance of the interpretive obligation implies not only a change in the script (to that of human rights), but also a change from local to European scenery.

Gathering together the dominant themes of his analysis, in the final chapter, Hunt sets out to show that the 'force of the argument for . . . recognition [of the interpretive obligation] is, at this particular point in political and constitutional history, irresistible' (p. 298). The demonstration (which, as I read it, silently employs Dworkinian interpretive methodology) starts by eliminating those accounts of the UK constitution that no longer satisfy the (unspecified) threshold of fit with practice (and not simply the practice of the judicial branch of the State: see pp. 308–11). This suffices to eliminate dogmatic dualism, sovereigntism, and their derivatives—hence, the customary international law account, presupposing 'the traditional constitutional picture' (p. 300), must also be rejected. However, at least two candidates survive to capture the essential idea that, in domestic practice, international human rights instruments are treated as 'soft' law, albeit falling short of 'hard' law giving rise to directly enforceable rights and obligations. One of these candidates, a rejuvenated common law presumption against unjustified interference with individual freedom, can be rejected as being too detached from ECHR jurisprudence as well as being liable to be backward-looking. Either way, there is a risk that such an 'indigenous' human rights jurisdiction would fail to do full justice to the moral ideal represented by human rights. Instead, Hunt suggests, a stronger base for the interpretive obligation is to be found in an indirect effect principle analogous to that developed in the context of EC law—although it is conceded that, if Article 13 of the ECHR is to anchor a jurisdiction comparable to that developed since *von Colson* (in the context of EC law), a more robust approach towards the concept of an effective remedy will be required at both European and domestic level.

What difference does incorporation of the ECHR make to Hunt's thesis? In one sense, it makes no difference. The interpretive obligation is argued for as part of a revised human rights-sensitive constitutional framework. To be sure, incorporation allows defenders of the traditional account to explain new commitments to human rights in an old-fashioned sovereigntist way. However, this misses the point. Hunt's argument is that sovereigntism has long been out of kilter with practice and it cannot be salvaged by incorporation of the ECHR (nor by any accompanying sovereigntist rhetoric). In another sense, incorporation renders more pressing Hunt's caveats about an indigenous human rights jurisdiction. If incorporation is not accompanied by a bolder judicial culture, the doctrine of proportionality will not be fully received, the deferential *Wednesbury* standard will be traded for a restrained 'margin of appreciation', and the onus will be on applicants rather than officials where it is alleged that there have been human rights violations. The challenge for the present generation of judges, Hunt concludes, is 'gradually to place domestic law into its international [human rights] setting' (p. 324).

To conclude: despite sharing Hunt's concern to promote acceptance of the interpretive obligation, we converge, I suspect, from rather different starting points. Hunt's new constitutionalism, as he puts it, 'embodies the spirit of the times' (ibid.). Undeniably, this is a time of regionalism and nation State interdependence, with European political culture being distinguished by its revitalized acceptance of human rights. Relative to such benchmarks, sovereigntism fails. However, drawing on a different (legal idealist) jurisprudential tradition, sovereigntism failed long before Europe started knitting closer together, long before a consensus began to form around international human rights instruments. The problem is not that Diceyan theory is in a time-warp; rather, it is that the legal positivism that underpins the traditional account is conceptually untenable. Quite simply, any constitutional theory that licenses a so-called legislative assembly to act in ways that are incompatible with respect for human rights fails the first test of legality (see Beyleveld and Brownsword, *Law as a Moral Judgment*, esp. ch. 7); and, without doubt, such a morally-dependent conception of law would need a much deeper defence than Hunt's fleeting reference to 'common humanity' (p. 308). Such differences, however, do not detract in the least from the overall judgment that this is an outstanding book, for the production of which both author and publisher are to be warmly congratulated.

ROGER BROWNSWORD

The Regime of Straits in International Law. By BING BING JIA. Oxford: Clarendon Press, 1998. lviii + 253 pp. including bibliography and index. £50.

The legal regime governing straits is surely one of the more important yet vexatious issues in the modern international law of the sea. Therefore, an extended treatment of the subject is to be commended, not least because it appears to be the first such treatment since the entry into force of the 1982 UN Convention on the Law of the Sea (1982 UNCLOS), and all the more so when such an endeavour is as comprehensive in its remit as this one is. For the public international lawyer no less than the law of the sea specialist, the international straits regime, especially post-UNCLOS III (Third UN Conference on the Law of the Sea, 1973–1982), is replete with questions of great import. Chief among these are gems such as the legal definition of what is meant by straits used for international navigation; and whether the transit passage regime is now part of customary international law. It is gratifying to note that both these questions and a plethora of related issues arising from them are tackled in chapters 3 and 8, respectively. The book commences with an introduction and also includes chapters on the geographical criterion of international straits (chapter 2), the relationship between straits and bays (chapter 4), the straits regime prior to UNCLOS III (chapter 5), special treaty-based passage regimes (chapter 6) and the advent and negotiation of the transit passage regime during UNCLOS III (chapter 7), and concludes in chapter 9. The lack of a comparative study of the legal regimes governing transit passage and archipelagic sea-lanes passage is perhaps the only lacuna discerned in the scope of this book, and even this observation may testify more to the idiosyncracy of the present reviewer rather than any obvious failing on the part of the author.

Throughout this study the discussion is enlivened by constant recourse to various examples of State practice and doctrinal writing in this subject area. This is particularly true in the case of the transit passage regime negotiated at UNCLOS III and now a cornerstone of the 1982 Convention that has to date spawned 125 ratifications (1 April, 1998). This synthesis of the primary and secondary sources of international law, the former having been culled from myriad different documentary sources and other materials, including the Official Record of the Conference itself, represents the culmination of an impressive piece of research, which in turn allows the author to make authoritative statements in respect of some of the more pressing questions arising within this issue area. For example, in relation to the legal status of the transit passage regime prior to UNCLOS III, Jia is able conclude with conviction that 'the right of transit passage was a *de lege ferenda* notion at the beginning of UNCLOS III' (p. 135).

More difficult perhaps is the question of how far the right of transit passage (as embodied in section 2 of Part III of the 1982 Convention) has passed into the corpus of customary law. In particular, the legal status and applicability of the transit passage regime *vis-à-vis* third States is important, despite the fewer numbers of non-party States compared to States parties. Here Jia points out that 'there is no indication that States interpret Article 38 as intending to grant the right of transit passage to third States, for the terms "all ships and aircraft" stress the type of ship and of aircraft rather than nationality' (p. 206). This finds agreement with the majority of writers on this issue who argue that the transit passage regime is a *sui generis* creature which was conceived during the UNCLOS III process and incorporated into the 1982 UNCLOS without much attendant State practice, unlike for example the exclusive economic zone (EEZ) concept. Drawing on State practice and the opinions of publicists on this issue, Jia answers this question in the negative (pp. 205–8), while conceding the possibility that the *concept* of transit passage (as opposed to the *right*) has been accepted by 'a proportion of States' (p. 204). However, Jia's attempt at making such a distinction is difficult to sustain given the fact that the recognition of the *concept* is inconceivable without at least some acknowledgement of the *right* that is provided for therein.

Further issues arising mainly concern the scope of the transit passage right, for example, in terms of whether it encompasses warships. In relation to this issue, Jia is of the view that both the *travaux préparatoires*, reflecting the general view at UNCLOS III, and the phrase 'all ships' in Article 38(1) include warships, and therefore clearly leave no room for doubt that the transit passage of warships is not to be made subject to either prior consent or authorization. Problems persist however, especially in respect of several different types of ships, notably warships carrying nuclear weapons, nuclear-powered ships be they warships or merchant vessels, and carriers of oil, nuclear and other hazardous or noxious cargoes. Although such ships may be confined to certain designated sea-lanes and are required to carry documents related to their safety status in the exercise of their innocent passage through territorial seas (Articles 22 and 23, respectively), these appear to be unnecessary in their exercise of transit passage. However, individual and regional State practice paint a different picture, particularly in relation to nuclear vessels and cargoes, with many States attempting to curb such passage through their territorial seas, whether or not these waters are included within the transit passage regime under the 1982 Convention. The reasons invoked for such constraints on transit passage by the littoral States mainly relate to security and environmental concerns. In this respect, the inclusion of the possibility of littoral State enforcement measures under Article 233 of the 1982 UNCLOS is apt to create complications for the exercise of transit passage rights by such vessels, as Jia points out (pp. 161–3).

Overall therefore this is a compelling study of an important area of the international law of the sea which not only provides a thorough analysis of the evolution of the straits regime in customary and treaty law but also relates this to examples in State practice which may influence the progressive development of the regime in the near future.

DAVID M. ONG

Manual of European Environmental Law. By A.C. KISS and D. SHELTON. 2nd edition. Cambridge: Cambridge University Press, 1997. 622 pp. Hardback, £90; paperback, £34.95.

The authors, in the preface, state that their intention has been to bring together material of interest not only to lawyers, but to those concerned with the protection of the environment within a range of disciplines. The text brings together material which provides a valuable introduction for those seeking to explore environmental law from a wider perspective, and those seeking information on the ever-increasing role of the law in environmental protection at both national and international level.

During the last ten years the number of books on various aspects of environmental law has increased dramatically, but most are limited to an explanation of the principles and policies operating at a national level, or environmental law developed by the European Community, and the policy factors affecting the formulation and application of the law. This book, written from an international law perspective, goes beyond this narrow definition of 'European environmental law', and includes discussion of material from countries outside the European Union, and from international law sources which have an impact in Europe, and on the relationships between European States and the wider world.

As befits a book intended to appeal to readers from a range of disciplines, Part 1 of the book is concerned with an exploration of the fundamental aspects of environmental law. It begins with an overview of European environmental law and the sources, national and international, from which it is drawn. It examines the various principles and concepts which have shaped modern environmental law, such as the polluter pays principle and the emphasis on the preventative approach to pollution control. It considers the 'players' on the stage of environmental protection: the role of the public, and the interest of the individual in a clean environment, and the various public agencies and institutions charged with the formation and implementation of law and policy in this area. The first part concludes with a discussion of the wide range of mechanisms which have been brought into the service of environmental protection—not only regulatory controls, but the use of economic instruments, civil law remedies and enforcement measures. The last decade has seen a shift away from an emphasis on regulatory controls alone as a means of environmental protection, and the greater emphasis placed on economic considerations, both here and later in the text, in this second edition is therefore to be welcomed.

The rest of the book is concerned with an examination of more specific issues in environmental protection. Part 2 adopts the traditional 'sectoral' approach, considering environmental protection on the basis of the media to be protected: nature conservation; soil protection; water; and the atmosphere. However, modern environmental law recognizes the fact that pollutants may have an impact on more than one environmental medium, and that an integrated approach may be required. Part 3 attempts to address this point by considering matters which may affect more than one environmental medium, such as tourism, military activities or waste management, and the role of an integrated approach to pollution control and environmental protection. At the Rio 'Earth Summit' in 1992 the need to balance economic development and environmental protection was recognized as one of the most important problems facing the world at the end of the twentieth century. The final chapter now reflects this important source of potential conflict, and the role of international trade and financial institutions.

Each chapter contains a discussion by the authors of the important issues raised, and includes extracts from important primary texts at national, European Community and international level, which serve to illustrate the various strategies and approaches adopted by different institutions within Europe. Many chapters also include 'case studies'. These are not, as the name might suggest, examples of how the law has been applied to specific pollution incidents (this could prove an interesting addition to future editions), but rather discussions of specific problems, often from a national perspective, by a variety of contributors. Given the authors' stated intention to produce a work which may act as a source of teaching material for university courses, the inclusion of a series of questions and problems at the end of each chapter serves to concentrate the mind of the reader (teacher or student) on the issues raised.

This text, which goes beyond simple environmental regulation to include such matters as human rights, and the impact of trade and armed conflict on the environment, presents a refreshing new outlook on the subject and a valuable addition to the texts on environmental law.

CAROLYN SHELBOURN

The United Nations System and its Predecessors. Edited by F. KNIPPING, H. VON MANGOLDT and V. RITTBERGER. Oxford: Oxford University Press, 1997. 2 volumes. 2,509 pp. £195.

This splendid publication has its origins in interdisciplinary teaching by the three editors who are, respectively, professors of contemporary history, public and international law and international relations at German universities. It is based on a bilingual (English or French and German) compilation of documents published in Germany and Switzerland in 1996.

Volume I, edited by Professors Mangoldt and Rittberger, deals with the United Nations system. Opening with the Atlantic Charter of 1941, the first section provides a set of basic documents on the origin and foundations of the United Nations. In addition to the UN Charter and the rules of procedure of the principal organs, the constituent instruments of all of the specialized agencies and many other United Nations bodies are included. So too are a selection of the most important resolutions of the world organization's first fifty years, particularly those of the Security Council and General Assembly, categorized according to subject-matter and then arranged chronologically. Considerable space is devoted to the major crises of recent times in which the UN has been heavily involved. The full texts of all Council resolutions adopted in relation to the Gulf Crisis of 1990–91 are provided, as are the most important of the numerous resolutions dealing with the UN's unhappy involvement in the Former Yugoslavia up to the end of 1995.

Coverage is impressively comprehensive. Nearly all UN documents to which reference is commonly made in international law and relations courses are to be found among the 140 contained in this volume. Each entry is accompanied by a concise commentary containing useful information on date of adoption, entry into force, State parties, voting record and so on as appropriate, together with reference to the original source from which the document was drawn. In many cases there are suggestions for further reading. The editors have also included in each volume a chronological list of documents which provides an interesting overview of the development of international law and world order over the course of the last two hundred years. Another helpful inclusion is a list of former names of States and dependent territories. Methodical cross-referencing and a full index make the volume easy to use in spite of its considerable bulk.

Volume II covers the period 1815 to 1946 and is the work of the professor of contemporary history, Franz Knipping. While perhaps of more direct value to scholars of history than of modern international law, it none the less makes fascinating reading.

Even those who have laboured long in this area will find much that is new among the 107 documents and Knipping's informative notes. Part A covers the century from the Congress of Vienna to the outbreak of the First World War. The much larger Part B affords to the League of Nations the same schematic treatment as Volume I does to the United Nations. Again, coverage is comprehensive, opening with President Wilson's fourteen points and concluding with the resolution for the dissolution of the League in 1946. As a former UN staff member, I was curious to see from the League Staff Regulations of 1926 how similar were conditions of service and how early UN 'entitlement-speak' was introduced. While current staffers will not envy their predecessors a six-day working week, 36 days' annual leave (compared to the modern 30) has its attractions, as does the possibility of adding, at the discretion of the Secretary-General, up to 56 days' travelling time to one's home country, travel by 'aerial navigation' being excluded.

As I finished this review, I wondered whether this collection did not lend itself to a loose-leaf format to facilitate updating. While Volume II will stand the test of time, the comprehensiveness of coverage, which is such a strength of Volume I, will quite quickly be eroded, especially if the current hyperactivity of the Security Council continues. That, however, is my only reservation. The price may deter all but the most committed of individual purchasers, but to institutions this book is a bargain, representing a veritable library on the law and history of world organizations in the space of two volumes. The editors are to be commended for the prodigious effort which must have gone into its compilation.

DOUGLAS ROSS

The Law of War Crimes: National and International Approaches. Edited by T.L.H. McCORMACK and G.J. SIMPSON. The Hague: Kluwer Law International, 1997. xxvii + 262 pp. £77.

The editors state that 'a principal objective of the book is to bring together two approaches to war crimes that are most commonly considered separately in the huge literature in the area. Accordingly, the book discusses both domestic and international approaches to war crime.' At the present time any book on the subject of war crimes can give but a snapshot view of a fast developing area of law, especially in relation to international proceedings. This book attempts to set out the position as at 31 December 1995. Much has happened since then at the *ad hoc* International Tribunal for the Former Yugoslavia, particularly in the Appeals Chamber, and in the preparations for an international criminal court. The book is therefore limited in value, to some extent, by this early cut-off date, even though it was published in 1997.

The book's chapter headings give a succinct overview of its coverage. These are: war crimes: a critical introduction; from Sun Tzu to the Sixth Committee: the evolution of an international criminal law regime; the politics of prosecution: European national approaches to war crimes; enforcing the lessons of history: Israel judges the holocaust; Australia's war crimes trials: all pity choked; laudable principles lacking application: the prosecution of war criminals in Canada; Nuremberg and Tokyo in contemporary perspective; atrocity and prosecution: the *ad hoc* tribunals for the Former Yugoslavia and Rwanda; and achieving the promise of Nuremberg: a new international criminal regime?

The chapters on national proceedings against alleged war criminals are well brought together. There is much useful detail given on the trials in Canada and in Australia. Marschik's chapter on contemporary trials in European States is particularly good, given that his approach is essentially comparative and analytical. The trials in Israel have been written about fairly extensively elsewhere; the author of this chapter might have gone on to explain his statement, when referring to the *Demjanjuk* case, that 'it simply becomes too difficult for the system of justice to extract the truth'. If this was a feature in the *Demjanjuk* case, is it relevant to other war crimes trials and what might be suggested to ensure that the system of justice *is* able to extract the truth? This issue is one of the essential problems with any war crimes trial. How can such trials ensure, at the same time, justice for both the individual defendant and the international community acting on its own and on the victims' behalf? The rules of procedure and the laws of evidence in such trials are as important as the substantive law itself, but they are often treated as subsidiary matters. The same may be said about defences to war crimes trials. If we leave aside head of State and superior orders as non-defences we might consider whether it is fair to try an individual without defining beforehand the availability and limits of any possible defences.

The chapter by Simpson, on war crimes: a critical introduction, is well thought out. This looks at war crimes trials in terms of partiality, legality, definitions of criminality and war crimes as history. He recognizes the problems imposed in ensuring procedural fairness and the value of war crimes trials in 'enlightening the present-day innocents'. He concludes that 'between 1945 and 1993 war crimes trials were held in municipal courts under domestic legislation . . . There is a sense that the international domain will be untainted by the biases and partialities of the municipal sphere. So, history is again turning to the international tribunal as a means of vindicating a universal notion of justice and global humanism.' There is, however, no analysis, for example, of the current international tribunal for the Former Yugoslavia to test this theory.

This book would have been improved had there been cross-referencing by the editors so that attention might have been directed to discussions of similar topics by different contributors. Thus, the Leipzig trials are discussed at pp. 49, 69 and 75, while defences to war crimes are at pp. 14 and 218, with no linkage. Although the editors state that the 'individual chapters confirm this intermingling of the national with the domestic', there is not much evidence in these chapters of any analysis of the differences between such jurisdictions. One might have expected, for instance, discussion of the differences between them of procedure, the admissibility of evidence and the availability of defences for the purpose of drawing out the most effective (and fair) form of trial. Given its limitations much of the book is, nevertheless, a useful contribution to the 'huge literature in the area'.

PETER ROWE

International Relations Law of the European Union. By DOMINIC MCGOLDRICK. London: Longman, 1997. xvii + 249 pp. Paperback, £16.99.

Given the increasing importance of the European Union's external relations, both in the political and in the commercial context, it is astonishing that until very recently there was no systematic overview of its principles and practice. Dominic McGoldrick suggests in his Introduction a number of reasons for this—including the arcane nature of the subject and the development of practice and doctrine 'for which legal justification seemed tenuous, if not downright dubious'. It may be, however, that the lacuna resulted from the increasing divergence between the 'new legal order' of European Community law and public international law. External relations law straddles the two, and in a period of virtual apartheid students may have been intimidated from studying it, and academic writers from explaining it, without having deep roots in both disciplines.

McGoldrick's book should help substantially to reduce suspicion and misunderstanding and even to generate enthusiasm for a subject necessarily on the cusp of law and international relations. It appeared the year after the substantial work by Macleod, Hendry and Hyett, *The External Relations of the European Communities: a Manual of Law and Practice*, and complements it admirably. *International Relations Law of the European Union* is the introductory book for the new student or the practitioner trying to acquire a general understanding of how disputes over the competence to conclude international agreements between Commission and Member States, or legislation on sanctions, for example, fit into the wider picture. *External Relations of the European Communites* is thc *vade mecum* for the insider needing advice on practice and precedents in specialized areas.

A major strength of McGoldrick's treatment is the proportion devoted to the Common Foreign and Security Policy, and the clear account of the relations between Second Pillar action and implementing Community legislation—now so frequent—within the First Pillar. This is a clearly thought through account of the post-Maastricht structure governing relations of the Union with the rest of the world. The dichotomy applied by insiders between 'external policies'—properly the concern of the Communities—and 'foreign policies'—properly the responsibility of the Member States with the European institutions given a merely co-ordinating role—was always an artificial one. It is no longer realistic to treat the CFSP as a minor appendage to an account of the European Communities' external relations. McGoldrick explains clearly how the CFSP now imposes binding legal obligations on the Member States, generated and enforced by institutional mechanisms which are for the most part those of classical international law. He gives a clear account of the distinction between formal common positions and joint actions, practical examples of where these new tools have been deployed, and an accurate (if brief) account of the successive methods by which the Community has imposed sanctions against third States. Increasingly the Council clarifies or goes beyond the opaque terms of United Nations Resolutions when it draws up what appear to be merely technical implementing measures, and does so under Article 228a of the European Community Treaty without scrutiny of its proposals either by the European Parliament or by national Parliaments. Given the impact which such measures can have—backed by the possibility of criminal charges against individual traders—it is of importance that the underlying European legal powers should be better understood.

The book went to press before the adoption of the Treaty of Amsterdam, but it includes extensive critical discussion of many of the proposals to improve the procedures and effectiveness of the CFSP which were discussed in the negotiations for the new Treaty. There is a brief account of the Third Pillar of the European Union with particular reference to those aspects with important international relations implications, such as asylum, immigration and combating international crime, and an equally brief account of international aspects of European Union citizenship. This notes that for third States it is curious to be presented 'with an assertion of a form of international citizenship of an entity which does not itself have international legal personality'—and questions whether they are under any obligation to recognize it. Here, as elsewhere, the brevity of the analysis is compensated for by the thoroughness and quality of the selection of recent literature cited in apposite footnotes.

In the final chapter—Appraisal and Prospectus—McGoldrick looks at the EU as model for the international community and the international law of the future. It is refreshing to read an assessment which is both positive and realistic on what has been and might be achieved by the Union's international actions, and one which does not regard as the main criterion of achievement progress towards a federal State overfulfilling its quota of decisions on anything and everything. He sees the European Union as exercising a benign leadership by example, as well as by specific external actions intended to promote human rights, democracy and economic liberalism. 'If the next century does herald a clash of civilizations then the EU represents a strong expression of western civilization.'

International Relations Law of the European Union is excellent value for the student of European Union law or international relations and a well-structured and illuminating guide for the practitioner or teacher.

EILEEN DENZA

Judge Sir Gerald Fitzmaurice and the Discipline of International Law. Opinions on the International Court of Justice, 1961–1973. By J. G. MERRILLS. The Hague: Kluwer Law International, 1998. xvi + 340 pp. £73.

This is the third in a series of volumes entitled *The Judges* and devoted to the judicial work of eminent judges on the International Court of Justice. The first two volumes covered the contributions of Judge Shigeru Oda and the late Judge Manfred Lachs and were reviewed together in an earlier edition of this *Year Book*: see volume 67 (1996), p. 522.

It is entirely fitting that this third volume should concentrate on the judicial activity of the late Sir Gerald Fitzmaurice, relating that judicial activity to the concept of the discipline of international law; for it was always central to Sir Gerald's vision of international law that it should be viewed as a discipline imposing necessary restraints on the liberty of States to pursue activities which might have adverse and injurious effects on the rights and interests of other States. Not for him what he regarded as the loose and dangerous credo of the Yale school with its attachment to visionary and imprecise notions of world order. His philosophy was altogether sterner, requiring a strict separation of legal from political considerations.

The present volume has been prepared by John Merrills, whose appreciation of Fitzmaurice's judicial (and indeed scholarly) activities has already been displayed in the two notable articles which he published in this *Year Book* on the role which Judge Fitzmaurice played in the International Court of Justice (see volume 48 of this *Year Book* (1975–6), at p. 183) and in the European Court of Human Rights (see volume 53 of this *Year Book* (1982), at p. 115). The book follows the pattern of the two previous volumes in this series, comprising a substantial biographical essay, followed by a reprint of the judge's separate or dissenting opinions, in full or in condensed form.

In his preface, Professor Merrills admits that he met Sir Gerald only towards the end of his life. The present reviewer suffers from what is perhaps a graver disability, namely, that he knew Sir Gerald well for the last thirty-two years of his life, having worked closely with him from 1950 to 1960 as one of the most junior of the small cadre of Foreign Office Legal Advisers at the time. He had an immense respect for the penetration of Fitzmaurice's analytical processes and for the clarity and elegance of his literary style. It was always a pleasure for a junior to discuss difficult international legal problems with Fitz (as he was known to all his colleagues in the Foreign Office); one could be assured of a patient hearing, followed by a quiet resumé of the principal elements of the problem and an indication of the best course of action to follow in the light of the applicable legal principles. Fitz may have been short of stature, but he had a towering intellect and a formidable capacity for work: it should not be forgotten that, during the seven and more years between 1952 and 1960 in which he served as Acting Legal Adviser (during the late Sir Eric Beckett's illness) and then Legal Adviser following Beckett's retirement on medical grounds, he succeeded in producing the majority of his memorable annual articles in this *Year Book* on the law and procedure of the International Court of Justice.

Lest it be thought that, during the 1950s there might have been a lull in Britain's diplomatic activities sufficient to reduce the pressure on Fitz in his capacity as Legal Adviser to the Foreign Office, few will need reminding that this decade witnessed, *inter alia*, the Suez adventure (where, as is well known, the views of the British Government's professional legal advisers were deliberately not sought during the final crucial month), the 1958 Geneva Conference on the Law of the Sea (where Fitz played a prominent role in the British delegation), and the beginnings of the movement towards European integration. To add to the burden upon him, Fitz was co-opted onto the International Law Commission in 1955 in succession to Sir Hersch Lauterpacht, also taking over from the latter as Special Rapporteur on the Law of Treaties, and leaving the Commission only on his election to the Court in November 1960, in consequence of Lauterpacht's untimely death. All his colleagues in the Foreign Office at this time knew that Fitz had a prodigious capacity for sustained endeavour, and that he was regularly accustomed to make copious notes on outstanding scholarly or other problems in the middle of the night. In the circumstances, his serenity and calm were remarkable features of a temperament which combined analytical skills of the highest order with the strong convictions of a major legal philosopher.

These then were the talents which Fitzmaurice brought to the International Court at The Hague and later to the European Court of Human Rights at Strasbourg. That he was thoroughly at home in the Hague and thoroughly uneasy in his later judicial activity in Strasbourg requires no demonstration. It is for his judicial work at the International Court of Justice that he will be remembered.. He had all the qualities required in an international judge; and yet he suffered a storm of criticism for the attitude which he took in the two *South West Africa* cases of 1962 and 1966, where he was represented by those who did not know him well enough as being sympathetic to *apartheid*. Nothing could have been further from the truth. The difficulty was that the line of argument espoused by those judges on the other side of the divide offended against some of Fitz's most deep-seated convictions as to the interpretation of international instruments and as to the role of the individual international judge. To characterize Fitz as the representative of a conservative and out-moded vision of international law, as some have done, is a misrepresentation. That he was not. More than thirty years on, it may be possible better to understand the manner in which Fitz's rule-oriented (as opposed to 'policy-oriented') approach to international law was an integral part of his legal philosophy and deeply embedded in his intellectual convictions.

In the final paragraph of his extended essay, Professor Merrills cites a passage from an address which Fitz made to the Grotius Society in 1952/53 on 'The United Nations and the Rule of the Law' about the task of lawyers in international affairs. I have always regarded that address as encapsulating the essence of Fitzmaurice's approach to the practice of international law, and I think it is appropriate to conclude this review of a stimulating work by recalling that, for Fitzmaurice (as he indicated in this address), it could be an error to seek for justice in the individual case; for him, justice was more likely to be found in the application of governing legal principles to the particular case. Let me put the thought in his own words:

> Justice is very seldom achieved by directly aiming at it: rather is it a by-product of the application of legal rules and principles, a consequence of the general order, certainty and stability introduced into human and international relationships through the regular and systematic application of known legal rules and principles, even if these rules and principles are not always perfect and do not always achieve ideal results in every case.
> (*Transactions of the Grotius Society*, 38 (1953), at p. 147.)

Some may view this as an ascetic and dangerous credo, but others, including the present reviewer, believe that it conveys a powerful message to the international lawyer—and a message which we neglect at our peril. It may in any event explain, at least in some measure, the view which Fitz took in the two *South West Africa* cases in the 1960s—a view which certainly troubled and pained him considerably, for he had no sympathy with the *apartheid* policies being pursued by successive South African Governments at the time. He was aware that his attitude would be misunderstood by many, but he felt it his duty to abide by his perception of the basic role of the international judge, whatever the cost to him personally. One may in fact disagree with some of the reasoning in his separate opinions in 1962 and 1966, and yet admire the fundamental integrity of the man. Professor Merrills does full justice to this multifaceted and brilliant international jurist whose commentaries on the jurisprudence of the International Court are still cited regularly by counsel before the Court in their written and oral pleadings.

IAN SINCLAIR

The International Court of Justice. Its Future Role after Fifty Years. Special issue of the *Leiden Journal of International Law.* Edited by A.S. MULLER, D. RAIČ and J.M. THURÀNSZKY. The Hague, Boston and London: Martinus Nijhoff, 1997. xxxiv + 433 pp. £86.

This is one of a number of collections of essays that have been published to celebrate the fiftieth anniversary (in 1996) of the International Court of Justice. A number of influential and authoritative scholars and practitioners have contributed to this volume. There are essays by judges of the ICJ as well as by academics, officials at the UN and the ICJ, and a diplomat. The editorial introduction explains that the aim of the collection is 'to make an assessment of the ICJ's fifty years' track record and, on the basis of that assessment, to provide some indications as to the future role the Court might fulfil' (p. xxvii). In order to carry out this task, a number of roles in which the Court functions have been identified. The contributors undertake an assessment of how successful the Court has been in carrying out these roles and suggest ways in which the Court's effectiveness in these role can be enhanced. The four roles identified are (1) the dispute settlement role; (2) the supervisory role; (3) the advisory role; and (4) the legislator role. In addition to sections devoted to each role of the Court, there is also an introductory essay and two concluding essays. By examining the functioning of the Court at these general levels rather than examining the contribution of the Court to specific areas of international law, the collection takes a different approach from other collections celebrating the anniversary of the Court. This collection addresses fundamental issues regarding the nature and effectiveness of judicial activity in international law. Is the ICJ a good place for dealing with 'political disputes'? Should it have a role in calling the Security Council to account in cases where that body is alleged to have violated international law? Should access to the Court be extended to non-State actors? These are some of the questions raised and sought to be answered by this volume.

The dispute settlement role of the Court is treated with an eye on the past and another on the future. The role of the Court in settling disputes between States is examined in four essays (by Sir Robert Jennings, Adede, Couvreur and Sugihara), but there is also contemplation of the possibility of international organizations (by Sztucki, Szasz and Siedl-Hohenveldern) and individuals (Janis) being given access to the Court's contentious jurisdiction. The issue of the relationship between the Court and United Nations Security Council and the possibility of review by the Court of Council decisions is one that is touched upon in a number of the essays but is given extensive and admirable treatment by Shaw as part of an assessment of the Court's supervisory role. The possibility of the Court exercising a supervisory jurisdiction over other international and national tribunals is considered by Schermers. However, by this time we are firmly casting an eye into the future—probably the distant future—role the Court might be asked to play in international society.

For the present, Shaw expresses the concern that the Security Council is increasingly tempted into a process of 'judicial drift' where it makes determinations or conclusions of law regarding the validity or legality of State action. For Shaw, the question of limits to Security Council action ought to be examined by reference to a threefold division. Determinations of a threat to the peace, breach of the peace or act of aggression fall into the first division, and in these matters the Council possesses 'the fullest discretion or widest attitude'. In the second division are actions taken with the *immediate object* of removing the threat or remedying the breach of peace. Here the Council also has an extensive discretion and there is little room for the application of international legal principles. However, those principles come into full effect in the third category where the Council is making a legal determination or taking secondary level action after the initial response to restore peace has been taken. It is here that the Court may enter into the picture in the exercise of its independent judicial function. This analysis raises a number of questions not fully explored by Shaw. For example, how is one to distinguish action taken with the immediate object of removing a threat from action which is secondary? Are there absolutely no legal limits to the powers of the Council when acting with the immediate object of removing a threat? Can the Council respond in absolutely any way it chooses or are there circumscribing boundaries? If there are circumscribing boundaries, why is the Court not able to point out those boundaries if it is admitted it has competence to restrain the Council in other areas?

The advisory jurisdiction of the Court is elegantly treated by Pomerance, who offers insight into the original conception of the advisory jurisdiction of the Permanent Court of International Justice, as well as an explanation of why that Court was more successful in its advisory function than the present Court. The point is made that at the time of the PCIJ, the advisory jurisdiction of the Court was usually utilized as part of its dispute settlement function and never sharply distinguished from its contentious role. The consequence was that the consent of the disputing parties (and of all the members of the Council of the League of Nations) was always sought and obtained before an advisory opinion was requested. The *Eastern Carelia* case is, of course, the one exception and there the Court firmly refused to render the opinion requested. ICJ/UN practice, on the other hand, has seen the transformation of the advisory role into one where it is mainly matters relating to international organizations that are in issue. Although these issues may be underlaid by inter-State disputes, the Court (and the political organs of the UN) have tended not to require the consent of those States. Instead, the Court has focused on the fact that it is providing a solution to the organizational problem. It is this departure from the practice of obtaining unanimity and consent before seeking an opinion from the ICJ that has, in Pomerance's view, led to the handing down of many 'ineffectual opinions'.

In relation to the Court's role as lawgiver, there are two essays by Gowlland-Debbas and Quintana. The former gives the reader a flavour of how the Court and individual judges view and have developed norms of international law which protect the fundamental values of the international community, whilst the latter examines the contribution of the Court to the development of the law of maritime delimitation. It is only in this section that the Court's contribution to substantive international law is examined. This is not a criticism of the work, but simply an indication of its focus.

In the first essay of the collection, intended as a general overview of the position of the Court, Judge Shahabuddeen attempts a description of the character of the Court. In doing so, he also tries to explain why the Court is much more active today than it was in earlier years. For Judge Shahabuddeen the two issues are linked. The main characteristic of the contemporary Court is its representativeness of universal society. This is also the reason for confidence in the Court today. Despite this apparent surge in confidence, Judge Shahabuddeen is right to point out that there is a lack of visibility of the Court in the international community. He gives explanations for this 'retiring image' (which is thought not correspond to the Court's importance) but falls short of offering a remedy. However, the point is made that there is now a tendency to regard recourse to the Court as a normal part of international life, and the hope is expressed that an increased workload will improve its image.

If the view one gets at the beginning of the volume is that the ICJ is at a high point from which it has begun to play a more central role in international affairs, the concluding remarks of the one political scientist among the contributors—David Forsythe—lead the reader to the opposite conclusion. In a very stimulating essay, Forsythe evaluates the other contributions and challenges a number of Shahabuddeen's conclusions. In Forsythe's view, 'the ICJ is, in fact, marginal to most of the structural issues of international relations' (p. 385). The Court is not 'fully occupied', as Shahabuddeen says, but still 'under-utilized'. The Court cannot, as argued by Shahabuddeen and other contributors, afford to render decisions without regard to prospects of compliance, but 'needs to pay attention to such "practical questions" as the likelihood of powerful states' co-operation' (p. 396).

This latter point relates to one of the issues which crop up throughout the volume: the distinction between legal and political disputes and whether it is relevant to the Court in its decision-making. This is an issue that forms the focal point of the essays that look at 'States as Litigants' under the Court's dispute settlement role. Sir Robert Jennings, a former President of the Court, takes the view that adjudication is a specific, technical and intellectual form of dispute settlement that is not appropriate for all types of disputes. For him, many disputes call for political decision-making and more attention should be paid to developing such procedures rather than to what Jennings sees as a naive over-concentration by international lawyers on judicial settlement. The alleged dichotomy between legal and political disputes is again taken up in detail by Sughira, who argues that though the Court's competence is not debarred by the fact that a case has political as well as legal aspects, there are two situations where political disputes are outside its purview. These two situations are (1) where there are no legal rules or they are inadequate and (2) where political factors predominate in the case. In both these cases, it is argued that it would be contrary to the Court's judicial function to decide the case. Whilst it may be acceptable that an absence of legal rules renders a particular question non-justiciable (if one accepts the possibility that on some issues there are no legal guidelines for decision-making), one may take issue with Sughira's other instances of non-justiciability. How is the Court to come to the conclusion that a legal rule is inadequate? What does inadequate mean? Inadequate for whom? To countenance the possibility of the Court sidestepping what it accepts to be the present law on the ground that it is 'inadequate' is precisely to ask the Court to engage in political decision-making. As Forsythe points out in his essay, a refusal by a court to rule on an issue is in fact 'a political act in favour of the actors that stand to benefit from the *status quo*' (p. 389). Furthermore, how is the Court to decide that political issues predominate in a case? If one accepts the definition quoted by Kooijmans in his concluding essay, a 'political dispute' is one 'of such a nature as to arouse violent national passions'; any dispute can fall into this category as long as the issue is seen as being sufficiently important to the country in question. How is the Court to make this assessment? It is an assessment that needs political skill and the exercise of political judgement, precisely the sort of skill and judgement that these writers are seeking to stop the Court from exercising!

Whilst the contributors and the editors deserve praise for putting together this collection, there are certain issues which this reviewer would also have liked to see dealt with. For example, the procedure of the Court is not touched upon at all, except in connection with the extension of standing to international organizations and individuals. It is felt in many quarters that the present rate at which the Court dispatches its business is too slow and certainly needs speeding up if the Court is to play a more central role in the international community. Judge Shahabuddeen's cursory statement that 'it seems doubtful that further simplification [of the Court's procedures] . . . would by itself attract additional business, and equally doubtful that possible litigation has been discouraged by fear of procedural difficulties' (p. 20) is open to challenge. The decision (in early 1998) of the Court to simplify certain aspects of its procedure with a view to a speedier dispatch of business is a sign that the Court has come to realize that more needs to be done.

Another problem with the work is that each writer seems to have written his or her piece in ignorance of what others in the project have done. Although a number of issues (the legal/political disputes debate, the question of judicial review of Security Council actions, *jus standi* of international organizations) are discussed in several different essays, the contributors fail to engage with each other and there is no cross referencing. Only the concluding essay of Forsythe attempts to respond to issues raised by others, and his essay demonstrates how much the work would have been improved with greater interaction.

Despite these quibbles there can be no doubt that any serious student of the functioning of the Court who ignores the essays in this collection does so at his or her own peril. The collection is definitely a valuable addition to any library (institutional or personal) that seeks to cover the work of the ICJ. Its contributors provide differing assessments of the past and raise challenging issues for the future. One may not always agree with the points of view but they are usually well argued. As we draw to the close of the United Nations Decade of International Law, the international community needs to look seriously at the continuing development of mechanisms for the peaceful settlement of international disputes. Amongst international lawyers, there is an assumption that the ICJ has a central role to play in this process. This work elucidates how the Court's role can be enhanced and where it can usefully act in the international community.

DAPO AKANDE

New Zealand Consolidated Treaty List as at 31 December 1996. By NEW ZEALAND MINISTRY OF FOREIGN AFFAIRS AND TRADE. Wellington, 1997. 2 volumes. 471+596 pp. Indices. NZ$25 per volume.

Treaties are central to the operation of the international political, economic, social and legal system. That appears from the determination of the peoples of the United Nations recorded in its Charter to establish conditions under which justice and respect for the obligations arising from treaties and other sources of international law can be maintained. One of the principles of the Organization is that all members shall fulfil in good faith the obligations assumed by them in accordance with the present Charter.

A generation later the Vienna Convention on the Law of Treaties recognized both the fundamental role of treaties in the history of international relations and their ever-increasing importance as a source of international law and as a means of developing peaceful co-operation among nations. It reaffirmed the principle of *pacta sunt servanda*: 'Every treaty in force is binding upon the parties to it and must be performed by them in good faith'. The Charter, like the Covenant of the League of Nations before it, recognizes that if those values and principles are to have real effect practical steps have to be taken in support of them. They reflect half of the first of President Woodrow Wilson's Fourteen Points, requiring that covenants be open, if not openly arrived at, with their stipulation that parties to treaties deposit them with the Secretariat, which is then to publish them (Article 102 of the Charter and Article 18 of the Covenant). Those obligations are the basis of the more than 1,800 volumes (up to 1991) of the *League of Nations* and *United Nations Treaty Series*, supplemented for the previous 270 years, back to the Treaties of Westphalia, by the 234 volumes of the *Consolidated Treaty Series*.

To be really useful, especially in particular contexts, those general collections must however be supplemented by national publications. Accordingly, many countries not only publish their treaties as State papers but also publish collections and lists of them. That activity was recorded over 40 years by the United Nations in its valuable *List of Treaty Collections* (1956)—and many would say a new edition would be of even greater help in this rapidly changing world.

As a small active member of the international community, the New Zealand Government in 1948 produced a treaty list and supplemented it in 1961. In 1997 it published the *New Zealand Consolidated Treaty List as at 31 December 1996* in two volumes—one on multilateral treaties, the other on bilaterals—extending to more than 1,000 pages or more than four times the length of the combined predecessor volumes.

The new volumes contain a valuable introduction which includes an historical overview, discussing among other things the application of treaties to acquired territory, and succession. Consider a seventeenth- or eighteenth-century British treaty which extended to New Zealand in 1840 when it became part of the British dominions, then became separately binding on New Zealand as independent State early this century and might now be distinctly applicable to Samoa, the Cook Islands and Niue. The other parties to the treaty may also have been through various vicissitudes, and other factors, such as war, may have affected the treaties. The *List* provides a great deal of helpful information on such matters both in relation to particular treaties and more generally. It is very easy to use—well organized, extensively referenced and with excellent indexes. It is a great credit to those who prepared it.

The *List* is wide-ranging in time, the oldest treaty dating back almost to the treaties of Westphalia: it is the Treaty of Peace and Commerce of 1654 between Sweden and the United Kingdom which was supplemented, confirmed, explained and amended in 1656 (twice), 1661, 1746, 1803, 1826, 1883 and 1911. During the union between Sweden and Norway the treaties became applicable to Norway. They were also expressly recognized as being applicable to the self-governing Dominions which in 1911 acquired separate rights to withdraw, a right which New Zealand exercised in 1933. The oldest multilateral treaty was concluded as recently as 1856, the Declaration of Paris respecting Maritime Law; the latest, it is rather gloomy to note, is also concerned with weaponry—the 1996 Comprehensive Nuclear Test Ban Treaty.

Notwithstanding that particular coincidence, the subject areas of the treaties are very diverse, as also appears from other national treaty collections and lists: peace as well as war, disarmament and arms control; international trade; international finance; international commercial transactions; international communications; international spaces (importantly for New Zealand including Antarctica); the environment; human rights; labour rights and conditions; international crimes; and many other areas of international economic and social co-operation.

The-subject matter indicates that the *List* is of value not only to those engaged as lawyers in government work—outside New Zealand as well as within it. It is also important for lawyers in private practice as more and more of their clients are governed or affected by international law. One measure is provided by recent decisions of the New Zealand Court of Appeal concerning the safety of civil aviation, liability for goods damaged in international air carriage, child abduction, refugees, immigrants, criminal law (including search and seizure, confronting witnesses, retrospectivity, sentencing and legal aid) and human rights (including the right to life, discrimination in relation to same sex marriage and the status of the Human Rights Committee). The judges must also become increasingly familiar with that material. And that is even more true of those in the university, teaching the lawyers of the next generation, as international rules take a more and more prominent role. The *List*, like many other national and international publications of treaty materials, helps give practical content to what otherwise might appear to be platitudes about 'the global village' or 'a borderless world'. Recent New Zealand Law Commission publications, *A New Zealand Guide to International Law and its Sources* (1996) and *The Treaty Making Process* (1997), provide further assistance, again not only for New Zealand users.

By emphasizing the pervasive effect on national policy and law of the international law-making process, the *List* also helps highlight questions about public and democratic participation in treaty-making and acceptance. It is significant that the New Zealand Minister of Foreign Affairs and Trade, when launching the publication, announced changes to the process for the ratification and acceptance of, or accession to, treaties to enable greater parliamentary and public debate before certain treaty decisions are finally taken by the executive. In New Zealand, as elsewhere, there is a growing recognition of the need, to return to President Wilson's First Point, not just that covenants be open, but that they be openly arrived at.

K.J. KEITH

Recognition of Governments: Legal Doctrine and State Practice, 1815–1995. By M. J. Peterson. Basingstoke: Macmillan Press, 1997. ix + 295 pp. £45.

Recognition is a long-established institution of international law and relations. In its essential character, it remains now much as when it started, a unilateral and, the facts remaining the same, irrevocable acknowledgement by the authorities of one State of the status of another entity as a State, or of the authorities within a State as a government. It is an act of political discretion, only lightly regulated by legal conditions, but with legal consequences flowing from the exercise of the discretion. There are some differences between recognition of States and recognition of governments. Professor Peterson restricts her study rigidly to the recognition of governments.

She has conducted an exhaustive trawl of the textbooks, studies and assemblies of State practice to find out what has gone on since 1815. The results are presented in a rather relentless way, but scholars and practitioners in future will have reason to be grateful for her work when they have a specific problem to pursue. Each chapter is concluded with a summary which seeks to encapsulate whatever lessons the practice reveals. Given that recognition has such high political overtones, it is hardly surprising that the uses to which it has been put reflect the overall situation in international relations of the time. Broadly, she divides her period into three: 1815 until the Russian Revolution; 1921 to the beginning of the Cold War; 1945 to 1992. In all the periods, there has been a substantial weight of practice in favour of 'effectivism', some based on principle (the need to keep out of the affairs of other States), some pragmatic (the need to have dealings with those in actual charge for the protection of a State's interests). As Professor Peterson shows, the generality of the practice is diluted by contrary considerations, when States have felt the need to express their approval for a displaced regime or their disapproval of an effective usurping one (or both).

In the last thirty years, an increasing number of States have avowed a policy of not recognizing governments, simply maintaining such contracts with a regime as seems expedient and allowing conclusions about the status of such authorities to be drawn by others if and when they need to do so. This abstentionism appeals to governments because it allows a spectrum of relations to be maintained with foreign authorities instead of the rather black and white alternatives presented by the recognize/not recognize dichotomy, and it avoids any apparent endorsement of a new regime which has come to power unconstitutionally (and, therefore, possibly bloodily). However, these advantages have not been enough to keep States to their self-denying ordinances. It seems that there will always be some circumstances when a State will want to make it clear that it does or does not recognize a foreign government—of which the British Government's stand on the recognition of the status of the elected but displaced government of Sierra Leone is a recent example.

Professor Peterson shows that the rise of unilateral institutions has had an impact on the use of and the fora for recognition decisions, but that there have not yet developed centralized standards which condition the exercise of the decision to recognize a foreign government. While this is true, the analysis would have been sharper if she had made a more nuanced sub-division of the category of decisions involved. While the decision to recognize speaks unequivocally (more or less), the decision not to recognize an authority comprehends a variety of positions, from mere abstention to positive (even compelled) non-recognition. Professor Peterson writes indiscriminately of the 'nonrecognition' decision. Further, although in general, the segregation of the recognition of States and governments is proper, recognition of State decisions sometimes have aspects to them which concern the qualities of the government of the State (the practice of the EC States with respect to 'Yugoslavia' is a prominent example) and, therefore, they may have something to add to the account of recognition of government decisions.

The range of inquiry in this work is impressive and its value to those with an interest in one of the fundamental institutions of international relations will be high. Professor Peterson has been justified in her continued pursuit of the recognition of governments in the face of its apparent abandonment in the recent past because States have found it too valuable an instrument to give up altogether. Her instincts, founded on a thorough study of the earlier practice, have been confirmed and should give those who use this book confidence in her judgment. This is as much true for lawyers as for political scientists, though lawyers will have further concerns about the consequences of the recognition decision which are only lightly touched upon here.

COLIN WARBRICK

The Law of the Sea: The European Union and its Member States. Edited by TULLIO TREVES and LAURA PINESCHI. The Hague: Martinus Nijhoff, 1997. 590 pp. £130.

This work, in the publisher's ocean development series, marks the milestone of the entry into force on 16 November 1994 of the United Nations Convention on the Law of the Sea, 1982. In his introduction, the principal editor, Professor (now also Judge) Treves states that its aim is 'to give a detailed study of the attitudes and practice concerning the law of the sea of the member States of the European Union and of the European Community as such'.

Each member State, with the exception of Luxembourg, has a chapter devoted to its practice, written by a national expert, and there is a chapter on the practice of the Community itself. Eleven chapters are in English and four (France, Spain, Portugal, together with Daniel Vignes' authoritative chapter on the Community's practice in the law of the sea) are in French. There is an appendix setting out the declarations concerning the Convention made by the member States and the Community, a list of principal multilateral conventions, and a general index. Each national chapter follows, more or less, a standard pattern corresponding to the main divisions of the subject. The matters covered are baselines, ports, territorial sea, straits, contiguous zone, EEZ and EFZ, continental shelf, high seas, delimitation, the preservation and protection of the marine environment, and marine scientific research. The national legislation and jurisprudence are described together with any relevant international practice in which the State has been involved. Some, but not all, chapters end with a short local bibliography.

It is impracticable to review each chapter here. As might be expected, they vary in length and depth. This reviewer was particularly pleased to see a contribution from Portugal, since there appears to be a dearth of academic writing about international law, let alone law of the sea, emanating from this country, other than, one optimistically assumes, in Portuguese. It is a feature of collective works like this that those who provide their contributions early have to endure the longest period of seeing their work become out of date. Promptness in meeting deadlines appears to have worked to the particular disadvantage of the United Kingdom contribution. Completed in 1993, it suffered the passage of the Merchant Shipping Act 1995, effecting considerable changes which have to be mentioned in a short postscript. Other contributions, perhaps those whose authors delayed submission, have managed to incorporate events up to mid-1996.

The book, which is substantial in size, information and price, will be useful both as a starting point for those undertaking research into the contemporary law of the sea in the EU States and as a historical bench-mark for the national positions at the time of the Convention's entry into force. The rapid development in national laws regarding the law of the sea, however, will mean that its use will be increasingly confined to the latter purpose.

GEOFFREY MARSTON

La Responsabilité des États membres en cas de violation du droit communautaire. By G. Vandersanden and M. Dony. Brussels: Établissements Émile Bruylant, 1997. 420 pp. Belgian Francs 2,750.

This book is premised on the argument that the doctrine of State liability, developed by the ECJ in *Francovich*, will be as useful or effective as the national remedies and procedures, through which individuals will rely on it, allow it to be. Furthermore, difficulties with and limitations on the operation of the doctrine will not necessarily be the same throughout the member States. Thus, this book is divided into three parts: a general introductory section on Community law; a second section subdivided into further sections each of which deals with one of six national legal systems; and finally a report synthesizing the findings of the national reports. This is a very good and timely idea: there has been much discussion of the doctrine of State liability, almost all of which focuses on the European law perspective, or, to a lesser degree, on the perspective of the individual member States. However, there has been no overview, and little consideration of how similar the remedy will be from State to State. This book, then, could provide a valuable contribution in supplying this deficiency, but does not completely succeed in doing so.

The first section provides a comprehensive introduction to the underlying themes in Community law from which State liability has developed. This puts State liability into the context of the need to ensure effectiveness of individuals' rights and the importance of judicial co-operation. The book then goes on to consider in some detail the basis of State liability and the conditions for its operation. This it does in a clear and coherent manner. None the less, although this latter section is thorough in terms of following the issues raised in *Brasserie de Pêcheur*, it is curiously unsatisfactory in that the discussion seems to be limited to only those issues. *Brasserie de Pêcheur* did not create an exhaustive list of problem issues. Indeed, some of the issues which *Brasserie de Pêcheur* dismissed as unproblematic are not necessarily without difficulty: for example, the question of causation may not be as straightforward or as uniform as the ECJ suggested.

Of the sections in the middle part of the book dealing with the control of public authority in Germany, Britain, Belgium, Spain, France and Italy, the reviewer is competent to criticize only the section on Great Britain. For the rest, it seems that a standardized approach has been adopted: a broad introductory section identifying the general approach to liability of public authorities and then an application of this in the context of State liability. Each part concludes with a brief summary section identifying the difficulties in each legal system and the degree to which the requirements of Community Law are likely to be satisfied. The British entry raises difficulties which illustrate some of the problems of comparative works such as this. It is unfortunate that Britain was defined to mean England and Wales;[1] this raises questions about both the degree of oversimplification necessary to fit a discussion of any legal system into a book this size, and the fact that the authors were not common lawyers. Despite their no doubt thorough research, the reviewer was not convinced that the authors of this section were comfortable with their discussion of the English legal system. In particular, the ordering of the section on fault seemed strange, perhaps the result of imposing civil law structures on common law reasoning. In reviewing the public law remedies and distinguishing them from the tortious actions, the authors might also have been hampered by the fact that public law has been developing apace in England of late. Taking an assessment from 1985, therefore, as to the role of public law remedies in England may be somewhat misleading. Despite this, the succeeding chapter on liability arising from Community law makes a noble attempt to explain some confusing, if not self-contradictory, cases on the appropriate cause of action: breach of statutory duty or misfeasance in public office. This

[1] The authors state, in speaking of the English legal system, that 'les solutions et principes qui y sont dégagés peuvent également être transposeś à l'Ecosse et à l'Ireland du Nord' (p. 95).

is an explanation which makes more sense than some English commentaries on the matter! This section, unfortunately, will be dated by not having dealt with the *Three Rivers* case and, more particularly, the High Court's views on *Factortame*.

The third section applies the first section to the results of the second section. This is a useful way to conclude, identifying the weaknesses of each member State's system in relation to the various elements of the doctrine. Again, though, some comments could be revised in the light of recent national case law. The problem of swiftly developing case law affects many law books, in particular those dealing with the EC, and these comments do not affect the validity of the book's conclusion. It seems that, after all, there are some similarities between the member States; that none of them have yet adapted their national legal system fully to the requirements of the ECJ. In summary then, the book serves a useful function. Although clearly not exhaustive in either its treatment of the State liability remedy at the European level, or of the national legal systems, it forms a useful starting-point for an enquiry in this area.

LORNA WOODS

Héctor Gros Espiell—Amicorum Liber. By VARIOUS AUTHORS. Brussels: Établissements Émile Bruylant, 1997. 2 volumes. lxiii + 1878 pp. No price stated.

This two volume work is a *Festschrift* to celebrate the 70th birthday of the celebrated Uruguayan international lawyer Héctor Gros Espiell. The 87 contributions are mainly in Spanish, although some are in English or French and one is in Portuguese. In content they mirror their subject's scholarly interests, dealing with both a range of issues of general international law and the advancement and protection of human rights in particular. Many of the authors will already be familiar to readers of this *Year Book* and although the quality of their contributions is somewhat uneven, there is much here that will be of interest.

Juan Alvarez Via has the privilege of contributing the first chapter, 'Derechos Humanos, Desarrollo y Cooperación', in which he calls for international co-operation and solidarity to combat global inequality in the development of human rights. Boutros Boutros-Ghali contributes a short chapter entitled 'L'ONU et l'impératif de democratisation', reflecting on the necessity for all States to embrace democracy, as well as the need for the United Nations system itself to become more democratic and decentralized. Mária del Luján Flores highlights the many difficulties that must be resolved before the international community can proceed to the creation of an international criminal court in 'La Corte Penal Internacional: Utopia o realidad'; and Jaime Ruiz de Santiago heaps praise on Gros Espiell for his work on the development of refugee law ('Contribución de Héctor Gros Espiell al desarrollo del Derecho Internacional de los Refugiados').

Space precludes mention of the many other valuable contributions. It suffices to say that the editors can be well satisfied that the present work not only provides a worthy tribute to its subject, but will also have wide appeal.

KISCH BEEVERS

The International Regime of Fisheries. From UNCLOS 1982 to the Presential Sea. By JOSÉ A. DE YTURRIAGA. The Hague: Martinus Nijhoff, 1997. xviii + 326 pp. £77.

International fisheries law has experienced a number of significant developments in recent years, such as the adoption of the FAO Compliance Agreement and the UN Straddling Fish Stocks Agreement and the establishment of a number of new regional organizations and arrangements. A new book on the subject is therefore in principle much to be welcomed, especially as many of the developments referred to have taken place since the publication in 1994 of the previous book on international fisheries law in English, Professor Burke's excellent *The New International Law of Fisheries*.

The present book consists of four chapters and takes a chronological approach. The first chapter traces the development of international fisheries law from the Hague Conference of 1930 down to the eve of the Third UN Conference on the Law of the Sea (UNCLOS) in 1972. The emphasis in this chapter is very much on the gradual extension of coastal State jurisdiction over fisheries. There is no discussion of the work of international fisheries commissions which in some areas, such as the North Atlantic, had a good deal of responsibility for such fisheries management as there was: it was the failings of such bodies which in part both prompted and made more acceptable proposals for extensive coastal State jurisdiction over fisheries made at UNCLOS.

Chapter 2 deals with the main proposals made at UNCLOS and the fisheries provisions of the successive negotiating texts. These first two chapters occupy some 40 per cent of the book. However, it might perhaps have been better if they had been more compressed so as to allow more space for the matters dealt with in the final two chapters. In particular, discussion of the proposals and the various negotiating texts could have been better integrated into the analysis of the provisions of the UN Convention on the Law of the Sea relating to fisheries which follows in chapter 3. This analysis is of somewhat variable quality, and in general lacks the depth and breadth of Burke's coverage. While the discussion of the high seas regime is good, the coverage of coastal States' rights and duties is rather brief (four pages only), and does not deal with some difficult issues, such as the extent of coastal States' legislative jurisdiction, or with State practice in relation to such matters as the access of foreign vessels and the management of shared stocks.

The final chapter, which discusses some recent developments, is the most interesting and informative. In particular there are good accounts of the Straddling Stocks Conference and Agreement and of the 'Presential Sea' doctrine espoused by Chile. The dispute between Canada and the EC/Spain over straddling stocks in the North-West Atlantic, written very much from a Spanish viewpoint, is less successful, not so much because of its perspective as because it does not give the uninformed reader enough on the background to the dispute and the role of the North-West Atlantic Fisheries Organization in order properly to understand the context of the dispute and its significance. The FAO Compliance Agreement also surely deserves more than the half-page treatment that it gets.

In general the style of the book tends to a descriptive narrative, rather than analytical, approach. It is also very much a legal text—there is nothing on the biological or economic background to fisheries, which is surely a disadvantage. The book also seems a little uneven in its treatment of recent law and practice. While many events of 1995 are discussed, the account of the ICJ's case law on maritime boundary delimitation surprisingly fails to mention its 1993 judgment in the *Jan Mayen/Greenland* case, which is its most significant maritime boundary case as far as fisheries are concerned. In addition, a number of the international fisheries commissions mentioned on pp. 163–4 no longer exist. A good feature of the book is a 40-page bibliography, but its utility is somewhat marred by the failure to give any page references to journal articles (these references do appear in the richly documented footnotes, however). There are also quite a lot of minor typographical errors.

Overall the book is likely to be found useful for anyone seeking a general introduction to international fisheries law. The more experienced reader is likely to find the book more uneven, but will nevertheless still benefit from it, especially parts of chapters 3 and 4.

R. R. CHURCHILL

DECISIONS OF BRITISH COURTS DURING 1998 INVOLVING QUESTIONS OF PUBLIC OR PRIVATE INTERNATIONAL LAW

A. PUBLIC INTERNATIONAL LAW*

On 25 November 1998 the House of Lords rendered judgment in *R* v. *Bow Street Metropolitan Stipendiary Magistrate and others, ex parte Pinochet Ugarte*, an appeal from a judgment of the Divisional Court of 28 October 1998. In normal circumstances both judgments would have been reviewed here. However, on 15 January 1999 the House of Lords set aside its judgment of 25 November 1998, holding that one of the Law Lords was disqualified because of an appearance of bias and that the case therefore had to be reheard. The new judgment, handed down on 24 March 1999, will be reviewed in the next issue of this *Year Book*.

Act of State doctrine—non-justiciability—relationship between the act of State doctrine and non-justiciability—whether an English court would recognize an Iraqi resolution transferring Kuwait Airways aircraft to Iraqi Airways

Case No. 1. Kuwait Airways Corporation v. *Iraqi Airways Company and another,* 29 July 1998, unreported, QBD. In English law, the act of State doctrine holds that the courts will not inquire into the validity of those acts or laws of a foreign State which purport to take effect within that State's territory. This doctrine prevents English courts from exercising jurisdiction in respect of such acts or laws even when the foreign State concerned is not a party to the suit. In other words, it applies *ratione materiae*: unlike State immunity, which was traditionally applied strictly *ratione personae*, the act of State doctrine is not dependent for its application on the identity of the parties.[1]

The act of State doctrine is related to the English doctrine of the non-justiciability of the rights and duties of States as between themselves. This related doctrine is often referred to as '*Buttes* non-justiciability' after the leading case on the point, *Buttes Gas and Oil Co.* v. *Hammer*.[2] Both the act of State doctrine and *Buttes* non-justiciability operate as substantive defences, as compared to immunities *ratione personae* which are preliminary objections to jurisdiction. The act of State doctrine and *Buttes* non-justiciability are questions of competence to adjudicate, rather than questions of an accorded privilege.[3]

[1] See generally *Blad* v. *Bamfield*, (1674) 3 Swans. 603, 36 ER 991; *Duke of Brunswick* v. *King of Hanover*, (1848) 2 HL Cas. 1, 21–2; *Luther* v. *Sagor*, [1921] 3 KB 532; *Princess Paley Olga* v. *Weisz*, [1929] 1 KB 718.

[2] [1982] AC 888, [1981] 3 WLR 787, [1981] 3 All ER 616, this *Year Book*, 53 (1982), pp. 259–68. See also *Cook* v. *Sprigg*, [1899] AC 572.

[3] See *Kuwait Airways Corporation* v. *Iraqi Airways Co.*, [1995] 1 WLR 1147 at 1167, [1995] 3 All ER 694 at 714–15, this *Year Book*, 66 (1995), pp. 496–501, HL.

They therefore arise at a later procedural stage than issues of diplomatic or State immunity.

This lengthy sole judgment, by Mance J in the ongoing Kuwait Airways Corporation ('KAC') litigation, contains one of the most rigorous and compelling considerations of the act of State doctrine and non-justiciability to be found anywhere.

After the Iraqi invasion of Kuwait in August 1990, the Revolutionary Council of Iraq ('RCC') passed Resolutions 312 and 313 designating Kuwait as a Governate forming an integral part of Iraq. The litigation arose out of a claim by KAC for wrongful interference with ten of its aircraft during the occupation. The aircraft, which had been at Kuwait airport at the time of the invasion, were seized and removed to Iraq. On 17 September 1990, the RCC passed Resolution 369, which purported to dissolve KAC and transfer its assets to Iraqi Airways Company ('IAC'). IAC then treated the aircraft as its own: six were flown to Iran where they were interned by the Iranian authorities and the remaining four were partially or wholly destroyed in air raids by the coalition forces.

In interlocutory proceedings the House of Lords held that IAC, as a separate entity acting in the exercise of sovereign authority, was, under section 14(2)(*a*) of the State Immunity Act 1978, entitled to immunity in respect of the taking and removal of the aircraft to Iraq. However, it also held that this immunity did not extend to any subsequent retention and use of the aircraft in consequence of the purported vesting in IAC of ownership by legislative decree. Lord Goff, speaking for the majority, said:

> Plainly, a separate entity of a state cannot ipso facto claim sovereign immunity in respect of a claim by the former owner, though it may well be able to plead, by way of defence, that its actions were not unlawful. Nor can it be said . . . that the acts done by IAC after 17 September 1990 were mere outward manifestations of a denial of title which occurred at the time of the seizure of the aircraft. As I understand the position, such acts constituted fresh acts of conversion, though the limitation period may, under the statute [a reference to the Limitation Act 1980, section 3(1)], run from an earlier date . . .
>
> Finally, I do not think it relevant that (as was very probably the case) the Iraqi government would not have tolerated return of the aircraft by IAC to KAC. For the fact remains that IAC in treating the aircraft as its own, was doing so pursuant to the Iraqi legislation which vested the aircraft in IAC; and by so doing it cannot be said to have acted in the exercise of sovereign authority.[4]

Lord Goff left open the possibility that IAC might have a defence based on its submission that the matters relied upon would involve the court in adjudicating on transactions of a foreign State in the conduct of foreign affairs, or on sovereign acts done by a foreign State in respect of persons or property within its jurisdiction which were non-justiciable in the English courts. It was this question—involving non-justiciability and the act of State doctrine—that now came before Mance J.

Before addressing the issue of non-justiciability, Mance J considered the basis for the plaintiff's tort claim. It was, he said, subject to the rule of double actionability, expressed in *Dicey and Morris* as follows:

> (1) As a general rule, an act done in a foreign country is a tort and actionable in England, only if it is both

[4] [1995] 1 WLR 1147 at 1163, [1995] 3 All ER 694 at 711.

(a) actionable as a tort according to English law, or in other words is an act which, if done in England, would be a tort; and
(b) actionable according to the law of the foreign country where it was done. [5]

He then quoted *Clerk and Lindsell* on the basic principle governing the English law of wrongful interference or conversion:

[C]onversion is an act of deliberate dealing with a chattel in a manner inconsistent with another's right whereby that other is deprived of the use and possession of it. To be liable the defendant need not intend to question or deny the plaintiff's rights; it is enough that his conduct is inconsistent with those rights . . . [6]

Although Iraqi law prohibited 'usurpation', that term was not specifically defined there. Mance J heard expert evidence on the relevant articles of the Iraqi Civil Code and concluded:

I find that all that is required for usurpation is a deliberate act affecting the property which objectively, whether or not this is intended or appreciated, manifests an attitude or claim inconsistent with its owner's title. . . . Article 193 regulates the responsibility of a usurper for loss or damage. Whether or not there is fault ('ta'adi'), the usurper is liable if the property usurped is lost or damaged. The only qualification that emerged and was eventually common ground in the expert evidence is that, in the case of a usurper acting in good faith, the owner must show that the loss or damage would not have occurred but for the usurpation . . . The test of good or bad faith is whether or not the usurper was aware that he was usurping another's property.[7]

IAC relied on this Iraqi law and Resolution 369 to argue that it had acted in good faith. It also pointed to a letter from the Head of the President of Iraq's Office, dated 10 September 1990, which read, in part: 'We enclose a copy of the Republican Decree number 369 issued on . . . 9.9.1990, requesting that all necessary action be taken to implement it. Thank you.'[8] IAC argued that this constituted an order to accept the hand-over of all KAC assets, including the aircraft, and to register them in its own name. It also argued that this was an order with which it was bound to comply under the Iraqi Constitution and which had the effect that it could not be regarded as acting illegitimately, or otherwise than in accordance with a legal requirement. In so far as this submission relied on Resolution 369, it raised the crucial question whether the court could and should refuse to recognize that Resolution on grounds of public policy. As Mance J explained:

KAC acknowledges that, if it is to succeed, it must overcome the apparent transfer of property in all ten aircraft to IAC by RCC Resolution 369. If IAC was owner of the aircraft, it cannot wrongfully have interfered with them by the conduct described.[9]

It is a general rule of English private international law that:

A governmental act affecting any private property right in any movable or immovable thing will be recognised as valid and effective in England if the act was valid and effective

[5] Approved Transcript at 4, quoting from Rule 203, Lawrence Collins (ed.), *Dicey and Morris on the Conflict of Laws* (12th edn., 1993).

[6] Approved Transcript at 4, quoting from *Clerk and Lindsell on Torts* (17th edn., 1995), ch.13, para.13–12.

[7] Approved Transcript at 18.

[8] Approved Transcript at 20.

[9] Approved Transcript at 29.

by the law of the country where the thing was situated (lex situs) at the moment when the act takes effect, and not otherwise.[10]

In *Buttes* v. *Hammer*,[11] Lord Wilberforce identified *Luther* v. *Sagor*[12] and *Princess Paley Olga* v. *Weisz*[13] as cases involving the act of State doctrine. This line of authority was, he explained, 'concerned with the applicability of foreign municipal legislation within its [a State's] own territory, and with the examinability of such legislation—often, but not invariably, arising in cases of confiscation of property'.[14]

There is, however, an exception to this rule based on grounds of public policy. As *Dicey and Morris* explain:

A foreign decree will not be recognised . . . if it is contrary to public policy. Thus legislation which constitutes a gross violation of human rights will not be recognised. Penal or discriminatory legislation may also be disregarded as contrary to public policy, if the court considers that, looking at all the circumstances, the law is so far-reaching in its scope and effect as really to offend against considerations of public policy of this country. In such cases the foreign law is treated as inapplicable and a title acquired under the foreign law is not recognised, even as regards property situate in the foreign country at the time of the legislation.[15]

In *Oppenheimer* v. *Cattermole*, the House of Lords considered whether an English court would recognize a Nazi decree depriving a Jew of his German nationality. Lord Cross expressed the view of the majority:

A judge should, of course, be very slow to refuse to give effect to the legislation of a foreign state in any sphere in which, according to accepted principles of international law, the foreign state has jurisdiction. He may well have an inadequate understanding of the circumstances in which the legislation was passed and his refusal to recognise it may be embarrassing to the branch of the executive which is concerned to maintain friendly foreign relations between this country and the foreign country in question. But I think . . . that it is part of the public policy of this country that our courts should give effect to clearly established rules of international law.[16]

Lord Wilberforce was, in *Buttes* v. *Hammer*, also careful to identify both a narrower act of State doctrine, concerning the acts of a foreign State within its own territory, and a broader principle of non-justiciability concerning 'a certain class of sovereign acts' on the part of a foreign State. In respect of the former he referred specifically to a public policy exception:

[10] Rule 122, *Dicey and Morris* (above, n. 5).

[11] [1982] AC 888 at 930–2, and cf. 933, [1981] 3 All ER 616 at 627–8, and cf. 629.

[12] [1921] 3 KB 532.

[13] [1929] 1 KB 718.

[14] [1982] AC 888 at 931, [1981] 3 All ER 616 at 628, this *Year Book*, loc. cit. above (n. 2). The traditional position in US law had been expressed by Chief Justice Fuller of the Supreme Court in the 1893 case of *Underhill* v. *Hernandez*, (1893) 65 Fed. 577: 'Every sovereign state is bound to respect the independence of every other sovereign state, and the courts of one country will not sit in judgement on the acts of the government of another done within its own territory. Redress of grievances by reason of such acts must be obtained through the means open to be availed of by sovereign powers as between themselves.' In the USA, the act of State doctrine has become somewhat more flexible over the course of the past century. See *Banco Nacional de Cuba* v. *Sabbatino*, (1964) 376 US 398; *Kirkpatrick* v. *Environmental Tectonics*, (1990) 493 US 403, 110 S Ct. 701.

[15] Op.cit. above (n. 5), p. 995.

[16] [1976] AC 249 at 277–8, this *Year Book*, 47 (1974–5), pp. 372–4.

It is quite one thing to assert that effect will not be given to a foreign municipal law or executive act if it is contrary to public policy, or to international law . . . and quite another to claim that the courts may examine the validity, under international law, or some doctrine of public policy, of an act or acts operating in the area of transactions between states.[17]

In light of all this, Mance J concluded:

I consider it to be clear that, in applying the act of state doctrine in its narrower sense, the English court is, as one element in its evaluation of public policy, entitled to take into account international law or . . . 'the usage of nations'. There may be cases where such law or usage is uncertain or open to different interpretations or where English public policy is shaped by other considerations. But there is no embargo or straight-jacket preventing its being considered at all.

. . . In *Oppenheimer* v. *Cattermole,* Lords Cross and Salmon regarded German legislation, singling out a section of the citizen body on racial grounds for the purpose of confiscating its property and depriving it of citizenship, as a grave infringement of human rights and of an immorality without parallel. Lord Cross expressly approved Upjohn J's view that it was part of the public policy of this country that our courts should give effect to clearly established rules of international law. Lord Cross's statement that the relevant Nazi law constituted 'so grave an infringement of human rights that the courts of this country ought to refuse to recognise it as a law at all' was formulated with reference to the particular circumstances of that case. General conceptions of morality and humanity can be seen also to have played their part in the assessment of public policy. Lord Cross did not have to consider whether public policy could ever lead to refusal of recognition in respect of a legislative or executive act relating to a corporation . . . Public policy may . . . require refusal of recognition in circumstances not involving individual human rights. The underlying test adopted by Lord Cross was one of public policy, having regard, inter alia, to established rules of international law.[18]

IAC, however, contended that the case called for the application of the broader principle of non-justiciability, on the grounds that the matters which KAC wished to raise in relation to Resolution 369 involved consideration of transactions between States and, in particular, matters concerning and arising from Iraq's invasion of Kuwait.

Mance J observed that, '[a]part from the *Buttes Gas* litigation itself, there is little in authority to assist on the scope or application of the wider principle of

[17] [1982] AC 888 at 931, [1981] 3 All ER 616 at 628, this *Year Book*, loc. cit. above (n. 2).

[18] Approved Transcript at 38–9. The same approach was adopted in the USA by the District Court of Columbia in *Letelier* v. *Chile*, (1980) 488 F Supp. 665. Mance J noted as well the following passage from Sir Robert Jennings and Sir Arthur Watts (eds.), *Oppenheim's International Law*, vol. 1 (9th edn., 1992), pp. 375–6, supporting the existence of an exception to the act of State doctrine on the grounds of public policy:

'Courts may be under a constitutional compulsion to give effect to the law of their own sovereign legislature even if violative of international law . . . but there is no compelling reason why they should assist in giving effect to violations of international law by a foreign legislature. In the absence of compulsory jurisdiction of international tribunals and having regard to the prohibition, under the Charter of the United Nations and elsewhere, of compulsory means of enforcement of international law by national action, municipal courts may on occasions provide the only means for securing respect for international law in this and other spheres. Principle does not countenance a rule which, by reference to international law, obliges courts to endow with legal effect legislative and other acts of foreign states which are in violation of international law; and in practice no such international obligation is regarded as existing.'

non-justiciability'.[19] In respect of the judgment of the House of Lords in that case, he wrote:

> Lord Wilberforce's speech demonstrates that whether in any particular case judicial restraint or abstention is required depends upon a close examination of the particular circumstances . . . Lord Wilberforce's speech proceeded not on or from any automatic assumption that, because the issues concerned international law or transactions between states, they were necessarily non-justiciable. He carefully analysed the nature of such issues and what their resolution would have involved, and he identified a number of potentially relevant considerations before him, concluding that the issues raised were non-justiciable.
>
> One relevant consideration is whether re-examination and perhaps condemnation by the domestic courts of another state would 'imperil the amicable relations between governments and vex the peace of nations'; . . . and a related consideration may be whether Her Majesty's Government has expressed a definite attitude on any issue arising, so that no evidential difficulty, potential breach of comity or possibility of embarrassment would arise if the English court were to deal with it.[20]

Mance J then identified the following passage as containing the 'actual reasons' give by Lord Wilberforce for concluding that the issues in *Buttes* v. *Hammer* were non-justiciable before English courts:

> Leaving aside all possibility of embarrassment in our foreign relations . . . there are . . . no judicial or manageable standards by which to judge these issues, or to adopt another phrase . . . ., the court would be in a judicial no-man's land: the court would be asked to review transactions in which four sovereign states were involved, which they had brought to a precarious settlement, after diplomacy and the use of force and to say that at least part of these were 'unlawful' under international law. I would just add, in answer to one of the respondents' arguments, that it is not to be assumed that these matters have now passed into history, so that they can now be examined with safe detachment.[21]

Mance J concluded:

> While *Buttes Gas* is authority for—and an instance of the application of—a wider principle of non-justiciability, it is, in my view, no authority that the English courts must automatically or invariably attribute to the conduct of a foreign state in its international relations a validity or legitimacy which it may in some cases be obvious that it does not bear. This is particularly—though not exclusively—true if Her Majesty's Government has expressed a clear attitude on the point. As to embarrassment or sensitivity, in clearcut cases it may involve a far greater affront to comity with other innocent sovereign states (not to mention elementary conceptions of justice and sound policy) if domestic courts refuse to address the reality, than if they do so squarely.[22]

In support of this conclusion Mance J quoted the following passage written by F.A. Mann:

> [I]f a State commits an international wrong and the court of another State, the forum, refuses recognition to that wrong, the latter does what international law expects it to do and what it must do in order not to become an accessory to the delinquency.[23]

[19] Approved Transcript at 40.
[20] Approved Transcript at 45.
[21] [1982] AC 888 at 938, [1981] 3 All ER 616 at 633, this *Year Book*, loc. cit. above (n. 2).
[22] Approved Transcript at 46.
[23] Approved Transcript at 46–7, quoting from Mann, 'International Delinquencies before Municipal Courts', *Law Quarterly Review*, 70 (1954), p. 181, at p. 198.

Mance J continued:

> The distinction which Lord Wilberforce drew raises the question how the doctrines of act of state and non-justiciability may inter-act. Subject to public policy, the doctrine of act of state calls for recognition of the validity of legislative and executive acts, primarily on a territorial basis. Non-justiciability involves a refusal to adjudicate upon an issue, and its effect may therefore depend upon who raises the issue and whether the issue is severable from the rest of the action . . . .
>
> That leads to the further question, how the doctrines of act of state and non-justiciability inter-act where one party invokes English public policy to examine foreign . . . [legislation] in the light of its compatibility with international law . . . .The basic principle of act of state is that domestic courts will give effect to legislative and executive acts of a foreign sovereign within its territory for reasons of comity and will only refuse to do so . . . where public policy requires. The second part of Lord Wilberforce's distinction [i.e. between act of State and non-justiciability] may be read as indicating that the conduct of states in their international relations is promoted to a yet higher level of immunity from review. Even assuming that this is so, and the principle of non-justiciability is potentially applicable in this situation, it is still only 'in suitable cases' that it should actually be applied . . . .The fact that non-justiciability is a flexible principle and depends for its application on a close analysis of the circumstances . . . probably enables the two doctrines to work sensibly together in a case such as the present.[24]

Mance J proceeded to apply these principles to the facts. In doing so, he held that he had to consider Resolution 369 as a whole and in its proper context.[25] He concluded, first, that Resolution 369, in seeking to dissolve a foreign corporation, was an exorbitant measure.

Second, he noted that the Secretary of State for Foreign and Commonwealth Affairs had, pursuant to an order of the court, been asked the following question: 'Has Her Majesty's Government recognized at any time that the State of Iraq exercised de facto sovereign power in Kuwait as at 17 September 1990 or at any time thereafter?'[26]

Sir Franklin Berman, the Legal Adviser to the Foreign and Commonwealth Office, wrote in response:

> I am instructed by the Secretary of State, in reply, to state that Her Majesty's Government in the United Kingdom have not at any time, throughout the period from [17 September 1990] until the expulsion of Iraqi forces from Kuwait on 26 February 1991, recognised Iraqi occupation or control over the territory of Kuwait.[27]

The letter went on to draw the court's attention to United Nations Security Council resolutions requiring the United Kingdom not to recognize Iraq as the *de facto* government in Kuwait.

[24] Approved Transcript at 47.

[25] He noted that Lord Cross had done likewise when considering the particular legislation at issue in *Oppenheimer* v. *Cattermole*, referring to it as 'legislation which takes away without compensation from a section of the body singled out on racial grounds all their property which the state passing the legislation can lay its hands on and, in addition, deprives them of their citizenship': Approved Transcript at 48, quoting from [1976] AC 249 at 278.

[26] Approved Transcript at 50.

[27] Approved Transcript at 50.

Mance J regarded this letter as decisive, notwithstanding the United Kingdom policy, adopted in 1980, of not according recognition to foreign governments.[28] He said:

In a particular case . . . Her Majesty's Government must remain free to take and to inform the court of a more categorical attitude regarding recognition, or non-recognition, of a foreign government . . . .[C]ircumstances may still arise where Her Majesty's Government's attitude to recognition of a suggested government is clear to a point where, if this court were to take a different attitude, the State would be speaking with two voices . . . .In a case like the present of purported annexation to which the Government categorically refuses recognition, it may, indeed, also be likely that the Government's answer will express a clear attitude to recognition of the annexing power as de facto sovereign . . . .

In a case where, outside or despite the scope of the 1980 announcement, Her Majesty's Government, in answer to the court's question, actually indicates unequivocally that it recognises or positively refuses to recognise a particular body as the government of a foreign state . . . .[p]ublic policy points compellingly towards the courts adopting the same attitude as Her Majesty's Government manifests.[29]

He continued:

The imperative to avoid the State speaking with two voices is at its most powerful, when the United Kingdom Government, responsible for foreign affairs, draws to the court's attention the obligations by which this country was and is bound under international law. . . . The strongest considerations thus combine to indicate that this court cannot accord to the Government of Iraq in Kuwait any de facto governmental status. I conclude for these reasons that this court cannot recognise the Government of Iraq as de facto Government of or in Kuwait.[30]

Mance J also stressed that Resolution 369 had been passed in the context of an invasion that was illegal under international law, including under the United Nations Charter. He said:

[28] See *Parliamentary Debates (Commons)*, vol. 983, *Written Answers*, cols. 277–9: 25 April 1980, reproduced in Geoffrey Marston, 'United Kingdom Materials on International Law 1980', this *Year Book*, 51(1980), p. 367; *Parliamentary Debates (Lords)*, vol. 408, cols. 1121–2: 28 April 1980; and *Republic of Somalia* v. *Woodhouse Drake & Carey (Suisse) SA*, [1992] QB 54, [1992] 3 WLR 744, [1993] 1 All ER 371, this *Year Book*, 63 (1992), pp. 501–5.

[29] Approved Transcript at 54–5.

[30] Approved Transcript at 55–6. It was argued by IAC that any conclusion that Iraq was not the *de facto* Government of Kuwait would mean that ordinary administrative or legal acts or transactions conducted within Kuwait during the period of the occupation might be deprived of legal effect to the detriment of even ordinary Kuwaiti citizens. Mance J (Approved Transcript at 58) referred with approval to the following passage by Sir John Donaldson MR in *Gur Corp.* v. *Trust Bank of Africa Ltd.*, [1987] QB 599 at 622, [1986] 3 All ER 449 at 463, this *Year Book*, 57 (1986), pp. 405–10, referring to *dicta* of Lord Wilberforce in *Carl Zeiss Stiftung* v. *Rayner & Keeler Ltd. (No. 2)*, [1967] 1 AC 853, [1966] 3 WLR 125:

'Lord Wilberforce . . . reserved for further consideration whether the non-recognition of a government or, I think, a state, would necessarily lead to the English courts treating all its legislative activities as being a nullity or whether, in the interests of justice and common sense, where no consideration of public policy to the contrary has to prevail, it might not be possible to take cognisance of the actual facts or realities found to exist in the territory in question and he instanced private rights, or acts of everyday occurrence or perfunctory acts of administration. I see great force in this reservation, since it is one thing to treat a state or government as being "without the law", but quite another to treat the inhabitants of its territory as "outlaws" who cannot effectively marry, beget legitimate children, purchase goods on credit or undertake countless day-to-day activities having legal consequences.'

Having removed KAC's aircraft from Kuwait by force of arms and in breach of international law, Iraq cannot claim the protection of any principle of international law which might allow a state in some circumstances to expropriate property, even though belonging to the nationals of other states, which happen to be within its jurisdiction.[31]

This conclusion was buttressed by the fact that the United Nations Security Council had passed a series of resolutions requiring Iraq to withdraw peacefully from Kuwait, which Iraq had ignored. Mance J concluded:

I revert to the factors which the House of Lords found persuasive in *Buttes Gas* in its decision that the issues there were not justiciable in a municipal court. The present case involves 'acts operating in the area of transactions between states' or 'in the international field'. But this is not a case where there is any absence of judicial or manageable standards nor, in my judgment, can or should it be treated as a judicial no-man's land. The court would not be setting itself up as the arbiter of disputed and sensitive issues, or at least not of any issues which could properly be disputed or upon which there can be any legitimate sensitivity to require the court to refrain from pronouncing upon them. It would, if anything, appear more likely to 'imperil amicable relations between governments' or 'vex the peace of nations' if this court refused to take notice of fundamental and incontrovertible wrongdoing at the international level. In addition, Her Majesty's Government has by its letter made clear that, in its eyes, the Security Council's resolutions were binding decisions, and that Iraq by its invasion and purported annexation never acquired any legitimate status in respect of Kuwait.

In short, this is a case where this court can and should properly conclude and proceed on the basis that there were clear and fundamental breaches of international law and of the United Nations Charter, both in the invasion and other steps taken towards Kuwait and in failing to rescind such actions in compliance with the Security Council's Resolutions. Iraq as a party to the Charter expressly agreed to submit itself to the Charter obligations and to Security Council decisions. It would run strangely contrary to this country's own international obligations, under the Security Council's Resolutions, if its courts, as an emanation of this country's sovereignty independently of the executive and legislature, adopted an approach contrary to that to which this country is committed under the Charter and as a result of Security Council Resolutions. . . .

Such conduct is, in the context of this case, justiciable and I consider that I am not only entitled, but bound to take it into account.[32]

This conclusion—that acts in violation of international law or contrary to the expressed policy of the United Kingdom Government cannot benefit from the act of State doctrine or '*Buttes* non-justiciability'— is to be commended as properly situating these doctrines of limited judicial restraint within the increasingly comprehensive and well-defined system of international law. At the same time, the judgment leaves at least some questions unanswered. Does the exception for acts in violation of international law apply to all such acts, or only to illegal uses of force and particularly serious human rights violations? If it only applies to some violations, how should the courts draw the line? Although

[31] Approved Transcript at 63.

[32] Approved Transcript at 66–7. It is interesting to note that Mance J also considered whether KAC could rely on factual matters stated in United Nations Security Council resolutions as 'public documents' falling within the scope of sections 9(1) and 9(2)(c) of the Civil Evidence Act 1968. Although he decided that it would not be appropriate to allow it to do so, since they had not been pleaded and insufficient notice had been given, he did comment that 'there is some attraction in a view of "public" documents which transcends the boundaries of the nation state, and takes account of pronouncements of one of the ultimate organs of the community of nations, especially when Her Majesty's Government has been party to them': Approved Transcript at 74.

Mance J was on solid ground given the facts of this case, future cases involving more difficult determinations of international law will require judges to do more than engage in a 'close examination of the particular circumstances' when determining that a particular violation cannot benefit from the act of State doctrine or '*Buttes* non-justiciability'.

Act of State doctrine—non-justiciability—effect of Cyprus Act 1960 in conferring independence upon the Republic of Cyprus—whether an English court is entitled to rule upon the constitutionality of a foreign government—whether the decision of the United Kingdom Government in voting in favour of opening negotiations for the accession of the Republic of Cyprus to the European Union was subject to judicial review

Case No. 2. R v. The Secretary of State for Foreign and Commonwealth Affairs, ex parte The British Council of Turkish Cypriot Associations, 19 March 1998, (1999) 112 ILR 735, QBD. In another case concerning the act of State doctrine and non-justiciability, the applicants sought leave to move for judicial review of the decision of the United Kingdom Government to vote in favour of the opening of negotiations for the possible accession of the Republic of Cyprus to the European Union. They argued that section 1 of the Cyprus Act 1960 and the Cyprus Order in Council 1960 had the effect of entrenching in English law the 1960 Cyprus Constitution and that, for the purposes of English law, the only lawful government of Cyprus was one which operated in accordance with that constitution. The government with which it was intended to engage in negotiations did not fulfil this requirement because it had been formed without Turkish Cypriot participation.

Section 1 of the Cyprus Act reads:

> Her Majesty may by Order in Council (to be laid before Parliament after being made) declare that the constitution designated in the Order as the Constitution of the Republic of Cyprus shall come into force on such day as may be specified in the Order; and on that day there shall be established in the Island of Cyprus an independent sovereign Republic of Cyprus, and Her Majesty shall have no sovereignty or jurisdiction over the Republic of Cyprus.

Crucial to the applicants' argument was the submission that, in legislating for Cyprus' independence, Parliament did not part with responsibility for upholding the 1960 Constitution.

In *Buck and others* v. *Attorney-General*, Diplock LJ had dealt with the contention that there was a moment in time when the Order in Council giving effect to the Sierra Leone Independence Act 1961 purported to be in force *before* Sierra Leone became an independent sovereign State, while the United Kingdom Government was still the sovereign government of the colony of Sierra Leone. It was argued that, since at this time the English court would have had jurisdiction to declare the Order in Council *ultra vires*, it did not lose that jurisdiction simply because Sierra Leone subsequently became independent. Diplock LJ responded:

> I should in any event reject this argument. In applying the rules of comity, one looks to the substance of the issue, not to its form. The Order in Council was, on the face of it,

intended to provide the constitution not of the colony of Sierra Leone, but of the new independent foreign state. The issue as to the validity of the Order in Council was thus, in substance, at the date of the writ, an issue as to the validity of the constitution of an independent sovereign state . . . .As soon as Sierra Leone became independent, the Order in Council ceased to have any effect as an Order in Council, that is, as an exercise of the sovereign power of the United Kingdom Government represented by the Attorney-General of England. Whatever effect it then had was as part of the law of a foreign sovereign state, into the validity of which this court has no jurisdiction to enquire.[33]

In the case at hand, Sedley J paraphrased this holding as follows: 'In other words, once cut free, a dependent State becomes an independent foreign State equipped with a constitution which belongs thenceforth to it and not to the United Kingdom.'[34]

Also crucial to the applicant's argument was the proposition that the government of Cyprus was acting unconstitutionally. The Secretary of State contended that this was the very class of issue on which, for well-established reasons of comity and non-justiciability, English courts would not adjudicate. Here Harman LJ's holding in *Buck and others* v. *Attorney-General* was of greatest relevance:

These courts cannot, in my view, make a declaration impugning the validity of the constitution of a foreign or independent state, at any rate where that is the object of the action. This may be put as a matter of international comity, or upon the ground of effectiveness. No relief effective in this country or anywhere else is sought by the action. Any declaration which the court might make may be ignored with impunity by the independent country into whose affairs it intends to pry, and I am of the opinion that it would be not only improper, but contrary to law in those circumstances to make such a declaration as is here sought.[35]

Sedley J also referred to the leading speech in *Buttes* v. *Hammer*[36] where Lord Wilberforce reasserted the act of State doctrine as articulated in *Duke of Brunswick* v. *King of Hanover*[37] and adopted the following language of Chief Justice Fuller of the United States Supreme Court in *Underhill* v. *Hernandez*:

Every sovereign state is bound to respect the independence of every other sovereign state, and the courts of one country will not sit in judgment on the acts of government of another done within its own territory.[38]

Having determined that this was the applicable common law, Sedley J went on to state that, on first principles, only clear statutory words could abrogate it.[39] He continued:

There is nothing in Section 1 of the Act of 1960 which diminishes or qualifies the decisive renunciation on the part of the United Kingdom of all claims to sovereign power or jurisdiction over Cyprus. There is no explicit reservation and no arguable basis for an

[33] [1965] Ch. 745 at 771, this *Year Book*, 41 (1965–6), pp. 435–8.
[34] (1999) 112 ILR 735 at 740.
[35] [1965] Ch. 745 at 768.
[36] [1982] AC 888, [1981] 3 All ER 616, this *Year Book*, 53 (1982), pp. 259–68.
[37] (1848) 2 HL Cas. 1.
[38] 168 US 250 (1897).
[39] (1999) 112 ILR 735 at 741.

implicit reservation of a continuing obligation in domestic United Kingdom law to take cognizance of the future constitutional course taken by the Republic of Cyprus.[40]

He also rejected a further submission, to the effect that this approach need not divest the courts of all power to enquire into the constitutionality of the actions of the newly sovereign State. In doing so, he distinguished between cases concerning a factual step (albeit a step involving a question of foreign law) on the path to a conclusion of national law, and cases where the necessary object of the action is to call into question what is now the constitution of a sovereign State by challenging the *vires* of the instrument bringing it into being. He concluded:

So here, the independence of Cyprus since 17 August 1960 forecloses any power in the United Kingdom courts to entertain issues which do not merely touch upon but are inseparable from the constitutionality of events in Cyprus. That the facts amounting to the asserted want of constitutionality are not themselves contentious cannot be an answer because it is not the evidence but the adjudication which in such a situation violates comity. If the Cyprus negotiation is finally successful, any necessary statutory authority, including an expressed or implied modification of the Cyprus Act 1960, will have to be given by Parliament in the form of an amendment of the European Communities Act 1972. But to accept this, as the Crown does, is not to accept that there is meanwhile no power to negotiate Cyprus' accession to the European Union. Negotiation is a function of diplomacy and therefore of the Prerogative. Unless a clear legal constraint is placed upon it, its conduct is not a matter for the courts.[41]

Diplomatic immunity—State immunity—immunity of State officials for official acts—relationship between State immunity and diplomatic immunity—Vienna Convention on Diplomatic Relations 1961, Articles 1, 31, 32 and 37

Case No. 3. P v. *P* , 22 January 1998, [1998] Times LR 119, [1998] 1 FLR 1026, (1999) 114 ILR (forthcoming), FD. This case, involving two sets of proceedings, concerned a child custody dispute between the father, a United States national who was a member of the United States diplomatic mission to the United Kingdom, and the mother, a German national. In the first set of proceedings, the mother, fearing the removal of the two children to the United States after she commenced divorce proceedings in Germany, applied to the High Court for orders under the Children Act 1989 restraining the father from removing the two children from the United Kingdom and seeking leave to take the children to Germany. The father and the United States, which intervened in the proceedings, maintained that the English courts lacked jurisdiction because

[40] (1999) 112 ILR 735 at 741.

[41] (1999) 112 ILR 735 at 742. The Divisional Court had another opportunity to consider the issue of non-justiciability in *Nuova Safim SpA* v. *The Sakura Bank Ltd.*, [1998] Lloyd's LR: Banking 142, [1998] CLC 306. In this case a Japanese bank claimed that the Law Decrees upon which the plaintiffs, a wholly owned subsidiary of the Italian State holding company Ente Partecipazioni e Finanziamento Industria Manifatturiera, relied in relation to a dispute over the termination of an interest rate and currency exchange agreement, were unconstitutional. The Court held that on the basis of the evidence of Italian law and arguments presented, it could not at this stage decide whether it was precluded from adjudicating upon the constitutionality of the Decrees. Thomas J applied *Buttes Gas* v. *Hammer* and concluded that non-justiciability can only be determined when there is evidence before the court of the precise nature of the challenge being made.

the father and the children all possessed diplomatic immunity. The High Court agreed and dismissed the application.

The following day, the father, mother and children left the United Kingdom for the United States. Although they travelled together, the mother maintained that she did not consent to the father taking the children to the United States. Child custody proceedings began in the United States, with the mother contending that the father had removed the children from the United Kingdom in violation of the 1980 Hague Convention on Civil Aspects of International Child Abduction. She also commenced a second set of proceedings in the High Court, seeking a declaration that the father had wrongfully removed the children from the United Kingdom in breach of the Hague Convention and the Child Abduction and Custody Act 1985.

The father and the United States now argued that the father's act was performed in the exercise of his functions as a member of a diplomatic mission and that he was therefore entitled to diplomatic immunity under Article 39(2) of the 1961 Vienna Convention on Diplomatic Relations notwithstanding that he was no longer a diplomat accredited in the United Kingdom. Article 39 reads:

> (1) Every person entitled to privileges and immunities shall enjoy them from the moment he enters the territory of the receiving State on proceeding to take up his post . . .
> (2) When the functions of a person enjoying privileges and immunities have come to an end, such privileges and immunities shall normally cease at the moment when he leaves the country, or on the expiry of a reasonable period in which to do so, but shall subsist until that time, even in case of armed conflict. However, with respect to acts performed by such a person in the exercise of his functions as a member of the mission, immunity shall continue to subsist.[42]

Article 37 extends this immunity to the members of a diplomat's family.

The father and the United States also contended that the removal of the children had been ordered by the United States, that the United States itself was immune from the jurisdiction of the English courts in respect of that act, and that the father benefited from that immunity.

The High Court again rejected the mother's application, this time drawing a distinction between diplomatic and State immunity. In respect of diplomatic immunity, it observed that this constituted immunity from jurisdiction, not immunity from legal liability. The fact that the father had been entitled to immunity from suit at the time he left the United Kingdom did not necessarily mean that the courts were still precluded from holding that he had acted illegally. Moreover, diplomatic privileges and immunities were functional in nature. Their purpose was to ensure the efficient performance of the functions of diplomatic missions as representing States; they were not directed at benefiting individual diplomats. The Court held that taking the children to the United States was a personal act performed at the end of a diplomatic posting, and could not be regarded as an exercise of the father's *official* functions as a diplomat within the meaning of Article 39(2). Accordingly, he was not now entitled to diplomatic immunity.

[42] The Convention was incorporated (as a schedule) into English law by the Diplomatic Privileges Act 1964.

However, he was entitled to State immunity. Sir Stephen Brown said:

> State immunity is a separate concept. The immunity usually applies in cases where the foreign State is named as a defendant. However it has been accepted by the Court of Appeal in the case of *Propend Finance Pty Ltd* v. *Sing* (unreported) 17 April 1997 that the agent of a foreign State will enjoy immunity in respect of his acts of a sovereign or governmental nature. Accordingly there may be cases where the diplomatic agent may enjoy both diplomatic and State immunity. These immunities will not be co-extensive.[43]

Since the act of taking the children back to the United States was performed under orders from the United States Government, it was of a sovereign governmental character.[44]

This case thus demonstrates the importance of maintaining a clear distinction between diplomatic immunity and State immunity, while at the same time again raising the question whether the courts should assume that all acts carried out under orders or in the exercise of governmental authority are necessarily acts of a 'sovereign governmental character'.[45] It is far from clear why the act of taking one's children out of the jurisdiction should be considered to be of a 'sovereign governmental character', whether that removal is ordered by a State or otherwise. Although the distinction between diplomatic and State immunity should be upheld, the court here fails to address the apparent paradox in its holdings that (i) for the purposes of diplomatic immunity, the act of taking the children to the United States was a personal act performed at the end of a diplomatic posting, and (ii) for the purposes of State immunity, the same act was of a sovereign character, carried out as an agent of a State.

[43] [1998] 1 FLR 1026 at 1034. The judgment in *Propend* was reviewed in this *Year Book*, 68 (1997), pp. 312–18.

[44] The mother appealed. The Court of Appeal dismissed the appeal on the grounds that it would serve no useful purpose for an English court to grant the declaration sought, prolonged proceedings in England might be contrary to the interests of the children, and the final decision had to be made by the courts of the United States.

[45] See discussion in this *Year Book*, 68 (1997), pp. 313–18.

Two other cases concerning State immunity were decided during the year under review. In *Holland* v. *Lampen-Wolfe*, [1998] Times LR 528, (1998) 95(36) LSG 32, the defendant in a libel action was a US citizen employed as an educational services officer at a US military base in Yorkshire by the US Government. He had published a memorandum listing complaints about the plaintiff who was also, as part of her employment by a US university, working at the base. The court held that, whereas s. 16(2) of the State Immunity Act 1978 excluded proceedings related to anything done by or in relation to the armed forces of a foreign State in the UK, the defendant benefited from State immunity under the common law. Applying *Littrell* v. *United States of America (No. 2)*, [1993] Times LR 589, [1994] 4 All ER 203, [1995] 1 WLR 82, this *Year Book*, 65 (1994), pp. 491–6, Hoffmann LJ concluded that the defendant's overall activity was closely enough connected to the central military activity of the US in maintaining the base to be clearly performed in the exercise of sovereign authority and not a private, commercial or even professional activity.

In *Malaysian Industrial Development Authority* v. *Jeyasingham*, (1998) ICR 307, the Employment Appeals Tribunal considered a complaint of unfair dismissal against an investment authority which was part of the State of Malaysia. On the advice of his solicitor, the director of the authority had entered a notice of appearance even though the High Commisioner had thought immunity should first be claimed. Only then did he claim immunity. At first instance, the tribunal decided it had jurisdiction to hear the complaint on the basis that immunity had been waived. The decision was reversed by the Appeals Tribunal, which held that under s. 2(7) of the State Immunity Act 1978, the High Commissioner was the only person who could waive immunity.

Recognition of foreign governments—criteria for determining whether the organizers of a military coup are now the government—degree, nature and stability of control required over the territory of the State—extent of international recognition required

Case No. 4. Sierra Leone Telecommunications Co. Ltd. v. *Barclays Bank plc*, 6 February 1998, [1998] 2 All ER 821, [1998] Times LR 102, [1998] CLC 501, QBD. This case, arising out of the military coup in Sierra Leone in 1997, represents a relatively straightforward application of the criteria for the recognition of foreign governments set out by Hobhouse J in the 1992 case of *Republic of Somalia* v. *Woodhouse Drake & Carey (Suisse) SA*.[46] The plaintiff company was incorporated in Sierra Leone and wholly owned and controlled by the Sierra Leone Government. Under the company's articles of association, its board of directors consisted of eight members appointed by the Government. The company held an account with the defendant bank in the United Kingdom and had completed a mandate authorizing four signatories to sign payment requests on its behalf, with two signatures being required for any payment.

Once the coup took place, in May 1997, it was condemned consistently by the United Kingdom, which continued to deal with the democratically elected government. In December 1997, however, the bank received a letter signed by the Sierra Leone Secretary of State, Transport and Communications notifying it that the company's board of directors had been dissolved, that a new board had been appointed and that three of the signatories had been suspended with immediate effect. A further fax communication from the company's executive chairman instructed the bank not to honour any payments without reference to the new board. The bank subsequently refused to meet several payment requests on the ground that they were ostensibly made without authority.

The company sought a declaration that the account remained subject to the terms of the original mandate on the grounds that the new mandate had not been determined under English law, which was the law governing the contract, and that the authority of the signatories had not been revoked properly since the new board had not in fact been appointed by the Government of Sierra Leone.

Cresswell J began by considering the established rules on the conflict of laws. In *Libyan Arab Foreign Bank* v. *Bankers Trust Co.* it was held that, as a general rule, the contract between a bank and its customer is governed by the law of the place where the account is kept, in the absence of any agreement to the contrary.[47] This rule was reaffirmed in *Libyan Arab Foreign Bank* v. *Manufacturers Hanover Trust Co.* where it was said that solid grounds are needed for holding that this general rule does not apply.[48] Cresswell J considered these cases in the light of the 1990 Rome Convention on the Law Applicable to Contractual Obligations, which was given the force of law in the United Kingdom by the Contracts (Applicable Law) Act 1990:

> The basic rule under the convention is that in the absence of a choice of law, a contract is governed by the law of the country with which it is most closely connected: art 4(1). The rule is qualified by a number of rebuttable presumptions. It is presumed that the

[46] [1993] 1 All ER 371, [1993] QB 54, this *Year Book*, 63 (1992), pp. 501–5.
[47] [1989] 3 All ER 252 at 266, [1989] QB 728 at 746, this *Year Book*, 60 (1989), pp. 502–6.
[48] [1988] 2 Lloyd's Rep 494 at 502.

contract is most closely connected with the country where the party who is to effect 'characteristic performance' has its central administration. In the case of a bank account, such party will be the bank . . . .It is the law of the country where the account is kept which governs the contract.[49]

Cresswell J then turned to the question whether the purported acts of the new board of directors were in fact valid. He quoted Rule 156 of *Dicey and Morris*, which states:

(1) The capacity of a corporation to enter into any legal transaction is governed both by the constitution of the corporation and by the law of the country which governs the transaction in question.
(2) All matters concerning the constitution of a corporation are governed by the law of the place of incorporation. [50]

Article 71(I) of the company's articles of association provided that: 'The Board of Directors of the Company shall consist of eight members appointed by the Government of Sierra Leone'. Furthermore, section 70 of the 1991 Constitution of Sierra Leone required all directors of parastatal companies to be appointed by the President and approved by Parliament. The military junta had neither lawfully set aside nor revised the constitution itself.

Turning to the question whether the military junta was in fact the Government of Sierra Leone, Cresswell J said:

In the field of foreign relations the Crown in its executive and judicial functions ought to speak with one voice and the recognition of a foreign state or government is a matter of foreign policy on which the executive is in a markedly superior position to form a judgment . . . .[51]

However, in 1980 the British Government had adopted a new policy towards the recognition of governments:

In future cases where a new regime comes to power unconstitutionally our attitude on the question whether it qualifies to be treated as a Government will be left to be inferred from the nature of the dealings, if any, which we may have with it, and in particular on whether we are dealing with it on a normal Government to Government basis.[52]

In *Republic of Somalia* v. *Woodhouse Drake & Carey*, Hobhouse J had stated:

[I]t is relevant to distinguish between regimes that have been the constitutional and established government of a state and a regime which is seeking to achieve that position either by displacing a former government or to fill a vacuum. Since the question is now whether a government *exists*, there is no room for more than one government at a time nor for separate de jure and de facto governments in respect of the same state. But a loss of control by a constitutional government may not immediately deprive it of its status, whereas an insurgent regime will require to establish control before it can exist as a government.[53]

[49] [1998] 2 All ER 821 at 827.

[50] Lawrence Collins (ed.), *Dicey and Morris on the Conflict of Laws* (12th edn., 1993), vol. 2, p.1111.

[51] [1998] 2 All ER 821 at 828.

[52] *Parliamentary Debates (Lords)*, vol. 408, cols. 1121–2: 28 April 1980; *Parliamentary Debates (Commons)*, vol. 983, *Written Answers*, cols. 277–9: 25 April 1980; ibid., vol. 985, *Written Answers*, col. 385: 23 May 1980. See also discussion of *Case No. 1*, above.

[53] [1993] 1 All ER 371 at 383, [1993] QB 54 at 67, this *Year Book*, loc. cit. above (n. 46) (emphasis in original).

He had gone on to elaborate the factors to be taken into account in deciding whether a government exists as the government of a State:

Accordingly, the factors to be taken into account in deciding whether a government exists as the government of the state are: (a) whether it is the constitutional government of the state; (b) the degree, nature and stability of administrative control, if any, that it of itself exercises over the territory of the state; (c) whether Her Majesty's government has any dealings with it and if so what is the nature of those dealings; and (d) in marginal cases, the extent of international recognition that it has as the government of the state.[54]

Cresswell J considered these factors in turn. Statements issued by the Minister of State at the Foreign and Commonwealth Office expressed British Government policy as follows:

We have consistently condemned the military coup of 25 May 1997 which overthrew the democratically elected government of Sierra Leone. We look forward to the restoration of constitutional order in that country. We continue to deal with the democratically elected government of Sierra Leone under President Kabbah. We have no dealings with the military junta in Freetown.[55]

The evidence further showed that the military junta in Sierra Leone was not in control outside the capital city and that forces loyal to the exiled government controlled larger parts of the country. Those areas under the control of the junta were devoid of law and order. Moreover, the United Nations Security Council had imposed sanctions and the coup had been condemned by the Commonwealth, the Organization of African Unity and the European Union. On the basis of these various factors, Cresswell J concluded—correctly—that the mandate to the bank was still valid, the 'new board' was invalidly appointed and the company was entitled to the declaration sought.

Refugees—past persecution—whether sufficient that individual originally fled country or remained abroad for well-founded fear of persecution—meaning of 'refugee' in the context of a civil war—1951 Geneva Convention relating to the Status of Refugees, Article 1A(2)

Case No. 5. R v. *Secretary of State for the Home Department, ex parte Adan*, 2 April 1998, [1998] 2 All ER 453, [1998] 2 WLR 702, [1998] INLR 325, (1998) 37 ILM 1090, *http://www.parliament.the-stationery-office.co.uk* (HL). In this case an applicant for asylum had fled Somalia in 1988 owing to a well-founded fear of persecution by the government then in power. In 1991 there was a change of government in Somalia, but clan and sub-clan-based civil war broke out in the north of that country. It was accepted by the Secretary of State that the warfare involved widespread killing, torture, rape and pillage, and that the country's infrastructure had broken down to the extent that the applicant would not obtain effective protection from any recognized State authority.

The Immigration Appeal Tribunal had held that the applicant was at no greater risk than others from the civil war. This decision was overturned by the

[54] [1993] 1 All ER 371 at 384, [1993] QB 54 at 68.

[55] Letter dated 28 November 1997 from the Foreign and Commonwealth Office to Messrs Stephenson Harwood, quoted in [1998] 2 All ER 821 at 830.

Court of Appeal, which held that it was unnecessary for the applicant to demonstrate a current well-founded fear of persecution provided that the original fear still played a causative part in his presence in the United Kingdom.[56] In its view, all those who might be identified with the interests of either side in a civil war were potential refugees entitled to protection under the 1951 Geneva Convention relating to the Status of Refugees.

Article 1A(2) of the 1951 Convention defines a refugee as any person who

> owing to well-founded fear of being persecuted for reasons of race, religion, nationality, membership of a particular social group or political opinion, is outside the country of his nationality and is unable or, owing to such fear, is unwilling to avail himself of the protection of that country; or who, not having a nationality and being outside the country of his former habitual residence as a result of such events, is unable or, owing to such fear, is unwilling to return to it.[57]

The first issue addressed by the House of Lords was whether a historic fear, that is a fear of persecution on the part of the applicant when he left his country of nationality, could suffice to found a claim of refugee status. Lord Lloyd, expressing the unanimous opinion of the Court, said that Article 1 must be interpreted in the light of the 1951 Convention as a whole and the purposes its framers sought to achieve. He continued:

> But having said that, the starting point must be the language itself. The most striking feature is that it is expressed throughout in the present tense: 'is outside', 'is unable', 'is unwilling'. Thus in order to bring himself within category (1) Mr Adan must show that he is (not was) unable to avail himself of the protection of his country. If one asks 'protection against what?' the answer must surely be, or at least include, protection against persecution. Since 'is unable' can only refer to current inability, one would expect that the persecution against which he needs protection is also current (or future) persecution. If he has no current fear of persecution it is not easy to see why he should need current protection against persecution, or why, indeed, protection is relevant at all.[58]

Lord Lloyd was of the view that the existence of the 'protection test', couched as it was in the present tense, leant positive support to the submission that 'owing to well-founded fear' was also confined to current fear. He relied on the following analysis by James Hathaway:

> In the Convention as ultimately adopted, therefore, persons determined to be refugees under earlier arrangements are not required to demonstrate a well-founded fear of being persecuted, and are not automatically subject to cessation of refugee status if conditions become safe in their homeland. It was the intention of the drafters, however, that all other refugees should have to demonstrate 'a present fear of persecution' in the sense that they 'are or may in the future be deprived of the protection of their country of origin'. Thus

[56] *Adan* v. *Secretary of State for the Home Department, and other appeals*, [1997] 1 WLR 1107, [1997] 2 All ER 723, [1997] Imm. AR 251, this *Year Book*, 68 (1997), pp. 319–23 and 328–9.

[57] *United Nations Treaty Series*, vol. 189, p. 137, Cmd. 9171, as modified by the 1967 Protocol relating to the Status of Refugees, Cmnd. 3906. The question of the application of the Geneva Convention in national law arose for determination on account of section 8(1) of the Asylum and Immigration Appeals Act 1993, which provides that: 'A person who is refused leave to enter the United Kingdom under the . . . [Immigration Act 1971] may appeal against the refusal to a special adjudicator on the ground that his removal in consequence of the refusal would be contrary to the United Kingdom's obligations under the [Geneva] Convention'.

[58] [1998] 2 WLR 702 at 707–8, [1998] 2 All ER 453 at 458.

it was agreed that the first branch of the IRO [International Refugee Organization] test which focused on past persecution should be omitted in favour of the 'well-founded fear of being persecuted' standard, involving evidence of a present or prospective risk in the country of origin. The use of the term 'fear' was intended to emphasize the forward-looking nature of the test, and not to ground refugee status in an assessment of the refugee claimant's state of mind. [59]

Lord Lloyd also relied on guidelines adopted by the Council of Ministers of the European Union in 1996 which reflected the view that the essential criterion for determining refugee status (other than refugees who are already covered by Article 1A (1)) was a current well-founded fear of persecution for a Convention reason.[60] Although the Council recognized that historic fear may be relevant to establishing evidence of present fear, it nevertheless considered the existence, or otherwise, of present fear to be determinative.

Lord Lloyd also noted the absence of any support for an alternative view, saying: 'So far as I am aware the suggestion that anything other than a current fear of persecution will suffice has never even been mooted'.[61]

The second issue dealt with by the House of Lords was whether a civil war involving widespread clan and sub-clan-based killing and torture could give rise to well-founded fear of persecution for Convention purposes, notwithstanding that the individual claimant is at no greater risk of adverse treatment than others owing to their clan membership. In theory, this question involved drawing a line between the persecution of individuals and groups, including very large groups, and the existence of a state of civil war.

Lord Lloyd held that the asylum seeker had to show fear of persecution for Convention reasons over and above the ordinary risks of clan warfare. Although he accepted that 'generalised oppression may indeed give rise to refugee status', he considered that this 'does not touch on the more difficult questions which arise when a country is in a state of war'.[62] He quoted with approval the following passage written by Hathaway:

Nonetheless, the Convention today remains firmly anchored in the notion of elevating only a subset of those at risk of war and violent conflict to the status of refugee. This general proposition is well-established in Canadian law by a variety of cases involving the victims of violence in Lebanon, Ethiopia, and Chile. Moreover, as the decision in *Elias Iskandar Ishac* [Immigration Appeal Board Decision M77–1040, 25 April 1977] makes clear, the mere fact that the conflict escaped is based on religion or politics is not relevant unless persons of a particular religion or political perspective are differentially at risk. In this case, the Board found the risk to be roughly equivalent for persons of all beliefs, and hence refused the claim of a citizen of Lebanon attempting to escape the civil war in that country: If the appellant is a refugee at all, he is a refugee from civil war in his country, and not a refugee protected by the Convention. . . . A civil war, even on religious grounds is not persecution as contemplated by the Convention.[63]

[59] *The Law of Refugee Status* (1991), pp. 68–9.

[60] Joint Position of the Member States of the European Union on the Harmonized Application of the Definition of the Term 'Refugee' (*Official Journal*, 1996, L63, 4 March 1996), pp. 3, 6.

[61] [1998] 2 WLR 702 at 710, [1998] 2 All ER 453 at 460.

[62] [1998] 2 WLR 702 at 712, [1998] 2 All ER 453 at 462.

[63] *The Law of Refugee Status* (1991), pp. 186–7. Lord Lloyd referred also to the UNHCR Handbook, para. 164, p. 39, and to the Joint Position of the Member States of the European Union on Procedures and Criteria for determining Refugee Status, loc. cit. above (n. 60), para. 6.

Lord Lloyd did emphasize that this theory applied only so long as the civil war continued, but on the basis of these considerations he concluded:

> I agree with the Court of Appeal that refugee status ought not to depend 'on casting around for the current underdog'.[64] But the difficulty of establishing the facts does not undermine the principle that those engaged in civil war are not, as such, entitled to the protection of the convention so long as the civil war continues, even if the civil war is being fought on religious or racial grounds.[65]

This judgment must be regarded with some concern in respect of both the issues with which it deals. The drafters of the 1951 Convention clearly considered that past persecution could be a sufficient basis for refugee status. This is evident in the fact that, prior to the 1967 Protocol, refugee status had to derive from events—and therefore persecution—occurring before 1 January 1951. Lord Lloyd's statement above as to the lack of any suggestions concerning the sufficiency of past persecution[66] must, therefore, in this context (and against the backdrop of Simon Brown LJ's judgment in the Court of Appeal) be regarded with some scepticism.

It is also important to remember that the Secretary of State accepted that the applicant's life was still very much at risk and that he would not obtain effective protection from any recognized State authority. The House of Lords, by adopting a *persecution* rather than a *protection*-based definition of 'refugee', would thus seem again to have gone against the clear intention of the drafters of the 1951 Convention—i.e. to *protect* individuals who, fearing death or worse because of who they are, have fled their country of nationality—in a situation where the serious humanitarian consequences of their decision could hardly have been more clear.[67]

The second issue, of whether persecution for a Convention reason can properly be said to arise in the context of a civil war, is equally important given that civil wars are now responsible for the largest outflows of refugees.[68] As Simon Brown LJ said in the Court of Appeal, the approach eventually adopted by the House of Lords requires that the 'putative refugee . . . must at the very least be able to point to some group within the area of civil war less at risk than his own'.[69] This increases the burden of proof on individual claimants in situations which, by their very nature, involve the very grounds of persecution set out in Article 1A(2)—i.e. divisions based on race, religion, membership of a

[64] Court of Appeal, [1997] 2 All ER 723 at 735, [1997] 1 WLR 1107 at 1120.

[65] [1998] 2 WLR 702 at 713, [1998] 2 All ER 453 at 463.

[66] [1998] 2 WLR 702 at 710, [1998] 2 All ER 453 at 460.

[67] It is possible that this aspect of the judgment will have other serious ramifications, for example in respect of asylum claims resulting from persecution (or the fear of persecution) at the hands of those who are not officials or agents of a State. For a more detailed analysis of this issue, see Storey, 'The "Internal Flight Alternative" (IFA) Test and the Concept of Protection', in Nicholson and Twomey, *Current Issues of UK Asylum Law and Policy* (1998), chapter 5, and Storey, 'The Internal Flight Alternative Test: The Jurisprudence Re-examined', *International Journal of Refugee Law*, 10 (1998), p. 499.

[68] Goodwin-Gill, *The Refugee in International Law* (2nd edn., 1996), p. 189. On refugees and civil wars, see generally Goodwin-Gill, ibid., pp. 75–6; Kälin, 'Refugees and Civil Wars: Only a Matter of Interpretation?', *International Journal of Refugee Law*, 3 (1991), p. 435; Bodart, 'Les réfugiés apolitiques: guerre civile et persécution de groupe au regard de la Convention de Genève', *International Journal of Refugee Law*, 7 (1995), p. 39.

[69] [1997] 2 All ER 723 at 735, [1997] 1 WLR 1107 at 1120.

particular social group or political opinion—and thus also seems to run contrary to the clear humanitarian intention of the drafters of the 1951 Convention. It is true that the drafters did not foresee the large-scale refugee movements that would result from the civil wars of the late twentieth century, and that national courts have properly dealt with some of the resulting *lacunae*, for example through the development of the concept of safe havens in international refugee law.[70] However, it is also true that other measures for dealing with these unforeseen challenges—such as the development of the concept of temporary protection—are best left to national legislatures and multilateral treaty negotiations.[71] Most importantly, the guiding principle in all efforts to improve international refugee law must be to uphold the obligations already set out in the 1951 Convention—for the simple reason that they are not just inter-State obligations, but also the mirror image of the existing human rights of individual refugees.[72]

Refugees—'safe third country'—whether Germany required too high a standard of proof to establish a well-founded fear of persecution—margin of appreciation—1951 Geneva Convention relating to the Status of Refugees, Article 33—Asylum and Immigration Act 1996, section 2

Case No. 6. R v. *Secretary of State for the Home Department, ex parte Iyadurai*, 10 June 1998, [1998] Imm. AR 470, [1998] INLR 472, [1998] Times LR 382, CA. By Article 33 of the 1951 Geneva Convention relating to the Status of Refugees the contracting States, including the United Kingdom, undertook not to 'expel or return (''*refouler*'') a refugee in any manner whatsoever to the frontiers of territories where his life or freedom would be threatened on account of his race, religion, nationality, membership of a particular social group or political opinion'.[73] However, section 2 of the Asylum and Immigration Act 1996 enables the Secretary of State to remove expeditiously from the United Kingdom claimants for asylum who have arrived from a 'safe third country'.

The applicant was a Tamil and citizen of Sri Lanka. In February 1996 he travelled to Germany where his claim for asylum was refused. He then travelled to Italy and from there to the United Kingdom. Following his claim for asylum

[70] See *R* v. *Secretary of State for the Home Department, ex parte Robinson*, [1997] 3 WLR 1162, [1997] Times LR 435, this *Year Book*, 68 (1997), pp. 323–5; *Attorney-General of Canada* v. *Ward*, [1993] 2 SCR 689 at 709, (1993) 103 DLR (4th) 1 at 12 (*per* La Forest J).

[71] See Donatella Luca, 'Questioning Temporary Protection', *International Journal of Refugee Law*, 6 (1994), p. 535; Goodwin-Gill, *The Refugee in International Law* (2nd edn., 1996), pp. 196–202; Khalid Koser, Martha Walsh and Richard Black, 'Temporary Protection and the Assisted Return of Refugees from the European Union', *International Journal of Refugee Law*, 10 (1998), p. 444.

[72] See Michael Byers, 'Review of Hathaway (ed.), *Reconceiving International Refugee Law* (1997)', *International and Comparative Law Quarterly*, 47 (1998), pp. 729–31.

[73] *United Nations Treaty Series*, vol. 189, p. 137, Cmd. 9171, as modified by the 1967 Protocol relating to the Status of Refugees, Cmnd. 3906. The question of the application of the Geneva Convention in national law arose for determination on account of section 8(1) of the Asylum and Immigration Appeals Act 1993, which provides that: 'A person who is refused leave to enter the United Kingdom under the . . . [Immigration Act 1971] may appeal against the refusal to a special adjudicator on the ground that his removal in consequence of the refusal would be contrary to the United Kingdom's obligations under the [Geneva] Convention'.

in the United Kingdom, Germany was asked to accept—and did accept—responsibility for examining his claim under the 1990 Dublin Convention.[73a] The applicant sought judicial review of the Secretary of State's decision.

Under section 2 of the 1996 Act, the Secretary of State has a discretion to remove an asylum claimant from the United Kingdom if he certifies that the following conditions have been fulfilled:

(*a*) That the person is not a national or citizen of the country or territory to which he is to be sent;
(*b*) That his life and liberty would not be threatened in that country or territory by reason of his race, religion, nationality, membership of a particular social group, or political opinion; and
(*c*) That the government of that country or territory would not send him to another country or territory otherwise than in accordance with the Convention [i.e. the 1951 Geneva Convention].

Lord Woolf MR referred to his decision in *R* v. *Secretary of State for the Home Department, ex parte Canbolat* where he had stated, for the Court of Appeal, in relation to section 2: '[I]t is for the Secretary of State to evaluate the material. If the Secretary of State could properly come to the decision which he did on that material then this court cannot intervene.'[74] In that case the Secretary of State was held to have acted within the scope of his discretion in deciding that France was a 'safe third country'. The standard of reasonableness required was held to extend beyond the simple *Wednesbury* standard:

> The court may not interfere with the exercise of an administrative discretion on substantive grounds save where the court is satisfied that the decision is unreasonable in the sense that it is beyond the range of responses open to a reasonable decision-maker. But in judging whether the decision-maker has exceeded this margin of appreciation the human rights context is important. The more substantial the interference with human rights, the more the court will require by way of justification before it is satisfied that the decision is reasonable in the sense outlined above.[75]

Lord Woolf MR referred as well to his judgment in *R* v. *Secretary of State for the Home Department, ex parte Kerrouche*, where it was argued that France took a narrower view of what constituted a political crime than the courts in the United Kingdom.[76] The Court of Appeal there held that, although a harmonious approach amongst the parties to the 1951 Convention was highly desirable, it was not a realistic expectation. Lord Woolf MR had said:

> Although it is highly desirable that the approach to the interpretation of the

[73a] Convention determining the State responsible for examining applications for asylum lodged in one of the Member States of the European Communities, reproduced in *International Legal Materials*, 30 (1991), p. 425.

[74] [1997] 1 WLR 1569 at 1579, [1998] 1 All ER 161 at 170.

[75] [1997] 1 WLR 1569 at 1579, [1998] 1 All ER 161 at 170, adopting a passage from *R* v. *Ministry of Defence, ex parte Smith, and other appeals*, [1996] 1 All ER 257 at 263, [1996] QB 517 at 554, this *Year Book*, 67 (1996), pp. 552–3, CA.

[76] [1997] Imm. AR 610, [1998] INLR 88.

Convention and Protocol should be the same in all countries which are signatories, this is not a realistic expectation in the absence of some supra-national court which is capable of giving authoritative interpretations to the provisions of the Convention and Protocol which are binding on the signatory countries. Absent such a body the fact that a particular country adopts an approach to the Convention which involves a difference in emphasis in the interpretation of one or more provisions from that which would be adopted under English law does not necessarily involve that country being regarded as one which does not adhere to the principles of the Convention and Protocol when, as in the case of France, it contends that it does do so.

. . . The difference in an approach to the interpretation of the Convention and Protocol has to be of such significance that it can be said that in making a decision affecting the position of a particular applicant for asylum, the third country would not be applying the principles of the Convention. For this to be the position, the third country's approach would have to be outside the range of tolerance which one signatory country, as a matter of comity, is expected to extend to another. While it is highly desirable that there should be a harmonised approach to the interpretation of international documents such as the Convention, until that harmonisation is achieved, one signatory must allow another signatory a margin of appreciation before treating that other country as being one which did not fulfil its obligations to adhere to the principles of the Convention.[77]

Lord Woolf had gone on to explain that to hold France's approach to be more restrictive than the approach in the United Kingdom would 'require the Secretary of State and special adjudicators to become deeply involved in a comparative analysis of the law of the different signatories to the Convention'.[78]

In the case at hand, he reaffirmed that a broad approach to the interpretation of section 2 was needed:

[W]hat it is important for the Secretary of State to decide is not whether the third country formulates its test in precisely the same language as that adopted by this country but whether the Secretary of State regards the third country on the material available to him as properly giving effect to the Convention.[79]

Lord Woolf then turned his attention to the difficult question of what constitutes a well-founded fear of persecution. The test for this had been elaborated by the House of Lords in *R* v. *Home Secretary, ex parte Sivakumaran*,[80] where Lord Keith of Kinkel said that 'there has to be demonstrated a reasonable degree of likelihood that he [i.e. the applicant] will be persecuted for a Convention reason if returned to his own country'.[81] In that same case, however, Lord Templeman said:

A danger from persecution is obviously a matter of degree and judgment. The Secretary of State accepts that an applicant who fears persecution is entitled to asylum in this

[77] [1997] Imm. AR 610 at 614–15, [1998] INLR 88 at 92–3.
[78] [1998] INLR 88 at 93.
[79] [1998] Imm. AR 470 at 475.
[80] [1988] 1 AC 958.
[81] [1988] 1 AC 958 at 994.

country unless the Secretary of State is satisfied that there is no real and substantial danger of persecution.[82]

In the case at hand, the applicant contended that, since the German courts did not apply the same language to the question of what constitutes a well-founded fear of persecution, this meant that they were not complying with their obligations under the 1951 Convention. Evidence was submitted that the standard of fear of persecution required by the jurisprudence of the German Federal Administrative Court was that of a 'clear probability'. However, the Secretary of State contended that this was achieved by comprehensive evaluation of all the circumstances of the case to determine whether, on balance, the factors indicating a danger of persecution weighed more heavily than those indicating the asylum seeker's safety.

Lord Woolf turned for assistance to the following passage in an expert opinion provided by Guy Goodwin-Gill:

> States may have some margin of appreciation in deciding whether certain types of treatment amount to persecution; . . . However, any such margin will be closely circumscribed given that fundamental human rights are at stake. Thus, while in some circumstances it might be possible for different views to be taken as to the factual situation in a particular country . . . the overriding question remains whether there is a serious risk of possibility of persecution. The concept of 'margin of appreciation' cannot apply to the standard by which such a risk has to be proved.[83]

He then implicitly rejected this guidance, concluding that the Secretary of State took reasonable steps to inform himself of the position in Germany and that no more was required of him. Differences in interpretation could often be attributed to linguistic difficulties if they were not of such a scale to indicate an approach outside the range of responses of a contracting State acting in good faith to fulfil its obligations under the 1951 Convention.

Buxton LJ took a slightly different approach to the issue, interpreting the judgment in *ex parte Kerrouche* as binding upon the Court in respect of the following propositions:

> 1. It is not possible for a national court to determine a single interpretation of the Convention that binds all other countries.
> 2. The question for the English jurisdiction, in a case where the likely conduct of a court of a third country is in issue, is whether the decisions of that court will be contrary to the terms of the Convention.
> 3. That question is not determined simply by asking whether the decision of the court in the third country would, on the same set of facts, be the same as the decision of the English court.[84]

He felt that the crucial question was not, however, whether the German court would breach its treaty obligations, but whether the opinion of the Secretary of

[82] [1988] 1 AC 958 at 996.
[83] Opinion dated 2 December 1997, quoted at [1998] Imm. AR 470 at 479.
[84] [1998] Imm. AR 470 at 484.

State in that regard was reasonable under the principle set out in *ex parte Canbolat*. Ignoring 'verbal infelicities', he concluded that it was.[85]

This case goes some way towards establishing the important principle that judges, when applying the concept of 'safe third country', must focus on whether the individual asylum seeker will *actually* be accorded his rights under the 1951 Convention, rather than on whether the third country is obligated to accord him those rights. This approach recognizes that 'more than one State may share joint responsibility for decisions which result in the *refoulement* of a refugee' and that 'a State may not rely on the obligation of another State party to the Convention, even where there are good grounds for saying that the latter State is indeed under a particular obligation with respect to the refugee, if that reliance is likely to result in a violation of Article 33'.[86] At the same time, however, the Court's discussion of the 'margin of appreciation' suggests a disturbing move away from the principle, established by the House of Lords in the case of *In re Musisi*[87] and followed by the Chief Adjudicator in *Mohammed A.S. Al-Mass'ari* v. *Secretary of State for the Home Department*,[88] that judges

[85] Three other cases decided during the year under review also concerned the concept of 'safe third country'. In *R* v. *Secretary of State for the Home Department, ex parte Demiraj and Ethemi*, 29 January 1998, [1998] INLR 451, QBD, the applicants were ethnic Albanians from Kosovo who had gone to Germany where their claim for asylum was refused. They then came to the UK and claimed asylum. The Secretary of State decided that Germany was a 'safe third country' responsible for examining their asylum claims under the 1990 Dublin Convention and issued certificates for their removal. The court dismissed their application for judicial review on the basis that, although a universally correct approach to determining an asylum seeker's claim under the 1951 Convention would be desirable, in the absence of some international agreement signatories to the Convention could properly differ in the way they required asylum seekers to establish their claim. The Secretary of State was entitled to consider Germany safe even if it had refused the applicants' claims, because the issue was whether the interpretation of the 1951 Convention applied by Germany was reasonable having regard to its language and purpose.

In *R* v. *Secretary of State for the Home Department, ex parte Elshani and Berisha*, 6 July 1998, [1998] INLR 638, QBD, the applicants were again ethnic Albanians from Kosovo who had first travelled to Greece before arriving in the UK. They argued that Greece was not a 'safe third country' because it did not comply with international standards and its refugee determination procedures were offensive to English notions of procedural and substantive justice. They also contended that by allowing asylum-seekers to remain on humanitarian grounds, Greece effectively deprived them of their right to refugee status. The court held that, although there might be some procedural criticisms of the Greek system, the Secretary of State had taken reasonable steps to acquaint himself with the relevant facts. The fact that Greece might reject their claims for refugee status did not of itself mean that he was not entitled to certify that Greece was a safe third country. He had merely to be satisfied that Greece would not return the applicants to Yugoslavia other than in accordance with the 1951 Convention.

Finally, in *R* v. *Secretary of State for the Home Department, ex parte Adan and Osman*, 24 November 1998, unreported, QBD, the applicant was a Somali national who had fled to Germany, where her claim for asylum was refused. She came to the UK and claimed asylum for herself and her child. The Secretary of State refused the claims on the basis that Germany was a 'safe third country' and their claims could be considered there. The applicant argued that Germany took an unduly restrictive view inconsistent with that of the majority of other parties to the 1951 Convention as it did not recognize as refugees those fearing persecution by non-State agents in the context of the civil war in Somalia. Rose LJ said Germany's interpretation was still a permissible one and there was no basis for concluding otherwise.

[86] Crawford and Hyndman, 'Three Heresies in the Application of the Refugee Convention', *International Journal of Refugee Law*, 1 (1989), p. 155, at p. 171.

[87] [1987] AC 514 at 531, [1987] 1 All ER 940 at 952, this *Year Book*, 58 (1987), pp. 433–8.

[88] This *Year Book*, 68 (1997), pp. 562–7.

are required to subject decisions of this kind by the Secretary of State to the 'most anxious scrutiny'.

Unimplemented treaties—relevance to the exercise of the royal prerogative—1950 European Convention for the Protection of Human Rights and Fundamental Freedoms—1989 United Nations Convention on the Rights of the Child

Case No. 7. R v. *Secretary of State for the Home Department, ex parte Ahmed and others,* 30 July 1998, [1998] INLR 570, CA. This case confirms a simple and logical proposition, that the exercise of the royal prerogative is not limited to any greater extent by unimplemented treaties than is the exercise of statute-based administrative discretion.

The appellants were illegal immigrants who married persons with indefinite leave to remain in the United Kingdom, had children here, and applied for leave to remain on the basis of their marriages. Their applications were refused on the basis of the Secretary of State's published marriage policy. They applied for judicial review of the decision, relying, *inter alia*, upon the United Kingdom's ratification of the 1950 European Convention on Human Rights ('ECHR')[89] and the 1989 United Nations Convention on the Rights of the Child.[90] They argued that there was a legitimate expectation that the Secretary of State would base decisions in deportation cases on these treaties and not upon the terms of his published marriage policy.

Lord Woolf MR considered the marriage policy and the facts of the individual cases before concluding:

> In the case of all the applicants, there is no suggestion that their marriages are otherwise [than] genuine. In each case, for the applicants to return home will undoubtedly result in hardship for the applicants and their families. While appreciating the position of the Secretary of State, it is difficult not to have considerable sympathy for their position . . . .
>
> But for the point as to the prerogative . . . it is difficult to see any basis on which any of the applicants could have been entitled to leave to apply for judicial review. Their cases all require the court to interfere with his [the Secretary of State's] application of what (apart from the ECHR) is a perfectly proper policy.[91]

Lord Woolf relied on Lord Ackner's statement, in *R* v. *Secretary of State for the Home Department, ex parte Brind*, that to require the Secretary of State to conform with the ECHR 'inevitably would result in incorporating the Convention into English domestic law by the back door'.[92] He also referred to the judgment of Hirst LJ in *R* v. *Secretary of State for the Home Department, ex parte Gangadeen and Jurawan; R* v. *Secretary of State for the Home Department, ex parte Khan,* which concerned the same marriage policy.[93] Hirst LJ had

[89] *United Nations Treaty Series*, vol. 213, p. 221; *UK Treaty Series*, No. 71 (1953) (Cmd. 8969).

[90] Reproduced in *International Legal Materials*, 28 (1989), p. 1457.

[91] [1998] INLR 570 at 581.

[92] [1991] 1 AC 696 at 761–2, [1991] 1 All ER 720 at 735, this *Year Book*, 62 (1991), pp. 437–41, HL.

[93] [1998] INLR 206.

applied the following *dicta* of Sir Thomas Bingham MR in *R* v. *Ministry of Defence, ex parte Smith and other appeals*:

It is, inevitably, common ground that the United Kingdom's obligation, binding in international law, to respect and secure compliance with this article [Article 8 of the ECHR] is not one that is enforceable by domestic courts. The relevance of the Convention in the present context is as background to the complaint of irrationality. The fact that a decision-maker failed to take account of Convention obligations when exercising an administrative discretion is not of itself a ground for impugning that exercise of discretion.[94]

The argument based on the 1989 United Nations Convention on the Rights of the Child also failed. Here an additional factor was of some relevance, namely that the United Kingdom had entered the following reservation to the relevant article (Article 3(1)) when ratifying the treaty:

The United Kingdom reserves the right to apply such legislation, insofar as it relates to the entry into, stay in and departure from the United Kingdom of those who do not have the right under the law of the United Kingdom to enter and remain in the United Kingdom, and to the acquisition and possession of citizenship, as it may deem necessary from time to time.

Lord Woolf concluded that the argument advanced on the prerogative:

would mean that the Secretary of State was not required to give direct effect to a Treaty which was not part of this country's domestic law when exercising his statutory powers, but he was required to do so when exercising in relation to the same statutory power an extra-statutory concession. The result would be that the obligations on the Secretary of State would be greater in relation to a residual discretion than they are in relation to the primary discretion. This would be a very strange result.[95]

However, at the same time he accepted that:

[T]he entering into a Treaty by the Secretary of State could give rise to a legitimate expectation on which the public in general are entitled to rely. Subject to any indication to the contrary, it could be a representation that the Secretary of State would act in accordance with any obligations which he accepted under the Treaty. This legitimate expectation could give rise to a right to relief, as well as additional obligations of fairness, if the Secretary of State, without reason, acted inconsistently with the obligations which this country had undertaken.[96]

In this case the Secretary of State had made his approach clear by making and publishing his marriage policy. Provided this policy was one that he could legitimately have, it could not be said that by entering into the treaties he had created a legitimate expectation that conflicted with it.

MICHAEL BYERS

[94] [1996] 1 All ER 257 at 266–7, [1996] 2 WLR 333 at 340, [1996] QB 517 at 558, this *Year Book*, 67 (1996), pp. 552–3, CA.
[95] [1998] INLR 570 at 583.
[96] [1998] INLR 570 at 583.

B. Private International Law*

1 *Injunctions to restrain proceedings before foreign courts: Airbus Industrie GIE* v. *Patel*[1]

The House of Lords reversed the decision of the Court of Appeal,[2] and set aside an injunction to restrain the further prosecution of an action in the courts of Texas which had been brought by the relatives of persons who had been killed in an aviation accident at Bangalore airport. The decision of the Court of Appeal was noted in 1996; and only the bare essentials of the facts need to be repeated here.

The Texas claim[3] was brought by plaintiffs having no connection whatever with the United States, against Airbus Industrie GIE (a French entity), the manufacturer of the aircraft (a French entity), in the courts of Texas, in accordance with local legislation which appeared to place few obstacles in the path of such naked and unashamed forum shopping. The defendant had obtained an anti-suit injunction from the court at Bangalore, but this the plaintiffs felt able to ignore, for though they had invoked and submitted to the jurisdiction of the Bangalore court, such a non-pecuniary order would not be enforceable outside India, and there were apparently no vulnerable assets within India. An application for an anti-suit injunction, made to the English courts and within the jurisdiction of which most of the plaintiffs were resident, was refused by Colman J, but succeeded before the Court of Appeal, which considered that the conduct of the plaintiffs in bringing the claim in Texas in accordance with the law of that State was vexatious or oppressive of Airbus. The court overcame the argument that the granting of such an injunction was none of its business—there was no action pending in England, and none likely to be—on the ground that oppression in the context of forum shopping was not confined to cases where any litigation should properly have been brought in England. The House of Lords considered that the principle for which the decision of the Court of Appeal stood was far too wide and failed to appreciate the proper limits upon the exercise of the court's discretion against a respondent admittedly subject to its personal jurisdiction. It set the order aside.

It had been clear at the time that though the Court of Appeal could be applauded for its robust reaction to oppressive behaviour committed by persons subject to its personal jurisdiction, there was nevertheless an intellectual chasm which separated the existence of jurisdiction from the grant of relief, and that the court had not been particularly specific about how this was to be bridged: the approach was almost one of *ubi forum, ibi remedium*. This could not be correct, though; there has to be some manner of limitation upon the granting of equitable relief. The traditional mechanism of the conflict of laws would have been to pose a question of choice of law, to ascertain that it was appropriate to apply English

[1] [1999] 1 AC 119, HL (Lords Goff of Chieveley, Slynn of Hadley, Steyn, Clyde and Hutton).

[2] [1997] ILPr. 230, [1997] 2 Lloyd's Rep. 8, CA; noted in this *Year Book*, 67 (1996), p. 601, and also at *Lloyd's Maritime and Commercial Law Quarterly*, 1997, p. 90.

[3] There had been prior proceedings brought in Bangalore, against the airline and the airport operator as well as against the manufacturer, Airbus Industrie GIE.

law (or equity) to the identification and vindication of rights claimed by a plaintiff. But the role of choice of law in the context of purely equitable rights has never been all that obvious;[4] and the Lords did not see fit to explore it. Alternatively, a contemporary, and more vital, mechanism might be fashioned by focusing on the naturalness or otherwise of England as the forum for resolution of the substantive dispute (as distinct, it appears, from being the natural forum for the disciplining of a forum shopper); and it was this means of control which Lord Goff of Chieveley, with whom the rest of their Lordships agreed, preferred to adopt. His Lordship explained at length, and with some passion, the many and real virtues of the discretionary approach to jurisdiction and its exercise which is the tradition of the common law, and contrasted this with the intellectual and practical limitations of the rigid scheme of the Brussels and Lugano Conventions. Applying the principles of the common law as he identified them, it was inconsistent with the principles of comity for an English court to interfere in the jurisdictional aspects of a claim before the courts of a foreign country, unless there were a sufficient connection to England to warrant the interference. Leaving temporarily aside those cases where there was a contractual choice of court for England, and those cases in which there appears to be only one court in which the action may be brought (these will be considered below), such a connection would exist if England were the natural forum for the dispute, but would be most unlikely to exist if this were not the case.[5] As the instant case was one in which litigation of issues arising out of the aviation accident had nothing to do with England, it was not for the English courts to interfere.

It is undeniable that the decision imposes limits upon the power of an English court to act, and that in reiterating the central role of the concept of the natural forum, it reasserts the general principles articulated by Lord Goff a decade before.[6] It was not clear that the Court of Appeal had recognized any general limitation upon its power to act; it must be counted as an advance that there is now some definition,[7] even if the price is that inequitable conduct may go unpunished if the court most closely connected to the problem declines or is unable to act. Moreover, the developing jurisprudence of the role of the natural forum, which is running in parallel with a related jurisprudence in Australia[8]

[4] The issue is briefly discussed in *Lloyd's Maritime and Commercial Law Quarterly*, 1997, p. 90.

[5] In particular, it was insufficient that the Texas court would, for its part, pay no, or no sufficient, attention to the demands of comity: at p. 700E: the judgment of Hobhouse LJ below was specifically disapproved on this point. It follows that this aspect of the analysis of Sopinka J in *Amchem Products Inc.* v. *Workers' Compensation Board*, [1993] 1 SCR 897, was also not approved.

[6] *Société Nationale Industrielle Aérospatiale* v. *Lee Kui Jak*, [1987] AC 871, PC.

[7] To contrary effect it might be contended that in the granting of provisional or protective relief, for example a *Mareva* injunction, the court simply acts when personal jurisdiction exists, and imposes no specific limitation upon the general discretion to act which it possesses. But the protective *Mareva* injunction is a very different animal from the anti-suit injunction, whether this is final or interlocutory.

[8] See in particular the High Court of Australia in *CSR Ltd.* v. *Cigna Insurance Australia Ltd.*, (1997) 189 CLR 345 (noted at *Law Quarterly Review*, 114 (1998), p. 27).

and Canada,[9] represents a firm basis upon which to ground the principles of limitation. But after the general applause for the decision, four points should perhaps be accorded closer attention.

First, Lord Goff identified comity as the reason why some restriction should be placed upon the right of the English court to act. It is not altogether clear that comity is sufficiently hard-edged to be useful, but as the principle of sufficient connection was developed, leaving comity as the motivation but not the mechanism, this is not a substantial criticism. It is perfectly understandable that his Lordship should consider that comity required to be recognized in relation to the courts of Texas, especially in light of the ill-tempered recent history of a case in which it was alleged that comity had been flouted.[10] But there were two foreign courts in *Airbus*: Texas, to be sure, but also that in Bangalore, undoubtedly the natural forum for the litigation which had in any event been commenced there, and which had made orders to restrain the plaintiffs from the proceedings they had felt advised to commence in Texas. Though a quirk of the common law rules on the enforcement of judgments led to the plain conclusion that the Indian injunctions could not be enforced in England,[11] one may wonder whether comity might not have lent a hand in helping the English court to act in general support of the Indian court. But this does not appear to have been pressed. It may be that any accepting of this argument would make the result depend upon the 'accident' of there being an Indian order obtained before the English application was made. But this may not be such an accident. Airbus had done what any reasonable defendant might have done, and what any English judge would have expected it to do: it applied to the court in which the plaintiffs had first commenced proceedings against it and sought relief there; this appears to have counted for nothing in reaching the conclusion that the assessment of comity lay only as between England and Texas. It is respectfully suggested that this particular aspect of the decision may be due for reconsideration.

Secondly, Lord Goff drew a weak distinction between cases in which the plaintiff was in a position to choose between courts (an 'alternative forum' case), and those in which the plaintiff could proceed only in one court (a 'single forum' case). The distinction is fairly characterized as weak, in that although Lord Goff saw the two sets of case as being intellectually distinct, he sought to formulate a principle which could accommodate both species of case, while recognizing their differences. In a single forum case, he said, sufficiency of connection might exist in a case in which the facts giving rise to the claim were much more closely connected to England than elsewhere; but the rightness of the granting of an

[9] See the decision of the Supreme Court of Canada in *Amchem Products Inc.* v. *Workers' Compensation Board*, [1993] 1 SCR 897. It is worth observing that this decision, and the earlier decision of the same court in *Morguard Investments Ltd.* v. *De Savoye*, [1990] SCR 1077, in the context of the recognition of foreign judgments, may suggest that a broad principle of naturalness of forum may be fashioned to link together the exercise of jurisdiction, the ordering of injunctions to restrain proceedings, and the recognition of foreign judgments. Clearly much work remains to be done, but the proposition is plainly an interesting one.

[10] In the general litigational battles in *British Airways Board* v. *Laker Airways Ltd.*, [1985] AC 58, HL; *Laker Airways Ltd.* v. *Sabena, Belgian World Airlines*, (1984) 731 F 2d 909.

[11] Only final and fixed money judgments can be enforced at common law. Matters stand differently, of course, when the judgment is given by the courts of a contracting State to the Brussels or Lugano Conventions.

injunction in *Midland Bank plc* v. *Laker Airways Ltd.*[12] was expressly left undecided.[13] With the concept of sufficiency of connection it is hard to take issue; but it remains very difficult indeed to accept that there is a distinction of any utility or principle between cases of so-called single or alternative forum. In truth, there is never[14] a single forum. It may be that a cause of action is available under the law applicable in one forum, which would be unavailable to the plaintiff as a result of the choice of law principles applied in the second: but this does not, cannot, mean that the plaintiff has only one forum in which to sue, as distinct from meaning that there is only one forum in which he may consider himself to have a realistic chance of success. Why is there such a concern with whether the plaintiff may win? There are two sides to any dispute; the fact that the defendant would be found to be free of liability if sued in a particular court does not suggest that the case is a single forum one, nor yet that the case is one which calls for treatment different in principle from that which applies when there are two places in which the plaintiff may believe that he has a chance of success. It is most regrettable that this spurious distinction has been allowed to complicate the picture. Surely the correct analysis of *Midland Bank* v. *Laker* should be that the natural forum for any claim against the Bank, which had done all and everything it did in and from England, and which had done nothing material in the United States, was England; the natural forum for any complaint which the liquidator of Laker Airways might have wished to raise was England, and it is nothing to the point that, as a matter of English law, he might have struggled to sustain a cause of action. One can only hope that this line of unreasoning will not be allowed to have an impact upon the decision required to be taken in an actual case.

Thirdly, Lord Goff went out of his way to say nothing about a case in which a choice of forum (or, one may suppose, arbitrators) had been contractually made by the parties.[15] If the parties have chosen English adjudication, it seems to follow that there will almost inevitably be a sufficient English interest to warrant an English court's enforcing the agreement, by injunction if necessary. If the parties have chosen the courts of a third country, it is much less clear that there is any justification for the intervention of the English courts: if inequitable misconduct does not by itself suffice to allow the court to exercise its discretion over a respondent who is subject to its personal jurisdiction, unlawful conduct which is, from the perspective of the English judge, similarly *res inter alios acta* ought not to justify the intervention of the court. But it is not certain that this, which would involve no more than an automatic application of the principles in

[12] [1986] QB 689, CA.

[13] At p. 698.

[14] The possibilities appear to be these. If there is a bar to justiciability of any and every claim against a defendant, or if the defendant enjoys personal immunity from the jurisdiction of the courts, this would be so. But the instances of non-justiciability, as opposed to a defeat inflicted by choice of law rules, are very rare. It may also be argued that in a case in which the foreign forum is barred to the plaintiff for exceptional reasons of the sort encountered in *Mohammed* v. *Bank of Kuwait and the Middle East KSC*, [1996] 1 WLR 1483, CA (and cf. the Note on *Lubbe* v. *Cape plc*, below), the case might be regarded as a single forum one. But these are all cases of genuine inability to commence proceedings in respect of any sort of claim, even under the domestic law of the foreign court. Cases where the courts are open to the plaintiff but he sees no point in suing there are different in kind, and are, it is submitted, undeserving of special treatment.

[15] At p. 138F.

Airbus, was what Lord Goff had in mind when he limited his statement of principle as operating without prejudice to that case.

Finally, it should be recorded that nothing was said by Lord Goff about any particular impact which might be felt in a case in which the other forum was that of another contracting State to the Brussels or Lugano Conventions. But the tenor of his Lordship's speech recognizes that the Conventions provide a different set of rules to govern a different world.[16] There is nothing in the speech to support the view that an anti-suit injunction may ever be granted to affect proceedings before the courts of another contracting State, and at least by implication, ground for thinking that this essential and tremendously valuable piece of common law finds no place within the intellectually stunted framework of the Conventions.

2 *The availability of the natural forum for the purposes of a stay of proceedings: Lubbe* v. *Cape plc*[17]

Five South African plaintiffs, alleged victims[18] of industrial injury caused by working in the defendant's asbestos mines and mills, brought proceedings against the English company. The mines and mills were located in South Africa; the defendant company had ceased to have any interest in them many years ago. Though sued in the courts for the place of its domicile, the defendant preferred to defend itself in South Africa rather than England, and sought a stay of proceedings upon the basis of the principle in *Spiliada Maritime Corporation* v. *Cansulex Ltd*.[19] A stay was ordered at first instance, it being concluded that the defendant had satisfied the *Spiliada* criteria; but the Court of Appeal reversed the judge and set the order aside. Though the Court noted that on the first limb of the test the defendant was required to show that South Africa was clearly and distinctly the more appropriate forum, two particular grounds motivated the decision that the defendant failed. First, South Africa was not, in the relevant sense, an available forum for the trial of the action, and secondly, the core of the defendant's alleged wrongdoing was its managerial misconduct in England, and not its implementation of those decisions at the mines in South Africa. The relationship between these factors is not clear, but their combination, at any rate, sufficed to refuse a stay. Whether either, and especially the first, would have justified that result by itself, is uncertain. But both points call for some comment.

It is well established that the first limb of *Spiliada* requires the defendant to show, clearly and distinctly, that there is another forum which is more appropriate than England for the trial of the action. It has latterly been explained that this condition cannot be satisfied unless the preferred forum is in some sense 'available' to the plaintiff.[20] A proposed forum is not rendered

[16] Esp. at pp. 692–4.

[17] [1999] ILPr. 113, CA (Evans, Millett, Auld LJJ).

[18] Four as workers, one as representative of a deceased worker.

[19] [1987] AC 460, HL.

[20] Although the requirement was mentioned without emphasis in the cases leading up to *Spiliada*, it emerged as a specific and discrete element of the first limb in *Mohammed* v. *Bank of Kuwait and the Middle East KSC*, [1996] 1 WLR 1483, CA (noted in this *Year Book*, 67 (1996), p. 587).

unavailable just because it would be financially impossible for the plaintiff to sue in it,[21] but it may[22] be contended that if he is prevented on political, or immigration, or similar grounds, from entering into the country, the court may be found to be unavailable, with the result that the defendant fails. In the present case there was no apparent difficulty, for the plaintiffs were South African, and the defendant had undertaken[23] to the court to submit to the jurisdiction of the South African courts. Yet the Court of Appeal accepted a submission that South Africa was not an available forum if all that could be said was that it was open to the plaintiff to sue there only by reason of the undertaking given by the defendant to the English court in the course of the proceedings for a stay. As a matter of South African law on civil procedure, the plaintiff had no right to invoke the jurisdiction of the South African courts over the defendant; that being so, South Africa was not an available forum in the relevant sense.

This was, perhaps, an unexpected conclusion. As the court recognized, it entails drawing a distinction between cases in which the jurisdiction of the proposed court exists independently of the volition of the defendant, and those where it exists by reason of the submission or concession of the defendant, and it is hard to see why this is right. Consider three cases: in the first, a writ may be served on the defendant, out of the jurisdiction if need be, as of right, with the defendant having a right to apply for the service to be set aside on discretionary grounds; in the second, the writ may be served only with the prior leave of the court; in the third, the defendant may be notified of a claim and invited to submit to the jurisdiction. In the first case, the court would appear to be available, for the right to sue does not depend upon the consent of the defendant, even though he may move to have service set aside and jurisdiction rescinded. In the second, jurisdiction no more depends upon the volition of the defendant, but is not available to the plaintiff as of right. In the third, it is not available, for it depends upon the volition of the defendant. In all cases the defendant may intervene in the jurisdictional phase with critical effect; in none does the plaintiff have an unassailable right to the jurisdiction of the court; but in two, but not three, the jurisdiction of the court is said to be available. It is very difficult to see why, for the purposes of the *Spiliada* test, there should be a fundamental difference grounded on this elusive and unpredictable point of foreign civil procedure. But it appears that there is. The alternative would have been to hold that if, at the date of the hearing, the defendant was subject to the jurisdiction of the foreign court, or would bind himself to accept its jurisdiction, the foreign forum was available for the purposes of the *Spiliada* test. The court appeared to be resistant to this interpretation, on the curious ground that it would appear to allow the *defendant* to forum shop by agreeing to submit to a foreign court, and laying the ground for a stay application as he went. With respect to those who think differently, this is banal. Given that a stay will not be ordered unless that foreign court is clearly more appropriate for the trial than is England, it is seriously misleading to suggest that the defendant would be able to obtain a stay by a strategic undertaking to submit. It does not follow at all; and in any case in

[21] *Connelly* v. *RTZ Corp. plc*, [1998] AC 834, HL (noted in this *Year Book*, 68 (1997), p. 357.

[22] If the decision in *Mohammed* is still good law outside the point determined in *Connelly*.

[23] It appears that it did so after the issue of the summons for a stay of proceedings.

which the undertaking does lead directly to a stay, this will only be because the court to whose jurisdiction the defendant has agreed to submit was the natural forum even before the submission. At the level of prejudice, it was, perhaps, a matter of comfort that the Court of Appeal was astute to protect the plaintiffs from the slippery manoeuvrability of the wealthy corporate defendant.[24] But it could have done so without accepting that the South African court, to which the defendant was willing to submit, was not an available, let alone the natural, forum.

One may wonder whether a jurisprudence of 'availability' is in any event a benefit to the law, or is even open for adoption by the court in any event. It made its debut in *Mohammed* v. *Bank of Kuwait and the Middle East KSC*,[25] and was not obviously accepted by the House of Lords when, in *Connelly* v. *RTZ Corp plc*,[26] they agreed that the first limb of *Spiliada* was satisfied even in a case in which suing in that court was, for the plaintiff, wholly impossible. It might have been supposed that this would have marked the departure from the legal stage of this requirement. It seems that this was too optimistic a prediction. Much more disconcertingly, it may yet come to be be argued that a case in which the plaintiff may seise a foreign court, but not with the cause of action of his preference, is one in which the foreign court is not available.[27] It is, after all, unclear that there is much difference between a 'single forum case' and one in which the foreign forum is 'not available'; but once issues such as this are noticed, the law will be off down a slippery slope: the even-handedness as between the parties and their prospects of success, which was the benchmark of *Spiliada* and the badge of principle, will be in danger of being lost for good. All this furnishes support for the view that the concept of a case being a 'single forum' one, or of the foreign forum being 'unavailable', is extremely dangerous to the rational development of the law. Moreover, Evans LJ accepted that the South African court would have been available if the defendant had written a letter, or made some other representation, agreeing to submit to its jurisdiction before the institution of proceedings by the plaintiff. At this point the supposed principle loses all rational content, for jurisdiction will still depend upon, and is still predicated upon, the consent of the defendant to being sued in the particular foreign court. Why anything should depend upon whether the agreement is embodied in a letter before proceedings, or in an undertaking to the court, is a mystery. The common law is not usually considered to be as mesmerized by the date of proceedings as is the jurisdictional scheme of the Brussels and Lugano Conventions. The Court of Appeal makes far too much turn upon the date upon which a defendant, whom we may presume always to have been willing, and always to have wanted, to be sued in the natural forum, makes plain his view and says so. It appears that defendants would do well to publish a virtual notice on their website to the effect that they are willing to be sued in, and to submit to, the named courts of their choice. It is absurd that the law should have come to this.

The court was concerned by the fact that, when they issued proceedings, the

[24] There are echoes in this of the sentiment of the majority of the House of Lords in *Connelly* v. *RTZ* (above, n. 21).

[25] [1996] 1 WLR 1483, CA.

[26] Loc. cit. above (n. 21).

[27] Cf. the previous note.

plaintiffs might not have been entitled to sue in South Africa and to issue and serve proceedings out of that court; and that if a manoeuvre by the defendants could have been used to penalize the plaintiffs for not doing something which the plaintiffs could never have done, this would be unsatisfactory. If this is the argument, it looks respectable enough. But the response to it may be to say that if a plaintiff has done nothing wrong, the defendant should pay the costs if the stay application is made and succeeds, so that the blameless plaintiff is not left out of pocket.[28] Such a disposition would not be impossible to countenance. As against that, if South Africa were the natural forum, and if the plaintiffs elected not to discover whether the defendant would submit and furnish a jurisdictional basis for the claim, one may wonder whether they (or their legal advisers) were as innocent of guile as all this might suggest. In summary, if there is a public interest in having cases heard and determined in their natural forum, the law should not create artificial obstacles to the furtherance of that aim, and should use its discretion as to costs to measure the conduct of a plaintiff who starts in England and then loses a stay application. It is suggested that this aspect of the decision in *Lubbe* should not be followed.

The court was on stronger ground in its conclusion that the natural forum for the dispute was not South Africa. Though the plaintiffs had sustained their injuries in South Africa, it did not follow from this that the place of the damage was the place of commission of the tort.[29] If, as the court accepted, the operational direction of the company was settled in London, and merely implemented in the various mines and mills, there was a good argument that London was an equally good, and possibly a better, place for the investigation whether these decisions had been careless of the plaintiffs and their welfare as employees. The proposition that the place of the tort may well be the natural forum for the litigation, previously proposed by the Court of Appeal, may be generally correct, but the subtlety required to locate the place where the tort was committed may make it a less reliable guide than may once have been supposed. If the allegation is that careless decision-taking and wrongful actions were conceived in London, there is a reasonable argument that England is where in substance the cause of action arose, and that England is therefore the natural forum for the litigation of it; the argument which the defendant would have had to advance, that South Africa was clearly the natural forum, was then impossible.

In the light of its conclusion that the stay of proceedings would be set aside, the court had no need to consider whether such an order would have been consistent with Article 2 of the Brussels Convention, which provides in effect that an English corporation shall be sued in England, and which is widely considered to allow for no common law discretion in determining whether to exercise a jurisdiction authorized and conferred by the legislative text. So the correctness of the decision in *Re Harrods (Buenos Aires) Ltd.*[30] remains in a state of uncertainty. Commentators have been making this observation for some years

[28] See, for an argument by analogy, Case C–275/94 *Van der Linden*, [1996] ECR I–1393, ECJ (noted at *Yearbook of European Law*, 16 (1996), p. 601).

[29] Though the test in *Metall & Rohstoff AG* v. *Donaldson Lufkin & Jenrette Inc.*, [1990] 1 QB 391, CA, locating the place of the tort is no longer part of the choice of law regime for tort claims. But it still has a persuasive role in the identification of the natural forum for a tort claim.

[30] [1992] Ch. 72, CA.

now; it cannot be much longer, surely, before the Court of Justice of the European Communities is asked to settle the doubt.

3 *Stays of proceedings and the injustice of having to proceed under the other forum's law: The Herceg Novi and the Ming Galaxy*[31]

The next decision can be noted briefly, but should not be overlooked, as it re-establishes an important point of principle in a context where it was in danger of being overlooked. The *Herceg Novi* and the *Ming Galaxy* collided in Singaporean waters; each side blamed the other for the accident (and the criminal courts in Singapore blamed and fined the masters of both vessels). The owners of the *Ming Galaxy* commenced an admiralty action *in rem* against the *Herceg Novi* and its owners, and related actions *in personam*, in Singapore; and a week later the owners of the *Herceg Novi* commenced an admiralty action *in rem* against the *Ming Galaxy* and its owners, in England. The owners of the *Ming Galaxy* sought a stay of proceedings, but though granting a partial stay, Clarke J refused to stay the English action as a whole. The result of this was that if the owners of the *Ming Galaxy* sought to limit their liability in the English action, this would have to be done under English law and the pecuniary limits fixed by the 1976 Convention.[32] These were significantly higher, and therefore much less attractive to the owners of the *Ming Galaxy*, than the corresponding provisions of the law of Singapore, under which the 1957 Convention[33] would be applied. The owners of the *Herceg Novi* contended that even if Singapore were the natural forum for the claim—which it plainly was—it was unjust to send them to a forum in which the level of limitation available to the owners of the *Ming Galaxy* would render the claim much less valuable. They supported this submission by the argument that the levels of limitation fixed by the 1976 Convention represented a form of international consensus which the English courts should regard as in some sense overriding the presumption in favour of a stay. The Court of Appeal was wholly unpersuaded by the argument and, reversing the Admiralty judge on this point, stayed the English action unconditionally. As well it might.

It is trite law that a stay under the *Spiliada* principles may be refused if it would be unjust to the plaintiff to impose it; it is also trite law that the courts do not favour submissions which contend—however much whitewash and flannel is applied—that the quality of justice available from the foreign court is inferior to the English equivalent; and Lord Goff in *Spiliada* made it plain that the prospect of higher damages from an English court was no indication that there was any injustice in consigning the plaintiff to the natural forum and its different, lower, quantification. So a submission that English law is in some sense internationally right in its approach to limitation and the recovery of damages, whereas the law in Singapore comes straight out of the dark ages,

[31] [1998] 2 Lloyd's Rep. 454, CA (Stuart-Smith, Brooke LJJ; Sir Christopher Staughton).

[32] Convention on Limitation for Maritime Claims 1976, set out in Merchant Shipping Act 1995, Sch. 7, Part 1.

[33] Convention relating to the Limitation of the Liability of Owners of Seagoing Ships 1957.

should never have found acceptance. Moreover, as there is no clear international agreement upon which limitation regime, if any at all, is to be preferred, the groundwork did not exist for a submission that the English approach represents an international standard; and the fact that the 1976 Convention enjoyed the support of the International Maritime Organization was nothing to the point: an interest group is not a sovereign State, and legal policy plainly varies from State to State. It was plainly impossible to say that the law of Singapore was such that substantial justice would be denied to the plaintiffs if required to make their claim there, and the prima facie case for a stay was not contradicted.

The surprise was that there had been other decisions which had taken the opposite view and which had accepted, in effect, that English law on damages and limitation was so superior that it should simply prevail, or that it had been elevated to the status of a rule of English public policy. Stays had been refused on this ground in *The Vishva Abha*,[34] *Caltex Singapore Pte. Ltd.* v. *BP Shipping Ltd.*,[35] *Caspian Basin Specialised Emergency Salvage Administration* v. *Bouygues Offshore SA*,[36] and *Bouygues Offshore SA* v. *Caspian Shipping Co.*[37] The only dissenting voice had been that of Waung J in the High Court of Hong Kong in *The Kapitan Shvetsov*.[38] But the Court of Appeal approved of Waung J's approach, and in effect overruled the earlier English decisions at first instance. It was, it is submitted, wholly right to do so, for the decision to stay proceedings in favour of the natural forum will get very quickly mired if the courts allow any real opportunity for an attack on the law which will be applied by the foreign court, or for the prospect of higher English damages to be taken to indicate injustice in the foreign court. In this respect, the decision of the Court of Appeal in *Baghlaf al Safer Factory Co. BR for Industry Ltd.* v. *Pakistan National Shipping Co.*,[39] which approved the bringing of an action in England when time-barred in the contractually agreed forum (Pakistan) and the Pakistani courts would have applied the limitation limits of the Hague Rules and not the Hague-Visby Rules (which case was not referred to in *The Herceg Novi* and which was presumably not cited to the court), seems almost completely inconsistent, and completely indefensible. It may well also be that the occasional temptation to justify disregarding limitation periods imposed under foreign laws should be similarly reconsidered. The Court of Appeal has issued a timely reminder that English judges should not allow themselves to be beguiled into believing that the way issues are dealt with in England is intrinsically superior to the different way they are dealt with in other courts, and making orders accordingly. From time to time it is no doubt necessary to remind judges of this fact, and to uproot the weeds which are beginning to take root in the flower beds. The clear, principled and intellectually honest judgment in *The Herceg Novi* does just that.

[34] [1990] 2 Lloyd's Rep. 312.

[35] [1996] 1 Lloyd's Rep. 286.

[36] [1997] 2 Lloyd's Rep. 507, though the point did not in fact arise for actual decision.

[37] [1997] 2 Lloyd's Rep. 533.

[38] [1998] 1 Lloyd's Rep. 199; decision reversed by a majority of the Court of Appeal of Hong Kong.

[39] [1998] CLC 716 (mentioned in this *Year Book*, 68 (1997), p. 359 n. 127).

4 *The limits upon the enforceability of jurisdiction agreements: Bouygues Offshore SA* v. *Caspian Shipping Co*;[40] *Hough* v. *P & O Containers (Bloem+Voss Holding AG, third parties)*[41]

A barge, owned by Bouygues Offshore SA, a French company, was being towed by a tug owned by Caspian, an Azerbaijani company, when the towline parted and the barge was driven onto rocks near to Cape Town. It was a total loss. The tug had been chartered to Ultisol Ltd., and was managed by a Dutch company. Bouygues claimed damages from Ultisol, with whom the towage contract had been made; from Caspian, on the ground that it was vicariously liable for the negligence of the tug's crew, and also on the basis of misrepresentation as to the capacity of the tug; and from the Cape Town harbour authority, Portnet. A claim for rescission of the towage contract was also made; issues of limitation of liability also arose. Proceedings were also instituted in South Africa; and anti-suit injunctions, and applications to join third parties, made the confusion greater. Evans LJ described the procedural history as 'complicated' which, to the average reader, will seem to be a piece of masterly understatement. On four occasions the interlocutory procedural battles in England had made their way into the law reports;[42] this appeal was, as far as one can tell, the culmination of all of them.

The point of interest for the conflict of laws is that the towage contract contained an exclusive jurisdiction agreement for the English courts, and Ultisol wished to hold Bouygues to it. This it had done by obtaining an anti-suit injunction to restrain Bouygues from claiming against it in the proceedings which Bouygues had brought in South Africa (where it had arrested the tug). It appeared that the South African courts would have had jurisdiction over all claims, but that the choice of court agreement in the towage contract, and the injunction obtained by Ultisol, stood in the way of this neat procedural result. As the history of the proceedings demonstrated the ample possibility of conflict and irreconcilability if the litigation were to be broken into pieces and determined in different countries, the question for the Court of Appeal was whether fidelity to the jurisdiction clause in the contract between Bouygues and Ultisol outweighed the case for getting all the litigation into one court. It was held, probably rightly, that it did not; the anti-suit injunction protecting the jurisdiction clause was lifted, permitting it, so far as the Court of Appeal was concerned, to be broken, and allowing the dispute to proceed to resolution in South Africa.

There may be an initial view that it was no business of the courts to re-write the terms of the towage contract, and that this is what was involved in lifting the injunction precisely in order to allow the agreement on choice of court to be

[40] [1998] 2 Lloyd's Rep. 463, CA (Evans, Mummery LJJ; Sir John Knox).

[41] [1998] 2 All E R 978, Rix J.

[42] [1996] 2 Lloyd's Rep. 140 (Clarke J); [1997] 2 Lloyd's Rep. 485 (Morison J); [1997] 2 Lloyd's Rep. 493 (Colman J); [1997] 2 Lloyd's Rep. 533 (Timothy Walker J). This was also an appeal against the decision of Rix J in a limitation action: [1997] 2 Lloyd's Rep. 507, in which he decided that the shipowner had a right to bring limitation proceedings where he himself chose, and could not be deprived of that right by an action brought by another interested party for a declaration that the shipowner was not entitled to limit his liability. Rix J was held to be correct in this analysis; it is not further examined here.

broken by Bouygues It may also be thought that were the enforcing of the agreement to present Bouygues with a rather unattractive lack of option, it should not have subscribed to a choice of court agreement in these terms: if it wished to have the right to sue outside England in a case such as this, it should have stipulated for it. Indeed, this uncompromising view would have been reached had the case arisen within the context of the Brussels or Lugano Conventions,[43] and it sets the highest premium on holding parties to the agreements they have made, without regard to the consequences. On the other hand, neither the English court nor Portnet nor Caspian was party to the choice of court agreement, and it is in keeping with a sense of privity that such an agreement should not bind those to whom it was *res inter alios acta*. As the court has a public responsibility to supervise the general administration of justice, and in particular the need to ensure consistency in judicial verdicts involving more than the parties to the agreement, the existence and exercise of a power to withhold specific[44] enforcement of the agreement must be right in principle. In this case, it would have been absolutely chaotic if the issues arising out of a single accident at sea were litigated in separate pieces. Whether it follows that a choice of court agreement should be seen as something less than a contractual term, but (for example) as a joint request to a court, is not certain. But if it is right that it be liable to be overridden, by what Sir John Knox called a 'special countervailing factor', this may actually be the right way to look at it.

The court did not furnish a verbal test by which to decide (or to predict the decision) whether a choice of court agreement should be overridden. But it made it clear that the impact on third parties of its enforcement was a legitimate part of the enquiry, and this is now to be regarded as settled. Presumably the same is true when the principles are those in *Spiliada* and the case does not concern a choice of court agreement: if third party concerns can override a contractual agreement on jurisdiction, they will certainly do so when there is no contract to take into account. It was less satisfactory for Evans LJ to observe that as Bouygues had commenced proceedings in South Africa by the 'proper' means of an arrest, the enforcing of the jurisdiction clause would have entailed the loss of the 'right' to sue where the arrest had taken place. This is, it is thought, a weak point: whenever a choice of court clause is enforced, the plaintiff loses the right, which he had thought to have, to sue somewhere else in accordance with the law of that court. As an observation which may tend to water down the strength of a choice of court agreement, it is not particularly helpful. Even so, this case settles, probably finally, that as a matter of common law, a choice of court agreement does not bind the court to act in its support, and where overall considerations of case management are put in issue, its significance will loom rather less large.

The decision contrasts oddly sharply with the interpretation of Article 17 of the Brussels Convention adopted by Rix J in *Hough* v. *P & O*, and raises the question whether it is desirable (and if it is not, whether it is avoidable) that the

[43] See the analysis of *Hough* v. *P & O Containers*, below.

[44] It has never been decisively stated whether a party in the position of Ultisol, whose jurisdiction agreement was to be broken, would have a claim for damages upon proof of loss. It is difficult to see why not, for if Bouygues proceeded against them in South Africa, this would be a breach of contract: the decision to lift the injunction did not mean that there was no breach, but just that the breach was not to be specifically restrained in equity.

common law and the Convention should be at odds on this point. In *Hough*, the plaintiff electrician, a New Zealander, sued the English defendant in respect of an industrial injury sustained while working on the defendant's ship then undergoing repair in dry dock in a German shipyard. Though the contract of repair provided that the courts of Hamburg should have exclusive jurisdiction, the defendant issued and served a third party notice on the yard, contending that Article 6.2 of the Convention allowed a third party claim to be brought where the main claim was pending. The yard argued that though Article 6.2 did just that, Article 17 gave it the right to defend itself in any claim brought by the defendant in Hamburg, displacing the application of Article 6.2. Rix J agreed. The result was that the defendant's liability to the plaintiff will be determined in England, and any claim for contribution or indemnity will have to be brought in Germany, and in proceedings in which the prior English judgment may not be taken as conclusive, as against the yard, of the defendant's liability to the plaintiff. Though the decision pays heed to the operation of the choice of court agreement and its vitality under Article 17 of the Convention, the decision does nothing for the coordination of the judicial effort to settle disputes. Rix J plainly regretted the conclusion he was compelled to reach,[45] but given the text of the Convention it was almost inescapable. The private policy of upholding agreements on jurisdiction overcame any countervailing public policy of not fragmenting legal proceedings.

In the hierarchy of rules under the Brussels Convention, an agreement on choice of court clearly outranks the special jurisdiction over third parties who are domiciled in another contracting State. Special jurisdiction is no more than an alternative to the general jurisdictional rule which requires a defendant to be sued where domiciled, and neither will arise if one of the superior rules of jurisdiction in Title II falls to be applied. Whether the judge was on firm ground when he sought to support this conclusion with the observation that Article 17 was worded as if mandatory ('shall have exclusive jurisdiction'), whereas Article 6.2 is not ('may also be sued') is open to question: Article 2 is, on this analysis, mandatory ('shall be sued'), yet it would be impossible to argue that Article 17 did not prevail over it. Moreover, such an approach to the interpretation of a text drafted in about a dozen languages of equal authenticity is not, whatever else it may be, teleological. His citation and agreement with Dicey and Morris,[46] and other textbooks, was more convincing. But the resultant fracturing of the litigational picture was plainly unattractive. It proceeds either from the uncritical respect accorded to Article 17, or from the fact that there is no provision in the Convention which allows jurisdiction to be taken when and because a claim is inseparably linked to one over which the court does have jurisdiction (the most recent attempt to discover whether the Court of Justice would accept this, on reference from the French Cour de Cassation, showed that the Court of Justice was having none of it[47]). And if ever a case cried out for sensible judicial

[45] At p. 988b. But for another decision which interpreted the Convention in a way almost guaranteed to generate irreconcilable judgments, see the case noted below, *Baltic Insurance Group* v. *Jordan Grand Prix Ltd.*, [1999] 1 All ER 289, HL.

[46] *The Conflict of Laws* (12th edn., 1993), Fourth Cumulative Supplement, p. 51; cited by the judge at p. 986.

[47] See Case C–51/97 *Réunion Européenne SA* v. *Spliethoff's Bevrachtingskantoor BV* (27 October 1998), where the referring court described the various claims as 'indivisible'.

discretion, of the sort which evidently causes apoplexy in many civilian jurisdictions, this was it. But in the context of the Conventions, that argument is apparently not winnable.

The result in *Hough* would have been substantially ameliorated if in any subsequent proceedings brought by the defendant for contribution or an indemnity, the German court would be obliged to accept as conclusive as against the third party any finding by the English court against the defendant. But it is unlikely that this would be the case. As a matter of common law, the decision in a claim between A and B is not binding if B sues C unless there was privity of interest between B and C, such that C is bound by the finding in A's favour; if the judgment is to be accorded in the State addressed the effect it has in the State of origin,[48] it will have no effect on a third party in Germany as it has none in England.

On the footing that Rix J was correct, the result is that the Convention appears, in this respect at least, to take jurisdiction agreements more seriously than does the common law, a conclusion which will come as a most unexpected surprise to common lawyers accustomed to believe that the civilians are pretty unsound on commercial agreements to sue in a particular place.

5 *Jurisdiction over counterclaims by insurers under the Brussels Convention: Baltic Insurance Group* v. *Jordan Grand Prix Ltd. and Quay Financial Software Ltd.*[49]

Another decision of the English courts propounded the view that fragmentation of legal proceedings was required by the provisions of the Brussels Convention, this time in the specialist context of claims in matters relating to insurance. Two sets of contractual relationships were involved. First, Jordan Grand Prix Ltd., a participant in the alleged sport of Formula 1 motor racing, had bound itself to make bonus payments to its employees in the event of the team faring well in the 1994 competition. As things turned out, these payments fell due, and Jordan, claiming that it had insured this contingent liability with Baltic Insurance Group, a Lithuanian company, sought to recover the sums due on its insurance. Baltic refused to pay, alleging fraud, conspiracy and concealment; and Jordan sued it in England. Second, Quay Financial Software Ltd., an Irish company, claimed that it had undertaken a conditional sponsorship of Jordan, that the money was now due and owing, that it too had insured this contingent liability with Baltic, and was now entitled to collect. Again, Baltic refused to pay, on the same grounds as before; but Quay did not institute proceedings against it. Indeed, when sued by Jordan, Baltic defended, and counterclaimed for the losses the alleged conspiracy had caused it. But it went on the offensive and advanced this counterclaim, not only against Jordan, but also against Quay and two of its directors, who were also domiciled in Ireland. Quay

[48] Cf. Case 145/86 *Hoffmann* v. *Krieg*, [1988] ECR 645.

[49] [1999] 1 All ER 289, HL (Lords Slynn of Hadley, Lloyd of Berwick, Steyn, Hoffmann and Millett).

and the directors (who are here referred to together as Quay) objected to being made to answer the allegations in England, relying on the rules of the Brussels Convention, and contended that if Baltic was to obtain a judgment against them, it would have to do so in Ireland. The House of Lords agreed; Lord Steyn gave the only speech.

Baltic contended that it was entitled to bring in Quay on two textual grounds. Both failed. Article 11, in dealing with actions brought by an insurer, provides that ' . . . an insurer may bring proceedings only in the courts of the contracting State in which the defendant is domiciled . . . '. But it goes on to state, in a second paragraph, that 'The provisions of this Section[50] shall not affect the right to bring a counterclaim in the court in which, in accordance with this Section, the original claim is pending'. It is important to notice that Article 11 is drafted in a distinctly unhelpful manner. Its first paragraph deals with the important jurisdictional rule which confines the insurer to suing where the defendant is domiciled; it is in this respect the counterpart of Articles 8 and 9, which define the jurisdictional privileges of the insured in suing the insurer. But its second paragraph contains a general rule, claiming to modify all the jurisdictional rules in Section 3, and allowing for counterclaims in the court seised of the original claim. It was for this reason that Article 11, ostensibly dealing with claims by an insurer, was relied on by the insurer to support its right to bring a counterclaim against Quay.

Baltic first sought to escape from the limitations of the first paragraph of Article 11 altogether, so that it did not require the claim against Quay to be advanced in Ireland, by contending that the insurer referred to was an insurer domiciled in a contracting State, and that as its domicile was Lithuanian, it was not limited to claiming against Quay where Quay was domiciled. This was quite hopeless, and leaves one wondering why leave to appeal on the point was granted in the first place. Within the context of Section 3 of Title II, Article 11's use of the word 'only'—a linguistic formulation found or echoed in all other language versions—explicitly limited the claim against Quay to the Irish courts. So how could Baltic reckon to escape from the shackles of the first paragraph of Article 11? Not, one might have thought, by contending that it was entitled to rely on other Sections of Title II, for this was inconsistent with the proposition that the courts of Quay's domicile *only* were competent to entertain a claim by an insurer. So instead it was argued that where the plaintiff insurer was not domiciled in a contracting State, a contracting State defendant insured should lose the protection of the Section 3 regime, and be left exposed to the rules of general and special jurisdiction in Sections 2 and 3 of Title II. Such desperation is beyond the help of rational supporting explanation. Why on earth an EU insured defendant should be jurisdictionally protected against an EU domiciled insurer, but left jurisdictionally unprotected against a non-EU insurer, is quite inexplicable; and Lord Steyn had no more difficulty than had the courts below in disposing of the submission with a notable economy of words. There was no

[50] Section 3 of Title II of the Convention, dealing with jurisdiction in cases of insurance.

conceivable justification for it, and there is nothing which can be said in its favour.

Whether Baltic was right on this point, however, was not critical to its submission. For the second paragraph of Article 11, as also Article 6.3, permitted the court hearing a claim to take jurisdiction over a counterclaim. Baltic contended that its claim against Quay, made by it as defendant and counterclaimant in the claim against it by Jordan, was therefore within the competence of the English courts.[51] On this point as well it lost, it being held that for the purposes of Article 11 at least, and almost certainly for the broader purposes of Article 6.3, a claim made by a defendant against new parties was not to be seen as a counterclaim. There is real difficulty in seeing the desirability of this limitation.

The definition of a counterclaim for the purposes of the Convention has not been exhaustively established. All that the Court of Justice had said was that a claim against a plaintiff by way of set-off, which did not exceed the value of the claim made by the plaintiff, was not to be seen as a counterclaim, but merely a defence to which no special jurisdictional rule applied.[52] It appeared that national laws take different views: English law allows counterclaims to bring in new parties, Belgian law evidently does not. Given the presumed diversity of national laws, Lord Steyn fell back on the alleged proposition that rules of special jurisdiction are to be given a narrow interpretation, and deduced that this militated against a claim against new parties being seen as a counterclaim for the purposes of the Convention. At first sight this might seem to be an orthodox interpretation of Article 6.3, and if the meaning of 'counterclaim' is common to Articles 6.3 and 11, it might have been sufficient as it stood. But it is not. The special jurisdictional rules in Article 5 properly deserve, and routinely get given, a narrow interpretation, for the only thing they really accomplish is to deprive a defendant of his right to defend at home in response to the particular preference of the plaintiff. But Article 6 is quite different. It is the Convention's only serious basis[53] for organizing and co-ordinating more complex situations, so that litigation which involves more than a single plaintiff suing a single defendant is, whenever possible, brought before a single court. Article 6 is a pretty imperfect tool for this task,[54] but an interpretation which weakens it still further is not welcome. Yet this is what results when it is said that Article 6.3 must be given a narrow interpretation. If one purpose of the Convention is—as it undoubtedly is—to procure the free movement of judgments and (to that end) to prevent inconsistent judicial decisions, which would entail non-recognition of judgments, flowing from separate trials, a broad and generous interpretation of Article 6 is indispensable. Only last year, the House of Lords in *Sarrio* v. *Kuwait*

[51] RSC, Order 15, rule 3, states the procedure in England.

[52] Case C–341/93 *Danvaern Production A/S* v. *Schuhfabriken Otterbeck GmbH & Co.*, [1995] ECR I–2053 (noted *Yearbook of European Law*, 15 (1995), p. 498).

[53] Article 22, which allows for proceedings to be dismissed for consolidation in proceedings before another court, does not itself confer jurisdiction over the proceedings which are proposed for dismissal.

[54] Not least because it does not confer jurisdiction over related actions as such.

Investment Authority[55] applied this perception to its interpretation of Article 22; the spirit of *Jordan* v. *Baltic* is strikingly at odds with it. It is, with respect, far too simplistic to equate Articles 5 and 6 and to require them all to be construed equally narrowly. Admittedly the Court of Justice has interpreted Article 6.1 as being applicable only when the link between the claims made against two defendants is such that they should be tried together to avoid the risk of irreconcilable judgments.[56] But the *raison d'être* of the power to make a claim against a third party (under Article 6.2) or to counterclaim (Article 6.3) is precisely this: and there is no pressing need for the approach to Article 6.3 to be one of judicial hostility to the counterclaimant. After all, Jordan sued Baltic, which alleged a conspiracy between Jordan and Quay. The prospect that Baltic's single allegation against the two conspirators must be separately tried in two messy parts, in the home court of each, is a recipe almost guaranteed to produce procedural muddle, substantive conflict, inconsistent judgments, and massive costs. Baltic may have been an insurer, but even insurers, and even Lithuanian ones, have a right to defend themselves according to procedures which are fundamentally rational. It appears that Baltic has no right to do so; that after it has defended and counterclaimed against Jordan it will face going to Ireland, with a judgment which affects it mightily but which is irrelevant to Quay, and bringing such proceedings as it may be advised. It is absurd, quite absurd, that Article 6.3, and Article 11, should be read in such a way that it maximises the chances of this.

Nor do his Lordship's two additional grounds in support of a narrow view of the second paragraph of Article 11 appear to carry much weight. He observed that it would be oddly asymmetrical if a defendant could make a counterclaim and join new parties, but a plaintiff had no right to join co-defendants. But it is far from clear that this would be so very odd. The structure of Section 3 is to confer jurisdictional privileges on the insured as plaintiff (he may often choose where to sue) and as defendant (he may defend at home); in this way the weaker party is given the advantage intended by those who drafted the Convention. But that having been secured, the defendant (whether insurer or insured) has the right to counterclaim. There is no asymmetry in this sense if both insured and insurer have the right when defending a claim by the other. Moreover, it would presumably be held that the national judge would be entitled to apply his own rules on the admissibility of counterclaims so long as their application did not prejudice the practical effect of the Convention: this is the law for third party

[55] [1999] 1 AC 32, HL (noted in this *Year Book*, 68 (1997), p. 339). It should be noted that the decision of the Court of Justice in Case C–51/97 *Réunion Européenne SA* v. *Spliethoff's Bevrachtingskantoor BV* (27 October 1998) appears to cast doubt on the proposition accepted by their Lordships in *Sarrio* that the proceedings in England and Spain were related. At para. 50 the Court said that 'two claims in one action for compensation, directed against different defendants and based in one instance on contractual liability and in the other on liability in tort or delict cannot be regarded as connected'. Given that the plaintiff's claim arose out of damage to goods in transit done either by the issuer of the bill of lading or the actual sea carrier, the claims were pertinently described as 'indivisible' by the referring court, the Cour de Cassation; but transposed to the context of *Sarrio*, it is very difficult to see that the actions in the English and Spanish courts would be properly seen as related. It is infuriating that the Court of Justice was blindly unpersuaded of the rational wisdom of accepting that these claims should be tried together. Even so, that observation does not affect the present point.

[56] Case 189/87 *Kalfelis*, [1988] ECR 5565.

claims under Article 6.2.[57] Admittedly, this might require some careful reflection in a case where the effect might be to undermine one aspect of the operation of Section 3 by requiring an insured to defend in a court not of his domicile; but it would place the decisional responsibility where it properly belongs, namely, on an appreciation of the purposes of the Convention taken by the national judge in the overall circumstances of the individual case.

Finally, Lord Steyn fell back on the proposition that if a defendant could bring in new parties, this would weaken the protection of the insured. But why should this be so ? If the defendant is the insured, it does not weaken him to be given a right which he may exercise if he wishes, and may ignore if he prefers. If the defendant is the insurer, he may counterclaim against the plaintiff insured in the court which the insured has selected from the menu available to him, or may claim against new parties in a way which does not obviously affect the claim against him of the plaintiff insured, and in the court which the plaintiff insured has chosen in any event.

This aspect of the decision in *Jordan* v. *Baltic* is, it must be said, highly unsatisfactory. It seems that the mantra of narrow construction has brought about a procedural chaos which is deeply regrettable, at least when viewed from the traditional English perspective of a rational and coherent resolution of all limbs of a dispute in a single trial binding on all concerned: loyalty to this one aspect of the Convention is being taken to lengths which are increasingly absurd and in conflict with its other, and surely equivalent, aims. This is not to say that the Court of Justice, whom their Lordships did not trouble in this case, would have disagreed with Lord Steyn. But that, as we all know, furnishes absolutely no warranty of quality.

6 *The extent of submission to the jurisdiction of a foreign court: Murthy* v. *Sivasjothi*[58]

It is one thing to say, as the common law does, that submission by voluntary appearance before a foreign court gives that court international jurisdiction in the eyes of the common law, and subjects the defendant to an obligation to recognize and obey the judgment duly given against him. It is another to be sure exactly how far such a submission extends. For it cannot be the case that the simple fact of appearance lays the defendant open—as a matter of English law on the recognition of judgments—to the unlimited power of the court over him, no matter the subject-matter of the claim in the summons to which he originally answered; neither can it easily be accepted that he can contend that he submitted to some but not to all of the claims actually made against him in the writ of summons to which he appeared. Broad common sense probably provides the basis for coming to a practical answer; this is what was brought to bear in *Murthy* v. *Sivasjothi*.

The plaintiff, a doctor of Indian extraction and living in Florida, met the defendant, and over the course of time was induced to transfer large sums of

[57] Cf. Case C–365/88 *Hagen*, [1990] ECR I–1845 (noted *Yearbook of European Law*, 10 (1990), p. 487.

[58] [1999] 1 WLR 467, CA (Evans, Morritt, Chadwick LJJ).

money to him, ostensibly for the establishing of a trust fund for the doctor's children. He was also induced to convey title to certain Florida land to him, as security for an alleged business venture of the defendant's . The money appears to have vanished without trace; and the land, mortgaged by the defendant, was foreclosed on by the mortgagee. In due course the plaintiff obtained judgment against the defendant in the United States District Court for sums in excess of $900,000 plus interest, covering all the pecuniary losses he had sustained in the transactions involving money and land, and in the English action he sought to enforce the Florida judgment. He succeeded.

The basis for asserting the international jurisdiction of the District Court over the defendant was that the defendant had submitted to its jurisdiction. The defendant, together with the plaintiff, was party to a 'stipulation for settlement', a document drawn up to settle or stay the foreclosure proceedings, which had been brought by the mortgagee against defendant and plaintiff, and which conceded the jurisdiction of the District Court over it. In due course the plaintiff recovered from the shock, advanced claims and cross-claims against the mortgagee and the defendant, and obtained his judgment in default against the defendant as a result of those claims. But when it came to the enforcing of the judgment in England, the defendant sought to contend that in acceding to the stipulation for settlement and the choice of court agreement within it, he was submitting to the jurisdiction of the District Court in relation to the mortgagee's foreclosure action, and not to the cross-claims made by the plaintiff against him. The question for the court was therefore this: assuming that the defendant was right, and that his submission was intended by him to be so limited, did it follow that he had also submitted to the claims which the District Court allowed to be added and advanced in the proceedings ? Evans LJ, with whom the others agreed, concluded that submission in the foreclosure action was to be seen as extending to 'related claims' advanced by other parties to the proceedings, and therefore covered the plaintiff's claim. Summary judgment was therefore ordered in the plaintiff's favour.

In the absence of English authority, Evans LJ was referred to a decision of the Supreme Court of the United States, *ex parte Indiana Transportation Co.*,[59] and to various passages from the *Restatement*. These cumulatively sought to use the concept of fairness to delimit the extent to which a defendant, who had voluntarily appeared, might be taken to have laid himself open to additional claims by the existing plaintiff, or new claims by additional parties. Prominent in the concerns of the American jurisprudence is the convenience of having a single and effective resolution of claims which should be resolved at once; where new claims are added, it is observed that the defendant should be given an opportunity to answer them; where new parties are added, to be (re-)served. Evans LJ used these as support for a common law rule which would extend the scope of a submission in two directions: to claims concerning the same subject-matter, and to related claims which ought to be dealt with in the same proceedings. Such claims would be within the scope of the submission if they were advanced against the defendant by the original plaintiff or by others parties[60] to the proceedings who were in at the date of the defendant's

[59] 244 US 456 (1917).
[60] Such as a co-defendant, seeking a contribution or an indemnity from the defendant.

submission to the court. Applying this principle to the facts of the case, the submission by the defendant in the foreclosure action, to which the plaintiff was already also party, constituted a submission to a separate but related claim by the plaintiff for damages for the whole of the fraudulent conspiracy of which the conveyance, mortgage, and foreclosure were part. The judgment was, it is submitted, absolutely correct.

Evans LJ noted, also surely correctly, that just because a foreign court has allowed amendment by addition of new claims, the English court is still entitled to decide for itself whether this will fall within the scope of the submission. In this regard it is reminiscent of the principle, now becoming accepted as uncontroversial,[61] that the fact that the foreign court considers there to have been a submission is a necessary, but not a sufficient, condition for there to be international jurisdiction in the foreign court.

In some ways, however, *Murthy* was not as difficult a case as it might have been, for the claims made were very closely connected, and the party advancing them was party to the foreign proceedings at the date of the critical submission. It is less obvious what the answer would properly have been had the plaintiff sought to become joined as a claimant only after the defendant had submitted to a claim by the mortgagee, and had taken no further step in the proceedings. Could it then have been said that he had not submitted to the claim by the new parties? Or what would the analysis be if a single plaintiff, to whose original summons the defendant has submitted, is permitted to add a new claim, the original inclusion of which might have led the defendant to not submit? The latter case seems to be answered by Evans LJ's formula, assuming that it is the same plaintiff and a connected cause of action. But the former is more difficult. To start with, it is not at all clear that as a matter of English domestic law a defendant may submit to some aspects of a claim but not to others, or to a claim made by only some of joined plaintiffs: submission to one is submission to all appears to be the rule. In fact, the jurisdiction of an English court does not depend on submission, but upon service of the writ. Once served, the defendant may acknowledge service and may, if so advised, contest the jurisdiction under RSC, Order 12, rule 8 (now replaced by Civil Procedure Rules 1999, Part 11). But if he fails, he has once again to decide whether to acknowledge service or to risk suffering judgment in default of appearance. He has no opportunity to make a selective or partial submission, not least because the jurisdiction of the English court to continue to hear the case does not depend on a process of submission, but appearance, and appearance must be to all of the writ or to none of it. But in relation to foreign judgments, this may not be directly applicable, and it may be that a defendant is entitled to say that he submitted to the adjudication of some claims, but maintained his stance of not submitting to others, even though the procedure of the foreign court did not permit him to do so formally. For this reason (though no doubt there are others as well) an English court does not deduce submission from the mere fact that the foreign court might have taken the defendant to have submitted, or otherwise acknowledged the authority of the court, according to its own law.[62] In the absence of English authority, it may be

[61] At the level of the Commercial Court, in any case: cf. *Adams* v. *Cape Industries plc*, [1990] Ch. 433, 461 (Scott J); *The Eastern Trader*, [1996] 2 Lloyd's Rep. 585, 599 (Rix J); *Akai Pty. Ltd.* v. *People's Insurance Co. Ltd.*, [1998] 1 Lloyd's Rep. 90, 97 (Thomas J).

[62] Cf. *Akai*, at p. 97.

hard to improve on Evans LJ's statement that the court will wish to be fair; it is rather more difficult to put flesh on the bones of so abstract a statement, and it is not proposed to try.

It may, however, be that there is a broader principle to be identified. The effect of a submission in *Murthy* was that it amounted to an inchoate submission to other claims, reasonably closely related to that one commenced by the writ. If the plaintiff were to have decided not to advance his claim in respect of the loaned money in the foreclosure action, but had done so by separate action in England, he might, in principle[63] at least, have been met by the plea that it was an abuse of the process of the English court to have saved up this cause of action which could have been advanced on the first occasion in Florida and properly disposed of there and then. If the action is one to which the defendant's first submission would have extended, so as to render a judgment upon this cause of action also enforceable in principle in England, it may well be that *Henderson* v. *Henderson*[64] should apply to it. But if it would not, it is less clear that it would be an abuse of process to keep the claims separate, for separate trial of the second cause of action. There is much complicated learning, and some fast-developing new law,[65] on the principles of abuse of process as these apply to participation in proceedings before foreign courts, and this is not the place to start to examine them. But intuitively it feels that the connections are there to be made when a suitable case provides the opportunity.

7 *Title to tangible movables in times of political trouble: City of Gotha* v. *Sotheby's and Cobert Finance SA*[66]

The year's one substantial case on choice of law dealt with title to a painting: *The Holy Family with Saints John and Elizabeth*, by Joachim Wtewael, painted in 1603 in the Dutch mannerist style. Measuring only 21 x 16 cm, this little treasure was collected by the Duke of Saxe-Coburg-Gotha, and housed in his picture gallery until the end of the First World War. Thereafter it led an extraordinarily exciting life, only to come to light in the hands of Sotheby's when offered for sale in 1992. At that point those claiming the painting were the defendants, Cobert Finance SA, the Panamanian corporation which had offered it for sale, and the two plaintiffs who alleged that the painting had been converted, the City of Gotha,[67] a corporate body claiming a possessory title, and the Federal Republic of Germany, claiming ownership. Sotheby's wisely stood back from the fray. Moses J, whose analysis of art history and political history was enthusiastically intricate, concluded that the title of the Federal Republic of Germany was recognized under English law, and that, its title being established in accordance with the rules of the English conflict of laws, its action in conversion should succeed. The decision is principally of interest because of the extremely difficult facts, rather than on account of problematic legal principles.

[63] Though the court chosen for the foreclosure action was not of the plaintiff's choice; it is not known whether this is material to the operation of *Henderson* v. *Henderson*, (1843) 3 Hare 100, in relation to an unadvanced counter- or cross-claim.

[64] (1843) 3 Hare 100.

[65] For a reference, see this *Year Book*, 67 (1996), pp. 596–9.

[66] 9 September 1998, Moses J.

[67] Gotha is a city in the former German Democratic Republic, in the *Land* of Thüringia.

But certain corners of the old science of choice of law were visited, and a few notorious problems were noticed along the way. Though the analysis of them was neither novel nor wrong, the manner of their intersection is of some interest. And any shortcoming in hard legal content is more than made up for by the thriller-like factual story, spellbindingly told by the judge.

To claim that their painting had been converted or wrongfully interfered with, the plaintiffs needed first to establish that the painting was theirs: a person relying on the torts of conversion or wrongful interference must make this step. Even though the tort was said to have taken place in England when Sotheby's offered it for sale, with the result that English law alone applied to determine liability,[68] a claimant still needs to establish title, and title, where acquired pursuant to a foreign law, requires proof and satisfaction of that foreign law. This does not mean that the plaintiff had to succeed under two laws, but just that the single cause of action had distinct parts, each governed by separate laws. It is therefore necessary to give a brief summary of the events which overtook the painting, in order to indicate how the plaintiffs claimed to have acquired, and to not have lost, title to it.[69] In November 1918 the workers' and soldiers' council of Gotha deposed the Duke. In 1919 the constitution of the German Reich required the dissolution of entailed estates, including that of the Duke, and it was duly voluntarily dissolved. In 1928 a law of the *Land* of Thüringia created 'The Duke of Saxe-Coburg-Gotha Foundation for Art and Science', which was to have its seat in the city of Gotha, and which had the preservation of the Ducal art collection as one of its cultural purposes. In 1939 the painting may have been evacuated to the countryside east of Gotha; and in the general chaos after the end of the war was taken to the Soviet Union. Precisely when this occurred was critical to any claim which depended upon the laws of Thüringia. The judge found that it was probably not touched in the days of American occupation of Gotha, but after the arrival of the Red Army in July 1945 there was an official acquisition of works of art on behalf of organs of the Soviet State, and (much more obscurely) an unofficial acquisition of chattels by self-help. In the 1980s the painting was smuggled out of the Soviet Union by a Mrs Sunzuga or Mrs Dikeni, and taken to West Berlin; it was acquired in 1988 by a Mina Breslav, who sold it to Cobert in 1989. The fortunes of the painting in the years between 1946 and 1980 were deeply obscure, and the cast of (real or imaginary) characters flitting across the stage and lurking in the shadows was quite extraordinary.

In order to determine title to the painting, the judge followed the Rule in Dicey and Morris,[70] and accepted that he had to apply German law, without reference to any of the possible exceptions mooted by Slade J in *Winkworth* v.

[68] Choice of law for a tort committed in England prior to the coming into force of Part III of the Private International Law (Miscellaneous Provisions) Act 1995 is English law: *Metall & Rohstoff AG* v. *Donaldson Lufkin & Jenrette Inc.*, [1990] 1 QB 391, CA. To this extent the rule in *Boys* v. *Chaplin*, [1971] AC 356, HL, was inapplicable. A separate choice of law rule for torts committed in England is believed to have been abolished by the 1995 Act, though the inept wording of the legislation leaves room for some doubt.

[69] In fact, we are concerned only with the claim of the Federal Republic to ownership; the City of Gotha maintained its claim to a possessory title only if the Federal Republic failed to establish ownership.

[70] *The Conflict of Laws* (12th edn., 1993), Rule 118.

Christie, Manson and Woods.[71] It was not suggested that the law of the Soviet Union had any bearing on the question of title, for Soviet law denied any effect to transfers without the consent of the lawful owner and no party saw fit to derive any advantage from a reference to Soviet law.[72] So what was the state of German law while the painting was still in Germany ? A picture of utter confusion prevailed, with various alleged authorities purporting to pass contradictory laws confiscating, sequestrating and expropriating property within and beyond the territory over which they claimed power; the judge's lengthy and detailed analysis does not lend itself to simplification. But in his opinion, two events may have succeeded in conferring title on the Federal Republic: one an expropriation, and one a succession.

As to the first of these, the judge concluded that title to the painting was acquired by the *Land* of Thüringia in October or December 1945, by virtue of an expropriatory decree passed while the painting was within the territory of Thüringia, following which the painting was taken into the possession of the *Land*'s trustee. On this analysis, the case was a simple one: the chattel was within the jurisdiction of the expropriating legislator, and title was duly acquired as a matter of the English conflict of laws. The fact that further laws were passed in 1946 by the Soviet Military Administration was irrelevant in the light of the judge's finding that the painting had by then been removed from the territory of the Soviet Military Administration. As the property of the *Land* vested in the German Democratic Republic, and then (on German unification) in the Federal Republic, the chain of title of the Federal Republic of Germany was secured. No difficult issue of the conflict of laws arose.

An alternative analysis was that the Ducal Foundation was dissolved in 1950 under the law of the *Land* of Thüringia, under which it had been created; and the consequences of its dissolution were likewise a matter for that law. On this view, the Federal Republic acquired title to the painting in 1950 by succession wherever it was. It is fairly clear that succession may[73] transfer title to a chattel by a process altogether distinct from the *inter vivos* transfer which is regulated by the *lex situs*, and the judge found that this was the effect of an act of the *Land* government in 1950, which was then successor *in universum jus*. It was contended that this conclusion could be gainsaid if the act could be characterized as governmental and intended to affect title to property outside the territorial jurisdiction of the legislator.[74] But whilst accepting that the distinction was sound in principle, the judge concluded that the act of dissolution was in substance just that, and that as the dissolution of a corporation is a matter of private law, rather than prerogative right, it was to be recognized as effective.

All that established that the Federal Republic was in principle able to establish

[71] [1981] Ch. 496. Accordingly the case does not cast light on the extent to which, if at all, these exceptions to the rule that the *lex situs* applies are soundly based.

[72] Accordingly the questions of conflict of laws which might have arisen in acute form, had someone claimed a title valid under Soviet law, did, not arise.

[73] It would depend upon the law dissolving the Foundation purporting to vest title to chattels outside the territory in the successor.

[74] Reflecting the distinctions drawn in *Adams* v. *National Bank of Greece and Athens SA*, [1958] 2 QB 59 (Diplock J); [1958] AC 509, HL, and in *Williams & Humbert Ltd.* v. *W & H Trade Marks (Jersey) Ltd.*, [1986] AC 369, HL.

its title as a matter of the English conflict of laws. The final obstacle was that if Germany was to establish its title to found its allegation of conversion,[75] a question of limitation arose. As, the Federal Republic had not acted in defence of its title for a very long time, the immediate question was which law governed limitation. Given that German law (for determining title) as well as English law (for determining the rights which followed from that title) fell to be taken into account in determining the claim for conversion, the Foreign Limitation Periods Act 1984, section 1(2), led to the result that German and English[76] limitation periods were both applicable. Though he noted the lamentably inept drafting of the Act, and the consequence that it would not be rarely that more laws than one had to be applied to limitation,[77] there was no way to overcome the proposition that English and German law on limitation had to be applied: to be taken into account in the determination of a matter was not a demanding, or a limiting, standard. But the judge found as a fact that the thirty-year limitation period of German law did not start to run until 1987, and that as a result title under German law was not extinguished by lapse of time. Had it been otherwise, he said, he would have found that German law, in allowing time to run even during a period of deliberate concealment, and in favour of a thief or *mala fide* acquirer from a thief, would be disapplied on grounds of its manifest inconsistency with English public policy.[78] This may be questioned, on the ground that the English law combination of a short period of limitation but (relatively) generous provisions which prevent the running of time in cases of theft or fraud should be taken as a whole; and the German law combination of a very long period but with fewer suspensory possibilities should also be taken as a whole; but that a plaintiff should not be able to pick and mix the most favourable elements from the two schemes and claim this to be the product of public policy.

In the result the case establishes little new law, re-establishes some old orthodoxies, and tells a rattling good tale. It makes for one of those occasions when the conflict of laws is pure, undiluted, fun. The reader may be left with more than a suspicion that the judge thought so too.[79]

[75] The casual suggestion by the judge that the claim of the Federal Republic might in some sense be restitutionary need not be pursued.

[76] There was no difficulty for the plaintiffs in the application of English limitation law, for as the painting had been stolen and had not been subsequently bought in good faith, Limitation Act 1980, s. 4, meant that time had not begun to run.

[77] So that in a single dispute, a variety of different laws may be applicable to separate parts of the cause of action, but every law so applied will be applicable to limitation. If one considers a tort claim to which a contractual defence is advanced, it being contended on various grounds (which will be referable to different laws) that the contract is invalid or ineffective in its own terms, or is inadmissible as a defence to the claim in tort, the list of laws to be taken into account in determining the matter is pretty long. A similar observation might have been appropriate if there had been a claim in the present case that under the law of the Soviet Union, something had occurred which had a bearing on the claim to title of the Federal Republic of Germany. It appears from section 1(2) of the Act that most, if not all, of these laws are used to determine whether limitation has bitten. Which principle of rational legal science created this nonsense has never been explained.

[78] Section 2 of the 1984 Act, as interpreted by the judge.

[79] Not least from the judge's cheerful admission that he had been permitted to sneak into Sotheby's for a judicial peek at the painting, then safely hidden in an envelope in a small office.

8 *Jurisdiction over claims concerning stolen foreign land: Re Polly Peck International (in administration) (No. 2)*[80]

The plaintiffs owned land and buildings in the northern part of the Republic of Cyprus, and had enjoyed possession until the invasion of the island by the armed forces of the Turkish Republic in 1974. Since that date the land had been expropriated, without the merest hint of compensation, by the authorities of the *soi-disant* 'Turkish Republic of Northern Cyprus', and had been let to Polly Peck International ('PPI') and/or companies associated with it. PPI having been placed in administration, the plaintiffs applied for leave[81] to commence proceedings against it and its administrators, in an action claiming that sums received by the administrators represented the profits and proceeds of wrongdoing by PPI,[82] which had been unjustly enriched at the expense of the plaintiffs, and which sums were subject to a 'remedial constructive trust' in the hands of the administrators for the benefit of the plaintiffs, so allowing them to jump the queue of unsecured creditors of the hopelessly insolvent PPI. PPI argued that the claim was bound to fail, and that leave should not be given. The Court of Appeal, reversing Rattee J,[83] agreed.

The plaintiffs faced three hurdles. The first was a jurisdictional one: there was a sense in which their claim raised a question which required determination of title to foreign land, and the rule in *British South Africa Co.* v. *Companhia de Moçambique*,[84] though modified by legislation,[85] established that the English courts had no jurisdiction to do such a thing. The second was whether English law[86] recognized such a thing as a 'remedial constructive trust'; and the third, whether such a thing, even if capable of being recognized in principle, could be asserted in the face of the scheme for distribution of assets established by the Insolvency Act 1986. The second and third of these lie beyond the scope of this note, though it is worth recording that the court was unanimous in rejecting the plaintiffs' contentions on both points, and for this reason refused leave to bring the action. But its treatment of the jurisdictional argument does call for comment.

The *Moçambique* rule has been amended, arguably twice, by statute. As a matter of direct amendment, section 30(1) Civil Jurisdiction and Judgments Act 1982 provides that 'the jurisdiction of any court in England . . . to entertain proceedings for trespass to, or any other tort affecting, immovable property shall extend to cases in which the property in question is situated outside [England]

[80] [1998] 3 All E R 812, CA (Nourse, Potter, Mummery LJJ).

[81] Under Insolvency Act 1986, s. 11(3)(*d*).

[82] Some of the sums were said to be comprised in the inflated value of the shares of the subsidiaries (which had gorged themselves on the expropriated land), which shares PPI had sold. This indirect location of the profits over which the trust was claimed made it very difficult for the plaintiffs to establish their claim as a matter of English law, but is of no immediate relevance to the issues addressed here.

[83] [1997] 2 BCLC 630.

[84] [1893] AC 602, HL.

[85] Civil Jurisdiction and Judgments Act 1982, s. 30.

[86] It was not argued, apparently, that the fact that the enrichment had originated in Cyprus allowed a law other than English to determine whether there was a maintainable proprietary or quasi-proprietary claim to the proceeds of that enrichment. It may be that the law of Cyprus was to the same effect as English law; but in any event, the decision contributes nothing to the debate on choice of law in relation to restitutionary claims.

unless the proceedings are principally concerned with a question of the title to, or the right to possession of, that property'. But there was also an argument to the effect that where the defendant was subject to the jurisdiction of the English courts by virtue of the Brussels Convention, it was not open to the court to apply a jurisdictional rule of the common law to contradict the Convention. Of this second, indirect, argument, more later.

Rattee J had concluded that the plaintiffs' claim was not principally concerned with a question of title to foreign land. His methodology was to list the legal issues which the court would have to decide, and to note that the issue of title was only one among many difficult points. As such, it could not be said that the question of title was the principal concern of the case. As it could not be said that the only real issue was that of title, Rattee J concluded that section 30(1) removed any jurisdictional obstacle. Further, he concluded that it was for him to decide the jurisdictional question at the preliminary stage, and was not necessary only for him to consider that there was a good arguable case as to jurisdiction. As to the latter point, Mummery LJ (with whom the others agreed) departed from the approach of the judge, preferring the view that a good arguable case (he called it a seriously arguable case; the significance of the difference in terminology was not explained) as to jurisdiction was sufficient to allow the case to proceed to trial.

As to the standard of proof point, there are difficulties with the view taken by Mummery LJ, but he is probably right. In the common form of jurisdictional objection, where a defendant applies under RSC, Order 12, rule 8 (now Civil Procedure Rules 1999, Part 11, and argues, for example, that the Brussels Convention, or RSC, Order 11, does not confer jurisdiction on the court, the plaintiff is required to show a good arguable case on the contested jurisdictional argument, and thereafter the court will proceed. In the ordinary course, the defendant then re-acknowledges service, and in doing so enters an appearance and submits to the jurisdiction of the court. His appearance provides the court with a distinct and new ground of jurisdiction over him; and if it should emerge at the end of the trial that the jurisdictional basis relied on by the plaintiff was in fact unfounded, it is too late: the court will not dismiss the action on jurisdictional grounds, for two reasons: it has already dealt with the jurisdictional question, and the defendant's appearance to the writ constitutes a new basis for confirming the existence of jurisdiction. In other words, the ruling on jurisdiction, though provisional in appearance, and low in standard of certainty, is unreviewable if shown to be wrong at trial. There are those who continue to believe that this has the potential to operate unfairly as against a defendant, and that the procedure to be found in some other contracting States to the Brussels and Lugano Conventions—that the judge makes only a provisional ruling *in limine*, and makes a final ruling on jurisdiction after the trial—is preferable[87] to the English system. Rattee J appears to have seen (correctly) that a jurisdictional objection based on the *Moçambique* rule is quite different, in that submission by a defendant cannot override it. He therefore decided that it was necessary to rule on jurisdiction on a balance of probabilities, and not to the lower level of a good arguable case, because

[87] It would be difficult to accommodate this within the existing structure of the Rules of the Supreme Court, but if the Brussels Convention were held to require it, no doubt a way could be found.

he was required to get the jurisdictional question right. But in this lay his mistake: because the *Moçambique* rule cannot be overcome by submission, in allowing the case to go to trial and encouraging the defendant to submit, the defendant's right to maintain the jurisdictional objection is not prejudiced. The defendant is entitled to fight the case through trial and still maintain that the court has no jurisdiction, without being estopped by his own appearance or submission. That being so, it was—contrary to the usual case—perfectly sensible to allow the case to proceed to trial on a provisional finding as to jurisdiction: any error in that provisional assessment could be put right later. Mummery LJ was therefore right to conclude that a good arguable case that section 30(1) conferred jurisdiction should have sufficed to allow the case to proceed to trial.

As to the interpretation of section 30(1), there is more room for doubt. It seems extraordinary that a case which would be excluded by the *Moçambique* rule may be within the jurisdiction of the court just because other issues pleaded and arising are themselves difficult and numerous. It is true that section 30(1) speaks of the 'proceedings' being 'principally concerned' with a question of title, but just because the procedural law will be complex, and the substantive and remedial issues difficult, are the proceedings any the less principally concerned with an issue as to title? It depends upon whether 'principally' connotes 'first and foremost', or 'first equally'. If the policy behind section 30(1) was to allow a court to deal with a trespass action when there was no substantial issue of foreign land law to grapple with, the fact that there are other issues as well will be irrelevant, and the approach preferred by Rattee J and Mummery LJ is not obviously correct. On the other hand, the wording used by section 30(1) is not blatantly inconsistent with the conclusion their Lordships reached, and if it is right to construe it as being no wider than necessary the exclusionary rule, the result follows as they decided. Even so, if the jurisdiction of the court depends upon the ability of the plaintiff (or the defendant, though in this respect acting contrary to his interests) to make the legal issues look complicated, this is curiously unsatisfactory.

A different approach would have been to ask whether there really was a question of title to the land in question. As a matter of English law, the *lex situs* was the law of the Republic of Cyprus, and not the regulations of the forces of illegal occupation in the north of the island, and according to it there was presumably no dispute whatever as to title.[88] If that were so, there would be no reason to apply the *Moçambique* rule. But such an argument may owe more to logic than to political reality: the truth was that there was disagreement, reinforced by thousands of Turkish soldiers, as to ownership of the land; and on that basis the *Moçambique* rule might have been properly applicable.

It followed from the fact that the plaintiff was denied leave to proceed on substantive grounds, rather than on jurisdictional ones, that it was unnecessary for the court to consider whether the fact that PPI and its administrators were domiciled in England led to the conclusion that the Brussels Convention gave the plaintiffs a right to invoke the jurisdiction of the English courts. Mummery LJ appeared to note that the decision of the Court of Appeal in *Re Harrods*

[88] An observation which would have been open to be made in the earlier case of *Hesperides Hotels Ltd.* v. *Muftizade*, [1979] AC 508, HL; as it was not made there it must be conceded that it is unsupported by authority.

(Buenos Aires) Ltd.[89] meant that it was open to an English court to stay proceedings in favour of the courts of a non-contracting State, and that as a result, it would be open to an English court to declare that the courts of the Republic of Cyprus (or the tribunals of the occupied zone) should exercise jurisdiction. In fact, his Lordship seemed to say that Article 2 did not apply at all, and could not be relied on, in a case where there was a competing forum in a non-contracting non-State, a proposition which must be regarded as a slip of the mind. But the rightness of *Re Harrods* has already arisen indirectly in those few other areas in which the jurisdictional rules of the common law held a dispute to be non-justiciable. In *Coin Controls Ltd.* v. *Suzo International (UK) Ltd.*[90] and *Fort Dodge Animal Health Ltd.* v. *Akzo Nobel*[91] it had been accepted that where the Brussels Convention gave personal jurisdiction over a defendant, a rule of the common law which denied that the substantive dispute was justiciable at all by the English courts was displaced. That conclusion may be controversial, but it supports the view that jurisdictional solutions reached by the common law are liable to be contradicted by the Convention. The same may be said of the rule of the common law which stays proceedings on the ground of *forum non conveniens*; it may also be that the common law right to invoke the jurisdictional rules of the Convention has superseded the common law power to not hear a case on the ground of *forum non conveniens*. But until the Court of Appeal or House of Lords refer to the Court of Justice a question designed to tease this out, the issue will remain one of uncertainty.

It was not said in the judgment, at least, that the *Moçambique* rule, in its application to the facts of the case, constituted a denial of rights secured to the plaintiffs by the European Convention on Human Rights. But Article 6 guarantees that everyone 'is entitled to a fair and public hearing within a reasonable time by an independent and impartial tribunal established by law'. In reaching the conclusion that the claim was doomed to fail on substantive grounds, the Court of Appeal may not have been depriving the plaintiffs of a hearing, any more than ever happens when a claim or a defence is struck out. But had the court reached the conclusion that the plaintiffs were shut out by the *Moçambique* rule, and were obliged on that account to go to the tribunals of the occupied zone of Cyprus and ask for an independent and impartial determination of their civil rights, a violation of Article 6 would have been easy to identify. It has been noticed before that the European Convention has the potential to affect the operation of jurisdictional rules;[92] and it has been held before that the enactment of an international convention may require rules on choice of law to be reconsidered.[93] When the Human Rights Act 1998 finally comes into force, the extent of rewriting which will be required in the field of the conflict of laws may be very substantial indeed. But that is another story.

ADRIAN BRIGGS

[89] [1992] Ch. 72, CA.

[90] [1997] 3 All E R 45 (Laddie J).

[91] [1998] FSR 222, CA: both decisions noted in this *Year Book*, 68 (1997), p. 349.

[92] *Connelly* v. *Rio Tinto Zinc Corporation plc (No. 2)*, 2 May 1996, CA (noted this *Year Book*, 67 (1996), p. 587, at p. 590), aff'd on different grounds [1998] AC 834, HL (noted this *Year Book*, 68 (1997), p. 357, at p. 360).

[93] *Pearce* v. *Ove Arup Partnership Ltd.*, [1997] Ch. 293, Ch. D.

DECISIONS ON THE EUROPEAN CONVENTION ON HUMAN RIGHTS DURING 1998*

In view of the number of decisions now being handed down by the European Court of Human Rights, the practice of providing a full note of each case has ceased to be practical. Thus, the survey will no longer cover all cases decided during the period under review, highlighting instead only a proportion of the cases. The present survey, departing from the approach of recent surveys, will also not be divided into parts, nor will the decisions be presented in strict chronological order.

Disclosure of medical records—right to private life—Article 8—no right in issue—applicability—Article 6(1)

Case No. 1. MS case.[1] In this case involving Sweden, the Court unanimously found that there had been no of violation of Article 8. Further, it found that Article 6(1) did not apply and that there was no separate issue under Article 13.

The applicant injured her back. Subsequently she claimed social security benefits payable in respect of industrial injuries. Her claim was then investigated, resulting in her medical records being released to the investigating officials. Those relating to the time of her back injury indicated that she had not had an industrial injury, the problem arising instead from a long-standing medical problem. Other records released, however, had not been requested from her doctor by the social security department, although they had some relevance to the applicant's back problem. These records included details of an abortion that the applicant had had some years after the back injury, the reason for the termination of the pregnancy having been severe back pain. Her claim was unsuccessful, as were all subsequent appeals. She then claimed that the disclosure of information from one public authority to another was in breach of her right to have her private life respected and was contrary to Article 8. Further, she claimed that there had been a breach of her right to a fair hearing in relation to the release of those medical records. Finally, she argued that, in breach of Article 13, she had had no remedy. The Commission, having declared the application admissible, suggested in its report that there had been no violation of Articles 8, 6 or 13.

This is one of a series of cases involving various aspects of Article 8. In this case, the protection of the individual's rights of confidentiality against invasion by State authorities was in issue. The first question was whether there had been an infringement of the applicant's rights under Article 8(1); the second, whether that could be justified under the terms of Article 8(2). The Court noted that the

[1] ECHR, judgment of 27 August 1997.

act of claiming social security could not constitute a waiver of individuals' rights of confidentiality as regards their medical records. Disclosure to another public authority still meant disclosure to a wider circle of civil servants and, furthermore, medical records were kept for different purposes from those for which the Social Security office wanted them. This clearly constituted an interference with the applicant's right under Article 8. The Court, however, then noted that this interference was allowed by domestic law and that the object of the disclosure was to serve a public interest, the allocation of public resources. So far, the actions of the authorities would seem to fall within the terms of Article 8(2). The final question, therefore, was whether the measure was proportional. As the release of the records was subject to safeguards (such as the personal liability of the relevant civil servants concerned), the Court held that there had been no violation of the applicant's rights under Article 8, despite the fact that not all the information disclosed to them had been requested by the authorities determining the question of allocation of resources. This case seems in line with the Court's reasoning in *Z* v. *Finland*,[2] but, given the sensitivity of the additional material disclosed, one might question the weight in such cases attributed to confidentiality of such records.

The Court then went on to consider the arguments under Article 6. It held that there was no right in issue here because the disclosure was subject to rules obliging the transfer of the medical records. Article 6 therefore did not apply.[3] It then went on to hold that no separate issue arose under Article 13.

Article 8 was considered in a number of cases in the period under review, a proportion of which dealt with the States' negative obligations under Article 8: see, for example, Case No. 2 *Mehemi*, Case No. 3 *Mentes* and Case No. 4 *Petrovik*. A number of cases also developed the positive aspect of Article 8, in particular Case No. 5 *Botta*, Case No. 6 *Sheffield and Horsham*, Case No.7 *Guerra*, Case No. 8 *McGinley and Egan* and Case No. 9 *LCB* v. *UK*.

Article 8—deportation for drug trafficking—right to family life

Case No. 2. Mehemi case.[4] In this case against France, the Court held unanimously that there had been a breach of Article 8 in respect of the applicant's right to a family life.

The applicant was an Algerian national born in France where he lived until his deportation in February 1995. All of the applicant's family live in France; some have French nationality. In 1986, he married a legally resident Italian national and they have children. In 1991 the applicant was imprisoned for six years for drug trafficking. This sentence was confirmed on appeal and an award was made permanently excluding the applicant from France. Appeals against the sentence relying on Article 8 failed. The Commission declared the application admissible and expressed the view in its report that there had been a violation of Article 8.

This case was one of several in which second generation immigrants were

[2] *Z* v. *Finland*, ECHR, judgment of 25 February 1997.

[3] See also *Andersson* v. *Sweden*, ECHR, judgment of 27 August 1997, and *Balmer–Schafroth* v. *Switzerland*, ECHR, judgment of 26 August 1997.

[4] ECHR, judgment of 26 September 1997.

seeking to challenge deportation orders made against them.[5] In this case, as in the others, the exclusion order clearly constituted an interference with the applicant's right to respect for his family life. The Court noted that the exclusion was in accordance with French law and it was aimed at the prevention of disorder or crime; the question then was whether the measure was necessary within a democratic society. Reprising previous case law, the Court noted that this meant that the measure must be justified by a pressing social need and must also be proportionate to the aim pursued. A balance between the competing interests of the individual's right and the prevention of crime or disorder must be sought. In this case, the applicant had a strong connection with France: he had been raised there and his parents, siblings, wife and children all lived there. Further, he had no links with Algeria other than his nationality. The French Government had suggested that the family could re-locate to Italy, given that the applicant's wife was Italian. This, however, would be a radical upheaval and there would certainly be obstacles to this course of action given the applicant's criminal record. Therefore, although the Court noted the severity of the offence, it held that the measure was disproportionate and that there had therefore been a violation of Article 8. In the other cases a similar approach was taken, although with a different outcome as, in each of the other three cases, no violation of Article 8 was found.

These cases highlight some difficulties for second generation immigrants. Obviously, the precise facts in the case will affect the outcome. One concern, however, is whether the Court is taking a consistent line in assessing these facts. Reviewing the Court's previous jurisprudence in *Boujlifa*,[6] Judges Baka and Van Dijk suggested that the applicant's crimes in that case, justifying deportation, were no more serious taken overall than those committed by previous applicants where a violation of Article 8 had been found.[7] They further commented that the Court should adopt a clear approach to the position of second generation immigrants as 'the present judgment does not provide the national authorities and the possible victims of future deportations with the certainty and clarity to which they are entitled'. The integrated immigrant without family might seem to be additionally disadvantaged by the Court's emphasis on family links in the host country, as opposed to other social links that an individual might form and which should also be protected by the right to private life.[8]

One might question further the emphasis that the Court seems to have placed on links with the State of origin and on nationality in particular. For example, in *Boujlifa*, the Court highlighted the fact that the applicant 'did not show any desire to acquire French nationality at the time when he was entitled to do so'. The Court has also shown a tendency to find no violation of Article 8 where the applicant has some relatives in the country of origin, or speaks the language of

[5] See also *El Boujaidi* v. *France*, ECHR, judgment of 26 September 1997, *Boujlifa* v. *France*, ECHR, judgment of 21 October 1997, and *Dalia* v. *France*, ECHR, judgment of 19 February 1998.

[6] *Boujlifa* v. *France*, ECHR, judgment of 21 October 1997.

[7] See *Moustaquim* v. *Belgium*, judgment of 18 February 1991, Series A, No. 193, *Beldjoudi* v. *France*, judgment of 26 March 1995, Series A, No. 234–A, and *Nasri* v. *France*, judgment of 13 July 1995, Series A, No. 320–B.

[8] See Judge Martens' comments in *Beldjoudi*, loc. cit. above (n. 7), reflecting the concerns raised by Wildhaber in *Nasri*, loc. cit. above (n. 7).

that country. This suggests that, in order to enjoy a certain security of family life over the long term in the host State, an individual must cut him or herself off from any family remaining in the State of origin, and also from the language and traditions of that State. In his dissenting opinion in *El Boujaidi*,[9] Judge Foighel noted the problems arising in respect of the second generation immigrant who was integrated into the host State. He commented that human rights should be available irrespective of nationality and that this treatment effectively constituted expulsion.

One final concern relates to the question of whether deportation constitutes an additional punishment imposed on immigrants, given that in these cases the immigrant has also served a term of imprisonment or received other punishment. Not only does this make a mockery of the idea of rehabilitating individuals who have committed offences, but it seems to be discriminating against the immigrant by in effect punishing him twice.

Destruction of village—right to home and family life—Article 8—lack of remedies—Article 13

Case No. 3. Mentes case.[10] In this case, one of many involving Turkey, the Court found, by sixteen votes to five, that there had been a violation of Article 8 in respect of the first three applicants. It unanimously decided not to examine the complaints under Articles 3, 5(1) and 6(1). By sixteen votes to five, the Court also held that there had been a violation of Article 13 in respect of the first three applicants. It unanimously held that there had been no violation of any of the above articles in respect of the fourth applicant. The Court finally made an award for costs and expenses under Article 50 but reserved the question of damages.

The four applicants were all of Kurdish origin. Since 1985 there had been serious disturbances in the area in which they lived as a consequence of the actions of the PKK. As a result of this action a number of villages had been deserted and destroyed. The facts in this case were disputed. The applicants claimed that security forces burnt the village deliberately in June 1993 as a punishment for the villagers allegedly having helped the PKK. The entire property of the villagers was destroyed in this action. The villagers themselves had been threatened with being burnt alive if they had tried to intervene. The only reason, according to the applicants, that the whole village had not been destroyed was that the commanding officer had arrived and prevented it. The Government claimed the destruction of the houses occurred later in the year as a result of actions taken against the PKK. It also claimed that the applicants had links to the PKK. Following the destruction of their village, the applicants complained to the national authorities but this resulted, after a brief investigation, in a decision not to prosecute.

The Commission declared the application admissible. After its own investigation of the facts, the Commission broadly accepted the applicants' version of events. In respect of the first three applicants, the Commission expressed the

[9] *El Boujaidi* v. *France*, ECHR, judgment of 26 September 1997.
[10] ECHR, judgment of 28 November 1997.

opinion that there had been a violation of Articles 8, 3, 6 and 13. It found that there had been no violation of Articles 5, 14 or 18.

The Court began by dismissing the Government's preliminary objection that the applicants had not exhausted their domestic remedies.[11] An individual should have no obligation to have recourse to inadequate or ineffective remedies. Given the context, this rule should be applied without excessive formalism, taking into account facts of the case. The Court referred back to its judgment in *Akdivar*.

> In such a situation it must be recognised that there may be obstacles to the proper functioning of justice. In particular, the difficulties in securing probative evidence for the purposes of domestic legal proceedings, inherent in such a troubled situation, may make pursuit of judicial remedies futile and the administrative inquiries on which such remedies depend may be prevented from taking place.[12]

Since there had been no previous successful action for compensation and given the vulnerability of the villagers, there was no reason to suppose the villagers should have tried to bring an action in the national courts. The Court then noted that the verification of facts is primarily a matter for the Commission and, although the Court is not bound by such findings, it would only be in exceptional circumstances, not applicable here, that the Court would deviate therefrom.

The Court found that the destruction of the applicants' homes and property constituted a grave interference with their right to respect for private life, family life and home under Article 8 and that there had been absolutely no justification for this interference. The Court noted the Commission's comments as regards Article 3 to the effect that the forced and immediate expulsion of the villagers in the circumstances of the case had led to physical and mental suffering and that this had been done with utter disregard for the safety and welfare of the applicants and their children, as it left them with no shelter and deprived them of their livelihood, possessions and homes. The Court, by contrast to its approach in *Selçuk and Asker* (Case No. 16), went no further in considering Article 3 in the light of the finding under Article 8. The boundary of what constitutes sufficiently severe treatment for the purposes of Article 3 is, however, discussed in a number of cases: Case No. 13 *Tekin*, Case No. 14 *Kurt*, Case No. 15 *Aydin*, and Case No. 16 *Selçuk and Asker*.[13]

As regards Article 6(1) and Article 13, the applicants did not dispute that rights theoretically existed under domestic law but argued that they were useless. In fact, the substance of the applicants' complaints was the lack of a proper investigation and was therefore an issue to be discussed under Article 13. The manner of investigation should be taken into account when assessing whether there had been an effective remedy and, in the Court's opinion, no thorough and effective investigation was conducted in this case. The issue of a

[11] See *Akdivar* v. *Turkey*, ECHR, judgment of 16 September 1996, paras. 65–9, and this *Year Book*, 68 (1997), p. 380. See also *Aksoy* v. *Turkey*, ECHR, judgment of 18 December 1996, paras. 51 –3, and this *Year Book*, 68 (1997), p. 397.

[12] Loc. cit. above (n. 11), para. 70.

[13] Contrast the position in *Raninen* v. *Finland*, ECHR, judgment of 16 December 1997, where the applicant was suffering from 'undefined psychological problems'; *Aerts* v. *Belgium*, ECHR, judgment of 30 July 1998, concerning detention in a prison psychiatric unit rather than in a medical facility; and also *Dalia* v. *France*, ECHR, judgment of 19 February 1998, in which the argument concerned the impact on a child of being deported with his mother.

proper investigation, or rather the lack thereof, was a constant theme in the cases brought against Turkey.

Right to parental leave allowance—right to family life—Article 8—discrimination—Article 14

Case No. 4. Petrovik case.[14] The Court held, in this case against Austria, that there had been no violation of Article 14 taken in conjunction with Article 8.

The applicant applied for a parental leave allowance so that he could look after his child, who had been born a couple of months previously, while his wife returned to her work. The application was turned down on the basis that, under the relevant Act, only mothers could claim such an allowance. He appealed, arguing that these provisions were discriminatory, unconstitutional and contrary to Article 8 of the Convention. The legislation was subsequently amended, allowing fathers to claim the allowance, but only in respect of children born after 31 December 1989. The Austrian Constitutional Court held that the changes in the law did not affect the applicant's position.

The Commission declared the application admissible and in its report expressed the opinion that there had been a violation of Article 14 taken in conjunction with Article 8.

The Court commenced by considering the applicability of Article 8, upon which the claim under Article 14 depended. The refusal to grant the applicant an allowance could not constitute a failure to respect family life, as Article 8 did not impose any positive obligation on States to provide such financial assistance. None the less, the allowance was intended to promote family life as it enabled one of the parents to stay at home and look after the children. By granting the allowance, the State was demonstrating its respect for family life and the provision therefore came within the scope of Article 8.

In this case it was not disputed that there had been a gender-based difference in treatment. The Court recalled, however, that contracting States enjoyed a certain margin of appreciation in assessing the extent to which situations deserved different treatment. The degree of the margin of appreciation depended on the circumstances, the subject matter and its background. In that respect, one relevant factor was the existence or lack of common ground between the States. In this field, there was no common approach. The parental allowance had been primarily aimed at mothers and society's opinions were only gradually adjusting towards a more equal sharing of childcare responsibilities between the sexes. It was therefore difficult to criticize the Austrian legislature for the approach it took to this question, as it reflects the gradual changes in society. Indeed, the Austrian legislation might be considered to have been very progressive. Given the wide disparity between the legal systems of the States as regards the position of fathers, the Government had in this case not exceeded its margin of appreciation. The question of the States' margin of appreciation (and the degree of consensus between contracting States) is of particular importance in Case No. 6 *Sheffield and Horsham*.

[14] ECHR, judgment of 27 March 1998.

Access to beach for the disabled—right to private life and personal development—Article 8—discrimination against the handicapped—Article 14

Case No. 5. *Botta* case.[15] In this case involving Italy, the Court found that neither Article 8 nor Article 14 was applicable.

The applicant was physically disabled, as was his friend. They went on holiday, but the resort was not equipped with facilities, such as special access ramps or bathing and washing facilities, so as to allow the applicant and his friend to go to the beach and sea. The lack of facilities was alleged to be in contravention of Italian legislation. The applicant complained, but the proceedings were discontinued as the judge had found no evidence of the relevant offence having been committed. The applicant complained that he had been subject to inhuman and degrading treatment (Article 3), had suffered restrictions on his right to liberty and security of person (Article 5(1)), had been the victim of discrimination (Articles 8 and 14), that his right to a fair trial had been infringed (Article 6(1)) and that there was no effective remedy (Article 13). The Commission declared the complaints on the first three issues admissible together with the facts underlying the complaints regarding the discrimination. The Commission the expressed the opinion in its report that there had been no violation of Article 8 either alone or in conjunction with Article 14.

This case is one of several in the period under review in which the States' positive obligations are considered. Depending on the interpretation given to Article 8 (and possibly also other articles), the States' obligations could be considerably widened. Here, the element of Article 8 in issue was the meaning of 'private life'. According to previous case law, this means 'a person's physical and psychological integrity', including the development of his personality.[16] In *X and Y*[17] the Court indicated the possibility of positive measures being required by such a definition, although this was not precisely defined. Indeed, as noted in the other cases in this area, States also enjoy a margin of appreciation. In this case, the Court noted that a State 'has obligations of this type where it has found a direct and immediate link between the measures sought by an applicant and the latter's private life'.[18] Thus in *Guerra* (Case No. 7), the toxic emissions from the factory had such a direct impact.[19] By contrast, the right asserted here 'concerns interpersonal relations of such broad and indeterminate scope that there can be no conceivable link between the measure the State was urged to take . . . and the applicant's private life'.[20] The Court therefore held that Article 8 was not applicable and that, because of the dependent nature of Article 14, that article was also inapplicable here. Although clearly boundaries have to be drawn limiting the obligations of States to provide facilities to allow individuals each to

[15] ECHR, judgment of 24 February 1998.

[16] See *Niemietz* v. *Germany*, Series A, No. 251–B, para. 29.

[17] *X and Y* v. *Netherlands*, Series A, No. 91, and this *Year Book*, 56 (1985), p. 344.

[18] Judgment, para. 34.

[19] See also *Airey* v. *Ireland*, Series A, No. 32, regarding legal aid in separation proceedings; *X and Y*, Series A, No. 91, and this *Year Book*, 56 (1985), p. 344, concerning the rape of a mentally handicapped person; and *Lopez Ostra* v. *Spain*, Series A, No. 303–C, and this *Year Book*, 66 (1995), p. 527, dealing with the harmful effects of pollution.

[20] Judgment, para. 34.

develop themselves, the position of specific groups who may be specifically disadvantaged, such as the disabled, needs to be considered carefully.[21]

Post-operative transsexual—no amendment to birth certificate possible—right to private life—Article 8

Case No. 6. Sheffield and Horsham case.[22] In this case against the UK, heard by a Grand Chamber, the Court held that there had been no violation of Article 8 and that no separate issue arose under Article 12. There had also been no violation of Article 14.

Both complaints were grounded in the fact that, under English law, it was not possible for a post-operative transsexual to have his or her birth certificate amended so as to reflect the transsexual's new gender. The applicants claimed that this caused them inconvenience and embarrassment. In numerous circumstances the first applicant had been required to reveal her former name and gender: when applying for a visa; standing surety for a friend; entering into insurance contracts. The second applicant had lived abroad since 1971, undergoing gender re-assignment surgery in 1992. That year she had requested that her birth certificate be amended, but this request was turned down in the light of domestic law. Further, she was informed that, as a matter of English law, she would not be regarded as married to her new partner, whether the marriage took place in the UK or elsewhere. This approach effectively precluded her from moving back to the UK.

The Commission declared the applications admissible as regards the majority of the applicants' complaints. In its report, the Commission took the view that there had been a violation of Article 8 but that there was no violation of Article 13 and no separate issues arose under Articles 12 or 14.

The main question in issue was whether the UK was in breach of any of its positive obligations under Article 8. The situation of transsexuals has been raised before the Court before[23] but, none the less, the meaning of 'respect' in this context was not clear cut, especially given the diversity of national practices. In determining the existence of a positive obligation, regard must be had to achieving a fair balance between the interests of the individual and those of the community.[24] In previous cases, the Court had held that the UK's approach did not constitute a failure to comply with its positive obligations under Article 8. The Court noted here that since its decision in *Rees* there have been no noteworthy scientific developments in this field that would compel the Court to depart from its previous case law.[25] In particular, the medical evidence referred to by the applicants as indicating such a change has not been universally

[21] Note that the Council of Europe Recommendation No. R (92) 6 urges States to guarantee rights to handicapped persons so as to ensure an independent and integrated life.

[22] ECHR, judgment of 30 July 1998.

[23] See, e.g., *Rees* v. *UK*, judgment of 17 October 1986, Series A, No. 106, and this *Year Book*, 57 (1986), p. 469; *Cossey* v. *UK*, judgment of 27 September 1990, Series A, No. 184, and this *Year Book*, 62 (1991), p. 467; *B* v. *France*, Series A, No. 232–C, and this *Year Book*, 63 (1992), p. 567; *X, Y and Z* v. *UK*, judgment of 22 April 1997, and this *Year Book*, 68 (1997), p. 404.

[24] See *Rees* judgment, loc. cit. above (n. 23), at para. 37, and *Cossey* judgment, loc. cit. above (n. 23).

[25] See *B* v. *France* and *Cossey* judgments, loc. cit. above (n. 23).

recognized. It should be noted however, as the dissenting judges pointed out, there has been a general acceptance of gender disphoria as a medical condition to the extent that the cost of surgery is in some places, including the UK, borne by the State. This constitutes in itself a change in attitude towards transsexuals. The Court did not consider this point, but stated that gender re-assignment surgery does not result in the acquisition of all biological characteristics of the new sex. Whether this is an appropriate criterion for determining the extent of the State's obligations is another question. None the less, the Court the concluded that:

> it continues to be the case that transsexualism raises complex scientific, legal, moral and social issues, in respect of which there is no generally shared approach among the Contracting States.[26]

In this context, Judges Bernhardt, Thór Vilhjálmsson, Spielmann, Palm, Wildhaber, Makarczyk and Voicu, in their partly dissenting joint opinion, disagreed with the degree of consensus needed. They referred to the judgment in *Marckx*,[27] suggesting that there had been no great degree of consensus throughout the contracting States regarding maternal affiliation when the Court gave judgment in that case.

The Court then considered whether the seriousness of the consequences would be sufficient to override the State's margin of appreciation. It observed that although the incidents referred to by the applicants might well be embarrassing and distressing, at the same time there were occasions when inquiries about gender might well be justified. The Court pointed out that life insurance contracts are *uberrimae fidei*; equally national authorities would need full details when checking for previous criminal records. The Court then noted that the occasions on which such inquires arose were infrequent and therefore could not be considered to impinge disproportionately into the applicants' private lives.[28] Finally, the UK had allowed the applicants to use their new identity on other documents, such as passports and driving licences, thus minimizing the interference with the applicants' private life. Having said this, the Court re-emphasized that the position needed to be kept under review and noted in this context that the legal position in the UK had not changed since the *Rees* decision.

One might question the Court's general approach here. By looking at the events complained of as a series of relatively insignificant, isolated events, the Court may have underestimated their cumulative impact. Indeed, in his dissenting opinion Judge Van Dijk characterized the issue in this way, noting that the applicants were not so much complaining about specific incidents, but rather of the continuous risk of having to reveal the pre-operative gender which had been abandoned deliberately and at great cost.

The Court moved on to consider the right to marry set out in Article 12. It confirmed that this right refers to the traditional conception of marriage between persons of the opposite biological sex; Article 12 makes it clear that it is concerned to protect marriage as the basis of the family. Furthermore, this right

[26] Judgment, para. 58, cross-referring *to X, Y and Z* v. *UK*, para. 52.

[27] *Marckx* v. *Belgium*, judgment of 13 June 1979, Series A, No. 31, at paras. 40–1.

[28] In his concurring opinion, Judge Sir John Freeland contrasted the position here with that in the case of *B* v. *France*, Series A, No. 232–C, and this *Year Book*, 63 (1992), p. 567.

is subject to national laws, although the very essence of the right must never be impaired by such laws. The legal impediment in the UK cannot be said to have this effect. The Court referred back to its judgment in *Cossey* and noted that it had held there that this traditional conception of marriage was sufficient reason for the continued use of the biological criteria for the determination of a person's sex. One might question if this is the conception of marriage that is commonly held, or is one that applies to all married couples. Consider, for example, the position of the infertile or those who choose not to have children. None the less, as Judges de Meyer, Valticos and Morenilla noted in their joint concurring opinions, even were medical science to progress to a point where all the physical attributes of the new gender were acquired, difficult legal, moral and ethical issues would remain, for example those arising out of previous marital and parental relationships.

The Court then noted that not every difference in treatment constituted a violation of Article 14. It must also be established that persons in analogous situations enjoyed preferential treatment with objective justification. The States enjoy a margin of appreciation in assessing this, as the Court noted in *Stubbings*.[29] The Court then commented that it had already been satisfied that a fair balance between the interests of the community and those of the applicants had been struck. These considerations applied also to the question of reasonable and objective justification for the purposes of Article 14, and therefore there had been no violation of this article.

Chemical factory—impact of pollution on health—failure of authorities to take steps or to inform local residents—Article 8—applicability of Article 10

Case No. 7. Guerra and others case.[30] In this case against Italy, the Court held by eighteen votes to two that Article 10 was not applicable. It found unanimously that Article 8 was applicable and that there had been a violation of that article, and that it was unnecessary to consider Article 2. Under Article 50, the Court awarded each of the applicants an amount in respect of non-pecuniary damage.

The applicants were residents of Manfredonia, approximately 1 km. away from a chemical factory. They claimed that the factory released large amounts of dangerous substances into the atmosphere and that accidents had occurred, the most serious resulting in 150 people being admitted to hospital with acute arsenic poisoning. In 1988, a committee of experts established that because of the factory's geographic position, emissions from it were channelled down into Manfredonia. It was noted in the experts' report that the emission treatment equipment at the factory was inadequate and the environmental-impact assessment incomplete. In 1989 the factory restricted production of some chemicals but continued to produce fertilizers and was still classified as a dangerous factory. In 1993, the Ministries for Environment and Health prescribed a number of improvements and provided the Prefect with an emergency plan and the measures for informing the local population of the improvements, although these

[29] *Stubbings* v. *UK*, ECHR, judgment of 22 October 1996, para. 72, and this *Year Book*, 68 (1997), p. 384.

[30] ECHR, judgment of 19 February 1998.

had still not been implemented by the time of the Commission's investigation. The factory permanently ceased fertilizer production in 1994, although a thermoelectric power station and a plant for waste treatment remained.

The applicants made a number of complaints to the Commission: the lack of practical measures to reduce the risk of accidents or pollution constituted an infringement of the right to respect for life (Article 2) and physical integrity (Article 8). They also argued that by not being informed of the dangers as required by domestic legislation, there had been a breach of the State's positive obligation under Article 10. The Commission declared the complaint under Article 10 admissible, declaring the remainder of the complaints inadmissible. It then suggested in its report that there had been a violation of Article 10.

One interesting issue in this case is the different characterization given to the issues by the Commission, the Court and, to a certain extent, the dissenting judges. In this context, the Court pointed out that it was not bound by the approach taken by others, whether this were that of the Commission, the applicants or the Government. A complaint would be characterized by the facts alleged and not by the legal grounds or arguments relied upon.[31] Here the grounds based on Articles 8 and 2 were not expressly set out in the application or in the proceedings lodged before the Commission, but they were closely linked with those pleaded. Given that the Commission had declared the complaint under Article 10, and the facts on which it was based, admissible, the Court held it had jurisdiction to consider Articles 8 and 2 as well as Article 10. Looking at the facts of the case, and the way the positive aspects of these rights were phrased, it is clear that there are close connections between these rights, if not potential overlap.

The Court first considered the applicability of Article 10. The Commission had argued that the existence of positive obligations under Article 10 as regards freedom of information had not been ruled out by the Court's previous case law. The Court disagreed with this. In the freedom of the press cases, the Court recognized that the public has the right to receive information as a corollary to the journalists' right to impart it. This could be distinguished from the present situation, which would impose on States a positive obligation to collect and disseminate information. Potentially, adopting the Commission's reasoning could create an onerous burden for States, especially as far as the obligation to collect information is concerned. Some judges,[32] although they concurred that there was no such obligation in the present case, did not rule out the possibility that States in some circumstances might be subject to such an obligation, though they did not identify when those circumstances would arise. Were this to happen, individuals (and pressure groups) would be given a powerful weapon for protecting their rights in this area.

The Court then went on to consider the position under Article 8. Given the direct effect of the toxins on the health of the people living in the area, it held that the right to respect for private and family life was applicable. Although Article 8 essentially protects individuals from arbitrary interference by public authorities, it does not merely compel States to abstain from such activities. Instead, the State may be under certain positive obligations inherent in the

[31] *Powell and Rayner* v. *UK*, Series A, No. 172.

[32] See opinion of Judges Palm, Bernhardt, Russo, Macdonald, Makarczyk and Van Dijk.

effective respect for private and family life.[33] The question is whether the authorities took the necessary steps to ensure this effective protection. The Court re-iterated that severe environmental pollution could affect individuals' well-being and prevent them from enjoying their homes in such a way as to affect their private and family life adversely. [34] In the instant case, the applicants had waited, right up until the production of fertilizers had ceased in 1994, for information that would have enabled them to assess the risks they and their families might run if they continued to live in Manfredonia. The Court consequently held that there had been a violation of Article 8.

Given this ruling, the Court held it unnecessary to consider Article 2. Judge Jambrek, in his concurring opinion, felt, however, that Article 2 was applicable[35] and that it was time to develop the case law on this article. Certainly, the scope of the States' obligations under that article to take steps to protect life (as opposed to refraining from taking it) is not clear. He suggested that a person's physical integrity had as close a link with the right to life as with respect for private and family life, arguing that

> [I]f information is withheld by a government about circumstances which foreseeably, and on substantial grounds, present a real risk of danger to health and physical integrity, then such a situation may also be protected by Article 2.[36]

This potentially far-reaching argument was also considered in *LCB* v. *UK* (Case No. 9).

Nuclear tests—impact on health—failure to disclose records—effective access to a tribunal—Article 6(1)—failure to comply with positive obligations—Article 8

Case No. 8. McGinley and Egan case.[37] In this case against the UK, the Court found by six votes to three, that there had been no violation of Article 6(1), and by five votes to four that there had been no violation of Article 8. Article 13 was not considered.

Between 1952 and 1967, the UK carried out atmospheric tests of nuclear weapons involving more than 20,000 servicemen near Christmas Island. No records exist of the servicemen's exposure to radiation, although the Government argued that experience from other tests had shown that the individuals involved had not been exposed to measurable levels of radiation. Some Government documents existed but were not produced. A summary of the surviving data was, however, published as a technical note in 1993.

Both applicants were in the Christmas Island area during the tests and claimed to have become ill as a consequence, although no contemporary medical records existed. Subsequently both were treated for various illnesses and discharged from military service. Both men continued to suffer ill health and

[33] Judgment, para. 58. See also *Airey* v. *Ireland*, Series A, No. 32.

[34] See *Lopez Ostra* v. *Spain*, Series A, No. 303–C.

[35] Judge Walsh expressed the view that there had been a violation of Article 2.

[36] The lack of a real risk was fatal to the applicants' claims in *Balmer-Schafroth* v. *Switzerland*, ECHR, judgment of 26 August 1997. There, however, the claim concerned Article 6(1) and the issue was whether the applicants had a civil right under domestic law.

[37] ECHR, judgment of 9 June 1998.

sought military pensions on this basis. The Department of Social Security investigated the claims, contacting the Ministry of Defence (MoD), which stated that the area in which the applicants had been had not been exposed to radiation. On this basis the applicants' claims were turned down. On appeal, the MoD's assurances in this respect were included with the medical evidence in the statement of case submitted to the Pensions Appeal Tribunal (PAT). The PAT disallowed both appeals in February 1988.

The Commission declared the applications admissible in so far as they related to the non-disclosure of records. The claims under Articles 2 and 3 were declared inadmissible. The Commission then evaluated the evidence, taking into account the clarity and completeness of the parties' responses to requests,[38] and finding the Government's arguments unconvincing. It commented that 'there is a co-existence of sufficiently strong, clear and consistent inferences allowing it to establish that radiation level records were created, are stored at the AWE Aldermaston and have not been released as yet into the public domain'.[39] Having established the facts, the Commission drew up a report in which it expressed the opinion that there had been a violation of Article 6(1) and a failure to fulfil the positive obligation of respect under Article 8.

The essence of the applicants' claim was that, because of the non-disclosure of portions of their medical records and the records of the radiation levels on Christmas Island, they had been denied effective access to a court in breach of Article 6(1) in relation to their pension applications. To succeed in their claims, the applicants needed to raise a reasonable possibility of the link between the tests and their illnesses; that is, they needed to challenge the MoD's statements. The Court noted that the applicants had, however, not proved the existence of the relevant documents and, moreover, had not requested that the PAT make a disclosure request, which it had the power to do. Where a procedure existed for the disclosure of documents and the applicants failed to utilize it, the State could not be said to have prevented the applicants from gaining access to or falsely denied the existence of relevant evidence. There was therefore no breach of Article 6(1).

The Court noted that, given their role and the absence of individual monitoring, the applicants were left in doubt as to the impact of the tests on their health, which was sufficiently closely linked to their private and family life to bring them within the scope of Article 8.[40] As in *Guerra* (Case No. 7), the question of Article 2 and the right to life was not considered, although they clearly are related issues. In determining whether a positive obligation under Article 8 existed, the Court had regard to the fair balance between the individual and the community in general. The Court distinguished this case from the *Guerra* case. In that case the risk was undisputed; here there was no documentary evidence substantiating the applicants' claims. Given the applicants' interest in obtaining access to the relevant material, however, and the fact that the Government stated that there was no pressing national security reason why they should not have access thereto, the Court held that a positive obligation under Article 8 still arose. Hazardous Government activities required effective

[38] See *Ireland* v. *UK*, Series A, No. 25.

[39] Opinion, para. 96. See *Ireland* v. *UK*, Series A, No. 25.

[40] See also the Commission's assessment: Commission opinion, para. 88.

and accessible procedures for individuals to seek relevant material. Despite this finding, the applicants' failure to use the disclosure mechanism was fatal to their claim. The Court, distinguishing the case from that of *Gaskin*,[41] therefore held that there was no violation of Article 8.

Four judges dissented from this approach. Judges De Meyer, Valticos and Morenilla focused on the obligations of the State given the serious nature of radiation, arguing that if there were no medical records then there should have been. The question of the need to monitor is also touched on in *LCB* v. *UK* (Case No. 9). Further, the disclosure mechanism was felt to be insufficient to satisfy the positive obligations under both Articles 6 and 8. Indeed, given the lack of candour in the MoD's approach noted by the Commission and the lack of records available, one might question how much use the disclosure order would have been. Judge Pekkanen noted that the absence of records distinguished the case from *Guerra*, but held that this did not remove the applicants' need for an effective and accessible procedure to obtain the information.

Nuclear testing—failure to advise as to potential impact—Article 2

Case No. 9. LCB case.[42] In this case involving the UK, the Court held unanimously that it had no jurisdiction in relation to the claim under Article 2 as regards the monitoring of the applicant's father and that there had been no violation thereof in respect of the failure to inform the applicant's parents. It further unanimously held that there had been no violation of Article 3. The Court held it had no jurisdiction in relation to the claim under Article 8 regarding contemporary records and it did not consider the other claims under Article 8.

The applicant's father was present at the Christmas Island tests detailed in relation to *McGinley and Egan* (Case No. 8). He was also involved in the subsequent clean-up operation. Again the servicemen were not individually monitored for radiation exposure. The applicant was born in 1966 and diagnosed with leukaemia in 1970. She argued that as a result of not being advised of her father's exposure to radiation, pre- and post-natal monitoring, which would have led to the earlier diagnosis and treatment of her illness, possibly improving her overall prognosis, was not carried out. She consequently argued that there had been violations of Articles 2, 3, 8 and 13. The Commission declared the complaints admissible as regards Articles 2 and 3 regarding the failure to advise and inform the applicant's parents about the exposure to radiation, and subsequently expressed the unanimous opinion that there had been no violation of those articles.

By contrast to the other cases, the Court considered this claim primarily under Article 2, rather than Article 8. Article 2(1) requires States to take appropriate steps to safeguard those within its jurisdiction.[43] Did the UK do all it should to prevent the applicant's life being put at risk? In the light of the lack of information regarding individual radiation doses, it was uncertain whether the

[41] *Gaskin* v. *UK*, Series A, No. 160, and this *Year Book*, 60 (1989), p. 549.
[42] ECHR, judgment of 9 June 1998.
[43] Contrast the reasoning in *Guerra* (Case No. 7).

applicant's father had been exposed to dangerous levels of radiation. In itself, this failure to monitor could raise questions as to whether the UK had done all it should. As the applicant had not raised the issue of the failure to monitor her father before the Commission, the Court could not consider the issue. In any event, these events pre-dated the UK's acceptance of the right of individual petition. From the information available, there was no evidence to show that the applicant's father reported any symptoms indicative of having been exposed to radiation. To the contrary, the records available from the date the UK accepted the right of individual petition and the date of LCB's diagnosis indicated that the UK authorities could reasonably have been confident that the applicant's father had not been dangerously irradiated. The Court suggested that, given that it seemed unlikely that the exposure of the father had engendered a real risk to health, the authorities were not obliged to provide advice to and monitor the health of his family. Since the Court was not satisfied that any causal link between the applicant's illness and her father's presence at the nuclear tests had been demonstrated in this case, it held that there had been no violation of Article 2. It seems implicit in this reasoning, however, that where there is a causal link then the State will be under an obligation to monitor individuals affected and to provide information to their families.

This is only one of a series of cases involving Article 2: see, for example, Case No. 10 *Andronicou and Constantinou*, Case No. 11 *Ergi* and Case No. 12 *Kaya*. These latter cases involve rather more direct action on the part of the State.

Article 2—accidental killing during police operation—level of planning—Article 6(1)—provision of legal aid

Case No. 10. Andronicou and Constantinou case.[44] In this case against Cyprus, the Court found by five votes to four that there had been no violation of Article 2 and unanimously found that there had been no violation of Article 6(1) regarding the provision of a legal aid scheme.

Following a quarrel between a couple, the woman involved was taken hostage by her partner. She claimed to have been beaten and that her fiancé had a gun. Attempts to secure the release of the woman were unsuccessful and the Police Special Forces were consequently involved. It was decided that, as it seemed likely that the man intended to kill his partner and then commit suicide around midnight, it would be necessary to storm the flat. The officers were told to use proportionate force and to fire only if either their own life or that of the woman were in danger. During the raid, one of the police officers was shot, triggering two of the other officers involved to start firing their automatic weapons. The man was killed in the flat and the woman died later in hospital. The families of the couple requested an investigation into the incident, which found that the rescue operation had been flawed. The inquiry also found, however, that the negotiations were conducted in the best manner possible under the circumstances, and that it was reasonable to assume that the man intended to stick by

[44] ECHR, judgment of 9 October 1997.

his midnight deadline. Given the findings of the inquiry, no criminal proceedings were instituted. The Government did, however, offer the applicants an *ex gratia* payment.

The applicants claimed that the killing of the couple was a violation of the right to life contained in Article 2 of the Convention. The Commission expressed the opinion that there had been a violation of Article 2 but that there had been no violation of Article 6(1).

The Government raised a preliminary objection, arguing that as the applicants had not instituted a civil action for compensation regarding the deaths, they had not exhausted their domestic remedies as required by Article 26. The Court noted that, given the results of the inquiry into the deaths, there was little likelihood that any such action would be successful. The Court therefore dismissed the objection.[45] The Government also argued that the application was an abuse of process. The Court disagreed, holding that:

> . . . an applicant's refusal either to enter into or continue negotiations with the authorities of a respondent State on the terms of a friendly settlement over an alleged abuse of a right guaranteed under the Convention cannot be construed as an abuse of the right of individual petition.[46]

Turning to the merits of the claim under Article 2, the Court began by re-stating the general principles in the application of Article 2. The right to life is one of the fundamental principles enshrined in the Convention; it admits of no derogation under Article 15 and any of the exceptions contained in Article 2(2) must be construed strictly. In particular, the reference to 'absolutely necessary' in Article 2(2) is a much stricter test that the 'necessary in a democratic society' requirement found, for example, in Article 8(2). In determining such an issue, all the circumstances surrounding the planning and control of the operation must be taken into account.[47]

The Court considered the planning and control of the rescue operation to identify whether the operation as a whole was managed so as to minimize the risk to the couple. The Court noted that it was not

> . . . appropriate to discuss with the benefit of hindsight the merits of alternative tactics . . . It is to be noted that alternative strategies were discussed and analysed before the domestic Commission of Inquiry and expert opinion differed as to their suitability in the circumstances.[48]

The Court balanced the various factors, such as the fact that this was a young couple rather than a pair of hardened criminals, against the knowledge that the man was armed and the fact that there had been a swift deterioration of the situation inside the flat. It concluded that it had not been shown that the rescue operation had not been planned and organized in such a way which minimized the risk to the couple to the greatest extent possible. Although judging actions with the benefits of hindsight is dangerous, one might question whether some

[45] The dissenting judges thought that it was improper to rely on *A* v. *France* (Series A, No. 277–B), as in this case the applicants had made no attempt to bring an action. The Cypriot courts therefore had no chance to rule on this issue, but their decision was pre-judged.

[46] Judgment, para. 165.

[47] See *McCann and others* v. *UK*, Series A, No. 324, and this *Year Book*, 67 (1996), p. 609.

[48] Judgment, para. 181.

unnecessary risks were not taken in this case. The dissenting judges suggested that in the circumstances arming a crack force with automatic weapons and sending them into a dark room was not an appropriate way to proceed.

Death of applicant's sister—Article 2—no investigation—Article 13—interview by authorities regarding application to Commission—Article 25

Case No. 11. Ergi case.[49] This case involved Turkey. The Court found unanimously that there had been a violation of Articles 2, 13 and 25. It did not examine Article 8 and found there had been no violation of Articles 14 and 18.

In 1993 the applicant's sister was killed while she was standing in a doorway leading on to the balcony of her house. The applicant claimed that this was an attack on the village by the security forces as a reprisal for the killing by the PKK of a villager who had 'collaborated' with the Government. The Government argued that the woman was caught in the crossfire resulting from an ambush of the PKK by the security forces. There was a brief investigation of the matter, but then the public prosecutor decided that, as it seemed likely that the bullet had been fired by a member of the PKK, the matter fell outside his jurisdiction. The matter was then referred to the National Security Court, where the case was at the time of judgment still pending. On 30 October and 3 November 1995, while this application was pending before the Court, the applicant was questioned by the anti-terrorist department of the police and by a public prosecutor concerning his legal aid application.

The Commission declared the application admissible. It heard evidence in the presence of the representatives of the parties. In its report, in which it established the facts, it expressed the opinion that there had been a violation of Article 2, but did not consider that any separate issue arose under Articles 8 or 13. It found no violation of Articles 14 or 18, but took the view that there had been a breach of Article 25.

The Court agreed with the Commission that there was insufficient evidence to show that the security forces shot the applicant's sister intentionally. None the less, under Article 2, States can be obliged to take steps to 'secure' an effective enjoyment of the right to life. This responsibility could also be engaged when agents of the State failed to take all reasonable precautions to minimize, if not avoid, incidental loss of civilian life. The Court considered that there had been real risk to the lives of the civilian population arising out of the crossfire between the PKK and the security forces. Since the Turkish authorities adduced no evidence as to the planning and conduct of the ambush, the Court agreed with the Commission that it could reasonably have been inferred that insufficient precautions had been taken.[50] Article 2 also requires a thorough and effective investigation, which is triggered by the mere knowledge of the occurrence of the killing. As in many of the cases involving Turkey, the authorities had not satisfied the obligation here. Thus, this also constituted a breach of Article 2.

[49] ECHR, judgment of 28 July 1998.

[50] Contrast Case No. 10 *Andronicou and Constantinou*.

As regards Article 13, the Court re-affirmed its case law on the need for an effective remedy where there was an arguable claim that there had been a violation of the Convention. The Court referred back to its findings regarding the investigation, and noted that failure to carry out a thorough investigation undermined any exercise of remedies available. There was thus a violation of Article 13. On the facts of the case, the Court did not find that the claims under Articles 14 or 18 were substantiated.

The Court then considered the fact that the applicant had been asked about the substance of his application and to provide an explanation for his application. The Court commented that there was no plausible excuse as to why he had been seen twice by the authorities concerned. The Court concluded that the applicant must consequently have felt intimidated, which must have interfered with his right of individual petition. The Court therefore held that the Turkish Government had not complied with its obligations under Article 25(1).

Right to life—effective investigation into circumstances of death—Article 2

Case No. 12. Kaya case.[51] The Court in this case involving Turkey unanimously held that there had been no violation of Article 2 in respect of the death of the applicant's brother. It further found, however, by eight votes to one, that there had been a violation of both Articles 2 and 13 in respect of the investigation of that death. The Court awarded the applicant an amount in compensation together with an amount for costs and expenses.

The applicant's brother was killed on 25 March 1993. The facts surrounding this death were disputed. The applicant claimed his brother was shot whilst unarmed by Turkish forces and that an assault rifle was planted on his body. The Government claimed that the body was found after a gun battle between the security forces and the PKK. That day a district government doctor and the public prosecutor for the region were flown to the scene of the incident. The doctor examined the body externally but concluded that a full autopsy was unnecessary. The public prosecutor initiated a preliminary investigation but then issued a decision of non-jurisdiction and transferred the matter to the State Security Court, where the matter was, at the time of this judgment, still pending.

The Commission declared the complaint admissible. In its report it expressed the opinion that it had not been established beyond reasonable doubt that the applicant's brother had been killed by security forces. It further opined that there had, however, been a violation of Article 2 and of Article 6(1) regarding the investigation. It expressed the opinion that there had been no violation of Articles 3 or 14 and that there was no separate issue under Article 13.

The Court referred to its earlier case law to the effect that determining questions of fact should primarily be a matter for the Commission. Here the Court agreed with the Commission's assessment of the facts and therefore held that there had been no violation of Article 2 as regards the death of the applicant's brother. As with the other cases concerning Article 2 under review this year, the Court noted that Article 2 additionally required the effective

[51] ECHR, judgment of 19 February 1998.

investigation of such a death. The prohibition on arbitrary killing would otherwise be ineffective, as in practice there would be no procedure for holding the authorities accountable. Even had this case concerned a clear case of a lawful killing, the investigation carried out would have been insufficient. As it was, there were uncertainties surrounding the death of the applicant's brother. In particular, the public prosecutor had taken it for granted that the applicant's brother was a terrorist killed whilst attacking security forces and took no concrete steps to find confirmatory evidence at the scene of the incident.

The applicant did not initiate legal proceedings for compensation because he believed he stood little chance of success. The Court took the view that his complaint under Article 6(1) was linked more to the complaint concerning Article 13. In this context, the Court noted that the nature of the right, the right to life, must have implications for the remedies available to the relatives. In particular, in addition to a right to compensation, it requires a thorough and effective investigation, which allows the relatives access to the procedure. These requirements are thus broader than those under Article 2. As noted above, the authorities had failed to carry out an effective investigation. The applicant was consequently denied an effective remedy in violation of Article 13. The applicant's other claims the Court found to be unsubstantiated.

Ill-treatment in police custody—Article 3—failure to investigate—Article 13

Case No. 13. Tekin case.[52] The Court held unanimously that in this case involving Turkey there had been no violation of Articles 2, 10, 14 and 18 but, by six votes to three, that there had been a breach of Article 3 and, by seven votes to two, of Article 13. The Court further held that it was not necessary to consider the complaints under Articles 5(1) and 6(1). The Court awarded a sum for non-pecuniary damage together with an amount for costs and expenses.

The applicant, a journalist, was arrested on suspicion of threatening village guards. According to the applicant, this happened on 15 February 1993, and to the Government, on 17 February. The applicant was taken to the gendarme station where, according to the applicant, he was kept in freezing conditions, interrogated whilst blindfolded, threatened with death and beaten by police officers. The applicant was then transferred on 19 February to the gendarme headquarters where he was allegedly tortured. On the same day he was taken before a public prosecutor, to whom he complained of ill-treatment. The prosecutor took no action. In December 1993, after the Commission had communicated his application to the Government, an investigation was commenced into the applicant's allegation, although this produced insufficient evidence to charge any of the officers involved.

The Commission declared the application admissible. It established the facts and, in its report, set forth the view that there had been a violation of Articles 3 and 13, that there had been no violation of Articles 2, 10, 14 and 18, and that it was not necessary to examine the other complaints.

The Government disputed the facts as established by the Commission, but the Court found it had been proved beyond reasonable doubt that the applicant

[52] ECHR, judgment of 9 June 1998.

had been treated as claimed. The Court noted in this context that the Commission had sent a delegation to Ankara to hear oral evidence. Although there was no independent evidence of the treatment that the applicant alleged he had suffered, the Court noted that the authorities had taken no steps to have him seen by a doctor despite his complaints to the public prosecutor. Further, those who had seen the applicant on his release had failed without good cause to attend the Commission's hearings. Given the obligations of the States under Article 28(1)(*a*) to 'furnish all necessary facilities', the respondent State, having failed to ensure the attendance of key witnesses, could hardly complain of the Commission's findings.

The Court did not find on the evidence that the applicant had been treated in such a way as to constitute a violation of his right to life. The Court, however, did find that the conditions in which the applicant was held and manner in which he was treated so as to leave wounds and bruises on his body constituted inhuman and degrading treatment contrary to Article 3. Further, the investigation into the complaints was not sufficiently thorough and effective to satisfy the requirements of Article 13. The Court did not, however, find the other claims substantiated.

Disappearance of family member—failure to act—Article 5—Article 3—Article 13—subsequent repudiation of petition—Article 25(1)

Case No. 14. Kurt case.[53] In this case against Turkey, the Court held, after unanimously dismissing of the Government's two preliminary objections, that there had been a violation of Article 5 (by six votes to three). The Court unanimously found that it was not necessary to decide on the applicant's complaint under Articles 2 and 3 in respect of her son but found, by six votes to three, that there had been a violation of Article 3 in respect of the applicant herself. Further, the Court found, by seven votes to two, that there had been a violation of Article 13. It unanimously held that there had been no violation of Articles and 14 and 18 but held, by six votes to three, that the State had failed to comply with its obligations under Article 25(1). The Court made an award under Article 50 for compensation in respect of non-pecuniary damage and for legal costs and expenses.

Following an operation carried out by security forces, which resulted in clashes with suspected terrorists, the applicant's son disappeared. The circumstances surrounding the disappearance were in dispute. The applicant claimed that she last saw her son in the custody of soldiers and village guards. She further claimed that he appeared to have been beaten. According to the Government, however, the applicant's son was never taken into custody and there were strong grounds for believing that he had either left the village during the operation to join the PKK or had been kidnapped by the PKK. Mrs Kurt's attempts to trace her son were unsuccessful. The district gendarme merely stated that her son had not been taken into custody. The public prosecutor issued a decision of non-jurisdiction on the grounds that the crime had been committed by the PKK. Further, the applicant claimed that since lodging her

[53] ECHR, judgment of 25 May 1998.

application with the Commission, she and her lawyer had been the target of a campaign by the authorities to make them withdraw the complaint. This the Government denied. To the contrary, it questioned whether she truly intended to bring an application and asserted that the applicant had been manipulated for political purposes by elements hostile to the State.

Having established the facts, the Commission adopted a report in which it expressed the opinion that there had been a violation of Article 5 regarding the applicant's son; that there had been a violation of Article 3 in respect the applicant; that it was not necessary to examine the complaints made under Articles 2 and 3 in relation to the applicant's son; that there had been a violation of Article 13 but that there had been no violation of Articles 14 and 18. Further, the Commission unanimously felt that Turkey had failed to comply with its obligations under Article 25(1).

Having regard to its own assessment of the evidence, the Court found that there were no exceptional circumstances which would justify its departure from the Commission's finding that the applicant had last seen her son surrounded by members of the security forces. The Court then held that, in the absence of concrete proof, the inference should not be drawn that the applicant's son met his death at the hands of the authorities. The Court also concluded that it was not necessary to decide whether the authorities had failed to protect his life, as it felt that the issues raised by the applicant in this context ought to be assessed from the standpoint of Article 5. It took a similar approach with regard to the applicant's claim under Article 3. Note, however, in this context that Judge Walsh in his dissenting opinion in *Brogan*[54] commented that

> [p]rolonged and sustained interrogation over periods of days, particularly without judicial intervention, could fall into the category of inhuman or degrading treatment.

As regards Article 5, the Court noted that the authorities are under a responsibility, once they have assumed control over an individual, to account for that individual's whereabouts. For this reason, Article 5 must be seen as requiring the authorities to take effective measures to safeguard against the risk of disappearance and, further, to conduct a prompt, effective investigation into an arguable claim that a person has been taken into custody and has not been seen since. The Court further noted that the detention of the applicant was never logged. That fact alone had to be considered a most serious failing as it enabled those responsible to conceal their involvement in a crime and thereby escape accountability for the fate of the detainee. The Court took the view that the absence of holding data was incompatible with the fundamental purpose of Article 5. Furthermore, in this case, the public prosecutor gave no real consideration to the merits of the applicant's complaint. Indeed, the Court felt that the authorities had failed to offer any credible or substantiated explanation of the whereabouts and the fate of the applicant's son after he was detained. The Court held that it must be accepted that he was in unacknowledged detention in the complete absence of the safeguards contained in Article 5. This, according to Court, gave rise to a particularly grave violation of the right to liberty and security of the person guaranteed thereby.

[54] *Brogan* v. *UK*, Series A, No. 145–B.

The applicant further contended that she had been the victim of inhuman and degrading treatment given the failure of the authorities to account for her son's disappearance. The Court noted that as a result of this failure, the applicant had endured over a prolonged period of time the anguish of knowing that her son had been detained but with no official information as to his subsequent fate. The Court thus found that there had been a violation of Article 3. This case differs from others in that the treatment at the base of the complaint was not aimed at the applicant but rather at her son. This re-emphasizes that the Court will consider the effects on the complainant in determining what behaviour is contrary to Article 3; here, intention on the part of the authorities is not a necessary element for the finding of a violation. Further, the ill-treatment complained of need not be physical.

Where there is an arguable claim that a relative has disappeared at the hands of the authorities, the notion of an effective remedy for the purposes of Article 13 entails, in addition to the payment of compensation where appropriate, a thorough and effective investigation capable of leading to the identification and punishment of those responsible. It includes effective access by the relatives to investigative procedure. On that understanding, given that the applicant's complaint was never given serious consideration, there had been a violation of Article 13.

The applicant had suggested that she had been subjected to pressure by the authorities to withdraw her application. The Court noted in this context that the applicant was interviewed on several occasions by the authorities after her application had been communicated by the Commission to the Government. In the wake of these interviews, she made statements repudiating all petitions made in her name. The Court was not persuaded that those statements were made on the initiative of the applicant. Furthermore, the Court found it noteworthy that when the applicant visited the notary for the purpose repudiating her petition, she was accompanied by a uniformed soldier and was not to required to pay the notary. The circumstances therefore suggested that the applicant was subjected to indirect and improper pressure to make statements in respect of her application and that this interfered with the free exercise of her right of individual petition guaranteed by Article 25. Further, although there was no follow-up to the threat to prosecute the applicant's lawyer, the threat to bring criminal proceedings against the lawyer must in itself be considered an interference with the exercise of the applicant's right of individual petition. For these reasons, the Court found that the State had failed to comply with its obligations under Article 25.

Ill-treatment by security forces whilst in custody—Article 3—failure to investigate—Article 13

Case No. 15. Aydin case.[55] In this case against Turkey, the Court found that there had been a breach of Articles 3 and 13. It also found that there had been no violation of Article 25 (1) and it did not consider the issues under Articles 6,

[55] ECHR, judgment of 25 September 1997.

28 or 53. The Court, under Article 50, awarded the sum of £25,000 plus costs.

The facts of the case were disputed. The applicant, aged 17, claimed that guards arrived in the village and questioned her family about the visits of the PKK. The applicant, her sister-in-law and father were driven away to the security force's headquarters. They were blindfolded. The applicant claimed she was separated from the other two and taken to a room where she was stripped, put in a tyre and spun round. She was then beaten and sprayed with cold water from high pressure jets. Subsequently she was raped and again beaten. The applicant was as a result in severe pain and covered in blood. The Government challenged this version of events on the basis that the applicant's details were not entered into the custody register and therefore she could not have been detained as she claimed.

On their release, the applicant and her family filed a complaint about this treatment. The public prosecutor took statements and sent the applicant and her family for a medical examination, which confirmed that the applicant had lost her virginity and that all three had wounds. The public prosecutor carried out some further inquiries, but the applicant's complaint was then declared inadmissible. The applicant also alleged that she and her family had been subject to harassment. The Government claimed the attention they received was no more than was necessary to investigate the complaint.

The application was declared admissible and in its report the Commission expressed the opinion that there had been a violation of Articles 3 and 6(1). It found that there was no separate issue under Article 13 and that there was a failure by Turkey to comply with Article 25. The Commission also had to make an evaluation as to the facts of the case. In the Commission's opinion, although there were inconsistencies in the applicant's evidence, these did not adversely affect her credibility.

As regards Article 3, the Court accepted the Commission's finding as to the facts. The Commission had applied the evidentiary test set out in *Ireland* v. *UK*:[56] that is, that the claim be proved beyond a reasonable doubt. It would be only in exceptional circumstances that the Court would substitute its judgment on the facts and here, reasonable doubt had been satisfied. Article 3 enshrines one of the fundamental values of the Convention and is expressed in absolute terms; it admits of no exceptions, not even under Article 15.[57] The Court then noted the distinction in Article 3 between 'torture' and 'inhuman or degrading treatment'. Torture is only applied to deliberate treatment causing very serious mental suffering.[58] This clearly constituted such a case. The Court felt that

> rape of a detainee by an official of the state must be considered to be an especially grave and abhorrent form of ill treatment given the ease with which the defendant can exploit the vulnerability and weakened resistance of his victim. Furthermore, rape leaves deep psychological scars on the victim which do not respond to the passage of time as quickly as other forms of physical and mental violence.[59]

[56] *Ireland* v. *UK*, judgment of 18 January 1978, Series A, No. 25.

[57] In circumstances where the State has been experiencing internal difficulties, the Court has been willing to be more flexible about what level of behaviour constitutes a violation of Article 3, but this has limits: see *Ireland* v. *UK*, loc. cit. above (n. 56), at para. 207.

[58] *Ireland* v. *UK*, judgment of 18 January 1978, Series A, No. 25.

[59] Judgment, para. 83.

The Court also referred to the pain the applicant had suffered and noted that she was 'debased and violated both physically and emotionally'. The accumulation of physical and mental violence, especially the rape, constituted torture. Indeed, the Court noted that any one of these incidents separately would constitute torture.[60]

The Court also considered whether the applicant had had effective access to the courts. The essence of the complaint was the failure of the public prosecutor to conduct an effective investigation which would have enhanced her prospects of a successful claim for compensation. This was more a question of an effective remedy than of access to the courts themselves. Given the nature of the allegations, Article 3 in conjunction with Article 13 imposes, without prejudice to other remedies, an obligation on States to carry out a thorough and effective investigation leading to the punishment of the individuals concerned. In this there are similarities to the obligations on authorities to conduct effective investigations where there has been an allegation of a violation of Article 2. The obligation in this case fell on the public prosecutor. The investigation was not, however, thorough. In particular, the medical examination focused on whether the applicant had lost her virginity, not on whether there was evidence of rape. For the Court, an allegation of rape whilst in custody would require the victim to be examined with all appropriate sensitivity by experienced, independent doctors. The examination in this case was clearly insufficient.

Finally, the Court noted that, by contrast to the position in *Kurt* (Case No. 14), there was insufficient evidence to substantiate the applicant's allegations under Article 25. Further, it was unnecessary to consider Articles 28 and 53.

Burning of property—inhuman treatment—Article 3—right to respect for private and family life and homes—Article 8—interference with peaceful enjoyment of property—Protocol 1, Article 1—lack of proper investigation—Article 13

Case No. 16. Selçuk and Asker case.[61] In this case against Turkey, the Court rejected the Government's preliminary objections and found, by eight votes to one, that there had been violations of Articles 3, 8 and 13 and of Protocol 1, Article 1. It unanimously found that there had been no violation of Articles 14 or 18. Under Article 50, the Court awarded the applicants a sum for damages together with costs and expenses.

Until June 1993, both applicants lived in Islamkoy, a village in the province of Diyarbakir. They alleged that on 16 June soldiers came to the village and burnt their homes. Ten days later the soldiers allegedly returned and burnt a mill partly owned by one of the applicants. The other applicant claimed that he submitted a petition to the District Governor in which he named the officer in charge and listed the property destroyed. The Government denied this. Following the communication of the applications by the Commission to the Government, an investigation was opened and statements were taken from the applicants. Thereafter, the investigation was transferred to the Kulp District Administrative Council.

[60] Judgment, para. 86.
[61] ECHR, judgment of 24 April 1998.

The Commission declared the applications admissible. It conducted an investigation into the facts and then adopted a report in which it expressed the opinion that there had been violations of Articles 3, 6(1), 8 and 13 and of Protocol 1, Article 1. It further expressed the opinion that there had been no violation of Articles 2, 5, 14 and 18.

Despite the Government's challenge to the Commission's finding as to the facts, the Court saw no reason to depart from the Commission's assessment, which it found to be proved beyond reasonable doubt. The Court also rejected the Government's preliminary objection that the applications were not valid, as the Court found no reason to doubt that these were valid and genuine expressions of the right of individual petition. The Court also concluded, given the extremely limited nature of the current investigation into the affair, that special circumstances existed which dispensed with the need for exhausting national remedies.[62]

The Court noted that the applicants, who were 54 and 60 at the time of the incident, had lived in Islamkoy all their lives. Their homes and most of their property were destroyed by the security forces, depriving them of their livelihood and forcing them to leave the village. The facts indicated that the attack was premeditated and carried out contemptuously, without regard to the feelings of the applicants. The applicants were taken unprepared and forced to watch the destruction of their property. Further, inadequate safeguards were taken to secure their safety and no assistance was offered to them afterwards. Taking into account the manner of the attack and the applicants' personal circumstances, the Court held it was clear that the applicants must have been caused suffering of sufficient severity to constitute inhuman treatment within Article 3.

As the claims under Articles 2 and 5 were not pursued by the applicants, the Court went on to consider the issues under Article 8 and Protocol 1, Article 1. Clearly the destruction of their homes, which obliged the applicants to leave Islamkoy, constituted a grave and unjustified interference with the applicants' right to respect for their private and family lives and homes and to the peaceful enjoyment of their possessions for which there was no justification. The Court therefore found violations of Article 8 and Protocol 1, Article 1.

Essentially, the applicants' complaint related to the lack of a proper investigation so the Court considered this issue under Article 13 rather than Article 6(1). The Court noted that, despite one of the applicant's petition to the Governor, it was not until the Convention institutions became involved that any investigation on this issue was set up. This investigation did not, however, even involve the interviewing of the officer named in the petition to the Governor. Further, no attempt was made to question the other villagers. The court was not provided with any information indicating any action by the Administrative Council following the transfer of investigation to it. The State could not be said to have carried out an effective and thorough investigation. Therefore there had been a violation of Article 13.

[62] See also, e.g., *Akdivar and others* v. *Turkey*, judgment of 16 September 1996, and this *Year Book*, 68 (1997), p. 380.

Retrospective legislation—loss of right of action—right to a court—Article 6(1)—Protocol 1, Article 1

Case No. 17. National and Provincial Building Society, Leeds Permanent Building Society and Yorkshire Building Society case.[63] In this case involving the UK, the Court held unanimously that there had been no violation of either Article 6(1) or Protocol 1, Article 1. It further held by eight votes to one that there had been no violation of either of these articles in conjunction with Article 14.

Transitional regulations were introduced covering a 'gap' between two accounting periods which resulted from a change in the tax system. The applicants claimed that this rendered them liable to pay tax in respect of a period for which their tax bill had already been fully discharged. After an action for judicial review, the regulations were found to be invalid. The applicants then commenced in 1991 an action for restitution and for judicial review of certain Treasury orders. The invalidated regulations were subsequently retroactively validated by section 53 of the Finance Act 1991, save that it did not apply to those building societies which had commenced their action for restitution prior to 18 July 1986, in effect only the Woolwich Building Society. Further, section 62 of the Finance (No. 2) Act 1992 provided that the challenged orders had always been effective, thus extinguishing the remaining proceedings lodged by the applicants.

The Commission declared the application admissible. In its report it suggested that there had been a violation of Article 6(1). The violation of Article 6(1) in conjunction with Article 14 was not examined. The Commission also found no violation of Protocol 1, Article 1, either alone or in conjunction with Article 14.

The Court noted the weakness of the applicants' claims to have had possessions within the meaning of Article 1, Protocol 1. As their claims were based on the outcome of two sets of proceedings, one of which was based on a principle of law not fully clarified at the time they commenced their proceedings, it could not be said that their rights were sufficiently established or based on any 'legitimate expectation'. None the less, given the intertwined nature of the claim for the existence of a possession and the argument that the possession had been interfered with, the Court stated that it would assume that there was a possession in issue.

Having accepted that the measures constituted interference, the issue then addressed by the Court was the justification for those measures. The Court reiterated the three rules contained in this article and their inter-connected nature.[64] It noted that the measures here were to secure the payment of tax; in passing section 52 of the 1991 Act, Parliament was concerned to restore its original intention which had been thwarted by the House of Lords' decision in the *Woolwich* case.[64a] Further, it was in the public interest to prevent entities from benefiting from loopholes in the taxation system. The same analysis was applied to the judicial review action. In neither instance was a violation found.

[63] ECHR, judgment of 23 October 1997.

[64] Judgment, para. 78.

[64a] *R* v. *Inland Revenue Commissioners, ex parte Woolwich Equitable Building Society*, [1990] 1 WLR 1400.

The Court considered the possibility of there having been a violation of Article 1, Protocol 1, in conjunction with Article 14 of the Convention. The applicants claimed that they were in the same situation as the Woolwich and should therefore have been treated the same. The Court noted that not every difference in treatment constituted discrimination. Although the applicants were in a substantially analogous position to the Woolwich, it was the Woolwich that took legal action and the Woolwich which consequently had the money repaid to it. The Court consequently found no violation of Article 14 in conjunction with Article 1, Protocol 1. Although the Court succeeded in drawing a distinction between the Woolwich on the one hand and the other building societies on the other, it is arguable that this approach did not fully take into account the way class actions work. Given the expense of taking legal action, it is not uncommon for individuals or companies facing a similar legal problem to pool their resources so as to minimize the risk and to avoid duplication. Against this backdrop, is it fair that the Woolwich should be the only society to receive the money back when all were (indirectly) involved in the litigation? To take this approach might be to discourage such actions leading to an increased number of cases coming through the courts, all based on the same legal question.

The Court questioned whether the dispute fell outside the scope of Article 6(1) as it concerned taxation. Referring back to the Commission's opinion, the Court noted that Article 6(1) would apply where the nature of the action was pecuniary and was founded on an infringement of rights which were also pecuniary and where the outcome was decisive for the private rights and obligations.[65] The action must still fall within the definition of civil law. Here the actions were described by the Commission as 'classic private law actions for recovery of monies alleged to have been wrongfully withheld'[66] and were therefore pecuniary. The Court agreed with this assessment, noting that the actions were determinative in respect of quantifiable sums and the fact that they had their origin in tax legislation did not affect this.[67] The judicial review actions were sufficiently interrelated with the strategy to assert the private law claims that they too fell within Article 6(1). The Court then noted that right to a court is not absolute and that States enjoy a margin of appreciation in regulating the right to a court, although not to the extent that they may impair the very essence of the right. The legislative action here was not such as to remove access to the courts themselves, but to remove any hope for the plaintiffs of ever winning the action. The Court then stated:

> . . . the Court is especially mindful of the dangers inherent in the use of retrospective legislation which has the effect of influencing the judicial determination of a dispute to which the State is a party, including where the effect is to make pending litigation unwinnable. Respect for the rule of law and the notion of a fair trial require that any such reasons adduced to justify such measures be treated with the greatest possible degree of circumspection.[68]

[65] See *Ortenberg* v. *Austria*, Series A, No. 295–B, at para. 28, and this *Year Book*, 66 (1995), p. 549.

[66] Commission opinion, para. 99.

[67] *Editions Periscope* v. *France*, Series A, No. 234–B, at para. 40, and this *Year Book*, 63 (1992), p. 574.

[68] Judgment, para. 112.

None the less, this did not mean that there could be no such interference. The Court contrasted the position here with the *Stran Greek Refineries* case[69] and noted that the litigation in this case was at a much earlier stage than in the *Stran Greek Refineries* case. Furthermore, the applicants had always known that government action of this sort was likely and, given the needs of the taxation system, there were public interest issues involved too. The Court therefore held that there was no violation of Article 6(1). The Court also dismissed the claim of the building societies under Article 14 in conjunction with Article 6(1) for reasons similar to those in its decision in respect of the claim under Article 1, Protocol 1, in conjunction with Article 14.

Article 10—freedom of expression—improper influence on outcome of criminal trial

Case No. 18. Worm case.[70] In this case against Austria, the Court, having dismissed the Government's preliminary objection, held, by seven votes to two, that there had been no violation of Article 10.

The applicant was a journalist. He wrote an article about the trial of a former minister of finance (Androsch) for tax evasion. In particular, he wrote: '[t]he flow of funds into and out of the seven undeclared accounts allow of no other interpretation than that Androsch was evading taxes. His defence in court was disgraceful; after so many years one would at least have expected properly constructed arguments.' The applicant was charged with having sought to exert improper influence on criminal proceedings. He was acquitted, but the prosecution appealed and the applicant was found guilty and fined. The applicant argued that there had been a violation of his freedom of expression. The Commission declared the application admissible and in its report expressed the opinion that there had been a violation of Article 10.

It was uncontested that there had been an interference with the applicant's freedom of expression. The question then was, did Austria's action fall within Article 10(2)? The Court noted that the Media Act was the basis for the sanctions imposed upon the applicant and, as it did not go beyond what was foreseeable, was lawful. It was aimed at protecting the independence of the judiciary and therefore fulfilled a legitimate aim for the purposes of Article 10(2). The final issue therefore was whether the action was 'necessary in a democratic society'. On the one hand, reporting and commentary on court proceedings contribute to the publicity of the proceedings and are therefore consonant with the requirements in Article 6(1) for 'public' hearings, especially when such a public figure was involved. None the less, public figures should still be entitled to a fair trial. In this, it is possible to distinguish this case from other cases in which public figures[71] were insulted. Freedom of expression is here being weighed against the interests of justice and not the rights of the insulted individual. The applicant clearly stated his view on Androsch's guilt and, taken in the context of the whole article, the Court held that it had the potential for

[69] *Stran Greek Refineries and Stratis Andreadis* v. *Greece*, judgment of 9 December 1994, Series A, No. 301B, and this *Year Book*, 66 (1995), p. 550.

[70] ECHR, judgment of 29 August 1997.

[71] See, e.g., *Oberschlick* v. *Austria (No. 2)*, ECHR, judgment of 1 July 1997.

influencing the trial, although there was no assessment as to the likelihood of this happening. The Court then concluded that the respective interests of the applicants and the public in the transmission of ideas did not outweigh the appeal court's considerations as to the adverse consequences for the authority and impartiality of the judiciary.[72] The Court argued:

> the public's becoming accustomed to the regular spectacle of pseudo trials in the news media in the long term have nefarious consequences for the acceptance of the courts as the proper forum for the determination of a person's guilt or innocence.

The Court therefore held that the authorities had 'sufficient' reasons for their interference. Finally, the imposition of the fine was not a disproportionate response. Although the concept of trial by media is a repugnant one, it is questionable whether judicial systems really need such automatic protection to function. Further, if the Court's previous jurisprudence is considered, it is debatable whether the Austrian authorities' actions have been subject to the same level of careful scrutiny as has been carried out in other cases concerning journalists' freedom of expression.[73]

Article 10—freedom of expression—press conference by lawyer

Case No. 19. Schopfer case.[74] In this case against Switzerland, the Court held unanimously that there had been no violation of Article 10.

The applicant was a lawyer who held a press conference at which he stated that in the local district authority the laws of the canton and human rights had been flagrantly violated for years. He gave an example, alleging that one of his clients had been arrested and detained without a warrant. Several newspapers published his statements. He was found to have committed professional misconduct by the Supervisory Board of the Lucerne Bar, as he had not referred his complaints to the appropriate authorities and because he had engaged in covert publicity and cheap showmanship. By this behaviour, he had disparaged the judicial authorities of Lucerne. The applicant's appeal against this finding was dismissed. The Commission suggested that there had been no violation of Article 10.

In this case the impact that respect for the law and the dictates of the proper administration of justice have on the right of freedom of expression can again be seen, albeit in completely different circumstances from the previous case. The Court noted that the special status of lawyers gave them a central position in the administration of justice, which justified certain restrictions on misconduct. Freedom of expression was available to lawyers, allowing them to comment on the administration of justice, but that comment could not overstep certain bounds. There must be a balance between the public's right to receive information; the proper administration of justice; and the dignity of the legal profession itself. Given that the applicant had commented on pending criminal proceedings (and that his appeal in that case was subsequently partially

[72] Contrast this with *De Haes and Gijsels* v. *Belgium*, ECHR, judgment of 24 February 1997.

[73] See, for example, *Sunday Times* case, Series A, No. 30; *Observer and Guardian* v. *UK*, Series A, No. 216; and *Sunday Times (No. 2)*, Series A, No. 217.

[74] ECHR, judgment of 20 May 1998.

successful), that the applicant had not applied to the other relevant supervisory authorities and the fine was not excessive, the Court found that there been no breach of Article 10.

Insulting the army—freedom of expression—Article 10—foreseeability of application—Article 7

Case No. 20. Grigoriades case.[75] The Court held in this case involving Greece, by twelve votes to eight, that there had been a violation of Article 10, but unanimously that there had been no breach of Article 7. The Court held that there was no causal link between the loss claimed and the incident but awarded a sum for costs and expenses under Article 50.

The applicant was a conscript reserve officer. He claimed to have discovered many abuses against conscripts, consequently coming into conflict with his senior officers. This resulted in the imposition of a disciplinary penalty and, as a consequence, the applicant had to serve extra time in the army, which he refused to do. Charges were brought against him for deserting. He wrote to his former commanding officer explaining his views on the army, describing it, *inter alia*, as a 'criminal and terrorist apparatus'. He was then charged with insulting the army and given a composite sentence of one year and ten months' imprisonment. On appeal the charge of desertion was quashed, but the finding concerning the insult was affirmed. He appealed, arguing that the term 'insult' was too vague. The appeal was unsuccessful. The Commission report contained the view that there had been a violation of Article 10, but that there had been no violation of Article 7.

There clearly had been an interference with the applicant's freedom of expression. The Government claimed that this was based in national law, but was the charge too vague to satisfy the requirement of foreseeability implied by the word 'lawful' in Article 10(2)? The term 'insult' was not defined in the relevant legislation and there was no case law on the point. None the less, on the ordinary meaning of the word the risk of falling within the scope of this offence must have been clear. The Court then noted that an effective military defence required discipline and that measures taken to attain this were pursuing the legitimate aim of protecting national security and public society. The last element required the measures to be necessary in a democratic society. Although States could impose restrictions where there was a threat to military discipline, such rules could not be applied for the purpose of frustrating the expression of opinions, even those directed against the army. Although the remarks made were very strong, they were made in the context of a much longer discourse. Further, the document had not been disseminated to a wider audience than the applicant's commanding officers. Finally, the insults had not been directed at individual officers.[76] Overall, the objective impact on military discipline must have been slight and therefore measures taken against the applicant were not necessary in a democratic society.

[75] ECHR, judgment of 25 November 1997.

[76] Insults aimed at individuals have received the protection of Article 10 before. See, for example, *Oberschlick* v. *Austria (No. 2)*, ECHR, judgment of 1 July 1997. Note, however, that these cases have tended to concern public figures rather than private individuals.

The Court dismissed the argument under Article 7 for the same reasons as it dismissed the argument about the certainty of domestic law under Article 10. Article 7 was also considered in *Larissis (*Case No. 26).

Article 10—freedom of expression—broadcasting licence

Case No. 21. Radio ABC case.[77] In this case against Austria, the Court unanimously held that there had been a violation of Article 10. A sum was awarded for costs and expenses but the remainder of the claim for just satisfaction under Article 50 was dismissed.

Radio ABC was a non-profit making association. It applied for a licence to set up and operate a radio station, and for the allocation of a frequency which would allow it to broadcast within the Vienna Region. The relevant body refused the application on the basis that the relevant broadcasting law required further legislation to authorize such activities. The only such legislation at that time enacted was in relation to the State broadcaster, ORF. ORF's monopoly had been held by the Austrian Constitutional Court to be compatible with Article 10. Subsequently the Regional Broadcasting Law came into force. Radio ABC requested one of the two frequencies reserved for private broadcasters. The application was rejected because Radio ABC's programming was too specialized. The Constitutional Court then ruled that certain provisions of the Regional Broadcasting Law were unconstitutional, consequently removing any legal basis upon which operating licences could be granted to other broadcasters. The Commission declared Radio ABC's complaint admissible, unanimously expressing the opinion that there had been a violation of Article 10.

The Court noted that it was uncontested ground that there was a restriction; the question was whether such a restriction was justified. In determining whether the restriction fell within Article 10(2), the Court referred to its judgment in the *Informationsverein Lentia* case.[78] As two of the three elements set out in 10(2) were satisfied (that the restriction was lawful and pursued a legitimate aim), the Court had to assess whether the restriction was necessary in a democratic society. The Court noted that although States do have a margin of appreciation, the supervision by the Convention institutions of its exercise is strict because of the importance of this right.

In this case, the Court noted the existence of four time periods. The first period under consideration resembled the situation in *Informationsverein Lentia*, and the Court therefore found that there had been a violation of Article 10. As regards the second, the Court noted that regulation of broadcasting is permitted within Article 10(1), often for technical reasons but also to regulate the nature and objectives of stations. The Government in this case justified regulation on the grounds of the need to preserve diversity, objectivity and impartiality. The Court noted that the need for such regulation would lessen in relation to the number of frequencies available. It should be noted, however, that the availability of more frequencies will not necessarily mean that all voices in society will

[77] ECHR, judgment of 20 October 1997.

[78] *Informationsverein Lentia* v. *Austria*, judgment of 24 November 1993, Series A, No. 276, and this *Year Book*, 65 (1994), p. 517.

have access to these frequencies, or that diversity of programming will necessarily result. Even in the age of digitization it may thus still be necessary to regulate broadcasters. The Court did not, however, consider the question of the limitation of the number of frequencies available as the ruling of the Constitutional Court returned the position to the same as that prior to the Regional Broadcasting Law's enactment. It therefore again found a breach of Article 10. The violation continued through the third period because the effect of the Constitutional Court's ruling was to prevent new licences being granted. The Court did not rule on the position in the fourth period as the applicant had not applied for a licence under the new laws and the Court would not rule on abstract problems.

Distribution of leaflets—criminal charge—Article 10—impartial tribunal—Article 6(1)

Case No. 22. Incal case.[79] The Court held unanimously that Turkey had violated its obligations under Article 10. It further held, by twelve votes to eight, that there had been a violation of Article 6(1). The Court awarded a specified sum for non-pecuniary loss together with an amount for costs and expenses.

The applicant was a member of the People's Labour Party (HEP). Following the decision of HEP to distribute leaflets campaigning against the municipality's decision to restrict the areas in which people could trade, HEP's local leaders were accused of disseminating separatist propaganda. The leaflets stated that the measures interfered with the rights of those of Kurdish origin, most of whom made their living through such small-scale trading. The National Security Court ordered the confiscation of the leaflets and they were handed over to the police. The public prosecutor commenced proceedings against the HEP leaders, including the applicant, for inciting hatred and hostility. The applicant was found guilty, fined and sentenced to a term of imprisonment. The applicant and his co-defendants appealed. The public prosecutor made submissions to the appeal court, which were not communicated to the applicant, requesting that the conviction be upheld. The Court of Cassation dismissed the appeal without hearing the applicant or the co-defendants. The Commission declared the application partly admissible. It drew up a report opining that there had been a violation of Article 6(1), Article 6(1) with 6(3)(*b*) and of Article 10.

The Court noted that freedom of expression included those opinions which shock or offend as well as those which are less contentious and was particularly important for political parties and their members (see also *United Communist Party*, Case No. 25). Interference in such cases called for the closest scrutiny on the part of the Court.[80] Although the Government referred to the duties and obligations mentioned in Article 10, the Court reiterated that any interference must satisfy the requirements set out in Article 10(2).[81] Having noted that the interference was prescribed by law and satisfied a legitimate aim, the Court

[79] ECHR, judgment of 9 June 1998.

[80] *Castello* v. *Spain*, judgment of 23 April 1992, Series A, No. 236, and this *Year Book*, 65 (1992), p. 581.

[81] See also *Thorgeir Thorgeirson* v. *Iceland*, judgment of 25 June 1992, Series A, No. 239, and this *Year Book*, 63 (1992), p. 587.

considered whether the interference was necessary in a democratic society. The Court noted that the leaflets contained a number of virulent remarks about the policy of the Turkish Government and that it appealed to the Kurds to band together to make certain political claims. These could not, in the opinion of the Court, be considered as incitement to the use of violence, hostility or hatred between citizens. It then emphasized the need for the acts or omissions of a government in a democratic system to be subject to public opinion. Further, given the dominant position of the Government, restraint must be shown in replying to the criticism of opponents; criminal action should not be used where other mechanisms were available.[82] In this case, when the HEP executive committee requested permission to distribute the leaflets, the Government could have requested changes to the text of the leaflets. Instead, the Government took the radical step of prosecuting criminal charges. The impact of the measure itself raised questions under Article 10.[83] In addition, however, the applicant had been sentenced to six months and twenty days' imprisonment and debarred from civil service and from taking part in a number of political activities. Although the Court noted the difficulties with terrorism existing in Turkey, the Court could not discern that the applicant was in any way responsible for any of these problems. In this way the Court distinguished the present case from the *Zana* case (Case No. 23). The Court then concluded that the conviction had been disproportionate to the end pursued and therefore in violation of Article 10. The Court considered the applicant's complaint under Article 9 to be subsumed within the complaint under Article 10.

The applicant also argued that he had not been tried before an independent and impartial tribunal. The Court noted that according to its previous decisions, such as *Findlay*[84] and *Gautrin*,[85] impartiality had two aspects: the existence of the personal conviction of a particular judge, and whether there were objective guarantees so as to exclude legitimate grounds for doubt about the tribunal's impartiality. It noted that appearances in this context are of a certain importance. Courts in a democratic society must inspire confidence both in the public in general and in the accused.[86] The court that convicted the applicant was made up of three judges, two civilian and one military. The independence of the two civilian judges was not in question. The Court thus had to determine the independence of the military judge. The law guaranteed that the military judges enjoyed the same training and constitutional safeguards as their civilian counterparts and they were required, according to the Constitution, to be independent. They were none the less part of the army, which took its orders from the executive, and the judges themselves remained subject to military discipline. Lastly, their term of office at the National Security Court was for four years only, although it could be renewed. The Court noted that it was significant that

[82] Although *Bowman* (Case No. 24) also concerned the distribution of leaflets, different arguments were used given the factual basis for the case. *Bowman* concerned elections and was not a response by the Government to try to stifle criticism.

[83] See *Vereniging Weekblad Bluf!* v. *Netherlands*, judgment of 9 February 1995, Series A, No. 306, at paras. 45 and 46, and *Vereinigung demokratischer Soldaten Österreichs and Gubi* v. *Austria*, judgment of 19 December 1994, Series A, No. 302, at para. 40.

[84] *Findlay* v. *UK*, ECHR, judgment of 25 February 1997.

[85] *Gautrin* v. *France*, ECHR, judgment of 20 May 1998.

[86] See *Hauschildt* v. *Denmark*, judgment of 24 May 1989, Series A, No. 154, at para. 48; *Pullar* v. *UK*, ECHR, judgment of 10 June 1996, at para. 38.

a civilian had to appear before a court composed partially of members of the armed forces. An individual could legitimately fear that a military person might be affected by considerations which had nothing to do with the nature of the case and therefore could doubt the independence and impartiality of that court, resulting in a violation of Article 6. Given this finding, the Court did not consider the proceedings before the Court of Cassation.

Right to a hearing in one's presence—Article 6(3)—length of proceedings—Article 6(1)—comments supportive of terrorists—limitations on freedom of expression—Article 10

Case No. 23. Zana case.[87] In this case involving Turkey, the Court held by twelve votes to eight that there had been no violation of Article 10 but, by seventeen votes to three, that there had been a violation of Article 6(1) in relation to the length of proceedings. Further, there had been a violation under Article 6(1) and (3)(*c*) regarding the applicant's absence at his trial. An award was made under Article 50.

The applicant made comments supportive of the PKK to journalists. As a result he was accused of defending an act punishable by law as a serious crime. In November 1987, he was committed for trial at the Diyarbakir Military Court, the jurisdiction of which he challenged. He refused to put forward a defence on the merits of the case and went on hunger strike. In December 1988 he again refused to address the court. In April 1989, the Military Court ruled that it lacked jurisdiction and the applicant was transferred to the high security civilian prison. At the hearing, the applicant insisted on speaking Kurdish and it was therefore put on the record that he had not put forward a defence. The trial continued and the applicant was represented, although he was not present. In March 1991 he was sentenced to twelve months' imprisonment, the majority of which was to be served on parole. On appeal the judgment was upheld. The Commission declared the application admissible and in its report expressed the opinion that there had been no violation of Article 10 but that there had been violations of Article 6(3) and Article 6(1).

Again, there had clearly been an interference with the applicant's freedom of speech. The question then to be considered was whether the measures fell within Article 10(2). The Court noted that the applicant's conviction was based on the Turkish Civil Code. Given the disturbances in south-east Turkey and given the applicant's status as a political figure, his comments could have had an impact sufficient to warrant the national authorities in taking measures to maintain national security. The measures therefore pursued a legitimate aim. Here, again, the Court can be seen to distinguish between the position of a public and a private person under Article 10. The Court then looked at whether the measures were necessary in a democratic society, that is: did they satisfy a pressing social need and were they proportionate? This must be assessed in the light of the prevailing circumstances. In this case, the statements had coincided with murderous attacks on civilians and the atmosphere in the area had consequently been tense. The applicant's comments, in the Court's opinion,

[87] ECHR, judgment of 25 November 1997.

were likely to exacerbate an already difficult situation. The Court therefore held that, in the light of the margin of appreciation, the requirements of Article 10(2) were satisfied. As the Court pointed out in other cases, the justification of internal difficulties would only apply in areas affected by these difficulties and would not constitute a *carte blanche* for the Government throughout the country.

The applicant was not requested to attend the hearing before the court that sentenced him. Pursuant to national law the assize court had taken evidence from him under powers delegated by the court trying the case. The raising of procedural objections and the insistence on the use of the Kurdish tongue in no way implied that the applicant had waived his right to defend himself and to appear before the court. Given the seriousness of the issue, the use of the 'indirect hearing' and the presence of the applicant's lawyers before the court trying the case did not compensate for the applicant's absence.

The Court noted finally that the proceedings had commenced in 1987 and lasted until 1991. The Court could take cognizance only of the period running from when Turkey accepted the right of individual petition, 22 January 1990. Given the relative simplicity of the case, the fact that the applicant had already been in custody and the fact that there was a period of relative inactivity prior to 22 January 1990 (which the Court could take into account for assessing reasonableness of proceedings), the Court held that there had been a breach of Article 6(1). The length of proceedings was the subject-matter of many cases in the period under review. This question is considered in particular in this review in *Parfitis* (Case No. 28).

Campaign expenses prior to election—limitations on amount spent—criminal offence—freedom of expression—Article 10

Case No. 24. Bowman case.[88] The Court held in this case against the UK, by fourteen votes to six, that there had been a violation of Article 10. The Court further held that the finding of a violation was just satisfaction and awarded the applicant a sum in respect of costs and expenses.

The applicant was the executive director of the Society for the Protection of the Unborn Child. Immediately prior to the 1992 elections in the UK, she arranged for the distribution of 1,500,000 leaflets detailing the various candidates' position on the abortion issue. The applicant was charged with and prosecuted for an offence under the Representation of the People Act 1983, which limits the amount that can be spent on campaigning. At the trial, the judge directed that she be acquitted as the time limit for bringing such a prosecution had not been complied with. The applicant had previously been convicted for similar offences under the same Act. Both Bowman and the society complained that this constituted interference with their freedom of expression. The Commission declared Bowman's, but not the society's, complaint admissible. In its report, it expressed the opinion that there had been a violation of Article 10.

The Government argued that the applicant had not been a victim within Article 25 as she had been acquitted of the offence. The Court disagreed as,

[88] ECHR, judgment of 19 February 1998.

although the applicant had not been convicted, the Commission had been satisfied that she had been affected by the charge. Further, her acquittal in this instance had been for technical reasons and the fact that proceedings had been commenced indicated that the applicant would be at risk of further criminal action unless she modified her behaviour.

The Court noted that the relevant provision did not restrict freedom of expression generally, but instead limited the amount that could be spent on publications and other means of disseminating information to £5. Furthermore, it only applied to transmission of information immediately prior to an election which was 'with a view to promoting or procuring the election of a candidate'. None the less, the provision constituted interference with the applicant's freedom of expression.

Considering Article 10(2), the Court noted that the fact that the provision was 'prescribed by law' was undisputed. Further, its purpose was to contribute to securing equality of candidates in elections. It therefore pursued a legitimate aim. The question then was whether it was necessary in a democratic society. The Court noted that this provision was only one of many making up the British electoral system. Consequently, Article 10 should be considered in this case in the light of Article 3, Protocol 1. Although the two provisions inter-relate, they may still come into conflict: freedom of expression may be limited to achieve the 'choice of the legislature' and the States may have a margin of appreciation in this context.[89] The Court noted that the limitation on expenditure in this case was very low, and that alternative means of communication would not be as effective. Although the applicant would be free to communicate her opinions at other times, at this time, when the electorate's minds were focused on the election of the government, she was effectively barred from doing so. The Court held that since the limit was not necessary to secure equality between candidates, it was disproportionate, resulting in a violation of Article 10.

There are some concerns about the impact of this judgment on the proper functioning of the electoral system. Judges Loizou, Baka and Jambrek dissented from the majority, emphasizing the importance of equality of arms within an electoral system. They felt that there must be some safeguards to protect candidates from manipulation by pressure groups and that the limitation here was narrow, and did not constitute a general impediment to freedom of expression. In any event, they disagreed with the Court's finding that the £5 limit[90] constituted a complete barrier to freedom of expression, as there were other ways in which the issues could be aired, especially as the press were not so limited. Another concern relates to the impact of single-issue politics, a point raised by Judges Levits and Sir John Freeland in their dissenting opinion. Referring to the *Mathieu-Mohin and Clerfayt* judgment,[91] they highlighted the need to counter the risk of a significant diversion from the main electoral debate which single-issue politics can constitute. Instead it was desirable to 'channel currents of thought so as to promote the emergence of a sufficiently clear and coherent political will'.

[89] See *Mathieu-Mohin and Clerfayt* v. *Belgium*, Series A, No. 113, especially paras. 52 and 54.

[90] Judge Valticos noted that the applicant could not have spent an insignificant sum to get 1,500,000 leaflets printed and distributed.

[91] Series A, No. 113.

Article 11—dissolution of political party—freedom of association

Case No. 25. United Communist Party of Turkey case.[92] In this case against Turkey, the Court held unanimously that there was a violation of Article 11, that it was unnecessary to consider Articles 9, 10 and 14 and Protocol 1, Articles 1 and 3, and dismissed the claim for just satisfaction. The applicants were awarded a sum in respect of costs and expenses.

The first applicant, TBKP, was a political party. The other applicants were chairman and secretary respectively of the party. The Principal State Counsel applied to the Constitutional Court requesting the dissolution of the TBKP on a number of grounds. Firstly, it was alleged that the TBKP sought to establish one social class over others; further, that it incorporated the word 'communist' into its name contrary to the law, that it carried out activities likely to undermine the territorial integrity of the State and the unity of the nation and, finally, that it declared itself to be the successor of another dissolved political party, the Turkish Workers' Party. The TBKP was dissolved on 16 July 1991 by the Constitutional Court in accordance with national law.

The Commission declared the complaint inadmissible as regards the complaint under Article 6(2), but admissible as regards the remainder of the complaint. In its report, the Commission expressed the unanimous opinion that there had been a breach of Article 11. No separate issues arose under Articles 9 and 10 and there was no need to consider separately the complaints under Articles 14 and 18 and Protocol 1, Articles 1 and 3.

The Government argued that Article 11 was not intended to cover political parties, indeed suggesting that the Convention did not apply at all. Its argument was that such issues were to be determined by the signatory States as part of their constitutional arrangements. The Government further suggested that if the Convention did apply, Article 17 should be considered, not Article 11.[93] The Court commenced by pointing out that the reference to 'trade unions' was an example, as was evidenced by the use of the conjunction 'including'. This reference to trade unions could not be taken to mean that political parties were excluded from the protection of Article 11. Furthermore, the Court emphasized the importance of political parties to the proper functioning of democracy. Parties which are regarded as undermining the constitutional order by national authorities are not thereby necessarily excluded from the protection of Article 11; any actions to protect the rule of law or to give effect to constitutional rights must comply with a State's obligations under the Convention and are subject to review by the Court.[94] Article 1, furthermore, requires the contracting States to 'secure to everyone within their jurisdiction the rights and freedoms defined in

[92] ECHR, judgment of 30 January 1998.

[93] It referred to the Commission's decisions in *Glimmerveen* and *Hagenbeek* v. *Netherlands*, Applications Nos. 8348/78 and 8406/78, *Decisions and Reports of the European Commission of Human Rights* (hereinafter *Decisions and Reports*), vol. 18, p. 187; *Kuhnen* v. *Germany*, Application No. 12194/86, *Decisions and Reports*, vol. 56, p. 205; *H, W, P and K* v. *Austria*, Application No. 12774/87 *Decisions and Reports*, vol. 62, p. 216; and *Remer* v. *Germany*, Application No. 15096/94, *Decisions and Reports*, vol. 82–B. p. 117.

[94] *Open Door and Dublin Well Woman* v. *Ireland*, Series A, No. 246–A, judgment of 29 October 1992, para. 69.

Section 1 of th[e] Convention'. Thus, it matters little whether the State measures in question are constitutional or legislative. [95] Indeed, to distinguish between the two may on occasions be difficult. This, the Court pointed out, did not mean that State authorities are powerless to protect the State's institutions. Compromises between the rights of the individual and the requirements of defending democracy were inherent in the system.[96] Such compromises, however, should comply with the requirements of Article 11(2). Finally, the Government's argument that a right to form an association did not prevent it from being disbanded was dismissed, as to have held otherwise would have rendered the right theoretical and illusory rather than practical and effective.[97] The Court confirmed that the right to form an association therefore lasts for an association's entire life.[98]

Having determined that Article 11 was applicable, the Court went on to apply it. The Court noted that there had been an interference with the right to form an association. Such interference would constitute a breach of Article 11 unless it was 'prescribed by law', pursued one of the aims specified in Article 11(2) and was 'necessary in a democratic society' for the achievement of those aims. The Court noted that it was common ground that Turkish national law permitted the dissolution of the party. The Government had suggested a number of legitimate aims between which the Commission distinguished in its opinion. For example, the ban on the use of the word 'communist' could not be said to be justified by any legitimate aim. By contrast, the distinction drawn in the party's programme between Turks and Kurds might have been seen as protecting the aim of territorial integrity and thus 'national security'. The Court concurred with this approach.[99]

The Court then considered whether such a measure was necessary in a democratic society. It started by outlining general principles relating to the application of Article 11. It noted that,

> notwithstanding its autonomous role and sphere of application, Article 11 must, in the present case, also be considered in the light of Article 10. The protection of opinions and the freedom to express them is one of the objectives of the freedoms of assembly and association as enshrined in Article 11.[100]

The Court argued that, given the essential role of political parties in ensuring pluralism and the functioning of democracy, this factor applied all the more. On this basis, as far as the application of Article 10 was concerned, even information and ideas that shock, offend or disturb should receive protection. As parties in themselves form part of a collective exercise of freedom of expression, they

[95] See *Gitonas* v. *Greece*, ECHR, judgment of 1 July 1997.

[96] *Klass and others* v. *Germany*, Series A, No. 28, judgment of 6 September 1978, para. 59.

[97] e.g. *Artico* v. *Italy*, Series A, No. 37, judgment of 13 May 1980, para. 33.

[98] Judgment, para. 33.

[99] Para. 41.

[100] Judgment, para. 42, citing, for example, *Young, James and Webster* v. *UK*, Series A, No. 44, judgment of 13 August 1981, para. 57, and *Vogt* v. *Germany*, Series A, No. 323, judgment of 26 September 1995, para. 64.

receive the protection of Articles 10 and 11; it is the existence of political parties which gives meaning to the right to vote. After reviewing the significance of democracy within the Convention, the Court then stated that the exceptions within Article 11 must be construed strictly. The contracting States, in determining 'necessity' in this context, have only a limited margin of appreciation, the subject of rigorous scrutiny. Although the Court should not substitute its own assessment for that of the national authorities, the Court must be convinced that the national authorities applied standards which were in conformity with the principles embodied in Article 11 and that they were also based on a reasonable assessment of the facts.[101]

Applying these principles to the facts, the Court noted that the TBKP was dissolved before it had started its activities. The dissolution was therefore based on the constitution and programme of the party. The party's choice of the name communist alone was not justification for the dissolution, a point the Court had already made earlier in its judgment. Further, it seemed that the party did not intend, by contrast to the position in Germany after the war when the German Communist party was held to be unconstitutional, to establish the domination of one social class over another. The party in this respect thus satisfied the requirements of democracy. The Court then considered whether the fact that the TBKP sought to promote separatism and the division of the Turkish nation would justify the dissolution of the party. It had been suggested by the Constitutional Court that, in distinguishing between the Turks and the Kurds, the TBKP was attempting the creation of a minority, which would have posed a threat to national territorial integrity. The Turkish Constitution for this reason proscribed self-determination and regional autonomy.[102] The Court noted that, to the contrary, the TBKP's programme did not refer to the Kurds as a minority, nor did it claim for them any special rights, still less a desire to secede. Indeed, the programme of the TBKP suggested it wanted to work within the democratic process so that Kurds and Turks could live peacefully together. This distinguished this case from other cases involving violence and terrorism.[103] The TBKP's practice might be different from its stated aims, but in any event the TBKP had had no opportunity to take action. Further, although the Court has in the past taken into account the difficulties in the fight against terrorism,[104] it noted that there was no evidence to conclude, in the absence of any activity by TBKP, that the party bore any responsibility for the problems which terrorism poses in Turkey. Finally, as regards Article 17, nothing in TBKP's constitution suggested that it was relying on the Convention to engage in acts aimed at the destruction of the rights of others. Similar issues were raised before the Court

[101] See *Jersild* v. *Denmark*, Series A, No. 298, judgment of 23 September 1994, para. 31.

[102] See judgment, para. 10, for details.

[103] The Turkish Government had cited *X* v. *Austria*, Application No. 5321/71, *Decisions and Reports*, vol. 42, p. 105; *T* v. *Belgium*, Application No. 9777/82, *Decisions and Reports*, vol. 36, p. 187; *Kuck* v. *Germany*, Application No. 19742/96; *Fleischle* v. *Germany*, Application No. 19744/96; and *Purcell* v. *Ireland*, Application No. 15404/89, *Decisions and Reports*, vol. 70, p. 262.

[104] *Ireland* v. *UK*, Series A, No. 25, and *Aksoy* v. *Turkey*, ECHR, judgment of 18 December 1996, and this *Year Book*, 68 (1997), p. 397.

during the period under review in the *Socialist Party case*[105] and in *Sidiropoulos*.[106]

Proselytizing of airmen and of civilians—freedom of religion—Article 9

Case No. 26. Larissis case.[107] In this case against Greece, the Court unanimously found that there had been no violation of Article 7 nor, by eight votes to one, of Article 9 in respect of the proselytizing of the airmen. The Court found by seven votes to two, however, that there had been a violation of Article 9 in relation to the proselytizing of the civilians. An award was made under Article 50 for non-pecuniary damage.

The applicants were followers of the Pentecostal Church and, at the material time, were officers in the Greek air force. For a period beginning in 1986 until 1989, they approached various airmen serving under them and spoke to those airmen about the teachings of the Pentecostal Church. Additionally, two of the three applicants also attempted to convert a number of civilians. They were charged with offences of proselytism for which they were convicted and sentenced to twelve, fourteen and eighteen months' imprisonment respectively, this sentence being convertible into pecuniary penalties. The penalties were suspended provided no further offences were committed for three years. All appeals were unsuccessful. The Commission adopted a report in which it expressed the opinion that there had been a violation of Article 9 regarding the proselytism of the civilians but not regarding the airmen.

The Court referred to the *Kokkinakis* case[108] and noted that the definition of proselytism in Greek law had satisfied the requirement of foreseeability prescribed by Article 7. The Court was not persuaded that the position had changed.

Moving on to Article 9, it was not disputed that there had been interference with the applicants' freedom to manifest their religious beliefs. The Court then considered whether the requirements of Article 9(2) had been satisfied. Given the ruling as regards the complaint under Article 7, the Court found the national measures to be sufficiently accessible and precise to satisfy the requirements of 'lawful' for the purposes of Article 9(2). The Court then noted that Article 9 included the right to try to convince one's neighbours about religious beliefs, but that it did not protect every act motivated by a religious belief, such as improper pressure being used to gain new members for a church. With regard to the proselytism of the airmen, the Court stated that States might wish to take measures to protect subordinate members of the armed forces from harassment or abuse of power, given the hierarchical nature of military structures. The evidence in this case suggested that the airmen had felt themselves subject to a degree of pressure. The Court further noted that the measures taken against the applicants had not been disproportionate, being more preventative than punitive

[105] *Socialist Party* v. *Turkey*, ECHR, judgment of 25 May 1998.
[106] *Sidiropoulos* v. *Greece*, ECHR, judgment of 10 July 1998.
[107] ECHR, judgment of 24 February 1998.
[108] *Kokkinakis* v. *Greece*, ECHR, judgment of 25 May 1993.

in nature. There had therefore been no violation of Article 9. The position was different with the proselytism of the civilians as they were not subject to the same pressures as the airmen. The measures in this instance were unjustified resulting in a violation of Article 9.

Failure to comply with time limits—non-exhaustion of domestic remedies—Article 26

Case No. 27. Bahaddar case.[109] In this case involving the Netherlands, the Court held, by seven votes to two, that the applicant had not exhausted the domestic remedies available.

The applicant applied for refugee status or a residence permit on humanitarian grounds, claiming to be a member of an illegal organization in his home country and in danger of persecution. His application was rejected. He appealed but, despite his lawyer being notified of the time limit that was applicable in respect of such appeals, the grounds for appeal were submitted approximately three months late without any explanation for their lateness. The appeal was declared inadmissible and subsequent applications were unsuccessful. He claimed that because his life would be in danger were he returned to his home country, there had been a violation of Articles 2 and 3. The Commission declared the complaint admissible, expressing the opinion in its report that there had been no violation of Article 2 but that there had been a violation of Article 3.

The Court considered the Government's preliminary objection that the applicant had failed to comply with procedural requirements despite being warned of the consequences and had therefore not exhausted the remedies available. The Court referred to its judgment in *Akdivar*,[110] noting that remedies must be sufficiently certain in practice. Although applicants must apply for any remedies in accordance with the time limits and other procedures, the applicant is under no obligation to exhaust ineffective remedies. Article 26 must be applied flexibly within the general legal and political context. The Court noted the seriousness of Article 3 and its absolute nature but held that applicants would still not be absolved from the need to exhaust effective domestic remedies. This was a question to be decided on the facts. No special circumstances came into play in this case; the applicant had had the opportunity to give grounds for the appeal and could have applied for an extension of the time limit within which the appeal had to be made. Further, the applicant could have availed himself of other remedies, meaning that there was no immediate danger of treatment contrary to Article 3. There had therefore been a failure to exhaust domestic remedies.

[109] ECHR, judgment of 19 February 1998.

[110] *Akdivar and others* v. *Turkey*, ECHR, judgment of 16 September 1996, at paras. 66–9, and this *Year Book*, 68 (1997,) p. 380.

Length of proceedings—reference to ECJ under Article 177 EC—impact of lawyers' strike—Article 6(1)

Case No. 28. Parfitis case.[111] In this case involving Greece, the Court found that there had been a violation of Article 6(1) in respect of two of the sets of proceedings involved, but not in respect of the others.

The share capital in the Bank of Central Greece was increased three times, leading to a stock exchange listing and a subsequent further increase in capital. The applicants sought to challenge these increases in share capital, leading to nine interconnected sets of proceedings. These proceedings were delayed because of numerous adjournments, some of the court's own motion, others as a result of a lawyers' strike. All cases were adjourned pending the decision of the European Court of Justice ('ECJ') in relation to a reference made to it under Article 177 of the EC Treaty. This article enables the ECJ to rule on questions of interpretation and/or validity of EC law. These rulings are then applied by the referring national courts to the proceedings before them. After several more adjournments, decisions dismissing all the actions were published on 27 February 1997. The applicants appealed, arguing that the Athens court had not taken into account the ECJ's ruling and had therefore violated Community law.

The Commission declared the complaint admissible and expressed the opinion that there had been a violation of Article 6(1) in respect of the first action but not in respect of the others.

The Court confirmed that Article 6(1) was applicable, there being a dispute over the applicants' civil rights and obligations, that is, the right under Greek and Community law to vote over an increase in share capital. The Court accepted that the case had been important and complex, but held that this alone could not justify the delay. It then stated that the conduct of the parties should be considered, and only those delays imputable to the relevant judicial authorities should be taken into account for determining whether the length of proceedings had exceeded a reasonable amount of time. The Court noted here that additional factors to be taken into account were the reference to the ECJ, the Bar strike and the close connection between the nine sets of proceedings. The Court held that it could not take the time elapsed as a result of the reference to the ECJ into account, as

> even though it may at first sight appear relatively long, to take it into account would adversely affect the system instituted by Article 177 of the EEC [*sic*] Treaty and work against the aim pursued in substance in that Article.[112]

Given that the European Communities have not yet acceded to the Convention, it is interesting to note that the Court actually considered the question of the length of time proceedings took before the European Court of Justice. One might have argued that the actions (or inaction) of the ECJ do not fall within the Court's jurisdiction. Indeed, the Commission has declared complaints against Community institutions inadmissible for this reason. Furthermore, it is not

[111] ECHR, judgment of 26 February 1998.
[112] Judgment, para. 95.

particularly clear why cases coming before the ECJ may take longer than, for example, those which come before constitutional courts.

As regards the Bar strike, this was organized by the Bar Association, an essentially professional association. In calling the strike, the association was trying to protect its members' interests rather than exercising the attributes of a public authority. The interconnection of the cases also had an impact on the length of time as all cases were stayed pending the outcome in one of them. Further, the Fourth Division of the Supreme Administrative Court had relinquished jurisdiction in favour of the plenary court. This constituted a fair balance between the need for expeditious proceedings and the more general principle of proper administration of justice.[113]

Of the various proceedings, the Court found that there had been a violation in respect of the judicial review action commenced on 1 January 1986 and finally determined on 17 April 1992, and in respect of Action 10429/1986 which was commenced on 22 December 1986 and which was, at the time of judgment, still pending. Taking into account only the delays that were attributable to the Supreme Court, these delays were unreasonable. In respect of the complaints regarding the other sets of proceedings, as only five months of the total time in each case was attributable to the Supreme Court, there had been no violation of Article 6(1). The Court made an award for non-pecuniary damage and for costs. In so doing, it noted that it was, in assessing damages, not bound by domestic rules on damages.[114]

Inadequate legal representation—right to a fair trial—Article 6(1)—Article 6(3)(c)

Case No. 29. Daud case.[115] In this case involving Portugal, the Court held unanimously that there had been a violation of Article 6(1) in conjunction with Article 6(3)(*c*) and that it was unnecessary to consider the complaint under Article 6(1) in conjunction with Article 6(3)(*e*). The Court further held that the finding of violation constituted just satisfaction for the non-pecuniary damage suffered.

The applicant was arrested as he arrived at Lisbon airport. He was carrying a false passport and a suitcase containing cocaine. He was interviewed by an investigating judge in the presence of an officially assigned lawyer and an interpreter and then was detained pending trial. The applicant requested that a judicial investigation be commenced. The reporting judge rejected this application because it did not comply with certain formalities, in particular being written in Spanish rather than Portuguese. On 16 November 1992, the file was sent to Lisbon Criminal Court. The applicant made further applications which the Court declined to consider as they were drafted in Spanish. On 14 January 1993, the officially assigned lawyer asked to be relieved of her duties for health reasons and another lawyer was assigned to the applicant. The trial began on 26

[113] See *Boddaert* v. *Belgium*, judgment of 12 October 1992, Series A, No. 235–D, at para. 39.

[114] See, for example, *Papamichalopoulos* v. *Greece*, judgment of 31 October 1995, Series A, No. 330–B, and this *Year Book*, 67 (1996), p. 653.

[115] ECHR, judgment of 21 April 1998.

January. On 8 February the applicant was sentenced to nine years' imprisonment. An appeal was lodged but was inadmissible on account of inadequate presentation of the grounds of appeal. The applicant complained that he had been denied a fair trial because of inadequate legal assistance, the refusal of his application for a judicial investigation and of his application to submit evidence.

The Commission declared the application admissible and adopted a report in which it expressed the opinion that there had been a violation of Article 6(3)(*c*) taken with Article 6(1) but no violation of Article 6(3)(*e*) in conjunction with Article 6(1).

The Court considered the general complaint regarding the level of legal assistance together with the refusal of his applications by the investigating judge and the court. The Court reiterated that the rights granted by the Convention were designed to be real and practical rather than illusory. Allocating counsel did not in itself ensure the effectiveness of the legal assistance thereby afforded. None the less, the State could not be held responsible for every shortcoming of a lawyer appointed by the State for legal aid purposes. The conduct of the defence was principally a matter between the defendant and his counsel. The competent authorities would be required to intervene under Article 6(3)(*c*) only if a failure by legal aid counsel were manifest or sufficiently brought to their attention. Here, the representation had not been effective. The first legally assigned lawyer had not taken any steps in the preparation of the case even before she stepped down due to ill health. Although a second counsel was appointed, this was very close before the commencement of a complex trial leading to a heavy sentence. The second lawyer had not, in the opinion of the Court, had enough time to study the file and prepare her client's defence. The Supreme Court had not remedied the situation, as it had held the appeal to be inadmissible.

Had the authorities been under an obligation to ensure, within the confines of the independence of the Bar, that the applicant received the benefit of this right? The refusal to grant the investigative methods requested by the applicant did not affect the fairness of the trial as these procedures had been carried out during the trial. The Court noted that one of the applications was a request for an interview with his lawyer, whom the applicant had not seen for eight months. This was rejected, as the other applications had been, because it was written in Spanish. This request should have alerted the authorities to a manifest shortcoming in the first State-appointed lawyer. Given this and the other applications made by the defendant himself, the court should have inquired into the manner in which the lawyer was fulfilling her duty. Further, after appointing the second lawyer, the Lisbon court could have adjourned the trial of its own motion. The fact that the lawyer did not make any such application herself did not affect this point. Taken as a whole, the Court held that there had been a violation of Article 6(3)(*c*). Given that no submissions had been made in respect of the quality of the interpreting, the Court did not feel it necessary to consider the issue of its own motion. Potentially, this reasoning could have far-reaching effects on the obligations of the judicial authorities to review the standard of legal representation before them. Given the close knit nature of most national legal communities, this could also give rise to difficult situations for the judiciary. In particular, when will a failure to provide adequate advice be manifest? This question also arose in *Twalib* (Case No. 30).

Right to free legal assistance—Article 6(1)—Article 6(3)(c)

Case No. 30. Twalib case.[116] In this case the Court found unanimously that Greece had been in violation of its obligations under Article 6(1) and 6(3)(*c*). The Court awarded the applicant a sum for non-pecuniary damage under Article 50.

The applicant was arrested on suspicion of drug-trafficking and was found to be in possession of a false passport. Criminal proceedings were instituted against him. When the trial against him and three others also accused opened, the applicant's lawyer was not present as a result of a lawyers' strike. The trial was adjourned, but the applicant's lawyer did not appear. The lawyer representing one of the co-accused offered to assist the applicant and the trial was adjourned for a short while to allow the lawyer time to study the file. The applicant was found guilty of various drugs-related offences on 16 July and was sentenced to life imprisonment. On appeal his sentence was reduced. The applicant lodged a further appeal, stating that the grounds of appeal would be presented through his lawyer. Three months later, he addressed a petition through the prison authorities requesting legal aid counsel to assist him with the preparation of his appeal. The Court of Cassation dismissed his appeal because no grounds of appeal had been submitted. He subsequently addressed a second petition concerning his financial situation and enquiring about the progress of his case. The prison authorities then informed him that his appeal had been unsuccessful.

The Commission declared the application admissible and adopted a report in which it expressed the opinion that there had been no violation of Article 5(2), of Article 6(1) and (3)(*b*) or of Article 6(1) and (3)(*e*). Finally, it suggested that there had been a violation of Article 6(1) and (3)(*c*).

The applicant argued that a lack of adequate time and facilities for the preparation of a defence during a criminal trial and the absence of legal aid during appeal proceedings had violated Article 6(1) taken in conjunction with Article 6(3)(*b*) and (*c*). The applicant did not pursue the other claims. Given that the Government's objection concerning non-exhaustion was closely linked with the substance of the applicant's claim, the Court decided to join it to the merits of the case. The Court noted that the applicant had been assigned a lawyer also representing one of his co-accused. Despite the complexity and seriousness of the case, the lawyer was given very little time to master the detail of the applicant's case. Given the possibility of a conflict of interest, this brevity could not be excused on the basis of the lawyer being familiar with the facts in issue. Clearly, there were shortcomings in the fairness of the trial. The Court then noted that the applicant was represented by a different lawyer in proceedings before the appeal court. Although that court had full jurisdiction to quash the impugned judgment, the applicant, through his new lawyer, did not request a retrial. The Court held that the appeal court could not have assumed there was

[116] ECHR, judgment of 9 June 1998.

a defect unless it had been specifically alerted to that fact. Given that the applicant, who was present at the appeal hearing, had had the opportunity to raise the alleged defect, there was nothing to suggest that the fairness of the appeal proceedings could be called into question. There had therefore been no violation of the relevant provision.

The Court found the applicant lacked the means to pay for his legal representation in respect of the appeal to the Court of Cassation. In view of the severity of the offences and of the sentence, and given that the procedure before the Court of Cassation was complex, the Court considered that the applicant, as a lay person, should have been granted legal aid to pursue the appeal. Given that Greek law made no such provision, the Court found that there had been a violation of Article 6(1) and (3)(*c*).

Undercover police operation—right to a fair trial—Article 6(1)

Case No. 31. Teixara de Castro case.[117] The Court held in this case involving Portugal that there had been a violation of Article 6(1) (by eight votes to one) and that it was unnecessary to consider Articles 3 or 8 (unanimously). The Court awarded a specified sum for damage and expenses.

The applicant was arrested when he was about to supply 20 grams of heroin to two undercover police officers. On the same day he was remanded in custody by the investigating judge. On 29 January 1993 he applied for his release on the ground he had been detained unlawfully, claiming that he had been incited to commit an offence. The investigating judge dismissed the application on 16 February 1993, a judgment which was upheld by the Oporto Court of Appeal on 21 April 1993. On 6 December 1993, the applicant was found guilty and sentenced to six years' imprisonment. His appeal was dismissed, the appellate court holding that the police officers had acted within the law and that their evidence was admissible. The Commission, having declared the application admissible, drew up a report in which it expressed the opinion that there had been a violation of Article 6(1) but that there had been no violation of Articles 3 or 8.

The Court restated that the admissibility of evidence and the assessment thereof was primarily a matter for the national authorities. The Court's task was to ascertain whether the proceedings taken as a whole had been fair. In particular, the Convention did not preclude, at the investigation stage, reliance on anonymous informants.[118] The subsequent use of their statements in court was a different matter. The use of undercover agents had to be restricted, even in the fight against drug-trafficking. The general requirement of fairness applied to all types of proceedings and the public interest could not justify the use of evidence obtained as a result of police incitement. Had the police in this case gone beyond what was acceptable for undercover agents?

The Court noted that the Government had not suggested that the officers had been part of an anti-drug trafficking operation ordered and supervised by a

[117] ECHR, judgment of 9 June 1998.

[118] See, e.g., *Ludi* v. *Switzerland*, judgment of 15 June 1992, Series A, No. 238, and this *Year Book*, 63 (1992), p. 584.

judge. Neither had the authorities any reason to suspect the applicant to be trafficking drugs; he had no previous criminal record and had only come to the attention of the police through the intermediacy of two other people. At the time of his arrest it did not seem as though the applicant had had more drugs, obtaining those he had from a third party who had obtained them from yet someone else. It did not seem as though he would be likely to commit further offences than those which he was incited to commit by the police. The inference was that the police officers in question had gone beyond passively investigating the applicant's criminal activity and had exercised an influence such as to incite the commission of the offence. The Court then noted that the applicant had been convicted mainly on the statements of the two police officers. The Court held that, taken together, these factors meant that the applicant had not had a fair trial and there had been a violation of Article 6(1).

Government certificate as to facts—access to a court—Article 6(1)

Case No. 32. Tinnelly and others case.[119] In this case against the UK, the Court held unanimously that there had been a violation of Article 6(1). The other complaints made by the applicants were not considered. The Court made an award under Article 50 in respect of lost opportunities and costs and expenses.

One of the applicants was a construction company, the managing director and secretary of which were also applicants. The other applicants, the McElduffs, were carpenters. All the individual applicants were Catholics. The applicants had all put in tenders for contracts, in respect of dismantling a power station and constructing a public building respectively. Although initially approved, the applicants in both cases were subsequently turned down without explanation in favour of another, less favourable contractor. The applicants complained to the relevant authorities, alleging discrimination on the grounds of religion and political opinion. In both cases the Secretary of State for Northern Ireland issued a certificate (a 'section 42 certificate') that the decision was, 'an act done for the purpose of safeguarding national security or the protection of public safety or order'. The section 42 certificate was conclusive proof that the act referred to had been done for the reasons stated. A judicial review action was commenced by the relevant authorities, claiming that the section 42 certificate had been issued for improper motives. During the proceedings the judge requested discovery of a number of documents, but a public interest immunity certificate was issued preventing the discovery of those documents relating to national security. Subsequently, the action for judicial review was dismissed, as it transpired that the decision had been based on information indicating a security risk supplied by the Royal Ulster Constabulary. The Commission, having declared the applications admissible, drew up a report in which it expressed the unanimous opinion that there had been a violation of the applicants' right to a court in Article 6(1).

[119] ECHR, judgment of 10 July 1998.

The Court commenced by examining the question of the applicability of Article 6(1). Contrary to the Government's arguments, the right in question was a pecuniary right as the applicants had a right not to be discriminated against in the job market and victims of discrimination were entitled to compensation. Further, section 42 could not operate so as to disapply rights against unlawful discrimination; the question of whether this had occurred was one for a court, even within the context of national security.

The effect of the section 42 certificate was to prevent the relevant authorities from scrutinizing the factual basis for the applicants' complaints. Even the judicial review proceedings had not given rise to a full scrutiny of the basis for the Secretary of State's decision to issue the certificate, as the judge felt himself constrained from going behind the face of the certificate to verify whether grounds existed for considering Tinnelly a security risk. Any substantive review would, in any event, have been hampered by not having had full access to the materials on which the Secretary of State based his decisions. Although the Court admitted there were security concerns regarding contracts for power stations and public buildings, the impact on the applicants' right of access to a court of the section 42 certificate was disproportionate. The right of access cannot be displaced by the statements of the executive even where there are valid security concerns. The Court finally observed that the Government had failed to show why normal proceedings could not have been modified so as to accommodate the rights of the parties and deal with the security concerns.[120]

More than one offence arising out of single incident—prohibition on double jeopardy—Protocol 7, Article 4

Case No. 33. Oliveira case.[121] The Court held in this case involving Switzerland by eight votes to eleven that there had been no violation of Protocol 7, Article 4.

The applicant lost control of her car whilst driving in icy conditions. She hit two cars, seriously injuring another driver. The file on the incident was sent for further investigation. The applicant was initially fined 200 Swiss francs for failing to control her vehicle. Subsequently, the District Attorney's Office issued a penal order in respect of the bodily injury caused and she was again fined. She challenged this and, although the court noted that the fact that she had been fined for a road traffic offence did not preclude her subsequent prosecution for a more serious offence, it annulled her earlier fine. The Commission drew up a report in which it expressed the opinion that there been an infringement of the applicant's right under Protocol 7, Article 4.

[120] This is not the first time that the use of such certificates has been criticized. The ECJ found a similar certificate to be incompatible with the right of access to a court in proceedings before it: Case 222/84, *Johnston* v. *Royal Ulster Constabulary*, [1986] ECR 1651.

[121] ECHR, judgment of 30 July 1998.

The applicant claimed that she had been convicted twice for the same offence. The Court noted, however, that this was an example of a single act constituting more than one offence and, in such cases, the greater offence would usually absorb the lesser one. This would not infringe Protocol 7, Article 4 because that article protects individuals against being tried twice for the same offence. The Court therefore held that there had been no violation of this provision.

LORNA WOODS

DECISIONS OF THE COURT OF JUSTICE OF THE EUROPEAN COMMUNITIES IN 1998*

I *External relations—TRIPS Agreement—Article 50 of the TRIPS Agreement—provisional measures—EEC/Yugoslavia Co-operation Agreement—suspension of trade concessions—Vienna Convention on the Law of Treaties—rebus sic stantibus clause*

I.1 *Case C–53/96, Hermès International* v. *FHT Marketing Choice BV*, 16 June 1998.[1] The Arrondissementsrechtsbank, Amsterdam, referred a question on the interpretation of Article 50(6)[2] of the Agreement on Trade-Related Aspects of Intellectual Property Rights ('the TRIPS Agreement').[3]

Hermès owned the registered trade mark for the name and device 'Hermès' in the Benelux. The trade mark was applied to, *inter alia*, neck ties which were marketed through a selective distribution agreement. Hermès commenced proceedings against FHT believing that FHT was marketing copies of its ties. It seized, with the leave of the President of the Arrondissementrechtsbank, Amsterdam, a number of ties, and then applied for an order requiring FHT to cease infringement of its copyright and trademark. An interim order was granted. In the same proceedings, Hermès requested the President to fix certain limits pursuant to Article 50(6) of the TRIPs Agreement during which FHT could request revocation of the President's decision and during which Hermès could commence proceedings on the merits. The President referred a question to the Court of Justice as to whether it had jurisdiction to fix a period within

[1] [1998] ECR I–3603.

[2] Article 50 of the TRIPS agreement provides, *inter alia*, as follows:

'1. The judicial authorities shall have the authority to order prompt and effective provisional measures:

(*a*) to prevent an infringement of any intellectual property right from occurring, and in particular to prevent the entry into the channels of commerce in their jurisdiction of goods, including imported goods immediately after customs clearance;

(*b*) to preserve relevant evidence in regard to the alleged infringement.

. . .

4. Where provisional measures have been adopted *in audita altera parte*, the parties affected shall be given notice, without delay after the execution of the measures at the latest. A review, including a right to be heard, shall take place upon request of the defendant with a view to deciding within a reasonable period after the notification of the measures, whether these measures shall be modified, revoked or confirmed.

. . .

6. Without prejudice to paragraph 4, provisional measures taken on the basis of paragraphs 1 and 2 shall, upon request by the defendant, be revoked or otherwise cease to have effect, if proceedings leading to a decision on the merits of the case are not initiated within a reasonable period, to be determined by the judicial authority ordering the measure where a Member's law so permits or, in the absence of such a determination, not to exceed 20 working days or 31 calendar days, whichever is the longer.'

[3] As set out in Annex 1C to the WTO Agreement approved on behalf of the Community in Council Decision 94/800/EC of 22 December 1994 (OJ, 1994, L336/1).

which Hermès should initiate proceedings. This would be required only if the measures ordered in the interim proceedings constituted a 'provisional measure' within the meaning of Article 50 of the TRIPS Agreement.

A number of Member States contended that the Court of Justice had no jurisdiction to answer the question submitted. This was rejected by the Court, which held that it did have jurisdiction, relying on the fact that pursuant to Article 99 of Council Regulation (EC) 40/94[4] rights arising from a Community trade mark might be safeguarded by the adoption of 'provisional, including protective, measures'. Thus even though the rules envisaged by Article 99 were those provided for by the Member State concerned:

> . . . since the Community is a party to the TRIPS Agreement and since that agreement applies to the Community trade mark, the courts referred to in Article 99 of Regulation 40/94 when called upon to apply national rules with a view to ordering provisional measures for the protection of rights arising under a Community trade mark, are required to do so, as far as possible, in the light of the wording and purpose of Article 50 of the TRIPS Agreement.[5]

Nor did it matter that the dispute concerned trade marks registered in the Netherlands. First, it was, in principle, for the national court to decide whether a preliminary ruling was necessary. Second, where a provision could apply to situations falling both within the scope of Community law and within the scope of national law, it was clearly in the interests of the Community that the provision should be interpreted uniformly, whatever the circumstances in which it was to apply.[6] In the present case, Article 50 of the TRIPS agreement applied both to Community trade marks and to national trade marks.

On the substance of the question referred, the Court of Justice held that a measure adopted to put an end to an alleged infringement of a trade mark was to be characterised as a 'provisional measure' if (*a*) it was characterised under national law as an 'immediate provisional measure' and its adoption was required on 'grounds of urgency'; (*b*) the opposing party was summoned and heard if he appeared before the court; (*c*) the decision adopting the measure was reasoned and given in writing following an assessment of the substance of the case by the judge hearing the interim application; (*d*) there was a procedure for appeal against the decision; and (*e*) although the parties remained free to initiate proceedings on the merits of the case, the decision was usually accepted by the parties as a 'final' resolution of their dispute.

I.2 *Case C–162/96, A. Racke GmbH & Co.* v. *Hauptzollamt Mainz*, 16 June 1998.[7] The Bundesfinanzhof referred questions to the Court of Justice concerning the validity of Regulation 3300/91 suspending the trade concessions provided for by the Co-operation Agreement between the European Economic Community and the Socialist Federal Republic of Yugoslavia ('the Suspending Regulation').[8] Under the Co-operation Agreement,[9] importers of wine from

[4] Of 20 December 1993 on the Community Trade Mark (OJ, 1994, L11/1).

[5] Paragraph 28 of the judgment.

[6] See, for example Case C–130/95, *Giloy* v. *Hauptzollamt Frankfurt am Main-Ost*, [1997] ECR I–4291, paragraph 28.

[7] [1998] ECR I–3655.

[8] OJ, 1991, L 315/1.

[9] OJ, 1983, L41/1.

Yugoslavia had been entitled to preferential customs duties. However, following the determination of a crisis in Yugoslavia which constituted a threat to international peace and security, the preferential duties under the Co-operation Agreement were suspended by the Suspending Regulation with effect from 15 November 1991. The questions referred by the Bundesfinanzhof to the Court of Justice were raised in proceedings brought by the Principal Customs Office, Mainz, against Racke GmbH, an importer of wine from the Kosovo wine-growing region, in order to recover the difference between the third-country rate of customs duty and the preferential rate under the Co-operation Agreement which had been suspended. Ranke challenged the validity of the Suspending Regulation as incompatible with Article 62 of the Vienna Convention on the Law of Treaties ('the Vienna Convention').[10] By way of preliminary observation, the Court of Justice noted that although the Vienna Convention does not bind either the Community or all its Member States, Article 62 reflects customary rules of international law.[11] The Court of Justice held that the European Community must respect international law in the exercise of its powers and must comply with the rules of customary international law when adopting a Regulation suspending a trade concession granted by an agreement which it had concluded with a non-Member country. The Court of Justice then set out the two conditions which customary international law (as codified in Article 62(1) of the Vienna Convention) lays down in order for it to be possible to contemplate the termination or suspension of an agreement by reason of a fundamental change of circumstances, namely (*a*) that the existence of the fundamental change of circumstances must have constituted an essential basis of the consent of the parties to be bound by the treaty, and (*b*) that the change of circumstances must have had the effect of radically transforming the extent of the obligations still to be performed under the treaty.

In application of the first condition to the facts, the Court of Justice held that in view of the wide-ranging objectives of the Co-operation Agreement:

> . . . the maintenance of a situation of peace in Yugoslavia, indispensable for neighbourly relations, and the existence of institutions capable of ensuring implementation of the co-operation envisaged by the [Co-operation] Agreement throughout the territory of Yugoslavia constituted an essential condition for initiating and pursuing that co-operation.[12]

[10] Article 62 of the Convention provides:
'1. A fundamental change of circumstances which has occurred with regard to those existing at the time of the conclusion of a treaty, and which was not foreseen by the parties, may not be invoked as a ground for terminating or withdrawing from the treaty unless:
 (*a*) the existence of those circumstances constituted an essential basis of the consent of the parties to be bound by the treaty; and
 (*b*) the effect of the change is radically to transform the extent of obligations still to be performed under the treaty.

. . .

3. If, under the foregoing paragraphs, a party may invoke a fundamental change of circumstances as a ground for terminating or withdrawing from a treaty it may also invoke the change as a ground for suspending the operation of the treaty.'

[11] The Court cited the judgment of the International Court of Justice in *Fisheries Jurisdiction (United Kingdom* v. *Iceland)*, *ICJ Reports*, 1973, p. 3, para 36.

[12] Paragraph 55 of the judgment.

With respect to the second condition, the Court of Justice held that it did not appear that the Council had made a manifest error of assessment by holding that the pursuit of hostilities, and their consequences on economic and trade relations, constituted a radical change in the conditions under which the Co-operation Agreement was concluded. Accordingly, the Court of Justice concluded that since both of the above conditions were fulfilled, the Suspending Regulation was compatible with international law and was therefore valid.

II *Free movement of goods—quantitative restrictions—European Convention on the Protection of Animals kept for Farming Purposes—Council Directive (EC) 91/629 laying down minimum standards for the protection of calves—export of calves to Member States complying with Directive but not Convention—validity of Directive*

II.1 *Case C–1/96, R* v. *Minister of Agriculture, Fisheries and Food, ex parte Compassion in World Farming Ltd. (CIWF)*, 19 March 1998.[13] CIWF, an animal welfare body, asked the Minister of Agriculture, Fisheries and Food to ban or restrict the export of veal calves intended for rearing in veal crates. This practice has been prohibited in the United Kingdom.[14] CIWF contended that the Minister had power under Article 36 of the EC Treaty[15] to restrict the export of veal calves to Member States which had implemented Council Directive (EC) 91/629 laying down minimum standards for the protection of calves[16] ('the Directive') where the veal crate system was still likely to be used during a transitional period.[17] CIWF also argued that the veal crate system was inconsistent with higher standards laid down by (*a*) the European Convention on the Protection of Animals kept for Farming Purposes[18] ('the Convention') adopted by the Council of Europe and approved by the EEC by Article 1 of Council Decision (EEC) 78/923;[19] and (*b*) the 1998 Recommendation concerning cattle adopted by the standing committee[20] ('the Recommendation').

The Minister responded to the request, stating that the United Kingdom had no power to restrict the export of veal calves and, even if it did, the Minister was

[13] [1998] ECR I–1251, [1998] All ER (EC) 302.
[14] Since 1 January 1990 by virtue of the Welfare of Cattle Regulations 1987, SI 1987/2021.
[15] Which provides, *inter alia*, as follows:
'The provisions on [free movement of goods] shall not preclude prohibitions or restrictions on . . . exports . . . justified on grounds of public morality, public policy . . . the protection of health and life of humans, animals or plants . . . '.
[16] OJ, 1991, L340/28.
[17] Pursuant to Article 3 of the Directive which provides, *inter alia*, as follows:
'(1) Member States shall ensure that from 1 January 1994 and for a transitional period of four years, all holdings newly built or rebuilt and/or brought into use for the first time after that date shall comply with at least the following requirements . . . where calves are housed in individual boxes or by tethering in stalls, the boxes or stalls shall have perforated walls and their width must be no less than 90 cms plus or minus 10%, or 0.80 times the height at the withers . . . (4) The duration of use of installations built before 1 January 1994 which do not meet the requirements of paragraph 1, shall under no circumstances extend beyond 31 December 2007, unless on that date they comply with the requirements of this Directive.'
[18] Of 17 March 1976 (OJ, 1978, L323/14).
[19] OJ, 1978, L323/12.
[20] Established by Article 9(1) of the Convention.

not minded to impose a ban for policy reasons. An application was made for judicial review of that decision and two questions were referred by the High Court to the Court of Justice for a preliminary ruling as to (*a*) whether the Minister had power under Article 36 of the EC Treaty to restrict the export of veal calves, and (*b*) if the effect of provisions of the Directive meant that the Minister did not have such power, whether those provisions of the Directive were valid.

The Court of Justice first considered the validity of the Directive. The Court pointed out that, although the Convention formed part of the Community legal order from its entry into force, the Convention's provisions were indicative only and granted the contracting parties considerable discretion when choosing which measures to adopt to implement the principles set out in it. The Recommendation provided expressly[21] that it was not directly applicable within the national law of the contracting parties. Thus, even if the Recommendation, and, in particular, its Annex C, which laid down provisions relating to the housing and diet of veal calves, were more precise, it could not contain legally binding rules for the contracting parties and therefore for the Community. On that basis, the Court concluded that the Directive was not invalid.

The Court then turned to consider the power of a Member State under Article 36 of the EC Treaty to restrict exports to other Member States which had implemented the Directive, but which did not apply the Recommendation. The Court began by repeating its well-known line of case law, namely that in a sector covered by a common organization of the market, Member States must refrain from taking any action which might affect that common organization or create exceptions to it.[22] Moreover, this rule applied even if the common organization of the market did not regulate exhaustively the sector in question.[23] Applying those principles to the facts,[24] the Court concluded that a ban on the export of veal calves would:

> . . . affect the structure of the market, and, in particular, would have a considerable impact on the formation of market prices, which would interfere with the proper functioning of the common organisation of the market.[25]

In 1992, in *Holdijk*,[26] the Court of Justice had ruled that a Member State was not precluded from maintaining or introducing higher standards for the installation of enclosures for fatting calves which were applicable both to calves intended for the national market and those intended for export. However, as the Court pointed out, that judgment related to measures which a Member State applied within its own territory. Further, the judgment was expressly based on the absence of any Community provisions for the welfare protection of cattle. Thus the Court was required to consider whether the Directive contained the

[21] Pursuant to Article 20.

[22] See, for example, Case 148/85, *Direction général des impôts* v. *Forest*, [1986] ECR 3449.

[23] See, for example, Case 218/85, *Association comité économique agricole régional fruits et légumes de Bretagne* v. *Le Campion*, [1986] ECR 3513.

[24] See also its decision in Case 83/78, *Pigs Marketing Board* v. *Redmond*, [1978] ECR 2347, where the Court of Justice held that any provisions which might alter the pattern of imports or exports by preventing producers from buying and selling freely within the Member State of establishment were not compatible with the common organization of the market.

[25] At paragraph 44 of the judgment.

[26] Joined Cases 141–143/81, [1982] ECR 1299.

necessary provisions for welfare protection of cattle with the result that it 'occupied the field' in the sector in question. This would mean that a Member State could no longer have recourse to Article 36. Instead it must rely on mutual trust that each Member State would carry out checks that the provisions of the Directive were being applied on its respective territories.[27]

The Court of Justice concluded that the Directive did indeed 'occupy the field' as it laid down exhaustive common minimum standards for the protection of cattle confined for the purposes of rearing and fattening.

Next, the Court considered the effect of Article 11(2) of the Directive.[28] The Court pointed out that this provision could only apply to measures taken within the territories of the Member States themselves and thus could not be used to justify an export ban. Nor did it mean that the Directive did not 'occupy the field' in the area of protection of veal calves.

Finally, the Court considered that it remained to be seen if Article 36 could be relied upon to restrict the export of veal calves for reasons related to public morality or public policy which were not covered by the Directive. In this respect, the Court noted that CIWF's reliance on public policy and public morality as separate justifications for invoking Article 36 were in reality an aspect of the justification relating to the protection of animal health, as they were based upon a section of national public opinion that the system put in place by the Directive was inadequate for the welfare protection of veal calves.

III *Practice and procedure—reference for preliminary ruling—dispute in main proceedings resolved after reference made—jurisdiction of Court to give reference—scope of the Court's review when hearing an appeal*

III.1 *Case C–314/96, Djabali* v. *Caisse d'Allocations Familiales de L'Essone*, 12 March 1998.[29] A request for a preliminary ruling was made by the Tribunal des Affaires de Sécurité Sociale d'Evry. The reference concerned the entitlement of an Algerian national resident in France[30] to a special allowance payable in France to disabled adults. After the reference was made, the Court of Justice was informed that the French authorities had decided to award the allowance to Mrs Djabali. However, upon being asked by the Court of Justice Registry whether it intended to withdraw the reference, the Tribunal stated that it had no power to do so under its procedural rules.

Somewhat unsurprisingly, the Court of Justice held that there was no need to

[27] See, most recently, Case C–5/94, *R* v. *Ministry of Agriculture, Fisheries and Food, ex parte Hedley Lomas*, [1996] ECR I–2553, [1996] All ER (EC) 493, where the Court of Justice rejected the proposition that Article 36 could have 'extra-territorial' application, i.e. that it could be invoked to restrict exports on the basis of animal welfare conditions existing in another Member State.

[28] Which provides that, from 1 January 1994, the Member States may, in compliance with the general rules of the Treaty, maintain or apply within their own territories stricter provisions for the protection of calves than those laid down in the Directive.

[29] [1998] ECR I–1149, [1998] All ER (EC) 426.

[30] Pursuant to the Co-operation Agreement between the EEC and the People's Democratic Republic of Algeria signed in Algiers on 26 April 1976 and approved on behalf of the Community by Council Regulation (EEC) 2210/78 (OJ, 1978, L263/1).

respond to the reference. Repeating its earlier case law,[31] the Court held that the purpose of the Article 177 reference procedure was to provide the national court with such interpretation of Community law as was necessary to give judgment in the case before it. Accordingly:

> The justification for a preliminary reference is not that it enables advisory opinions on general or hypothetical questions to be delivered but rather that it is necessary for the effective resolution of a dispute.[32]

III.2 *Case C–7/95P, John Deere Limited* v. *European Commission*, 28 May 1998.[33] This case concerned an appeal against a judgment by the Court of First Instance ('CFI')[34] which dismissed John Deere's application for annulment of Commission Decision (EEC) 92/157 relating to a proceeding under Article 85 of the EC Treaty. The judgment is of interest because the Court took the opportunity to outline the principles applicable to such appeals.

The Court noted that, pursuant to Article 168a of the EC Treaty and Article 51 of the Statute of the Court of Justice, an appeal must be limited to points of law and must be based on the following three grounds, namely (*a*) lack of competence of the CFI; (*b*) breach of procedure before the CFI which adversely affected the interests of the appellant; (*c*) infringement of Community law by the CFI. Further, pursuant to Article 112(1)(*c*) of the Court of Justice's Rules of Procedure,[35] an appeal must contain the pleas in law and legal arguments relied upon.

Accordingly, the Court noted that first, the appeal must indicate precisely those elements of the judgment that the appellant wished to have set aside and the legal arguments relied upon. Second, that this requirement was not satisfied merely by repeating the arguments and submissions made to the CFI as this amounted to a request for a re-hearing which the Court of Justice had no jurisdiction to undertake.[36]

The Court then went on to consider its jurisdiction to hear appeals based on the facts found by the CFI. It held that the CFI had exclusive jurisdiction, first, to establish the facts except where the substantive inaccuracy of its finding was apparent from the documents submitted to it, and second, to assess those facts. Once the CFI had found the facts, the Court of Justice had jurisdiction pursuant to Article 168 of the EC Treaty to review the legal characterization of those facts by the CFI and the legal conclusions that it had drawn from them. The Court thus concluded it had no jurisdiction to establish the facts or, in principle, to examine the evidence accepted by the CFI in support. Unless the evidence had been fundamentally misconstrued, the appraisal by the CFI of the evidence

[31] See, in particular, Case 244/80, *Foglia* v. *Novello*, [1981] ECR 3045; Joined Cases C–297/88 and C–197/89, *Dzodzi* v. *Belgium*, [1990] ECR I–3763; Case C–231/89, *Gmurzynska-Bscher* v. *Oberfinanzdirektion Köln*, [1990] ECR I–4003; Joined Cases C–422–424/93, *Zabala Erasun* v. *Instituto Nacional de Empleo*, [1995] ECR I–1567.

[32] See paragraph 19 of the judgment.

[33] [1998] ECR I–3111, [1998] All ER (EC) 481.

[34] Reported at [1994] ECR II–957.

[35] OJ, 1991, L176/7.

[36] See paragraph 38 of the order in Case C–19/95P, *San Marco* v. *Commission*, [1996] ECR I–4435.

before it did not constitute a point of law which was subject to review by the Court of Justice.[37]

IV *Principles of Community law—recovery of sums paid but not due—procedural time limits under national law*

IV.1 *Case C–231/96, Edilizia Industriale Siderurgica Srl (Edis)* v. *Ministero delle Finanze*, 15 September 1998.[38] Edis applied to the competent Italian finance administration for the refund of certain registration charges payable for the registration of companies in Italy. The request was refused and Edis applied to the President of the Tribunale di Genova for an injunction requiring the Ministry of Finance to refund the sum in question. In *Ponente Carni and Cispadana Costruzioni*,[39] the Court of Justice had held that, subject to certain exceptions, annual charges paid to register companies were contrary to Article 10 of Council Directive 69/335/EEC.[40]

Under Italian law, a taxpayer might request repayment of charges wrongly paid within three years from the date of payment, failing which the action was time-barred. The President of the Tribunale di Genova considered that this time limit might be incompatible with the case law of the Court of Justice on the refunding of charges levied in breach of Community law, and referred three questions to the Court of Justice.

By its first question, the Italian court asked whether a Member State could resist repayment of charges levied in breach of Community law where the effect of that time limit would restrict the effects in time of a preliminary ruling by the Court of Justice. The Court held that it could. The Court noted its well-known case law that, in the absence of Community rules governing the refund of national taxes levied though not due, it was for the domestic legal system to safeguard the rights which individuals derived from Community law providing that such rules were not less favourable than those governing similar actions under domestic law and did not render virtually impossible or excessively difficult the exercise of rights conferred by Community law.[41] The Court also noted that it had recognized that the laying down of reasonable limitation periods for bringing proceedings was compatible with Community law in the interests of legal certainty.[42] Accordingly the Court ruled that:

> . . . the fact that the Court has given a preliminary ruling interpreting a provision of Community law without limiting the temporal effects of its judgment does not affect the right of a Member State to impose a time-limit under national law within which, on

[37] See Case C–53/92P, *Hilti* v. *European Commission*, [1994] ECR I–667 (paragraph 42 of the judgment).

[38] Not yet reported.

[39] [1993] ECR I–1915.

[40] Of 17 July 1969 concerning indirect taxes on the raising of capital (OJ, English Special Edition, 1969 (II), p.412).

[41] See, most recently, Case C–312/93, *Peterbroeck* v. *Belgian State*, [1995] ECR I–4599, paragraph 12 of the judgment.

[42] See, for example, Case 33/76, *Rewe* v. *Landwirtschaftskammer Saarland*, [1976] ECR 1989; see also Case C–261/95, *Palmisani* v. *INPS*, [1997] ECR I–4025, paragraph 28 of the judgment.

penalty of being barred, proceedings for repayment of charges levied in breach of that provision must be commenced.[43]

In its second question, the national court asked whether Community law precluded a Member State from resisting actions for repayment of charges levied in breach of Community law by relying on a three-year time limit in circumstances where the normal rule under national law governing the repayment of sums paid but not due was more favourable. Thus, in essence, the Court was asked to clarify its case law according to which national procedural rules governing actions for safeguarding rights which individuals derived from Community law could not be less favourable than those governing similar actions under national law. The Court noted that there was a considerable diversity between the rules applied in different Member States for the repayment of charges levied unlawfully, and considered that the diversity between national systems derived mainly from the lack of Community rules on the subject. In principle, it was for the national legal systems to lay down their own rules so long as they respected the principles of equivalence (i.e. claims based upon Community law were not treated less favourably than claims based on national law) and effectiveness (i.e. the rules did not render virtually impossible or excessively difficult the exercise of rights conferred by Community law).

On the principle of effectiveness, the Court noted that a time limit of three years from the date of contested payments appeared reasonable. As for the principle of equivalence the Court of Justice considered that:

> That principle cannot, however, be interpreted as obliging a Member State to extend its most favourable rules governing recovery under national law to all actions for repayment of charges or dues levied in breach of Community law.[44]

Further, the Court noted that the time limit at issue applied not only to repayment of the contested registration charge but also to all governmental charges of that kind. Thus the Court held that the time limit was not in breach of the principle of equivalence so long as it applied to actions based on Community law in the same way as to those based on national law.

Finally, the Italian court asked whether the Member State could resist actions for repayment by relying on a three-year time limit in circumstances where it had not properly transposed the directive at the time when the time limit began to run. Edis relied on the Court's decision in *Emmot*,[45] where the Court ruled that a Member State could not rely on a national limitation period to defeat a claim so long as the directive had not been properly implemented. However, in *Fantask*,[46] the Court had expressly ruled that *Emmot* was to be restricted to its own facts. In the present case, the Court applied its decision in *Fantask*, where it had held that the fact that the directive had not been properly transposed did not prevent a Member State from relying on a limitation period of five years. The Court noted that the decision in *Emmot* was justified by the particular circumstances of that case, namely that the time bar had the effect of depriving the plaintiff of any opportunity whatever to rely on her right to equal treatment.

[43] See paragraph 26 of the judgment.
[44] See paragraph 36 of the judgment.
[45] Case C–208/90, *Emmot* v. *Minister for Social Welfare*, [1991] ECR I–4269.
[46] Case C–188/95, [1997] ECR I–6783, noted in this *Year Book*, 68 (1997), p. 455.

Thus, the Court ruled that the three-year time limit imposed by Italian law was permissible even if the limitation period began to run before the directive was properly transposed.

It is to be noted that exactly the same decision was reached in Case C–260/96, *Ministero delle Finanze* v. *Spac SpA*.[47] Further, in two later decisions in 1998, Joined Cases C–10/97 to C–22/97, *Ministero delle Finanze* v. *IN.CO.GE.'90 Srl and others*,[48] and Case C–228/96, *Aprile Srl, en liquidation* v. *Amministrazione delle Finanze dello Stato*,[49] the Court of Justice covered essentially the same subject-matter as that covered in *Edis* and arrived at the same result.

V *Equal treatment of men and women—equal treatment on grounds of sexual orientation—Council Directive (EC) 75/117 — EC Treaty, Article 119*

V.1 *Case C–249/96, Grant* v. *South West Trains Ltd.*, 17 February 1998.[50] In this reference from the Southampton Industrial Tribunal, the Court of Justice considered whether the same-sex partner of the employee of a railway company, Ms Grant, was entitled to travel concessions. It was common ground that had Ms Grant's partner been of the opposite sex, travel concessions would have been granted.[51]

The Court began its judgment by repeating its decision in *Garland* v. *British Rail Engineering Ltd.*,[52] that travel concessions granted by an employer to former employees, and their spouses or dependants, constituted pay within the meaning of Article 119 of the EC Treaty.[53] The Court then went on to consider whether the refusal to grant travel concessions to Ms Grant's same sex-partner was unlawful discrimination.

Ms Grant's first argument was that the refusal was direct discrimination based on sex as her employer's decision would have been different had her partner been a man. This was rejected by the Court of Justice which held that the refusal to grant the travel concessions was based upon the fact that she did not have a 'spouse' or person of the opposite sex with whom she had had a 'meaningful relationship' for more then two years. Accordingly,

> That condition, the effect of which is that the worker must live in a stable relationship with a person of the opposite sex in order to benefit from the travel concession is, like the other alternative conditions prescribed in the undertaking's regulations, applied regardless of the sex of the worker concerned. The travel concessions are refused to a male

[47] Judgment of 15 September 1998, not yet reported.

[48] Judgment of 22 October 1998, not yet reported.

[49] Judgment of 17 November 1998, not yet reported.

[50] [1998] ECR I–621, [1998] All ER (EC) 193.

[51] The applicable regulations provided that 'privilege tickets' were available for unmarried partners who enjoyed 'a meaningful relationship' of two years or more.

[52] Case 12/81, [1982] ECR 359.

[53] Article 119 provides, *inter alia*, as follows:

'Each Member State shall during the first stage ensure and subsequently maintain the application of the principle that men and women should receive equal pay for equal work.

For the purposes of this Article, "pay" means the ordinary basic or minimum wage or salary and any other consideration, whether in cash or in kind, which the worker receives, directly or indirectly, in respect of his employment from his employer.'

worker if he is living with a person of the same sex, just as they are to a female worker if she is living with a person of the same sex.[54]

Next, Ms Grant argued that the refusal to grant travel concessions constituted discrimination based on 'sexual orientation', which was included in the concept of 'discrimination based on sex' found in Article 119 of the EC Treaty, and that the difference in treatment was not objectively justified. This submission was also rejected by the Court of Justice. After reviewing a number of relevant decisions of the European Commission of Human Rights and the European Court of Human Rights, the Court concluded[55]:

> . . . in the present state of the law within the Community, stable relationships between two persons of the same sex are not regarded as equivalent to marriages or stable relationships outside marriage between persons of opposite sex. Consequently, an employer is not required by Community law to treat the situation of a person who has a stable relationship with a partner of the same sex as equivalent to that of a person who is married to or has a stable relationship outside marriage with a partner of the opposite sex.

Next, the Court considered the impact of its decision in *P* v. *S*[56] where it held that the dismissal of an employee on the grounds of a sex change was to be regarded as 'discrimination on grounds of sex' within the meaning of Council Directive (EEC) 76/207.[57] In this respect, the Court held, with somewhat unconvincing reasoning, that its decision in *P* v. *S* was based essentially on the sex of the person involved. Accordingly:

> That reasoning, which leads to the conclusion that such discrimination is to be prohibited just as is discrimination based on the fact that a person belongs to a particular sex, is limited to the case of a worker's gender reassignment and does not therefore apply to differences of treatment based on a person's sexual orientation.[58]

Finally, Ms Grant argued that, like certain provisions of national or international law, Community provisions on equal treatment should be interpreted so as to cover discrimination on the grounds of sexual orientation. She relied upon the International Covenant on Civil and Political Rights[59] in which, according to the view of the Human Rights Committee established under that instrument, the term 'sex' includes sexual orientation.[60]

The Court considered that, although the Covenant was one of the international human rights instruments which it took into account in applying fundamental principles of Community law, and respect for fundamental rights was a condition for the legality of Community acts, those rights could not have

[54] At paragraph 27 of the judgment.

[55] At paragraph 35 of the judgment.

[56] Case C–13/94, [1996] ECR I–2143, [1996] All ER (EC) 397.

[57] On the implementation of the principle of equal treatment for men and women as regards access to employment, vocational training and promotion and working conditions (OJ, 1976, L39/40).

[58] See paragraph 42 of the judgment.

[59] New York, 16 December 1966; TS No. 6(1977); Cmnd. 6702.

[60] See *Toomen* v. *Australia Communication*, [1994] 1–3 IHRR 97.

the effect of rewriting the EC Treaty.[61] Moreover, the Human Rights Committee, in the communication relied on (which was of no binding force), merely stated that in its view the reference to 'sex' in Articles 2, paragraph 1 and 26 is to be taken as including sexual orientation. Therefore:

> Such an observation, which does not in any event, appear to reflect the interpretation so far generally accepted of the concept of discrimination based on sex which appears in various international instruments concerning the protection of fundamental rights, cannot, in any case, constitute a basis for the court to extend the scope of article 119 of the Treaty.[62]

The Court thus concluded that Community law at present did not cover discrimination based on sexual orientation of the type covered by Ms Grant's case. However, the Court noted that the Treaty of Amsterdam, once it entered into force, would contain a new provision, Article 6a, which would permit the EC Council to take appropriate action to eliminate certain forms of discrimination, including discrimination based on sexual orientation.

VI *Free movement of persons—promotion on grounds of seniority—professional experience acquired in another Member State—Act of Accession 1972—Protocol concerning the Channel Islands*

VI.1 *Case C–15/96, Kalliope Schöning-Kougebetopoulou* v. *Freie und Hansestadt Hamburg*, 15 January 1998.[63] In this reference from the Arbeitsgericht, Hamburg, the Court of Justice considered whether the refusal to take into account professional experience acquired in another Member State was contrary to the right to free movement guaranteed by Article 48 of the EC Treaty and Articles 7(1) and (4) of Council Regulation (EEC) 1612/68.[64]

Mrs Schöning-Kougebetopoulou, a Greek national, was employed by the Freie und Hansestadt Hamburg as a doctor. She had previously worked in the Greek public service for six years as a specialist doctor employed under the staff regulations applicable to civil servants in that State. Under the Federal Collective Wage Agreement for Contractual Employees ('the BAT') her professional experience acquired in Greece could not be taken into account in assessing her seniority and thus her wage. She argued that this period should be

[61] See, in this regard *Opinion 2/94*, [1996] ECR 1–1759 (paras. 34–35); noted in this *Year Book*, 67 (1996), p. 657.

[62] At paragraph 49 of the judgment.

[63] [1998] ECR I–47.

[64] On freedom of movement for workers within the Community (OJ, Special Edition, 1968 (II), p. 475). Article 7(1) and (4) of Regulation 1612/68 provides as follows:

> '(1) A worker who is a national of a Member State may not, in the territory of another Member State, be treated differently from national workers by reason of his nationality in respect of any conditions of employment and work, in particular as regards remuneration, dismissal, and should he become unemployed, reinstatement or re-employment.
>
> . . .
>
> (4) Any clause of a collective or individual agreement or of any other collective regulation concerning eligibility for employment, employment, remuneration and other conditions of work or dismissal shall be null and void in so far as it lays down or authorises discriminatory conditions in respect of workers who are nationals of the other Member State.'

taken into account and contended that the failure to do so was indirectly discriminatory.

On the question of discrimination, the Court's response was succinct. The conditions for promotion on the grounds of seniority laid down in the BAT, which did not permit periods of employment completed in other Member States to be taken into account,

> . . . manifestly work to the detriment of migrant workers who have spent part of their careers in the public service of another Member State. For that reason they are such as to contravene the principle of non-discrimination laid down by article 48 of the Treaty and articles 7(1) and (4) of Regulation 1612/68.[65]

The Court then went on to consider whether the discrimination found was objectively justified. The German Government had argued that one purpose of the BAT was to reward an employee's loyalty to his employer and to motivate him by the prospect of improving his financial position. At the oral hearing, the German Government had explained that the BAT covered not only the majority of government institutions but also undertakings performing public interest tasks. Accordingly, the Court considered that, given the multiplicity of employees covered, the provision could not be justified by the desire to reward employee loyalty. Rather the system encouraged considerable mobility within the group of employees covered by the BAT.

Finally, the Court had to consider the effect of a finding that a provision such as the clause in the BAT governing seniority infringed Community law. The Court held that pursuant to Article 7(4) of Council Regulation 1612/68, the clause was null and void. Pending the requisite amendments, the German Government should, by analogy with the Court's case law on the principle of equal pay for men and women,[66] apply the same rules to the members of the group disadvantaged, i.e. workers with relevant professional experience acquired in another Member State, as those it applied to other workers.

VI.2 *Case C–171/96, Rui Alberto Pereira Roque* v. *His Excellency the Lieutenant Governor of Jersey*, 16 July 1998.[67] Mr Roque, a Portuguese national, arrived in Jersey in February 1992. He was admitted without restriction pursuant to section 7(1) of the United Kingdom Immigration Act, 1988.[68] He was employed as a hotel worker and convicted of a number of thefts. In December 1994, the Lieutenant Governor of Jersey issued a deportation order against Mr Roque. Mr

[65] See paragraph 23 of the judgment.

[66] See, most recently, Case C–154/92, *Van Cant* v. *Rijksdienst voor Pensionen*, [1993] ECR I–3811, paragraph 20 of the judgment.

[67] [1998] ECR I–4607.

[68] Which provides as follows:

'a person shall not under the [Immigration Act 1971] require leave to enter or remain in the Bailiwick of Jersey in circumstances in which he would not be entitled to enter or remain in the United Kingdom by virtue of an enforceable Community right . . . '.

Roque contended that the deportation order was contrary to the principle of equal treatment contained in Article 4 of Protocol No. 3.[69]

The Royal Court of Jersey referred three questions to the Court of Justice for a preliminary ruling.

By its first question, the Court asked whether the effect of the rule on equal treatment was to prohibit the deportation of nationals of other Member States from Jersey, since British citizens, including those who are not Channel Islanders, are not liable to be deported from Jersey.[70] The Court held that in so far as Mr Roque's situation fell under the rules on free movement of workers in areas where the Treaty was fully applicable, the principle of equal treatment contained in Article 4 of Protocol No. 3 was applicable to him even if Community nationals could not obtain in the Channel Islands the benefit of the rules on free movement.[71] However, the Court noted that pursuant to Article 48(3) of the EC Treaty, a Member State could restrict the rights to free movement of nationals from other Member States in certain circumstances.[72] It was unable to do so in relation to its own nationals owing to the rule of international law which precluded a State from denying to its own nationals the right to enter its territory and reside there. The EC Treaty could not be assumed to disregard this rule. The Court accepted that Protocol No. 3 distinguished citizens of the United Kingdom having certain links with the Channel Islands from other citizens of the United Kingdom. However, the Court considered that since Channel Islanders are British citizens, the distinction between them and other citizens of the United Kingdom could not be likened to the difference in nationality between the nationals of two Member States. Thus, the Court concluded that the difference in treatment between nationals of other Member States who could be deported, and United Kingdom citizens, including those who were not Channel Islanders, who could not, did not infringe the principle of equal treatment contained in Article 4 of Protocol No. 3.

[69] Protocol No. 3 (OJ, English Special Edition of 27 March 1972, p. 164) provides, pursuant to Article 227(5)(*c*), for the application of certain provisions of the EC Treaty to Jersey.

Article 1 of that Protocol provides, *inter alia*, that Community rules on customs matters and quantitative restrictions are applicable to the Channel Islands under the same conditions as they apply to the United Kingdom.

Article 2 provides as follows:

'The rights enjoyed by Channel Islanders or Manxmen in the United Kingdom shall not be affected by the Act of Accession. However, such persons shall not benefit from Community provisions relating to the free movement of persons and services.'

Article 4 provides that:

'The authorities of these territories shall apply the same treatment to all natural and legal persons of the Community.'

[70] Within the meaning of Article 6 of Protocol No. 3, which provides as follows:

'In this Protocol, Channel Islander or Manxman shall mean any citizen of the United Kingdom and Colonies who holds that citizenship by virtue of the fact that he, a parent or grandparent was born, adopted, naturalised or registered in the island in question; but such a person shall not for this purpose be regarded as a Channel Islander or Manxman if he, a parent or grandparent was born, adopted, naturalised or registered in the United Kingdom. Nor shall he be so regarded if he has at any time been ordinarily resident in the United Kingdom for five years.

The administrative arrangements necessary to identify these persons will be notified to the Commission.'

[71] By reason of Article 2 of Protocol No 3.

[72] Namely if the restrictions are justified on the grounds of public policy, public security or public health.

Next the Jersey Court asked whether Article 4 of Protocol No. 3 limited the reasons for which a national of another Member State could be deported to those contained in Article 48(3) of the Treaty, namely public policy, public security or public health. The Court held that the principle of equal treatment, even if it permitted a difference in treatment between citizens of the United Kingdom and nationals of other Member States, prohibited the Jersey authorities from basing the exercise of their powers on factors which would result in the application of an arbitrary distinction to the detriment of nationals of other Member States. Such an arbitrary distinction would occur if a deportation order were made against a national of another Member State on the basis of an assessment of conduct which, when attributable to nationals of the United Kingdom, would not give rise to repressive measures or other effective measures intended to combat such conduct. In the case of Jersey, the Court considered that the relevant comparison was between the circumstances when a person from another Member State would be the subject of a deportation order and the measures which would be taken if the same type of conduct was to be attributed to a citizen of the United Kingdom.

Finally, the Jersey Court asked whether a national of another Member State could be deported when the public policy considerations relied upon would not in practice result in the deportation of that person from the United Kingdom. In response, the Court noted that even if the Channel Island authorities might rely on considerations other than those laid down in Community law to deport a national from another Member State, the extension of a deportation order to the mainland territory of the United Kingdom might have the indirect consequence of making the provisions of Community law on the freedom of movement of persons no longer fully applicable there. The Court considered that it was clear from Article 227(5) of the EC Treaty,[73] as well as the provisions of Protocol No. 3, that those are not intended to affect the free movements of nationals of other Member States in the territory of the United Kingdom. Accordingly, the Court concluded that Protocol No. 3 could not be interpreted so that a deportation order made against a national of another Member State could prohibit that person's right to enter and reside in the territory of the United Kingdom for reasons other than those for which the United Kingdom authorities could restrict the free movement of persons under Community law.

[73] Which provides, *inter alia*, as follows:
'(*c*) . . . this Treaty shall apply to the Channel Islands and the Isle of Man only to the extent necessary to ensure the implementation of the arrangements for those islands set out in the Treaty concerning the accession of new Member States to the European Economic Community and the European Atomic Energy Committee signed on 22 January 1972.'

VII *Brussels Convention—Article 21—lis alibi pendens provisions—definition of 'same parties'—interpretation of Article 5(1),(3) and Article 6—claim for compensation by the consignee or insurer of the goods on the basis of the bill of lading against a defendant who did not issue the bill of lading but is regarded by the plaintiff as the actual maritime carrier—arbitration clause—interim payment—provisional measures*

VII.1 *Case C–351/96, Drouot Assurances SA* v. *Consolidated Metallurgical Industries (CMI Industrial Sites)*, 19 May 1998.[74] This reference from the French Cour de Cassation considered the interpretation of the *lis alibi pendens* provisions contained in Article 21[75] of the Brussels Convention.[76] CMI arranged to transport cargo from the Dutch port of Rotterdam to the French port of Garlingham-Aire-la-Lys on the Rhine on board the vessel *Sequena*. The vessel foundered during the voyage. The vessel's hull insurer, Drouot, had the vessel refloated at its own expense and CMI's cargo was salvaged.

In December 1990, Drouot brought proceedings before the Paris Tribunal de Commerce, against CMI, Protea (the cargo insurers) and GIE Réunion (Protea's agent at the time of the incident) seeking a contribution to general average.

Four months previously, in August 1989, CMI and Protea had commenced proceedings against the vessel's owner and charterer before the Arrondissementsrechtsbank, Rotterdam, seeking, *inter alia*, a declaration that they were not liable to contribute to general average. Before the French Courts, they sought to argue that, pursuant to the *lis alibi pendens* provisions contained in Article 21 of the Brussels Convention, the French Court was obliged to stay its proceedings as the court second seised. CMI argued that the only reason why Drouot were not a party to the Dutch proceedings was a rule of Dutch procedure according to which insurers were not permitted to be joined to proceedings. Further, the subject-matter of the Dutch proceedings encompassed the proceedings before the French Court. Accordingly, the subject-matter of the two proceedings was the same.

The question was referred to the Court of Justice. The question for the Court was whether, in the context of the Dutch and French proceedings, the hull insurer could be deemed to be the same person as the insured for the purposes of Article 21 of the Convention.

Repeating its previous decision on Article 21 in *The Tatry*,[77] the Court repeated that the purpose of the *lis alibi pendens* provisions contained in Articles 21 and 22 of the Brussels Convention was to prevent the risk of parallel proceedings and to avoid conflicts in decisions between them. Thus the object of

[74] [1998] ECR I–3075, [1998] All ER (EC) 483.

[75] Article 21 provides, *inter alia*, as follows:

'Where proceedings involving the same cause of action and between the same parties are brought in the Courts of different Contracting States, any court other than the court first seised shall of its own motion decline jurisdiction in favour of that court.

A court which would be required to decline jurisdiction may stay its proceedings if the jurisdiction of the other court is contested.'

[76] The Convention on Jurisdiction and the Enforcement of Judgments in Civil and Commercial Matters, 1968.

[77] Case 406/92, *The Maciej Rataj, Tatry (cargo owners)* v. *Maciej Rataj (owners)*, [1994] ECR I–5439, paragraphs 32–33 of the judgment; [1995] All ER (EC) 229.

the rules was to prevent, so far as possible, the need to apply Article 27(3) of the Convention.[78]

On the issue of the identity of interests between the insurer and the insured and whether they may be deemed the same person for the purposes of Article 21 of the Convention, the Court of Justice distinguished two different situations. The Court considered, on the one hand, that:

> 19. . . . there may be such a degree of identity between the interests of the insurer and those of its insured that a judgment delivered against one of them would have the force of res judicata against the other. That would be the case, inter alia, where an insurer, by virtue of its right of subrogation, brings or defends an action in the name of its insured without the latter being in a position to influence the proceedings. In such a situation, insurer and insured must be considered to be one and the same for the purposes of the application of the Convention.

On the other hand, the Court of Justice noted that:

> 20. . . . the application of Article 21 of the Convention cannot have the effect of precluding the insurer and its insured, where their interests diverge, from asserting their respective interests before the courts as against the other parties concerned.

Applying those principles to the facts before it, the Court noted that the interests of the insurer and the insured did not appear to be identical in the two proceedings. In the Netherlands action, CMI and Protea sought to have the owner of the vessel declared exclusively liable for the foundering and Drouot, the hull insurer, took the view that it could not be held liable for the fault of its insured and thus had no interest in the Netherlands proceedings. Further, before the French courts, Drouot was acting not in its capacity as representative of the insured but as a direct participant in the refloating of the vessel.

The Court concluded, however, that it was for the national court to determine whether this was the case. Article 21 would only require the French courts to decline jurisdiction if:

> . . . with regard to the subject matter of the two disputes, the interests of the insurer of the hull of the vessel are identical to and indissociable from those of its insured, the owner and the charterer of that vessel.[79]

VII.2 *Case C–51/97, Réunion Européenne SA and others* v. *Spliethoff's Bevrachtingskantoor BV and Capitaine Commandant le Navire 'Alblasgracht V002'*, 27 October 1998.[80] A consignment of pears was carried from Melbourne to Rotterdam aboard the vessel *Alblasgracht V002* under a bearer bill of lading issued by Refrigerated Container Carriers Pty. Limited ('RCC') whose registered office was in Sydney. The goods were then carried by road under an international consignment note to Rungis in France where Brambi Fruit, the receivers, discovered the damage. Proceedings were commenced by Brambi's insurers against RCC, Spliethoff's Bevrachtingskantoor BV ('Spliethoff') and against the Master of the vessel before the Tribunal de Commerce in Créteil,

[78] Article 27(3) of the Convention provides for the non-recognition of a judgment on the grounds of its irreconcilability with a judgment given in a dispute between the same parties in a State in which recognition is sought.

[79] At paragraph 25 of the judgment.

[80] Not yet reported.

where Rungis is situated. The Tribunal de Commerce considered that it should decline jurisdiction in favour of Rotterdam, on the basis that Rotterdam was the place of performance of the obligation in question for the purposes of Article 5(1) of the Brussels Convention.[81] In the alternative, the Court considered that it should decline jurisdiction in favour of Amsterdam or Sydney pursuant to Article 6(1) of the Convention.[82] The French Cour de Cassation decided to refer four questions to the Court of Justice.

In its judgment, the Court of Justice first considered the scope of Articles 5(1) and (3) of the Convention. Both the Master of the vessel and Spliethoff submitted that the dispute was a 'matter relating to a contract' for the purposes of Article 5(1) of the Brussels Convention, since the action against them was based upon the bill of lading, the document containing the combined transport document. This argument was rejected by the Court. Repeating its decision in *Handte*,[83] where the Court held that the phrase 'matters relating to a contract' was not to be understood as covering a situation in which there was no obligation freely assumed by one party towards the other, the Court of Justice held that the bill of lading disclosed no contractual relationship between Brambi, the receivers, and Spliethoff's and the Master, who, according to the insurers, were the actual carriers of the goods. The Court thus concluded that the action was not covered by Article 5(1) of the Convention.

Next, the Court went on to consider whether the action fell within the scope of Article 5(3). The Court considered that the action did fall within Article 5(3), basing its decision on *Kalfelis* v. *Schröder*[84] where it held that the concept of matters relating to tort, delict or quasi-delict was an independent concept which was apt to cover all actions which seek to establish the liability of a defendant and which are not related to a contract within the meaning of Article 5(1).

By the third question referred, the Court had to consider the scope of the phrase 'place where the harmful event occurred' in Article 5(3) of the Convention. In previous cases,[85] the Court had held that the phrase must be understood as being intended to cover both the place where the damage occurred and the place of the event giving rise to it, so that the defendant might be sued, at the option of the plaintiff, in the courts of either place. In a restrictive interpretation of Article 5(3),[86] the Court held that the term could not be construed so extensively as to encompass any place where the adverse consequences could be felt of an event which had already caused damage actually arising elsewhere. Thus, in an international transport operation, the place where the damage

[81] Article 5(1) and (3) of the Convention provides as follows:

'A person domiciled in a Contracting State may, in another Contracting State, be sued:

(1) in matters relating to a contract, in the courts for the place of performance of the obligation in question . . .

. . .

(3) in matters relating to tort, delict or quasi-delict, in the courts for the place where the harmful event occurred.

[82] Article 6(1) provides that where such a person is one of a number of defendants, he may also be sued in the courts where any one of them is domiciled.

[83] Case C–26/91, [1992] ECR 3967.

[84] Case 189/87, [1988] ECR 5565.

[85] See, in particular, Case 21/76, *Bier* v. *Mines de Potasse d'Alsace*, [1976] ECR 1735, and Case C–68/93, *Shevill and others* v. *Presse Alliance*, [1995] ECR I–415.

[86] See, for a similarly restrictive interpretation, Case C–364/93, *Marinari* v. *Lloyds Bank*, [1995] ECR I–2719.

occurred could not be either the place of final delivery, which could be changed mid-voyage, or the place where the damage was discovered. Moreover, the Court noted that to permit the consignee to bring his action before the courts of the place of final delivery, or before those of the place where the damage was ascertained, would in most cases mean granting jurisdiction to the place of the plaintiff's domicile which was against the object of the Convention, save in the cases in which it was expressly provided for. The Court thus concluded that:

> . . . the place where the damage arose in the case of an international transport operation of the kind at issue in the main proceedings can only be the place where the actual maritime carrier was to deliver the goods.[87]

Finally, the Court considered the possible application of Articles 22[88] and 6(1) of the Brussels Convention.[89] This was in response to a question from the national court as to whether a defendant domiciled in the territory of a Contracting State may be brought before the court in another Contracting State hearing an action against a co-defendant not domiciled in the territory of any Contracting State, on the grounds that the disputes in question were indivisible, rather than merely displaying a connection.

The Court noted that Article 22 could only apply where related actions are brought before courts of two or more Contracting States. There was no evidence that separate actions had been brought before the courts of different Contracting States. Further, Article 6(1) could only apply if the proceedings were brought before the courts for the place where one of the defendants was domiciled. This was similarly not the case here. For Article 6(1) to apply, the Court considered:

> there must exist between the various actions brought by the same plaintiff against different defendants a connection of such a kind that it is expedient to determine the actions together in order to avoid the risk of irreconcilable judgments resulting from separate proceedings.[90]

Further, the Court noted its decision in *Kalfelis* where it held that a court only had jurisdiction under Article 5(3) of the Convention over an action to the extent that it was based on tort or delict. Thus, the Court of Justice concluded that:

> . . . two claims in one action for compensation, directed against different defendants and based in one instance on contractual liability and in the other on liability in tort or delict cannot be regarded as connected.[91]

The Court noted that although disadvantages might arise from different aspects of the same dispute being decided by different courts, it was always open to a plaintiff to bring the entirety of his claim in the courts where the defendant was domiciled.

[87] Paragraph 35 of the judgment.

[88] Which provides as follows:

'Where related actions are brought in the courts of different Contracting States, any court other than the court first seised may, while the actions are pending at first instance, stay its proceedings.'

[89] Which provides that a person may also be sued, 'where he is one of a number of defendants, in the courts for the place where any one of them is domiciled'.

[90] Paragraph 48 of the judgment.

[91] Paragraph 50 of the judgment.

VII.3 *Case C–391/95, Van Uden Maritime BV, agissant sous le nom Van Uden Africa Line/Kommanditgesellschaft in Firma Deco-Line ea*, 17 November 1998.[92] Van Uden Maritime BV ('Van Uden') and Deco-Line concluded a 'slot/space charter agreement' pursuant to which Van Uden undertook to make available to Deco-Line cargo space on vessels operated by Van Uden. In return, Deco-Line was to pay charterparty hire. Van Uden instituted arbitration proceedings in the Netherlands on the grounds that Deco-Line had failed to pay certain invoices submitted by Van Uden. Van Uden also applied to the President of the Rechtsbank, Rotterdam, for an interim payment. Following appeals to the Gerechtshof te s'Gravenhage and then to the Hoge Raad der Nederlanden, a number of questions were referred to the Court of Justice on the scope of Article 5(1) of the Brussels Convention, the scope of the arbitration exclusion contained in Article 1 of the Brussels Convention[93] and Article 24 of the Brussels Convention.[94]

In summary, the national court wished to know whether (*a*) it could assume jurisdiction over the application for an interim payment pursuant to Article 5(1) of the Convention or, alternatively, (*b*) jurisdiction could be assumed on the basis that the application was for a 'provisional measure' within the meaning of Article 24.

First, the Court of Justice considered the impact of the arbitration exclusion contained in Article 1 of the Convention and its interrelationship with Article 5(1). The Court concluded in this respect that:

> Where the parties have validly excluded the jurisdiction of the courts in a dispute arising under a contract and have referred that dispute to arbitration, there are not courts of any State that have jurisdiction as to the substance of the case for the purposes of the Convention. Consequently, a party to such a contract is not in a position to make an application for provisional or protective measures to a court that would have jurisdiction under the Convention as to the substance of the case.[95]

The Court then went on to consider the effect of Article 24. The Court noted that the object of the arbitration exclusion contained in Article 1 was to exclude arbitration in its entirety, including proceedings before national courts.[96] However, the Court considered that provisional measures were not in principle ancillary to arbitration proceedings as they concerned not arbitration as such but the protection of a wide variety of rights. Thus, the Court concluded that:

> . . . where . . . the subject matter of an application for provisional measures relates to a question falling within the scope *ratione materiae* of the Convention, the Convention is applicable and Article 24 thereof may confer jurisdiction on the court hearing that application even where proceedings have already been, or may be, commenced on the

[92] Not yet reported.

[93] Which provides that the Convention does not apply to arbitration.

[94] Which provides as follows:

'Applications may be made to the courts of a Contracting State for such provisional, including protective, measures as may be available under the law of that State even if, under this Convention, the courts of another Contracting State have jurisdiction as to the substance of the matter.'

[95] At paragraph 24 of the judgment.

[96] See, in this respect, Case C–190/89, *Rich* v. *Società Italiana Impianti*, [1991] ECR I–3855.

substance of the case and even where those proceedings are to be conducted before arbitrators.[97]

Next, the Court considered the conditions necessary for the grant of provisional measures under Article 24. In this respect, it held that the granting of provisional or protective measures was subject to the requirement of a real connecting link between the measures sought and the territorial jurisdiction of the court before whom the request was made.

Finally, the Court considered whether an interim payment order could be classified as a provisional measure. Deco-Line, the United Kingdom Government and the German Government argued that it could not. The Commission and Van Uden on the other hand submitted that provisional measures within the meaning of Article 24 could comprise positive acts such as the handing over of property or the payment of a sum of money.

The Court considered that an interim payment order could by its very nature pre-empt the decision on the merits of the case. Further, in circumstances where the plaintiff could secure such an order in his State of domicile even if that court did not have jurisdiction over the substance of the case, and thereafter have that order recognized in the defendant's State of domicile, this could undermine the whole scheme of the Convention and, in particular, the jurisdictional rules laid down in Articles 2 to 18. Accordingly, the Court ruled that an interim payment order was not a provisional measure for the purposes of Article 24 of the Convention unless repayment to the defendants was guaranteed if the plaintiff lost the case on the merits, and also if the measure related only to assets located within the territorial jurisdiction of the court where the application was made.

SARA MASTERS

[97] At paragraph 34 of the judgment.

UNITED KINGDOM MATERIALS ON INTERNATIONAL LAW 1998*

Edited by GEOFFREY MARSTON[1]

[*Editorial Notes*:
1. From its start in 1978 and up to and including 1996, the materials in UKMIL were classified on the basis of the *Model Plan for the Classification of Documents concerning State Practice in the Field of Public International Law* adopted by the Committee of Ministers of the Council of Europe in its Resolution (68) 17 of 28 June 1968. The Committee of Ministers considered that developments in public international law since 1968 made it necessary to amend the Model Plan. Accordingly, by Recommendation (97)11 of 12 June 1997, it adopted an Amended Model Plan as a contribution by the Council of Europe towards implementing General Assembly Resolution 2099(XX) on technical assistance to promote the teaching, study, dissemination and wider understanding of international law and to the United Nations Decade of International Law from 1990 to 1999. The present issue of UKMIL is based on the Amended Model Plan.
2. Attention is drawn to the editorial note in UKMIL 1983, p. 361. Delay in the appearance of the bound volumes of the *Parliamentary Debates* has not made it possible to make any corrections which might be necessary to the column references in volumes 319 to 322 of the House of Commons Debates and in volumes 593 to 595 of the House of Lords Debates.]

INDEX

Part One: International Law in general — *Page*

I. Nature, basis, purpose
- A. General
- B. *jus cogens* — 443
- C. 'Soft law'

[1] LL M, Ph.D (Lond.): Lecturer in Law, University of Cambridge; Fellow of Sidney Sussex College, The assistance of Ms S. C. Hulton of the Legal Advisers, Foreign and Commonwealth Office, of the Treaty and News Departments, Foreign and Commonwealth Office, and of the staff of the Official Publications Department, University Library, Cambridge, is gratefully acknowledged.

II. History

Part Two: Sources and Codification of International Law

I. Sources of international law
A. Treaties
B. Custom 443
C. General principles of law
D. Unilateral acts (including acts and decisions of international organizations and conferences)
E. Judicial decisions
F. Opinions of writers
G. Equity
H. Comity
II. Acquisition, retention and loss of rights (see also Part Nine: III. B., below) 444
III. Codification and progressive development 444

Part Three: The Law of Treaties

I. Definition, conclusion and entry into force
A. Definition
B. Conclusion, including signature, ratification and accession 447
C. Reservations, declarations and objections 454
D. Provisional application and entry into force
II. Observance, application and interpretation
A. Observance
B. Application
C. Interpretation
D. Treaties and third States
III. Amendment and modification
IV. Breach and its consequences 455
V. Invalidity, termination and suspension of operation
A. General rules
B. Invalidity
C. Termination and suspension of operation, denunciation and withdrawal 456
D. Procedure
E. Consequences of invalidity, termination and suspension of operation
VI. State succession in respect of treaties (see Part Five: I.D.5.(b).(iii).)
VII. Depositaries, notifications, corrections and registration
VIII. Consensual arrangements other than treaties

Part Four: Relationship between International Law and Internal Law

I. General
II. Application and implementation of international law in internal law
A. Treaties 462
B. Custom
C. Sources other than treaty and custom
III. Remedies under internal law for violation of international law (see also Part Six: IX. and Part Seventeen: V.) 472
IV. Non-justiciability, including public interest immunity

Part Five: Subjects of International Law

I. States
A. Status and powers
1. Personality
2. Territorial integrity 474
3. Sovereignty and independence 474
4. Non-intervention 475
5. Domestic jurisdiction 476
6. Equality of States
7. State immunity (see Part Seven: IV. A.)
8. Treaty-making power
9. Powers other than treaty-making
B. Recognition
1. Recognition of States 476
2. Recognition of governments 477
3. Types of recognition
(a) *de facto/de jure*
(b) conditional/unilateral
4. Acts of recognition
(a) express/implied
(b) unilateral/collective
5. Effects of recognition
6. Non-recognition and its effects 478
7. Withdrawal of recognition
C. Types of States
1. Unitary States
2. Personal and real unions
3. Federal States and confederations
4. Protected States
5. The Holy See
D. Formation, continuity, extinction and succession of States
1. Conditions for statehood

2. Formation
3. Identity and continuity 479
4. Extinction
5. Succession
(a) Situations of State succession
(i) Union with or without demise of predecessor State
(ii) Dismemberment
(iii) Separation
(iv) Succession
(b) Effects of State succession
(i) Territory and other areas under national jurisdiction
(ii) Nationality
(iii) Succession in respect of treaties 479
(iv) Archives
(v) Debts 488
(vi) Property 488
(vii) Responsibility
(viii) Other rights and obligations
II. International organizations
A. General
1. Status and powers
(a) Personality
(b) Privileges and immunities of the organization
(c) Treaty-making power
(d) Other powers
2. Participation of States and international organizations in international organizations and in their activities
(a) Admission
(b) Suspension, withdrawal and expulsion
(c) Obligations of membership
(d) Representation of States and international organizations, including privileges and immunities
3. Legal effect of the acts of international organizations 488
4. Personnel of international organizations, including privileges and immunities 488
5. Responsibility of international organizations (see Part Thirteen: III. B.)
6. Succession of international organizations
B. Particular types of organizations
1. Universal organizations

2. Regional organizations
3. Organizations constituting integrated (e.g. economic) communities
4. Other types
III. Entities and groups other than States and international organizations
A. Mandated and trust territories
B. Dependent territories 490
C. Condominia
D. Special regimes
E. Self-determination units and the concept of self-determination 495
F. Insurgents
G. Belligerents
H. Others (e.g. indigenous peoples, minorities, national liberation movements)

Part Six: The Individual (including the Corporation) in International Law

I. Nationality
II. Diplomatic and consular protection (see Part Thirteen: II.C.)
III. Aliens
IV. Members of minorities
V. Stateless persons
VI. Refugees
VII. Immigration and emigration, extradition, expulsion, asylum
A. Immigration and emigration 498
B. Extradition 498
C. Expulsion
D. Asylum
VIII. Human rights and fundamental freedoms 506
IX. Crimes under international law (see also Part Seventeen: IV) 512
X. Responsibility of the individual (see Part Thirteen: III.D.)

Part Seven: The State and its Organs

I. The composition of the State
A. Heads of State
B. Ministers
C. Departments of the State
D. Diplomatic missions and their members 522
E. Consulates and their members

F. Special missions
G. Trades and information offices, trade delegations, etc.
H. Armed forces
I. Police and security services
II. Protecting Powers
III. State property
IV. Privileges and immunities
A. State immunity (including Head of State immunity) 523
B. Diplomatic privileges and immunities 524
C. Consular privileges and immunities 527
D. Visiting forces 527
E. Other privileges and immunities

Part Eight: Jurisdiction of the State

I. Bases of jurisdiction
A. Territorial principle
B. Personal principle
C. Protective principle
D. Universality principle
E. Other bases
II. Types of jurisdiction
A. Jurisdiction to prescribe
B. Jurisdiction to adjudicate
C. Jurisdiction to enforce
III. Extra-territorial exercises of jurisdiction
A. General 530
B. Consular jurisdiction
C. Military and other personnel abroad
D. Others (e.g. artificial islands, *terrae nullius*)
IV. Limitations upon jurisdiction (e.g. servitudes, leases)
V. Concurrent jurisdiction

Part Nine: State Territory

I. Territory
A. Elements of territory
1. Land, internal waters, lakes, rivers and land-locked seas (see also Parts Ten and Eleven: I.)
2. Sub-soil
3. Territorial sea (see Part Eleven: II.)
4. Airspace (see Part Twelve: I.)
B. Good neighbourliness 534
II. Boundaries and frontiers
A. Delimitation 535
B. Demarcation
C. Stability

III. Territorial sovereignty
A. General
B. Acquisition and retention 536
C. Loss 539

Part Ten: International Watercourses

I. Rivers and lakes
A. Definition
B. Navigation
C. Uses other than navigation
D. Protection of the environment
E. Institutional aspects
II. Groundwaters
III. Canals

Part Eleven: Seas and Vessels

I. Internal waters (including ports and harbours) 540
II. Territorial sea 542
III. Straits
IV. Archipelagic waters
V. Contiguous zone 549
VI. Exclusive economic zone
VII. Exclusive or preferential fisheries zone 549
VIII. Continental shelf
IX. High seas
A. Freedom of the high seas 550
B. Visit and search
C. Hot pursuit
D. Piracy
E. Conservation of living resources
X. Islands, rocks and low-tide elevations
XI. Enclosed and semi-enclosed seas
XII. International Seabed Area
XIII. Land-locked and geographically disadvantaged States
XIV. Protection of the marine environment
XV. Marine scientific research
XVI. Cables and pipelines
XVII. Artificial islands, installations and structures
XVIII. Tunnels
XIX. Vessels
A. Legal regime
1. Warships
2. Public vessels other than warships
3. Merchant vessels
B. Nationality

C. Jurisdiction over vessels
1. Flag State
2. Coastal State
3. Port State
4. Other exercises of jurisdiction
XX. International law of the sea in general

Part Twelve: Air Space, Outer Space and Antarctica
I. Air space
A. Status and limits
B. Uses
C. Legal regime of aircraft
II. Outer space and celestial bodies
A. Status and limits 550
B. Uses
C. Legal regime of spacecraft
III. Antarctica
A. Limits and status
B. Uses
C. Protection of the environment

Part Thirteen: International Responsibility
I. General concept 551
II. General issues of international responsibility
A. The elements of responsibility (e.g. wrongfulness of the act, imputability) 552
B. Factors excluding responsibility (e.g. self-defence, necessity, counter-measures) 553
C. Procedure
1. Diplomatic protection 557
(a) Nationality of claims
(b) Exhaustion of local remedies 557
2. Consular protection
3. Peaceful settlement of disputes (see Part Fourteen)
D. Consequences of responsibility
1. Reparation 559
2. Other consequences
III. Responsible entities
A. States
1. Criminal responsibility 561
2. Responsibility other than criminal 563
B. International organizations
C. Entities other than States and international organizations
D. Individuals (including corporations) 564

Part Fourteen: Peaceful Settlement of Disputes

I. The concept of an international dispute
II. Means of settlement
A. Negotiations 564
B. Good offices
C. Enquiry (fact-finding)
D. Mediation
E. Conciliation
F. Arbitration
1. Permanent Court of Arbitration
2. Arbitral tribunals and commissions other than the Permanent Court of Arbitration 565
G. Judicial settlement
1. International Court of Justice 567
2. Courts and tribunals other than the International Court of Justice
H. Settlement within international organizations
1. United Nations
2. Organizations other than the United Nations 569
I. Other means of settlement

Part Fifteen: Coercive Measures short of the Use of Force

I. Unilateral measures
A. Retorsion
B. Counter-measures 569
C. Pacific blockade
D. Intervention (see also Part Five: I. A. 4.)
E. Other unilateral measures 571
II. Collective measures
A. United Nations 572
B. Outside the United Nations 582

Part Sixteen: Use of Force

I. Prohibition of the use of force
II. Legitimate use of force
A. Self-defence 585
B. Collective measures
1. United Nations 586
2. Outside the United Nations
C. Legitimate uses other than self-defence and collective measures 592
III. Disarmament and arms control

Part Seventeen: The Law of Armed Conflict

I. International armed conflict
A. Definition
B. The law of international armed conflict
1. Sources
2. Commencement of international armed conflict and its legal effects
3. Land warfare
4. Sea warfare
5. Air warfare
6. Distinction between combatants and non-combatants
7. Belligerent occupation 594
8. Conventional weapons 600
9. Nuclear, bacteriological and chemical weapons 601
10. Treaty relations between combatants (e.g. armistices)
11. Termination of international armed conflict, treaties of peace 604
II. Non-international armed conflict
III. International humanitarian law 605
IV. War crimes (see also Part Six: IX. and Part Thirteen: III. D.) 606

Part Eighteen: Neutrality and Non-belligerency

I. The laws of neutrality
A. Land warfare
B. Sea warfare
C. Air warfare
II. Permanent neutrality
III. Neutrality in the light of the United Nations Charter
IV. Policy of neutrality and non-alignment
V. Non-belligerency

Appendices

I. Multilateral Agreements signed by the UK in 1998 608
II. European Communities Agreements signed by the UK in 1998 611
III. Bilateral Agreements signed by the UK in 1998 623
IV. UK Legislation during 1998 concerning matters of International Law 628

Abbreviations

HC Debs.	*Hansard*, House of Commons Debates (6th series)
HL Debs.	*Hansard*, House of Lords Debates (5th series)
Cmnd.	Command Paper (5th series)
Cm	Command Paper (6th series)
UKMIL	*United Kingdom Materials on International Law*
TS	*United Kingdom Treaty Series*
EC	European Community
EU	European Union
FCO	Foreign and Commonwealth Office
WA	Written Answers

Part One: I. B. *International law in general—nature, basis, purpose—jus cogens*

(See Part Thirteen II. B. (paragraph 86 of comments by UK Government on International Law Commission's draft articles on State responsibility) and Part Thirteen: III. A. 1. (ibid., paragraph 52), below)

Part Two: I. B. *Sources and codification of international law—sources of international law—custom*

(See also Part Thirteen (comments by UK Government on ILC draft articles on State responsibility), below)

The following question was asked of Her Majesty's Government:

What action they took, as holders of the presidency of the European Union, to persuade the Serbian authorities to honour their international obligations under the Code of Conduct on Politico-Military Aspects of Security of the Organisation for Security and Co-operation in Europe?

The Parliamentary Under-Secretary of State, FCO, Baroness Symons of Vernham Dean, replied:

. . . the Federal Republic of Yugoslavia is not a participating state in the OSCE. As presidency of the EU, the UK has therefore not specifically raised compliance with the Code of Conduct on Politico-Military Aspects of Security with the Federal Republic of Yugoslavia. However, we have frequently reminded the Yugoslav authorities of their need to show commitment to the process of democratisation, respect for human rights and the rule of law.

The questioner then asked:

. . . is not the code simply a restatement of customary international law? Is it not a gross breach of customary international law to kill several hundred civilians and forcibly displace 60,000 people from their homes?

The Minister responded in part:

. . . the noble Lord often poses important questions and I shall try to deal with them. The Code of Conduct on Politico-Military Aspects of Security is politically binding. It enshrines a number of international agreements and conventions, mainly concerning the democratic control of armed forces. Since the FRY suspension from the OSCE, there is no mechanism available to ensure compliance with the Code.

(HL Debs., vol. 591, col. 669: 1 July 1998)

Part Two: II. *Sources and codification of international law—acquisition, retention and loss of rights*

(See Part Nine: III. B. (item of 9 December 1997), below)

Part Two: III. *Sources and codification of international law—codification and progressive development*

Speaking in the Sixth Committee of the UN General Assembly on 17 November 1998, the representative of Austria, on behalf of the EU, stated in part:

I have the honour to speak on behalf of the European Union. The Central and Eastern European countries associated with the European Union, Bulgaria, Czech Republic, Estonia, Hungary, Latvia, Lithuania, Poland, Romania, Slovakia and Slovenia, and the Associated country Cyprus, as well as the EFTA countries members of the EEA, Iceland and Norway, align themselves with this statement.

The item concerning the United Nations Decade on International Law is now in its ninth year. The resolution which the GA will adopt at the conclusion of the consideration of this item will be the tenth in a row. The Decade on International Law in now drawing to a close. The year 1999 will see the final activities of the Decade.

It is therefore altogether timely at this stage to proceed to a stocktaking, to reflect on what has been done and achieved during the Decade and also to look back for a moment to the beginning. When the General Assembly on 17 November 1989 adopted resolution 44/23 setting in motion the Decade and a variety of related programmes and projects on which it subsequently decided in a step by step procedure, it was conscious not only of the general feeling that there was an overall need to strengthen the rule of law in international relations, but also of the fact that in the last decade of the twentieth century important anniversaries would be celebrated related to the adoption of certain international legal documents of great impact and importance. The 50th anniversary of the UN Charter, mentioned in resolution 44/23, is already history as is the twenty-fifth anniversary of the Declaration on Principles of International Law concerning Friendly Relations and Co-operation among States in accordance with the Charter of the United Nations. What lies before us on the other hand is the centenary of the first International Peace Conference, held at The Hague in

1899, which adopted the Convention for the Pacific Settlement of International Disputes and created the Permanent Court of Arbitration. For celebration of the latter anniversary promising preparations are under way. I shall come to that later.

As the Decade enters its final year, we ought to recall its main purposes which are:

– to promote acceptance of and respect for the principles of international law;

– to promote means and methods for the peaceful settlement of disputes between States, including resort to and full respect for the International Court of Justice;

– to encourage the progressive development of international law and its codification;

– to encourage the teaching, study, dissemination and wider appreciation of international law;

How and to what extent have those purposes been achieved?

In the world of today there is certainly a greater awareness than ever before of the role which international law is designed to play in international relations. State authorities and the public at large realize the potential of international law and the need to apply the rule to inter-State relations.

This, we think, is at least partly a result of the relevant activities undertaken in this field by the United Nations, within the framework of the Decade or with the Decade in mind. The European Union had occasion to comment on those activities as they evolved over the years and as they were reported to the General Assembly by the Secretary-General in his successive reports. Last year we had occasion to state that the implementation of the Decade activities has indeed contributed to giving life to the aspirations expressed at the start of the Decade. We emphasized that the Legal Office and in particular the Codification Division deserved praise for the skill and energy with which they have conducted their tasks under the Decade programme. One of the main objectives of the Decade was to introduce the themes of international law to a much broader public than only to the very few scholars and practitioners of international law. Among others, many well respected lawyers, professors, diplomats and officials of various international organizations, both governmental and non-governmental, were alerted and have played a role towards the fulfilment of this particular objective of the Decade. In every year since 1987 people and organizations all over the world were involved in the organization of activities related to the realization of objectives of the Decade.

This year the Secretary-General has again submitted a report on the relevant action undertaken by him, and we wish to thank him for the overview contained in his note A/53/492. Some of the activities carried out by the Secretariat deserve our highest praise. I shall just mention a few of them.

The European Union welcomes the determined effort which has been made to eliminate the backlog in the publication of the United Nations Juridical Yearbook. All those who use the Juridical Yearbook as an essential repertory of UN procedures and practices will appreciate that the editions will soon be complete up to 1995. Moreover, the cumulative index for the Yearbook covering the period 1962–1986 will be issued in the near future. We are aware of the amount of painstaking work which went into the preparation of these Yearbooks and we readily express our appreciation. Similarly we welcome the issuance of the Summaries of Judgments, Advisory Opinions and Orders of the International Court of Justice 1992–1996. The Secretariat is thus continuing a very laudable policy of publishing, in abbreviated form and more accessible to a broader range of interested people, legal texts of great importance. In a similar vein the proceedings of the Colloquium on the Progressive Development and Codification of International Law held in New York in October 1997 have been issued. An analytical guide to the work of the International Law Commission 1949–1997 was published recently as were the proceedings of the seminar held in celebration of the 50th anniversary of the ILC and, we hope, will soon be made available in more than one linguistic version. All these publications serve the purpose to facilitate research into the Commission's work on the codification and progressive development of international law during the first fifty years of its existence, thus again fulfilling one of the goals of the Decade.

Of particular importance are two publications which are now seeing the light of the day. One is the study entitled 'The United Nations and the Development of International Law during the 1990's' analyzing as it does legal instruments emanating from the various law-generating processes within the United Nations during the current decade and assessing their contribution to the development of international law. This study, prepared by the Codification Division, is further proof of the outstanding capacity for research and legal analysis available in that Division and of the readiness of the Division's Director and staff to make a contribution of their own, appreciated by delegations and scholars alike. The other publication is the collection of essays to be issued next year. That collection, foreseen in the programme of the final term of the Decade, will provide a perspective on international law as viewed from the practical viewpoint to those who are involved in the actual practice of international law.

Besides publications mentioned explicitly because of their direct relationship with the process of establishing and disseminating general public international law, one is also bound to note several other publications of no lesser importance but restricted to specific areas, such as trade law or the Law of the Sea.

Needless to say, the European Union feels encouraged by those activities of the Secretariat. But it is not the United Nations alone which is active under the Decade programme. We should like to pay tribute to scholars as well as research and teaching institutions, such as the Hague Academy of International Law for having addressed in their respective activities the issues of the state of international law at the turn of the millennium. In this respect we should like to mention that the Hague Academy organized—in 1998—a thought provoking course on 'Le droit international à la veille du 21e siècle: valeurs et faits'.

The Secretary-General's report also reflects the wide range of technical and in particular electronic measures taken within the Secretariat in order to improve the dissemination of information concerning United Nations activities in the field of international law. Various websites have been newly created, others have been expanded, such as the Treaty data base. We note that the Codification Division is actively co-operating with the Global Legal Information Network (GLIN). It is also in this context that we are appreciative of the note on multilateral treaties deposited with the Secretary-General (A/53/525).

This year has also witnessed the adoption of the Rome Statute of the International Criminal Court which is an historic achievement breaking new ground in the field of the application of international law. The European Union wishes to emphasize its commitment to the cause of the ICC and expresses the hope that the Court will become operational soon.

Turning now to the upcoming commemoration of the centennial of the Hague Peace Conference of 1899 which represented a milestone in the development of international law, the European Union is aware of the promising preparatory process which will lead to the holding of important events in The Hague and in St. Petersburg. Those events are designed to highlight the main purposes of the Decade. The European Union commends the Netherlands and the Russian Federation for their efforts and initiatives in that regard. Some interesting documents are already being elaborated by prominent scholars for presentation and discussion at those events. The agenda is taking shape. The peaceful settlement of disputes and the question of disarmament will figure prominently on it. So will international humanitarian law to which the International Red Cross Movement is preparing a substantial contribution through the holding of the 27th International Red Cross Conference in the fall of 1999 thereby giving a special hallmark to the 1999 events which in turn can be seen as the final touchstones of the United Nations Decade of International Law.

The manifold activities undertaken within the framework of the Decade have underlined and are underlining the importance of international law in the world of today. They show that the idea of calling for a 'Decade of International Law', as expressed by the General Assembly in 1989 fell on fertile ground and constituted an additional element in the ongoing process of strengthening international law and creating an appropriate awareness, worldwide, for this important regulatory system.

(Text provided by the FCO; see also A/C.6/53/SR. 31, pp. 2–3)

Part Three: I. B. *The law of treaties—definition, conclusion and entry into force—conclusion, including signature, ratification and accession*

In reply to the question in what circumstances may persons who are not members of Her Majesty's Privy Council sign treaties on behalf of Her Majesty, the Minister of State, FCO, wrote:

Most treaties are signed with Governmental Full Powers either by Ministers or Ambassadors. Membership of the Privy Council is not a factor in the issuing of Full Powers.

The Vienna Convention on the Law of Treaties provides that Heads of State, Heads of Government and Ministers for Foreign Affairs are eligible to sign treaties by virtue of their office. Anyone else signing a treaty in articled form requires a formal document known as a Full Power.

In the United Kingdom, the Treaty-making power is vested in the Crown as part of the Royal prerogative. The exercise of that power is the concern of my right hon. Friend the Secretary of State for Foreign and Commonwealth Affairs.

The United Kingdom has three types of Full Power: (i) Queen's General Full Powers, which are signed by Her Majesty The Queen and empower the Secretary of State for Foreign and Commonwealth Affairs, FCO Ministers of State, FCO Under-Secretaries of State to sign any treaty; and the UK

Permanent Representatives to the UN and the EC to sign treaties in their respective fields. (ii) Queen's Special Full Powers, which are issued for the signing of a specific treaty drawn up between Heads of State. (iii) Governmental Full Powers, which are signed by the Secretary of State for Foreign and Commonwealth Affairs and are issued for the signing of specific inter-governmental and inter-state treaties.

(HC Debs., vol. 306, WA, col. *247*: 11 February 1998)

In reply to a question, the Parliamentary Under-Secretary of State, FCO, wrote:

Since 1 January 1997, all treaties which have been concluded subject to ratification or to which we intend to accede, and which are laid under the Ponsonby Rule, have been accompanied by an Explanatory Memorandum.

The Explanatory Memorandum contains a description of the subject matter of the treaty and an account of the reasons why it is proposed that the United Kingdom should become a party to the treaty. It further highlights the benefits for the United Kingdom from participation as well as any burdens on the United Kingdom which would result.

So far, 21 Explanatory Memoranda have been laid before Parliament. They are published on the Foreign and Commonwealth Office's Internet site at www.fco.gov.uk/treaty.

(HL Debs., vol. 588, *WA 203*: 21 April 1998)

The following memorandum was presented by the FCO to the HC Select Committee on Procedure on 30 November 1998:

THE PRESENTATION OF TREATIES TO PARLIAMENT: THE PONSONBY RULE

Introduction

1. The purpose of this memorandum is to examine the background to the current position on the Ponsonby Rule. The term 'treaty' will be used to describe all international agreements, whatever their title (whether 'Convention', 'Protocol', 'Charter'), intended to bind the United Kingdom under international law; it does not cover 'Memoranda of Understanding' or other informal instruments which do not constitute binding international agreements.

2. The power to make treaties is a Prerogative power vested in the Crown. It is exercised on the advice of the Secretary of State for Foreign and Commonwealth Affairs, who, in turn, consults with other Departments of Government whose responsibilities would be engaged in executing the provisions of particular treaties.

3. Since 1924 all treaties subject to ratification (with limited exceptions) have been laid before Parliament for 21 sitting days in accordance with the Ponsonby Rule (see paragraphs 6–14 below). The laying is done by means of a Command Paper in the Country, Miscellaneous or European Communities Series. Upon entry into force all treaties binding the United Kingdom are published in the Treaty Series of Command Papers.

4. Following an undertaking by Ministers on 16 December 1996, all treaties signed after 1 January 1997 and laid before Parliament under the Ponsonby Rule are now accompanied by an Explanatory Memorandum (see paragraphs 15–19 below).
5. In the period January to December 1997, 36 treaties were laid before Parliament in accordance with the Ponsonby Rule. In the same period 77 treaties were published in the Treaty Series of Command Papers (26 of which had previously been published in the Country, Miscellaneous or European Communities Series). In the period January to October 1998, 22 treaties were laid before Parliament in accordance with the Ponsonby Rule. In the same period 47 were published in the Treaty Series (10 of which had previously been published in the Country, Miscellaneous or European Communities Series).

The Ponsonby Rule of 1924

6. Since March 1892, it had been the practice to present to Parliament the texts of treaties binding the United Kingdom. This was done in a numbered series of Command Papers known as the Treaty Series. But treaties were published in that series only after they had entered into force, so that at that stage no Parliamentary approval, tacit or express, could be sought or given.
7. On 1 April 1924, during the Second Reading Debate on the Treaty of Peace (Turkey) Bill, Mr Arthur Ponsonby (Under-Secretary of State for Foreign Affairs in Ramsay MacDonald's first Labour Government) made the following statement: 'It is the intention of His Majesty's Government to lay on the table of both Houses of Parliament every treaty, when signed, for a period of 21 days, after which the treaty will be ratified and published and circulated in the Treaty Series. In the case of important treaties, the Government will, of course, take an opportunity of submitting them to the House for discussion within this period. But, as the Government cannot take upon itself to decide what may be considered important or unimportant, if there is a formal demand for discussion forwarded through the usual channels from the Opposition or any other party, time will be found for the discussion of the Treaty in question. . . . During our term of office, we shall inform the House of all agreements, commitments, and understandings which may in any way bind the nation to specific action in certain circumstances. . . . This is our intention. There is no method by which we can bind future Governments'. He also warned that: 'Resolutions expressing Parliamentary approval of every Treaty before ratification would be a very cumbersome form of procedure and would burden the House with a lot of unnecessary business. The absence of disapproval may be accepted as sanction, and publicity and opportunity for discussion and criticism are the really material and valuable elements which henceforth will be introduced' (H.C. Deb. (1924) 171, c. 1999–2005).
8. The statement responded to the demands of some of the Government's supporters for a Parliamentary practice that would render impossible the 'secret Treaties and secret clauses of Treaties' of the kind which were then generally supposed to have helped bring about the First World War. Since then, the practice of secret treaties has been largely abolished by change in diplomatic practice, reinforced in turn by specific obligations in the Covenant of the League

of Nations and then in the United Nations Charter requiring all treaties to be deposited with the Organisation, which then published them. Moreover, many states, including the United Kingdom, have published treaty series of their own. The Ponsonby Rule was withdrawn during the subsequent Baldwin Government, but was reinstated in 1929 and gradually hardened into a practice observed by all successive Governments.

Application of the Ponsonby Rule

9. The Ponsonby Rule requires that every treaty signed by the United Kingdom subject to ratification should be laid before Parliament for 21 sitting days (although they need not be continuous). The FCO interprets the Ponsonby Rule as applying to acceptance, approval and accession as well as to ratification. 'Acceptance' and 'approval' have the same legal effect as ratification and 'accession' arises when the British Government consents to be bound by a treaty of which it was not an original signatory.

10. In its Response of July 1982 to the 6th Report of the Joint Committee on Statutory Instruments (Session 1981–82), the Government confirmed that 'International agreements (including agreements amending international agreements) that are subject to ratification are, under the Ponsonby rule, laid before Parliament before they are ratified.' However, 'Sometimes an international agreement is amended, and the amendment, which may or may not be in the form of an international agreement, though it is not subject to ratification, does require the making of a statutory instrument for its implementation. In such a case, the Government accepts that the text of the agreement or amendment should be made available to Parliament, preferably when the statutory instrument is laid but in any case before it enters into force unless urgent or other important considerations make this impracticable' [Cmnd. 8600]. Therefore, in practice the Ponsonby Rule has also been applied to (a) amendments to multilateral treaties which are themselves subject to ratification and (b) amendments which, although subject to the silent procedure, require legislation.

11. Moreover, since January 1998 it has been the FCO's consistent practice to apply the Ponsonby Rule to treaties which are not subject to formal ratification (or acceptance or approval) but simply to the mutual notification of the completion of constitutional and other procedures by each Party.

Exceptions to the Ponsonby Rule

12. On 6 May 1981 the Lord Privy Seal announced in a written answer to a parliamentary question that: 'In order to effect economies in the publication of Command Papers, it has been decided that the texts of bilateral double taxation agreements should no longer be tabled in Parliament as White papers in the country series of Command Papers. They will however continue to be published in the treaty series of Command Papers after entry into force. These new arrangements will necessitate a limited departure from the strict terms of what has become known as the Ponsonby rule—namely, the practice whereby the texts of all international agreements concluded subject to ratification are laid

before Parliament for a period of 21 sitting days after signature and before ratification. The purpose of the Ponsonby rule is to afford Parliament the opportunity of considering commitments which the Government of the day are proposing to enter into. In the case of bilateral double taxation agreements, that purpose is already served by the statutory requirement that the draft of any Order in Council providing for double taxation relief shall be laid before the House of Commons for approval by affirmative resolution, it being the invariable practice that the text of any bilateral double taxation agreement falling within the scope of the Ponsonby rule should be scheduled to the draft Order designed to implement the agreement. It will accordingly be seen that the new arrangements are wholly consistent with the spirit of the Ponsonby rule.' [WA 82].

13. There are, in practice, a handful of other exceptions to the Ponsonby Rule. For example, International Labour Organisation (ILO) Conventions are laid by the DfEE as Command Papers, rather than by the FCO under the Ponsonby Rule. The DTI lays Universal Postal Union (UPU) and International Telecommunications Union (ITU) Conventions. Amendments to satellite agreements (e.g. Eutelsat and Inmarsat) are also laid by the DTI. Whereas amendments to the Agreement on the International Carriage of Perishable Foodstuffs and on the Special Equipment to be used for such Carriage (ATP) are laid by the DETR.

14. With the growth of practice over the years, the Ponsonby Rule has been understood to allow for exceptions from its operation in special cases, when other means of consulting or informing Parliament can be used instead. Alternative procedures are:

- adopting a Motion;
- passing a Bill;
- making an announcement in a debate;
- adopting a resolution or a Motion as part of the Affirmative Resolution procedure for making an Order in Council;
- answering a Parliamentary Question;
- consulting leaders of the Opposition and other parliamentary parties.

However, in practice departures from the Ponsonby Rule are rare.

The Introduction of Explanatory Memoranda in 1997

15. Since January 1997 all treaties which are laid before Parliament under the Ponsonby Rule have been accompanied by an Explanatory Memorandum (EM). It contains a description of the subject matter of the treaty and an account of the reasons why it is proposed that the United Kingdom should become a party to the treaty. It further highlights the benefits for the United Kingdom from participation in the treaty as well as any burdens which would result.

16. The system of EMs followed the tabling of a Private Member's Bill, the Treaties (Parliamentary Approval) Bill in the House of Lords on 9 January 1996 [HL Bill 27, 51/4]. During the second reading of the Bill on 28 February, Baroness Chalker of Wallasey (then Minister of State at the FCO) stated that: 'there would be a significant additional amount of parliamentary time required

under the noble Lord's Bill without necessarily demonstrably contributing to the better scrutiny of the treaty-making process'. However, she considered its proposal for EMs 'worthy of further consideration whether or not this Bill becomes law', adding, 'I shall want to examine it further with my colleagues before giving a definitive answer, but it seems a sensible way to proceed' [c. 1530–1564].

17. The Bill was in due course withdrawn in exchange for the Government's undertaking to introduce a system of EMs by administrative, non-statutory means. After consultation of other Government Departments with an interest in treaty matters, the FCO produced a note for Departments entitled *Guidelines on Explanatory Memoranda for Treaties*, which is now available in the Library of the House and on the FCO web site for treaty information: www.fco.gov.uk/directory/treaty.asp.

Availability of EMs

18. On 12 April 1998, in a written answer to Lord Lester's question whether HMG would publish EMs before ratifying international conventions so as to facilitate effective parliamentary scrutiny, Baroness Symons of Vernham Dean stated that EMs are published on the FCO's internet site [WA 202–203]. In response to a second question from Lord Lester enquiring whether HMG would introduce a procedure to give Lords notice of the publication of EMs, Baroness Symons wrote on 30 July 1998: 'Notice of the publication of an Explanatory Memorandum (EM) is given in the Minutes of Proceedings and Votes with each entry for a treaty laid under the Ponsonby Rule. Paper copies are available in the Printed Paper Office on the day after the treaty is laid together with copies of the relevant Command Paper' [WA 222–223].

19. In order to ensure that EMs are readily available to Members of Parliament, the system has been refined in the course of the past year. The FCO sends two copies of a Command Paper and its accompanying EM (one set is stamped 'Printed Paper Office') to the Clerk in Charge, Votes and Proceedings Office, House of Commons, and the Clerk of the Parliaments, House of Lords, respectively, on the day of laying. The documents are sent under a cover note (in triplicate, one copy of which is returned stamped and initialled to acknowledge receipt). It is the FCO's understanding that the Clerks flag the availability of EMs in the Minutes of Proceedings and Votes by adding 'with an Explanatory Memorandum' to the entry for each treaty laid in this way and that paper copies of EMs are made available from the Printed Paper Office. Electronic copies are available on the FCO's web site.

EU Treaties

20. European Union business is the subject of a sophisticated and comprehensive scrutiny system. Most of the documents submitted to the scrutiny committees of the two Houses relate to Community secondary legislation, but they include several types of international agreement as well, in particular:

(i) agreements concluded with non-Member States or international organisations by one of the Communities (with or without Member States also being parties);

(ii) conventions and other legally-binding instruments to be concluded amongst Member States under the Third Pillar;

(iii) at least under the new scrutiny arrangements, legally-binding CFSP instruments.

The scrutiny committees were also continually sent draft treaty texts throughout the IGC leading up to Amsterdam and regularly took evidence from FCO Ministers and officials.

21. Moreover, many agreements concluded in the EU context require legislation for their implementation in the UK and thus some form of parliamentary process. Primary legislation is required for amendments or additions to the corpus of basic Community Treaties (most recently the Treaty of Amsterdam); and subordinate legislation is often required for mixed agreements (Orders under section 1(3) of the European Communities Act 1972). Some Third Pillar conventions also require UK legislation for their implementation.

The Practice of other States

22. In the majority of OECD countries, parliamentary approval is required for all treaties or for certain types of treaty. But in such countries, unlike the United Kingdom, treaties so approved normally take effect directly in national law upon ratification. In the United Kingdom treaties do not take effect in national law except to the extent that their terms are specifically incorporated by statute. It is the practice never to ratify a treaty until all the domestic legislation and administrative provisions required for its proper execution in the United Kingdom are in place.

Summary

23. Treaties not yet binding on the United Kingdom may be debated by Parliament under a variety of procedures. In addition to the laying of all treaties requiring ratification, accession, acceptance or approval before Parliament for 21 sitting days under the Ponsonby Rule, there are special cases in which, by convention, treaties are not entered into without parliamentary sanction. For example, Parliament expressly provided in the European Assembly Elections Act 1978 that no treaty which provides for an increase in the powers of the European Parliament may be ratified by the United Kingdom unless it has been approved by an Act of Parliament.

24. In addition, treaties are not concluded without Parliamentary approval, usually in the form of statute, if they require an amendment to United Kingdom law; affect private rights; create a charge on public funds; attribute new powers to the Crown; or cede British territory. In other cases, Parliament sanctions in advance, by general legislation, the conclusion of bilateral treaties in particular fields, within the limits laid down. Examples are: extradition treaties, double taxation treaties and reciprocal social security benefit treaties. Here it is often

provided that the terms of the treaty take immediate effect on being scheduled to an Order in Council.

(Text provided by the FCO)

Part Three: I. C. *The law of treaties—definition, conclusion and entry into force—reservations, declarations and objections*

(See also Part Seventeen: I.B.8. and I.B.9. (item of 28 January 1998), below)

The following question was asked of Her Majesty's Government:

Whether they will review the reservation registered by the Conservative Government regarding the United Kingdom's ratification of the United Nations Convention on the Rights of the Child, with particular reference to nationality, immigration, asylum and detention and the practical effects of the reservation since 1991?

In reply, the Parliamentary Under-Secretary of State, Home Office, wrote:

We do not intend to review the reservation. We take the view that the United Kingdom's immigration and nationality law is entirely consistent with the thrust of the convention, but believe it is necessary to retain this reservation, which makes it clear that nothing in the convention is to be interpreted as affecting the operation of our immigration and nationality legislation.

(HL Debs, vol. 587, *WA 256*: 26 March 1998; see also HL Debs., vol. 588, *WA 216*: 22 April 1998)

The following letter, dated 29 July 1998, was addressed to the UN Secretary-General by the UK Permanent Representative to the UN in New York:

I have the honour to enclose for deposit the Instrument of Ratification by the Government of the United Kingdom of Great Britain and Northern Ireland in respect of the Convention on the Prohibition of the Use, Stockpiling, Production and Transfer of Anti-personnel Mines and of their Destruction, opened for signature at Ottawa on 3 December 1997.

I also have the honour to lodge with you, as the depositary of the said Convention, the following statement in respect of the ratification of that Convention by the United Kingdom:

It is the understanding of the Government of the United Kingdom that the mere participation in the planning or execution of operations, exercises or other military activity by the United Kingdom's Armed Forces, or individual United Kingdom nationals, conducted in combination with the armed forces of States not party to the Convention on the Prohibition of the Use, Stockpiling, Production and Transfer of Anti-personnel Mines and of their Destruction, opened for signature at Ottawa on 3 December 1997, which engage in activity prohibited under that Convention, is not, by itself, assistance, encouragement or inducement for the purposes of Article 1, paragraph 1(c) of the Convention.

(Text provided by the FCO)

Part Three: IV. *The law of treaties—breach and its consequences*

In the course of an affidavit sworn on 19 June 1998 in the case of *R* v. *Foreign and Commonwealth Office, ex parte International Transport Workers Federation* in the Divisional Court of the Queen's Bench, Mr M.C. Wood, Deputy Legal Adviser, FCO, referred to an argument by the applicants that there had been a breach by the Russian Federation, Ukraine or Georgia of the Protocol of 1 March 1974 to the treaty on merchant navigation concluded by the UK and the USSR on 3 April 1968. He went on:

21. Further, in point of fact, Her Majesty's Government is not aware of any breach of Article 2 having been committed by the Russian Federation, Ukraine or Georgia, since it is not aware of any judgment or settlement which has benefited from the immunity where the claim has thereafter not been paid. In the decisions of the Scottish and English courts referred to by the Applicants in the Form 86A, namely the Coreck, MV Inessa Armand and Bridge Oil cases, it was decided that there was no immunity. There are thus no grounds for asserting that the Russian Federation, Ukraine or Georgia are or have been in breach of Article 2 of the Protocol.

22. Even if there had been a breach of the Protocol (there has been none), under international law such breach does not automatically lead to suspension or termination of the Protocol. The relevant rules of international law are set out in articles 60 and 65 to 67 of the Vienna Convention on the Law of Treaties (Cmnd 7964). It is only in the case of a 'material breach' of the treaty in question that the question of termination may arise in the case of bilateral treaties. A 'material breach' is defined in Article 60(2) of the Vienna Convention as either 'a repudiation of the treaty not sanctioned by the present Convention' or 'the violation of a provision essential to the accomplishment of the object or purpose of the treaty'. It is Her Majesty's Government's view that the high threshold established by these provisions could not be met in the instant case.

23. In any event, Article 60 only provides that a material breach of a bilateral treaty by one of the parties 'entitles' the other to invoke the breach as a ground for terminating the treaty or suspending its operation in whole or in part. If a State wishes to exercise its option to invoke the breach in this way, the Vienna Convention provides a clear procedure to be followed. Article 65 states that a party which wishes, inter alia, to invoke a ground for terminating the treaty or suspending its operation 'must notify the other parties of its claim. The notification shall indicate the measure proposed to be taken with respect to the treaty and the reasons therefor'. If the other party raises no objection within a specified period (not less than three months) after receipt of the notification, the party making the notification may carry out the measure which it has proposed.

If the other party does object, the parties are to seek a solution through the means indicated in Article 33 of the United Nations Charter.

24. In the instant case, as explained in paragraph 21 above, it does not appear that Ukraine or Georgia have committed any breach of the Protocol, still less a material breach. But even if such breach had taken place, Her Majesty's Government have not sought to invoke such breach in order to seek termination of the treaty or suspension of its operation. Therefore, on any view, the United Kingdom remains bound by Article 2 of the Protocol.

(Text provided by the FCO)

Part Three: V. C. *The law of treaties—invalidity, termination and suspension of operation—termination and suspension of operation, denunciation and withdrawal*

(See also Part Fifteen: II.A. (item of 16 September 1998), below)

In December 1997, the Department of the Environment, Transport and the Regions issued a consultation paper on the review of the Treaty on Merchant Navigation concluded between the UK and the USSR in 1968. Relevant passages from the paper are as follows:

REVIEW OF TREATY ON MERCHANT NAVIGATION BETWEEN THE UK AND USSR 1968 AND RELATED PROTOCOLS

Introduction

1. The Department is reviewing whether the UK should retain or withdraw from the Treaty on Merchant Navigation between the UK and USSR of 1968 and related Protocols, which are still in force and partly govern our maritime relations with the Russian Federation, Ukraine and Georgia. The Treaty and the Protocols all provide individually for termination by either contracting party after giving 12 months notice in writing. Before reaching a decision we are seeking the views of interested parties.

2. The Department believes that the need for the Treaty has diminished, chiefly due to the end of cold war relations, the greatly increased extent of liberalisation in the international shipping policies of Russia, Ukraine and Georgia, and the lack of current reported difficulties experienced by UK shipping companies and UK shippers in these countries. In addition, under the terms of a Protocol to the Treaty, state-owned merchant ships of Russia, Ukraine and Georgia are immune from seizure in connection with legal proceedings in the UK, which, in the case of Ukraine, has led to difficulties for UK creditors in recovering their claims.

3. Annex 1 lists the relevant related Protocols and statutory instruments connected with the 1968 Treaty. . . .

Historical background

4. The main reason for the conclusion of the 1968 Treaty, from the UK point of view, was to set a framework for maritime relations given the state of cold war relations with the USSR, and a desire to strengthen non-discriminatory shipping undertakings which had previously been included in general trade agreements. The Treaty was therefore aimed at furthering the UK policy of assisting UK commercial shipping interests by enabling UK shipping to participate, on equitable terms, on all routes in the carriage of Soviet trade.
5. When the USSR broke up in 1991, Russia (as the continuing State) continued all of the former USSR's treaty obligations with the UK. Ukraine and Georgia, as successor States, also assumed all of the former USSR's treaty obligations to the UK. These treaty obligations included the 1968 Treaty and related Protocols.
6. As for the rest of the former USSR, the 3 Baltic States (Lithuania, Latvia and Estonia) were not regarded as successor States. It is unclear whether the 1968 Treaty applies to the remaining Republics of the former USSR (see Annex 2), as there has been no contact with these countries on this matter and they play no, or only a minor role, in international shipping.

Summary of Main Provisions of the 1968 Treaty

7. The main provisions of the 1968 Treaty provide for freedom of navigation, access to markets on the basis of the principle of free and fair competition, the same treatment of each other's flag-vessels as afforded to national vessels in respect of access to ports and their facilities and in respect of port charges, and the maintenance of working relationships between shipping administrations. The Treaty also provides for: mutual recognition of shipping documentation, tonnage certificates and seaman's certificates; taxation of shipping companies; procedures in cases of accident or shipwreck; immigration of seamen; and procedures in cases of civil proceedings involving ship's crew members.
8. The Consular Relations (Merchant Shipping) (USSR) Order 1970 gives effect in the UK to the relevant provisions of the 1968 Treaty concerning the procedures in cases of civil proceedings. This limits the jurisdiction of UK courts to entertain proceedings relating to the remuneration or any contract of service of the master or a member of the crew, and over offences committed on board USSR merchant ships.

European Union Partnership & Cooperation Agreements

9. The European Union has signed Partnership and Co-operation Agreements with Russia (1994), Ukraine (1994) and Georgia (1996), which include maritime articles. These make provision for unrestricted access to international shipping markets and for national treatment for Member States' and the three former USSR States' flag-vessels.

1974 Protocol

10. A Protocol signed in 1974 (which entered into force 1977) to the 1968 Treaty on shipping, provides for immunity from seizure for state-owned vessels of each Contracting Party and the cargoes therein, in connection with the execution of court judgements. The contracting parties are nevertheless obliged to take steps to give effect to judgements in respect of vessels enjoying immunity—essentially this means they are required to honour the debts of vessels immune from arrest.
11. This treaty obligation concerning immunity was first implemented in the UK by the State Immunity (Merchant Shipping) (USSR) Order 1978. In order to remove doubts that had arisen, as a result of court proceedings, as to whether the 1978 Order continued to give effect in the UK to this treaty obligation in connection with the Russian Federation, Ukraine, and Georgia, a new Order was made in 1997, coming into force on 1 November 1997. The base statute for this is the State Immunity Act 1978 (as amended).
12. Russian and Georgian shipping has largely now been privatised. The Department is aware, however, that several UK companies have recently been involved in civil proceedings with the Republic of Ukraine in connection with unpaid debts owed by the Republic's state-owned Black Sea Shipping Company (Blasco). This has led to the arrest of a number of Blasco's vessels as UK creditors have attempted to execute against the capital assets with which Blasco trades, represented by the ships in its fleet. The Government of Ukraine has claimed state immunity in respect of Blasco vessels, which would prevent the arrest and sale of such vessels. In connection with recent particular proceedings the Admiralty Judge ruled on 23 November that a Blasco ship could nevertheless be sold.

1986 Protocol

13. In 1986 the UK and the USSR negotiated an Additional Protocol to the 1968 Treaty. This came into effect in January 1987. Article 5 of the Protocol provided for reciprocal Port Notification schemes, whereby vessels were required to give 96 hours notice prior to entering a port of the other government. The Soviet authorities never enforced the reciprocal obligation on British merchant shipping, and formally rescinded it in 1989.
14. The UK ceased to operate the scheme in 1991 as regards all former USSR States in the light of improved relations. As regards the Russian Federation, the scheme was formally dissolved when Article 5 of the Protocol was terminated by exchange of diplomatic notes in 1993.
15. The rest of the Protocol remains in force. This provides for regular meetings of a Joint Maritime Commission (JMC), consisting of senior officials and representatives of the shipping industry, from the UK and the former USSR. Although not currently sitting, the JMC is tasked to consider various maritime topics such as third country protectionism, Soviet cross-trading, International Maritime Organisation matters and problems that may affect the operations of vessels in the two countries' respective territories. It is not a

decision making body and does not control the allocation of cargoes. The last meeting of the JMC was in 1990.

What would be our position on maritime relations vis-à-vis former USSR States if the Treaty and related Protocols were terminated?

16. If the 1968 Treaty were terminated, the provisions on market access and national treatment included in the EU Partnership & Cooperation Agreements with Russia, Ukraine and Georgia would continue to apply. Other than this, commercial shipping relations would proceed without recourse to treaty, as do existing UK shipping relations with the overwhelming majority of the world's countries (it has been the UK's long-standing policy not to enter into bilateral maritime agreements unless there are exceptional circumstances). Current international shipping policies in Russia, Ukraine and Georgia are based on open markets, and few difficulties have been reported by UK companies.

17. State immunity in the UK for merchant ships owned by Ukraine (and also Russia and Georgia) would be lost.

18. The limitations on jurisdiction by UK courts on civil proceedings involving crews on these countries' vessels would also be removed, as would immunity for crews on UK vessels in former USSR States. (Certain other aspects of consular relations affecting merchant shipping are governed by the Consular Relations Convention between the UK and USSR signed in 1965, which entered into force 1968. This is still in force between the UK and the successor States of the former USSR. Under this Convention consular officers are entitled to assist with matters arising from, or investigate into, incidents on vessels. These provisions would remain in force.)

Annex 1

Treaty and related Protocols

- Treaty on Merchant Navigation between the United Kingdom of Great Britain and Northern Ireland and the Union of Soviet Socialist Republics 1968
- Protocol to the Treaty, signed in 1974 (Treaty Series No. 104 (1977))
- Additional Protocol to the Treaty, signed in 1986 (Treaty Series No. 26 (1987)) (—except Article 5 on 'port notification scheme', which was terminated by exchange of diplomatic notes in 1993).

Statutory Instruments

- The State Immunity (Merchant Shipping) Order 1997 (SI 1997 No. 2591)
- The State Immunity (Merchant Shipping) (Union of Soviet Socialist Republics) Order 1978 SI 1978 No. 1524—superseded and revoked by 1997 Order

- The Consular Relations (Merchant Shipping) (Union of Soviet Socialist Republics) Order 1997 SI 1970 No. 1916

Annex 2

Country	*Fleet*
Russia	yes
Ukraine	yes
Georgia	yes
Belarus	—
Moldova	—
Armenia	—
Azerbijan	yes
Tajikistan	—
Turkmenistan	very small fleet
Kazakhstan	very small fleet
Uzbekistan	—
Kyrgystan	—

** *Latvia, Lithuania* and *Estonia* are not regarded as *successor* States to the USSR (all three countries have fleets).

(Text provided by the FCO with the consent of the Department of the Environment, Transport and the Regions)

On 1 May 1998, the Department of the Environment, Transport and the Regions wrote to the International Transport Workers' Federation about the Department's review of the Treaty on Merchant Navigation 1968 between the UK and the USSR with its related Protocols. The letter stated in part:

I am pleased to inform you that we have now completed our review and, having taken the consultation responses into account, have concluded that the Treaty and Protocols should be terminated, given the productive modern shipping ties which the UK now enjoys with states of the former USSR. Ministers have agreed to denunciation by the UK of those instruments, as explicitly provided for in the relevant articles therein. The states of the former USSR were notified formally on 30 April of the UK's decision to terminate those instruments. In accordance with the terms of the Treaty and Protocols, termination will take effect 12 months from the date of notification unless earlier dates can be agreed with the states concerned.

The text of the Note Verbale from the British Embassy in Georgia to the Ministry of Foreign Affairs of Georgia, delivered on 30 April 1998, read as follows:

Her Britannic Majesty's Embassy presents its compliments to the Ministry of Foreign Affairs of Georgia and has the honour to refer to the Treaty on

Merchant Navigation between the United Kingdom of Great Britain and Northern Ireland and the Union of Soviet Socialist Republics signed at London, 3 April 1968; to the Protocol to the Treaty signed at Moscow, 1 March 1974; and the Additional Protocol to the Treaty signed at Moscow, 30 December 1986 which are currently in force between the United Kingdom and Georgia.

In accordance with Article 17 of the Treaty, Article 5 of the Protocol and Article 6 of the Additional Protocol, the United Kingdom hereby notifies Georgia with effect from 30 April 1998 of its desire to terminate the above agreements. The three agreements will therefore terminate on 29 April 1999, unless the United Kingdom and Georgia agree to terminate them at an earlier date.

Her Britannic Majesty's Embassy avails itself of this opportunity to renew to the Ministry of Foreign Affairs of Georgia the assurance of its highest consideration.

(Texts provided by the FCO. A Note in similar terms was delivered to the Ministry of Foreign Affairs in Ukraine on 24 April 1998)

In the course of an affidavit sworn on 19 June 1998 in the case of *R.* v. *Foreign and Commonwealth Office, ex parte International Transport Workers Federation* in the Divisional Court of the Queen's Bench Division, Mr M.C. Wood, Deputy Legal Adviser, FCO, referred to the Treaty on Merchant Navigation concluded between the UK and the USSR in 1968 and its Protocol of 1974. He continued:

Review and termination of the Treaty and Protocol

30. In the Form 86A (paragraph 9(2)), the Applicants refer to the review of the 1968 Treaty, 1974 Protocol and 1986 Additional Protocol. The position is that in December 1997 the Department of the Environment, Transport and the Regions commenced the review since they considered that the need for the Treaty and its Protocols had diminished 'chiefly due to the end of Cold War relations, the greatly increased extent of liberalisation in the international shipping policy of Russia, Ukraine and Georgia, and the lack of current reported difficulties experienced by UK shipping companies and UK shippers in these countries'. (Consultative paper annexed to the DETR letter of 9 December 1997, exhibited to the affidavit of P A Newdick . . . [reproduced in part above]). The review concluded that the Treaty and Protocols should be terminated given the productive modern shipping ties which the United Kingdom now enjoys with the states of the former USSR. A copy of the letter dated 1 May 1998 notifying the outcome of the review is at pages 22–23 of MCW1 [for its relevant text, see above].

31. Following the review, the Russian Federation and the eleven successor States (including Georgia and Ukraine) to the Union of Soviet Socialist Republics were notified formally of the United Kingdom's decision to terminate the Treaty and Protocols, pursuant to Article 17 of the Treaty and the corresponding provisions of the protocols, with effect from 30 April 1998. A true copy of the text of the Notes Verbales delivered to Ukraine and Georgia is at

pages 24–25 of MCW1 [text of the Note to Georgia reproduced above]. Termination will take effect in respect of each State one year later, unless the State concerned agrees to earlier termination.

(Text provided by the FCO)

Part Four: II. A. *Relationship between international law and internal law—application and implementation of international law in internal law—treaties*

(See also Part Four: III., Part Six: VIII. (item of 20 April 1998), and Part Seventeen: I.B. 8. and 9., below)

Speaking in the House of Lords during the Report stage of the Human Rights Bill, the Lord Chancellor, Lord Irvine of Lairg, stated:

We believe that the purpose of the Bill can be readily understood from the scheme of the Bill, which is well understood, as was demonstrated in Committee. The Bill provides a clear and coherent scheme by which the convention rights are to be given further effect in our domestic law. The purpose of the Bill is obvious: it is to enable convention rights to be asserted directly in our domestic courts. The medium of achieving that is, among others, Clause 3, the interpretative principle that, so far as possible, the courts are to construe primary legislation and subordinate legislation compatibly with convention rights.

(HL Debs., vol. 584, col. 1261: 19 January 1998)

Later in the debate, the Lord Chancellor remarked:

The Bill sets out a scheme for giving effect to the convention rights which maximises the protection to individuals while retaining the fundamental principle of parliamentary sovereignty. Clause 3 is the central part of this scheme. Clause 3(1) requires legislation to be read and given effect to so far as it is possible to do so in a way that is compatible with the convention rights. Clause 3(2) provides that where it is not possible to give a compatible construction to primary legislation or to subordinate legislation whose incompatibility flows from the terms of the parent Act, that does not affect its validity, continuing operation or enforcement. This ensures that the courts are not empowered to strike down Acts of Parliament which they find to be incompatible with the convention rights. Instead, Clause 4 of the Bill, together with Clauses 10 to 12, introduces a new mechanism through which the courts can signal to the Government that a provision of legislation is, in their view, incompatible. It is then for Government and Parliament to consider what action should be taken. I believe that this will prove to be an effective procedure and it is also one which accords with our traditions of parliamentary sovereignty. That is why the Bill adopts it.

The position under the Bill is that, where pre-existing legislation cannot be construed by the courts compatibly with the convention, the intention of the Government is that the courts may make a declaration of incompatibility and then Parliament may make a remedial order.

(Ibid. col. 1294)

In the course of a later debate upon the Report stage of the Human Rights Bill in the House of Lords, the Lord Chancellor, Lord Irvine of Lairg, stated:

I have to make this point absolutely plain. The European Convention on Human Rights under this Bill is not made part of our law. The Bill gives the European Convention on Human Rights a special relationship which will mean that the courts will give effect to the interpretative provisions to which I have already referred, but it does not make the convention directly justiciable as it would be if it were expressly made part of our law. I want there to be no ambiguity about that.

(HL Debs., vol. 585, col. 421: 29 January 1998)

In reply to an oral question, the Parliamentary Under-Secretary of State, Home Office, Mr Michael O'Brien, stated:

The Human Rights Bill gives effect to our manifesto commitment to incorporate the convention. It will enable everyone in the United Kingdom to enforce their convention rights before our courts. It will bring rights home to the British people. Our judges must be trained and our courts ready to implement the convention's incorporation.

(HC Debs., vol. 305, col. 715: 2 February 1998)

During the third reading of the Bill, the Lord Chancellor observed:

Let us remember that the European Convention was drawn up after the Second World War in response to the devastation it caused, accompanied by the grossest denials of human rights. It is a convention for the protection of human rights and fundamental freedoms. I emphasise the word 'fundamental'. For nearly 50 years the United Kingdom has been bound under international law to observe those basic human rights of people within its jurisdiction. . . . Over the some half century that we have been signed up to the convention, the Church has not experienced any problem whatever—that I am aware of—with the convention. It has been the clear desire of all the main political parties, and has had their general assent, that we comply with our convention obligations. That has been so for 50 years. The purpose of this Bill is to bring those rights home. It is to enable people to enforce their human rights in the courts of the United Kingdom rather than having to take their case to Strasbourg. The Bill does not create new human rights or take any existing human rights away. It provides better and easier access to rights which already exist.

(HL Debs., vol. 585, col. 755: 5 February 1998)

Later in the third reading debate, the Lord Chancellor stated:

The Bill provides for all legislation, past and future, to be interpreted as far as possible in a way which is compatible with the convention rights. The convention rights are the magnetic north and the needle of judicial interpretation will swing towards them.

The noble Lord knows, and I am sure accepts, that the courts are not to set aside primary legislation under the Bill, but the principle of statutory construction is a strong alternative. It will be unlawful for public authorities to act in a way which is incompatible with the convention rights and that also is a strong and far-reaching provision. Taken together, those measures provide for the convention rights to have a great effect in our domestic law. I go further; in 99 per cent. of the cases that will arise, there will be no need for judicial declarations of incompatibility.

What the Bill does not do is make the convention rights themselves directly a part of our domestic law in the same way that, for example, the civil wrongs of negligence, trespass or libel are part of our domestic law. Claims in those areas are all actionable in tort in cases between private individuals. But, as the noble Lord knows, we have not provided for the convention rights to be directly justiciable in actions between private individuals. We have sought to protect the human rights of individuals against the abuse of power by the state, broadly defined, rather than to protect them against each other. That is the only practical difference between the full incorporation of the convention rights into our domestic law and the actual effect of the Bill. I hope that we can put to one side what is really a theological dispute in relation to the meaning of the word 'incorporation' and concentrate on what the Bill was designed to achieve, which is a real enhancement of the human rights of people in this country.

(Ibid., col. 840)

In moving the second reading in the House of Commons of the Human Rights Bill, the Secretary of State for the Home Department, Mr Jack Straw, stated:

Three hundred and nine years ago, Parliament enacted the 1689 Bill of Rights. That Bill delineated the relationship between Parliament, the Crown and the courts. It was a foundation stone of representative government, curbing unelected power and establishing a constitutional monarchy. One reflection of that is in the mutual respect shown by Her Majesty and the House. So I have it in command from Her Majesty the Queen to acquaint the House that Her Majesty, having been informed of the purport of the Human Rights Bill, has consented to place her prerogative and interest, so far as they are affected by the Bill, at the disposal of Parliament for the purposes of the Bill.

This is the first major Bill on human rights for more than 300 years. It will strengthen representative and democratic government. It does so by enabling citizens to challenge more easily actions of the state if they fail to match the standards set by the European convention. The Bill will thus create a new and better relationship between the Government and the people.

Nothing in the Bill will take away the freedoms that our citizens already enjoy. However, those freedoms alone are not enough: they need to be complemented by positive rights that individuals can assert when they believe that they have been treated unfairly by the state, or that the state and its institutions have failed properly to protect them. The Bill will guarantee to everyone the means to enforce a set of basic civil and political rights, establishing a floor below which standards will not be allowed to fall. The Bill will achieve that by giving further effect in our domestic law to the fundamental rights and freedoms contained in the European convention on human rights.

The convention is a treaty of the Council of Europe, now a body of some 40 countries. The Council was established at the end of the second world war as part of the allies' programme to reconstruct civilisation on the mainland of Europe. The United Kingdom was a prime mover in the convention and played a major and dignified part in its drafting. One of its draftsmen, David Maxwell Fyfe, later became, as Lord Kilmuir, a distinguished Lord Chancellor in the Conservative Government from 1954 to 1962. The United Kingdom was also among the first countries to sign the convention, which we did on the first available day. We were the first to ratify it, in March 1951.

The United Kingdom's international commitment to the convention has continued ever since. In 1966, we accepted the right of individuals to bring cases against the United Kingdom. The United Kingdom has also set a good example in responding to any adverse findings of the European Court of Human Rights in Strasbourg. For nearly 50 years, there has been broad political support for what the convention does and what it stands for, with a fundamental recognition that, in practice, decisions of the Strasbourg court must be implemented.

. . .

Since the convention's drafting nearly 50 years ago, almost all the states that are party to it have gradually incorporated it into their domestic law. Ireland and Norway have not done so, but Ireland has a Bill of Rights which guarantees rights similar to those of the convention, and Norway is in the process of incorporating the convention. Several other countries with which we share our common law tradition, such as Canada and New Zealand, have provided similar protection for human rights in their legal systems.

The effect of non-incorporation on the British people is a practical one. The rights, originally developed by Britain, are no longer seen as British, and enforcing them takes far too long and costs far too much—on average five years and £30,000 to get an action into the European Court at Strasbourg once all domestic remedies have been exhausted. Bringing these rights home will mean that the British people will be able to argue for their rights in the British courts, without inordinate delay and cost. It will also mean that the rights will be brought much more fully into the jurisprudence of the courts throughout the United Kingdom, and their interpretation will thus be far more woven into our common law.

There will be another benefit: British judges will be enabled to make a distinctively British contribution to the development of the jurisprudence of human rights across Europe. It is also now plain that the approach that the United Kingdom has so far adopted towards the convention has not stood the test of time. The most obvious proof of that lies in the number of cases in which the European Court has found that there have been violations of convention rights in the United Kingdom. It is only natural that people of all political persuasions have asked, 'Why do individuals in the United Kingdom have to go to Strasbourg to enforce their British rights? Why can they not rely on them before our domestic courts?'

. . .

Alongside the Bill, which had its First Reading in another place on 23 October, I published a White Paper entitled 'Rights Brought Home', setting out the case for the Bill and how it would work. The Bill does not create new substantive rights, but it makes the existing convention rights more immediate and relevant. Under the Bill, all courts and tribunals will be required to have regard to these rights.

Having decided that we should incorporate the convention, the most fundamental question that we faced was how to do that in a manner that strengthened, and did not undermine, the sovereignty of Parliament. Some had argued that the courts should have power to set aside primary legislation, whether past or future, on the ground of incompatibility with the convention. That is a feature of many, though by no means all, government systems with a basic law enshrined in a written constitution. It is also true that, under the European Communities Act 1972, enacted by the then Conservative Government, European law with direct effect automatically takes precedence over our domestic law and Parliament, whatever Parliament wants to do otherwise.

That is not the road that we are going down. The Bill, important though it is, has the limited function of bringing the British people's rights home. It is no part of the project to call into question constitutional arrangements that have evolved in this country to make us one of the world's most stable democracies.

(HC Debs., vol. 306, cols. 769–70: 16 February 1998)

The Visiting Forces and International Headquarters (Application of Law) (Amendment) Order 1998 (Statutory Instruments 1998, No. 253) entered into force on 12 February 1998. An explanatory note, attached to but not forming part of the Order, read:

This Order amends article 3(3) of the Visiting Forces and International Headquarters (Application of Law) Order 1965 by inserting Albania, Bulgaria, the Czech Republic, Estonia, Hungary, Latvia, Lithuania, Poland, Romania, the Slovak Republic, Slovenia and Sweden as countries to whose forces the 1965 Order applies. This is done in pursuance of the Agreement, dated 19th June 1995, made between Member States of the North Atlantic Treaty Organisation and those other States which have accepted the invitation to take part in the Partnership for Peace (Miscellaneous No. 12 (1996), Cm. 3237).

The Order also amends article 7(c) of the 1965 Order by adding to the categories of persons who may be excepted under that article from the provisions of Part I of the Wireless Telegraphy Act 1949.

In reply to a question, the Minister of State, FCO, wrote:

The European Communities (Amendment) Bill will not incorporate Article K7 into UK law.

There is no question of Article K7 binding future Parliaments.

(HC Debs., vol. 308, WA, col. *611*: 18 March 1998)

In reply to the question what legislative changes are needed to enable the UK to ratify Protocol No. 7 to the European Convention on Human Rights, the Parliamentary Under-Secretary of State, Home Office, wrote:

Legislation is needed to amend three rules of family law in England and Wales which we do not think are capable of being interpreted consistently with Article 5 of Protocol 7 ('Equality between spouses'). These rules are:

(i) At common law a husband has a duty to maintain his wife, but not vice versa.

(ii) Under Section 1 of the Married Women's Property Act 1964, if the wife gives her husband a housekeeping allowance any goods bought with it remain his wife's, but if the husband gives his wife a housekeeping allowance it belongs to them in equal shares unless they agree otherwise.

(iii) A common law presumption of 'advancement'—where a husband makes a payment or puts property in his wife's name it is presumed to be a gift to her, but if the wife does the same the presumption does not apply.

(HL Debs., vol. 588, *WA 197*: 21 April 1998)

The Federal Republic of Yugoslavia (United Nations Sanctions) Order 1998 (Statutory Instruments 1998, No. 1065) entered into force on 24 April 1998. An explanatory note, attached to but not forming part of the Order, read:

This order, made under the United Nations Act 1946, imposes restrictions pursuant to a decision of the Security Council of the United Nations in Resolution 1160 of 31st March 1998 on the export to the Federal Republic of Yugoslavia and the supply to persons in the Federal Republic of Yugoslavia of arms and related matériel, and petroleum and petroleum products. It restricts certain related activities including the carriage of prohibited goods in ships, aircraft and vehicles.

See also to the same effect the Federal Republic of Yugoslavia (United Nations Sanctions) (Dependent Territories) Order 1998 (Statutory Instruments 1998, No. 1064), the Federal Republic of Yugoslavia (United Nations Sanctions) (Channel Islands) Order 1998 (Statutory Instruments 1998, No. 1072) and the Federal Republic of Yugoslavia (United Nations Sanctions) (Isle of Man) Order 1998 (Statutory Instruments 1998, No. 1073).

In reply to a question, the Minister of State, FCO, wrote:

The European Communities (Amendment) Bill, the passage of which will allow the United Kingdom to ratify the Treaty of Amsterdam, incorporates into domestic law those parts of the Treaty of Amsterdam which give rise to Community rights and obligations. It does not incorporate the Treaty's provisions dealing with Pillars II and III (such as Article K7), since these are intergovernmental provisions which do not give rise to Community rights and obligations.

(HC Debs., vol. 312, WA, col. *140*: 13 May 1998)

During the committee stage of the Human Rights Bill in the House of Commons, the Secretary of State for the Home Department, Mr Jack Straw, stated:

The case for incorporation, among others, is that British judges can be involved in the development of jurisprudence. I happen to think that that will be extremely helpful, both because they obviously have a better understanding of circumstances in this country than judges from other jurisdictions, and because we have a body of people in the higher judiciary with a degree of skill and professionalism that is in some ways unrivalled throughout the world. It is important that that skill should be utilised in the interpretation of a profoundly important convention and a profoundly important Bill.

Secondly, the right hon. and learned Gentleman felt that it was right that we should incorporate the convention in a way that fashioned the law through the combined efforts of the judiciary and Parliament. In opposition, when we first looked into the matter, we certainly tried to achieve that.

On the third point, we did not want to incorporate the convention in a way that challenged the supremacy of Parliament and its sovereignty. I have noticed some correspondence and articles in the newspapers suggesting that we should have gone down that route, and that, if we did not, it would be a milk-and-water version of incorporation.

When reference is made to Bills of Rights not only in the United States but in jurisdictions such as Canada, what is forgotten is that those jurisdictions have written constitutions and that there is what amounts to a superior law, which is brought into effect by the procedures for change in the constitution itself. We do not have that facility, and I do not suggest that we should. As an alternative, we have the sovereignty of Parliament, and therefore it is of profound importance that the ultimate judge of what should or should not be a right and a responsibility in the United Kingdom must be this Parliament and no other body.

(HC Debs., vol. 312, col. 980: 20 May 1998)

Speaking later in the committee debate, the Parliamentary Secretary, Lord Chancellor's Department, Mr Geoffrey Hoon, was asked whether UK courts would follow the jurisprudence of the European Court of Human Rights. He replied:

Clearly, it is important because the UK is bound internationally by the convention's provisions, that our law should be consistent with the general provisions of the European convention. That is already the law of the UK in relation to the international position. The Government are seeking to incorporate those international obligations into our domestic law. Therefore, it is important, ultimately, that the law of the UK, as applied by UK courts, is broadly consistent with the jurisprudence of the Strasbourg court.

That is something that, if cases were pressed to their logical and ultimate conclusion, is already necessary. Having been bound internationally to satisfy the terms of the convention, there is an obligation on the UK, as a signatory state to the European convention, to translate those decisions into our domestic legislation, so there is no legal distinction between the position today and the position that will obtain once incorporation has taken place.

(Ibid., vol. 313, col. 403: 3 June 1998)

The Merchant Shipping (Control of Pollution) (SOLAS) Order 1998 (Statutory Instruments 1998, No. 1500), which came into force on 1 July 1998, was accompanied by the following explanatory memorandum:

This Order enables regulations to be made to give effect to the International Convention for the Safety of Life at Sea Convention 1974 (and its Protocol of 1978, and amendments) ('SOLAS') so far as the Convention relates to the prevention, reduction or control of pollution of the sea or other waters by waste matter from ships. (The Convention relates primarily to safety, but recent amendments also contain provisions for the protection of the environment.)

In reply to a question, the Minister of State, FCO, wrote in part:

The FCO has introduced three pieces of legislation in the current session: to implement the Comprehensive Nuclear Test Ban Treaty, the Treaty of Amsterdam and the Ottawa Convention on Landmines. These implement internationally negotiated treaties in the United Kingdom.

(HC Debs., vol. 315, WA, col. *687*: 10 July 1998)

In the course of a debate on the subject of the procedures for election of judges to the European Court of Human Rights, the Lord Chancellor, Lord Irvine of Lairg, stated:

I agree with the noble Lord, Lord Lester, that the European Convention is the jewel in the crown of the Council of Europe. For nearly 50 years, the convention has been the bedrock of European human rights law. For 50 years the convention has stood as the objective framework of values against which governments measured their commitment to democracy and freedom. Britain has worked throughout those 50 years to uphold the values in the convention. We were there at the beginning in the drafting of the convention, and we were first to ratify in 1951.

That commitment to the convention continues today. This Government, 50 years after the convention was drafted, introduced legislation to incorporate the convention into law and so to make its provisions accessible to all in our domestic courts. The Human Rights Bill, now nearing the end of its progress in another place, reminds us that the convention remains a powerful instrument, as relevant today as it was 50 years ago. The Bill is a major pillar of the Government's programme of constitutional change. But while the rights and freedoms guaranteed by the convention remain broadly the same as those drafted 50 years ago, their relevance in post-war history has a new dimension.

(HL Debs., vol. 592, cols. 94–5: 13 July 1998)

In moving the second reading in the House of Lords of the Landmines Bill, the Parliamentary Under-Secretary of State, FCO, Baroness Symons of Vernham Dean, referred to the Ottawa Convention on the subject. She went on:

Britain was closely involved in negotiating the convention in Oslo last September. Securing agreement on a final text in less than three weeks honoured the memory of Diana, Princess of Wales, who died so tragically on the conference's eve. We were delighted to be among the first countries to sign the Ottawa convention last December. There are now 128 signatories: a truly remarkable achievement in so short a period.

Having helped write the convention, we now want to help bring it into effect. That is why we are here today. In passing this legislation now, we should ensure that Britain is among the first 40 countries whose ratification will secure the convention's entry into force; 24 states have already ratified. Several more are expected to announce their ratification soon.

If we and others can take this step quickly, the convention will be in effect early next year. That would be a wonderful tribute to the hard work and dedication of all involved in the campaign to rid the world of this deadly scourge. It would also send a powerful signal to those who have not signed the convention. It would make clear that the world community will not tolerate the continued use of anti-personnel landmines.

We need this legislation to implement the Ottawa convention. The Bill is entirely consistent with the convention.

(HL Debs., vol. 592, cols. 499–500: 17 July 1998)

Later in the debate, the Minister stated:

The noble Lord, Lord Moynihan, asked a number of questions about consistency between the convention and the legislation. He is quite right. Some of the language used in the definitions and in the Bill is different from the definitions used in the convention. We have sought greater clarity where appropriate but without changing the substance of the definitions. We believe that, if anything, the language in the Bill is tighter than that used in the convention. For example, the Bill covers components which the convention does not.

It is the Government's view that our legislation is in accordance with the aims and conventions of the Ottawa Convention. The kinds of things that have been described as possible abuses of the convention, because of the protection afforded by Clause 5, are not in the Government's view a correct understanding of the legislation before your Lordships. The legislation faithfully and fully puts the Ottawa convention into British legislation. Let me repeat this to your Lordships. It prohibits from using, developing, producing, possessing or transferring anti-personnel landmines or assisting, encouraging or inducing anyone else to do so. That provision will be clearly expressed in the rules of engagement for British troops.

(Ibid., cols. 539–40)

During the committee stage in the House of Lords, the same Minister stated:

First, I shall deal head-on with the question as to whether or not Clause 5 is legal and whether it is legally compatible with the Ottawa Convention. All I can say to your Lordships is that the Government have taken the best legal advice available and have received assurances that there is nothing in Clause 5 that is either likely to be challenged at international law or is incompatible with the Ottawa Convention. I have the benefit of the sagacity of my noble and learned friend the Solicitor-General, who is sitting beside me. I am sure that if I get any of this wrong he will be happy to intervene so that we can have two people speaking from the Front Bench, just to preserve a little symmetry in the proceedings.

So far as I know, there have been no challenges offered, suggested or mooted to this legislation. I am advised that, were any challenges so to emerge, they would not result in any delay to our ratification.

(HL Debs., vol. 592, col. 1171: 24 July 1998)

The Solicitor-General, Lord Falconer of Thoroton, later observed:

The convention bans certain activities, including assisting in the laying of landmines. Subject, *inter alia*, to Clause 5 of the Bill, anyone, either in Britain or abroad, who does such a thing is guilty of a criminal offence. Clause 5 provides a defence in special circumstances. That defence is where somebody is engaged in activity of a joint military nature. What is being said in Clause 5 is that, simply because we are engaged in a joint military operation where some other country which has not signed the convention is laying landmines, will not of itself constitute a criminal offence. It is a defence; it is not a permission to do specific things.

Even that defence excludes from it the act of laying landmines itself. That is an unequivocal act which is banned by the convention. There will be grey areas where it will not be clear precisely whether it was banned or not by the convention. I am sure we all agree that in relation to the individual soldier he must know precisely where he stands. However, it is the Government's unequivocal intention to stand by the aims of the convention. We want to do that but at the same time leave the soldier knowing where he stands.

Therefore, in relation to those cases where there may be abuses, we say that that will be dealt with by the rules of engagement and standing orders. That is how we intend to comply with the convention. There is an underlying misconception in many of the questions in relation to international law. Britain could be taken to the international court—I cannot say the procedural way in which it would reach there—but the question would not be: does Clause 5 constitute a breach of international law? The question would be whether, on the facts of a specific case, it would constitute a breach of international law.

(Ibid., cols. 1175–6)

The following question was asked of Her Majesty's Government:

When [do] they expect legislation to be introduced to incorporate the rights and freedoms guaranteed by the European Convention of Human Rights into the domestic laws of the Isle of Man and the Channel Islands; and whether they will ensure the equal protection of the law for everyone within the jurisdiction of the United Kingdom?

In reply, the Parliamentary Under-Secretary of State, Home Office, wrote:

The Insular Authorities in Jersey, Guernsey and the Isle of Man all hope to have legislation in draft by the end of the year.

Insular legislation will incorporate the Convention fully into domestic law and will be drafted to take account of local circumstances and institutions.

(HL Debs., vol. 592, *WA 153*: 27 July 1998)

An explanatory memorandum accompanying the presentation to Parliament in September 1998 of the Convention on combating Bribery of Foreign Public Officials in International Business Transactions, which the UK signed on 17 December 1997, read in part:

The domestic legislation which will enable the United Kingdom to implement the Convention is already in place, and does not require amendment. The United Kingdom's obligations are met by the scope of the Public Bodies Corrupt Practices Act 1889, the Prevention of Corruption Act 1906 and the Prevention of Corruption Act 1916.

(Text provided by the FCO)

In reply to a question, the Parliamentary Under-Secretary of State, Home Office, wrote:

Ratification of Protocol 4 will be possible only if potential conflicts with our domestic laws can be resolved. There is a particular concern in relation to Article 3(2) of the Protocol which protects the right of nationals not to be excluded from their home state. This could be taken as conferring the right of abode in the United Kingdom on various categories of British nationals who do not have it.

(HC Debs., vol. 318, WA, col. *578*: 4 November 1998)

Part Four: III. *Relationship between international law and internal law—remedies under internal law for violation of international law*

Her Majesty's Government was asked to list the occasions when it was obliged to bring forward (a) primary legislation and (b) secondary legislation, in order to comply with the UK's treaty obligations to keep its internal law in conformity with the European Convention on Human Rights. In reply, the Minister of State, FCO, wrote:

Primary legislation has been brought forward in order to implement the judgments of the European Court of Human Rights in the following cases:

Sunday Times (1979)
Young, James and Webster (1981)
X (Mental patient) (1981)
Campbell and Cosans (1982)
Malone (1984)
O, H, W, B and R (Parental access) (1987)
Thynne, Wilson and Gunnell (1990)

Boner and Maxwell (1994)
Hussain and Singh (1996)
Chahal (1996)

Secondary legislation has been brought forward in order to implement the judgments of the European Court of Human Rights in the following cases:

Golder (1975)
Dudgeon (1981)
Silver and Others (1983)
Abdulaziz, Cabales and Balkandali (1985)
McCallum (1990)
Campbell (1992)
McMichael (1995)
Benham (1996)

In relation to the cases of Fox, Campbell and Hartley (1990), Findlay (1997) and Coyne (1977), changes in primary legislation had already been made which in the Government's view ensured that United Kingdom law was compatible with the judgments of the European Court of Human Rights.

Primary and secondary legislation may have also been enacted in order to implement decisions of the Committee of Ministers in cases where reports of the European Commission of Human Rights have been transmitted to them under Article 32 of the Convention, but this information could be provided only at disproportionate cost.

(HC Debs., vol. 305, WA, cols. *544–5*: 2 February 1998)

In reply to a question asking for more detailed information about the above, the Minister of State wrote:

The primary legislation brought forward in order to implement the judgments of the European Court of Human Rights was as follows:

Sunday Times (1979): Contempt of Court Act 1981;
Young, James and Webster (1981): Employment Act 1982, sections 2–14;
X (Mental patient) (1981): Mental Health (Amendment) Act 1982, section 28 and Schedule 1.
Campbell and Cosans (1982): Education (No. 2) Act 1986, section 47;
Malone (1984): Interception of Communications Act 1985;
O, H, W, B and R (Parental Access) (1987): Children Act 1989, sections 22 and 34;
Thynne, Wilson and Gunnell (1990): Criminal Justice Act 1991, section 34;
Boner and Maxwell (1994): Criminal Justice (Scotland) Act 1995, section 42;
Hussain and Singh (1996): Crime (Sentences) Act 1997, section 28;
Chahal (1996): Special Immigration Appeals Commission Act 1997.

The subordinate instruments brought forward in order to implement the judgments of the European Court of Human Rights were as follows:

Golder (1975): Prison (Amendment) Rules 1976 (S.I. 1976/503);

Dudgeon (1981): Homosexual Offences (Northern Ireland) Order 1982 (S.I. 1982/1536; N.I. 19);
Silver and Others (1983): Prison (Amendment) Rules 1983 (S.I. 1983/568);
Abdulaziz, Cabales and Balkandali (1985): Statement of Changes in Immigration Rules, laid before Parliament on 15 July 1985 (HC 503);
McCallum (1990); Campbell (1992): Prison (Scotland) Amendment Rules 1993 (S.I. 1993/2227);
McMichael (1995): Children's Hearings (Scotland) Amendment Rules (S.I. 1996/1199);
Benham (1996): Legal Advice and Assistance (Scope) (Amendment) Regulations 1997 (S.I. 1997/997).

The primary legislation already brought forward which in the Government's view ensured that United Kingdom law was compatible with subsequent judgments of the European Court of Human Rights was as follows:

Fox, Campbell and Hartley (1990): Northern Ireland (Emergency Provisions) Act 1987, section 6;
Findlay (1997); Coyne (1997): Armed Forces Act 1996, section 5 and Schedule 1; section 15; section 16 and Schedule 5; section 17.

In some cases, the action taken to ensure the compatibility of United Kingdom law with a judgment of the European Court of Human Rights may have been a combination of the above and other measures.

(HC Debs., vol. 306, WA, cols. *490–1*: 16 February 1998)

Part Five: I. A. 2. *Subjects of international law—States—status and powers—territorial integrity*

(See Parts Five: I. A. 3. (item of 12 January 1998) and Five: I. A. 4., below)

Part Five: I. A. 3. *Subjects of international law—States—status and powers—sovereignty and independence*

In reply to a question, the Parliamentary Under-Secretary of State, FCO, wrote:

It is generally accepted that the oil reserves in the Caspian Sea are substantial, but estimates vary considerably. Our principal policy objectives in the Transcaucasus are underpinning the countries' independence and territorial integrity, supporting efforts to resolve conflicts, encouraging political and economic reform, and increasing bilateral trade. These objectives are unaffected by the level of Caspian oil reserves.

(HL Debs., vol. 584, *WA 128*: 12 January 1998)

The EU Presidency issued the following statement in London on 14 February 1998:

On the ninth anniversary of the publication of the *fatwa* condemning the British author Salman Rushdie to death and calling for his assassination, the European Union recalls and repeats the affirmations it has made on previous anniversaries of the *fatwa*. These said that the *fatwa* remained null and void because it violated the Universal Declaration on Human Rights and the principle of the sovereignty of states, who have responsibility for the protection of their nationals.

The European Union also expresses its grave concern over the continuing threats to the life of individuals associated with the work of Salman Rushdie.

Recalling previous resolutions of European Councils, the European Union calls upon Iran to abide by international law and urges the Iranian authorities to work with the EU to find a satisfactory solution in respect of Salman Rushdie. The European Union welcomes the new Iranian Government's stated commitment to respect the rule of law and their emphasis on the need for a dialogue of civilisations. The European Union hopes that this will take us towards the assurances that we need to remove the threat to Salman Rushdie's life.

The Central and Eastern European countries associated with the European Union, the associated country Cyprus, and the EFTA countries members of the European Economic Area align themselves with this declaration.

(*Bulletin of the European Union*, 1998–1/2, p. 86)

During a meeting on 16 February 1998 between Mr Salman Rushdie and the Secretary of State for Foreign and Commonwealth Affairs, Mr Robin Cook, the Secretary of State observed:

The new President of Iran has stressed that he wants to work within the rule of law and has called for a dialogue between civilisations. In our view, a clear test of these commitments will be whether he is willing to work with us to remove the threat to Mr Rushdie's life, which is plainly in breach of international law, and any dialogue with the people of Britain must be based on a willingness to recognise that.

(Text provided by the FCO)

Part Five: I. A. 4. *Subjects of international law—States—status and powers—non-intervention*

On 11 August 1998 the EU Presidency issued a statement on events in the Democratic Republic of Congo. It stated in part:

The European Union is . . . greatly preoccupied by the information regarding the possibility of foreign interference in the country's internal affairs and agrees with the United Nations Charter and the OAU's fundamental principles in support of the territorial integrity of the Democratic Republic of Congo and the territorial integrity of neighbouring countries.

(*Bulletin of the European Union*, 1998–7/8, p. 80; see also the EU statement of 16 August 1998 on the same subject (ibid., pp. 80–1)).

Part Five: I. A. 5. *Subjects of international law—States—status and powers—domestic jurisdiction*

In reply to the question what representations had been made by Her Majesty's Government to the Israeli Government about the imprisonment in Israel of Mr Mordechai Vanunu, the Parliamentary Under-Secretary of State, FCO, wrote:

We have no formal standing to intervene in this case as there is no evidence of any illegality prior to his departure from the United Kingdom. Mr. Vanunu appears to have been treated in accordance with the normal judicial process in Israel. Nevertheless, on humanitarian grounds, we regularly raise with the Israelis the length of Mr. Vanunu's solitary confinement and did this most recently with the Israeli Ministry of Foreign Affairs on 17 December.

(HL Debs., vol. 584, *WA 127*: 12 January 1998)

In reply to a question about a claim being pursued by Mr Patel, of London, in Tanzania in respect of the settlement of moneys owed under British aid projects, the Minister of State wrote:

Mr. Patel is pursuing a private commercial claim against his former local representative in Dar-es-Salaam and the Government of Tanzania, following the supply of goods to a nationalised Tanzanian company. We have assisted attempts to expedite the claim since 1993. In October 1996 we were informed that a payment of 84 million Tanzanian Shillings, out of a total claim of 92 million Shillings, had been paid to Mr. Patel's local representative. Mr. Patel now appears to be in dispute with this representative. We have no jurisdiction to intervene in this dispute and have advised Mr. Patel to pursue his claim through the appropriate legal channels.

(HC Debs., vol. 305, WA, col. *381*: 29 January 1998)

In the course of an interview in Luxembourg on 3 October 1998, the Secretary of State for Foreign and Commonwealth Affairs, Mr Robin Cook, stated:

First of all I think that I am obliged to say that Gibraltar is not a domestic Spanish issue.

(Text provided by the FCO)

Part Five: I. B. 1. *Subjects of international law—States—recognition—recognition of States*

(See also Part Five: I. D. 3 and Part Five: I. D. 9. (b). (iii) (affidavit of 19 June 1998), below)

The following question was asked of Her Majesty's Government:

Whether their policy on dealing with regimes which came into power unconstitutionally remains as stated by Lord Carrington on 28 April 1980 . . . ?

In reply, the Parliamentary Under-Secretary of State, FCO, wrote:

It does. We recognise states, not governments. We decide the nature of our dealings with regimes which come to power unconstitutionally in the light of our assessment of whether they are able of themselves to exercise effective control of the territory of the state concerned, and seem likely to continue to do so.

(HL Debs., vol. 584, *WA 125*: 12 January 1998; see also UKMIL 1980, pp. 367–8)

Part Five: I. B. 2. *Subjects of international law—States—recognition—recognition of governments*

In his judgment in *Sierra Leone Telecommunications Co. Ltd.* v. *Barclays Bank plc*, given on 6 February 1998, Cresswell J. set out the following extract from a letter dated 28 November 1997 sent by the FCO to the plaintiff's solicitors, Messrs Stephenson Harwood:

You asked me to set out the British Government's policy towards Sierra Leone . . . The British Government welcomed the election in Sierra Leone of President Ahmad Tejan Kabbah in February 1996. We have consistently condemned the military coup of 25 May 1997 which overthrew the democratically elected government of Sierra Leone. We look forward to the restoration of constitutional order in that country. We continue to deal with the democratically elected government of Sierra Leone under President Kabbah. We have no dealings with the military junta in Freetown.

([1998] 2 All ER 821, 830)

The following question was asked of Her Majesty's Government:

What criteria they apply in deciding whether to support governments in exile, either politically or financially; and why they have given £130,000 to former President Ahmed Tejan Kabbah of Sierra Leone and nothing to former President Pascal Lissouba of Congo Brazzaville?

In reply, the Parliamentary Under-Secretary of State, FCO, wrote:

Where democratic governments have been overthrown by violence we have often worked with them in exile as part of our global support for democracy. Tejan Kabbah is not the 'former' President of Sierra Leone; he remains the legitimate leader of that country, whereas the outbreak of civil war in June 1997 in Congo (Brazzaville) resulted in the cancellation of the presidential election and the subsequent expiry of President Lissouba's mandate in August 1997. Moreover, although the UK was a principal donor to Sierra Leone before the coup—and hopes to be again after the restoration of constitutional order there—we have not had a bilateral aid relationship with the Republic of the Congo for many years.

(HL Debs., vol. 584, *WA 126*: 12 January 1998)

In the course of answering a question, the Minister of State, FCO, wrote:

It is our view that the legitimate government of President Kabbah should be restored to power in Sierra Leone. We have called for the restoration of the democratically elected President, the establishment of a broadly based government and for all parties to move to a process of disarmament and demobilisation.

(HC Debs., vol. 307, WA, col. *385*: 27 February 1998)

In reply to a question, the Secretary of State for Foreign and Commonwealth Affairs wrote:

This Government have consistently supported the peaceful restoration of the legitimate government of Sierra Leone.

(HC Debs., vol. 312, WA, col. *361*: 19 May 1998)

In reply to a question, the Secretary of State for Foreign and Commonwealth Affairs wrote:

Following the military coup, like the rest of the international community, the United Kingdom continued to regard President Kabbah as the head of the legitimate Government of Sierra Leone. We were in the lead in efforts to achieve the peaceful restoration of that Government.

Although the junta was in power in Freetown, large parts of Sierra Leone were under control of forces loyal to President Kabbah, and it was widely expected that the junta would not remain in power. It was important to remain in close contact with the President and to maintain the High Commissioner's strong relationship with him. Ministers therefore agreed that the High Commissioner should, on a temporary basis, stay in Conakry, where he had been evacuated after the coup in Freetown.

(HC Debs., vol. 316, WA, col. *693*: 23 July 1998)

Part Five: I. B. 6. *Subjects of international law—States—recognition—non-recognition and its effects*

(See also Part Six: VII. A., below)

In travel advice issued to the public on 26 January 1998 by the Consular Division of the FCO, the following passage was included in the material on Western Sahara:

The territory of the Western Sahara is disputed between Morocco and the Polisario Front, and the United Kingdom regards sovereignty as undetermined.

(Text provided by the FCO)

In the course of a debate on the subject of the future of the Western Sahara, the Minister of State, FCO, Mr Derek Fatchett, stated:

We neither support the Moroccan claim to sovereignty over the territory, nor recognise the Polisario's self-proclaimed Saharwi Arab Democratic Republic.

(HC Debs., vol. 313, col. 339: 3 June 1998)

Part Five: I. D. 3. *Subjects of international law—States—formation, continuity, extinction and succession of States—identity and continuity*

In the course of an affidavit sworn on 19 June 1998 in the case of *R* v. *Foreign and Commonwealth Office, ex parte International Transport Workers Federation* in the Divisional Court of the Queen's Bench, Mr M.C. Wood, Deputy Legal Adviser, FCO, stated:

The effect of the break up of the USSR
5. In 1991, upon the break-up of the Union of Soviet Socialist Republics, the Russian Federation continued the legal personality of the former USSR. This was the basis for the continuation of the Russian Federation as a permanent member of the United Nations Security Council. The legal situation was recognized by other States, and was confirmed not only by the attitude and practice of the Russian Federation but also that of other components of the former USSR and, indeed, other States more generally to whom rights and duties were owed. For example, it was confirmed by members of the Commonwealth of Independent States as is shown by the decision of the Council of Heads of States of the Commonwealth of Independent States done at Alma Ata on 21 December 1991. A copy of the decision as translated and published in 31 International Legal Materials is at page 1 of MCW1 [not reproduced]. This legal situation was and is accepted by Her Majesty's Government, as is clear from various statements made in Parliament by the Secretary of State for Foreign and Commonwealth Affairs and Ministers of State in the Foreign and Commonwealth Office. I refer to written answers to Parliamentary Questions given on 15, 20, 21, 23 and 24 January, 5 February, and 16 March 1992; and a House of Lords Debate on 29 January 1992. . . . The Russian Federation is thus accepted as the continuation of the Union of Soviet Socialist Republics under another name and within altered boundaries. As a matter of international law, the Russian Federation continued in principle to be the bearer of the rights and obligations of the Union of Soviet Socialist Republics. This position was confirmed by the Russian Federation, as is evidenced by a Diplomatic Note No 11/UCP dated 13 January 1992 which was delivered to, inter alia, the Embassy of the United Kingdom in Moscow [not reproduced].

Part Five: I. D. 5. (b). (iii). *Subjects of international law—States—formation, continuity, extinction and succession of States—succession—effects of State succession—succession in respect of treaties*

(See also Part Three: V. C., above)

On 2 January 1998, Mr Tony Lloyd, Minister of State, FCO, replied to Ms Joan Walley MP, who had written to the Secretary of State for Foreign and Commonwealth Affairs on the subject of the State Immunity (Merchant Shipping) Order 1997. His reply stated in part:

The State Immunity (Merchant Shipping) Order 1997 was made to remove any doubt over the implementation in domestic law of the 1974 Protocol to the

Treaty on Merchant Navigation [between the UK and the USSR]. The Order was prepared as a matter of urgency after it came to our attention that doubts about the domestic implementation of the Protocol could at any time lead to the UK being placed in breach of its international obligations. For this reason the Order came into force immediately, without waiting the normal 21 days, as was perfectly proper given the urgency of the situation. The Order concerned existing international obligations and so was prepared within the Foreign and Commonwealth Office.

The UK has obligations under the Protocol towards Ukraine because, when the UK recognised Ukraine, it was confirmed that treaties between the UK and the USSR such as the 1974 Protocol would remain in force with Ukraine. The continued application of the 1974 Protocol between the UK and Ukraine was provided for in an Exchange of Notes in 1995.

(Text provided by the FCO)

In the course of answering oral questions on the subject of the Middle East, the Secretary of State for Foreign and Commonwealth Affairs, Mr Robin Cook, stated:

. . . we shall continue to condemn any breach of the Oslo accords. In particular, we call on the Government of Israel to honour the agreement entered into by the previous Israeli Government, which, because it has the force of a treaty, is binding on successor Governments.

(HC Debs., vol. 306, col. 131: 10 February 1998)

The following record of a meeting signed in Belgrade on 3 March 1998 and in London on 3 April 1998 respectively was printed in the *UK Treaty Series*:

1. Representatives of the Foreign and Commonwealth Office of the United Kingdom of Great Britain and Northern Ireland and the Federal Ministry of Foreign Affairs of the Federal Republic of Yugoslavia met in Belgrade on 14 October 1996 to consider the position of bilateral agreements and arrangements between the two countries.
2. It was recalled that, in a Declaration of 27 April 1992 the Federal Government of the Federal Republic of Yugoslavia had affirmed that it would strictly abide by all commitments that the Socialist Federal Republic of Yugoslavia had assumed internationally. It was also recalled that, on 10 April 1996, the Secretary of State for Foreign and Commonwealth Affairs had sent a message to the President of the Federal Republic of Yugoslavia in which inter alia the United Kingdom had confirmed that, as appropriate, it regarded treaties and agreements in force to which the United Kingdom and the Socialist Federal Republic of Yugoslavia were parties as remaining in force between the United Kingdom and the Federal Republic of Yugoslavia.
3. In light of paragraph 2 above, representatives of the Foreign and Commonwealth Office of the United Kingdom of Great Britain and Northern Ireland and the Federal Ministry of Foreign Affairs of the Federal Republic of Yugoslavia confirmed that the bilateral agreements and arrangements that were in force between the United Kingdom of Great Britain and Northern Ireland

and the Socialist Federal Republic of Yugoslavia and which are listed below [list not reproduced] remain in force between the United Kingdom of Great Britain and Northern Ireland and the Federal Republic of Yugoslavia, without prejudice to the possibility that other bilateral agreements and arrangements might remain in force between the two countries in accordance with international law.

(TS No. 28 (1998); Cm 4005, p. 62)

The following letter, dated 1 October 1997, was addressed to the UK Embassy in Sarajevo, Republic of Bosnia and Herzegovina:

The Ministry for Foreign Affairs of Bosnia and Herzegovina presents its compliments to the Embassy of the United Kingdom of Great Britain and Northern Ireland and has the honour to recall the discussions in Sarajevo on 15 June 1997 between the Ministry for Foreign Affairs and the Foreign and Commonwealth Office concerning succession to bilateral agreements and arrangements.

The Ministry confirms that the bilateral agreements and arrangements that were in force between the Socialist Federal Republic of Yugoslavia and the United Kingdom of Great Britain and Northern Ireland and which are listed below remain in force between Bosnia and Herzegovina and the United Kingdom of Great Britain and Northern Ireland, without prejudice to the possibility that other bilateral agreements and arrangements may remain in force between the two countries in accordance with international law.

[list not reproduced]

The Agreements concluded between the former Socialist Federal Republic of Yugoslavia and the United Kingdom of Great Britain and Northern Ireland on certain Commercial Debts were not discussed, since they are being dealt with in the negotiations on the assumption by the Government of Bosnia and Herzegovina of certain foreign debts of the former Socialist Federal Republic of Yugoslavia within the framework of the Paris Club.

If this is acceptable to the Government of the United Kingdom of Great Britain and Northern Ireland, the Ministry suggests that this Note and the Embassy's reply to that effect will constitute joint confirmation that the bilateral agreements and arrangements listed above remain in force between Bosnia and Herzegovina and the United Kingdom of Great Britain and Northern Ireland.

(Text provided by the FCO)

The following letter, dated 28 May 1998, was addressed to the Ambassador of the UK in Ljubljana, Slovenia, by the Slovenian Foreign Minister:

I have the honour to recall the discussions in Ljubljana on 10 February 1997 between the Ministry for Foreign Affairs of the Republic of Slovenia and the Foreign and Commonwealth Office of the United Kingdom of Great Britain and Northern Ireland concerning succession to bilateral agreements and arrangements, and to confirm that the bilateral agreements and arrangements that were in force between the former Socialist Federal Republic of Yugoslavia and the United Kingdom of Great Britain and Northern Ireland and which are listed

below remain in force between the Republic of Slovenia and the United Kingdom of Great Britain and Northern Ireland, without prejudice to the possibility that other bilateral agreements and arrangements might remain in force between the two countries in accordance with international law.
[list not reproduced]

By a letter dated 8 June 1998, the Ambassador of the UK stated 'that your Excellency's letter and this reply constitutes joint confirmation that the aforementioned agreements and arrangements remain in force between the United Kingdom of Great Britain and Northern Ireland and the Republic of Slovenia'.

(Text provided by the FCO; see also TS No. 39 (1998); Cm 4046, p. 35)

In the course of an affidavit sworn on 19 June 1998 in the case of *R* v. *Foreign and Commonwealth Office, ex parte International Transport Workers Federation* in the Divisional Court of the Queen's Bench, Mr M.C. Wood, Deputy Legal Advisor, FCO, stated:

6. A number of successor States emerged from the USSR, including the Republic of Ukraine ('Ukraine') and Georgia. The question therefore arose for Her Majesty's Government and other States that were in bilateral treaty relations with the former USSR as to whether the successor States should be treated as having also succeeded to the bilateral treaties to which the former USSR had been party. Various doctrines of succession to treaties have been put forward by writers in international law, none of which has gained universal acceptance. Her Majesty's Government have consistently over the years advocated in their international practice the greatest measure of succession to treaties, as they have taken the view that continuity in treaty relations is an important element in stability of international relations.
7. The key determinant in practice, and this is fully recognized in international law, is the view adopted by the relevant States themselves, that is those States that are parties to the bilateral treaties with the predecessor State and the successor States. Consistent with their general approach Her Majesty's Government has taken the position with regard to the former USSR that successor States have succeeded to the bilateral treaties of the USSR.
8. One such successor State was Ukraine. On 31 December 1991 the then Prime Minister of the United Kingdom, Mr John Major, wrote to the President of Ukraine . . . [for the letter's complete text see below]. That letter placed on record the United Kingdom's recognition of Ukraine as an independent sovereign State. Recognition of a State is an exercise of the prerogative of the Crown. The letter went on to state that:

> 'I can confirm that, as appropriate, we regard treaties and agreements in force to which the United Kingdom and the Union of Soviet Socialist Republics were parties as remaining in force between the United Kingdom and Ukraine.'

The word 'confirm' was deliberately used because Her Majesty's Government considered that such treaties and agreements were already in force between the

United Kingdom and Ukraine and had been in force between those countries from the date of the succession of States which had been part of the former USSR.

9. In a letter from Mr Major to Mr Shevardnadze, Chairman of the State Council of Georgia, dated 23 March 1992, the exact same language was used to confirm that treaties remain in force between the United Kingdom and Georgia. A true copy of that letter as reproduced in United Kingdom Materials on International Law 1992 [UKMIL 1992, pp. 640–1] is exhibited to the affidavit of PA Newdick . . .

10. Neither Ukraine nor Georgia made any objection to the letters from Mr Major, and both have positively affirmed that they are parties to the Treaty and Protocol, as follows.

11. On 21 December 1991 Ukraine signed the Alma Ata Declaration along with Azerbaijan, Armenia, Belarus, Kazakhstan, Kyrgyzstan, Moldova, Russian Federation, Tajikistan, Turkmenistan, and Uzbekistan. A true copy of that Declaration as translated and published in 31 International Legal Materials is at pages 15–16 of MCW1 [not reproduced]. The Declaration provides that:

> 'The States participating in the Commonwealth guarantee in accordance with their constitutional procedures the discharge of the international obligations deriving from treaties and agreements concluded by the former Union of Soviet Socialist Republics.'

It will be noted that the States parties to the Alma Ata Declaration used the word 'guarantee' in relation to the obligations that they would continue to discharge, a word that imports a clear intention that all the world should be entitled to rely upon this statement. This is certainly the view which Her Majesty's Government has taken of the declaration. The continuance of such obligations was not restricted to the States emerging from the former USSR *inter se*, but was on the contrary phrased so as to apply to all 'international obligations deriving from treaties and agreements concluded by the former Union of Soviet Socialist Republics'.

12. The Embassy of Ukraine in the United Kingdom delivered a Diplomatic Note dated 6 November 1995 to the Foreign and Commonwealth Office. A true copy of that Note is exhibited to the affidavit of PA Newdick . . . [not reproduced]. That Note refers to the 'British-Soviet Treaty of 1968 on Merchant Navigation' and certifies that a vessel which had been arrested is the property of Ukraine. The reference to the 1968 Treaty was made in the context of Ukraine asserting State immunity in respect of the vessel, and is regarded by Her Majesty's Government as clear evidence that Ukraine accepts that the Treaty and Protocol are in force between Ukraine and the United Kingdom. The United Kingdom responded by Diplomatic Note dated 28 December 1995, a true copy of which is exhibited to the affidavit of PA Newdick . . . [for text of Note see below]. The United Kingdom position was made clear in the Note, which states:

> 'The Department would like to inform the Embassy that in accordance with the Protocol to the Treaty of Merchant Navigation between the United Kingdom and Union of Soviet Socialist Republics, which entered into force on 15 June 1977, United Kingdom law provides that no warrant of arrest shall

be issued against a ship owned by the Ukraine until notice has been served on a consular officer of the Ukraine.'

13. A further clear statement of Ukraine's position was provided in June 1997. At that time the Foreign and Commonwealth Office were contacted by solicitors for both parties in respect of proceedings regarding the MV Inessa Armand, a ship owned by the Black Sea Shipping Company which had been arrested in Belfast. In relation to those proceedings the Foreign and Commonwealth Office received a fax from Messrs Lawrence Graham, Solicitors acting on behalf of Ukraine, dated 13 June 1997 which enclosed a copy letter dated 10 June 1997 from the Ukraine Embassy to Messrs Lawrence Graham regarding those proceedings. A true copy of the letter dated 10 June 1997 is exhibited to the affidavit of PA Newdick . . . [not reproduced].

14. The letter of 10 June 1997 states that Ukraine regards itself as a party to the Treaty, and points out that this is reflected in domestic legislation in Ukraine. Firstly, reference is made to the Ukraine Law of 1991 entitled 'On Succession of Ukraine', in terms of which 'Ukraine is the successor in respect of rights and duties derived from the international treaties of the Union of SSR which are not contradicting to the Constitution of Ukraine and its state interests'. Ukraine's assertion that it is a party to the Treaty must be assumed to mean that the Treaty does not contradict the Ukrainian constitution or State interests. Secondly, reference is made to the Merchant Shipping Code of Ukraine, which affirms that 'international treaties of Ukraine on merchant shipping are applicable to Ukraine in accordance with the provisions of the law of Ukraine on International Treaties of Ukraine'.

15. A further statement of the position of Ukraine is provided by a Diplomatic Note from Ukraine to the Embassy of the United Kingdom in Ukraine dated 12 March 1998, a true copy of which is at page 17 of MCW1 [not reproduced]. That Note states that:

> 'The Government of Ukraine is of the opinion that the provisions of the Treaty on Merchant Navigation between the USSR and the United Kingdom of Great Britain and Northern Ireland signed on 3 April 1968 and the Protocol to that Treaty signed on 1 March 1974 are in force as between Ukraine and Britain.'

16. Georgia, for its part, signed the Alma Ata Declaration at Tbilisi on 9 December 1993. A true copy of the Declaration signed by the President of Georgia, together with a translation, is at pages 18–19 of MCW1 [not reproduced]. Thus, Georgia's position in respect of the Alma Ata Declaration is the same as that explained in paragraph 11 of this affidavit in respect of Ukraine. This makes clear the position of Georgia that she is a party to the Treaty and Protocols.

17. On 28 April 1998 the British Ambassador in Tbilisi handed to the Head of the Legal Department of the Ministry of Foreign Affairs of Georgia ('the MFA') a Note Verbale denouncing the Treaty and Protocols . . . . In response, the Head of the Legal Department said that he had no difficulty with unilateral denunciation. The MFA had already written to the competent ministries and was still awaiting a reply. These remarks from the Head of the Legal Department of the

MFA were clearly made on the footing that Georgia accepted that the Treaty and its Protocols were in force between Georgia and the United Kingdom.

. . .

United Kingdom litigation and the making of the 1997 Order

25. Earlier in this affidavit (paragraph 13) I mentioned proceedings in the High Court in Belfast concerning the arrest of the MV Inessa Armand. On 16 June 1997 the Foreign and Commonwealth Office were requested by the parties to those proceedings to state whether the Treaty and Protocol applied between the United Kingdom and Ukraine. The Foreign and Commonwealth Office replied the same day to the effect that Her Majesty's Government and, to the best of the belief of the Foreign and Commonwealth Office, Ukraine regarded the Treaty and Protocol as being in force. A true copy of that letter is exhibited to the affidavit of PA Newdick . . . [for its text see below]. The FCO learned in October 1997 that this case had been concluded without deciding the point.
26. The Foreign and Commonwealth Office heard nothing more until 16 October 1997, when Messrs Lawrence Graham, solicitors for Ukraine, contacted the Foreign and Commonwealth Office about the case of *Bridge Oil Limited* v. *The owners of the ship 'Guiseppe di Vittorio'*. In their letter . . . [not reproduced], the solicitors informed the Foreign and Commonwealth Office that Ukraine was appealing against the order of Clark[e] J of 15 July 1997 affirming the arrest of the vessel and ordering her to be sold. The letter stated that Clark[e] J had held that the State Immunity (Merchant Shipping) (Union of Soviet Socialist Republics) Order 1978 did not apply to Ukraine, and that the matter was now before the Court of Appeal. The solicitors further said that they would pass the letter of the Foreign and Commonwealth Office of 16 June 1997 in relation to the Inessa Armand case to the court, and in addition that the appeal was to conclude the next day. In response to this letter, the Foreign and Commonwealth Office confirmed in a letter of 16 October 1997 [not reproduced] exhibited to the affidavit of PA Newdick . . . that they had nothing to add to the letter of 16 June 1997. The Foreign and Commonwealth Office further stated that it was clearly desirable to avoid any doubt that there might be concerning the effect of the 1978 Order in respect of Ukraine, and that it was therefore intended that a further Order be made, at the earliest opportunity, expressly applying provisions identical to those of Articles 3 and 4 of the 1978 Order to ships owned by Ukraine.
27. Since further vessels might be arrested at any time, with consequent uncertainty and court proceedings, with the result that the United Kingdom would be in breach of its treaty obligations, it was considered by the Foreign and Commonwealth Office at this stage (mid-October 1997) that a further Order in Council should be made and brought into force as soon as possible. Accordingly, the State Immunity (Merchant Shipping) Order 1997 was drafted as a matter of urgency, approved by the Minister, and transmitted to the Privy Council Office on 23 October 1997. It was made on 30 October 1997 and came into force on 1 November 1997.
28. On 29 October 1997, the Court of Appeal upheld the decision of Clark[e] J to the effect that the 1978 Order did not apply to Ukraine.

29. In the Guiseppe di Vittorio case, the judgment of Clark[e] J referred to the provisional conclusion of the Court of Session in the case of *Coreck Maritime Gmbh v. Sevybokhodflot* [1994] SLT 893 on the separate question of whether the 1978 Order applied to the Russian Federation. I am not aware that the judgment of the Court of Session was drawn to the attention of the Foreign and Commonwealth Office before October 1997.

(Text provided by the FCO)

The letter from the Prime Minister to the President of Ukraine of 31 December 1991 read as follows:

With other Member States of the European Community, the United Kingdom has today issued a statement on the changes which have taken place in your country and in neighbouring Republics.

I am writing to place on record that the British Government formally recognises Ukraine as an independent sovereign state. We have noted that Ukraine, by the terms of its accession to the Commonwealth of Independent States, has assumed its share of the legal and financial obligations of the former USSR. I believe it is essential for Ukraine to cooperate fully in international efforts to service the debts and financial obligations of the former Soviet Union. I look forward to the establishment of diplomatic relations in the very near future in addition to our newly established consular relations. I can confirm that, as appropriate, we regard Treaties and Agreements in force to which the United Kingdom and the Union of Soviet Socialist Republics were parties as remaining in force between the United Kingdom and Ukraine. Recognition shall not be taken to imply acceptance by Her Majesty's Government of the position of any of the Republics concerning territory which is the subject of a dispute between two or more Republics.

The United Kingdom has separately recognised as independent sovereign states, the Republics of Armenia, Belarus, Kazakhstan, Moldova, Turkmenistan, Uzbekistan, and the Azerbaidzhan Republic.

The changes in what was previously the Soviet Union mark a new relationship between our countries. I take this opportunity to send the best wishes of the British people to the people of Ukraine. We firmly support your efforts to achieve political and economic reform and to bring about lasting progress for your people. We welcome the establishment of the Commonwealth of Independent States, and shall do all in our power to help the development of stable, peaceful and prosperous relations between the States formerly part of the Soviet Union.

The Diplomatic Note to the Embassy of Ukraine in London dated 28 December 1995 read as follows:

Note No. AMDNV 263/95

The Aviation and Maritime Department of the Foreign and Commonwealth Office present their compliments to the Embassy of Ukraine and have the honour to refer to the Embassy's Note No. KB/95–289 of 6 November regarding the arrest of the motor vessel 'Zorinsk'.

The Department would like to inform the Embassy that in accordance with the Protocol to the Treaty of Merchant Navigation between the United Kingdom and the Union of Soviet Socialist Republics, which entered into force on 15 June 1977, United Kingdom law provides that no warrant of arrest shall be issued against a ship owned by the Ukraine until notice has been served on a consular officer of the Ukraine. Notice is given by the solicitors for the party seeking to have the ship arrested, in this case Messrs Clyde & Co. The Marine Safety Agency is not involved in proceedings related to the detention of ships unless the detention is for reasons of maritime safety or marine pollution.

The Department notes that the vessel has now been released from arrest.

The letter dated 16 June 1997 from the FCO to solicitors read as follows:

Re: M.V. Inessa Armand

We understand that you are the legal representatives of the parties involved in the litigation currently before the High Court in Belfast concerning the arrest of the M.V. 'Inessa Armand', and that it is a material question in those proceedings whether the Treaty on Merchant Navigation between the United Kingdom of Great Britain and Northern Ireland and the Union of Soviet Socialist Republics, done at London on 3 April 1968, together with its Protocol, done at Moscow on 1 March 1974, applies between the United Kingdom of Great Britain and Northern Ireland and the Republic of Ukraine.

I am instructed to state in that connection:

(a) that when Her Majesty's Government recognised Ukraine, on 31 December 1991, as an independent sovereign State, they did so on the following terms (which were formally conveyed to the Government of Ukraine): '[We] confirm that, as appropriate, we regard all Treaties and Agreements in force to which the United Kingdom and the Union of Soviet Socialist Republics were parties as remaining in force between the United Kingdom and Ukraine';

(b) that pursuant to the above Her Majesty's Government regard the said Treaty and Protocol as being in force between the United Kingdom and Ukraine, subject only to such minor adjustments (which have not been expressly agreed between the two Governments) as are necessary for their application in the new circumstances;

(c) that, to the best of the belief of the relevant Departments of Her Majesty's Government, the Government of Ukraine adopt a corresponding attitude to the application of the Treaty and Protocol between the two States.

While the Foreign and Commonwealth Office has done its best to provide an adequate response to the request posed within the very limited time allowed, I am to request, in the event that the Court requires further or other assistance to enable it to dispose of the matter before it, that sufficient time be allowed to permit the Office to certify in properly considered form.

(Above texts provided by the FCO)

Part Five: I. D. 5. (b). (v). *Subjects of international law—States—formation, continuity, extinction and succession of States—succession—effects of State succession—debts*

In reply to the question what steps the Secretary of State for Foreign and Commonwealth Affairs has taken 'to trace the assets of the former Socialist Federal Republic of Yugoslavia under the control of Serbia and to ensure that these are returned on an equitable basis to the successor nations', the Minister of State, FCO, wrote:

None. It is for the five successor States to resolve questions of succession to assets and liabilities of the former Socialist Federal Republic of Yugoslavia. Negotiations continue under the auspices of the High Representatives special negotiator, Sir Arthur Watts, whose fees we cover.

(HC Debs., vol. 316, WA, col. *31*: 13 July 1998)

Part Five: I. D. 5. (b). (vi). *Subjects of international law—States—formation, continuity, extinction and succession of States—succession—effects of State succession—property*

(See Part Five: I. D. 5. (b). (v), above)

Part Five: II. A. 3. *Subjects of international law—international organizations—general—legal effect of the acts of international organizations*

During a press conference held on 24 August 1998, the Secretary of State for Foreign and Commonwealth Affairs, Mr Robin Cook, stated:

Almost seven years ago warrants were issued for the arrest of two Libyan terrorists. Since that date Libya has persistently failed to carry out its obligations to hand over the two accused for trial despite binding resolutions of the Security Council requiring it to do so.

(Text provided by the FCO)

Part Five: II. A. 4. *Subjects of international law—international organizations—general—personnel of international organizations, including privileges and immunities*

In reply to a question, the Minister of State, FCO, wrote:

Under the 1965 Protocol on Privileges and Immunities of the European Communities, 26 members of staff at the European Commission based in London enjoy Diplomatic Immunity. This is only in respect of acts carried out in their official capacity.

(HC Debs., vol. 309, WA, col. *535*: 1 April 1998)

The following written statement, dated October 1998, was submitted by the Government of the UK to the International Court of Justice in respect of the request for an advisory opinion by the UN Economic and Social Council (*Difference relating to Immunity from Legal Process of a Special Rapporteur of the Commission on Human Rights*):

1. By decision 1998/297 of 5 August 1998 the United Nations Economic and Social Council has requested, on a priority basis, pursuant to Article 96 of the Charter of the United Nations and in accordance with General Assembly resolution 89(I) of 11 December 1946, an advisory opinion from the International Court of Justice on the legal question of the applicability of Article VI, Section 22, of the Convention on the Privileges and Immunities of the United Nations ('the General Convention') in the case of Dato' Param Cumaraswamy as Special Rapporteur of the Commission on Human Rights on the independence of judges and lawyers and on the legal obligations of Malaysia in this case.

2. Pursuant to the provisions of Article 66(2) of the Statute of the International Court of Justice ('the Court') and in response to the invitation of the Registrar contained in his letter of 10 August 1998, the Government of the United Kingdom hereby submit a written statement in this case.

3. The Government of the United Kingdom welcome the submission of this matter to the Court and fully support the Secretary-General's efforts to resolve this difference in accordance with the provisions of Article VIII, Section 30 of the General Convention. In the view of the Government of the United Kingdom this provision is an essential mechanism for ensuring that the privileges and immunities conferred under the General Convention are respected and that any uncertainty as to its interpretation or application can be resolved by conclusive adjudication.

4. It is of fundamental importance that experts performing missions for the United Nations are able to act with independence and impartiality. It is well established that Special Rapporteurs are 'experts on missions' within the terms of Article VI, Section 22 of the General Convention and therefore essential that they be accorded the privileges and immunities provided for under that Section. The United Kingdom is a firm supporter of the system of Special Rapporteurs developed by the Commission on Human Rights. It is essential for the proper functioning of their mandates that Special Rapporteurs receive the full co-operation of governments and are not impeded in their ability to receive or communicate information relevant to their work. For these reasons the European Union raised their concerns about Mr Cumaraswamy's situation with the Government of Malaysia in August 1997.

5. Section 22(b) of the General Convention states that experts on missions shall be accorded:

> 'In respect of words spoken or written and acts done by them in the course of the performance of their mission, immunity from legal process of every kind . . . '.

The Government of the United Kingdom believe that it is vital that full and proper effect be given to this provision in the light of the stated purpose of Article VI, which is to accord such privileges and immunities as are necessary for the independent exercise of an expert's functions.

6. Where a question arises as to whether or not an individual is entitled to immunity under Section 22 in a particular case, any views expressed by the Secretary-General will be crucial. The Government of the United Kingdom consider it to be essential that all due weight is given to such views by the national courts. The expert is after all on mission *for the United Nations* and the Secretary-General will therefore be aware of the scope of the mission and can provide an authoritative view as to whether the expert is in the course of performing the mission in particular circumstances. The United Kingdom would not expect a national court to take a different view from the Secretary-General except for the most compelling reasons. The United Kingdom is not aware of any such reasons in the present case.

7. In this context, the practice of the United Kingdom is that the Secretary of State for Foreign and Commonwealth Affairs may issue certificates for the purpose of court proceedings under domestic legislation on privileges and immunities. These certificates are limited to stating facts relating to the question of entitlement to privileges and immunities, and are conclusive evidence as to the facts which they certify; they cannot address questions of law or interpretation. In the case of persons connected with international organisations, for example, section 8 of the International Organisations Act 1968 provides that:

> 'If in any proceedings a question arises whether a person is or is not entitled to any privilege or immunity by virtue of this Act or any Order in Council made thereunder, a certificate issued by or under the authority of the Secretary of State stating any fact relating to that question shall be conclusive evidence of that fact.'

8. In conclusion, the United Kingdom recalls that under Article 56 of the United Nations Charter, all Members of the United Nations have pledged themselves to take joint and separate action in co-operation with the United Nations for the achievement of the purpose of the promotion of universal respect for and observance of human rights and fundamental freedoms in accordance with Article 55 of the Charter. In the United Kingdom's view, the thematic procedures established by the Commission on Human Rights are a vital element of the agreed United Nations machinery for the protection of human rights.

(Text provided by the FCO)

Part Five: III. B. *Subjects of international law—entities and groups other than States and international organizations—dependent territories*

(See also Part Four: II. A. (item of 27 July 1998), above, and Part Six: VIII. (item of 20 April 1998), below)

The FCO supplied the following Supplementary Memorandum, dated January 1998, to the Foreign Affairs Committee of the House of Commons reviewing the dependent territories:

Supplementary memorandum by the Foreign and Commonwealth Office

THE ILOIS

Background

1. The 'Ilois' are the former contract workers who worked on the copra plantations in the British Indian Ocean Territory (BIOT). They were removed from the Territory when the plantations were closed and the defence facility built, and now mainly reside in Mauritius.
2. The British Government paid £650,000 to the Government of Mauritius in 1973 to help meet the cost of resettling the Ilois in Mauritius, and a further ex gratia payment of £4 million in 1982 into a specially set-up Ilois Trust Fund.

Current Position

3. There are both legal and pragmatic difficulties in permitting Ilois to return to live on the outer islands of BIOT.
3.1 First, a 1966 Agreement between Britain and the United States makes provision for the whole of the Territory to be made available to meet the possible defence needs of both Governments until, at least, 2016.
3.2 Secondly, there is no prospect of re-establishing the copra plantations on any commercially viable scale; the plantations were already becoming untenable in the 1960s, before their final closure in the early 1970s.
3.3 Thirdly, there is no infrastructure left on any of the outer islands to support a settlement.
4. The Secretary of State made these points to Prime Minister Ramgoolam when they met in October. Given that it is now some 30 years since the Ilois left the Territory and most would have little memory of life there, the Secretary of State concluded that the only viable prospect for the remaining Ilois was better integration into Mauritian life.
5. In the same meeting, the Secretary of State stressed that there was nothing to prevent Ilois working on Diego Garcia as part of the contractor work force to the US military. On the contrary, the contractors had been actively seeking to employ more Mauritians, Ilois or otherwise.

(*Parliamentary Papers*, 1997–98, HC, Paper 347, p. 80)

The following questions were answered by the Parliamentary Under-Secretary of State, Home Office:

Q. Whether they consider that they have international obligations to: (a) secure rights under the European Convention on Human Rights; and (b) provide effective remedies for breaches of those rights, for everyone within the Isle of Man and the Channel Islands; and if so, what steps have been taken by the Government to give effect to those obligations.
A. The obligation on Her Majesty's Government is to ensure that the Crown Dependencies comply with the European Convention on Human Rights. All Channel Islands Laws and Isle of Man Acts are scrutinised to ensure that they comply with this and other international obligations.

Q. Whether the courts of the Isle of Man and the Channel Islands respectively have given effect to the European Convention on Human Rights in their decisions; and if so, in which cases this has been done.

A. The convention has not been incorporated into domestic law in the Crown Dependencies. It is applied by the Island courts only in limited circumstances, as is presently the case in the United Kingdom.

Q. Whether the courts of the Isle of Man and the Channel Islands respectively are required or authorised to provide effective remedies for breaches of the European Convention on Human Rights by public authorities within their jurisdiction; and if so, how such a requirement or authorisation is prescribed by law.

A. The courts in the Isle of Man and the Channel Islands are not required or authorised directly to provide remedies for breaches of the European Convention on Human Rights. People in the Crown Dependencies may petition the European Commission of Human Rights in the same way as people in the United Kingdom may do.

Q. Whether they have renewed the right of individual application under the European Convention on Human Rights in respect of the Isle of Man and the Channel Islands; and if not, why not.

A. The right of individual petition was renewed on 3 June 1993 in respect of the Isle of Man and with effect from 14 January 1996 in respect of the Channel Islands.

(HL Debs., vol. 584, *WA 167–8*: 12 January 1998)

During the committee stage of the debate in the House of Commons on the Human Rights Bill, the Secretary of State for the Home Department, Mr Jack Straw, stated:

As we have heard, the amendments would apply the Bill's provisions in various ways to the Channel Islands and the Isle of Man. My hon. Friend has pointed out that the United Kingdom is obliged to ensure that the islands comply with the convention and that there is a right of individual petition to the convention institutions in Strasbourg in respect of the islands, but that the convention does not at present have effect in their domestic law. I am happy to tell the Committee that the island authorities have made it clear that they want to bring rights home to the islands, just as we are doing in the United Kingdom.

Before I move on to the detail of that, it may assist the Committee if I say something about the constitutional relationship between the United Kingdom and the islands. That was set out in detail in the report of the royal commission on the constitution in 1973—the Kilbrandon report. My hon. Friend referred in particular to paragraph 1494 and the conclusions in paragraph 1513.

Briefly, the conclusion of the Kilbrandon report is that the United Kingdom Government are responsible for the defence and international relations of the islands, and the Crown is ultimately responsible for their good government. It falls to the Home Secretary to advise the Crown on the exercise of those duties and responsibilities. The United Kingdom Parliament has the power to legislate for the islands, but it would exercise that power without their agreement in relation to domestic matters only in the most exceptional circumstances.

A domestic circumstance that also affected all the countries that make up the United Kingdom—and, to some extent, had international effects—which was cited at length in the Kilbrandon report, was the issue, which those of us of a certain age remember only too well, of the so-called pirate radio stations that were set up off the shore of the Isle of Man in the early 1960s. Some of us still remember the catch tune of Radio Caroline. Much of the noise harassment that some of us now suffer could be said to have flowed from that experiment. Those were exceptional circumstances: legislation on domestic matters usually takes the form of laws enacted by the island legislatures, although they are subject to endorsement by me as Secretary of State for the Home Department and by the Privy Council.

United Kingdom laws are sometimes extended to the islands with their agreement. We consulted the island authorities about the extension of the Bill to them. All three said that they did not wish it to be so extended, and, as we want to maintain satisfactory relations with the islands, we paid careful attention to their views, as always.

The Committee will be glad to know that my noble Friend Lord Williams, the Minister with responsibility for the Channel Islands and the Isle of Man, has undertaken a series of visits to find out from the island authorities what plans they have in the human rights field. I am pleased to say that their responses have all have been positive. Each of the island authorities has made clear its intentions with respect to the Bill and the incorporation in its domestic law of the European convention. I have placed copies of their public statements and letters in the Library and have made them available to the official Opposition, to the Liberal Democrats and to my hon. Friend the Member for Great Grimsby.

It is worth pointing out that Jersey has fairly said that, six years ago, under the previous Administration, a proposal that the island should enact legislation to incorporate the European convention was raised with Home Office officials and was discussed informally with the Secretary-General of the Commission in Strasbourg. The island's Attorney-General was informed at that time by officials that the Home Office did not favour the island acting in advance of the United Kingdom, so the matter was shelved. Consultation goes both ways, and the previous Government, for reasons that I understand, but do not agree with, decided that they did not want incorporation of the convention in the United Kingdom of Great Britain and Northern Ireland, and asked the island authorities to follow suit.

The Bailiff of Jersey has now made it clear that the insular authorities

> 'wish to confirm their previously declared intention to progress the matter of legislation to incorporate the European Convention on Human Rights into Jersey law, having regard to the particular circumstances of the Island, once the United Kingdom Bill has completed its progress through Parliament in Westminster.'

The Bailiff's letter goes on:

> 'The Insular Authorities confidently expect to have a draft law with the Home Office for pre audit in the normal way by the end of this year.'

The States of Guernsey issued a public statement on 22 May. The President of the Advisory and Finance Committee said:

'The States Advisory and Finance Committee intends to recommend to the States of Guernsey that legislation be enacted'—

to incorporate the convention—

'having regard to the particular circumstances of the Island'.

He said that once the Bill has become law, recommendations will be laid before the States of Guernsey. He added:

'The Committee is confident that it will be possible to submit a draft law to the Home Office for pre-audit before the end of this year.'

In December 1997, the Isle of Man made it clear that it intended to introduce legislation to give effect in Manx law to the convention on human rights. It says:

'Before any Government Bill is introduced in the House of Keys, a draft is always sent to the Home Office for their comments, if necessary after consultation with other United Kingdom Departments, and appropriate measures are taken to consult local interests.'

In the light of those statements, I hope that the Committee will recognise that the Governments of each of the three islands are committed to introducing legislation fully to incorporate the European convention into their own law and to consult me, my officials and the Government more widely on the precise terms of that incorporation.

I believe that that is a satisfactory outcome.

(HC Debs., vol. 313, cols. 471–3: 3 June 1998)

Mr Straw continued:

My hon. Friend asked whether any of the island authorities could incorporate into their domestic law the fourth protocol of the convention, even though it is not being incorporated into the Bill. The answer is that they cannot incorporate any part of the convention that the United Kingdom and the Crown, as high contracting party to the convention, have not accepted. That important part of our relationship with the islands gives the Crown and the United Kingdom Parliament ultimate authority over them: we, and not they, enter into all international obligations, which are then binding on the islands.

That said, it would none the less be open to each of the island authorities and Parliaments, should they want to, to write the terms of the fourth protocol, or of any other protocol not incorporated into the Bill, into their domestic law.

(Ibid., col. 473)

In the course of a debate on the subject of offshore financial centres in the Channel Islands and the Isle of Man, the Minister of State, Home Office, Lord Williams of Mostyn, stated:

. . . the Channel Islands and the Isle of Man are not fully part of the European Union, as the noble Lord rightly implies. The constitutional position in the Channel Islands and the Isle of Man remains the same as that I described, I think last week. They are Crown dependencies. They have internal legislatures; and the United Kingdom, let alone any other party, is only entitled to intervene and impose legislative solutions as a matter of last resort.

(HL Debs., vol. 595, col. 236: 30 November 1998)

In reply to an oral question on the subject of the Channel Islands' relationship with the European Union, the same Minister stated:

The constitutional arrangements between Her Majesty's Government and the Channel Islands are plain: we have a power of last resort to interfere with their domestic matters, which includes taxation. It would be unprecedented for Her Majesty's Government to interfere with their domestic legislation, which includes taxation. I cannot make the position any clearer than that.

(HL Debs., vol. 595, cols. 928–9: 9 December 1998)

Part Five: III. E. *Subjects of international law—entities and groups other than States and international organizations—self-determination units and the concept of self-determination*

(See also Part Fifteen: I.E., below)

In reply to oral questions, the Secretary of State for Foreign and Commonwealth Affairs, Mr Robin Cook, stated:

Gibraltar is a British dependent territory whose relationship with the United Kingdom is defined by the provisions of the 1969 constitution. Britain has repeatedly confirmed to the Spanish Government that there can be no change to that constitution without the democratic agreement of the people of Gibraltar.

. . .

We are a democratic House elected on democratic principles, and we must respect the same democratic right of the people of Gibraltar to decide their own future. In December, I expressed forcibly to the Spanish Foreign Minister the importance to us of respecting the wishes of the people of Gibraltar.

(HC Debs., vol. 304, col. 128: 13 January 1998)

In reply to a question, the Parliamentary Under-Secretary of State, FCO, wrote:

We support the right or principle of self-determination reflecting the wishes of the people concerned. It should be exercised in accordance with the other principles and rights in the UN Charter and with other treaty obligations. In Gibraltar's case that includes Article X of the Treaty of Utrecht. This has been the long-standing position of successive British Governments.

(HL Debs., vol. 586, *WA 107*: 26 February 1998)

In reply to a question, the Minister of State, Ministry of Defence, wrote:

The Government remain fully committed to defending the right of the Falkland Islanders to determine their own future. Force levels in the Falklands and the South Atlantic are kept under review to ensure that the resources necessary to guarantee the security of the Islands in the most appropriate and effective manner are available.

(HL Debs., vol. 588, *WA 72*: 2 April 1998)

In the course of a debate on the subject of the future of the Western Sahara, the Minister of State, FCO, Mr Derek Fatchett, stated:

My hon. Friend asked about the Government's policy towards Western Sahara. It is very simple: we seek a just and lasting settlement and we support the United Nations' efforts to bring one about. We want to see a clean, fair and transparent referendum that will give the people of the territory the opportunity to decide whether their future lies with Morocco or as an independent state.

(HC Debs., vol. 313, col. 336: 3 June 1998)

In reply to a question, the Government spokesman in the House of Lords wrote:

We are committed to ensuring the security of all UK overseas territories and to promoting their prosperity. In the case of Gibraltar, we have made it clear that there can be no change in sovereignty without the consent of its people.

(HL Debs., vol. 590, *WA 100*: 11 June 1998)

Speaking in the Third Committee of the UN General Assembly on 23 October 1998, the representative of Austria, on behalf of the EU, stated:

18. I should like to turn now to agenda item 109, entitled 'Right of peoples to self-determination'.
19. The right of peoples to freely determine their political status and pursue their economic, social and cultural development, is well established. Figuring prominently in the UN Charter and the catalogue of rights contained in the International Covenants on Economic, Social and Cultural Rights, as well as on Civil and Political Rights, it has been reiterated in the Vienna Declaration and Programme of Action five years ago.
20. This right is of continuing importance today as part of the framework of international human rights. Its realisation is a continuing process that requires the effective guarantee, observance and promotion of all human rights by all States. Violations of this right constitute a threat to the freedom and dignity of persons, and run counter to the principles and standards laid down in the relevant human rights instruments. The Universal Declaration of Human Rights, adopted 50 years ago, the International Covenants, and numerous other international and regional human rights instruments provide the framework for the realisation of the ideal of free human beings enjoying freedom from fear and want.
21. Central in this regard is the right of everybody to take part in the public affairs of his or her country, directly or through freely chosen representatives. Governments must be elected through genuinely free and periodic elections. States must provide channels for participation of people in decisions which affect their lives. Moreover, effective popular participation is an essential

component of successful and lasting development. Participation of all, including persons belonging to minorities and indigenous populations, requires full respect of the principle of non-discrimination, as well as of the right to freedom of expression and freedom of peaceful assembly and association. Free pursuance of economic, social and cultural development is impossible if ideas and aspirations cannot be voiced and be brought forward, individually and in association with others. Democracy, the rule of law and human rights empower people to shape the society in which they live. States must create an environment where these fundamental rights and freedoms are fully ensured.

22. The European Union believes that democracy and good governance are essential for the protection of all human rights. The holding of free and fair elections by secret ballot and universal suffrage is one of the prerequisites for actually implementing the right of a people to determine its own destiny. Free and fair elections are necessary for the establishment of a democratic order, but democratisation is a long term process and not a one-time event. Results of genuine elections must be respected; elected representatives must be allowed to take office; they must fulfil their mandate with full accountability. Today, the world speaks out unanimously against any change of government by undemocratic means, such as coups d'etats, and does not accept regimes that rule against the expressed will of the people.

(Text provided by the FCO; see also A/C.3/53/SR. 23, pp. 6–7)

In reply to a question asking about Her Majesty's Government's reply to the proposals on Gibraltar presented by the Foreign Minister of Spain in the round of the Brussels agreement talks on 10 December 1997, the Parliamentary Under-Secretary of State, FCO, wrote in part:

Her Majesty's Government have said that we will study the proposals and reply in due course. We have also said that we stand by the commitment enshrined in the preamble to the 1969 Constitution. There can be no change in sovereignty over Gibraltar without the consent of its people. That remains the position.

(HL Debs., vol. 593, *WA 141*: 20 October 1998)

In reply to a question, the Parliamentary Under-Secretary of State, FCO, wrote:

As set out in the Preamble to the 1969 Gibraltar Constitution Order, it is Her Majesty's Government's policy that there can be no alteration in Gibraltar's status as a United Kingdom's Overseas Territory without the consent of the people of Gibraltar.

(HC Debs., vol. 318, WA, col. *85*: 26 October 1998)

The following declaration was made on 29 December 1998 on behalf of the EU:

The EU reiterates its full support for the Settlement Plan proposed by the United Nations Secretary General for Western Sahara, which aims at the holding of a free, fair and impartial referendum on the self-determination of the people of Western Sahara.

(Text provided by the Austrian Presidency)

In reply to a question, the Minister of State, FCO, wrote:

The Government's policy on this issue is clear. We, in line with EU partners, support the right of the Palestinian people to self-determination, not excluding the option of a state. Palestinian statehood is an issue for final status negotiations. We hope both sides will concentrate their efforts on implementation of the Wye River Memorandum, which calls for the immediate resumption of final status talks aimed at completion before 4 May. We will do our utmost, both bilaterally and within the EU, to help both sides implement this agreement and assist the negotiations between the parties on final status issues.

(HC Debs., vol. 319, WA, col. *646*: 18 November 1998)

Part Six: VII. A. *The individual (including the corporation) in international law—immigration and emigration, extradition, expulsion, asylum—immigration and emigration*

In reply to the question what are the entry requirements of holders of travel documents issued by the 'Turkish Republic of Northern Cyprus', the Parliamentary Under-Secretary of State, Home Office, wrote:

Under the immigration rules, holders of travel documents which are not issued by a recognised national authority are required to obtain a visa if they wish to come to the United Kingdom. Despite this, while not recognising the authorities of the so-called 'Turkish Republic of Northern Cyprus' (TRNC) we have in the past accepted TRNC travel documents as proof of identity. This has meant that holders of TRNC documents were up till now not required to obtain a visa if visiting the United Kingdom for a short period. This operated under a concession.

We are today bringing the arrangements concerning holders of these documents into line with our standard practice by withdrawing this concession. There have been significant numbers of asylum claims by passengers travelling with this document which, when determined, have all been unfounded. With effect from midnight tonight, holders of documents issued by the authorities of the so-called 'Turkish Republic of Northern Cyprus' will be required to obtain visas to the United Kingdom, regardless of the purpose of their journey.

We have also today laid an amendment to the Immigration (Transit Visa) Order 1993, requiring holders of such documents to obtain a visa when in transit through the United Kingdom. This requirement will apply from 5 February.

(HL Debs., vol. 584, *WA 205*: 15 January 1998)

Part Six: VII. B. *The individual (including the corporation) in international law—immigration and emigration, extradition, expulsion, asylum—extradition*

In the course of a press conference held in Sofia, Bulgaria, on 20 October 1998, the Secretary of State for Foreign and Commonwealth

Affairs, Mr Robin Cook, was asked a question about the likelihood of the extradition to Spain of Senator Augusto Pinochet of Chile. He replied:

First of all, the legal process in the courts in Britain are totally separate from the government and that is as it should be. Our politicians and our government have no rights to instruct the courts, nor have we any wish to interfere with due judicial process. General Pinochet has been detained on the basis of a warrant following a request from Spain for the extradition of General Pinochet to Spain. We have well tried and well established means for the courts to process an extradition request, in the first instance Spain has 40 days in which to provide fuller details of the basis for its request for extradition, they will then be tested through our courts. We are very content that this is a matter which should be established by due legal process. There have been some suggestions to us that we should intervene for political or diplomatic reasons. I want to make it clear that first of all we have no powers to do so; and secondly we have no wish to do so, to do so would be wrong, this is a matter that must be resolved in the appropriate legal manner, as it would with anybody else on whom an extradition request was served in Britain.

(Text provided by the FCO)

In reply to questions about the detention in London of Senator Pinochet, the Minister of State, FCO, wrote:

There was no consultation between the Foreign and Commonwealth Office and the Spanish Government prior to the issuing of the request for a provisional warrant for the arrest of Senator Pinochet.

. . .

We have received the following representations from the Chilean Government since 1 May 1997 concerning General Pinochet: (i) The Chilean Embassy in London contacted the Foreign and Commonwealth Office in September 1998 ahead of Senator Pinochet's visit to request the use of VIP facilities on his arrival at Heathrow Airport; (ii) The Chilean Foreign Minister, Sr. Jose Miguel Insulza, handed over a formal Note protesting the arrest of Senator Pinochet to the British Ambassador in Chile on 17 October 1998. The Chilean Embassy in London also passed a Note making the same points to the Foreign and Commonwealth Office on 19 October 1998. A second Note was passed to the British Embassy in Santiago on 23 October 1998; (iii) The Chilean Foreign Minister, Sr. Jose Miguel Insulza telephoned my right hon. Friend the Foreign Secretary on 17 October 1998. The Chilean Deputy Foreign Minister, Sr. Mariano Fernandez, called on my right hon. Friend the Foreign Secretary on Saturday 24 October.

. . . FCO officials were kept informed of events leading up to the arrest. The only consultation that took place was between the Metropolitan Police and the FCO on the technical question of whether Senator Pinochet would be entitled to diplomatic immunity.

(HC Debs., vol. 318, WA, cols. *81–2*: 26 October 1998)

In the course of replying to oral questions on the subject of the detention in London of Senator Pinochet, the Secretary of State for Foreign and Commonwealth Affairs, Mr Robin Cook, stated:

Of course we have had no contact on the question with the Spanish Government. It would be deeply improper to do so. The extradition request has been processed by entirely competent legal authority in Spain. It is for the Spanish authorities to decide whether they wish to withdraw it, not for us to decide whether we should ignore it. The Home Secretary was entirely proper in allowing the due process of law to proceed.

. . .

It is a matter for the Spanish legal authorities to decide whether to proceed with this, just as it is a matter for the British courts to decide how to proceed on it. Of course, areas of discretion are available to the Home Secretary after due process and after the matter has been before the courts.

(HC Debs., vol. 318, cols. 141–2: 27 October 1998)

In reply to a question on the subject of the detention in London of Senator Pinochet, the Secretary of State for the Home Department wrote:

Requests made by judicial and law enforcement authorities overseas for persons in the United Kingdom to be interviewed on a voluntary basis in connection with criminal investigations or proceedings are made through the United Kingdom Central Bureau of Interpol (Interpol London) at the National Criminal Intelligence Service and executed directly by the police or other law enforcement agencies. Where such requests are made directly to the Home Office they are referred to the police to execute.

The 5th Central Magistrate's Court in Madrid contacted the Metropolitan Police via Interpol on 14 October.

Requests made by courts overseas for statements to be made on oath or to be conducted before a judicial authority in England and Wales are made directly or indirectly to the Home Office. The Secretary of State may, if he thinks fit, nominate a court in England and Wales under section 4 of the Criminal Justice (International Co-operation) Act 1990 to receive such of the evidence requested as the court considers appropriate for the purpose of executing the request.

On 19 October, Interpol London received a request for Augusto Pinochet to make a statement. The request was made under the 1959 European Convention for Mutual Assistance in Criminal Matters, for which the Home Secretary is the designated United Kingdom Central Authority.

As the Secretary of State I will consider whether the request is for evidence to be taken before a court in England and Wales and one for which the exercise of his powers under section 4 of the 1990 Act would be appropriate. If the Secretary of State considers the request is not one for which the nomination of the court would be appropriate, or the requesting authority clarifies that a voluntary statement would be sufficient for its purpose, the request will be passed to the Metropolitan Police to execute.

(HC Debs., vol. 318, WA, cols. *123–4*: 27 October 1998)

In reply to a question on the same subject, the Secretary of State for the Home Department stated:

Ministers and civil servants in the Home Office were kept informed by the Metropolitan Police of events leading up to Senator Pinochet's arrest on 16 October.

The decision to issue a provisional warrant for the arrest of Senator Pinochet was taken by the Bow Street Magistrate under section 8(1)(b) of the Extradition Act 1989 in response to a request from an extradition partner.

(HC Debs., vol. 318, WA, col. *184*: 28 October 1998)

In the course of a debate on the subject of relations with Chile, the question arose of whether the Home Secretary has a residual discretion not to give effect to an order of the court in the extradition process in respect of Senator Pinochet. The Parliamentary Under-Secretary of State, FCO, Baroness Symons of Vernham Dean, stated in reply:

Yes, my Lords. The Home Secretary will consider the formal request which must be certified with the seal of the Spanish Ministry of Justice, against the requirements of the Extradition Act 1989. I am sure that the noble and learned Lord is aware of that. My right honourable friend must decide—usually within seven days of receipt of a formal request—whether to issue an authority to proceed. He will consider, among other issues, whether the offences are extradition crimes; whether the request is properly authenticated; whether the offences are of a political character; and whether there are any compassionate circumstances. He does so on every request.

(HL Debs., vol. 593, col. 1916: 28 October 1998)

In reply to questions, the Secretary of State for the Home Department wrote:

I have received no formal request for the extradition of Senator Pinochet from the Spanish Government, or any other government, or from any competent authority in Spain or any other country.

The Metropolitan Police received, on Friday 16 October, via Interpol, a request for the provisional arrest of Senator Pinochet issued by the 5th Magistrates' Court in Madrid. Disclosure of that document is a matter for the Metropolitan Police.

. . .

The Extradition Section at the Home Office received notification on 19 October of the first provisional warrant for Senator Pinochet issued on 16 October by the Bow Street Magistrate under section 8(1)(b) of the Extradition Act 1989 and received notification on 23 October of a further provisional warrant issued on 22 October by the Bow Street Magistrate.

I was invited, on 21 October, by Senator Pinochet's legal representatives to exercise my discretionary power under section 8(4) and to cancel the first provisional warrant issued on 16 October. I had taken no decision before legal proceedings were launched in the Divisional Court on 22 October. The Divisional Court, in its judgment of 28 October, dismissed application for leave to move for judicial review of my failure to exercise my discretionary powers under section 8(4) of the Act.

(HC Debs., vol. 318, WA, col. *579*: 4 November 1998)

In reply to a question, the Minister of State, Home Office, wrote:

We received a formal request for the extradition of Senator Pinochet from the Spanish Government on 11 November. The request was submitted through diplomatic channels.

(HL Debs., vol. 594, *WA 110*: 12 November 1998)

In reply to a question, the Secretary of State for the Home Department, Mr Jack Straw, wrote:

I signed an authority to proceed in respect of Senator Pinochet today. The Spanish request for his extradition will now be considered by the courts. The reasons for my decision were sent to all the parties concerned in a letter from one of my officials as set out:

'1. I am writing to inform you that the Secretary of State has today signed an authority to proceed in respect of Senator Pinochet. The authority to proceed and supporting documentation are being transmitted to Bow St. I am notifying the Deputy Chief Clerk of this decision by fax. I enclose a copy of the authority to proceed for your information.

2. The Secretary of State is not under an obligation to provide reasons for his decision to sign an authority to proceed. However, in this case, and in the light of the matters raised by the representations, he has agreed to give his reasons at this stage.

Representations

3. The Secretary of State received notification, before the House of Lords judgment on 25 November, that he would be receiving representations for and against the issue of an authority to proceed.

4. Although there is no provision in the Extradition Act ("the Act") for representations at this stage in extradition proceedings, he has taken careful account of these in making his decision; in particular representations made to him by legal representatives of Senator Pinochet, the Spanish Government, the Chilean Government and legal representatives for "the Interveners" before the House of Lords. He also received material from the Foreign and Commonwealth Office and the Ministry of Defence.

5. The decision to issue an Authority to Proceed was taken personally by the Secretary of State.

Requests from the French and Swiss Governments

6. The Secretary of State received formal extradition requests for Senator Pinochet from the Spanish Government on 11 November 1998, from the Swiss Government later the same day, and from the French Government on 13 November 1998.

7. The Secretary of State has considered these requests, and further material

made available by the Swiss Government, under section 12(5) of the Act and Article 17 of the European Convention on Extradition ("ECE"). He has given precedence to the Spanish request, and notified the French and Swiss Governments accordingly.

The Secretary of State's approach to his decision

8. He has taken his decision under section 7(4) of the Act, which provides:

> (4) On receipt of any such request the Secretary of State may issue an authority to proceed unless it appears to him that an order for the return of the person concerned could not lawfully be made, or would not in fact be made, in accordance with the provisions of this Act.

9. The Secretary of State has taken the approach that if it already appears to him that no order for the return of Senator Pinochet to Spain could lawfully be made, or would in fact be made, then he should not issue an authority to proceed. If those conditions do not exist he has a discretion whether or not to issue an authority to proceed.

10. He has had regard to the relevant extradition arrangement, namely the ECE. The UK's obligation is to extradite Senator Pinochet to Spain consistently with the ECE. That is a consideration to which the Secretary of State gives particular weight.

11. In reaching his decision, the Secretary of State has considered the application of the Act to the Spanish request and all the general restrictions on surrender in sections 6 and 12 of the Act.

Extradition crimes

12. Section 1 of the Act provides that where, as in the case of Spain, extradition procedures under Part III of the Act are available, a person in the United Kingdom who: "is accused in that state of the commission of an extradition crime" may be arrested and returned to that state in accordance with those procedures.

13. The Secretary of State considers that Senator Pinochet is accused, in Spain, of offences equivalent to UK offences of attempted murder, conspiracy to murder, torture, conspiracy to torture, hostage taking and conspiracy to take hostages.

14. Senator Pinochet is also charged, under Spanish law, with genocide, and the CPS advised, on behalf of the Spanish Government, that murder is also disclosed by the request. The Secretary of State does not consider that the contents of the extradition request satisfied the definition of an extradition crime under section 2 of the Act in respect of these offences, and has therefore not included them in the authority to proceed.

15. The relevant test under the Act was explained by the Lord Chief Justice in the Divisional Court (with whom the other judges agreed) who said: "What is necessary [for the definition of extradition crime in s.2] is that *at the time of the extradition request* (rather than at the time of the conduct alleged; emphasis supplied) the offence should be a criminal offence here, . . . "

16. The Secretary of State has proceeded on the basis that he is entitled, at this stage of the extradition proceedings against Senator Pinochet, to treat the Spanish request as well-founded as a matter of Spanish law.

Sovereign or diplomatic immunity

17. The Secretary of State has also proceeded on the basis that Senator Pinochet does not enjoy any immunity in relation to the offences in question. He has not accepted a representation made on behalf of Senator Pinochet that he should disregard the House of Lords judgment on the grounds of alleged bias on the part of one of the law lords. Nor does it appear to him that Senator Pinochet is entitled to diplomatic immunity or protection as the head of a special mission.

General restrictions

18. The Secretary of State has considered all the general restrictions on surrender in sections 6 and 12 of the Act. In particular, he has had regard to:

Political Offences (section 6(1)(a))

19. Section 24 of the Act provides that no offence to which section 1 of the Suppression of Terrorism Act applies can be regarded as an offence of a political character. Since Spain is a designated country for the purposes of section 24, the Secretary of State considers that all the offences that are to be included in the authority to proceed fall within this provision. In any event it does not appear to him that the offences charged are of a political character.

Punishment for political opinions (sections 6(1)(c) and (d))

20. The Secretary of State does not consider that there are good grounds for concluding that the request has been issued for this purpose.

The passage of time (section 12(2)(a)(ii))

21. The Secretary of State has not been notified by the Spanish Government that any of the offences for which extradition is sought are time barred from prosecution, and considers that it is reasonable to proceed at this stage on the footing that no relevant time bar appears to apply.

22. Nor does the Secretary of State consider that the passage of time would render it unjust or oppressive to issue an authority to proceed in this case. It does not appear that Senator Pinochet is unfit to stand trial. The offences for which return has been sought are serious, and in the nature of those for which domestically, passage of time would not be regarded as restricting prosecution. The case is an accusation case and, ordinarily, the reliability of witnesses' memories may properly be regarded as a matter for the court of prosecution.

Accusation not made in good faith in the interests of justice (section 12(2)(a)(iii))

23. The Secretary of State does not believe that there are good grounds for concluding that the request has been issued other than in good faith in the interests of justice.

The Secretary of State's discretion

24. The Secretary of State has considered the ambit of his discretion under section 7(4) and his residual general discretion under section 12 of the Act, which would apply in relation to the return of Senator Pinochet were he to be committed by the Bow Street magistrate under section 9 of the Act. Contrary to certain of the representations made to him, he has been advised that the discretion conferred upon him is wide, and he has therefore taken a range of factors into consideration.

25. A large number of points were raised in representations concerning the Secretary of State's discretion, including aspects of issues that fall to be considered under the general restrictions on return contained in the Act. In particular, the Secretary of State has had regard to the following:

Humanitarian considerations

26. Representations were made on behalf of the Senator that his age and health would render it unjust or oppressive to issue an authority to proceed. The Secretary of State has considered these carefully, but concluded that it does not appear that the Senator is unfit to stand trial and concluded that in all the circumstances it would not be unjust or oppressive for him to stand trial in relation to the offences with which he is charged. The Secretary of State also has in mind that this question, among others, can be re-examined in the light of any developments, at the stage when he comes to exercise his final discretion at the end of the extradition process, under section 12 of the Act.

Pending proceedings in Chile

27. The Chilean Government argued that Senator Pinochet should be returned to Chile where he could stand trial. However, there is no extradition request from the Chilean Government, which the Secretary of State could consider under section 12(5) of the Act. Moreover, there is no provision of international law which excludes Spain's jurisdiction in this matter. The Secretary of State does not consider the possibility of a trial in Chile to be a factor which outweighs the UK's obligations under the ECE to extradite Senator Pinochet to Spain.

Other factors

28. The Secretary of State has also considered other factors, under his general discretion, including:

(i) the possible effect of extradition proceedings on the stability of Chile, and its future democracy; and

(ii) the possible effect of extradition proceedings on the UK national interest.

29. He has concluded that the material and representations put before him do not amount to sufficient grounds not to issue an authority to proceed.

Conclusion

30. In the event that Senator Pinochet is committed to await the Secretary of State's decision on his return, the Secretary of State will consider the extradition request afresh under section 12 of the Act. At that stage he will be able to take into account any findings in the committal proceedings and any habeas corpus proceedings as well as any further representations which Senator Pinochet may wish to make against return.
31. If Senator Pinochet decides to apply for leave to move for judicial review of the Secretary of State's decision, he reserves the right to expand upon the reasons given in this letter in an affidavit to be sworn by one of his officials.'

(HC Debs., vol. 322, WA, cols. *213–17*: 9 December 1998)

Part Six: VIII. *The individual (including the corporation) in international law—human rights and fundamental freedoms*

(See also Part Five: I. A. 2 (item of 14 February 1998) and Part Five: III. B. (items relating to Channel Islands and Isle of Man), above)

The FCO presented a memorandum, dated October 1997, to the Foreign Affairs Committee of the House of Commons considering foreign policy and human rights on 6 January 1998. Part of the memorandum read as follows:

SECTION (1): PRINCIPLES AND OBJECTIVES

2. The FCO Mission Statement says the UK will work through international forums and bilateral relationships to spread the values of human rights, civil liberties and democracy which we demand for ourselves.
3. Human rights standards are universal. They are enshrined in the 1948 United Nations Universal Declaration of Human Rights (UDHR), drafted by representatives from around the world, and adopted without a dissenting vote (and only eight abstentions) by the UN General Assembly. The UDHR was reaffirmed, again without dissent, at the Vienna World Conference on Human Rights in 1993. The rights are rights of individuals; both civil and political rights, and economic, social and cultural rights. The UDHR was the starting point in constructing a framework of international instruments and mechanisms.
4. All categories of human rights are of equal importance, and interdependent. Sustainable economic growth and protection of economic rights are enhanced by respect of civil and political rights. Societies ensuring freedom for their people are more likely to develop, through innovative and enterprising work-forces.

5. We do not dictate Western values to developing countries. As the Vienna Conference recognised, promotion and protection of human rights in individual countries is a legitimate concern of the international community. It is up to governments to decide whether to accede to legally binding international human rights instruments. But, failing to accede cannot exempt a country from international attention and criticism.
6. The Government is committed to human rights at home and in our Dependent Territories. We are open to scrutiny and aware of the need to respect international commitments.
7. UK foreign policy has to project UK values, including respect for democracy, justice and the rule of law, if it is to be acceptable at home and persuasive abroad. The protection of human rights is also crucial to UK interests: securing peace, stability and prosperity in the world.
8. We have initiated major reviews on arms sales criteria, on additional UK adherence to UN and Council of Europe human rights instruments, and on outstanding ILO 'core' labour conventions.

(*Parliamentary Papers*, 1997–98, HC, Paper 369–III, p. 40)

Speaking in the UN Commission on Human Rights on 19 March 1998, the UK representative, Mr Lloyd, on behalf of the EU and the States associated with it, stated:

. . . the adoption of the Universal Declaration of Human Rights had been a defining moment for the United Nations. The greatest achievement of the Declaration had been to establish universal standards for all peoples and nations. It listed rights which applied to all individuals and which had been reaffirmed by all nations as recently as the 1993 World Conference on Human Rights.

. . .

The Union was committed to the universality of human rights and had taken action against activities, such as racism and xenophobia, which undermined a just, tolerant and pluralistic society.

. . .

Universal human rights standards were the basis on which the Union sought engagement with other countries on human rights.

(E/CN.4/1998/SR. 2, p. 8)

In reply to a question, the Parliamentary Under-Secretary of State, Home Office, wrote:

In December last year, the Isle of Man Government announced its intention to introduce legislation to incorporate the European Convention on Human Rights into the law of the Isle of Man. A Bill will be introduced in the House of Keys, when the legislative timetable permits, based upon the equivalent United Kingdom legislation when enacted.

(HL Debs., vol. 588, *WA 192*: 20 April 1998)

In reply to a question, the Minister of State, FCO, wrote:

We regard bonded labour as an intolerable form of labour akin to slavery, forced labour and compulsory labour. The international human rights instruments to which the United Kingdom is a party and which specifically prohibit or require the suppression of slavery, forced and compulsory labour are as follows:

(*a*) The International Covenant on Civil and Political Rights. Article 8 of the Covenant states that no one shall be held in slavery; that slavery and the slave trade in all their forms shall be prohibited; that no one shall be held in servitude; and that no one shall be forced to perform forced or compulsory labour;

(*b*) The United Nations Supplementary Convention on the Abolition of Slavery, the Slave Trade, and Institutions and Practices Similar to Slavery. Article 1 of the Convention requires States parties to take all practicable and necessary legislative and other measures to bring about progressively and as soon as possible the complete abolition or abandonment of, among other institutions and practices, debt bondage, serfdom and any institution or practice whereby a child or young person under the age of 18 years is delivered by either or both of his natural parents or by his guardian to another person, whether for reward or not, with a view to the exploitation of the child or young person or of his labour.

(*c*) The International Labour Organisation Convention (No 29) Concerning Forced Labour. Article 1 of the Convention requires each State party to suppress the use of forced labour or compulsory labour in all its forms within the shortest possible period;

(*d*) The International Labour Organisation Convention (No 105) Concerning the Abolition of Forced Labour. Article 1 of the Convention requires each State party to suppress and not to make use of forced or compulsory labour.

Any State which ratified these human rights instruments would be in breach of its legally binding obligations if it did not fulfil its undertakings in respect of these Articles.

(HC Debs., vol. 310, WA, cols. *721–2*: 24 April 1998)

In reply to a question on the subject of the Armenian massacres, the Parliamentary Under-Secretary of State, FCO, wrote:

The British Government condemned the 1915 massacres at the time, and view the sufferings of the Armenian people then as a tragedy of historic proportions. However, in the absence of evidence to show that the Turkish Government took a specific decision to eliminate the Armenians under their control at the time, the British Government have not recognised the events of 1915 as a genocide.

(HL Debs., vol. 591, *WA 42*: 25 June 1998; see also ibid., *WA 63–4*: 30 June 1998)

Speaking in a debate in the House of Lords on the subject of the European Court of Human Rights, the Lord Chancellor, Lord Irvine of Lairg, remarked:

The Court and Commission of Human Rights established under the Convention have done a fine job in entrenching the Convention as a living and effective instrument. I pay tribute to their work. But times have changed, and with them the scale of the challenge facing the Court. The Court has needed to adapt to retain its capacity to meet the challenges of an enlarged Europe and to deliver proper service to the swelling numbers of those who have access to the protection afforded by the Convention. That is why we continue to support the comprehensive reform process under way in Strasbourg which will bring the new Protocol 11 Court of Human Rights into operation on 1st November this year. . . . We recognise the hugely important role that this new court will have to play in the newly enlarged Council of Europe. The people of Russia and the Ukraine now have access to the rights and freedoms contained in the Convention. This means that judgments of the Court will help shape human rights across the European continent. This is why the Government made the election to the Court of high quality judges a matter of major importance.

(HL Debs., vol. 592, col. 95: 13 July 1998)

In reply to a question about events in the Democratic Republic of Congo, the Minister of State, FCO, wrote:

The United Nations Secretary-General's Investigative Team's report was published on 30 June. We regret that the investigation was not able to be completed. The team was therefore unable to establish the accuracy of many allegations of violations of international humanitarian law or international human rights law. It is nonetheless clear from such work as the team were able to conduct that serious violations did take place, and were carried out by a variety of groups. We are carefully considering the report's recommendations and the possibilities for further investigation.

We continue to call upon all countries in the region to acknowledge their international legal obligation to respect human rights. We have urged regional Governments to take appropriate legal action if members of their forces are shown to have been involved in any violations.

(HC Debs., vol. 316, WA, cols. *151–2*: 14 July 1998)

The following Presidency statement was issued on behalf of the EU on 22 October 1998:

The EU condemns the execution of 24 soldiers by firing squad, which took place on 19 October 1998 in Sierra Leone.

The EU recognises that the military junta overthrew, temporarily, the democratically elected government of Sierra Leone, that it committed appalling atrocities upon the civilian population and that the remnants of the junta/RUF forces continue to commit gross abuses. The EU understands that those responsible for these crimes must be brought to justice.

However, the soldiers had been sentenced to death by a court martial and thus did not have the right to appeal to a higher court, which is contrary to Article 14(5) of the International Covenant for Civil and Political Rights (ICCPR), stating that 'Everyone convicted of a crime shall have the right to his conviction and sentence being reviewed by a higher tribunal according to law'. The EU had appealed to the Government of Sierra Leone to establish a channel for appeals from court martial proceedings in order to comply with its international obligations.

The EU is particularly concerned that the executions were carried out, although 17 of the 34 soldiers sentenced to death had submitted applications to the Human Rights Committee under the optional Protocol. Under the first optional Protocol to the ICCPR, which Sierra Leone ratified in 1996, those sentenced to death are entitled to petition the UN Human Rights Committee to complain of any violations of their rights under the ICCPR. The death sentences should not have carried out while the cases were pending before the Human Rights Committee.

The EU has been following carefully the trials of those accused of participating in the coup which overthrew, temporarily, the legitimate government of Sierra Leone. The EU is convinced that the executions which have just been carried out will not be conducive to fostering the peace and reconciliation process, which the international community is aiming to encourage.

(*Bulletin of the European Union*, 1998–10, p. 64)

Speaking in the Third Committee of the UN General Assembly on 23 October 1998, the representative of Austria, on behalf of the EU, stated:

1. I have the honour to speak on behalf of the European Union on agenda item 108 entitled 'Elimination of racism and racial discrimination' and agenda item 109 entitled 'Right of Peoples to Self-determination'. The Central and Eastern European countries associated with the European Union, Bulgaria, Czech Republic, Estonia, Hungary, Latvia, Lithuania, Poland, Romania, Slovakia, Slovenia, and the associated country Cyprus as well as the EFTA country member of the EEA, Iceland, align themselves with this statement.

2. Respect for human rights and fundamental freedoms without distinction of any kind is a fundamental rule of international human rights law. The Universal Declaration of Human Rights asserts that all human beings are born free and equal in dignity and rights. Racism and racial discrimination fundamentally contradict these basic principles. Moreover, racist phenomena contribute to the disruption of social cohesion. Racist attitudes have their basis in cultural and socio-economic factors, often exacerbated by a lack of recognition of diversity and of understanding.

. . .

5. Regional organisations play an important role in this regard. In this context, the EU would like to highlight the work done by the Council of Europe, and its European Commission against Racism and Intolerance, including the drafting of an additional protocol to the European Convention on Human Rights broadening the field of application of the non-discrimination clause in Article 14 of the Convention. Other important steps have been the entry into force, earlier this year, of the Framework Convention for the protection of National Minorities and of the European Charter for Regional or Minority Languages.

6. The legal basis for the principle of non-discrimination is the Universal Declaration of Human Rights, the International Covenants and the International Convention on the Elimination of All Forms of Racial Discrimination and is further laid down in a number of regional instruments. At the universal

level, the Convention on the Elimination of All Forms of Racial Discrimination forms the important legal basis for translating the world-wide rejection of phenomena of racism and racial discrimination into concrete obligations.
7. The EU believes that ratification of, or accession to, the Convention on a universal basis is necessary for the realisation of the goals of the Third Decade as well as for the promotion of the Convention's global objective. The achievement of universal ratification of this core human rights treaty, as soon as possible, should also be on top of the agenda of the World Conference against Racism, Racial Discrimination, Xenophobia, and related Intolerance, which will be held not later than in the year 2001.

(Text provided by the FCO; see also A/C.3/53/SR. 23, pp. 6–7)

In reply to a question, the Minister of State, FCO, wrote in part:

We are mindful of the obligation of all parties to the European Convention on Human Rights under Article 53 of the Convention to abide by European Court of Human Rights judgments.

(HC Debs., vol. 318, WA, col. *541*: 3 November 1998)

The following question was asked of Her Majesty's Government:

Whether they consider that the obligations imposed upon the United Kingdom by ratification of the International Covenant on Civil and Political Rights include:

(a) securing equality before the law and the equal protection of the law without discrimination on any ground in all parts of the United Kingdom; and
(b) providing effective remedies for alleged breaches of the right to equality of treatment without discrimination?

In reply, the Minister of State, Home Office, wrote:

Under the International Covenant on Civil and Political Rights, the United Kingdom is obliged to respect and ensure the rights recognised in the covenant, which include equality before the law and the equal protection of the law without any discrimination, and the right to an effective remedy where rights or freedoms recognised in the covenant are violated.

(HL Debs., vol. 594, *WA 74*: 9 November 1998)

In reply to a question, the Minister of State, FCO, wrote:

We continue to have many serious concerns about human rights in China. During his visit to China earlier this year my right hon. Friend the Foreign Secretary raised these concerns with Chinese leaders, as did my right hon. Friend the Prime Minister. Recently, the Chinese Government has taken some positive steps in this field, which we have welcomed, while repeating our desire to address issues of concern through the continuing bilateral and EU/China Human Rights Dialogues.

Since the commencement of the bilateral UK/China Dialogue, and the resumption of the EU/China Human Rights Dialogue, last year, China has taken several positive steps which will bring about its closer integration into the UN human rights system, and should in time help to strengthen protection of human rights in China. It has signed the International Covenants on Civil and Political Rights and on Economic Social and Cultural Rights; agreed to report to the UN on Hong Kong under these two Covenants; admitted the UN High Commissioner for Human Rights, Mrs. Robinson, as well as the UN Working Group on Arbitrary Detention; and welcomed a possible visit by the UN Special Rapporteur on Torture.

In addition, China has allowed a visit by a delegation of EU Troika Ambassadors to Tibet and accepted the participation in the Dialogue of critical NGOs such as Amnesty International. It is also noteworthy that the Dialogue has allowed us to discuss privately and frankly with the Chinese authorities a range of concerns from Tibet, to the death penalty, freedom of association and torture.

Both Britain and the EU have now established substantial co-operation programmes with China, funded respectively by DFID and the Commission, and these seek among other things to promote judicial exchanges and legal reform.

We shall encourage the Chinese Government to ratify the International Human Rights Covenants, with as few reservations as possible, as soon as possible. We want to see further reform in China's capital punishment regime, leading ultimately to abolition, as well as improvements in its systems of detention. At the same time we shall continue to raise the cases of individuals, as we did on 2 December, when we expressed our concern to the Chinese Government at the recent detention of Mr. Xu Wenli, a prominent dissident. We look forward to discussing these and other points with the Chinese Government.

(HC Debs., vol. 322, WA, cols. *166–7*: 8 December 1998)

Part Six: IX. *The individual (including the corporation) in international law—crimes under international law*

(See also Part Two: III. and Part Six: VIII. (items of 25 June, 14 July and 22 October 1998), above, and Part Seventeen: IV., below)

The Secretary of State for Foreign and Commonwealth Affairs was asked if he had requested legal advice on whether the massacre in Rwanda in 1994 constituted genocide under the terms of the Genocide Convention. In reply, the Minister of State, FCO, wrote:

Since 1 May 1997, we have not had cause to seek legal advice on whether the massacre in Rwanda in 1994 constituted genocide under the terms of the Genocide Convention.

The UN Security Council resolution establishing the International Criminal Tribunal for Rwanda (ICTR) makes the strong presumption that genocide, as defined in the relevant UN Convention, took place in Rwanda. The UK fully supports action through the ICTR and by the Government of Rwanda, to bring to justice those responsible for acts of genocide.

(HC Debs., vol. 305. WA, col. *385*: 29 January 1998)

In reply to a question, the Minister of State, FCO, wrote:

The UK supports proposals for the Court to be able to try war crimes which are recognised under customary international law. The use as such of nuclear weapons or land mines does not come into this category. But nuclear weapons and land mines, like any other weapon, might be used in a way that would contravene international law. Under the proposals we support, this could well lead to the user being prosecuted at the International Criminal Court.

(HC Debs., vol. 306, WA, col. *140*: 10 February 1998)

The following written statement, dated 24 February 1998, was issued by Her Majesty's Government:

INTERNATIONAL CRIMINAL COURT: STATEMENT OF GOVERNMENT POLICY

1. The Government fully supports the establishment of an effective International Criminal Court to try the most serious crimes of international concern. We are working energetically, at the Preparatory Committee and elsewhere, to advance the negotiations on the subject. . . .
2. We shall send a delegation of senior officials from the FCO, Ministry of Defence and the Home Office to the Diplomatic Conference. The delegation will be led by Sir Franklin Berman, Legal Adviser to the FCO. Tony Lloyd, Minister of State at the FCO, hopes to address the Conference.
3. The world needs an International Criminal Court for three reasons. First, justice should be done. Those who commit the most serious crimes of international concern should not be able to do so with impunity. Second, it will have a deterrent effect, persuading at least some of those tempted to commit atrocities in the future to think twice before doing so. Third, we hope that the knowledge that those who have committed atrocities are being brought to justice may help their victims to put the past behind them and participate in a process of reconciliation. The time has come for a permanent International Criminal Court. Periodic calls either for new *ad hoc* Tribunals or for the extension of the mandate of the existing Tribunal for Rwanda make the need clear.
4. There is general agreement that the Court should have jurisdiction over genocide, crimes against humanity and war crimes. Today, many of the worst conflicts take place within rather than between states. We therefore support the inclusion within the Court's jurisdiction of grave crimes committed in the course of such conflicts. Rape and other crimes of sexual violence committed in armed conflict should be properly defined and explicitly listed as war crimes in the Court's Statute. We also support the inclusion in the list of war crimes of recruitment of children under 15 into armed forces or groups. The Court will need appropriate procedures to handle cases involving children and gender-based violence.
5. It would be appropriate for the Court also to have jurisdiction over atrocities committed against UN personnel and peacekeeping forces operating under the UN Charter. And we would support it also having jurisdiction over crimes of aggression, in cases where the UN Security Council has determined that an act of aggression has taken place, provided that a satisfactory definition of aggression can be agreed for inclusion in the Statute.

6. The Court is not intended to substitute for national legal processes. It should have jurisdiction only where national systems are unable or unwilling genuinely to investigate a crime and to bring a prosecution if the results of the investigation warrant one. We would expect states parties not to seek to avoid the political or financial burden of holding trials themselves where they were able to do so.
7. We hope that all states will eventually adhere to the Treaty establishing the Court, to give it a global remit. But it would not be right or practical to give the Court jurisdiction over crimes which took place in the territory of states which had not adhered to the Treaty, unless they specifically agreed to that in a particular case. But the agreement of relevant non-parties would not be necessary in cases where the Security Council, in pursuit of its obligation under the UN Charter to maintain international peace and security, had referred a situation to the Court.
8. The Court would have a Prosecutor, who would be appointed by states parties to the Treaty but who should be independent of them. Some countries propose that the Prosecutor should only be able to investigate incidents if requested to do so by the Security Council or states parties, others that the Prosecutor should himself or herself to able to decide which investigations to initiate. Consultations within Whitehall on these proposals are still proceeding. In any event the Prosecutor should be responsible for deciding whether, following an investigation, a prosecution should be brought. It should not be necessary to obtain the consent of the state party where the alleged crime took place or of the state party of which the accused is a national. The Security Council should have the power to ask for the suspension of an investigation by the Prosecutor if it decided that this was impeding its mandate to maintain international peace and security. We support the proposal which emerged from the August 1997 meeting of the Prepcom providing for such a power of suspension for a limited but renewable period.
9. States parties to the Treaty should be obliged to cooperate with the Court in enabling investigations to be carried out, to surrender persons whom the Prosecutor has indicated, and to assist the Court at trial. We support the simplest possible procedures for the transfer of the accused by Governments to the Court. Full extradition proceedings should not be required. We will need fair and effective procedures if the Court is to operate properly once cases have begun. We are not wedded to one of our own domestic legal systems or to any other; we think the Court should adopt the best features of all.
10. The Court will inevitably be costly. In negotiating its Statute, we will press for the least expensive arrangements consistent with its effective functioning. It should start off small and expand as and when it needs to.

(Text provided by the FCO)

The Secretary of State for Foreign and Commonwealth Affairs, Mr Robin Cook, made the following statement in the House of Commons:

It has been the Government's policy to back the creation of an effective International Criminal Court. I am pleased to report to the House that in Rome on Friday, Britain was part of the overwhelming majority that agreed to set up such a court. It has been a paradox of our century that those who murder one person are more likely to be brought to justice than those who plot genocide against millions. The International Criminal Court will put on notice the Pol Pots and Saddam Husseins of the future that they may be held to account personally for their crimes against humanity. It will also offer justice to the victims who have no means at present of bringing their suffering before any court.

I ask the House to record its appreciation of the hard work by the British team through five weeks of difficult and intensive negotiations. Britain's firm support for the principle of an International Criminal Court and the leading role that was played by our delegation in brokering consensus contributed to the successful outcome of the Rome conference.

The result is a strong court with wide powers. It will have the power to try cases of genocide, war crimes and crimes against humanity, including crimes of sexual violence, such as the use of mass rape as an instrument of ethnic cleansing, as was practised in Bosnia. The conscription of children under 15 into military service will also be an offence liable to prosecution before the court.

The British delegation played a key part in securing a definition of war crimes that embraced internal conflicts, not only wars between states. That is of great importance, as most of the violence of the past two decades has arisen from internal, not external, conflicts.

The British team also took the initiative in proposing that the court should have power to order those who are guilty to pay reparations to their victims. That is a new power, which is not available to the tribunals on the former Yugoslavia and Rwanda. It reflects the fact that those who abuse their power to commit crimes against others often also abuse their power to make themselves wealthy.

We consistently rejected attempts by other countries to give the court the power of the death penalty, and we were successful in maintaining a majority against any international body having the power to order the death penalty.

Much of the debate in the period running up to the Rome conference revolved around the independence of the prosecutor. I am pleased to report that the prosecutor will have the power to initiate investigations leading to prosecution on his or her own authority. States that are party to the treaty may also refer alleged crimes for investigation, but the prosecutor can take the initiative without waiting for such a referral.

From the start, our objective has been to secure maximum support for the International Criminal Court. To be credible, such a court must command substantial support in the international community. The final vote in support of the court—120 votes to seven—exceeded our expectations. The large number voting in favour was, in part, a reflection of the comprehensive international presence at the Rome conference, which was brought about by the financial support that Britain and others provided towards meeting the attendance costs of 50 of the smaller and poorer states.

To build that overwhelming support, it was necessary to meet the concerns of a number of countries that supported an International Criminal Court in principle, but had reservations about the proposed procedures. In particular, it was necessary to agree that countries signing up to the court should have the right to claim immunity from prosecution for war crimes for up to seven years.

That immunity is time limited; it does not extend to the other crimes in the court's remit, such as crimes against humanity, and it can, in any event, be overriden by a Security Council resolution. It is much more restricted than the initial bid by a number of countries that wanted an indefinite right to opt out from any of the crimes in the court's remit. I understand the regrets of those who would have preferred that no such concession were granted, but I firmly believe that it was right to make a limited compromise to secure wider support for the court and thereby achieve greater credibility for its authority.

I am sorry that, at the end of the Rome conference, the United States felt unable to support the compromise proposals. I understand its concerns about the security of its service men who are posted abroad, but we believe that those concerns are misplaced. Britain, too, has a large number of service men in posts abroad, and we and other major NATO allies are satisfied that the safeguards that are built in to the International Criminal Court will protect our service men against malicious or politically motivated prosecution.

In particular, it is a clearly established principle that the court will be able to prosecute only when there is no remedy in national law. We are confident that we can demonstrate that there is a remedy in British justice—and, for that matter, in United States justice—for accusations that are made against our service men in good faith. The screening of cases by the pre-trial chamber of the International Criminal Court will provide a safeguard against accusations that are brought in bad faith.

We shall continue, through close dialogue, to seek to bring our United States partners on board in support of this improvement to international justice, which has gained such overwhelming support from the rest of the international community.

Later this year, the world will celebrate the 50th anniversary of the signing of the universal declaration of human rights. There can be no more fitting way in which to mark that anniversary than for us to sign up to this agreement, which, for the first time, creates an international court to enforce the most fundamental of those rights. I hope that the support that the court will secure in the House will be as overwhelming as the support that it has already received in the international community.

(HC Debs., vol. 316, cols. 803–4: 20 July 1998)

In the course of the following debate, the Secretary of State made these observations:

The hon. Lady also raised the territorial application and jurisdiction of the court. It is indeed the case that one of the tests of whether the jurisdiction of the court would apply is whether the country that contains the territory in which the alleged crime took place consents. In practice, it is very difficult to imagine the court operating on any other basis. It is hard to see how a case could succeed without access to the scene of the crime, and the court has no powers to try people in absentia, a legal principle which most hon. Members would support. Therefore, it is difficult to see how the court could proceed against existing tyrants still in power, but there is, of course, power for the Security Council, by resolution, to refer any country or individual to the court without any consent by that country or its Government.

(Ibid., col. 809)

There is already legal provision for those guilty of war crimes of a Nazi character during the second world war to be brought to justice. As the House well knows, Britain is at the forefront of insisting that those legal provisions should be honoured. I must be clear with the House—I do not want there to be any misunderstanding on this point—that, as a general principle, the International Criminal Court will not have a retrospective character. However, in future, it will be able to try those who commit crimes against humanity, war crimes or genocide. We hope that—by the very fact of its existence—the court will provide deterrence against such crimes, as tyrants will know not only that those whom they send out to commit such evil work may succumb to justice, but that they themselves may personally be held responsible.

(Ibid.)

The EU Presidency issued the following statement on 22 July 1998:

The European Union expresses its deep appreciation for the successful completion of the Conference for the Establishment of the International Criminal Court which is an achievement of historical dimensions sending a signal that the world can be made a safer and more just place to live in.

The European Union fully endorses the outcome of the Rome conference as reflected in the statute adopted by an overwhelming majority of participating states on July 17, 1998. Although not all aspirations could be fully accommodated, this statute lays the foundation for an effective and credible court as an institution to fight impunity of the most heinous crimes and to deter their commission. The European Union is pleased that complicated and difficult issues such as the definition of crimes, the principle of complementarity, the scope of jurisdiction, the independence of the prosecutor, and the relationship with the United Nations were resolved in a satisfactory manner acceptable to all EU-member-states.

The European Union is well aware that not all tasks to make the court a reality have been accomplished yet. In particular, the Preparatory Commission has still to carry out its work as set out in the statute such as the elaboration of the rules of procedure and evidence. The European Union stands ready to do its utmost to contribute to the accomplishment of this task. The European Union expressed the hope that the required number of sixty ratifications will be reached soon in order for the court to become operative.

(*Bulletin of the European Union*, 1998–7/8, p. 83)

The FCO issued a press statement on 18 September 1998 in the following form:

LOCKERBIE: SIGNING OF THE UK/DUTCH AGREEMENT

The Agreement between the Government of the Kingdom of the Netherlands and the Government of the United Kingdom of Great Britain and Northern Ireland on a Scottish trial in the Netherlands in respect of the Lockerbie bombing was signed today in The Hague.

This Agreement regulates the sitting of the Scottish Court in the Netherlands and the matters arising out of the trial of the 2 Libyan suspects and the proper functioning of the Scottish Court.

Foreign Secretary Robin Cook said:

> 'This is a significant step forward for the joint UK/US strategy to resolve the Lockerbie issue which the Lord Advocate and I outlined last month. We are extremely grateful to Jozias van Aartsen and the Dutch Government for their cooperation in enabling the Scottish Court to sit in the Netherlands. I hope that the signing of this Agreement will also be a further indication to the victims' families of our determination to end their long wait for justice. We now look to the Libyan Government to respond positively to the unanimously expressed will of the UN Security Council.'

Notes for Editors

1. The Agreement was signed by Foreign Minister Jozias van Aartsen on behalf of the Dutch Government and British Ambassador Rosemary Spencer on behalf of the Government of the United Kingdom.
2. The Court will be Scottish and will follow normal Scots law in every respect except for the replacement of the jury by a panel of 3 Scottish High Court Judges. The Scottish rules of evidence and procedure, and all the guarantees of fair trial provided by the law of Scotland, would apply. Arrangement will be made for international observers to attend the trial.
3. Formal Libyan response to the initiative is still awaited. The UK and the US have always made it clear that their proposal is not open to negotiation. But we are of course fully prepared to clarify any legal or technical points, provided that Libya seeks such clarification through the Office of the United Nations Secretary-General, whose assistance we greatly appreciate.

(Text provided by the FCO)

In the course of a joint press conference given by Mr Cook and the Lord Advocate, Lord Hardie, following the above signing, the Lord Advocate observed that in respect of a suggestion that the proposed trial of the two Libyan suspects should be held before an international panel of judges:

It has never been explained how such a court would work. It would not operate under international law because there is no body of international criminal law and procedure under which it could operate.

(Text provided by the FCO)

In reply to questions on the subject of the situation in Kosovo, the Minister of State, FCO, wrote in part:

We are among the first 120 states which decided on 17 July this year to establish the International Criminal Court. However, the Court will come into effect only when sixty States have ratified its Statute and will not have jurisdiction over events which take place before then.

The International Criminal Tribunal for the former Yugoslavia has jurisdiction to investigate and prosecute war crimes against humanity throughout the territory of the former Yugoslavia, including Kosovo.

(HC Debs., vol. 318, WA, col. *200*: 28 October 1998)

In reply to a question, the Minister of State, FCO, wrote:

The International Criminal Tribunal for the former Yugoslavia (ICTY) has conducted initial investigations in Kosovo following the announcement in July by Justice Arbour that in her view the conflict there falls within the Tribunal's mandate. Along with our EU Partners we have formally protested to the authorities of the Federal Republic of Yugoslavia following their recent decision not to issue the necessary visas to Justice Arbour and her officials to enable them to carry out further investigations in Kosovo. We have made it clear to Belgrade that their actions constitute non-compliance with UN Security Council Resolutions 1160, 1199 and 1203. We are supporting the adoption of a new UN Security Council Resolution demanding the full cooperation of the Federal Authorities with the ICTY. A draft resolution is currently being discussed in New York.

(HC Debs., vol. 319, WA, col. *415*: 16 November 1998)

In reply to the question what representations Her Majesty's Government have made through the UN, concerning the refusal of the authorities in the Federal Republic of Yugoslavia to allow the Chief Prosecutor of the UN War Crimes Tribunal to investigate alleged Serbian atrocities in Kosovo, the Minister of State, FCO wrote:

Along with our EU Partners we have formally protested to the FRY Authorities following their recent decision not to issue the necessary visas to Justice Arbour and her officials to enable them to carry out further investigations in Kosovo. We have made it clear to Belgrade that we view their actions as non-compliance with UN Security Council Resolutions 1160, 1199 and 1203. We are also supporting the adoption of a new UN Security Council Resolution demanding the full cooperation of the FRY Authorities with the ICTY. A draft resolution is currently being discussed in New York.

(Ibid.)

Speaking in the UN General Assembly on 2 December 1998, the representative of Austria, on behalf of the EU, stated:

I have the honour to speak on behalf of the European Union on agenda item 46(b), entitled 'Fiftieth anniversary of the adoption of the Convention on the Prevention and Punishment of the Crime of Genocide'. The Central and Eastern European countries associated with the European Union—Bulgaria, the Czech Republic, Estonia, Hungary, Latvia, Lithuania, Poland, Romania, Slovakia, Slovenia—and the associated country Cyprus, as well as the European Free Trade Association country member of the European Economic Area—Iceland—align themselves with this statement.

This year marks not only the fiftieth anniversary of the Universal Declaration of Human Rights but also that of the Convention on the Prevention and Punishment of the Crime of Genocide, which was adopted by the General

Assembly 50 years ago on 9 December 1948, one day before the adoption of the Universal Declaration.

The European Union very much welcomes this opportunity to commemorate the adoption of the Genocide Convention. This is first of all the moment to honour the millions of victims of acts of genocide throughout history and to keep their memory alive. In the wake of the horror of the Holocaust, the conviction that such events must never occur again was a crucial element in the foundation of the United Nations and guided the work of this Organization from its very inception. It was the same conviction that led to the inclusion of the promotion and encouragement of respect for human rights among the purposes of the United Nations.

As the Universal Declaration of Human Rights was the beginning of an impressive development of the body of international human rights law, the adoption of the Convention on the Prevention and Punishment of the Crime of Genocide was an important first step towards the effective prevention and punishment of war crimes and crimes against humanity.

Towards the end of the Second World War, the full horror of the obscenity of the suffering and extermination endured in concentration camps and elsewhere and the full extent and inhuman nature of the horrible crimes committed became public knowledge. It was said that the world was confronted with 'a crime that has no name'. While the Charter of the Nuremberg Tribunal referred to the concepts of war crimes and crimes against peace and humanity, the notion of genocide was introduced only subsequently. Genocide is a crime on a different scale than all other crimes against humanity, since it implies an intention to exterminate, in whole or in part, a particular group of human beings. The international community gave it special priority in order to take steps to prevent acts of genocide for all time.

The elaboration of a legally binding instrument for the prevention and punishment of genocide became a crucial standard-setting initiative in the early work of the United Nations. The Genocide Convention constituted major progress because of its general applicability. Under the Convention, all States parties are held to prevent and punish genocide in times of peace and war, in regard to the defeated and victors alike as well as in regard to nationals and non-nationals, no matter whether they are private individuals or constitutionally responsible rulers.

When the Genocide Convention was being prepared and discussed in the General Assembly, the question of an international criminal tribunal to prosecute and punish acts falling under the Convention was high on the agenda. Some argued that the creation of such a tribunal was necessary to reach the lofty goals embraced by the Convention.

However, at that time the international community was reluctant to take such a step. A general reference to an international penal tribunal to try persons charged with genocide was included in article VI of the Convention, but no provision for the immediate setting up of such a tribunal was made. Instead, the General Assembly, after unanimous adoption of the Convention, requested the International Law Commission to further pursue the question of the establishment of an international criminal court. Thus the adoption of the Genocide Convention also had a catalytic impact on the further development of international humanitarian and criminal law.

Today, we must acknowledge that despite the establishment of a basic framework of human rights and humanitarian law 50 years ago, the world continues to witness massive violations of human rights, war crimes, crimes against humanity, and genocide. From Cambodia to the Balkans to the Great Lakes region in Africa, unbelievable atrocities occur on a large scale. The international community has to date more often than not failed to prevent and stop such acts. As the High Commissioner for Human Rights rightly pointed out, we have lacked the means, the political will and an effective weapon against a culture of impunity.

Finally, a decisive step was taken by the international community, shocked by the cruel and outrageous crimes committed in the course of the violent break-up of Yugoslavia and the genocide in Rwanda. The establishment of ad hoc tribunals to prosecute and try the perpetrators of such crimes was and is a strong signal that individual responsibility is being taken seriously. The European Union will continue to support the work of the ad hoc tribunals, and it calls on all States to do likewise. The mission entrusted to these institutions must be fulfilled. The European Union also welcomes the Secretary-General's establishment of a group of experts charged, *inter alia*, with exploring options for bringing Khmer Rouge leaders to justice for the most serious human rights violations committed in Cambodia in the years 1975 to 1979.

In this fiftieth anniversary year, the idea of an international penal tribunal contained in the Genocide Convention [has] at long last become a reality. The Rome Statute for the International Criminal Court, adopted last July, concludes a long and sometimes cumbersome process initiated 50 years ago. The European Union strongly supported the creation of an international criminal court, and it is extremely satisfied with the outcome of the Rome conference. Building on the experiences and achievements of the ad hoc tribunals for the former Yugoslavia and Rwanda, the results obtained in Rome hold the genuine promise of achieving a world where the interests of peace and justice will not be seen as contradictory.

We should keep in mind that the purpose of the International Criminal Court will not only be to prosecute and punish those who commit the most heinous crimes, but, through its mere existence, to deter and prevent individuals from committing them in the first place. The earliest possible entry into force of the Statute of the International Criminal Court is therefore of utmost importance. The European Union reiterates its call on all States to sign and ratify the Statute as soon as possible. It will be one of the lasting achievements of this General Assembly to have prepared the ground for a speedy follow-up to the Rome conference, so that the Court will become a reality as soon as possible.

Indeed, the Court will add a new and most important dimension to international relations in general and to the effectiveness of international law in particular. It will reinforce individual responsibility.

The time when cruelties and atrocities go unpunished must come to an end. Let us renew today this commitment that inspired the founders of the United Nations. Let us strongly reaffirm the 'never again' expressed 50 years ago.

(A/53/PV. 77, pp. 1–3)

Part Seven: I. D. *The State and its organs—the composition of the State—diplomatic missions and their members*

The following statement was made on 16 November 1998 in the Sixth Committee of the UN General Assembly by the representative of Austria on behalf of the EU:

I have the honour to speak on behalf of the European Union. The Central and Eastern European countries associated with the European Union, Czech Republic, Hungary, Latvia, Lithuania, Poland, Romania, Slovakia and Slovenia, and the Associated country Cyprus, as well as the EFTA countries members of the EEA, Iceland and Liechtenstein align themselves with this statement.

Item 147 entitled 'Consideration of effective measures to enhance the protection, security and safety of diplomatic and consular missions and representatives' has been with the Sixth Committee since 1980 when it was included in the General Assembly's agenda at the request of the Nordic countries. The explanatory memorandum presented then noted that there had been increasingly frequent violations of or failures to observe the relevant provisions of international law, including physical safety of diplomatic and consular personnel and the inviolability of their premises. In the light of this development, it was urgent that the Assembly consider ways of enhancing respect for the rules of international law governing diplomatic and consular relations. This is the issue we are again facing.

In the last debate which took place in the General Assembly on this item two years ago, the European Union emphasized the importance of the topic, referring to the fact that it not only addresses the effective conduct of diplomatic and consular relations but is also relevant to relations between States in general. The privileges and immunities of diplomatic and consular missions and personnel are not for personal benefit. They are granted to ensure that diplomatic and consular functions can be exercised without hindrance and thus to facilitate normal healthy exchanges between States over a wide range of subjects. Diplomatic and consular missions play a very special role in this process which is to the benefit of the exchanging States and their citizens. The collective beneficial effect in international relations in general of smoothly running diplomatic and consular relations between individual States is obvious. Considerations such as these underline the need to ensure that the relevant privileges and immunities, as recognized in general international law and as provided for in international agreements, are issued in practice. In this respect the obligation to ensure the protection, security and safety is the most vital. The EU is unreservedly committed to upholding this obligation. It welcomes further efforts, particularly through international cooperation, to ensure that the right to adequate protection, security and safety, as well as the other relevant rights and immunities, are in fact enjoyed.

After this general consideration, let me express our gratitude for the report which the Secretary-General is submitting under this item (A/53/279). As in previous reports, the text of the most recent General Assembly resolution on this subject (i.e. resolution 51/156) is given in full. Like the Secretary-General we would refer to the wording of that resolution and in particular to one of its central paragraphs, i.e. operative paragraph 3 which, we believe, sums up our common sense of purpose: 'The General Assembly urges States to strictly observe, implement and enforce the principles and rules of international law governing diplomatic and consular relations and, in particular, to ensure, in conformity with their international obligations, the protection, security and safety of the missions, representatives and officials officially present in territories under their jurisdiction, including practical measures to prohibit in their territories illegal activities of persons, groups and organizations that encourage, instigate, organize or engage in the perpetration of acts against the security and safety of such missions, representatives and officials'. This call emanating from the General Assembly reminds all Governments of their binding obligation to provide adequate protection to foreign missions and representatives and certainly is reflective of the general consideration I have presented earlier. It is absolutely essential that every government does its utmost to prevent infringements on the inviolability of internationally protected premises and persons.

While the Secretary-General's report this year lists only one single serious incident reported by a Government, this does not necessarily mean, that the overall situation worldwide has improved. In fact, the number and gravity of violent incidents involving foreign diplomatic personnel and premises has increased, taking a growing toll of human lives. The barbaric bombing of the US embassies in Kenya and Tanzania, the cold-blooded murder of Iranian diplomats in Afghanistan are a vivid reminder of a deteriorating situation. I would like on behalf of the European Union to convey its condolences to the families of those who died and to those who were injured as a result of such heinous activities directed against the personnel of diplomatic and consular missions. We find it absolutely unacceptable that a principle existing since time immemorial should be so brutally violated. In this connection we should like to express our appreciation and support to the Governments concerned for their efforts to bring the perpetrators to justice.

Finally I wish to refer to the useful tabulations as to the ratification of, accession and succession to, the relevant multilateral agreements contained in the Secretary-General's report. The European Union has taken note with interest of that information which shows that the main conventions are experiencing a fairly high degree of ratification. However, as universal acceptance of the rules contained in those instruments is our common goal, the European Union hopes that more States will become parties to them. In this respect the European Union, as repeatedly stated in the past, is of the view that adherence to and observance of the provisions of these instruments by the international community should lead to significant improvements in the safety of diplomatic premises and, most importantly, in the safety of human beings, namely the diplomatic and consular personnel and their families.

(Text provided by the FCO; see also A/C.6/53/SR. 30, pp. 2–3)

Part Seven: IV. A. *The State and its organs—privileges and immunities—State immunity (including Head of State immunity)*

(See Part Three: V. C. and Part Five: I. D. 5. (b). (iii). (affidavit of 19 June 1998), above)

Part Seven: IV. B. *The State and its organs—privileges and immunities—diplomatic privileges and immunities*

(See also Part Seven: I.D., above)

In reply to a question asking what are the rules and guidance governing diplomats and consular officials giving evidence in foreign courts, the Minister of State, FCO, wrote:

Under Article 31(2) of the Vienna Convention on Diplomatic Relations (1961), 'a diplomatic agent is not obliged to give evidence as witness'.

Article 44(1) of the Vienna Convention on Consular Relations (1963) states that 'a consular employee or a member of the service staff shall not, except in the cases mentioned in paragraph 3 of this Article, decline to give evidence. If a consular officer should decline to do so, no coercive measure or penalty may be applied to him'. Article 44(3) goes on to state that 'Members of a consular post are under no obligation to give evidence concerning matters connected with the exercise of their functions or to produce official correspondence and documents [in] relation thereto. They are also entitled to decline to give evidence as expert witnesses with regard to the law of the sending State'.

Internal guidance to FCO staff, however, is that Her Majesty's Government would normally expect all staff to assist local police and judicial authorities if called upon to do.

(HC Debs., vol. 305, WA, col. *386*: 29 January 1998)

In reply to a question, the Parliamentary Under-Secretary of State, FCO, wrote:

According to Protocol Department's record, there are presently 10 persons accredited to 10 of the London Diplomatic missions as diplomatic agents who are dual nationals, holding UK nationality in addition to that of the sending state, and who are eligible for limited immunity associated with diplomatic status in accordance with Article 38(1) of the Vienna Convention on Diplomatic Relations. No persons of UK nationality alone are eligible for this status.

(HL Debs., vol. 590, *WA 16*: 1 June 1998)

In reply to a question, the Minister of State, FCO, wrote:

From a diplomatic community of over 17,000 persons, seventeen alleged serious offences by persons entitled to immunity were drawn to the attention of the Foreign and Commonwealth Office in 1997. 'Serious offences' are defined in accordance with the Report to the Foreign Affairs Committee 'The Abuse of Diplomatic Immunities and Privileges (1985)' as offences which fall into the category which in certain circumstances attract a maximum penalty of 6 months imprisonment or more: the majority involved drinking and driving and shop-lifting.

In relation to this question, I refer my hon. Friend to the answer my noble Friend the Parliamentary Under-Secretary of State gave to the noble Lord, Lord Marlesford on 1 June 1998, *Official Report, House of Lords*, column *16*, that one diplomat was withdrawn at the Department's request from his post in the United Kingdom as a result of alleged offences, compared with six the previous year.

(HC Debs., vol. 315, WA, cols. *160–1*: 30 June 1998; see also HL Debs., vol. 591, *WA 67–8*: 30 June 1998)

In reply to the question 'whether all persons listed in the London Diplomatic List enjoy (a) diplomatic immunity and (b) diplomatic privileges of a fiscal nature', the Parliamentary Under-Secretary of State, FCO, wrote:

Yes. The London Diplomatic List gives details of all category A and category B diplomatic agents accredited to diplomatic missions in the United Kingdom. Category A diplomatic agents are heads of mission of the sending state and category B diplomatic agents are senior members of their support staff. Diplomatic agents enjoy immunity from civil and administrative jurisdiction of the receiving state under Article 31 of the Vienna Convention on Diplomatic Relations. Category A and category B diplomatic agents are entitled to immunity in this respect as a result of this provision.

Under Article 34 of the Vienna Convention on Diplomatic Relations, diplomatic agents are exempt from all dues and taxes, personal or real, national, regional or municipal, with certain exceptions which are set out in the convention.

The London Diplomatic List also incorporates a directory of international organisations and honorary consuls. Staff of international organisations benefit from privileges and immunities negotiated individually under the auspices of the International Organisations Act 1968. Honorary consuls benefit from limited diplomatic immunity when on official duty. They do not enjoy privileges of a fiscal nature.

(HL Debs., vol. 591, *WA 64–5*: 30 June 1998)

On 9 July 1998, the Council of the EU adopted a 'Common Position' concerning Belarus, on the basis of Article J.2 of the Treaty on European Union. The recital to the Common Position read as follows:

THE COUNCIL OF THE EUROPEAN UNION,

Having regard to the Treaty on European Union, and in particular Article J.2 thereof;
Whereas the Government of Belarus has taken certain measures or allowed certain measures to be carried out affecting the residences of Ambassadors from several Member States of the European Union at the Drozdy diplomatic compound in Minsk;
Whereas these measures, in particular the beginning of construction and repair work on the site, the interruption of power and water supply, and the blocking of access for cars, make any use of the residences concerned impossible and therefore severely impede the performance of the diplomatic missions concerned;
Whereas the European Union considers that these measures taken by or with the consent of the Government of Belarus constitute an infringement of the Vienna

Convention on Diplomatic Relations and are contrary to the principle of friendly relations among States;
Whereas the Member States of the European Union, in a spirit of loyalty and mutual solidarity, have decided to react to the behaviour of the Government of Belarus;
Whereas the Member States of the European Union have decided to recall their Ambassadors from Minsk for consultations;
Whereas the Member States of the European Union have also decided to request Belarusian Ambassadors accredited to them to return to Minsk for reporting;
Whereas the Government of Belarus has subsequently allowed the premises of the Missions of several Member States to be entered without the consent of the Heads of Mission concerned;
Whereas these actions constitute a further violation of the Vienna Convention on Diplomatic Relations;
Whereas the European Union, while reaffirming its interests in a continued constructive dialogue with Belarus, considers the behaviour of the Government of Belarus unlawful and unacceptable;
Whereas the European Union has decided to adopt the measures indicated below as a reaction to the violation of the premises of the missions concerned;
Whereas the European Union will closely monitor the development of the situation in Belarus, with a view to take further measures if necessary,
HAS DEFINED THE FOLLOWING COMMON POSITION:
. . .

(Text provided by EU Presidency press service)

In reply to a question, the Minister of State, FCO, wrote:

We, our EU partners and other countries affected by the Belarusian decision to exclude Ambassadors from their residencies at Drozdy are in regular contact with the Belarusian authorities. The Troika of EU chargés d'affaires met Deputy Foreign Minister Gerasimovich on 20 July. They underlined the need for the Belarusian authorities to comply with international law on the inviolability of diplomatic premises, and called on the Belarusian authorities to put forward concrete proposals to resolve the problem.

(HC Debs., vol. 317, WA, col. *683*: 31 July 1998)

During a debate on the subject of relations with Chile, the detention in London of Senator Pinochet was mentioned. The Parliamentary Under-Secretary of State, FCO, Baroness Symons of Vernham Dean, remarked:

Senator Pinochet's diplomatic passport did not entitle him to diplomatic immunity. Under the Vienna Convention only members of a permanent diplomatic mission are entitled to diplomatic immunity.

(HL Debs., vol. 593, col. 1915: 28 October 1998)

In reply to the question asked of the Secretary of State for Foreign and Commonwealth Affairs 'from whom and when he obtained advice on

Senator Pinochet's entitlement to diplomatic immunity', the Minister of State, FCO, wrote:

> My right hon. Friend the Foreign Secretary was told on the evening of 16 October of the advice on this subject that had been given by FCO officials to the Metropolitan Police.

In reply to the further question 'what advice his Department gave the Metropolitan Police on Senator Pinochet's entitlement to diplomatic immunity', the Minister of State wrote:

> This Department informed the Metropolitan Police that there were no grounds on the basis of immunity for not proceeding with the provisional arrest warrant.

(HC Debs., vol. 318, WA, col. *601*: 4 November 1998)

Part Seven: IV. C. *The State and its organs—privileges and immunities—consular privileges and immunities*

(See Part Seven: IV. B. (item of 29 January 1998), above)

In reply to the question whether the British Vice-Consul in Istanbul will be permitted to give evidence to a Turkish court regarding incidents in Istanbul on 2 September 1997, the Minister of State, FCO, wrote:

> As set out in the answer given by the Minister of State, Foreign and Commonwealth Office, my hon. Friend the Member for Manchester, Central (Mr. Lloyd) on 29 January 1998, *Official Report*, column *385*, our guidelines are that we generally expect British officials to co-operate with local judicial authorities. In this particular instance, no request has been made by the local courts. Under Article 44(3) of the Vienna Convention on Consular Relations members of a consular post are not obliged to give evidence on matters encountered in the exercise of their functions. We have concluded that it would be inappropriate for the British Vice Consul (Information) to give evidence because of the need for him to retain the status of impartial observer in attending subsequent court cases in his consular capacity.

(HC Debs., vol. 306, WA, cols. *35–6*: 9 February 1998)

Part Seven: IV. D. *The State and its organs—privileges and immunities—visiting forces*

On 29 January 1998, evidence was taken by the Defence Committee of the House of Commons on the subject of the draft Visiting Forces and International Headquarters (Application of Law) (Amendment) Order 1998. The following passage is from the evidence given by Mr M. Fuller, Head of Secretariat (Air Staff):

The subject matter does not lend itself to a very short and succinct explanation, so I hope the Committee will bear with me. If I can take you back 50 years following the Second World War: the allies agreed on arrangements for jurisdiction and application of domestic law to visiting forces based on the soil of the host country. This was enshrined in the 1951 NATO Status of Forces Agreement between the allies. The two points, perhaps, for the Committee to focus on in that agreement are, first of all, its provisions for reciprocity. In other words, that the parties to the agreement enter into the agreement and offer various privileges and benefits to visiting forces, on the understanding that their own forces will enjoy the same privileges and benefits reciprocally from other countries. The second point to make is the issue of equivalence: that the host country can only extend to visiting forces the sort of privileges and benefits that it extends to its own home forces. So the arrangements that were set up were intended to facilitate proper military co-operation between the NATO allies. That provision was put into domestic legislation by means of the 1952 Visiting Forces Act, which provides for various exclusions and exemptions, and provides a power to make statutory instruments in relation to visiting forces with the intention that visiting forces would be put, very broadly, on all fours with the home force in terms of application of domestic law. The most important statutory instrument under the 1952 Act is the 1965 Visiting Forces Order: a fairly lengthy Order which lists the countries to which it applies—essentially Commonwealth countries and NATO countries—and goes on to specify a range of domestic legislation which will not apply to visiting forces. The Schedules to the Order list a great many of these statutes. The Order before you, to bring us completely up-to-date, is an amending Order to the 1965 Order and happily this is rather short and straightforward. So this is the legislative framework in which arrangements for visiting forces can be made. It generally facilitates the sort of exchanges that you will be familiar with: with forces from other countries coming here to exercise in co-operation with our own forces. It also facilitates the sort of exercising and training that our forces do in other countries that are party to these reciprocal agreements, because we expect our forces when they exercise in partner countries to have the same privileges and benefits. So that is the framework. The forces that we are talking about could be any forces that are from the countries listed in the Order. In this country we have, of course, American forces that are based here on a fairly long-term basis; and we have forces from NATO countries or Partnership for Peace countries that would come here for a shorter length of time to do specific exercises.

The following question was then asked of Mr N. Beach, Legal Adviser, Ministry of Defence:

Is the legal basis in relation to United States forces, or does this merely supplement other legislation relating to the United States?

(*Mr Beach*) Yes. The legal basis for both—what one might call those who are permanently based here and those who just come here for short exercises—is exactly the same. It is the Visiting Forces Act 1952 and subordinate legislation made under it.

(*Parliamentary Papers*, 1997–98, HC, Paper 521, pp. 1–2)

The following question was then put to Mr Fuller:

. . . Could you summarise for us, in laymen's terms, the privileges and immunities granted to visiting forces under the 1965 Order, which this draft Order will extend to the countries listed.

(*Mr Fuller*) The 1965 Order covers a great range of activities and statutes, as I said. The intention behind the Order was to make it possible for visiting forces to operate. For example, the Firearms Acts' provisions are relevant. You need to allow both our own forces, and those that they are training with, to carry firearms in the course of their duty. So there needs to be an exemption in relation to that. But also in relation to other more mundane matters connected with the jurisdiction over members of a visiting force, the application of the Road Traffic Acts and so on will apply to quite a considerable range of measures.

(Ibid., p. 2)

In moving the approval by the House of Lords of the draft Visiting Forces and International Headquarters (Application of Law) (Amendment) Order 1998, the Minister of State, Ministry of Defence, Lord Gilbert, stated:

First, this is merely an extension to some long-standing arrangements which we have enjoyed on a mutual basis with members of NATO and with certain Commonwealth countries. We propose to extend these exemptions from certain British laws to troops of countries that are signing up to the Partnership for Peace who will be training here, just as they are extending these immunities to our troops who are training or are stationed in their countries.

(HL Debs., vol. 585, col. 851: 5 February 1998; see also HC Second Standing Committee on Delegated Legislation, 3 February 1998, col. 3)

The Visiting Forces (Designation) Order 1998 (Statutory Instruments 1998, No. 1268), made on 19 May 1998, was accompanied by an explanatory note which read as follows:

This Order designates Armenia, Austria, Azerbaijan, Belarus, Finland, Georgia, Kazakhstan, Kyrgyzstan, the Former Yugoslav Republic of Macedonia, Moldova, Russia, Switzerland, Turkmenistan, Ukraine and Uzbekistan as countries to which the Visiting Forces Act 1952 applies.

The Order partially implements, in relation to the countries designated by it, the obligations imposed on the United Kingdom by the Agreement, dated 19 June 1995, made between Member States of the North Atlantic Treaty Organisation (NATO) and those other States which have accepted the invitation to take part in the Partnership for Peace (Miscellaneous No. 12 (1966), Cm 3237). The effect of this Order, together with the Visiting Forces (Designation) Order 1997, is to designate as countries to which the Visiting Forces Act 1952 applies all those States which have accepted the invitation of NATO to take part in the Partnership for Peace and which are parties to the Agreement of 19 June 1995.

In moving the consideration in the House of Commons Second Standing Committee on Delegated Legislation of the draft Visiting

Forces and International Headquarters (Application of Law) (Amendment) Order 1998, the Minister for the Armed Forces, Dr John Reid, stated on 3 February 1998:

I hope that the order meets with the approval of all quarters in the House. Generally speaking, we can agree that this is of benefit not only to those . . . forces with whom we are now acting either through liaison, action, friendship or alliance but to the country as a whole. Hon. Members will be aware that the purpose of the draft order is to amend a 1965 Order in Council. They will also be aware that it has already been scrutinised by the Defence Select Committee, which approved and commended it to the House.

The statutory instrument provides exemptions for visiting forces and international headquarters from certain elements of our domestic legislation to the extent that similar exemptions may be enjoyed by our armed forces. The visiting forces concerned are those from commonwealth countries and North Atlantic Treaty Organisation members, which either maintain troops in this country or send personnel or contingents here for training and joint exercises.

The principle of granting such exemptions is well established, and historically NATO countries have extended legal immunities to visiting forces from other member states. We now wish to extend this to those with whom we are working in partnership through NATO's Partnership for Peace programme.

(HC Debs., Second Standing Committee on Delegated Legislation, 3 February 1998, col. 3)

Part Eight: III. A. *Jurisdiction of the State—extra-territorial exercises of jurisdiction—general*

During a press conference held in Brussels on 26 January 1998, the Secretary of State for Foreign and Commonwealth Affairs, Mr Robin Cook, stated in respect of US legislation directed against Cuba:

. . . this is an extra-territorial legislation and we cannot accept the United States or any other power taking penalty action against a European company for carrying out an act which is entirely lawful in its domestic legislation and entirely lawful in international law . . .

(Text provided by the FCO)

In reply to a question, the Prime Minister wrote:

I have raised US extraterritorial legislation with President Clinton on a number of occasions. I and my colleagues continue to take every opportunity to make it clear to the US Administration and Congress that we reject such legislation.

(HC Debs., vol. 306, WA, col. *778*: 19 February 1998)

At a press conference held in Luxembourg on 27 April 1998, the Secretary of State for Foreign and Commonwealth Affairs, Mr Robin Cook, referred to US legislation providing for measures against Cuba (Helms-Burton Act) and Iran and Libya (D'Amato Act). He stated:

In both cases Europe cannot accept the extra-territorial principle at the bottom of that legislation, but also we do believe that they are counter-productive.

(Text provided by the FCO)

In reply to a question, the Parliamentary Under-Secretary of State, FCO, stated:

The UK and EU believe constructive dialogue and co-operation, not isolation, is the way to promote change towards pluralist democracy in Cuba. Since 1996, we have voted in favour of the Cuban resolution at the UN condemning the US blockade. We and the EU particularly reject the extra-territorial extension of US sanctions legislation to non-US companies.

(HL Debs., vol. 589, *WA 66–7*: 5 May 1998)

At a press conference held on 24 August 1998, the Secretary of State for Foreign and Commonwealth Affairs, Mr Robin Cook, referred to impending arrangements with the Netherlands for the trial before a Scottish court sitting in the Netherlands of two Libyans alleged to have caused the destruction of Pan Am flight 103 over Scotland. He continued:

The agreements are complex and comprehensive; they represent an historic innovation in international legal practice to enable the court of one country to conduct a trial in another country.

(Text provided by the FCO)

In moving that the Criminal Justice Bill be read a second time in the House of Lords. the Minister of State, Home Office, Lord Williams of Mostyn, stated:

Conspiracy is dealt with in Clause 5 and subsequent clauses. These provisions are designed to close off a gap which has been recognised for some time in our response to international terrorism and other international crime. In our country it is not always an offence to conspire to commit criminal acts outside this country. This section of the Bill deals with those people who try to use our country as a safe place to plot the commission of terrorist offences or other crimes abroad. Terrorism and other forms of organised crime cannot be contained by a line on a map. Crime in one country is often instigated and planned in another. We think that there should not be a hiding place in our jurisdiction for terrorists, those who traffic in arms, drug smugglers, money launderers or counterfeiters. We have a tradition of tolerance in this country—I hope we have borne that in mind—but we do not propose to tolerate criminals who want to use our jurisdiction as a safe place for planning crimes abroad.

Some powers already exist in this field. Extra-territorial jurisdiction is available for some offences such as computer misuse and sexual offences against children. Other offences are covered, but only in relation to certain countries, under the Suppression of Terrorism Act. I give an example. If the recent murderous, terrorist attacks in Kenya, Tanzania and South Africa had been plotted and planned here and uncovered at an advanced stage of planning, the hands of our police would probably have been tied. I cannot justify that. We have thought about these provisions. I hope I may again quote the noble and learned Lord, Lord Lloyd, who said,

> 'The most significant additional measure which the Government can take is to amend the law of conspiracy so as to facilitate the prosecution of those who conspire here to commit terrorist offences abroad'.

(HL Debs., vol. 593, col. 14: 3 September 1998)

The following joint UK/US letter, dated 18 September 1998, was sent to the UN Secretary-General for circulation as a document of the UN Security Council:

1. The Governments of the United Kingdom of Great Britain and Northern Ireland and the United States of America are gravely concerned that almost ten years after the terrorist bombing of Pam Am flight 103 over Lockerbie, those accused have not yet stood trial. Several years have passed since the Security Council, in resolutions 731 (1992), 748 (1992) and 883 (1993) required the Libyan Arab Jamahiriya to ensure the appearance of the two accused for trial in the appropriate United Kingdom or United States court.

2. Our two Governments consider that it is essential for the promotion of international peace and security that justice is done and is seen to be done before the eyes of the international community in the appropriate Scottish or United States court. Despite the comprehensive assurances given as to the fairness of a trial in these jurisdictions, the report of those independent legal experts appointed by you to look at the Scottish judicial system (S/1997/1991) and the offer made by the Government of the United Kingdom to accommodate international observers at a Scottish trial, Libya has failed to ensure the appearance of the two accused. Our two Governments reiterate their profound concern at this disregard of the Security Council's demands.

3. Nevertheless, in the interest of resolving this situation in a way which will allow justice to be done, our Governments are prepared, as an exceptional measure, to arrange for the two accused to be tried before a Scottish court sitting in the Netherlands. After close consultation with the Government of the Kingdom of the Netherlands, we are pleased to confirm that the Government of the Kingdom of the Netherlands has agreed to facilitate arrangements for such a court. It would be a Scottish court and would follow normal Scots law and procedure in every respect except for the replacement of the jury by a panel of three Scottish High Court judges. The Scottish rules of evidence and procedure, and all the guarantees of fair trial provided by the law of Scotland, would apply. Arrangements would be made for international observers to attend the trial. Attached is the text of the intended Agreement between the Government of the Kingdom of the Netherlands and the Government of the United Kingdom.

4. The two accused will have safe passage from Libya to the Netherlands for the purpose of the trial. While they are in the Netherlands for the purpose of the trial, we shall not seek their transfer to any jurisdiction other than the Scottish court sitting in the Netherlands. If found guilty, the two accused will serve their sentence in the United Kingdom. If acquitted, or in the event of the prosecution being discontinued by any process of law preventing any further trial under

Scots law, the two accused will have safe passage back to Libya. Should other offences committed prior to arrival in the Netherlands come to light during the course of the trial, neither of the two accused nor any other person attending the court, including witnesses, will be liable for arrest for such offences while in The Netherlands for the purposes of the trial.

5. The two accused will enjoy the protection afforded by Scottish law. They will be able to choose Scottish solicitors and advocates to represent them at all stages of the proceedings. The proceedings will be interpreted into Arabic in the same way as a trial held in Scotland. The accused will be given prior medical attention. If they wish, they can be visited in custody by the international observers. The trial would of course be held in public, adequate provision being made for the media.

6. Our two Governments are prepared to support a further Security Council resolution for the purpose of the initiative (which would also suspend sanctions upon the appearence of the two accused in the Netherlands for the purpose of trial before the Scottish court) and which would require all States to cooperate to that end. Once that resolution is adopted, the Government of the United Kingdom will legislate to enable a Scottish court to hold a trial in the Netherlands. The necessary United Kingdom legislation has already been prepared and is attached (annex II).

7. This initiative represents a sincere attempt by the Governments of the United Kingdom and the United States to resolve this issue, and is an approach which has recently been endorsed by others, including the Organization of African Unity, the League of Arab States, the Movement of Non-Aligned States and the Organization of the Islamic Conference (S/1994/373, S/1995/834, S/1997/35, S/1997/273, S/1997/406, S/1997/497, S/1997/529). We are only willing to proceed in this exceptional way on the basis of the terms set out in the present letter (and its annexes), and provided that the Libyan Arab Jamahiriya cooperates fully by:

(a) Ensuring the timely appearance of the two accused in the Netherlands for trial before the Scottish court;
(b) Ensuring the production of evidence, including the presence of witnesses before the court;
(c) Complying fully with all the requirements of the Security Council Resolutions.

8. We trust that the Libyan Arab Jamahiriya will respond promptly, positively and unequivocally by ensuring the timely appearance of the two accused in the Netherlands for trial before the Scottish court. If it does not do so, our two Governments reserve the right to propose further sanctions at the time of the next Security Council review. They also reserve the right to withdraw this initiative.

9. We have the honour to request that you convey the text of the present letter and its annexes to the Government of the Libyan Arab Jamahiriya. We would be grateful if you would agree to give the Libyan Arab Jamahiriya any assistance it might require with the physical arrangements for the transfer of the two accused directly to the Netherlands.

(S/1998/795 (annexes not reproduced))

In the course of a speech on 14 October 1998 in the UN General Assembly debating US sanctions against Cuba, the representative of Austria, speaking on behalf of the EU, stated:

The European Union believes the United States trade policy towards Cuba is principally a matter for those two Governments. But the European Union has made clear its opposition to the extraterritorial extension of the so-called Cuban Democracy Act 1992 and the Helms-Burton Act of 1996.

Furthermore, we wish to reaffirm that the European Unions's strong opposition, based both on law and on principle, to the imposition of secondary boycotts and legislation with extraterritorial effect and retroactivity remains unchanged.

In November 1996, the Council of Ministers of the European Union adopted a regulation and a joint action to protect the interests of natural or legal persons resident in the European Union against the extraterritorial effects of the Helms-Burton legislation, which prohibits compliance with that legislation.

On 18 May 1998, at the European Union/United States summit in London, a package was agreed with regard to United States sanction laws including a commitment by the United States Administration to resist future extraterritorial legislation of this kind and an understanding with respect to disciplines for the strengthening of investment protection.

(A/53/PV. 37, p. 17)

Part Nine: I. B. *State territory—territory—good neighbourliness*

The following statement was issued by the EU Presidency in Luxembourg on 15 December 1997:

L'Union européenne a pris note avec intérêt des initiatives de la Fédération de Russie sur les aspects de sécurité, les mesures de confiance et la coopéeration régionale dans la région de la Mer baltique. Elle rappelle son attachement aux principes d'indivisibilité de la sécurité européenne et du droit fondamental de l'Estonie, de la Lettonie, de la Lituanie et de tous les autres Etats souverains de choisir librement leurs arrangements de sécurité.

L'Union européenne se félicite de la volonté de la Fédération de Russie de développer de manière constructive ses relations avec les Etats de cette région et notamment avec les trois Etats baltes en engageant entre Etats souverains une politique de bon voisinage, basée sur la coopération et la confiance mutuelle. L'Union européenne note avec satisfaction l'intention annoncée par le Président de la Fédération de Russie de réduire sensiblement ses forces armées dans les régions adjacentes aux Etats baltes.

L'Union européenne prend note de la disponibilité de l'Estonie, de la Lettonie et de la Lituanie à entrer dans la voie de l'établissement respectivement du renforcement des relations de bon voisinage, du dialogue politique bilatéral et, dans le cadre des enceintes existantes, de mesures de confiance et de la coopération mutuellement bénéfique dans tous les domaines d'intérêt commun.

L'Union européenne encourage fortement l'Estonie, La Lettonie, la Lituanie et la Fédération de Russie à entamer respectivement à poursuivre, tant bilatéralement que de concert avec d'autres Etats de la région, des discussions sur la coopération régionale mutuellement bénéfique dans les domaines d'intérêt commun et notamment dans les domaines économique, social et de l'environnement. Elle considère que le Conseil des Etats de la Mer Baltique a un rôle important à jouer dans la mise en œuvre de cette coopération.

L'Union européenne estime que suite à la signature de l'accord frontalier avec la Lituanie, une signature rapide d'accords similaires avec la Lettonie et l'Estonie apporterait la preuvre de la volonté de la Fédération de Russie d'entrer dans des relations basées sur la sécurité multidimensionnelle et la confiance réciproque.

(Text provided by the Presidency press service)

Part Nine: II. A. *State territory—boundaries and frontiers—delimitation*

The following question was asked of Her Majesty's Government:

Whether they believe that the Russian Federation has done all in its power, in accordance with its request for membership of the Council of Europe, 'to settle outstanding international border disputes according to the principles of international law, abiding by the existing international treaties'?

The Government Minister in the House of Lords, Lord Whitty, replied:

Her Majesty's Government share the Council of Europe's assessment of 22nd June that the Russian Federation has made significant progress towards meeting its membership commitments. There are a number of outstanding questions, including the borders with China and Japan, where Russia has worked hard to find a solution, and those with the Baltic States. The Government have encouraged Russia to sign border agreements with Latvia and Estonia, without linkage to other issues, as soon as possible. We shall continue to watch the situation closely.

The Minister was then asked whether he agreed that 'since the Baltic States regained their independence, the Russian Federation has put every obstacle in the path of recognising the borders that Lenin recognised in 1920 in the Treaty of Riga and the Treaty of Tartu respectively'. The Minister replied in part:

The 1920 treaties do not involve exactly the same borders as have now been technically agreed. Those borders have been agreed at the technical level, but the Russians are not signing the treaties. However, while we do not want any explicit linkage with other issues, it is also the case that in Estonia and Latvia the treatment of the Russian minorities is an important issue both in this context and in the context of application to join the European Union.

(HL Debs., vol. 592, col. 101: 14 July 1998)

Part Nine: III. B. *State territory—territorial sovereignty—acquisition and retention*

(See also Part Nine: III. C., below)

Giving evidence on 9 December 1997 to the Foreign Affairs Committee of the House of Commons in a review of the dependent territories, Mr P. Westmacott, Director, Americas, FCO, stated:

It is clearly understood between ourselves and the Argentine Government that every negotiation, conversation and discussion with them on South Atlantic issues is conducted under what we term the 'sovereignty umbrella'; that is, there is no implication of any kind on the part of either government as to the sovereignty of the Falkland Islands. Therefore, when we talk to the Argentines about, say, Antarctica, oil, fish, or even environmental considerations, all of that is on the clear understanding that it has no implications at all for our clearly defined position on sovereignty.

(*Parliamentary Papers*, 1997–98, HC, Paper 347: p. 37)

In the course of the same evidence, Mr Westmacott stated:

There are two fundamental principles which the new Government have espoused and which are precisely the same as those of the previous government: first, that sovereignty is not negotiable; and, secondly, that there cannot be any change in the status of the Falkland Islands without it being in accordance with the wishes of the people who live there.

(Ibid., p. 36)

In reply to the question 'if [the Secretary of State for Foreign and Commonwealth Affairs] will list those countries in the European Union which have a claim in their constitutions over the territory of another member of the Union', the Secretary of State, Mr Robin Cook, wrote:

The only such case I know of concerns the Irish Constitution, Article 2 of which asserts that the national territory consists of the whole island of Ireland. The Irish Government has undertaken to introduce and support proposals to change the constitution, so as fully to reflect the principle of consent, as part of an overall settlement in Northern Ireland.

(HC Debs., vol. 304, WA, col. *188*: 13 January 1998)

In Travel Advice for Western Sahara issued in January 1998 by the Consular Division of the FCO it is stated:

The territory of the Western Sahara is disputed between Western Morocco and the Polisario Front, and the United Kingdom regards sovereignty as undetermined.

(Text provided by the FCO)

During an address on 4 February 1998 to the Dependent Territories Association, the Secretary of State for Foreign and Commonwealth Affairs, Mr Robin Cook, stated:

I would like to use this forum to restate publicly Britain's commitment to the people of Gibraltar. We will continue to respect their wishes. There can be no change in the sovereignty over Gibraltar without their assent.

(Text provided by the FCO)

In reply to a question about the possible application of UN General Assembly Resolution No. 1514 to the former residents of Diego Garcia, the Minister of State, FCO, wrote:

The islands of the British Indian Ocean Territory are British, and have been since 1814 when ceded by France. We do not accept that they were ever an integral part of Mauritius. We do not therefore consider that General Assembly Resolution 1514, which was concerned with the partial or total disruption of the national unity and territorial integrity of a country, has any application to the Territory.

(HC Debs., vol. 307, WA, col. *192*: 24 February 1998)

In reply to a question, the Minister of State, FCO, wrote:

We have no plans to discuss the transfer or sharing of the sovereignty of the Falkland Islands with the Argentine Government. We do not regard the sovereignty of the Islands as negotiable.

(HC Debs., vol. 312, WA, col. *106*: 12 May 1998)

During a debate on the subject of oil and gas exploration in the waters of the Falkland Islands, the Government spokesman, Lord Whitty, observed:

. . . as regards the joint co-operation area, there is a willingness on the part of both Governments to state their sovereignty claims, to put them to one side and to co-operate in that area. The Falklands' territorial claim stems from the sovereignty of the Falkland Islands. Argentina has not accepted that claim. However, the British Government continue to assert it.

(HL Debs., vol. 590, col. 999: 10 June 1998)

In reply to a question, the Minister of State, FCO, wrote:

The Philippines, Malaysia and Brunei claim specific parts of the South China Sea, while China, Taiwan and Vietnam claim all of its islands, islets and reefs.

The South China Sea is regularly discussed at meetings under the auspices of the ASEAN Regional Forum and in a series of Indonesian-initiated regional workshops.

The UK takes no position on respective claims, but hopes disputes can be resolved peacefully.

(HC Debs., vol. 315, WA, col. *70*: 29 June 1998)

In the course of a debate on the subject of the impending official visit of President Menem of Argentina, the Minister of State, FCO, Mr Tony Lloyd, stated:

I shall talk in more detail later about the strength of our relationship, but first I must acknowledge the serious disagreement that remains in our relations with Argentina—over sovereignty over the Falklands. Argentina still disputes our claim. When we invited President Menem, we made it clear that the visit would not be an occasion to negotiate our sovereignty of the Falklands. Our position remains that we have no doubt about our sovereignty over the islands, and we remain fully committed to protecting the right of the Falkland islanders to determine their future.

(HC Debs., vol. 316, col. 1096: 22 July 1998)

On 13 July 1998, the Government of the Kingdom of the Netherlands, as depositary of the Convention on the Civil Aspects of International Abduction, 1980, received the following objection by the Government of the Republic of Argentina to the extension of the application of the Convention to the Falkland Islands by the UK:

The Argentine Republic disavows the designation, by the United Kingdom, of the illegitimate government of the Malvinas Islands as central authority, as well as any other act which derives or could derive from that illegitimate extension to the Malvinas Islands. The Argentine Republic reaffirms its sovereign rights over the Malvinas, South Georgia and South Sandwich Islands and its surrounding maritime areas, which form an integral part of its national territory.

On 22 July 1998, the UK Government notified the following declaration to the Netherlands Government:

With reference to the declaration made by the Republic of Argentina rejecting the extension of the Convention to the Falkland Islands, South Georgia and the South Sandwich Islands, the position of the United Kingdom is well known and remains unchanged. The United Kingdom has no doubt about its sovereignty over the Falkland Islands (which is the correct title for the territory recognised by the Administrative Power), and over South Georgia and the South Sandwich Islands and its consequent right to extend treaties to them.

(TS No. 1 (1999): Cm. 4185, pp. 23–4)

In reply to a question, the Minister of State, FCO, wrote:

We have no doubt about our sovereignty over the Falklands. This is not negotiable. There will be no change in the status of the Islands unless that is the wish of the Islanders themselves. In inviting President Menem we have made clear to the Argentines that his visit will not be an opportunity to negotiate sovereignty over the Falklands.

(HC Debs., vol. 318, WA, col. *275*: 20 October 1998)

During a television interview on 25 October 1998, the Secretary of State for Foreign and Commonwealth Affairs, Mr Robin Cook, stated:

Sovereignty will only change if the Falkland Islanders want to change it. That has been the position of this Government and the position of the previous

Governments. It will remain our position. There will be no change in the sovereignty of the islands unless the Falkland Islanders ask for it.

(Text provided by the FCO)

In reply to questions on the subject of the Falkland Islands, put after a visit to London by President Carlos Menem of Argentina, the Minister of State, FCO, wrote:

The Government of Argentina have repeatedly called on us to enter into negotiations on sovereignty over the Falkland Islands. In response we have made it clear that the United Kingdom does not regard sovereignty over the Falklands as negotiable.

. . .

. . . We do not regard the sovereignty of the Falkland Islands as negotiable. Moreover, the United Kingdom Permanent Representative to the United Nations at New York told the General Assembly on 22 September:

> 'we have no doubt about Britain's sovereignty over the Falkland Islands and the other British Dependencies in the South Atlantic'.

. . .

. . . We do not regard the sovereignty of the Falklands as negotiable. There will be no change in the status of the Islands unless that is the wish of the Islanders themselves.

. . . We did not enter into any discussion on sovereignty over the Falkland Islands during the recent visit of President Menem. The President and his delegation reiterated to us the Argentine view on the Falklands. In response we made it clear that the UK does not regard its sovereignty over the Falklands as negotiable.

(HC Debs., vol. 319, WA, col. *416*: 16 November 1998)

In reply to a question, the Minister of State, FCO, wrote:

The Government of Argentina have repeatedly asserted their view that Argentina has a claim to sovereignty over the Falkland Islands, and have called on us to enter into negotiations. In response, we have made it clear that the United Kingdom has no doubt about its sovereignty over the Falklands and does not regard this as negotiable. It remains our position that there will be no change in the status of the Falklands unless that is the wish of the Islanders themselves.

(HC Debs., vol. 321, WA, col. *161*: 1 December 1998)

Part Nine: III. C. *State territory—territorial sovereignty—loss*

(See also Part Nine: III. B. (item of 24 February 1998), above)

The following oral question was asked of Her Majesty's Government:

Whether they have any proposals to change their policy on the sovereignty of the British Indian Ocean Territory and in particular whether they will agree to the return of the former inhabitants to those islands from Mauritius?

In reply, the Parliamentary Under-Secretary of State, FCO, Baroness Symons of Vernham Dean, stated:

Our policy remains that the territory will be ceded to Mauritius when it is no longer required for defence purposes. It is possible for the Ilois to apply for contract work at the defence facility on Diego Garcia. But, given the lack of infrastructure needed to sustain inhabitation, a wider return by them to the other islands of the British Indian Ocean Territory is not a realistic prospect.

(HL Debs. vol. 586, col. 543: 24 February 1998)

Later in the debate, the Minister remarked:

The Government can reaffirm, as publicly stated in 1992 under the previous administration, that the territory will be ceded to Mauritius when no longer required for the defence purposes for which it is needed at the moment.

(Ibid., col. 545; see also UKML 1992, pp. 722–3)

Part Eleven: I. *Seas and vessels—internal waters (including ports and harbours)*

[*Editorial note*: the following two items should be regarded as part of UKMIL 1994]

A *démarche* dated 14 December 1994 from the German Embassy in Tehran (on behalf of the EU) addressed to the Ministry of Foreign Affairs of Iran read as follows:

The Embassy of the Federal Republic of Germany in Tehran presents its compliments to the Ministry of Foreign Affairs of the Islamic Republic of Iran and, on behalf of the European Union, has the honour to invite its attention to the following:

The European Union has examined the Act on the Marine Areas of the Islamic Republic of Iran in the Persian Gulf and in the Oman Sea adopted by the Islamic Republic of Iran on 2 May 1993.[1] The Act refers, in the matter of baselines, to Decree No. 2/250–67 dated 31 Tir 1352 (22 July 1973) of the Council of Ministers.

The European Union notes that the Islamic Republic of Iran has employed the method of straight baselines along practically the entire coastline, even where it is not deeply indented and cut into and there is no fringe of islands along the coast in its immediate vicinity.

The European Union considers that although the United Nations Convention on the Law of the Sea, which entered into force on 16 November 1994, does not stipulate any maximum length for baseline segments, several of the segments

[1] *Law of the Sea Bulletin*, No. 24 (1994), p. 10.

where the straight baseline method has been employed by the Islamic Republic of Iran are excessively long.

The European Union would further recall that the islands may only be used in defining internal waters where they form part of a genuine system of straight baselines or where they constitute the line which delimits a bay.

It also notes that the Islamic Republic of Iran does not consider the passage of foreign vessels through its territorial sea to be innocent if they engage in any act aimed at collecting information prejudicial to the economic interests of the Islamic Republic of Iran (although article 19, paragraph 2 (c), of the United Nations Convention on the Law of the Sea merely refers to the collecting of information to the prejudice of the defence or security of the coastal State) or any act of pollution of the marine environment contrary to the rules and regulations of the Islamic Republic of Iran (although article 19, paragraph 2 (h), of the United Nations Convention on the Law of the Sea merely refers to any act of wilful and serious pollution contrary to this Convention); that the Islamic Republic of Iran is subjecting the entry into its territorial sea of warships, submarines, nuclear-powered ships and vessels or any other floating objects or vessels carrying nuclear or other dangerous or noxious substances harmful to the environment to prior authorization, and that the Islamic Republic of Iran prohibits any activity in its exclusive economic zone and continental shelf that is inconsistent with its rights and interests.

The European Union considers that the aforementioned provisions of the Act of 2 May 1993 are not in conformity with the rules of international law, in particular articles 5, 7, 19, 56, 58 and 78 of the United Nations Convention on the Law of the Sea. Consequently, the States members of the Union reserve their position and their rights in respect of those provisions.

The acceding States, namely Austria, Finland and Sweden, endorse this démarche.

(*Law of the Sea Bulletin*, No. 30, pp. 60–1)

A *note verbale* dated 23 December 1994 from the German Embassy in Bangkok (on behalf of the EU) addressed to the Ministry of Foreign Affairs of Thailand read as follows:

The Embassy of the Federal Republic of Germany in Bangkok presents its compliments to the Ministry of Foreign Affairs of Thailand and, on behalf of the European Union, has the honour to request its kind attention to the matter set out below.

The European Union has taken cognizance of the announcement by the Prime Minister's Cabinet on 17 August 1992 concerning Thailand's straight baselines and internal waters in area 4.[1]

The European Union wishes to point out that, in accordance with international law and in particular the United Nations Convention on the Law of the Sea, which entered into force on 16 November 1994, the normal baseline for measuring the breadth of the territorial sea is the low-water line along the coast, as shown by the appropriate symbol on charts officially recognized by the coastal State, and that the coastal State may employ the method of straight baselines

[1] *Law of the Sea Bulletin*, No. 25, p. 82.

joining appropriate points only in localities where the coastline is deeply indented and cut into or if there is a fringe of islands along the coast in its immediate vicinity.

The European Union has observed that Thailand has used straight baselines along its entire coastline in area 4, even where the coastline is not deeply indented and cut into or if there is not a fringe of islands along the coast in its immediate vicinity.

The European Union considers that, even if the United Nations Convention on the Law of the Sea does not set a maximum length for baseline segments, the segments determined by Thailand are excessively long. They are in fact 81 miles long between points 1 and 2, 98 miles long between points 2 and 3 and 60 miles between points 3 and 4.

The European Union wishes finally to point out that islands may be used for defining internal waters only where they form part of a valid system of straight baselines or where they form the line delimiting a bay.

The acceding States, namely Austria, Finland and Sweden, endorse the present *démarche*.

(*Law of the Sea Bulletin*, No. 28, p. 31)

In response to questions about confrontations between the Royal Navy or Royal Gibraltar Police and the sea-borne Spanish Civil Guard since 1 May 1997, the Minister of State, FCO, wrote:

There have been no incidents during this period involving the Royal Navy or Royal Gibraltar Police and marine units of the Spanish Civil Guard. However, the Royal Navy was involved in two incidents in British waters around Gibraltar, on 22 October 1997 and 5 April 1998, involving incursions by Spanish naval patrol vessels. The Royal Gibraltar Police and the Royal Navy were involved in three incidents, on 5 July 1997 and on 13 March and 4 April 1998, involving incursions by vessels of the Spanish coastguard service.

. . .

There was no incident on 6 April. However, on 5 April, a Spanish naval patrol vessel was observed moving within British waters off Gibraltar. When the Spanish vessel failed to respond to calls, HMS Nottingham, which was approaching Gibraltar at the time, requested her to leave. The Spanish vessel was escorted out of British waters by a patrol craft of the Gibraltar Squadron. Our Ambassador in Madrid later protested to the Spanish Ministry of Foreign Affairs over this incident.

(HC Debs., vol. 312, WA, col. *363*: 19 May 1998)

Part Eleven: II. *Seas and vessels—territorial sea*

(See also Part Eleven: I. (item of 14 December 1994), above)

[*Editorial note*: the following item should be regarded as part of UKMIL 1994]

A *note verbale* dated 14 December 1994 from the German Embassy in

San José (on behalf of the EU) addressed to the Ministry of Foreign Affairs of Costa Rica read as follows:

The Embassy of the Federal Republic of Germany in San José presents its compliments to the Ministry of Foreign Affairs of the Republic of Costa Rica and, on behalf of the European Union, has the honour to request its kind attention to the matter set out below.

The European Union has taken cognizance of the regulations adopted by the Republic of Costa Rica on 15 June 1993 concerning the passage of foreign fishing vessels through its territorial sea.

It has noted that, under articles 2, 7, 8, 9 and 22 of the said regulations, the Republic of Costa Rica is subjecting the entry into and passage through its territorial sea of foreign fishing vessels to prior authorization, and that the request for such authorization must be submitted at least 24 hours before the intended date of entry into the territorial sea.

The European Union considers that these provisions are not in conformity with regulations under international law, in particular article 19 of the United Nations Convention on the Law of the Sea, which the Republic of Costa Rica ratified on 21 September 1992 and which entered into force on 16 November 1994.

The acceding States, namely Austria, Finland and Sweden, endorse the present *démarche*.

(*Law of the Sea Bulletin*, No. 28, pp. 31–2)

In reply to a question on the subject of infringement of Gibraltarian waters by Spanish fishermen and Spanish armed forces, the Minister of State, FCO, wrote:

There has been an increase in incursions into British waters around Gibraltar by Spanish fishermen since the beginning of this year. The Royal Gibraltar police has routinely requested vessels fishing illegally in British waters around Gibraltar, both Spanish and other, to refrain from doing so. In extreme cases, offenders have been arrested. Spanish military or law enforcement vessels entering British waters, unless exercising a right of innocent passage or co-operating with the Gibraltar authorities, are routinely asked to leave.

(HC Debs., vol. 318, WA, col. *86*: 26 October 1998)

In reply to a question on the subject of the protection of the integrity of British territorial waters around Gibraltar against the incursion of Spanish fishing boats and armed militia, the Minister of State, FCO, wrote:

We have assured the Governor that HMG will provide whatever support is necessary to protect the integrity of British territorial waters around Gibraltar.

(HC Debs., vol. 318, WA, col. *413*: 2 November 1998)

The Territorial Sea (Amendment) Order 1998 (Statutory Instruments 1998 No. 2564) which came into force on 15 November 1998, was accompanied by the following explanatory note:

This Order amends the Schedule to the Territorial Waters Order in Council 1964 by adding a new baseline between the Mull of Kintyre and Laggan, as well as by making minor changes to points 5, 9 and 22, which result from the publication of a new, larger scale chart of the area.

The following notice was issued by the UK Hydrographic Office on 1 January 1999:

12/99 NATIONAL CLAIMS TO MARITIME JURISDICTION.

Former Notice 2406/98 is cancelled.

The following list shows the breadth of sea (measured from the appropriate baselines) claimed respectively as territorial sea (TS), contiguous zone (CZ), exclusive economic zone (EEZ) and fishery zone (FZ), where no EEZ is claimed, as being under the state's jurisdiction. The information is compiled from various, sometimes unofficial sources, the absence of a limit from this list indicates that the information is not held.

The claims are published for information only. Her Majesty's Government does not recognise claims to territorial seas exceeding twelve nautical miles, to contiguous zones exceeding twenty four nautical miles or to exclusive economic zones and fisheries zones exceeding two hundred nautical miles.

Country	*TS*	*CZ*	*EEZ*	*FZ*
Albania[1]	12**	—	—	12
Algeria[1]*	12**	—	—	52[23]
Angola*	20	—	—	200
Antigua and Barbuda[2]*	12**	24	200	—
Argentina[1]*	12	24	200	—
Australia[1]*	12[11]	24	200	—
Australian Antarctica	12	—	—	12
Bahamas[2]*	12	—	200	—
Bahrain	12	24	—	—
Bangladesh[4]	12**	18	200	—
Barbados*	12**	—	200	—
Belgium	12	—	—	200
Belize[1]*	12[17]	—	200	—
Benin*	200	—	—	200
Brazil*[1]	12**	24	200	—
Brunei*	12	—	200	—
Bulgaria*	12**	24	200	—
Burma[1]*	12**	24	200	—
Cambodia*	12**	24	200	—
Cameroon*	50	—	—	—

Country	*TS*	*CZ*	*EEZ*	*FZ*
Canada[1]	12	24	200	—
Cape Verde Islands[2]*	12	24	200	—
Chile[1]*	12	24	200	—
China				
PRC[1]*	12**	—	—	—
ROC (Taiwan)	12	—	—	200
Colombia[1]	12	—	200	—
Comoros[2]*	12	—	200	—
Congo*	200	—	—	200
Cook Islands*	12	—	200	—
Costa Rica*	12	—	200	—
Croatia[1]*	12	—	—	—
Cuba[1]*	12	—	200	—
Cyprus*	12	—	—	12
Denmark[1]	3**	—	200	—
Greenland[1]	3	—	—	200
Færoe Islands[1]	3	—	—	200
Djibouti[1]*	12	24	200	—
Dominica*	12	24	200	—
Dominican Republic*	6	24	200	—
Ecuador[1]	200	—	—	200
Egypt[1]*	12**	24	200	—
El Salvador	200	—	—	200
Equatorial Guinea*	12**	—	200	—
Eritrea*	12[13]	—	—	—
Estonia	12**[21]	—	200	—
Federated States of Micronesia*	12	—	200	—
Fiji[2]*	12	24	200	—
Finland[1]*	12**[14, 21] 14		—	12[22]
France[1]*	12	24	200[15]	12[15]
French Antarctica	12	—	—	—
Gabon*	12	24	200	—
Gambia*	12	18	200	—
Georgia*	12	—	200	—
Germany[1]*[9]	12	—	200	—
Ghana*	12	24	200	—
Greece*	6	—	—	6
Grenada*	12**	—	200	—
Guatemala*	12	—	200	—
Guinea*	12	24	200	—
Guinea Bissau[1]*	12	—	200	—
Guyana*	12**	—	200	—

Country	*TS*	*CZ*	*EEZ*	*FZ*
Haiti*	12	24	200	—
Honduras*	12	24	200	—
Iceland[1]*	12	—	200	—
India*	12**	24	200	—
Indonesia[2]*	12	24	200	—
Iran[1]	12**	24	200	—
Iraq*	12	—	—	—
Irish Republic[1]*	12	—	—	200
Israel	12[18]	—	—	—
Italy[1]*	12	—	—	12
Ivory Coast*	12	—	200	—
Jamaica[2]*	12	—	200	—
Japan[1]*	12	—	200	—
Jordan*	3	—	—	3
Kenya[1]*	12	—	200	—
Kiribati[2]	12	—	200	—
Korea (North)	12**	—	200	—
Korea (South)[1]*	12[6]**	24	200	—
Kuwait*	12	—	—	—
Latvia	12	—	200	—
Lebanon*	12	—	—	—
Liberia	200	—	—	200
Libya[5]	12**	—	—	20
Lithuania	12	—	200	—
Madagascar[1]	12	24	200	—
Malaysia[1]*	12	—	200	—
Maldives[3]	12[3]**	—	200[3]	—
Malta[1]*	12**	24	—	25
Marshall Islands[2]*	12	24	200	—
Mauritania[1]*	12	24	200	—
Mauritius[1]*	12**	—	200	—
Mexico[1]*	12	24	200	—
Monaco[3]*	12	—	—	12
Morocco[1]	12	24	200	—
Mozambique[1]*	12	—	200	—
Namibia*	12	—	200	—
Nauru*	12	—	—	200
Netherlands[1]*	12	—	—	200
Netherlands Antilles	12	—	—	12
Aruba	12	—	—	12

Country	*TS*	*CZ*	*EEZ*	*FZ*
New Zealand*	12	—	200	—
Ross Dependency	12	—	—	—
Nicaragua	200**	—	—	200
Nigeria*	12**	—	200	—
Norway[1]*	4	—	200	—
Svalbard	4	—	—	200
Oman[1]*	12	24	200	—
Pakistan[1]*	12**	24	200	—
Panama*	200	—	—	200
Papua New Guinea[2]*	12[16]	—	200	—
Peru	200	—	—	200
Philippines[2]* [3]	12	—	200	—
Poland	12**	—	200	—
Portugal[1]*	12	—	200	—
Qatar	12	24	—	to median lines
Republic of Belau (Palau)	3	—	—	200
Romania[1]*	12**	24	200	—
Russia[1]*	12	—	200	—
St. Kitts-Nevis*	12	24	200	—
St. Lucia*	12	24	200	—
St. Vincent and the Grenadines[2]*	12**	24	200	—
Sao Tome and Principe[2]*	12	—	200	—
Saudi Arabia[1]*	12	18	—	—
Senegal[1]*	12	24	200	—
Seychelles*	12	24	200	—
Sierra Leone*	200	—	—	200
Singapore*	3	—	—	3
Slovenia*	12	—	—	—
Solomon Islands[2]*	12	—	200	—
Somalia*	200*	—	—	200
South Africa*	12	—	—	200
Spain[1]*	12	24	200[15]	to median lines[15]
Sri Lanka*	12**	24	200	—
Sudan*	12**	18	—	—
Surinam*	12	—	200	—
Sweden[1]*	12	—	200	—
Syria	35**	41	—	—
Tanzania*	12	—	200	—
Thailand[1]	12	—	200	—
Togo*	30	—	200	—

Country	*TS*	*CZ*	*EEZ*	*FZ*
Tonga*	12	—	200	—
Trinidad and Tobago[2]*	12	24	200	—
Tunisia[1]*	12	24	—	12[8]
Turkey[1]	12[7]**	—	200[19]	12[7]
Tuvalu[2]	12	24	200	—
UAE[1]	12**	24	200	—
UK[1]*	12	—	—	200
Anguilla*	3	—	—	200
Bailiwick of Guernsey*	3	—	—	12
Bailiwick of Jersey*	12	—	—	3
Bermuda*	12	—	200	—
British Antarctic Territory*	3	—	—	3
British Indian Ocean Territory*	3	—	—	200
British Virgin Islands*	3	—	—	200
Cayman Islands*	12	—	—	200
Cyprus (Sovereign Base Areas)	3	—	—	3
Falkland Islands[1]*	12	—	—	200[10]
Gibraltar*	3	—	—	3
Isle of Man*	12	—	—	12
Montserrat*	3	—	—	200
Pitcairn*	3	—	200	—
St. Helena and Dependencies*	12	—	—	200
South Georgia[1]*	12	—	200	—
South Sandwich Islands*	12	—	200	—
Turks and Caicos Islands[1]*	12	—	—	200
Ukraine[1]	12	—	200	—
Uruguay*	200[12]	—	—	200
USA	12	—	200	—
Vanuatu[2]	12	24	200	—
Venezuela[1]	12	15	200	—
Vietnam[1]*	12**	24	200	—
Western Samoa*	12	—	200	—
Yemen*	12**	24	200	—
Yugoslavia[1]*[20]	12	—	—	12
Zaire*	12	—	—	200

Limits of depedent territories have not been listed unless they differ from those of the metropolitan state.

1 employs straight baseline systems along all or a part of the coast.

2 claims archipelago status.

3 claims waters within limits defined by geographic co-ordinates not related to distance from the coastline.

[4] claims straight baseline system between points along the 18 metre isobath.
[5] claims all water south of 32° 30'N. in the Gulf of Sirte as internal waters.
[6] claims 3 nm in Korea Strait.
[7] claims 6 nm in Aegean Sea.
[8] fishery limit extends to 50 metre isobath off the Gulf of Gabes.
[9] special claim extends limit to include the deep water anchorage west of Helgoland.
[10] 150 nm in west with a rhumb line between 52° 30'.00S, 63°19'.25W and 54° 08'.68S, 60° 00'.00W.
[11] certain islands in the Torres Strait retain 3 nm territorial sea limit.
[12] freedom of navigation and overflight is not curtailed beyond 12 nm.
[13] jurisdiction claimed to the limit of the pearl and sedentary fishery grounds.
[14] Bogskar has a 3 nm territorial sea limit.
[15] does not claim an EEZ in the Mediterranean, France only claims a 12nm fishery limit and Spain a fishery limit to median lines.
[16] reduced to 3 nm in the Torres Strait area.
[17] reduced to 3 nm in the Gulf of Honduras.
[18] reduced to 3 nm off Gaza.
[19] only claims an EEZ in the Black Sea.
[20] Republic of Serbia and Montenegro.
[21] TS limit reduced in parts of the Gulf of Finland to preserve a 6nm wide high seas corridor.
[22] to maritime boundaries in areas exceeding 12 nm.
[23] reduced to 32 nm west of the longitude of Ras Térés.

* indicates a state which has ratified or acceded to the U.N. Convention of the Law of the Sea, which came into force on 16 November 1994.

** indicates a state which requires prior permission or notification for entry of foreign warships into territorial sea. The United Kingdom government does not recognise this requirement.

(Published in *Annual Summary of Admiralty Notices to Mariners in Force on 1 January 1999*, pp. 1-81–1-85)

Part Eleven: V. *Seas and vessels—contiguous zone*

(See Part Eleven: II. (table of 1 January 1999), above)

Part Eleven: VII. *Seas and vessels—exclusive or preferential fisheries zone*

(See also Part Eleven: II. (table of 1 January 1999), above)

In reply to a question on the subject of proposals for the protection of coral reefs around fishing grounds in the British Indian Ocean Territory, the Minister of State, FCO, wrote:

Administering the British Indian Ocean Territory's (BIOT) 200 mile Fisheries Conservation and Management Zone is the responsibility of the BIOT Government. It is alert to the need to provide protection for the coral reef fishery.

(HC Debs., vol. 316, WA, col. *398*: 20 July 1998)

In reply to a question, the Minister of State, FCO, wrote in part:

Argentina has no competence to authorise fishing in Falklands waters.

(HC Debs., vol. 318, WA, col. *545*: 3 November 1998)

Part Eleven: IX. A. *Seas and vessels—high seas—freedom of the high seas*

In reply to a question, the Parliamentary Under-Secretary of State, FCO, wrote in part:

The freedom of the high seas, which is codified in the United Nations Convention on the Law of the Sea, includes freedom of navigation for military vessels and the right to engage in lawful military activities.

(HL Debs., vol. 588, *WA 135*: 8 April 1998)

Part Twelve: II. A. *Air space, outer space and Antarctica—outer space and celestial bodies—status and limits*

In reply to the question whether Her Majesty's Government consider that it is desirable to set up an internationally agreed framework to develop and enforce international law in space, the Parliamentary Under-Secretary of State, FCO, wrote:

An international framework governing such activities in space already exists and is primarily based upon the United Nations Treaty on Principles Governing the Activities of States in the Exploration and Use of Outer Space, including the moon and other celestial bodies.

Details of this treaty and other relevant international agreements are contained in the United Nations publication *Treaties and Principles on Outer Space* . . .

(HL Debs., vol. 593, *WA 41*: 3 September 1998)

The following question was asked of Her Majesty's Government:

Whether they recognise any definitions of the terms 'airspace', 'outer space', 'deep space' and 'interstellar space'; whether they will detail such definitions; and whether these are the same definitions as used by the United States Government?

In reply, the Parliamentary Under-Secretary of State, Department of Trade and Industry, wrote:

HMG recognise and use the term 'airspace'. The principle of airspace sovereignty is defined in the Chicago Convention on International Civil Aviation (1944), which states that a country has complete and exclusive sovereignty over the airspace above its territory, including its territorial sea. This airspace starts immediately above the surface of the earth.

There is no internationally agreed definition of where 'outer space' starts. The most commonly used boundary between airspace and outer space is functional. This means, for instance, that the launching of satellites or other space objects is deemed to be an 'outer space' activity and that the flight of aircraft is considered to be an activity in airspace. The use of 'outer space' is governed by the United Nations Treaty on Principles Governing the Activities of States in the Exploration and Use of Outer Space, including the Moon and other Celestial Bodies (known as the Outer Space Treaty, 1967) which covers all activity beyond sovereign airspace. Both the UK and the US have ratified the Outer Space Treaty and UK legislation regulating such activity (the Outer Space Act 1986) is based on its principles.

'Deep space' and 'interstellar space' are terms sometimes used by space scientists and astronomers. 'Deep space' is a phrase often used to describe space missions to other planets, beyond the combined gravitational field of the earth and the moon. 'Interstellar space' is not commonly used but could, for example, denote the space between stars within a galaxy.

(HL Debs., vol. 593, *WA 130*: 19 October 1998)

Part Thirteen: I. *International responsibility—general concept*

On 9 February 1998, the UK Permanent Mission to the UN in New York presented to the UN Secretary-General the comments of the UK Government on the draft articles on State responsibility prepared by the International Law Commission. The comments contained the following observation:

3. Given the fundamental place occupied by State responsibility in the system of international law, the United Kingdom considers it essential that the outcome of the project should encourage stability and certainty in international relations. To warrant approval, the principles must be sufficiently flexible to accommodate changes in the nature of international legal relations, such as those arising from the development of international environmental law. Flexibility for future development should however be clearly distinguished from innovation. Conscious innovation may indeed be required, for example in respect of new problems or areas of concern; but such innovation is most effectively achieved by the considered negotiation of specific instruments in particular contexts, and not by changing the underlying principles of international responsibility. To change the underlying principles may have unpredictable effects and may prove to be undesirable in particular contexts. Accordingly, the United Kingdom believes it to be of crucial importance that the Commission's draft, in its final form, reflect the established principles of customary international law grounded in the practice of States.

4. The United Kingdom Government do not consider it necessary or helpful to discuss in these comments the theoretical debates concerning the nature of State responsibility. States may come to an agreement on legal principles by a variety of routes; but the crucial question is whether the principles do in fact command the assent and respect of the international community. It is, therefore, necessary that the draft articles should not contain elements that render them unacceptable in principle to a significant part of the international community. It is also necessary that the draft articles are sufficiently practical and resilient to work effectively as the framework for day-to-day international relations. On both grounds the United Kingdom Government have concerns about parts of the current draft.

5. The United Kingdom Government consider that there is room for considerable improvement in the drafting of the articles. Some draft articles (such as draft articles 1, 2, 16 and 51) might usefully be combined with neighbouring draft articles or even omitted entirely. Other draft articles (such as draft articles 18, 20–26) introduce a fineness of detail and distinction which, while valuable as an analytical tool, is unnecessarily complex, and unhelpful, in an instrument that is to lay down the principles of responsibility applicable in the daily dealings between States. In yet other cases (notably the provisions on international crimes and certain provisions on countermeasures and on settlement of disputes) it seems necessary to jettison elements of the draft in their entirety if there is to be any hope of a final product which reflects what States would find acceptable.

(Text provided by the FCO)

Part Thirteen: II. A. *International responsibility—general issues of international responsibility—the elements of responsibility*

On 9 February 1998, the UK Permanent Mission to the UN in New York presented to the UN Secretary-General the comments of the UK Government on the draft articles on State responsibility presented by the International Law Commission. In its comments, the UK Government observed:

34. Draft article 5 establishes that acts of organs that are, under the municipal law of a State, organs of that State are acts of that State. If that law itself designates the organ as an organ of the State, it may be appropriate for international law to adopt a similar position. If, however, the municipal law of a State does *not* treat an organ as part of the State, it does not necessarily follow that the organ's acts are not attributable to the State. The municipal law cannot have determinative effect in this context: attribution is a matter for international law. The United Kingdom also observes that the principles developed in the context of State immunity are not necessarily applicable in the context of State responsibility. The United Kingdom Government hope that the International Law Commission will clarify these points in the Commentary, and consider whether any change to the drafting of the draft articles is necessary.

(Text provided by the FCO)

Speaking on 27 October 1998 in the Sixth Committee of the UN General Assembly debating the annual report of the International Law Commission, the FCO Legal Adviser, Sir Franklin Berman, stated:

Let me turn briefly to the two specific points on which the Commission has sought States' guidance:

i. The Commission asks [in paragraph 35] whether all conduct of an organ of a State is attributable to that State under article 5 of the draft articles, irrespective of the *jure gestionis* or *jure imperii* nature of the conduct.

The short answer to this, in our view, is yes. The question whether acts are attributable to the State is independent of the question of the nature of those acts. All acts of an organ of the State, when acting officially, are attributable to the State. There is no relationship, as the terms used in the question might suggest, between whether an act is attributable to a State and whether the State enjoys immunity from the jurisdiction of foreign courts.

. . .

(Text provided by the FCO; see also A/C.6/53/SR. 14, p. 3)

Part Thirteen: II. B. *International responsibility—general issues of international responsibility—factors excluding responsibility*

On 9 February 1998, the Permanent Mission of the UK to the UN in New York presented to the Secretary-General of the UN the comments of the UK Government on the International Law Commission's draft articles on State responsibility. In its comments, the UK Government wrote:

CHAPTER V: CIRCUMSTANCES PRECLUDING WRONGFULNESS

Article 29: Consent

77. The decision of the International Law Commission that the exculpatory 'defences' in draft articles 29–34 should preclude wrongfulness and not merely preclude responsibility entails the conclusion that a State that takes action which causes loss to another State or its nationals is, because its action is not unlawful, under no duty to pay compensation. The United Kingdom Government consider that this is entirely appropriate in circumstances where a State is acting with the consent of the State harmed (draft article 29) or is exercising in accordance with international law its right to take countermeasures (draft article 30) or its right of self-defence (draft article 34). In the case of consent validly given, there is no violation of international law, and therefore no question of wrongfulness should arise. In the case of exercises of the right to take countermeasures or to act in self-defence, the conduct of the State is by definition a consequence, specifically permitted by international law, of a prior wrongful act by another State. It is appropriate that a State that exercises these rights given to it by international law to protect its interests against the wrongful

acts of another State should not be regarded as acting wrongfully, any more than it would if it were to exercise any other right under international law.

78. The United Kingdom Government also accept that it might be appropriate to regard as being in principle 'not wrongful' conduct resulting from irresistible forces creating a situation in which performance of the international obligation in question is materially impossible (draft article 31, because the 'conduct' is by definition involuntary.

79. The United Kingdom Government think, however, that it would be useful to consider whether this approach to defences in international responsibility should operate in exactly the same manner in the context of the remaining circumstances precluding wrongfulness: i.e., distress (draft article 32), and necessity (draft article 33). In those cases, the State has a choice as to whether it complies with its international obligations or, in order to protect important interests, violates those obligations. In those circumstances, it may be preferable to adopt the view that the defences may excuse the wrongful conduct and in some circumstances release the State in question from the duty to make reparation for injury caused by it, but do not entirely preclude the *wrongfulness* of the conduct. On this basis the legal obligation would clearly survive, as would the obligation in principle to make reparation for any injury caused, and the State would be under a clear duty to return to compliance with the obligation. This possibility is one that the United Kingdom Government hope the Commission will consider.

. . .

80. The United Kingdom Government support the principle in draft article 29(1), that consent precludes the wrongfulness of (or at least, responsibility for) an act, but consider that it would be helpful for the International Law Commission to give further consideration to two issues.

81. The first is the question of the person or organ by which the consent of the State must be given. The Commentary (97–02583, p. 216, paragraph 15) suggests that consent may validly be expressed by anyone whose acts are attributable to the State. The United Kingdom Government, however, consider that there is no necessary identity between the category of persons whose acts are attributable to the State and the category of persons competent to bind the State. Minor officials, for example, belong to the first but not the second category. It is hoped that the International Law Commission might give further consideration to this question. In particular, the questions of the extent to which consent may be given on behalf of a State by (a) minor officials, and (b) insurrectionists who subsequently become the government of the State, require clarification.

82. A further aspect of the question, who may give the State's consent?, arises in the context of revolutionary groups. Under draft article 15, the acts of insurrectional movements that become the new government of a State are to be regarded as acts of the State. A desire for theoretical consistency might suggest that expressions of 'consent' by insurrectional governments be treated in the same way. Typically, that consent might relate to intervention by forces of a third State in support of the insurrection, or to the non-fulfilment of a treaty obligation owed by a third State to the insurrectionists' State. It is generally neater to have all aspects of international responsibility that concern the acts of insurrectionists determined on the basis of the same principles. The policy considerations are, however, different in the two cases.

83. It is desirable that a new government should not be able to escape international responsibility for the acts that brought it to power, especially as there is a particular likelihood of injury to foreign States and nationals during an insurrection. On the other hand, to entitle, as it were, successful insurrectionists to consent to departures from legal obligations owed to their national State might be thought to promote the non-observance of such obligations at a critical juncture for the State, and even to encourage intervention by third States in its internal affairs. It might, therefore, be thought preferable, in the interest of stability, to adopt the position that only the incumbent government may consent to departures from legal obligations. Certainly, the new insurrectional government could have no cause for complaint if third States did adhere to their legal obligations to the insurrectional State.

84. The policy argument against counting acts of successful insurrectionists as consent on behalf of the State is supported by another practical consideration. The Vienna Convention on the Law of Treaties makes no provision for the conclusion of international agreements by insurrectionists; and to the extent that the Vienna Convention is relevant to cases of insurrection, its provisions (notably article 8 and 46) clearly suggest that insurrectionists cannot make treaties binding on the State. It is hard to see why insurrectionists should be entitled to achieve a modification of duties owed to their State by way of consent to departure from those obligations, when they could not do so by concluding a treaty modifying the same obligations. There are, then, arguments on both sides of this issue. There does not seem to be a decisive argument favouring either side. It is, however, desirable that the problem be addressed further by the Commission.

85. The second issue concerns the manner in which consent may be expressed. There are emergency situations in which it is appropriate to allow a State to take action to protect persons in another State from imminent and serious danger (for example, from risk of death from fire or flood), but where there may be insufficient time to obtain the consent of that other State. There may be a need to address, in the draft article itself or in the Commentary, the possibility of implied or retrospective consent. The United Kingdom Government hope that the International Law Commission will consider whether it is possible, either in draft article 29 or elsewhere, to make express provision for a right to take such humanitarian action in emergency situations, with appropriate safeguards to protect the interests of the State in whose territory the action is taken.

86. The United Kingdom Government are unable to support the inclusion of draft article 29(2) which precludes consent to a rule of *jus cogens*. The uncertainty which continues to surround the content of the category of *jus cogens*, and the lack of any practical mechanism for resolving that uncertainty, make the provision impractical.

. . .

Article 31: Force majeure and fortuitous event

88. The principle of the defence of *force majeure* and fortuitous event in draft article 31 is not controversial, but the United Kingdom Government consider that it should be explicitly confined to circumstances in which (a) there is a

situation in which it is materially impossible for the State to comply with its international obligations, which situation (b) derives directly from factors or events that are both (c) exceptional and (d) beyond the control of the State. For instance, there is a clear distinction between circumstances where a State loses control of part of its territory, to insurgents for example, and circumstances where the State is unable to compel persons within the territory which *is* under its control to conduct themselves as they ought—perhaps because key workers are on strike. The former is an exceptional circumstance, and if it causes a State not to comply with its obligations it is appropriate that the wrongfulness be precluded. The latter is a constant risk which affects all States, all of the time; and it should not form the basis of a circumstance precluding wrongfulness. It is not apparent from the Commentary that the Commission has taken this view; indeed, it may be that the Commission has decided not to take this view . . . . The United Kingdom Government urge the Commission to consider the explicit adoption of this distinction, either in the Commentary or in the draft article itself.

Article 32: Distress

89. The United Kingdom Government support the principle of the defence of distress, set out in this draft article, but recall the comment made in relation to draft article 29, that it is desirable that an explicit provision be made somewhere in the draft articles for emergency humanitarian action to be taken without risk of international responsibility.

90. In draft article 32, the reference to the availability of a defence in circumstances where an international obligation is breached in order to save the lives of 'persons entrusted to [the] care' of the actor limits the applicability of the draft article in humanitarian situations. There is no defence if the conduct is aimed at saving the lives of persons who have not been entrusted to the care of the actor, whether or not there was anyone else in the vicinity who could have saved those lives. The United Kingdom Government recognise the danger that the extension of the principle of distress might lead to abuse. Nonetheless, they consider that the benefits of facilitating humanitarian action have to be balanced against the risk of abuse, and that it would be regrettable if no formula could be devised to enable cross-frontier actions to save life *in extremis*.

Article 33: State of necessity

91. The United Kingdom Government view with extreme circumspection the introduction of a right to depart from international obligations in circumstances where the State has judged it necessary to do so in order to protect an interest that it deems 'essential'. A defence of necessity would be open to very serious abuse across the whole range of international relations. There is a grave risk that the provision would weaken the rule of law.

92. The United Kingdom accepts all the same that further consideration is required as to whether there is a need for a provision concerning action taken by a State to cope with environmental emergencies which pose an immediate threat

to its territory (as envisaged in the Commentary, 97–02583, p. 246 paragraph 16). If so, this would be akin to *force majeure* or distress, and might be considered in that context. It would not however, in the United Kingdom's view, provide in itself a sufficient basis for any wider provision concerning necessity.

(Text provided by the FCO)

Part Thirteen: II. C. I. *International responsibility—general issues of international responsibility—procedure—diplomatic protection*

Speaking on 27 October 1998 in the Sixth Committee of the UN General Assembly debating the annual report of the International Law Commission, the FCO Legal Adviser, Sir Franklin Berman, observed:

As to the topic of *Diplomatic Protection*, while noting the Commission's view, as the Chairman put it yesterday, that 'hardly any topic . . . was as ripe for codification', a sense of perplexity, or even disappointment, remains. Certainly the idea put forward by the Special Rapporteur, that Diplomatic Protection should now be recognised not as an inter-State institution of international law but of an arrangement under which the State acts as agent for its injured national, would not be codification at all but a radical reformulation from which it is hard to see what benefit would flow.

(Text provided by the FCO: see also A/C.6/53/SR. 14, pp. 2–3)

Part Thirteen: II. C. 1. (b). *International responsibility—general issues of international responsibility—procedure—diplomatic protection—exhaustion of local remedies*

On 9 February 1998, the UK Permanent Mission to the UN in New York presented to the UN Secretary-General the comments of the UK Government on the draft articles of the International Law Commission on the topic of State responsibility. In its comments, the UK Government made the following observations:

The Exhaustion of Local Remedies Principle

30. In the view of the United Kingdom Government the draft articles are in one respect based upon an incorrect interpretation of the rules of customary international law. The Commentary on certain draft articles, notably draft article 22, indicated that the effect of the rule concerning the exhaustion of local remedies is that no international wrong arises until the moment that the local remedies have definitively failed to redress the wrong. The United Kingdom Government are not persuaded that this is correct. They hope that the International Law Commission will give further consideration to the question whether as a matter of customary international law the exhaustion of local

remedies is not merely a procedural precondition to the making of an international claim, rather than a precondition to substantive responsibility arising. This is a question of some practical importance, particularly in the context of time-limited compromissory clauses and of the determination of the quantum of compensation due for breaches of international obligations. It is desirable that the draft articles accurately reflect current customary law on this point.

. . .

Article 22: Exhaustion of local remedies

58. The views of the United Kingdom Government concerning the exhaustion of local remedies principle have already been noted. Draft article 22 adopts the view that the duty to exhaust local remedies is not a 'merely procedural' rule. In the United Kingdom Government's view, however, the duty to exhaust local remedies is indeed merely a procedural rule. There are rules of international law which are, in the International Law Commission's terminology, 'obligations of conduct'. The rule forbidding the physical mistreatment of aliens by persons whose actions are imputable to the State is an example. In such cases, the breach plainly arises at the time that the State fails to act in conformity with the rule. Where the alien initially seeks a remedy in the local courts, the claim before the local courts is a step in the exhaustion of the local remedies. It takes place after the violation has occurred and before a claim in respect of the violation may be pursued on the international plane.

59. There may appear to be exceptional cases in which unsuccessful recourse to the local courts is indeed necessary in order to 'complete' the violation of international law. Thus, some rules of international law permit what might at first appear to be 'mistreatment' of aliens and their property, provided that the alien is compensated. The rules permitting the expropriation of alien property for a public purpose are an example. On a proper analysis of the precise nature of the obligation in these rules, however, it is clear that they do not constitute exceptions to the analysis applied above to 'obligations of conduct'. It is true that the breach does not arise until local procedures have definitely failed to deliver proper compensation (or, more accurately in the case of expropriation, have so failed within the time limits implied by the requirement of promptness). But this is not because the breach arises only when local remedies have been exhausted. It is because the duty is, strictly, not to refrain from expropriation for public purposes, but to compensate (by whatever procedure the State might choose) if property is expropriated—or, to put it another way, to refrain from uncompensated expropriations.

60. The category of rules of this second kind, where the breach arises only after a definitive position is taken by the courts or other organs of the State, is approximately the same as the International Law Commission's category of 'obligations of result'. The International Law Commission has drafted article 22 so as to make plain that it applies only to such obligations. Draft article 22 states that there is a breach only if local remedies have been exhausted without redress. But this embodies, in the view of the United Kingdom Government, a fundamental conceptual confusion. The recourse to 'local remedies' is in this

context not at all of the same nature as recourse to local remedies as a procedural precondition for the taking over of the individual's claim and its pursuit on the international plane by his national State. The United Kingdom Government do not accept the approach adopted by the International Law Commission in draft article 22. Indeed, they consider that draft article 21 states all that is necessary in this context in relation to obligations of result, and that draft article 22 could advantageously be omitted.

(Text provided by the FCO)

Part Thirteen: II. D. 1. *International responsibility—general issues of international responsibility—consequences of responsibility—reparation*

In reply to a question, the Government Minister in the House of Lords wrote:

We have already told the Government of Zimbabwe that we expect any acquisition of land to proceed in accordance with Zimbabwe's laws, its constitution and its international obligations. Zimbabwe's 1992 Land Acquisition Act requires the Government to pay compensation, and provides access to the courts if the amount of compensation is disputed.

(HL Debs., vol. 584, *WA 257*: 22 January 1998)

On 9 February 1998, the UK Permanent Mission to the UN in New York presented to the UN Secretary-General the comments of the UK Government on the draft articles on State responsibility prepared by the International Law Commission. In its comments, the UK Government wrote:

113. The United Kingdom Government consider that it would be helpful to have a statement of principle concerning the making of reparation and that the point should be made that an injured State cannot *insist* upon a particular kind or level of reparation. They believe that draft article 42 could usefully be modified. There might be a separate article stipulating that the right to reparation, in whatever form, is to be implemented taking into account, *inter alia*, the importance of the rule and of the interest protected by it, the seriousness of the breach (and perhaps the degree of negligence or wilful misconduct involved), and the need to maintain international peace and security and to bring about settlement of international disputes in conformity with principles of international law and justice. The article might then state that when a determination is made as to the precise form that reparation should take, account should be taken of the principle that the form of reparation imposed should not impose a burden on the State making reparation out of all proportion to the benefit that the injured State would derive from some other form of reparation.

. . .

Article 44: Compensation

115. The United Kingdom Government considers that, to the extent that it represents the actual loss suffered by the claimant, the payment of interest is not an optional matter but an obligation. Draft article 44 should be amended accordingly.

(Text provided by the FCO)

On 24 April 1998, the Governments of the UK and Uganda concluded an Agreement for the Promotion and Protection of Investments. Its Articles 4 and 5 read as follows:

ARTICLE 4

Compensation for Losses

(1) Nationals or companies of one Contracting Party whose investments in the territory of the other Contracting Party suffer losses owing to war or other armed conflict, revolution, a state of national emergency, revolt, insurrection or riot in the territory of the latter Contracting Party shall be accorded by the latter Contracting Party treatment, as regards restitution, indemnification, compensation or other settlement, no less favourable than that which the latter Contracting Party accords to its own nationals or companies or to nationals or companies of any third State. Resulting payments shall be freely transferable.
(2) Without prejudice to paragraph (1) of this Article, nationals or companies of one Contracting Party who in any of the situations referred to in that paragraph suffer losses in the territory of the other Contracting Party resulting from:
(a) requisitioning of their property by its forces or authorities, or
(b) destruction of their property by its forces or authorities, which was not caused in combat action or was not required by the necessity of the situation, shall be accorded restitution or adequate compensation. Resulting payments shall be freely transferable.

ARTICLE 5

Expropriation

(1) Investments of nationals or companies of either Contracting Party shall not be nationalised, expropriated or subjected to measures having effect equivalent to nationalisation or expropriation (hereinafter referred to as 'expropriation') in the territory of the other Contracting Party except for a public purpose related to the internal needs of that Party on a non-discriminatory basis and against prompt, adequate and effective compensation. Such compensation shall amount to the genuine value of the investment expropriated immediately before the expropriation or before the impending expropriation became public knowledge, whichever is the earlier, shall include interest at a normal commercial rate until the date of payment, shall be made without delay, be effectively realisable and be freely transferable. The national or company affected shall have a right, under the law of the Contracting Party making the expropriation, to prompt review, by

judicial or other independent authority of that Party of his or its case and of the valuation of his or its investment in accordance with the principles set out in this paragraph.
(2) Where a Contracting Party expropriates the assets of a company which is incorporated or constituted under the law in force in any part of its own territory, and in which nationals or companies of the other Contracting Party own shares, it shall ensure that the provisions of paragraph (1) of this Article are applied to the extent necessary to guarantee prompt, adequate and effective compensation in respect of their investment to such nationals or companies of the other Contracting Party who are owners of those shares.

(TS No. 33 (1998); Cm 4037)

In the course of a debate on the subject of the respect for property rights by States in eastern Europe, the Government spokesman in the House of Lords, Lord Whitty, stated:

As noble Lords are aware, it is a basic principle of international law that a state ought not to expropriate the property of foreign nationals except for genuine public purposes, and with prompt, adequate, and effective compensation. The Government expect all countries to abide by those principles and, in particular, to respect the property rights of British nationals. That is particularly true, of course, of our fellow members of the EU and the 10 former Communist countries of central Europe which have embraced the free market and private property, and have sought membership of the EU.

(HL Debs., vol. 589, col. 373: 29 April 1998)

On 26 November 1998, the Minister of State, FCO, Mr Derek Fatchett, commented on a decision of a court in Japan rejecting a claim for compensation brought against the Japanese Government by British former prisoners of war. The Minister stated in part:

We are not in a position to comment on the detail of a judicial decision taken in another country. The Government's legal advice is clear: we are not able to re-open the question of compensation under the 1951 Peace Treaty. More than 40 years ago, the then Government decided against pursuing the matter further. This is a matter of public record.

(Text provided by the FCO)

Part Thirteen: III. A. 1. *International responsibility—responsible entities—States—criminal responsibility*

On 9 February 1998, the UK Permanent Mission to the UN in New York presented to the UN Secretary-General the comments of the UK Government on the draft articles on State responsibility prepared by the International Law Commission. The comments contained the following observations:

International crimes

11. The United Kingdom remains firmly persuaded that it would be damaging and undesirable to attempt to distinguish in the draft articles between international delicts in general and so-called 'international crimes'. This view has been expounded over many years in the debates in the Sixth Committee on the Commission's annual Reports. The United Kingdom has seen nothing to cause it to deviate from the views then expressed; quite the contrary. In essence therefore, the position of the United Kingdom remains that the provisions concerning international crimes should be omitted from the draft articles. While reaffirming that position, the United Kingdom wishes merely to add the following.

12. There is no basis in customary international law for the concept of international crimes. Nor is there a clear need for it. Indeed, it is entirely possible that the concept would impede, rather than facilitate, the condemnation of egregious breaches of the law. The proposed draft articles are likely to make it more difficult for the international community to frame the terms of the condemnation so as to match precisely the particular circumstances of each case of wrongdoing. By establishing the category of international crimes, the danger of polarising moral and political judgments into a crude choice between crimes and delicts is increased. There is a real possibility of dissipating international concern with the causes and consequences of wrongful acts by focussing debates on the question whether or not those acts should be classified as international crimes, rather than on the substance of the wrong. There is also a serious risk that the category will become devalued, as cases of greater and lesser wrongs are put together in the same category, or as some wrongs are criminalised while others of equal gravity are not.

13. The legal circumstances of the designation of an international wrongful act as an international crime appear to the United Kingdom Government to be of little practical significance and, to the extent that they do have significance, to be unworkable.

. . .

17. Given the controversial nature of the concept, and the possibility that its adoption might lead to adverse consequences, the United Kingdom is opposed to the creation of a separate category on international crimes. Further, more detailed, criticisms of the Commission's proposal are made below.

Later in its comments, the UK Government wrote:

Article 19: International crimes and international delicts

50. Draft article 19 introduces the controversial category of international crimes. It was indicated above that the United Kingdom Government do not support this provision. Without prejudice to that position, they wish to make two more specific points concerning the approach adopted in draft article 19.

51. First, the category of international crimes depends upon the identification of international obligations that are 'so essential for the protection of fundamental interests of the international community' that their breach is recognised by that

community as a crime. Yet there is no coherent account given of the manner in which 'the international community as a whole' may 'recognise' such rules. How, and by whom, is it to be determined what 'the international community as a whole' is, and whether it has recognised a particular norm as 'so essential for the protection of fundamental interests' as to render its breach an international crime?

52. Secondly, there is a tension between paragraphs (2) and (3) of draft article 19. Paragraph (2) defines a crime as 'the breach by a State' of what might be called an 'essential obligation'. Paragraph (3) states that crimes may result from a '*serious* breach' of certain obligations. It should at least be made clear whether it is the importance of the rule, or the seriousness of the conduct violating the rule, which is decisive. It seems probable that the International Law Commission intended the approach represented by paragraph (3) to be followed, since the Commentary emphasises that a breach of a rule of *jus cogens* does not necessarily constitute an international crime. If that be so, and the essential question is not the nature of the rule but rather the seriousness of the conduct constituting the violation, it may be asked again whether there is a need for a distinct category of 'international crimes'.

(Text provided by the FCO)

Part Thirteen: III. A. 2. *International responsibility—responsible entities—States—responsibility other than criminal*

In reply to a question, the Minister of State, FCO, wrote:

We have no plans to ask the Argentines for compensation for the damage done during the Falklands conflict.

(HC Debs., vol. 312, WA, col. *531*: 21 May 1998)

The following question was asked of Her Majesty's Government:

Whether they and the Governments of France, Germany, Italy and other countries which have taken part in peacekeeping operations approved by the United Nations are considering taking the Government of the United States to court over the monies due to them from the unpaid United States dues to the United Nations?

In reply, the Parliamentary Under-Secretary of State, FCO, wrote:

No. However, we have made it clear to the US Administration on several occasions that we expect the US to pay its UN arrears and future contributions promptly, in full and without conditions. The EU Troika, led by the UK as Presidency, reiterated this to the US Administration on 9 June.

(HL Debs., vol. 591, *WA 41*: 25 June 1998)

In reply to a question, the Minister of State, FCO, wrote:

The disciplines on investment in expropriated property agreed as part of the EU/US Understanding signed on 18 May include a denial of government support to new investment in properties expropriated in contravention of international law. Each case would have to be considered on an individual basis. There are no specific provisions concerning properties which belonged to individuals who were Cuban citizens at the time of their expropriation and who subsequently became US citizens.

(HC Debs., vol. 316, WA, col. *31*: 13 July 1998)

Part Thirteen: III. D. *International responsibility—responsible entities—individuals (including corporations)*

The following question was asked of Her Majesty's Government:

Why they have not detained General Augusto Pinochet, former dictator of Chile, now on a visit to Britain, using the powers in the Criminal Justice Act 1988, which embody in our law the obligation under Article 6 of the Convention Against Torture and Other Cruel, Inhuman and Degrading Treatment or Punishment, to take into custody and prosecute any person within our jurisdiction who is alleged to have committed torture or an act which constitutes complicity or participating in torture?

In reply, the Minister of State, Home Office, wrote:

The offence of torture contained in Section 134 of the Criminal Justice Act 1988 provides that a United Kingdom court has jurisdiction to prosecute for an offence of torture committed by any person of any nationality committed in any part of the world. The police may arrest or detain a suspect in connection with an offence under Section 134 only if they have sufficient evidence to do so. If the noble Lord believes he has evidence of an offence under Section 134, he should place it in the hands of the police.

(HL Debs., vol. 593, *WA 199*: 26 October 1998)

Part Fourteen: II. A. *Pacific settlement of disputes—means of settlement—negotiations*

On 15 May 1998, the Minister of State, FCO, Mr Tony Lloyd, made the following statement as a EU Presidency Statement:

The EU is concerned at reports of recent military clashes in the Ethiopian/Eritrean border region.

We urge both governments to show the utmost restraint and to resolve any disagreement by peaceful means.

(Text provided by the FCO)

In reply to a question, the Parliamentary Under-Secretary of State, FCO, wrote:

We are gravely concerned by the border conflict between Ethiopia and Eritrea, which undermines the stability of a region already prone to conflict. We have deplored the escalation of hostilities and the loss of innocent civilian lives on both sides. We have urged both parties to implement an immediate ceasefire, and to solve this dispute by peaceful negotiations. In this respect, we and our partners on the United Nations Security Council support the US/Rwandan facilitation efforts, together with those of the OAU.

(HL Debs., vol. 591, *WA 41*: 25 June 1998)

In the course of answering oral questions on the subject of Kashmir, the Minister of State, FCO, Mr Derek Fatchett, stated:

The international community is naturally concerned about the developments in relation to Kashmir and the threats that those pose for regional stability and security. The best current approach is through the bilateral talks between India and Pakistan. We wish those well. The obvious parties to resolve these difficulties are the two Governments. If they can come to an understanding, that is the best way for the peace of the area and for the people of Kashmir.

(HC Debs., vol. 318, col. 149: 27 October 1998)

Part Fourteen: II. F. 2. *Peaceful settlement of disputes—means of settlement—arbitration—arbitral tribunals and commissions other than the Permanent Court of Arbitration*

On 24 April 1998, the Governments of the UK and Uganda concluded an Agreement for the Promotion and Protection of Investments. Its Articles 8 and 9 read as follows:

ARTICLE 8

Reference to International Centre for Settlement of Investment Disputes

(1) Each Contracting Party hereby consents to submit to the International Centre for the Settlement of Investment Disputes (hereinafter referred to as 'the Centre') for settlement by conciliation or arbitration under the Convention on the Settlement of Investment Disputes between States and Nationals of Other States opened for signature at Washington on 18 March 1965 any legal dispute arising between that Contracting Party and a national or company of the other Contracting Party concerning an investment of the latter in the territory of the former.
(2) A company which is incorporated or constituted under the law in force in the territory of one Contracting Party and in which before such a dispute arises the majority of shares are owned by nationals or companies of the other Contracting Party shall in accordance with Article 25(2)(b) of the Convention be treated for the purposes of the Convention as a company of the other Contracting Party.
(3) If any such dispute should arise and agreement cannot be reached within three months between the parties to this dispute through pursuit of local remedies or otherwise, then, if the national or company affected also consents in

writing to submit the dispute to the Centre for settlement by conciliation or arbitration under the Convention, either party may institute proceedings by addressing a request to that effect to the Secretary-General of the Centre as provided in Articles 28 and 36 of the Convention. In the event of disagreement as to whether conciliation or arbitration is the more appropriate procedure the national or company affected shall have the right to choose. The Contracting Party which is a party to the dispute shall not raise as an objection at any stage of the proceedings or enforcement of an award the fact that the national or company which is the other party to the dispute has received in pursuance of an insurance contract an indemnity in respect of some or all of his or its losses.

(4) Neither Contracting Party shall pursue through the diplomatic channel any dispute referred to the Centre unless:

(a) the Secretary-General of the Centre, or a conciliation commission or an arbitral tribunal constituted by it, decides that the dispute is not within the jurisdiction of the Centre; or

(b) the other Contracting Party should fail to abide by or to comply with any award rendered by an arbitral tribunal.

ARTICLE 9

Disputes between the Contracting Parties

(1) Disputes between the Contracting Parties concerning the interpretation or application of this Agreement should, if possible, be settled through the diplomatic channel.

(2) If a dispute between the Contracting Parties cannot thus be settled, it shall upon the request of either Contracting Party be submitted to an arbitral tribunal.

(3) Such an arbitral tribunal shall be constituted for each individual case in the following way. Within two months of the receipt of the request for arbitration, each Contracting Party shall appoint one member of the tribunal. Those two members shall then select a national of a third State who on approval by the two Contracting Parties shall be appointed Chairman of the tribunal. The Chairman shall be appointed within two months from the date of appointment of the other two members.

(4) If within the periods specified in paragraph (3) of this Article the necessary appointments have not been made, either Contracting Party may, in the absence of any other agreement, invite the President of the International Court of Justice to make any necessary appointments. If the President is a national of either Contracting Party or if he is otherwise prevented from discharging the said function, the Vice-President shall be invited to make the necessary appointments. If the Vice-President is a national of either Contracting Party or if he too is prevented from discharging the said function, the Member of the International Court of Justice next in seniority who is not a national of either Contracting Party shall be invited to make the necessary appointments.

(5) The arbitral tribunal shall reach its decision by a majority of votes. Such decision shall be binding on both Contracting Parties. Each Contracting Party shall bear the cost of its own member of the tribunal and of its representation in the arbitral proceedings; the cost of the Chairman and the remaining costs shall

be borne in equal parts by the Contracting Parties. The tribunal may, however, in its decision direct that a higher proportion of costs shall be borne by one of the two Contracting Parties, and this award shall be binding on both Contracting Parties. The tribunal shall determine its own procedure.

(TS No. 33 (1998); Cm. 4037)

On 21 October 1998, the Presidency on behalf of the EU made the following declaration:

The EU welcomes the acceptance of the first ruling by the . . . Arbitration Committee by the Republic of Yemen and the State of Eritrea on their territorial dispute and recognises that France has made an important contribution to the definition and the implementation of the arbitration process leading to this ruling of 9 October. The EU particularly notes the fact that both countries have started a new policy of reconciliation and improved neighbourhood immediately after the Committee's ruling. The Union hopes that these developments will contribute to the maintenance of peace and stability in the region and considers that both countries deserve recognition of the international community for the peaceful solution of their territorial conflict.

(*Bulletin of the European Union*, 1998–10, p. 65)

Part Fourteen: II. G. 1. *Peaceful settlement of disputes—means of settlement—judicial settlement—International Court of Justice*

The following statement was issued as an EU Presidency statement in April 1998:

The European Union and its Member States welcome the invitation contained in paragraph 4 of UN General Assembly Resolution 52/161 of 15 December 1997 to UN Member States to comment on the consequences that the increase in the volume of cases before the International Court of Justice has on its operation.

The European Union and its Member States are strong supporters of the International Court of Justice as the 'principal judicial organ' of the United Nations. They commend the International Court of Justice for its notable role in the peaceful settlement of international disputes.

The recent increase in the workload of the International Court of Justice has been considerable. The Court is likely to remain extremely busy. The European Union and its Member States believe that the International Court of Justice should have at its disposal the necessary resources, both human and financial, to enable it to fulfil its functions, and to do so efficiently in both of its working languages.

(Text provided by the FCO)

In reply to the question what role does Her Majesty's Government see for the International Court of Justice in resolving the range of disputes between Greece and Turkey, the Parliamentary Under-Secretary of State, FCO, wrote:

Her Majesty's Government believe that it is for Greece and Turkey to agree upon the most effective forum in which to discuss their bilateral issues. We continue to urge both sides to adopt an open and flexible approach, including . . . recourse to the International Court of Justice.

(HL Debs., vol. 593, *WA 121*: 15 October 1998)

Speaking in the Sixth Committee of the UN General Assembly on 16 October 1998 on the Report of the Special Committee on the Charter of the United Nations and on the Strengthening of the Role of the Organisation, the representative of Austria, on behalf of the EU, stated in part:

Let me now turn to the Secretary-General's report on the workload of the International Court of Justice (A/53/326): The picture which emerges from that report, i.e. from the detailed and well structured comments and observations presented by the Court itself, is a fairly pessimistic one. The financial and personal resources of the Court have so far not kept pace with the increased number of cases with which the Court is seized. Obviously the Court which is one of the six principal organs of the United Nations and its principal judicial organ, must at all times be able to exercise the functions entrusted to it if the terms and intent of the Charter are to be implemented. Also, the entire raison d'être of the Court is to deal with the cases submitted to it by Member States and with the requests for advisory opinions made by United Nations organs or specialized agencies. These statutory duties of the Court mean that it does not have programmes which may be cut or expanded at will, even if such possibilities do exist for other UN organs.

The workload of the Court is, therefore, not a self generated one, and the Court has no influence on it. It is within that framework that one has to assess the fact, that over the last years—and I have already referred to this tendency as a very commendable one—more and more issues have been brought before the Court for judicial assessment. As a matter of fact it would appear both from the history of the Permanent Court of International Justice and of the present Court, that judicial recourse is resorted to more frequently in times of détente rather than of tension.

The increasing tendency these days to bring cases to the Court by Special Agreement would seem to be testimony to this. Further, more and more multilateral conventions include reference clauses to the Court for the settlement of disputes. Moreover, more and more States today accept the 'Optional Clause' under Article 36, paragraph 2, of the Statute, allowing cases to be brought against them by States accepting the same obligations. The conclusion of the Court is, therefore, that there is every reason to suppose that the rise in the number of cases coming to the Court represents a fundamental change, which is likely to endure and perhaps expand.

We share this conclusion and believe that the legitimate demands of the Court in terms of budgetary resources ought to be fulfilled. Otherwise the judicial branch of the UN would not only be discriminated against, there might also be serious implications of a political nature if cases submitted by States or legal opinions sought by major organs of the UN cannot be dealt with in a timely fashion. The whole credibility of the judicial dispute settlement system is at stake in this area. Again and again the General Assembly has recommended that States make full use of the potential of the Court and that legal inter-State disputes be submitted to that organ.

(Text provided by the FCO; see also A/C.6/53/SR. 5, pp. 2–3)

Part Fourteen: II. H. 2. *Peaceful settlement of disputes—settlement within international organizations—organizations other than the United Nations*

In reply to a question, the Minister of State, Department of Trade and Industry, wrote:

The UK and EU consider that the Massachusetts Burma Selective Purchase Law breaks the United States' obligations under the World Trade Organisation's Government Procurement Agreement. On 8 September, after lengthy efforts to resolve the problem informally, the EU (and Japan) requested a formal WTO Panel. This request was agreed at the meeting of the Dispute Settlement Body on 21 October.

(HC Debs., vol. 318, WA, col. *129*: 27 October 1998)

Part Fifteen: I. B *Coercive measures short of the use of force—unilateral measures—counter-measures*

On 9 February 1998, the UK Permanent Mission to the UN in New York presented to the Secretary-General of the UN the comments of the UK Government on the draft articles on State responsibility prepared by the International Law Commission. The comments contained the following observations:

Countermeasures

18. The United Kingdom Government welcome the acknowledgement in draft article 30 that States are entitled to resort to countermeasures. Were draft article 30 to stand alone, it would constitute a clear statement of that right; and the exercise of that right would be subject to the limitations that have emerged in State practice and to rules specially agreed by States (such as the relevant rules of the Vienna Convention on the Law of Treaties). In this respect draft article 30 would be comparable to draft article 34 on the right of self-defence. The United Kingdom Government commend this approach to the Commission.

19. It appears both unnecessary and undesirable to single out countermeasures as the one 'circumstance precluding wrongfulness' whose content purports to be fixed by the draft articles. The United Kingdom Government would prefer that draft article 30 stand as the only provision on countermeasures, and that the context of the law on countermeasures be considered on another occasion. The United Kingdom Government do not consider that the elaboration of the content of the rules on countermeasures reflects the current state of customary

international law, or that the draft articles represent a desirable development of it.

20. First, the limitations which draft article 50 sets upon lawful countermeasures are not satisfactory. The notion of countermeasures involving 'extreme economic or political coercion', which draft article 50(b) seeks to prohibit, is vague and altogether too subjective. The wording lacks precision, but there is in any case no obvious way in which a definition of 'extreme' measures might be approached. Furthermore, if the original wrong were the application of 'extreme economic or political coercion' to the injured State, it is hard to see why that State should not respond in kind against the wrongdoing State.

21. Again, the prohibition that draft article 50(d) seeks to set on countermeasures that would 'derogate from basic human rights' strikes a sympathetic chord but is, all the same, difficult to grasp and unacceptably wide. Principles such as the sanctity of human life and freedom from slavery or torture are of course fundamental, and their preservation has the United Kingdom's firm support. The fact remains, however, that most countermeasures are not directed at individuals, but are measures taken by one State against another State. It is therefore far from clear how any recognisable countermeasure in the understood sense of the term could amount to 'conduct which derogates from' fundamental rights of this kind. Whether the same would be true of other generally recognised human rights, such as freedom of association, is not immediately apparent; but nor is it apparent whether they would or would not be within the proposition in the draft article. The United Kingdom notes, moreover, that the Commentary on draft Article 50(d) cites as an illustration of the proposition the exclusion from asset freezes and trade embargoes of items necessary for basic subsistence and humanitarian purposes. This is however a subject of some current controversy which is under discussion in the Security Council and General Assembly within the framework of Article 50 of the UN Charter.

. . .

24. The proposal in draft article 58(2) for compulsory arbitration at the option of a State that is the target of countermeasures is unacceptable. It has no basis in customary international law, and is inequitable and undesirable in principle. It is inequitable that the wrongdoer should be given a right to demand compulsory arbitration when the victim of the original wrong is given no such right. It is also predictable that, were draft article 58(2) to be adopted, it would lead to an increase in the use of countermeasures, as States sought to provoke the wrongdoing State into referring to arbitration the dispute arising out of the original wrong.

25. Finally, the United Kingdom Government are concerned that the principles in the draft articles concerning countermeasures may be particularly ill-suited to situations where the dispute is not bilateral. Questions of proportionality, for instance, are much complicated if the initial obligation breached is an obligation *erga omnes*, or in some other way owed to several States. Several States may take countermeasures, but the State principally affected may decide to take none, or even to consent to the breach.

26. For all these reasons, the United Kingdom Government are strongly of the view that it is inappropriate to include any provision other than draft article 30

in these draft articles, and that the question of countermeasures needs careful and separate consideration.

Later in its comments, the UK Government wrote:

Article 48: Conditions relating to resort to countermeasures

118. The United Kingdom Government believe that it is correct in principle, and desirable as a matter of policy, that a State should not resort to countermeasures after a lapse of time which clearly implies that the State has waived its right to do so. They suggest that, if this chapter of the draft articles is to be retained, the International Law Commission should consider the addition of a provision corresponding to article 45 of the Vienna Convention on the Law of Treaties, barring recourse to countermeasures by a State after it has acquiesced in a breach of its rights. Once more, the United Kingdom Government note that the question of countermeasures in the context of multilateral disputes needs particular attention.

(Text provided by the FCO)

Part Fifteen: I. E. *Coercive measures short of the use of force—unilateral measures—other unilateral measures*

In reply to a question, the Minister of State, FCO, wrote:

Since 3 April 1982 the UK has maintained a national arms embargo on Argentina. It has been the policy of the UK to deny all applications for licenses to export goods specified in Part III of Schedule I to the Export of Goods (Control) Order 1994, commonly known as the Military List. We have decided to replace this embargo with new arrangements, with immediate effect.

Licences will only be granted for exports that we are satisfied would not, now or in the foreseeable future, put at risk the security of our Overseas Territories in the South Atlantic or our forces operating there. We will assess all applications for licences to export goods to Argentina on a case-by-case basis against our national export licensing criteria and those in the EU Code of Conduct on Arms Exports. This will also be the case with applications for advance approvals for promotion prior to a formal application for an export licence.

This is a logical modernisation of our export control arrangements. It reflects the changed circumstances since the embargo was put in place.

There has been no change in the resolve of the Government to protect our Overseas Territories in the South Atlantic. The Government remains committed to defend them, and the right of self-determination of their people.

(HL Debs., vol. 595, *WA 182*: 17 December 1998)

The FCO issued the following explanatory notes to editors in respect of the above answer:

1. The terms of the embargo have not been revised since it was introduced on 3 April 1982 following the Argentine invasion of the Falkland Islands. The

embargo was referred to in Ministerial statements to Parliament on 5 April 1982 by Mr Biffin, Lord Trefgarne and Mr Pattie.
2. Dual-use items were not embargoed. Applications to export such items will continue to be assessed case-by-case against our national criteria and the EU Code of Conduct when there are grounds for believing that the end-user will be the Argentine armed forces or internal security forces.
3. Diplomatic relations between the United Kingdom and Argentina were restored in 1990. In a lecture at Lancaster House during his recent visit to London on 27 October to 1 November, President Menem of Argentina disavowed the use of force against the Falklands, as he had already done on several occasions in Argentina. During talks at No. 10 the Prime Minister welcomed this and told President Menem that we would review the embargo in a positive light, mindful of our security considerations.
4. The Government has in the past granted some exceptions to the embargo for strong policy reasons, such as to help Argentina perform UN work, or in certain anomalous situations which technically fall within the embargo, such as the recent application to export shotgun cartridges. These exceptions met our standard export licensing criteria and were announced to Parliament by Foreign Office Ministers. They did not constitute a change to the embargo.

(Text provided by the FCO)

Part Fifteen: II. A. *Coercive measures short of the use of force—collective measures—United Nations*

(See also Part Four: II. A. (Statutory Instruments of 24 April 1998), above)

In reply to a question asking for a list of all arms embargoes currently implemented by the UK, the Minister of State, FCO, wrote:

The United Kingdom currently enforces eighteen arms embargoes. Under the United Nations Charter, we have a legally binding obligation to enforce arms embargoes imposed by the Security Council under Article 41 of the Charter. Other embargoes are imposed on a national basis or following agreement within the European Union (EU) or the Organisation for Security and Co-operation in Europe (formerly CSCE).

Under UK law, binding UN embargoes are implemented by prohibiting the export of goods and technology on the Military List which forms Part III to Schedule 1 of the Export of Goods (Control) Order 1994, as amended. In addition, the supply of such items from the UK or supply abroad by UK registered companies and nationals is prohibited by Orders in Council under the United Nations Act 1946. From time to time, the contents of the Military List may change, for example, to reflect technological advances or continuing international efforts to counter the proliferations of weapons of mass destruction. Orders in Council extend such embargoes to the Crown Dependencies and the Dependent Territories. A licence is required for each export or supply from the UK or abroad by a UK registered company or national.

National embargoes and those agreed in the EU and the OSCE prohibit only the export of goods covered by the embargo. With the exception of the embargoes on China and Iran, the UK interprets the scope of all such embargoes to cover goods and technology on the Military List as defined above.

There are currently seven binding UN arms embargoes:

Angola (a), Iraq (b), Liberia (c), Libya (d), Rwanda (e), Somalia (f) and Sierra Leone (g).

There are currently seven EU embargoes:

Afghanistan (h), Bosnia and Herzegovina, Croatia and the Federal Republic of Yugoslavia (i), Burma (j), China (k), Nigeria (l), Sudan (m) and *Democratic Republic of Congo (formerly Zaire) (n).*

The UK currently implements two embargoes as a result of decisions by the OSCE:

Armenia (o) and *Azerbaijan (p).*

There are currently two national embargoes:

Argentina (q) and *Iran (r).*

I shall keep the House informed of current arms embargoes and their scope on a yearly basis. All new embargoes or any amendments to existing embargoes will be announced at the time. We shall also shortly be laying in the Library of the House a revised list of all UK policy commitments to control strategic exports, including embargoes. An updated version will be laid in the Library annually (or more frequently if policy changes require a revision). This statement will be used to inform British industry.

Footnotes:

(a) Implemented in the UK on 1 October 1993. Products covered by the scope of the embargo can be supplied through named points of entry on a list provided by the Government of Angola;

(b) Implemented in the UK on 9 August 1990 as part of comprehensive trade sanctions;

(c) Implemented in the UK on 22 July 1993;

(d) Implemented in the UK on 15 April 1992 as part of a range of sanctions (following an EU arms embargo imposed on 14 April 1986);

(e) Implemented in the UK on 24 June 1994. The embargo does not apply to the sale or supply of arms and related material if under licence to the Government of Rwanda. But it does cover the sale or supply of arms and material to persons in States neighbouring Rwanda (i.e., Burundi, Tanzania, Uganda and the Democratic Republic of Congo) if that sale or supply is for the purpose of the use of such arms or material within Rwanda;

(f) Implemented in the UK on 22 July 1993;

(g) Implemented in the UK on 1 November 1997;

(h) Implemented in the UK on 17 December 1996;

(i) Implemented in the UK on 26 February 1996. This embargo does not extend to transfers of equipment need for demining activities;

(j) Implemented in the UK on 29 July 1991;

(k) Implemented in the UK on 26 June 1989 (although a national embargo was announced on 6 June 1989). In the absence of agreement amongst EU partners on its scope, interpretation of the embargo was left to national discretion. The UK interprets this embargo to include:

lethal weapons such as machine guns, large calibre weapons, bombs, torpedoes, rockets and missiles;

specially designed components of the above, and ammunition;

military aircraft and helicopters, vessels of war, armoured fighting vehicles and other such weapons platforms; and

any equipment which is likely to be used for internal repression

(l) Implemented in the UK on 20 November 1995 (although a national embargo was announced on 11 November 1995);

(m) Implemented in the UK on 15 March 1994;

(n) Implemented in the UK on 7 April 1993;

(o) Implemented in the UK on 28 February 1992;

(p) Implemented in the UK on 28 February 1992;

(q) Implemented on 3 April 1982

(r) Implemented on 1 March 1993. In addition to the Military List as defined above, the scope of this embargo also covers items entered in Group O in Annex 1 of European Council Decision 94/942/CFSP on the export of dual-use goods, as amended.

There are two exceptions to this embargo:

goods essential for the safety of civil aircraft and air traffic control systems;

radioactive material in the form of sources for medical equipment and deuterium labelled compounds for medical use.

Licences are not approved for any equipment where there is knowledge or reason to suspect that it would go to a military end-user or be used for military purposes. The exception is equipment which would not normally require an export licence but is deemed licensable under the Weapons of Mass Destruction (WMD) end-use control and where WMD concerns are not subsequently substantiated.

(HC Debs., vol. 305, WA, cols. *273–4*: 28 January 1998)

In reply to a question, the Parliamentary Under-Secretary of State, FCO, wrote:

The EU already imposes an arms embargo on the Federal Republic of Yugoslavia. The UK's interpretation of this embargo covers all goods and technology in Part III of Schedule I to the Export of Goods (Control) Order 1994, as amended (the so-called 'Military List').

Following the adoption by the UN Security Council on 31 March of Resolution 1160 as a result of the recent violence in Kosovo, the Privy Council has made Orders in Council giving full effect to the action which the UK is required to take. The Federal Republic of Yugoslavia (United Nations Sanctions) Order 1998; the Federal Republic of Yugoslavia (United Nations Sanctions) (Dependent Territories) Order 1998; the Federal Republic of Yugoslavia (United Nations Sanctions) (Channel Islands) Order 1998; and the Federal Republic of Yugoslavia (United Nations Sanctions) (Isle of Man) Order 1998 were approved by the Privy Council on 22 April and will come into force on 24 April. As a result of these orders, a licence will be required to supply any goods on the Military List to the FRY, so bringing under control such supplies abroad by UK-registered companies or nationals.

(HL Debs., vol. 589, *WA 6*: 27 April 1998)

In reply to a question asking what conditions contained in UN Security Council resolutions require to be fulfilled before sanctions on Iraq can properly be lifted, the Minister of State, FCO, wrote:

United Nations Security Council resolution 687 provides that the Security Council will consider lifting the sanctions imposed on Iraq 'in the light of the policies and practices of the Government of Iraq, including the implementation of all relevant resolutions of the Security Council'. These of course include resolution 687 itself which imposed obligations on Iraq with regard to the elimination under international supervision of weapons of mass destruction.

(HC Debs., vol. 311, WA, col. *343*: 5 May 1998)

In making a statement on the subject of reports of British arm sales to Sierra Leone in breach of UN Security Council resolution, the Secretary of State, FCO, Mr Robin Cook, remarked:

President Kabbah, the democratically elected leader of Sierra Leone, was deposed in a military coup. In October, the UN Security Council passed resolution 1132, which imposed an arms embargo on Sierra Leone. It was promptly implemented in this country by an Order in Council prepared by the Foreign Office.

(HC Debs., vol. 311, col. 721: 6 May 1998)

At the end of his statement, the Secretary of State observed:

This Government have consistently supported the legitimacy of the United Nations. This Government abide by the resolutions of the Security Council and are committed to the rule of international law. I assure the House that we have not, and we will not, condone any breach of international law.

(Ibid., col. 722)

During the debate which followed, the Secretary of State remarked in response to a question:

There was no Government policy or UN support for military intervention to restore President Kabbah. Resolution 1132 and consistent ministerial statements on Sierra Leone stressed that we supported President Kabbah, but wanted him to be restored through diplomatic negotiation, not military intervention. The hon. Gentleman is wildly out of touch with reality if he suggests that a breach of a UN Security Council resolution that we ourselves voted for was somehow going along with ministerial policy.

(Ibid., col. 727)

In reply to a question, the Secretary of State wrote:

Our policy is clear. We were instrumental in drawing up UN Security Council Resolution 1132, which prohibits the sale of arms and related material of all types to Sierra Leone.

(Ibid., WA, col. *540*: 8 May 1998)

In a television interview on 10 May 1998, the Secretary of State for Foreign and Commonwealth Affairs, Mr Robin Cook, referred to the situation in Sierra Leone. He went on:

We are a government that stands by international law. We have worked hard, as we did during the Iraqi confrontation, to restore the legitimacy of the United Nations. We will not condone any breach of international law or anything that undermines the legitimacy of the United Nations resolutions.

(Text provided by the FCO)

In a memorandum presented to the House of Commons Foreign Affairs Committee discussing arms deliveries to Sierra Leone, the FCO wrote:

UN mandatory sanctions are imposed by the UN Security Council under Chapter VII of the UN Charter. In the United Kingdom, the sanctions are implemented in domestic law by Orders in Council made under the United Nations Act 1946. In the case of Sierra Leone, UN Security Council Resolution 1132 was implemented in UK Law by the Sierra Leone (United Nations Sanctions) Order 1997 (No 2592), which was laid before Parliament on 31 October and came into force on 1 November 1997. Corresponding Orders were made for the Crown Dependencies and the Overseas Territories.

(*Parliamentary Papers*, 1998–99, HC, Paper 116–II, p. 34 (hearing of 14 May 1998))

Attached to the above memorandum was the following undated opinion of the FCO Legal Advisers:

FCO LEGAL OPINION ON THE APPLICABILITY OF THE UN SECURITY COUNCIL RESOLUTION 1132 (1997) TO THE LEGITIMATE GOVERNMENT OF SIERRA LEONE

The issue is whether the arms embargo imposed by the Security Council in resolution 1132 (1997) applied to the legitimate government in exile.

Paragraph 6 of resolution 1132 reads as follows: '*Decides* that all States shall prevent the sale or supply to Sierra Leone, by their nationals or from their territories, or using their flag vessels or aircraft, of petroleum and petroleum products and arms and related *matériel* of all types, including weapons and ammunition, military vehicles and equipment, paramilitary equipment and spare parts for the aforementioned, whether or not originating in their territory.'

No exceptions were provided to the arms embargo. The effect therefore was that any sale or supply of arms to Sierra Leone was prohibited by the resolution.

In implementing arms embargoes in domestic law it is standard practice to include provisions which will enable the embargoes to be effectively applied. Thus the Sierra Leone (United Nations Sanctions) Order 1997 prohibited the sale or supply of arms etc., to 'any destination for the purpose of delivery directly or indirectly, to or to the order of a person connected with Sierra Leone', unless the delivery was licensed by the President of the Board of Trade.

'Person connected with Sierra Leone' was defined as including the Government of Sierra Leone and any other person in or resident in Sierra Leone.

(Ibid., p. 38)

In reply to a question on the subject of arms exports, the Minister of State, FCO, wrote in part:

The UK takes seriously its obligations to implement UN Arms Embargoes and expects other countries to do the same.

(HC Debs., vol. 312, WA, col. *205*: 14 May 1998)

In reply to a question on the application of Security Council Resolution 1132 to the Nigerian-led military observers group of the Economic Community of West African States at the time 'when it was seeking to restore democracy to Sierra Leone', the Secretary of State for Foreign and Commonwealth Relations wrote:

Operative paragraph 6 of Security Council Resolution 1132 provides that the Security Council 'Decides that all States shall prevent the sale or supply to Sierra Leone, by their nationals or from their flag vessels or aircraft, of petroleum and petroleum products and arms and related matériel of all types, including weapons and ammunition, military vehicles and equipment, paramilitary equipment and spare parts for the aforementioned, whether or not originating in their territory'. No exceptions were made to the embargo.

Now that the conditions set out in SCR 1132 for the lifting of the embargo have been met United Nations Security Council Members have agreed that a new resolution is required. This should lift the arms embargo on the Sierra Leone Government and ECOMOG but maintain it on non-governmental forces. Urgent discussions on the precise terms of the resolution are underway in New York.

(HC Debs., vol. 313, WA, cols. *345–6*: 4 June 1998)

In reply to a question on the subject of the UN Security Council resolution of 5 June 1998 concerning Sierra Leone, the Government spokesman in the House of Lords wrote:

The new resolution supersedes part of UN Security Council Resolution 1132. It ensures that the arms embargo to Sierra Leone applies to non-governmental forces and makes explicit exception for the Military Observer Group of the Economic Community of West African States (ECOMOG) and the United Nations.

Following the adoption by the UN Security Council on 5 June of the new resolution, Orders in Council are now being prepared giving full effect in our law to the arms embargo imposed by the new resolution.

(HL Debs., vol. 590, *WA 124*: 16 June 1998)

In reply to questions, the Secretary of State for Foreign and Commonwealth Affairs wrote:

At no stage during the drafting of Security Council Resolution 1132 did the draft under consideration in New York refer to the arms ban applying to both the Government in exile of President Kabbah and its replacement. The earliest and all subsequent drafts referred only to a ban on the sale or supply of arms and related material to Sierra Leone. Sir Thomas Legg has access to all documents germane to his investigation, including those relating to the drafting of Security Council Resolution 1132.

. . .

Our interpretation of SCR 1132 was set out in my reply to a question from the hon. Member for Reigate (Mr Blunt) 4 June 1998, *Official Report*, columns *345–46*. The legal advice on which this interpretation is based has been made available to the Select Committee on Foreign Affairs. The Government's interpretation has not been affected by the advice sent to the Chairman of the Sierra Leone Sanctions Committee of the United Nations by the UN's Legal Counsel. Subsequent discussion in the Sanctions Committee revealed that different member states held differing views on the Legal Counsel's advice.

(HC Debs., vol. 314, WA, col. *304*: 18 June 1998)

The United Nations Arms Embargoes (Amendment) (Sierra Leone) Order 1998 (Statutory Instruments 1998, No. 1501) which came into force on 26 June 1998 was accompanied by the following explanatory memorandum:

This Order, made under the United Nations Act 1946, amends the United Nations Arms Embargoes (Liberia, Somalia and the former Yugoslavia) Order 1993 by imposing restrictions on the delivery and supply of arms and related matériel to Sierra Leone, pursuant to a decision of the Security Council of the United Nations in Resolution No. 1171 of 5th June 1998, which terminated earlier restrictions related to Sierra Leone and re-imposed more limited restrictions. The Order also revokes the Sierra Leone (United Nations Sanctions) Order 1997. In addition, the opportunity has been taken to bring the definition of 'prohibited goods' into line with recent legislation.

In reply to questions, the Minister of State, FCO, wrote:

UNITA's representative in the United Kingdom conducted UNITA business from his commercial premises in London. Following the adoption of United Nations Security Council Resolution 1127 (1997), Mr. Kandeya was immediately ordered to leave the United Kingdom. He has submitted an application to remain in the United Kingdom which is being considered by the Home Office. Officials have visited Mr. Kandeya's commercial premises and satisfied themselves that there was no sign of any continuing association with UNITA. As far as we are aware, there are no offices or premises being maintained in the United Kingdom under the name of UNITA.

. . .

The Government have prepared Orders in Council to implement United Nations Security Council Resolution 1173, which it expects to be laid before Parliament on 22 July and enter into force on 23 July. When it is passed, the Bank of England will simultaneously write to the relevant UK financial institutions asking them to implement the United Nations' financial sanctions against UNITA.

(HC Debs., vol. 316, WA, col. *358*: 17 July 1998)

In reply to the question what measures have Her Majesty's Government taken to implement UN Security Council Resolution 1173, the Parliamentary Under-Secretary of State, FCO, wrote:

Resolution 1173 imposed a freeze on the funds and financial resources of UNITA, its officials and their immediate families; a ban on most official contacts in Angola with UNITA, a prohibition on the import of diamonds outside the governmental certificate of origin regime; and prohibitions on the sale or supply of equipment which may be used in mining transportation, and on transportation services.

We have instructed all our diplomatic mission overseas to avoid any contract with UNITA, whether locally or in Angola.

The prohibition on the importation of diamonds will be given effect in the United Kingdom by amendment to the Open General Import Licence.

The remainder of the prohibitions are to be implemented in the UK by the Angola (United Nations Sanctions) Order 1998 and in the Overseas Territories by the Angola (United Nations Sanctions) (Dependent Territories) Order 1998 made on 21 July and laid yesterday. Similar orders have been made to give effect to the resolution in the Crown Dependencies. These orders restrict the sale or supply of certain goods which may be used in mining or transportation and the supply of transportation services; impose a freeze on the funds and financial resources in relation to UNITA and persons connected with UNITA, and for the Overseas Territories and Channel Islands, restrict the importation of diamonds exported from Angola on or after 1 July 1998. There is provision for medical and humanitarian exceptions.

(HL Debs., vol. 592, *WA 127*: 23 July 1998)

In reply to a question, the Parliamentary Under-Secretary of State, FCO, wrote:

It is clear that the Kosovo Liberation Army has procured significant quantities of arms in Albania. Media and other reports also suggest that Kosovo Albanians living in Europe and elsewhere are actively involved in fundraising for the KLA. United Nations Security Council Resolution 1160 adopted on 31 March 1998 condemned all external support for terrorist activity in Kosovo and decided that states should prevent arming and training for terrorist activity there. At its meeting in Bonn on 8 July, the Contact Group requested all states to pursue, as a matter of urgency, all means consistent with their domestic laws and relevant international law, to prevent funds collected on their behalf being used to contravene the resolution.

(HL Debs., vol. 592, *WA 181*: 28 July 1998)

The following question was asked of Her Majesty's Government:

To ask the Secretary of State for Foreign and Commonwealth Affairs if he will make a statement on the extent to which the end-use control, relating to goods which may be used in connection with the development of weapons of mass destruction, applies to the supply of goods to destinations subject to binding UN arms embargoes.

In reply, the Minister of State, FCO, wrote:

Council Regulation (EC) No. 3381/94 and the Dual-Use and Related Goods (Export Control) Regulations 1996 prohibit the export from the UK to any destination of dual-use or other goods which the exporter has been informed by a competent authority are or may be intended, wholly or in part, or which the exporter knows are intended, wholly or in part, to be used in connection with the development, production, handling, operation, maintenance, storage, detection, identification or dissemination of chemical, biological or nuclear weapons or the development, production, maintenance or storage of missiles capable of delivering such weapons, and also where the exporter has grounds for suspecting that the goods might so be used. These provisions are known as the end-use control.

Under UK law, all binding UN embargoes are implemented by prohibiting the export of goods and technology on the Military List which forms part III of Schedule I to the Export of Goods (Control) Order 1994, as amended.

In addition, the Orders in Council implementing in UK law the binding UN embargoes against Liberia, Somalia, Libya, Angola and Rwanda also prohibit the supply [by] persons in the UK or by UK nationals or companies overseas of goods which are or may be intended to be used in connection with the development, production, handling, operation, maintenance, storage, detection, identification or dissemination of chemical, biological or nuclear weapons or the development, production, maintenance or storage of missiles capable of delivering such weapons.

This statement supplements the information given in another place on the scope of arms embargoes observed by the UK by the Minister of State, Foreign and Commonwealth Affairs, Baroness Chalker of Wallasey, on 20 March 1997, *Official Report, House of Lords*, columns 75–77; and by the Parliamentary Under-Secretary of State Baroness Symons, on 28 January 1998, *Official Report, House of Lords*, columns *36–39*. An updated version of the list of the Government's commitments regarding the application of strategic export controls, covering this point and other recent changes, has been laid in the Library.

(HC Debs., vol. 317, WA, cols. *523–4*: 30 July 1998)

The Secretary of State for Foreign and Commonwealth Affairs, Mr Robin Cook, issued the following statement on 16 September 1998:

The Government is today ordering that all flights by Yugoslav carriers to the UK be banned with immediate effect.

The UK had firmly backed the flight ban against the Federal Republic of Yugoslavia (FRY) from the beginning, and under the terms of the bilateral UK/Yugoslavia Air Services Agreement we gave 12 months notice of termination.

On my return from leave, I instituted an immediate review of the timing of implementation of the flight ban, given the potentially conflicting obligations under the EC Regulation and our bilateral Air Services Agreement, and given the continued repressive activities of President Milosevic's troops in Kosovo, and the sharply deteriorating humanitarian situation. In the changed circumstances, we have concluded that it would be right to proceed with an immediate ban. President Milosevic's current behaviour, and in particular his worsening record on human rights, means that, on moral and political grounds, he has forfeited the right of his Government to insist upon the 12 months notice which would normally apply.

The UK has taken the lead in pressing for international action against the Federal Republic of Yugoslavia (FRY), both as a member of the Contact Group and within the EU. In addition to the flight ban and the UN arms embargo the EU under British Presidency agreed a ban on investment in the FRY; freezing of the funds held abroad by the FRY and Serbian governments; suspension of export credit guarantees; a ban on the sale of repressive equipment and a selective visa ban on FRY officials.

The UK is determined to strengthen the sanctions regime: we are pressing for a UN Security Council Resolution, which would include a worldwide flight ban on the FRY. We are also pressing for action within the EU to tighten the freeze on FRY Government funds to include funds held overseas by state controlled companies and banks.

(Text provided by the FCO)

In reply to the question of what measures Her Majesty's Government has taken to implement United Nations Security Council Resolution 1173 (1998), the Minister of State, FCO, wrote:

Resolution 1173 imposed a freeze on the funds and financial resources of UNITA, its officials and their immediate families; a ban on most official contacts in Angola with UNITA; a prohibition on the import of diamonds outside the government certificate of origin regime; and prohibitions on the sale or supply of equipment which may be used in mining or transportation, and on transportation services.

We have instructed all our diplomatic mission overseas to avoid any contact with UNITA, whether locally or in Angola. There is one exception: our Embassy in Luanda may continue to have contacts with UNITA officials in areas of Angola to which State Administration has been extended. This is in accordance with UN Security Council Resolution 1173 (1998) which prohibits certain official contacts with UNITA.

The prohibition on the importation of diamonds will be given effect in the United Kingdom by amendment to the Open General Import Licence.

The remainder of the prohibitions are to be implemented in the UK by the Angola (United Nations Sanctions) Order 1998 and in the Overseas Territories by the Angola (United Nations Sanctions) (Dependent Territories) Order 1998 made on 21 July and laid on July.

Similar Orders have been made to give effect to the Resolution in the Crown Dependencies. These orders restrict the sale or supply of certain goods which may be used in mining or transportation and the supply of transportation services; impose a freeze on the funds and financial resources in relation to UNITA and persons connected with UNITA, and for the Overseas territories and Channel Islands, restrict the importation of diamonds exported from

Angola on or after 1 July 1998. There is provision for medical and humanitarian exceptions.

(HC Debs., vol. 319, WA, col. *35*: 9 November 1998)

Part Fifteen: II. B. *Coercive measures short of the use of force—collective measures—outside the United Nations*

(See also Part Fifteen: II. A. (items of 27 April and 16 September 1998), above)

In reply to questions, the Minister of State, FCO, wrote:

Following the transfer of sovereignty over Hong Kong to China on 1 July 1997, we have conducted a detailed review of the applicability to the Hong Kong Special Administrative Region (HKSAR) of the European Union arms embargo against China. In view of the HKSAR's autonomy from mainland China in customs, trade and economic matters and its well-established strategic trade control system, we have concluded that its access to a broad range of strategic commodities from the UK for civil end-use should be preserved. The DTI will therefore issue a new Open General Export Licence and Open General Transhipment Licence to allow the continued export and transhipment of dual-use goods to the HKSAR for civil end-use.

As for the export of strategic goods for military end-use, we have concluded that, in order to fulfil our obligations under the EU embargo, goods which we would not approve for export to the Chinese armed forces in mainland China should not be permitted for export for military end-use in the HKSAR. Goods for military end-use will therefore be subject to individual licensing requirements.

These changes will take effect on 23 January.

(HC Debs., vol. 304, WA, col. *220*: 14 January 1998)

In reply to a question on the subject of the EU arms embargo on Afghanistan, the Minister of State, FCO, wrote:

We remain committed to the EU arms embargo against Afghanistan which the UK interprets as covering all goods and technology entered on Part III to schedule 1 to the Export of Goods Order 1994, as amended.

Following consultation with this Department and the Ministry of Defence, the Department of Trade and Industry recently approved a licence for the export of mine clearance equipment for use by the United Nations Office for the Co-ordination of Humanitarian Assistance to Afghanistan in its demining operations. The grant of this licence is for humanitarian purposes, and is consistent with the purpose of the embargo.

(HC Debs., vol. 308, WA, cols. *679–80*: 19 March 1998)

In reply to a question, the Parliamentary Under-Secretary of State, FCO, wrote:

The EU introduced a ban on arms sales to China on 26 June 1989, but the scope of that ban has, in the absence of agreement on a common interpretation, been left for national interpretation. The UK interprets this ban to include:

lethal weapons such as machine guns, large calibre weapons, bombs, torpedoes, rockets and missiles; specially designed components of the above, and ammunition;
military aircraft and helicopters, vessels of war, armoured fighting vehicles and other such weapons platforms;
any equipment which might be used for internal repression.

All applications are considered case by case in the light of these criteria as well as the overall criteria governing defence exports announced on 28 July 1997 by the Foreign Secretary. (*Official Report*, Commons, cols. 26–29)

(HL Debs., vol. 590, *WA 41*: 3 June 1998)

In reply to a question, the Parliamentary Under-Secretary of State, FCO, wrote:

Her Majesty's Government remain committed to the EU arms embargo against Afghanistan.

Following discussion with this department and the Ministry of Defence, the Department of Trade and Industry recently approved a licence for the export of mine-clearance suits for use by the United Nations Office for the Co-ordination of Humanitarian Assistance to Afghanistan in its demining operations. The grant of this licence is for humanitarian purposes, and is consistent with the purpose of the embargo.

(HL Debs., vol. 590, *WA 66*: 8 June 1998)

In reply to a question, the Minister of State, FCO, wrote:

The EU agreed a Common Position on Nigeria on 20 November 1995 which includes a full-scope arms embargo. The UK interprets the embargo to include all goods and technology on the Military List (part III of Schedule 1 of the Export of Goods (Control) Order 1994). The Government enforced the embargo rigorously.

(HC Debs., vol. 313, WA, col. *459*: 8 June 1998)

In a press conference held in Luxemburg on 8 June 1998, the Secretary of State for Foreign and Commonwealth Affairs, Mr Robin Cook, spoke about measures taken against the Federal Republic of Yugoslavia. He stated:

On the question of a freezing of assets, we have already resolved to freeze the assets of the state outside the Federal Republic; to achieve a freeze on assets of individuals would require a United Nations Security Council resolution because the legality of that, without such a resolution, would be difficult to apply.

(Text provided by the FCO)

In reply to a question, the Minister of State, FCO, wrote:

Bank accounts of the former Socialist Federal Republic of Yugoslavia remain frozen pending the resolution of succession negotiations which are continuing under the auspices of the High Representative's special negotiator. UK banks and other financial institutions holding assets which are subject to the resolution of third party claims are not required under current legislation to reveal their existence. We have no plans to ask the United Nations or the EU to intervene in this matter.

(HC Debs., vol. 316, WA, col. *184*: 15 July 1998)

In reply to a question, the Minister of State, FCO, wrote:

There was no embargo on the export of defence equipment to Croatia in 1989 and 1990. The European Union and its Member States decided on 5 July 1991 to impose an embargo on armaments and military equipment applicable to the whole of the Socialist Federal Republic of Yugoslavia (SFRY). UNSCR 713 (1991) established a general and complete embargo on all deliveries of weapons and military equipment to the SFRY with effect from 25 September 1991. The embargoes included anti-tank weapons for export to Croatia. The EU embargo remains in force in respect to Croatia.

(HC Debs., vol. 319, WA, col. *227*: 11 November 1998)

In reply to questions, the Minister of State, FCO, wrote in part:

We will continue to implement rigorously the EU arms embargo against Nigeria. The UK interprets this as covering all goods and technology on the UK Military List which forms Part III to Schedule 1 to the Export of Goods Order 1994, as amended.

. . .

In recognition of the progress being made towards respect for human rights and the restoration of a democratic civilian Government in Nigeria, on 1 November the EU adopted a new Common Position, replacing the Common Positions of 20 November 1995 and 4 December 1995. The UK was at the forefront of those advocating this change of policy. As a result the following measures have now been lifted:

all visa restrictions;
the ban on high level visits;
the ban on sporting contacts;
the ban on the appointment of European military personnel to diplomatic missions in Nigeria and Nigerian military personnel in the European Union.

The following measures continue to apply:

suspension of military co-operation;
cancellation of training courses for all Nigerian military personnel, except for non-combative courses to encourage respect for human rights and to prepare the military for the democratic control by a civilian Government of the armed forces;
an embargo on arms, munitions and military equipment. A dialogue on development co-operation may now be resumed with a view to re-engagement after the installation of a democratically elected civilian Government.

The European Union also re-affirmed its willingness to strengthen a constructive dialogue with Nigeria and to support the electoral process. It also re-iterated its support for Nigeria's regional peacekeeping activities.

The new Common Position will be reviewed no later than 1 June 1999. Should there be any deterioration in the respect for human rights or the democratic processes, the Council will immediately review the Common Position with a view to adopting additional measures.

(HC Debs., vol. 319, cols. *818–19*: 19 November 1998)

In reply to a question, the Parliamentary Under-Secretary of State, Department of the Environment, Transport and the Regions, wrote:

Her Majesty's Government remain committed to the EU arms embargo against Afghanistan, which the UK interprets as covering all goods and technology entered on Part III to Schedule 1 to the Export of Goods Order 1994, as amended.

Following consultations with this department and the Ministry of Defence, the Department of Trade and Industry recently approved two export licences: the first for the export of mine-clearance suits for use by the United Nations Office for the Co-ordination of Humanitarian Assistance to Afghanistan in its demining operations and the second for the export of mine clearance equipment for use by the Halo Trust to aid their demining activities also in Afghanistan. The grant of these licences is for humanitarian purposes, and is consistent with the purpose of the embargo.

(HL Debs., vol. 595, *WA 3*: 26 November 1998)

In reply to a question, the Minister of State, FCO, wrote in part:

We remain committed to the EU arms embargo against Afghanistan which the UK interprets as covering all goods and technology entered on Part III to Schedule 1 to the Export of Goods Order 1994, as amended.

(HC Debs., vol. 321, WA, col. *11*: 26 November 1998)

Part Sixteen: II. A. *Use of force—legitimate use of force—self-defence*

(See also Part Sixteen: II. B. 1. (items of 23 February and 30 December 1998) and Part Seventeen: I.B.9. (item of 29 October 1998), below)

Giving evidence to the Foreign Affairs Committee of the House of Commons the Minister of State, FCO, Mr Derek Fatchett, was asked for his view on what was said to be a right of the United States to take a unilateral decision to take military action for the protection of US military interests. He stated:

The decision that we must take is one that is based on international law, and Security Council resolutions. We are going into very technical grounds. Under the United Nations Charter a country has the right within legally defined terms to protect its own national interests. But these interests are very clearly defined in international law. The crucial point in relation to Saddam Hussein is that we act collectively and base our actions on the United Nations Security Council resolutions and international law.

(*Parliamentary Papers*, 1997–98, HC, Paper 582–i, p. 4: 24 February 1998)

The Minister was then asked: 'What is [Her Majesty's Government's] position in relation to the Turkish troops who are presently stationed on Iraqi soil?'. He replied:

We have said constantly that while we recognise that Turkey has the right to defend its own territorial integrity, whatever action it takes in northern Iraq must be proportionate to the threat.

(Ibid., p. 5)

In reply to a question, the Parliamentary Under-Secretary of State, FCO, wrote in part:

The use of force, including in self-defence, is governed by general international law and in particular the Charter of the United Nations.

(HL Debs., vol. 588, *WA 135*: 8 April 1998)

Part Sixteen: II. B. 1. *Use of force—legitimate use of force—collective measures—United Nations*

The following question was asked of Her Majesty's Government:

Whether they agree with the United States Administration that further military action against Iraq does not need further United Nations Security Council authority, or with the French Government, which says that it does?

In reply, the Parliamentary Under-Secretary of State, FCO, wrote:

If Saddam Hussein reverted to a policy of obstructing UNSCOM operations, as witnessed in November, this would be a clear breach of Iraq's obligations under Security Council resolutions. We would continue to pursue a diplomatic solution but could not rule out military action as a last resort.

(HL Debs., vol. 584, *WA 125*: 12 January 1998)

In the course of a debate on the subject of Iraq, the Parliamentary Under-Secretary of State, FCO, Baroness Symons of Vernham Dean, stated:

Iraq's failure to comply with UNSCOM is a clear breach of its obligations under Security Council resolutions, particularly Security Council Resolution 687, which was the ceasefire resolution. Iraq has threatened regional peace and security many times over the past 20 years. Its weapons of mass destruction programme is a clear threat to regional neighbours. Past experience shows that Saddam Hussein would not hesitate to turn the weapons against his neighbours or his own people.

The question of exactly what would happen in relation to military action would of course depend on the circumstances in which Her Majesty's Government and our allies find ourselves, should our discussions through diplomatic channels fail.

(HL Debs., vol. 585, col. 46: 26 January 1998)

In reply to the following question asked of Her Majesty's Government:

Whether they or the United States are seeking a Resolution in the United Nations Security Council which would find Iraq 'in material breach of the ceasefire' that ended the Gulf War, and would legitimate attacks on Iraqi targets; and whether they are prepared to support United States unilateral action against Iraq in the event of such a Resolution not securing United Nations Security Council approval?

the Parliamentary Under-Secretary of State, FCO, wrote:

We are still pursuing a diplomatic solution to the crisis with Iraq, but cannot rule out military action if Saddam fails to back down.

Iraq's obstruction of UNSCOM is a clear breach of its obligations under SCRs. Iraq has threatened regional peace and security many times over the last 20 years. Its WMD programme is a clear threat to its neighbours in the region.

The main purpose of the action we are promoting in the Security Council is to send a tough and united message to Saddam Hussein. If he fails to heed that, then the legal justification for the use of force would depend on the precise circumstances at that time.

(HL Debs., vol. 585, *WA 152*: 10 February 1998)

In the course of a debate in the House of Lords on the subject of Iraq, the Parliamentary Under-Secretary of State, FCO, Baroness Symons of Vernham Dean, stated:

In our previous discussions in this House, some of your Lordships asked about the legality of our action. Any action involving UK forces would be based on international law. The Charter of the United Nations allows for the use of force under the authority of the Security Council. The Security Council resolution adopted before the Gulf conflict authorised the use of force in order to restore international peace and security in the region. Iraq is in clear breach of Security Council Resolution 687 which laid down the conditions for the ceasefire at the end of the conflict. Those conditions included a requirement on Iraq to eliminate its weapons of mass destruction under international supervision. Those conditions have been broken.

The international community has been accused of applying double standards between Iraq and Israel. Indeed, one or two of your Lordships raised anxieties on that point. This is not the case. In the case of both countries, we insist on respect for international legality and support the implementation of UNSCRs. We must remember too that Iraq is led by an aggressive dictator who persistently flouts UN resolutions and who has used weapons of mass destruction against his own people and against his own neighbours. Israel is a democracy which has engaged in a wide-ranging and potentially fruitful negotiating process.

(HL Debs., vol. 586, col. 148: 17 February 1998)

Later in the debate, the Minister of State, Ministry of Defence, Lord Gilbert, stated:

I turn now to the position with regard to legal advice. I know that I put myself at risk in talking about legal matters but, as I understand it—different countries receive different legal advice on such matters—we do not need an additional Security Council resolution, but we would far prefer to have one if possible.

(Ibid., col. 216)

The following question was asked of Her Majesty's Government:

Whether they accept the United States interpretation of international law which would allow it to attack Iraq in the absence of either an immediate threat to its security or a specific Security Council Resolution; and whether this indicates a change in the British Government's interpretation of the Charter of the United Nations?

In reply, the Parliamentary Under-Secretary of State, FCO, wrote:

The Government's interpretation of the Charter of the United Nations has not changed. Any use of force requires to be justified under international law, notably the United Nations Charter. It is well established that, under the Charter, force may be used in self-defence or under the authority of the Security Council.

(HL Debs., vol. 586, *WA 59–60*: 23 February 1998)

The EU Presidency issued the following statement in London on 3 March 1998:

The EU welcomes the unanimous adoption of Security Council Resolution (SCR) 1154 on 2 March.

This Resolution commends the initiative by the UN Secretary-General to secure commitments from the government of Iraq on compliance with its obligations under the relevant Resolutions and endorses the Memorandum of Understanding signed by the Deputy Prime Minister of Iraq and the UN Secretary-General on 23 February 1998.

The EU calls on the Iraqi authorities to comply fully with the Memorandum of Understanding and with the relevant Security Council Resolutions.

The EU notes that under the terms of SCR 1154 any violation by Iraq of its obligations would have the severest consequences. On the other hand, compliance by Iraq with its obligations, repeated in the Memorandum of Understanding, to accord immediate, unconditional and unrestricted access to the Special Commission and the IAEA would allow the Security Council to act in accordance with the relevant [provision] of SCR 687 on the lifting of sanctions. The EU notes that, in accordance with its responsibility under the Charter, the Security Council will remain actively seized of the matter, in order to secure the implementation of this Resolution and to secure peace and security in the area.

The EU meanwhile remains determined to ensure that the arrangements for bringing increased humanitarian assistance to the Iraqi people under SCR 1153 are fully and effectively implemented.

The following questions were put to Her Majesty's Government and answered by the Parliamentary Under-Secretary of State, FCO:

Q. Whether they have agreed to take part in any unilateral military action which the United States might take in pursuit of its interpretation of the United Nations Security Council Resolution 1154 (1998), or to support such action?
A. Her Majesty's Government would prefer to ensure compliance by Iraq with its obligations to the United Nations without the resort to force. But, as Security Council Resolution 1154 makes clear, if Iraq violates the agreement signed in Baghdad with the UN Secretary-General the severest consequences will follow. It is not sensible to speculate at this stage on what those consequences might be.
Q. What are the implications for international law if Resolution 1154 (1998) (or any other United Nations Security Council Resolution) is interpreted by one or more, but not by all, permanent members of the United Nations Security Council as authorising them to take 'unilateral (military) action', and if they will urgently refer the matter to the World Court for an opinion on the lawfulness of any such unilateral military action?
A. All members of the United Nations are required to comply with mandatory resolutions of the Security Council. Security Council Resolution 1154 was adopted unanimously by the Security Council. All members agreed that further violations of Iraq's obligations under relevant Security Council Resolutions and the Memorandum of Understanding signed in Baghdad would be followed by the severest consequences. It is not sensible at this stage to speculate on what those might be, nor to seek to involve the World Court in this matter.
Q. What they consider are the implications for other United Nations Resolutions, which establish various prohibitions relating to Iraq, of a decision by the United States to interpret Resolution 1154 (1998) unilaterally, and whether embargoes, sanctions etc., may in future be unilaterally interpreted and acted upon by all members of the Security Council in accordance with their feelings?
A. All members of the United Nations are required to comply with mandatory resolutions of the Security Council. It is not sensible to speculate on the consequences of hypothetical decisions by other members of the Council.

(HL Debs., vol. 587, *WA* 94–5: 16 March 1998)

The following question was asked of Her Majesty's Government:

Whether they consider that the Charter of the United Nations permits, and the international rule of law can survive, claims by individual member states to a right of unilateral interpretation of UN Security Council Resolutions, and a right to engage in military operations under such unilateral interpretations?

In reply, the Parliamentary Under-Secretary of State, FCO, wrote:

The legal basis for any use of force depends upon all the circumstances at the time. These may include authorisation by the UN Security Council, whose resolutions must be interpreted and applied in good faith.

(HL Debs., vol. 593, *WA 213–14*: 27 October 1998)

Speaking in the UN Security Council on 5 November 1998, the UK Permanent Representative to the UN in New York, Sir Jeremy Greenstock, stated:

By its decisions of 5 August and 31 October, Iraq has put itself in flagrant violation of its obligations under the relevant resolutions of the Council. It is right that the Council should react formally and unanimously to this latest attempt to challenge its authority and that of the United Nations as a whole.

This resolution reiterates the Council's full support for the Special Commission and the IAEA. Their work is absolutely vital. Iraq's constant attempts to undermine them and avoid its obligations only delay the moment when the decision can be taken on the lifting of sanctions. Cooperation, not confrontation, is the only way out from sanctions for Iraq.

Certain speakers have given their views on the meaning of this resolution as regards the possible use of force. Let me set out briefly the view of the United Kingdom. It is well established that the authorization to use force given by the Security Council in 1990 may be revived if the Council decides that there has been a sufficiently serious breach of the conditions laid down by the Council for the ceasefire.

In the resolution we have just adopted, the Council has condemned the Iraqi decision to cease all cooperation as a flagrant violation of its obligations.

This resolution sends a clear message to Iraq: resume cooperation now. If Iraq does so, the Council has spelt out unambiguously that it stands ready to conduct a comprehensive review of Iraq's compliance with its obligations under the relevant resolutions and what steps remain to be taken. We hope Iraq will respond positively and resume full cooperation soon.

(S/PV. 3939, p. 10)

In the course of a debate on the subject of Iraq's non-compliance with weapon inspection obligations, the Parliamentary Under-Secretary of State, FCO, Baroness Symons of Vernham Dean, stated:

My Lords, I know that the legal basis for the projected action has been a matter of concern in your Lordships' House, and understandably so. We have discussed it on a number of occasions. It is important to remember that we are considering a highly complex network of United Nations Security Council resolutions. Perhaps I may remind your Lordships that there is Resolution 678 demanding that Iraq left Kuwait. There is Resolution 687, which set out the ceasefire arrangements, the position of UNSCOM and the necessity for Iraq to comply with it on an unconditional basis. There is also Resolution 1154, which concerns the memorandum of understanding with the United Nations Secretary General and which speaks of the severest consequences if that memorandum was broken. There is Resolution 1205, which speaks of the flagrant violation which the United Nations Security Council believes has been committed by Iraq.

I believe I have been very clear that Her Majesty's Government were not in any doubt that there was a clear legal basis for the planned military action at the weekend. Similarly, I give your Lordships an undertaking that any action taken by Her Majesty's Government in the future will be lawful. I am sure that Her Majesty's Government recognise the very important point made by my noble friend Lord Judd that it is enormously important that we do everything we can to keep the members of the United Nations Security Council as close to each other as we can in what I believe are bound to be some difficult days, and possibly weeks, ahead regarding this crucial matter of international stability.

(HL Debs., vol. 594, col. 1031: 16 November 1998)

Speaking in the UN Security Council on 16 December 1998 in announcement of the armed action of UK and US forces against targets in Iraq, the UK Permanent Representative, Sir Jeremy Greenstock, stated in part:

In this, our objectives are clear: to degrade Iraq's capability to build and use weapons of mass destruction, and to diminish the military threat Iraq poses to its neighbours. The targets chosen, therefore, are targets connected with his military capability, his weapons of mass destruction and his ability to threaten his neighbours.

There is a clear legal basis for military action in the resolutions adopted by the Security Council. Resolution 1154 (1998) made it clear that any violation by Iraq of its obligations to allow the Special Commission and the International Atomic Energy Agency unrestricted access world have the severest consequences. That was three resolutions and nine months ago. Resolution 1205 (1998) established that Iraq's decision of 31 October 1998 to cease cooperation with the Special Commission was a flagrant violation of resolution 687 (1991), which laid down the conditions for the 1991 ceasefire. By that resolution, therefore, the Council implicitly revived the authorization to use force given in resolution 678 (1990). And Ambassador Butler's report makes clear that, despite its undertakings to rescind the decision of 31 October, Iraq has not only failed to resume full cooperation with the Special Commission but has imposed new restrictions on its work.

The British Prime Minister said in his statement earlier this evening,

> 'This action could have been avoided. Since the Gulf war, the entire international community has worked to stop Saddam Hussein from keeping and developing nuclear, chemical and biological weapons and from continuing to threaten his neighbours. For the safety and stability of the region and the wider world, he cannot be allowed to do so. If he will not, through reason and diplomacy, abandon his weapons of mass destruction programme, it must be degraded and diminished by military force. Having exhausted all other avenues, there is no realistic alternative'.

(S/PV. 3939, pp. 6–7)

Announcing British participation in a US-UK military airstrike against targets in Iraq, the Prime Minister, Mr Tony Blair, observed:

I have no doubt that we have the proper legal authority, as it is contained in successive Security Council resolution documents.

(HC Debs., vol. 322, col. 1110: 17 December 1999)

The following press release was made by the Ministry of Defence on 30 December 1998:

IRAQ MISSILE AGGRESSION

At around 06.20 GMT this morning six Iraqi SAM-6 surface to air guided missiles were fired at aircraft taking part in coalition operations to patrol the no-fly zone over southern Iraq. These included UK Tornado GR1 aircraft. The missiles were launched from a site around 20 miles west of Talil. US F–16 aircraft flying with the Tornadoes responded by attacking the SAM–6 site with HARM anti-radar missiles and laser guided bombs. All coalition aircraft returned safely to base.

Commenting on the incident, Defence Secretary George Robertson said:

'Saddam's war machine was badly damaged by the recent campaign of military action against his regime, and this latest gesture of arrogance and defiance is a sign of his weakness. It will make no difference to the way in which we police the no-fly zones. They were set up in support of UN Security Council Resolution 688 to bring protection to the Kurds in the north and the Shia in the south, and as long as that humanitarian need remains, we will continue to enforce the no-fly zones. Saddam knows that coalition pilots will respond to threats to their safety in self-defence, in accordance with international law.'

The following Note for Editors was appended to the release:

The no-fly zones were established in April 1991 and August 1992 respectively, in support of UN Security Council Resolution 688 which demanded an end to the Iraqi regimes repression of Kurds in the north and Shia in the south. Coalition aircraft help protect the interests of these minorities by ensuring that Iraqi aircraft are unable to fly north of the 36th parallel or south of the 33rd parallel.

Part Sixteen: II. C. *Use of force—legitimate use of force—legitimate uses other than self-defence and collective measures*

The following question was put to Her Majesty's Government:

Whether they will detail the provisions in the Charter of the United Nations, or elsewhere in international law, under which a NATO attack on Serbia is permissible and, if it is permissible, what rules of war, relating to 'proportionality', contingent damage to civilians (especially in relation to attacks on facilities suspected of being used to make chemical or biological weapons) and other matters apply?

In reply, the Parliamentary Under-Secretary of State, FCO, wrote:

The legal basis for the use of force can only be considered in the light of all the circumstances at the time. In the exceptional circumstances of Kosovo it was considered that the use of force would be justified on the grounds of overwhelming humanitarian necessity, without Security Council authorisation. The rules of international humanitarian law would of course apply.

(HL Debs., vol. 594, *WA 11*: 2 November 1998)

The following questions were asked of Her Majesty's Government:

Whether the concept of 'overwhelming humanitarian necessity' (as now used by the Government in connection with the possible use of force by NATO in the context of Kosovo) is recognised in international law; and, if so, in what form; and

What is their own definition of 'overwhelming humanitarian necessity'; and whether there is a consensus within the United Nations Security Council:

(a) on the meaning and legal validity of the concept;
(b) on the authority it may confer on states or groups of states proposing to use military force in the absence of a United Nations Security Council Resolution specifically requiring or permitting the use of force; and

Whether 'overwhelming humanitarian necessity' overrides other principles of international law; and, if so, how are the circumstances in which it may do so to be recognised by the international community; and by whom should they be recognised if military action is lawfully to follow; and

Whether unilateral declarations alleging 'overwhelming humanitarian necessity' may confer legality on threats or uses of force or interference within sovereign states that would otherwise be unlawful; and

Whether the concept of 'overwhelming humanitarian necessity' and related legal doctrines have been considered by the International Court at The Hague.

In reply, the Parliamentary Under-Secretary of State, FCO, wrote:

The prohibitions on the use of force contained in the UN Charter do not preclude the use of force by a state or group of states in self-defence in accordance with Article 51 or under the authorisation of the Security Council acting under Chapter VII of the Charter. There is no general doctrine of humanitarian necessity in international law. Cases have nevertheless arisen (as in northern Iraq in 1991) when, in the light of all the circumstances, a limited use of force was justifiable in support of purposes laid down by the Security Council but without the Council's express authorisation when that was the only means to avert an immediate and overwhelming humanitarian catastrophe. Such cases would in the nature of things be exceptional and would depend on an objective assessment of the factual circumstances at the time and on the terms of relevant decisions of the Security Council bearing on the situation in question.

(HL Debs., vol. 594, *WA 139–40*: 16 November 1998)

Part Seventeen: I. B. 7. *The law of armed conflict—international armed conflict—the law of international armed conflict—belligerent occupation*

In the course of a debate on the subject of the Middle East, the Parliamentary Under-Secretary of State, FCO, Baroness Symons of Vernham Dean, stated:

We and our EU partners believe that Israeli settlement activities in the Occupied Territories are both illegal and damaging to the prospects of peace.

. . .

Questions were asked about the status of Jerusalem. Questions have been raised in your Lordships' House recently. Perhaps I can make Her Majesty's Government's view clear again. The status of Jerusalem should be determined in the final status talks. Neither side should seek to pre-empt this. We have condemned Israeli policies aimed at altering the demographic balance of East Jerusalem, including settlement building and confiscation of Palestinian ID cards. Pending agreement, we recognise *de facto* Israeli control of West Jerusalem but consider East Jerusalem to be illegally occupied. We recognise no *de jure* sovereignty over the city.

(HL Debs., vol. 584, cols. 1240–1: 15 January 1998)

The following statement by Mr Derek Fatchett, Minister of State, FCO, was issued on 4 February 1998 as an EU Press Release:

Expansion of Israeli settlements in the West Bank

I am disturbed to hear reports that the Israeli Interior Ministry has given final approval for the construction of 132 housing units for Jewish residents in the Ras Al Amoud area of East Jerusalem. This development is particularly unhelpful at a time when the US and the international community are intensifying their efforts to achieve a breakthrough in the peace process.

I understand that Prime Minister Netanyahu's office have said that the Israeli Government will not allow this construction. We look to the Israeli Government to prevent it from going ahead.

The EU position on settlement building in the Occupied Territories is clear. It is both illegal under international law, and damaging to the peace process. At the European Council on 26 January, European leaders reiterated their view that, if we are to make progress in the negotiations, both sides must avoid unilateral actions which pre-empt final status talks, in particular on settlements and Jerusalem.

In the course of answering questions on the subject of Israel, the Secretary of State for Foreign and Commonwealth Affairs, Mr Robin Cook, stated:

The EU position on settlement building in the occupied territories is clear. It is both illegal under international law, and damaging to the peace process. The building of settlements pre-empts final status talks and destroys hard-won trust between Israelis and Palestinians.

. . .

Two issues of great concern to the Palestinian people arise from the Ras al-Amud development—first, the illegal continuing occupation and building of settlements on territory occupied by military force; and, secondly, the longer-term implications for Jerusalem, as it appears to be part of a strategy to make sure that Jerusalem does not continue to be a mixed city with a division between the two peoples there. For those reasons it is very important, if Israel wants the peace process to proceed, that it halts that particular expansion and refrains from all further settlement development.

(HC Debs., vol. 306, col. 141: 10 February 1998)

At a press conference held in Jerusalem on 17 March 1998, the Secretary of State for Foreign and Commonwealth Affairs, Mr Robin Cook, stated:

As to the issue of sovereignty, our understanding is that part of the construction at Har Homa is beyond the green line and therefore is what we have always recognised as occupied territory.

(Text provided by the FCO)

Speaking in an emergency special session of the UN General Assembly on 17 March 1998, the UK Permanent Representative to the UN in New York, Sir John Weston, stated in part:

I have the honour to take the floor on behalf of the European Union. The Central and Eastern European countries associated with the European Union (. . .) and the Associated Country Cyprus, as well as the EFTA countries members of the EEA (. . .) align themselves with this statement.

The European Union regrets the fact that the General Assembly has had to meet again to examine the question of 'illegal Israeli actions in occupied East Jerusalem and the rest of the Occupied Palestinian Territory'.

The Union deplores Israel's failure to respond to the appeals made by the United Nations General Assembly and the international community to cease construction work in Jabel Abu Ghneim/Har Homa in the Occupied West Bank and, in general, to suspend the development of settlements in the Occupied Territories, including Jerusalem.

These activities are contrary to the provisions of the Fourth Geneva Convention.

. . .

According to resolution ES-10/3, the General Assembly recommends to the High Contracting Parties to the Fourth Geneva Convention to convene a conference on measures to enforce the Convention in the Occupied Palestinian Territory, including Jerusalem, and to ensure its respect.

The European Union reaffirms that the Geneva Convention relative to the Protection of Civilian Persons in Time of War applies to the Occupied Palestinian Territory, including Jerusalem, and to the other Arab territories occupied by Israel since 1967. We call on Israel to recognize that the Convention applies de facto and de jure to those territories and to comply with its provisions.

The EU thanks Switzerland for its actions in following up resolution ES-10/4. The EU suggests that resolution ES-10/4 might be taken forward in the following way: the mandate of the experts meeting should be to follow up resolution ES-10/4, notably OP4 and OP5. It should aim to make recommendations on dates, locations, participants etc and commission any reports necessary.

It should also discuss substance, notably the situation in the Occupied Territories relative to the Fourth Geneva Convention, and the political and legal implications of the conference, taking into account the obligations of Israel and other States Parties under this Convention. The European Union also believes that the meeting should take place in Geneva, on an informal basis, with participation to include expert level representatives of the High Contracting Parties, as well as the International Committee of the Red Cross and the Palestinian Liberation Organisation.

(A/ES–10 PV. 8, pp. 15–16)

Speaking in the UN Commission on Human Rights on 22 March 1998, the UK representative, Ms A. Glover, on behalf of the EU and the States associated with it, stated:

The Union was gravely concerned about the continuing expansion of Israeli settlements in the territories occupied in 1997. Such settlements were both illegal under international law and damaging to the peace process.

. . .

Palestinian residents of Jerusalem were also facing problems as a result of discriminatory measures adopted by the Israeli Government and judiciary. They risked losing their Jerusalem identity cards if they were dual citizens or if, despite meeting previous residence requirements, they had lived or worked for extended periods outside the city. Such blatant attempts to change the demographic composition of Jerusalem were contrary to international law and to the spirit of the peace process; they must cease immediately.

(E/CN.4/1998/SR. 8, p. 15)

Replying in a debate on the subject of the Israeli-occupied territories, the Minister of State, FCO, Mr Derek Fatchett, stated:

My hon. Friend clearly set out his views on the international legal position on settlements. Until a final settlement is agreed, we will base our position on the United Nations Security Council resolutions. International humanitarian law will remain the basis for our policy on the occupied territories. The key to that, as my hon. Friend said, is the fourth Geneva convention of 1949. Again, we have consistently called upon Israel to comply fully with its provisions. Israel ratified it in 1951, so we are asking Israel to do no more than what it has committed itself to for the past 47 years. Successive UK Governments have never accepted the Israeli argument that the convention does not apply to occupied territories. That has been the UK position for many years—many people would say too many years in relation to progress on the issue.

Article 49 of the fourth Geneva convention clearly states: 'The Occupying power shall not deport or transfer parts of its own civilian population into the territory it occupies.' It appears difficult not to agree that the purpose of the

Israeli settlers, and perhaps of the present Government of Israel, is to change demographically the population and structure throughout the occupied territories. Following that through logically, as my hon. Friend did, it appears to be inconsistent with article 49.

My hon. Friend also asked what action the UK had taken in relation to the fourth Geneva convention. We have constantly reminded Israel of its obligations under the convention. More recently, the United Kingdom, in its EU presidency, supported the UN resolution in March calling for a full conference of the high contracting parties to the fourth Geneva convention to discuss the Israeli violations.

(HC Debs., vol. 314, WA, cols. *955–6*: 23 June 1998)

In reply to a question on the subject of the expansion of Jewish settlements on the West Bank, the Parliamentary Under-Secretary of State, FCO, wrote in part:

. . . settlements in the occupied territories are illegal under international law. They are also an obstacle to peace, pre-empting final status talks and destroying hard won trust between Israelis and Palestinians. EU missions in Tel Aviv and Jerusalem carefully monitor the situation on the ground and produce quarterly reports summarising settlement activity. Those reports are then put to the Israeli Government.

As EU presidency, we issued a statement on 21st June expressing concern at the Israeli Government's endorsement of plans to expand the boundaries of the Jerusalem area. We also issued a statement on 12th June urging the government to take urgent measures to prevent provocative settlement activity in East Jerusalem.

(HL Debs., vol. 591, col. 348: 25 June 1998)

In reply to a question about the construction of Israeli settlements at Har Homa, the Parliamentary Under-Secretary of State, FCO, wrote:

Our Ambassador in Tel Aviv has registered our disapproval with senior officials at the announcement by the Israeli Ministry of Construction and Housing on 12 November to issue tenders for construction of 1,025 building plots at Har Homa. We will continue to monitor the situation closely. We regard settlement activity in the Occupied Territories and East Jerusalem as illegal under international law and an obstacle to peace. The US has also said it regards settlement activity as unhelpful to the peace process.

(HL Debs., vol. 594, *WA 218*: 19 September 1998)

In reply to a question about the Israeli settlement of Ariel, the same Minister wrote:

The decision to give Ariel city status was announced on 11 June and this was formally conferred by Prime Minister Netanyahu on 7 October. Belated action at this sensitive stage of the pease process would be counter productive. But our position on settlements is clear and well known to the Israelis. Settlements in the Occupied Territories and East Jerusalem are illegal under international law and an obstacle to peace. The Israeli Cabinet ratified the Wye River Memorandum on 11 November. We expect Israel to abide by the letter and spirit of this agreement and refrain from any unilateral or provocative acts.

(Ibid., *WA 213*)

The following observations were made by Mr M. Eaton, Deputy Legal Adviser, FCO, at an Experts' Meeting on the Fourth Geneva Convention on Humanitarian Law, held in Geneva on 27–29 October 1998:

Greatest problem in relation to implementation of the GCIV is that of refusal to recognise its applicability. As ICRC says 'when confronted with situations in which the Convention should be applied, the state party to it almost invariably cite some grounds or other on which in their view it is not applicable'.

Has also been rightly said 'The law of belligerent occupation has had a poor record of compliance for most of the twentieth century. The principal problem has been the reluctance of states to admit that the law applies at all'. This is not a problem of a single situation of occupation – it is a widespread and long-observed phenomenon. But, since a particular current occupation situation has frequently been mentioned here, I wish to state that the British position on the *de jure* application of the Convention to the territories occupied by Israel after 1967 is well-known, and does not need to be rehearsed.

Unfortunately the question of applicability of GCIV is very frequently bedevilled and confused by that of title to the territory in question. If applicability of the law were dependent on the resolution of underlying questions of title it would almost never be applied.

In fact the law does not make it a precondition that the territory occupied must have belonged to the displaced sovereign prior to the occupation. It might appear so from GCIV Article 2(2): 'The Convention shall also apply in all cases of partial or total occupation of the territory of an ACP, even if the occupation meets with no armed resistance'.

But this is not the primary criterion for application. It is, rather, a residual role. The *primary* rule is in Article 2(1): 'The Convention shall apply to all cases of declared war or other armed conflict'.

So if, during an armed conflict, a state takes military control of territory it did not control before the conflict the Convention is applicable, whatever the underlying disputes about title.

To restate a very well-known, yet often not-respected, principle of IHL [International Humanitarian Law], the application of IHL is not concerned with the rights and wrongs and origins of the conflict. The sole question is, is there an armed conflict, international or internal? If so, the relevant rules of IHL apply. Of course, that question itself is not always easy to answer, but my point is that the application of IHL depends upon a factual situation of occupation. For the sake of the civilians caught up in the situation it needs to be applied notwithstanding legal arguments over status, whether of territory or of parties to the conflict. The drafters of the Convention did their best to exclude such arguments. It is sad that they are still used to justify its non-application.

If I may be permitted a personal reminiscence of the Protocol I negotiations in the Third Committee of the Diplomatic Conference of 1974–77 (in this very room): there was a proposal to characterise occupation as inherently wrong.

It was resisted by the Rapporteur, Ambassador George Aldrich of the USA, who recalled that his country, with France, the Soviet Union and UK was an occupying power in Berlin and he saw nothing wrong in that. The proposal was promptly dropped.

So it is not occupation per se that offends against IHL (I leave aside other legal questions of use of force etc). It is refusal of occupants fully to apply the rules of IHL to the occupied territory as a matter of law. There is no particular weakness in the law, save that it is not applied.

To state this is easy. To put it into practice very hard, because neither the Fourth Convention nor Additional Protocol I sets up an independent arbiter to determine when they apply. It is not the job of the ICRC. The international community and HCPs individually or collectively, indeed, should say what they think. But ultimately it depends on the political will of the HCP concerned in any given situation of occupation.

Of course it is welcome when the Convention is applied voluntarily and *de facto* in situations where there is dispute as to its application *de jure*, even if such application is only partial. If civilians *in practice* are protected that is the most important thing. But it can never be a completely satisfactory substitute for *de jure* application, being both partial and dependent upon a consent which can always be withdrawn.

Finally, it has been suggested that the law of belligerent occupation is ill-suited to long-running occupations of the kind we have seen relatively often since 1945, being essentially designed for temporary situations. There is some force in that. It is possible to pick out particular GCIV provisions which are hard to apply in a long-running occupation. But what do you put in its place? Any change which recognises a permanency to the situation, or gives occupying power greater powers to make changes there, would tend to legitimize the substitution of the occupant for the former sovereign power.

So, once again it does not seem to my delegation that there is any need to embark on the difficult exercise of trying to agree new provisions to apply in long-running occupations. Better to apply the existing law, which is in our view elastic enough. None of the difficulties of application is insuperable.

(Text provided by the FCO)

In reply to a question, the Minister of State, FCO, wrote:

We have made no formal representation to the Israeli government specifically about the announcement of the addition of further housing units to the settlement of Kiryat Arba near Hebron. But our position on settlements is clear and well known to them. Settlements in the Occupied Territories and East Jerusalem are illegal under international law and an obstacle to peace. We note the clarification given by Prime Minister Netanyahu's Office on 1 November that no new building permits have been issued in Jerusalem. We expect the Israeli government to continue to refrain from granting such permits, and to abide by the new spirit of cooperation forged at Wye.

(HC Debs., vol. 319, WA, col. *33*: 9 November 1998)

In reply to the question what assurances the FCO has received from the Israeli Government that no new building permits will be issued for

Jewish housing units in (a) Gaza and (b) the Occupied West Bank, the Minister of State, FCO, wrote:

We have received no further assurances from the Israeli government that no new building permits will be issued for Jewish housing units in Gaza and the West Bank. But the Israeli Cabinet endorsed the Wye River Memorandum on 12 November and we expect the Israeli government to abide by the letter and the spirit of the agreement, which prohibits either side from taking any steps to change the status of the West Bank and the Gaza Strip. We have made it clear to Israel that we regard the initiation and encouragement of settlement activity as a violation of international law and an obstacle to peace, and we recently informed them of our concern at the issuing of tenders for construction at Har Homa in East Jerusalem.

(HC Debs., vol. 319, WA, cols. *568–9*: 17 November 1998)

Part Seventeen: I. B. 8. *The law of armed conflict—international armed conflict—the law of international armed conflict—conventional weapons*

In September 1998, the FCO published a Briefing Paper entitled *The Ottawa Convention on Anti-Personnel Mines: A British Perspective.* It read in part as follows:

On 31 July 1998, Britain became the 29th country to ratify the Ottawa Convention on anti-personnel mines (APLs), and, on 16 September 1998, the Convention achieved its 40th ratification. It will now enter into force on 1 March 1999, demonstrating the international community's determination to rid the world of these weapons.

OTTAWA CONVENTION

The Convention on the Prohibition of the Use, Stockpiling, Production and Transfer of Anti-Personnel Mines and on their Destruction (or Ottawa Convention) provides for a ban on the use, production and transfer of APLs immediately upon its entry into force and for the destruction of stockpiles of these weapons within four years of this date. It will enter into force on the first day of the sixth month after the 40th ratification.

Its provisions apply to all APLs*, but not to other categories of mine (whether or not equipped with anti-handling devices), nor booby traps (unless they also fall within the definition of an anti-personnel mine). These weapons are covered by other international agreements.

The Ottawa Landmines Conference, to which Canada invited countries supporting a ban on APLs and leading non-governmental organisations (NGOs) from the International Campaign to Ban Landmines, was held from 2–5 October 1996. Participants agreed to negotiate a ban on APLs, and Canadian Foreign Minister, Lloyd Axworthy, called for the ban to be implemented by December 1997. The text was agreed at Oslo on 18 September 1997 and the Convention opened for signature at Ottawa on 3 December 1997. By the end of August 1998, 130 countries had signed the Convention.

* Article 2, paragraph 1 of the Convention reads: 'Anti-personnel mine' means a mine designed to be exploded by the presence, proximity or contact of a person and that will incapacitate, injure or kill one or more persons. Mines designed to be detonated by the presence, proximity or contact of a vehicle as opposed to a person, that are equipped with anti-handling devices, are not considered anti-personnel mines as a result of being so equipped.

BRITISH LEGISLATION

The Landmines Act 1998 makes it a criminal offence, punishable by up to 14 years' imprisonment, for any person to engage in any activity prohibited by the Ottawa Convention. The Act also contains provision for fact-finding missions to Britain to investigate alleged violations of the Convention.

Not all NATO States*have signed the Ottawa Convention. Canada made a declaration on 3 December 1997, setting out her understanding that the Convention does not prohibit joint operations with the armed forces of a non-State Party which use APLs. On ratification, Britain issued a similar interpretative statement. This recorded Britain's understanding 'that the mere participation in the planning or execution of operations, exercises or other military activity by the United Kingdom's Armed Forces, or individual United Kingdom nationals, conducted in combination with the armed forces of States not party to the Ottawa Convention which engage in activity prohibited under the Convention, is not by itself assistance, encouragement or inducement for the purposes of Article 1 paragraph 1(c) of the Convention'.

* Turkey and the United States have not signed. Greece has signed, but does not expect to ratify the Convention for some time.

Part Seventeen: I. B. 9. *The law of armed conflict—international armed conflict—the law of international armed conflict—nuclear, bacteriological and chemical weapons*

In reply to a question, the Minister of State, FCO, wrote:

I am pleased to be able to inform the House that the United Kingdom instruments of ratification of the two Additional Protocols of 1997 to the Geneva Conventions of 1949 for the Protection of War Victims are today being deposited with the Swiss authorities in Berne.

The necessary legislation, the Geneva Conventions (Amendment) Act 1995, received the Royal Assent on 19 July 1995.

A copy of the note accompanying the instrument of ratification has been placed in the Library of the House. The note contains the statements made by the United Kingdom on ratification of Additional Protocol I on International Conflicts. In most cases these reflect similar statements made by the United Kingdom on signing Protocol I in 1997.

I wish to draw the attention of the House in particular to the statement concerning nuclear weapons, which is in the following terms: 'It continues to be the understanding of the United Kingdom that the rules introduced by the Protocol apply exclusively to conventional weapons without prejudice to any other rules of international law applicable to other types of weapons. In particular, the rules so introduced do not have any effect on, and do not regulate or prohibit the use of nuclear weapons.'

Statements to similar effect have been made by NATO partners and others ratifying Protocol I. They reflect the basis upon which the Conference which drew up Additional Protocol I took place and statements made at the Conference by the United Kingdom delegation among others.

I would also draw the attention of the House to statement (m) on Articles 51 to 55 and statement (n) on Articles 56 and 85, paragraph 3c. These statements reserve our right to threaten reprisals if attacks were launched against our own civilians or civilian targets and remove the virtual immunity under the Protocol for attacks on dams, dykes and certain nuclear facilities such as nuclear power stations, even when they are a significant part of the enemy's war effort. Both reservations have been drafted with great care to show that these would be measures of last resort, to be decided upon only if all else had failed, and requiring high level authorisation. Our actions would still be subject to the classic rule of proportionality.

I would also draw the attention of the House to statement (d) concerned with Article 1, paragraph 4 and Article 96, paragraph 3, which extend the application of the Protocol to armed conflicts 'in which peoples are fighting against colonial domination and alien occupation and against racist regimes in the exercise of their right of self-determination.'

To guard against the possibility that terrorist organisations may seek to misuse these provisions the statement makes clear that the term 'armed conflict' is understood as denoting something clearly beyond the commission of ordinary crimes including acts of terrorism, and that the United Kingdom will not be bound, in relation to any situation in which the United Kingdom itself is involved, unless it expressly recognises the adversary as genuinely an authority representing a people engaged in an armed conflict of the type referred to in these Articles.

In accordance with the powers conferred in Section 7 of the 1957 Geneva Convention Act, as amended by Section 4 (7) of the Geneva Conventions (Amendment) Act 1995, the Government will certify in an Order in Council the terms of the statements made in ratification.

Article 90 of Additional Protocol I establishes an International Fact-finding Commission and provides that the High Contracting Parties may at the time of ratification or subsequently declare that they recognise, in relation to any other High Contracting Party accepting the same obligation, the competence of the Commission to inquire into allegations by such other party of facts alleged to be a grave breach or serious violation of the Conventions or the Protocol. The Government intend to make a declaration of acceptance of the competence of the Fact-finding Commission. It will be necessary first to bring before the House legislation to confer upon the members of the Commission and their staff the necessary privileges and immunities.

(HC Debs., vol. 305, WA, cols. *270–2*; 28 January 1998)

In the course of answering questions on the subject of a proposal for an international peace police, the Parliamentary Under-Secretary of State, FCO, Baroness Symons of Vernham Dean, stated:

The United Kingdom Government believe in universal adherence to and compliance with both the Chemical Weapons Convention and the Biological and

Toxin Weapons Convention. As I said, we have detected shortcomings in the second convention, which is why we are eagerly pursuing improvements to it. As to the longer term, suggestions about examining these issues will be considered appropriately by Her Majesty's Government.

(HL Debs., vol. 587, col. 815: 19 March 1998)

The following question was asked of Her Majesty's Government:

Whether they agree with the [interpretation of the] International Court of Justice Opinion given by Mr Rupert Ticehurst that, 'At the very least the United Kingdom must accept that the legality of its Trident programme is brought into considerable doubt by the ICJ Opinion. Its continued deployment raises very important legal and military issues which must as a matter or urgency be addressed'?

In reply, the Parliamentary Under-Secretary of State, FCO, wrote:

The ICJ did not consider nuclear weapons, as such, to be unlawful. The legality of the use of nuclear weapons would depend on all the circumstances at the time. The Opinion does not require a change in [the] United Kingdom's entirely defensive nuclear deterrence policy.

(HL Debs., vol. 588, *WA 202:* 21 April 1998)

In reply to the question whether the UK chemical defence programme is in compliance with the terms of the Chemical Weapons Convention, the Minister of State, Ministry of Defence, wrote in part:

The Chemical Weapons Convention, with which the United Kingdom is fully compliant, permits activities which protect against the use of chemical weapons. The UK chemical defence programme has been constructed to meet that need.

(HL Debs., vol. 589, *WA 1*: 27 April 1998)

In reply to the question whether the use of anti-personnel mines will be included in the jurisdiction of the International Criminal Court, the Minister of State, FCO, wrote:

Our intention is get landmines universally banned.

The Statute of the International Criminal Court is still being negotiated. We support proposals for the Court to be able to try war crimes which are recognised under customary international law. Despite the signature of the Ottawa Convention, the use of anti-personnel landmines does not at present come into this category. But landmines, like any other weapon, might be used in a way that would contravene international law. Under the proposals which we support this could well lead to the user being prosecuted at the International Criminal Court.

(HC Debs., vol. 315, WA, cols. *579-80*: 9 July 1998)

In reply to a question, the Minister of State, FCO, wrote:

Until such time as the use of Anti-Personnel mines become subject to a comprehensive prohibition under international law, it cannot be classified as a war crime. This is not a matter of policy but what is currently possible under international law.

The abhorrence with which the Government view the use of Anti-Personnel land mines should be in no doubt to anyone. This is reflected by the Government's introduction of domestic legislation to fulfil our obligations under the Ottawa Convention. We shall continue to encourage as many countries as possible to sign and ratify the Ottawa Convention.

(HC Debs., vol. 317, WA, col. *539*: 30 July 1998)

In the course of a debate on the subject of events in Kosovo, the Parliamentary Under-Secretary of State, FCO, Baroness Symons of Vernham Dean, stated:

I am sure I speak for the whole House when I say that we are appalled at the recent massacres at Gornje Obrinje and near Vucitern. As I am sure we are all aware, most of those killed were women [and] children. This was not an act of war; it was plain, cold-blooded murder. We know what happened; we have seen the appalling evidence with our own eyes. UNSCR 1199 affirms the role of the International Criminal Tribunal for the Former Yugoslavia in Kosovo.

(HL Debs., vol. 593, col. 716: 12 October 1998)

In reply to a question, the Government Minister in the House of Lords wrote:

The use of chemical or biological weapons by any state would be a grave breach of international law. A state which chose to use chemical or biological weapons against the United Kingdom should expect us to exercise our right of self defence and to make a proportionate response.

(HL Debs., vol. 593, *WA 224*: 29 October 1998)

Part Seventeen: I. B. 11. *The law of armed conflict—international armed conflict—the law of international armed conflict—termination of international armed conflict, treaties of peace*

In reply to a question on the subject of compensation for the treatment of British prisoners of war by Japan, the Minister of State, FCO, wrote in part:

Since taking office last May, we have held a series of high-level discussions with the Japanese Government on ways to help the former prisoners of war. Throughout these talks, the Japanese Government referred to the 1951 San Francisco Peace Treaty which legally settled the question of compensation at governmental level. It is clear that there is no prospect of a new round of compensation.

(HC Debs., vol. 308, WA, col. *259*: 11 March 1998)

Part Seventeen: III. *The law of armed conflict—international humanitarian law*

(See also Part Sixteen: II. C. (item of 2 November 1998), above)

The following statement was made by Mr M. Eaton of the UK delegation to the First Periodical Meeting of States Parties to the Geneva Conventions on Humanitarian Law, held in Geneva in January 1998:

Mr Chairman, the UK's comments fall into two parts. First some comments on the legal situation in 'anarchic conflicts'. Secondly, and at greater length, some proposals for action that States Parties to the Geneva Conventions can usefully take in relation to such conflicts: to help prevent them, resolve them, and rebuild countries after them.

I can be relatively brief as to the law because we largely share the analysis of the ICRC in its paper—both as to the characteristics of such conflicts in disintegrating states and as to the law which applies. We agree that in all such conflicts Common Article 3 will apply (as the ICJ has said). More rarely it may be that Protocol II will apply.

Some speakers have referred to the proposal for a new instrument on minimum humanitarian standards. We have every respect for the motives of those promoting this proposal. But we continue to doubt whether that is a worthwhile exercise. If even the modest standards of Common Article 3 are often not applied, what realistic chance is there than an instrument with more extensive obligations will be, even if ratified? Let us work with what we have—provisions which as the spokesman for the Federation said yesterday, reflect principles, customs and values universally accepted in all parts of the world.

We do however agree strongly that the ICC will fill a big gap in the present machinery, namely the lack of credible and effective ways of bringing war criminals to justice especially in situations where local courts have ceased to function properly.

What is the result of Common Article 3? Yesterday at least two distinguished representatives took issue with the ICRC's view that it could and should deal with armed factions as 'parties to the conflict'. It was said that terrorists could never have that status, and that the ICRC could only deal with such factions with the government's consent. The UK has every sympathy for the concerns of these delegations but, with respect, they seem to be based on a confusion between two different situations. It is true that, for Article 3 to apply at all, there must be an 'armed conflict'. That term, as the ICRC rightly say, excludes situations of isolated and sporadic acts of violence. Terrorist situations normally fall into that category. My country has suffered from such acts for some time—though I hope and pray that they will soon be a thing of the past.

But the type of anarchic conflicts with which we are dealing today are a quite different and more serious situation, where there is undoubtedly an internal armed conflict with armed factions fighting each other and the structures of the state disintegrating. In that situation Article 3 applies. One of the provisions of Article 3 is that 'An impartial body such as the ICRC may offer its services to the Parties to the conflict'. That must mean all those fighting. There is no mention of the ICRC needing Government consent to make such an offer to non-Governmental parties. It has that right under the Convention. We certainly agree that it is desirable for it to do so with Government consent, and we understand it is ICRC practice to seek it. The important point is that the Government has no veto. There is an important reassurance in the last sentence of Common Article 3, that 'the application of the previous provisions shall not affect the legal status of the Parties to the conflict'. So those who may well remain, in the Government's eyes, 'terrorists' are not in any way legitimised by the ICRC's approach. But the ICRC must remain free to approach them; how can it otherwise carry out its humanitarian work to care for victims of the conflict? It must deal with those wielding *de facto* power.

(Text provided by the FCO)

On 19 May 1998, the EU Presidency issued a statement about events in Sierra Leone. It stated in part:

The European Union and the United States express the gravest concern at the violent attacks by the Revolutionary United Front and the deposed Military Junta on the civilian population of Sierra Leone.

. . .

This unspeakable cruelty is a gross violation of human rights and international humanitarian law.

(*Bulletin of the European Union*, 1998–5, p. 74)

On 23 September 1998, the EU Presidency issued a statement on Afghanistan which read in part as follows:

The European Union asks all parties to fully respect international humanitarian law and human rights in all parts of Afghanistan and would welcome an international presence, particularly in Bamyan province, to observe compliance with these rights. The non-compliance with the basic principle of international humanitarian law is a major factor in an alarming situation of tensions in the region, in particular between Iran and the Taliban.

(*Bulletin of the European Union*, 1998–9, p. 55)

Part Seventeen: IV. *The law of armed conflict—war crimes*

In reply to a question, the Parliamentary Under-Secretary of State, FCO, wrote:

Her Majesty's Government attach the highest priority to seeing all those who have been indicted for war crimes face trial in The Hague. The primary responsibility for bringing the remaining 32 war crimes indictees to justice lies with the parties to the Dayton Peace Agreement themselves. We shall continue to press them to fulfil this, and all other, Dayton obligations. However, the international community has also shown its willingness to act where others do not. The action in April by British SFOR troops to detain a further two indictees in Prijedor is the latest reaffirmation of this commitment.

(HL Debs., vol. 590, *WA 18*: 1 June 1998)

The Secretary of State for Foreign and Commonwealth Affairs,

Mr Robin Cook, made the following statement at a press conference in Brussels on 13 July 1998:

> . . . we have noted the very welcome recent statement by the Prosecutor at the International Criminal Tribunal on Yugoslavia that her remit does extend to Kosovo and that she regards Kosovo as being in a state of armed conflict; which is significant because it triggers her writ. That puts on notice all those taking part in armed conflict in Kosovo that they may well be held individually responsible for their actions and therefore must take great care not to carry out war crimes particularly against the civilian population of Kosovo.

(Text provided by the FCO)

APPENDICES

I. Multilateral Agreements Signed by the United Kingdom in 1998[1]

Title	*Place and Date*	*UK Signature*	*Text*[2]
Terms of Reference of the International Copper Study Group	New York, 24.2.1989	26.6.1998 (provisional acceptance)	
Convention for the Establishment of the European Telecommunication Office (ETO)	Copenhagen, 1.9.1996	2.7.1998	
Convention on the Prohibition of the Use, Stockpiling, Production and Transfer of Anti-Personnel Mines and on their Destruction	Oslo, 18.9.1997	3.12.1997	TS No. 18 (1999) (Cm 4308)
Kyoto Protocol to the United Nations Framework Convention on Climate Change	Kyoto, 11.12.1997	29.4.1998	
International Convention for the Suppression of Terrorist Bombings	New York, 15.12.1997	12.1.1998	
Protocol to the North Atlantic Treaty on the Accession of the Czech Republic	Brussels, 16.12.1997	16.12.1997	Misc. No. 3 (1998) (Cm 3930)
Protocol to the North Atlantic Treaty on the Accession of the Republic of Hungary	Brussels, 16.12.1997	16.12.1997	Misc. No. 4 (1998) (Cm 3931)

[1] Information supplied by the Foreign and Commonwealth Office. The table includes some agreements signed by the United Kingdom before 1998, where information was not previously available. The information is correct as at January 1999, although in some cases information available since that time has been included.

[2] Publication is in the Miscellaneous Series (Misc.) and Treaty Series (TS) of UK Command Papers. Cm = Command Paper number.

Title	*Place and Date*	*UK Signature*	*Text*
Protocol to the North Atlantic Treaty on the Accession of the Republic of Poland	Brussels, 16.12.1997	16.12.1997	Misc. No. 2 (1998) (Cm 3929)
Convention on Combating Bribery of Foreign Public Officials in International Business Transactions	Paris, 17.12.1997	17.12.1997	Misc. No. 6 (1998) (Cm 3994)
Agreement relating to the Commission established by the Convention for the Protection of the Marine Environment in the North-East Atlantic 1992	London, 18.12.1997	18.12.1997	TS No. 13 (1999) (Cm 4277)
1998 Amendments to the International Convention on Maritime Search and Rescue, 1979 (MSC 70(69))	London, 18.5.1998	18.5.1998	
1997 Amendments to the International Convention for the Safety of Life at Sea, 1974, as amended (MSC 65(68))	London, 4.6.1998	4.6.1998	
Protocol to the 1979 Convention on Long-Range Transboundary Air Pollution on Heavy Metals	Aarhus, 24.6.1998	24.6.1998 (confirmation awaited)	
Protocol to the 1979 Convention on Long-Range Transboundary Air Pollution on Persistent Organic Pollutants	Aarhus, 24.6.1998	24.6.1998 (confirmation awaited)	
Protocol of Amendment to the European Convention for the Protection of Vertebrate Animals used for Experimental and other Scientific Purposes (ETS No. 170)	Strasbourg, 22.6.1998	8.9.1998	

Title	*Place and Date*	*UK Signature*	*Text*
Convention on Access to Information, Public Participation in Decision-Making and Access to Justice in Environmental Matters	Aarhus, 25.6.1998	25.6.1998	
Rome Statute of the International Criminal Court	Rome, 17.7.1998	30.11.1998	
Protocol relating to an Amendment to the Convention on International Civil Aviation	Montreal, 1.10.1998	1.10.1988	

II. European Communities Agreements Signed by the United Kingdom in 1998[1]

Title	*Place and Date*	*UK Signature*	*Text*[2]
Economic Partnership, Political Coordination and Co-operation Agreement between the European Community and its Member States, of the one part, and the United Mexican States, of the other part, with Annex, Declarations and Final Act	Brussels, 8.12.1997	8.12.1997	EC No. 4 (1998) (Cm 4097)
Protocol establishing the Fishing Possibilities and the Financial Compensation provided for in the Agreement between the European Economic Community and the Government of the Revolutionary People's Republic of Guinea on Fishing off the Guinean Coast for the period 1 January 1998 to 31 December 1999	Brussels, 11.12.1997		Not to be published
Convention drawn up on the basis of Article K.3 of the Treaty on European Union, on Mutual Assistance and Co-operation between Customs Administrations	Brussels, 18.12.1997	18.12.1997	Not yet published
Agreement in the form of an Exchange of Letters concerning the Provisional Application of the Protocol establishing the Fishing	Brussels, 20.1.1998		Not to be published

[1] Information supplied by the Foreign and Commonwealth Office. The information is correct as at January 1999, although in some cases information available since that time has been included.

[2] Publication is in the European Communities Series of UK Command Papers (EC). Cm = Command Paper number.

Title	*Place and Date*	*UK Signature*	*Text*
Rights and Financial Contribution provided for in the Agreement between the European Economic Community and the Republic of Côte d'Ivoire for the period 1.7.1997 to 30.6.2000	Brussels, 20.1.1998		Not to be published
Agreement in the form of an Exchange of Letters on the Provisional Application of the Protocol establishing, for the period 6.9.1997 to 5.9.2000, the Fishing Rights and the Financial Contribution provided for by the Agreement between the European Economic Community and the Republic of Cape Verde on Fishing off the Coast of Cape Verde	Brussels, 20.1.1998		Not to be published
Agreement among the Government of Canada, Governments of Member States of the European Space Agency, the Government of Japan, the Government of the Russian Federation, and the Government of the United States of America concerning Co-operation on the Civil International Space Station	Washington, 29.1.1998	29.1.1998	
Protocol setting out, for the period 28.2.1998 to 27.2.2001, the Fishing Opportunities and Financial Contribution provided for in the Agreement between the European Economic Community and the	Brussels, 27.2.1998		Not to be published

Title	*Place and Date*	*UK Signature*	*Text*
Islamic Federal Republic of the Comoros on Fishing off the Comoros	Brussels, 27.2.1998		Not to be published
Agreement in the form of an Exchange of Letters between the European Community and the Republic of Poland regarding the Modernization of the Polish Oil Sector within the framework of the Europe Agreement establishing an Association between the European Communities and their Member States, of the one part, and the Republic of Poland, of the other part	Brussels, 3/24.3.1998		Not to be published
Agreement between the European Community and the United States of America on Sanitary Measures to Protect Public and Animal Health in Trade in Live Animals and Animal Products	Brussels, 16.3.1998		Not to be published
Agreement in the form of an Exchange of Letters amending the Agreement in the form of an Exchange of Letters between the European Community and the Republic of Bulgaria on the Reciprocal Establishment of Tariff Quotas for Certain Wines	Brussels, 19.3.1998		Not to be published
Agreement between the European Community and the Russian Federation on Trade in Textile Products	Brussels, 28.3.1998		Not to be published
Agreement between the European Community and the Gabonese Republic on Fishing off the Coast of Gabon	Libreville, 1.4.1998		Not to be published

Title	*Place and Date*	*UK Signature*	*Text*
Agreement in the form of an Exchange of Letters amending the Agreement in the form of an Exchange of Letters between the European Community and Romania on the Reciprocal Establishment of Tariff Quotas for Certain Wines	Brussels, 7.4.1998		Not to be published
Agreement on Mutual Recognition between the European Community and Canada	London, 14.5.1998		Not to be published
Agreement in the form of an Exchange of Letters between the European Community and the Republic of Georgia maintaining in force the Agreement between the European Economic Community and the Republic of Georgia on Trade in Textile Products initialled in Brussels on 17.11.1993 as amended by an Agreement in the form of an Exchange of Letters initialled on 15.6.1995	Brussels, 15.5.1998		Not to be published
Protocol setting out the Fishing Opportunities and Financial Contribution provided for in the Agreement between the European Economic Community and the Republic of Madagascar on Fishing off Madagascar for the period from 21.5.1998 to 20.5.2001	Brussels, 21.5.1998		Not to be published
Partnership and Co-operation Agreement establishing a Partnership between the European Communities	Brussels, 25.5.1998	25.5.1998	

Title	*Place and Date*	*UK Signature*	*Text*
and their Member States, of the one part, and Turkmenistan, of the other part, with Declarations, Protocol, Exchange of Letters, and Final Act	Brussels, 25.5.1998	25.5.1998	
Protocol setting out the Fishing Opportunities and Financial Compensation provided for in the Agreement between the European Economic Community and the Republic of Madagascar on Fishing off Madagascar for the period from 21.5.1998 to 20.5.2001	Luxembourg, 25.5.1998		Not to be published
Convention drawn up on the basis of Article K3 of the Treaty on European Union on Jurisdiction and the Recognition and Enforcement of Judgments in Matrimonial Matters	Brussels, 28.5.1998	28.5.1998	
Protocol drawn up on the basis of Article K3 of the Treaty on European Union on the Interpretation by the Court of Justice of the European Communities of the Convention on Jurisdiction and Enforcement of Judgments in Matrimonial Matters	Brussels, 28.5.1998	28.5.1998	
Agreement between the European Communities and the Government of the United States of America on the Application of Positive Comity Principles in the Enforcement of their Competition Laws	Brussels/ Washington, 3.6.1998		Not to be published

Title	*Place and Date*	*UK Signature*	*Text*
Convention drawn up on the basis of Article K3 of the Treaty of the European Union on Driving Disqualifications	Brussels, 17.6.1998	17.6.1998	
Agreement between the European Community, the European Space Agency and the European Organization for the Safety of Air Navigation on a European Contribution to the Development of a Global Navigation Satellite System (GNSS)	Luxembourg, 18.6.1998		Not to be published
Agreement on Mutual Recognition in relation to Conformity Assessment between the European Community and New Zealand	Luxembourg, 18.6.1998		Not to be published
Agreement on Mutual Recognition in relation to Conformity Assessment, Certificates and Markings between the European Community and Australia	Canberra, 24.6.1998		Not to be published
Agreement on Mutual Recognition in relation to Conformity Assessment between the European Community and New Zealand	Wellington, 25.6.1998		Not to be published
Agreement in the form of an Exchange of Letters between the European Community and the Republic of India on the Guaranteed Prices for Cane Sugar for the 1997/98 Delivery Period	Brussels, 26.6.1998		Not to be published

Title	*Place and Date*	*UK Signature*	*Text*
Agreement in the form of an Exchange of Letters between the European Community and the Republic of Guinea concerning the Provisional Application of the Protocol establishing the Fishing Possibilities and the Financial Compensation provided for in the Agreement between the European Economic Community and the Government of the Revolutionary People's Republic of Guinea on Fishing off the Coast for the period 1.1.1998 to 31.12.1999	Brussels, 29.6.1998		Not to be published
Protocol adjusting Trade Aspects of the Europe Agreement establishing an Association between the European Communities and their Member States, of the one part, and the Republic of Lithuania, of the other part, to take account of the Accession of the Republic of Austria, the Republic of Finland and the Kingdom of Sweden to the European Union and the Outcome of the Uruguay Round Negotiations on Agriculture, including Improvements to the Existing Preferential Arrangements	Brussels, 16.7.1998		
Protocol setting out, for the period 28.2.1998 to 27.2.2001, the Fishing	Brussels, 20.7.1998		Not to be published

Title	*Place and Date*	*UK Signature*	*Text*
Opportunities and Financial Contribution provided for in the Agreement between the European Economic Community and the Islamic Federal Republic of the Comoros on Fishing off the Comoros	Brussels, 20.7.1998		Not to be published
Agreement in the form of an Exchange of Letters between the European Community and the Republic of Poland regarding a Protocol on a European Conformity Assessment Agreement	Brussels, 30.7.1998		Not to be published
Accession by the European Community and the European Atomic Energy Community, acting as one party, to the Agreement to establish a Science and Technology Centre in Ukraine, of 25.10.1993, between Canada, Sweden, Ukraine and the United States of America	Brussels, 30.7.1998		Not to be published
Agreement in the form of an Exchange of Letters between the European Community and the Republic of Poland regarding a Protocol on a European Conformity Assessment Agreement	Brussels, 30.7.1998		Not to be published
Agreement in the form of an Exchange of Letters amending and extending the Agreement between the European Community and	Brussels, 10.9.1998		Not to be published

Title	Place and Date	UK Signature	Text
the Socialist Republic of Vietnam on Trade in Textile and Clothing Products initialled on 15.12.1992, as last amended by the Agreement in the form of an Exchange of Letters initialled on 1.8.1995	Brussels, 10.9.1998		Not to be published
Protocol for the Adaption of the Trade Aspects of the Europe Agreement between the European Communities and their Member States, of the one part, and Romania, of the other part, to take into account the Accession of the Republic of Austria, the Republic of Finland and the Kingdom of Sweden to the European Union and the Results of the Agricultural Negotiations of the Uruguay Round, including the Improvements of the Existing Preferential Regime	Brussels, 13.10.1998		Not to be published
Protocol for the Adaption of Trade Aspects of the Europe Agreement between the European Communities and their Member States, of the one part, and the Slovak Republic, of the other part, to take into account the Accession of the Republic of Austria, the Republic of Finland and the Kingdom of Sweden to the European Union and the Results of the Agricultural Negotiations of the	Brussels, 19.10.1998		Not to be published

Title	*Place and Date*	*UK Signature*	*Text*
Uruguay Round, including the Improvements of the Existing Preferential Regime	Brussels, 19.10.1998		Not to be published
Exchange of Letters between the European Community and the Republic of Hungary on Certain Import Arrangements for Agricultural Products	Brussels, 20.10.1998		Not to be published
Protocol for the Adaption of Trade Aspects of the Europe Agreement between the European Communities and their Member States, of the one part, and the Czech Republic, of the other part, to take into account the Accession of the Republic of Austria, the Republic of Finland and the Kingdom of Sweden to the European Union and the Results of the Agricultural Negotiations of the Uruguay Round, including the Improvements of the Existing Preferential Regime	Brussels, 27.10.1998		Not to be published
Additional protocol to the Interim Agreement on Trade and Trade-related Matters between the European Community, the European Coal and Steel Community and the European Atomic Energy Community, of the one part, and the Republic of Slovenia, of the other part, and to the Europe Agreement between the European Communities	Brussels, 30.10.1998		Not to be published

Title	Place and Date	UK Signature	Text
and their Member States, of the one part, and the Republic of Slovenia, of the other part	Brussels, 30.10.1998		Not to be published
Agreement in the form of an Exchange of Letters between the European Community and Barbados, Belize, the Republic of Congo, Fiji, the Co-operative Republic of Guyana, the Republic of Côte d'Ivoire, Jamaica, the Republic of Kenya, the Republic of Madagascar, the Republic of Malawi, the Republic of Mauritius, the Republic of Suriname, Saint Kitts and Nevis, the Kingdom of Swaziland, the United Republic of Tanzania, the Republic of Trinidad and Tobago, the Republic of Uganda, the Republic of Zambia and the Republic of Zimbabwe on the Guaranteed Prices for Cane Sugar for the 1997/98 delivery period	Brussels, 3.11.1998		Not to be published
Protocol setting out the Fishing Opportunities and Financial Compensation provided for in the Agreement between the European Community and the Gabonese Republic on Fishing off the coast of Gabon	Brussels, 9.11.1998		Not to be published
Agreement between the European Community and the Lao People's Democratic Republic on Trade in Textile Products	Brussels, 9.11.1998		Not to be published

Title	*Place and Date*	*UK Signature*	*Text*
Agreement between the European Community and the Republic of Chile on Precursors and Chemical Substances frequently used for the Illicit Manufacture of Narcotic Drugs and Psychotropic Substances	Brussels, 24.11.1998		Not to be published
Agreement in the form of an Exchange of Letters between the European Community and the People's Republic of China amending the Agreement between the European Community and the People's Republic of China on Trade in Textile Products as last amended by Agreements initialled on 13.12.1995	Brussels, 9.12.1998		Not to be published
Agreement between Canada and the European Atomic Energy Community for Co-operation in the Area of Nuclear Research	Ottawa, 17.12.1998		Not to be published

III. Bilateral Agreements Signed by the United Kingdom in 1998[1]

Country and Title	*Place and Date*	*Text*[2]
AUSTRALIA		
Exchange of Letters constituting an Agreement to amend the Agreement on Health Services between the United Kingdom and Australia	London, 29.5.1998	
BAHRAIN		
Agreement concerning Air Services	London, 29.4.1998	TS No. 4 (1999) (Cm 4250)
BELGIUM		
Agreement relating to the Transmission of Natural Gas through a Pipeline between the United Kingdom and Belgium	Brussels, 10.12.1997	Belgium No. 1 (1998) (Cm 3943)
BRAZIL		
Exchange of Notes concerning the Abolition of Visas	London, 2.7.1998	
CHINA, PEOPLE'S REPUBLIC OF		
Amendment to the Protocol on Scientific and Technological Co-operation with the Government of the People's Republic of China	Peking, 17.9.1998	
CROATIA		
Agreement for the Promotion and Protection of Investments	London, 11.3.1997	TS No. 29 (1998) (Cm 4013)
CZECH REPUBLIC		
Agreement concerning Air Services	Prague, 20.3.1998	TS No. 34 (1998) (Cm 4038)
Agreement on International Road Transport	Copenhagen, 27.5.1998	

[1] Information supplied by the Foreign and Commonwealth Office. The table includes some agreements signed by the United Kingdom before 1998, where information was not previously available. The information is correct as at January 1999, although in some cases information available since that time has been included.

[2] Publication is in various series of UK Command Papers, including Miscellaneous Series (Misc.) and Treaty Series (TS) of UK Command Papers. Cm = Command Paper number.

Country and Title	Place and Date	Text
FRANCE		
Agreement concerning the European Air Group	London, 6.7.1998	TS No. 10 (1999) (Cm 4270)
GEORGIA		
Agreement on International Road Transport	London, 13.11.1997	Georgia No. 1 (1998) (Cm 4016)
GUINEA		
Exchange of Notes concerning Certain Commercial Debts (UK/Guinea Debt Agreement No. 6 (1997))	Dakar/Conakry, 23.4.1998	TS No. 48 (1998) (Cm 4077)
HONG KONG SAR		
Agreement concerning Air Services	Hong Kong, 25.7.1997	TS No. 27 (1999) (Cm 4336)
Agreement for the Transfer of Sentenced Persons	Hong Kong, 5.11.1997	TS No. 51 (1998) (Cm 4099)
Agreement for the Surrender of Fugitive Offenders	Hong Kong, 5.11.1997	TS No. 30 (1998) (Cm 4034)
Agreement concerning Mutual Legal Assistance in Criminal Matters	Hong Kong, 23.1.1998	
Agreement for the Promotion and Protection of Investments	Hong Kong, 30.7.1998	Hong Kong No. 4 (1998) (Cm 4173)
IRELAND, REPUBLIC OF		
British-Irish Agreement	Belfast, 10.4.1998	
Protocol amending the Convention for the Avoidance of Double Taxation and the Prevention of Fiscal Evasion with respect to Taxes on Income and Capital Gains signed at Dublin on 2.6.1976, as amended by the Protocols signed at Dublin on 28.10.1976 and at London on 7.11.1994	London, 4.11.1998	TS No. 23 (1999) (Cm 4322)
Agreement concerning Mutual Assistance in relation to Criminal Matters	Dublin, 26.11.1998	

Country and Title	*Place and Date*	*Text*
ITALY		
Agreement concerning the Co-Production of Films	London, 5.5.1998	Italy No. 1 (1998) (Cm 4029)
JAPAN		
Agreement for Co-operation in the Peaceful Uses of Nuclear Energy, with Agreed Minutes	Tokyo, 25.2.1998	Japan No. 1 (1998) (Cm 3948)
NETHERLANDS		
Agreement concerning a Scottish Trial in the Netherlands	The Hague, 18.9.1998	
NORWAY		
Exchange of Notes concerning the Disposal of the 'Brent Spar' Offshore Installation	Oslo, 7.8.1998	TS No. 46 (1998) (Cm 4070)
Framework Agreement relating to the Laying, Operation and Jurisdiction of Inter-connecting Submarine Pipelines	Oslo, 25.8.1998	
Agreement relating to the Amendment to the Agreement of 10.5.1976 relating to the Exploitation of the Frigg Field Reservoir and the Transmission of Gas therefrom to the United Kingdom	Oslo, 25.8.1998	
OMAN		
Agreement for the Avoidance of Double Taxation and the Prevention of Fiscal Evasion with respect to Taxation on Incomes and Capital Gains, with Exchange of Notes	London, 23.2.1998	TS No. 22 (1999) (Cm 4318)
QATAR		
Agreement concerning Air Services	London, 24.6.1998	TS No. 15 (1999) (Cm 4289)
RUSSIAN FEDERATION		
Agreement on Co-operation in Fighting Crime	Moscow, 6.10.1997	

Country and Title	*Place and Date*	*Text*
SENEGAL		
Exchange of Notes amending the UK/Senegal Debt Agreement No. 11 (1995) (UK/Senegal Debt Agreement No. 11 (1995) Amendment)	Dakar, 15/26.5.1998	TS No. 50 (1998) (Cm 4096)
SOUTH AFRICA		
Protocol to the Agreement for the Promotion and Protection of Investments, signed at Cape Town on 20.9.1994	London, 25.11.1997	TS No. 35 (1998) (Cm 4039)
SRI LANKA		
Agreement concerning Air Services	Colombo, 22.4.1998	TS No. 19 (1999) (Cm 4319)
TANZANIA		
Exchange of Notes concerning Certain Commercial Debts (UK/Tanzania Debt Agreement No. 5 (1997))	Dar es Salaam, 20/23.1.1998	TS No. 17 (1998) (Cm 3933)
UGANDA		
Agreement for the Promotion and Protection of Investments	Kampala, 24.4.1998	TS No. 33 (1998) (Cm 4037)
UNITED STATES OF AMERICA		
Agreement with the United States concerning Maritime and Aerial Operations to Suppress Illicit Trafficking by Sea in Waters of the Caribbean and Bermuda	Washington, 13.7.1998	United States No. 1 (1998) (Cm 4145)
URUGUAY		
Exchange of Notes concerning the Transfer of the Hut located in Hope Bay (Bahía Experanza) in the Antarctic Peninsula	Montevideo, 8.12.1997	TS No. 16 (1998) (Cm 3932)
MISCELLANEOUS		
Draft Headquarters Agreement between the Government of the UK and the OSPAR Commission	London, 18.12.1997	Misc. No. 11 (1997) (Cm 3796)

Country and Title	*Place and Date*	*Text*
Protocol additional to the Agreement between the UK and the European Atomic Energy Community and the International Atomic Energy Agency for the Application of Safeguards in the UK in connection with the Treaty on the Non-Proliferation of Nuclear Weapons	Vienna, 22.9.1998	

IV. United Kingdom Legislation During 1998 Concerning Matters of International Law[1]

The Criminal Justice (Terrorism and Conspiracy) Act 1998 (c.40), *inter alia*, amends the Criminal Law Act 1977 by making it an offence in England or Wales to conspire to pursue a course of conduct which is intended to take place in a country or territory outside the UK and which amounts to an offence under the law of that country or territory. It contains amendments of similar effect to the laws of Northern Ireland and Scotland. (See UKMIL 1997, pp. 575–80.)

The European Communities (Amendment) Act 1998 (c.21) amends the European Communities Act 1972 so as to include the Treaty of Amsterdam of 2 October 1997 in the definition of 'the Treaties' and 'the Community Treaties'. It also approves the Treaty of Amsterdam for the purpose of section 6 of the European Parliamentary Elections Act 1978, which requires approval by Act of Parliament before ratification by the UK of any treaty which increases the powers of the European Parliament.

The Government of Wales Act 1998 (c.38) provides for the establishment of a National Assembly for Wales and for changes in administrative authorities in Wales. Sections 106–8 contain provisions relating to the obligations, powers and functions of the Assembly in relation to European Community law, the European Convention on Human Rights and other international obligations.

The Human Rights Act 1998 (c.42) gives effect to certain rights and freedoms guaranteed under the European Convention on Human Rights and the First and Sixth Protocols to the Convention, and makes provision with respect to holders of certain judicial offices who become judges of the European Court of Human Rights. (See Parts Four: II. A. and Five: III. B., above.)

The Landmines Act 1998 (c.33) prohibits any use, development, production, acquisition or possession of anti-personnel mines which is in contravention of the Ottawa Convention of 3 December 1997 on the Prohibition of the Use, Stockpiling, Production and Transfer of Anti-Personnel Mines and on their Destruction. It applies to conduct by any person in the UK, or to conduct outside the UK by a UK national, Scottish partnership or body incorporated in any part of the UK. Possession or transfer of objects is lawful if undertaken for the development of techniques of mine detection or destruction. No offence is committed if the conduct is part of an international military operation (which is defined as a military operation wholly or mainly outside the UK involving both members of Her Majesty's armed forces and members of the armed forces of a State other than the UK). The Act empowers the Secretary of State to authorize entry of premises to remove, immobilise or destroy objects where there is reasonable cause to do so. It also provides for rights of entry and inspection for members of fact-finding missions under the Ottawa Convention and for the privileges and immunities of members of such missions. (See Parts Four: II. A. and Seventeen: I. B. 8., above.)

[1] Compiled by C. A. Hopkins.

The Nuclear Explosions (Prohibition and Inspections) Act 1998 (c.7) implements certain provisions of the Comprehensive Nuclear-Test-Ban Treaty of 10 September 1996. It creates an offence of knowingly causing a nuclear explosion, where such act is done in the UK, or outside the UK by a UK national, Scottish partnership or body incorporated in any part of the UK. It also provides for rights of entry for purposes of on-site inspections in accordance with the Treaty, and for privileges and immunities of members of inspection teams and observers. (See UKMIL 1997, pp. 583 and 641–2.)

The Petroleum Act 1998 (c.17) consolidates the Petroleum (Production) Act 1934, the Petroleum and Submarine Pipelines Act 1975, the Oil and Gas (Enterprise) Act 1982, and Parts I and II of the Petroleum Act 1987. It deals with proprietary rights in, and licences required for the extraction of, any mineral oil, relative hydrocarbon or natural gas. The Act imposes civil and criminal law on offshore activities, and introduces an authorization and decommissioning system with respect to submarine pipelines.

The Scotland Act 1998 (c.46) provides for the establishment of a Scottish Parliament and Administration and for other changes in the government of Scotland. *Inter alia*, it contains the following provisions in relation to European Community law and the European Convention on Human Rights:
(1) Section 29 provides that any provision which is incompatible with any of the Convention rights (as defined in the Human Rights Act 1998) or with Community law is outside the legislative competence of the Scottish Parliament.
(2) Section 57 provides for functions relating to observing and implementing obligations under Community law to be shared between Ministers of the Crown and Scottish Ministers. It also provides that a member of the Scottish Executive has no power to make any subordinate legislation, or do any other act, so far as the legislation or act is incompatible with Convention rights or Community law.
(3) Section 100 contains provisions to ensure that proceedings in relation to Convention rights brought under the Scotland Act are subject to the same restrictions (requiring a litigant to be a 'victim' and limiting the award of damages) as those imposed by the Human Rights Act 1998.

TABLE OF CASES

A *v*. France, 376
Aaland Islands Case, 93, 105–6
Abdulaziz, Cabales and Balkandali *v*. UK, 473, 474
Adams *v*. Cape Industries plc, 351
Adams *v*. National Bank of Greece and Athens SA, 354
Adan *v*. Secretary of State for the Home Department, and other appeals, 322
Aegean Sea Continental Shelf Case, 16, 36, 45, 53–4
Aerial Incident of 27 July 1955 Case, 74–7, 78, 80, 82
Aerial Incident of 3 July 1988 Case, 37
Aerts *v*. Belgium, 365
Airbus Industrie GIE *v*. Patel, **332–6**
Airey *v*. Ireland, 367, 372
Akai Pty. Ltd. *v*. People's Insurance Co. Ltd., 351
Akdivar and others *v*. Turkey, 365, 385, 401
Aksoy *v*. Turkey, 365, 399
Alabama Arbitration, 87
Al-Mass'ari (Mohammed A.S.) *v*. Secretary of State for the Home Department, 329
Ambatielos Case, 17, 20, 30, 40, 57, 62, 73
Amchem Products Inc. *v*. Workers' Compensation Board, 333, 334
Andersson *v*. Sweden, 362
Andronicou and Constantinou *v*. Cyprus, **375–7**
Anglo-Iranian Oil Co. Case, 16, 22, 23
Antarctica Cases (UK *v*. Argentina, UK *v*. Chile), 11
Appeal relating to the Jurisdiction of the ICAO Council, 8, 13–14, 28–9, 30, 31–2, 57, 58–61, 67, 68, 79
Application for Review of Judgment No. 158 of the UN Administrative Tribunal (Fasla Case), 28, 57
Application for Review of Judgment No. 273 of the UN Administrative Tribunal (Mortished Case), 57, 59–60
Application for Review of Judgment No. 333 of the UN Administrative Tribunal (Yakimetz Case), 57
Application for Revision and Interpretation of the Judgment of 24 February 1982 in the Continental Shelf (Tunisia/Libya) Case, 26
Application of the Convention on the Prevention and Punishment of the Crime of Genocide (Bosnia and Herzegovina *v*. Yugoslavia) (Counter-Claims), 19
Application of the Convention on the Prevention and Punishment of the Crime of Genocide (Bosnia and Herzegovina *v*. Yugoslavia (Serbia and Montenegro)) (Further Requests for the Indication of Provisional Measures), 21
Application of the Convention on the Prevention and Punishment of the Crime of Genocide (Bosnia and Herzegovina *v*. Yugoslavia (Serbia and Montenegro)) (Request for the Indication of Provisional Measures), 6, 26, 29–30
Application of the Vienna Convention on Consular Relations (Paraguay *v*. US) (Request for the Indication of Provisional Measures), 21
Aprile Srl, en liquidation *v*. Amministrazione delle Finanze dello Stato, 420
Arbitral Award of the King of Spain Case, 26, 57, 61–3, 64, 65, 67
Arbitral Award of 31 July 1989 (Guinea-Bissau/Senegal) Case, 5, 19, 57, 63–72
Artico *v*. Italy, 398
Associated Provincial Picture Houses Ltd. *v*. Wednesbury Corporation, 283, 285, 326
Association comité économique agricole régional fruits et légumes de Bretagne *v*. Le Campion, 415
Attorney-General of Canada *v*. Ward, 325
Aydin *v*. Turkey, 365, **382–4**

B *v*. France, 368, 369
Baghlaf al Safer Factory Co. BR for Industry Ltd. *v*. Pakistan National Shipping Co., 341
Bahaddar *v*. Netherlands, **401**
Balmer-Schafroth *v*. Switzerland, 362, 372
Baltic Insurance Group *v*. Jordan Grand Prix Ltd. and Quay Financial Software Ltd., 344 **345–9**
Banco Nacional de Cuba *v*. Sabbatino, 308
Barcelona Traction, Light and Power Co. Ltd. Case (Preliminary Objections), 26–7, 77–80, 82
Barcelona Traction, Light and Power Co. Ltd. Case (Second Phase), 37, 281
Beef Hormones Case, 188–92
Beldjoudi *v*. France, 363
Bendone-Derossi *v*. Iran, 67
Benham *v*. UK, 473, 474
Bier *v*. Mines de Potasse d'Alsace, 428
Blad *v*. Bamfield, 305
Boddaert *v*. Belgium, 403
Boner and Maxwell *v*. UK, 473

[1] The figures in heavier type indicate the pages on which cases are reviewed.

Border and Transborder Armed Actions Case (Nicaragua *v.* Honduras), 15
Bosnia and Herzegovina *v.* Yugoslavia (Application of the Convention on the Prevention and Punishment of the Crime of Genocide) (Counter-Claims), 19
Bosnia and Herzegovina *v.* Yugoslavia (Serbia and Montenegro) (Application of the Convention on the Prevention and Punishment of the Crime of Genocide) (Further Requests for the Indication of Provisional Measures), 21
Bosnia and Herzegovina *v.* Yugoslavia (Serbia and Montenegro) (Application of the Convention on the Prevention and Punishment of the Crime of Genocide) (Request for the Indication of Provisional Measures), 6, 26, 29–30
Botta *v.* Italy, 362, **367–8**
Boujlifa *v.* France, 363
Bouygues Offshore SA *v.* Caspian Shipping Co., 341, **342–5**
Bowman *v.* UK, 393, **395–6**
Boys *v.* Chaplin, 353
Brasserie du Pêcheur SA *v.* Germany, 301
Brcko Arbitration, 219, 233
Bridge Oil Ltd. *v.* Owners of the Ship *Guiseppe di Vittorio*, 455, 485–6
British Airways Board *v.* Laker Airways Ltd., 334
British South Africa Co. *v.* Companhia de Moçambique, 356, 357, 358, 359
Brogan *v.* UK, 381
Brunswick (Duke of) *v.* King of Hanover, 305, 315
Buck and others *v.* Attorney-General, 314–15
Burkina Faso/Mali (Frontier Dispute) Case, 54, 66, 91
Buttes Gas and Oil Co. *v.* Hammer (Nos. 2 and 3), 305, 308–10, 311, 313–14, 315, 316

Caltex Singapore Pte. Ltd. *v.* BP Shipping Ltd., 341
Cameroon *v.* Nigeria (Land and Maritime Boundary) (Preliminary Objections), 3, 8, 14, 54
Campbell *v.* UK, 473
Campbell and Cosans *v.* UK, 472, 473
Carl Zeiss Stiftung *v.* Rayner & Keeler Ltd. (No. 2), 312
Caspian Basin Specialised Emergency Salvage Administration *v.* Bouygues Offshore SA, 341
Castello *v.* Spain, 392
Certain Phosphate Lands in Nauru Case (Nauru *v.* Australia), 34, 35, 48–50
Chahal *v.* UK, 473
Chorzów Factory Case (Jurisdiction), 15–16
CJEC Opinion 2/94, 422
Clipperton Island Arbitration, 262
Coin Controls Ltd. *v.* Suzo International (UK) Ltd., 359
Colorado *v.* New Mexico, 184–5
Connelly *v.* RTZ Corp. plc (No. 2), 337, 338, 359
Continental Shelf (Tunisia/Libya) Case, Application for Revision and Interpretation of the Judgment of 24 February 1982 in the, 26
Cook *v.* Sprigg, 305
Coreck Maritime GmbH *v.* Sevybokhodflot, 455, 486
Corfu Channel Case (Merits), 35, 37, 136, 137
Corfu Channel Case (Preliminary Objection), 5, 27, 28, 29
Cossey *v.* UK, 368, 370
Costa *v.* ENEL, 283
Coyne *v.* UK, 473, 474
CSR Ltd. *v.* Cigna Insurance Australia Ltd., 333

Dalia *v.* France, 363, 365
Danvaern Production A/S *v.* Schuhfabriken Otterbeck GmbH & Co., 347
Daud *v.* Portugal, **403–5**
De Haes and Gijsels *v.* Belgium, 389
Deere (John) Ltd. *v.* European Commission, **417–18**
Demjanjuk Trial, 289–90
Difference relating to Immunity from Legal Process of a Special Rapporteur of the Commission on Human Rights, 489–90
Direction général des impôts *v.* Forest, 415
Djabali *v.* Caisse d'Allocations Familiales de l'Essone, **416–17**
Drouot Assurances SA *v.* Consolidated Metallurgical Industries (CMI Industrial Sites), **426–7**
Dudgeon *v.* UK, 473, 474
Dzodzi *v.* Belgium, 417

East Timor Case, 34, 39, 50–2, 53
Eastern Carelia Case, 295
Eastern Trader, The, 351
EC Arbitration Commission on Yugoslavia, Opinions of, 100–5, 106, 109
Edilizia Industriale Siderurgica Srl *v.* Ministero delle Finanze, **418–20**
Editions Periscope *v.* France, 387
El Boujaidi *v.* France, 363, 364
El Salvador/Honduras (Land, Island and Maritime Frontier Dispute) Case (Application for Permission to Intervene), 48
Emmott *v.* Minister for Social Welfare, 419
Ergi *v.* Turkey, 375, **377–8**

Fantask A/S and others *v.* Industriministeriet (Erhvervsministeriet), 419
Fasla Case (Application for Review of Judgment No. 158 of the UN Administrative Tribunal), 28, 57
Findlay *v.* UK, 393, 473, 474

Fisheries Jurisdiction Case (Federal Republic of Germany *v.* Iceland) (Jurisdiction), 7
Fisheries Jurisdiction Case (Federal Republic of Germany *v.* Iceland) (Merits), 7
Fisheries Jurisdiction Case (UK *v.* Iceland) (Jurisdiction), 413
Fleischle *v.* Germany, 399
Foglia *v.* Novello, 417
Fort Dodge Animal Health Ltd. *v.* Akzo Nobel NV, 359
Fox, Campbell and Hartley *v.* UK, 473, 474
Francovich *v.* Italy, 301
Free Zones of Upper Savoy and the District of Gex Case, 5
Frontier Dispute Case (Burkina Faso/Mali), 54, 66, 91

Gabčíkovo-Nagymaros Project Case, 11, 124
Garland *v.* British Rail Engineering Ltd., 420
Gaskin *v.* UK, 374
Gautrin *v.* UK, 393
Genocide Case: *see* Application of the Convention on the Prevention and Punishment of the Crime of Genocide (Bosnia and Herzegovina *v.* Yugoslavia (Serbia and Montenegro))
Giloy *v.* Hauptzollamt Frankfurt am Main-Ost, 412
Gitonas *v.* Greece, 398
Glimmerveen *v.* Netherlands, 397
Gmurzynska-Bscher *v.* Oberfinanzdirektion Köln, 417
Golder *v.* UK, 473
Gotha (City of) *v.* Sotheby's and Cobert Finance SA, **352–5**
Grant *v.* South West Trains Ltd., **420–2**
Grigoriades *v.* Greece, **390–1**
Guardianship of Infants Case, 5
Guerra and others *v.* Italy, 362, 367, **370–2**, 373, 374
Guinea/Guinea-Bissau Maritime Delimitation Arbitration, 125
Guinea-Bissau/Senegal (Arbitral Award of 31 July 1989) Case, 5, 19, 57, 63–72
Guiseppe di Vittorio, The (Bridge Oil Ltd. *v.* Owners of the Ship *Guiseppe di Vittorio*), 455, 485–6
Gulf of Maine Case, 182–3
Gur Corporation *v.* Trust Bank of Africa Ltd., 312

H, W, P and K *v.* Austria, 397
Hagen *v.* Zeehaghe BV, 349
Hagenbeek *v.* Netherlands, 397
Handte & Cie. GmbH *v.* Traitements mécano-chimiques des surfaces, 428
Harrods (Buenos Aires) Ltd., *Re,* 339, 358–9
Hauschildt *v.* Denmark, 393
Haya de la Torre Case, 28
Henderson *v.* Henderson, 352
Herceg Novi, The, and The Ming Galaxy, **340–1**
Hermès International *v.* FHT Marketing Choice BV, **411–12**
Hesperides Hotels Ltd. *v.* Muftizade, 358
Hilti *v.* European Commission, 418
Hoffmann *v.* Krieg, 345
Holdijk Case, 415
Holland *v.* Lampen-Wolfe, 318
Hostages Case (US Diplomatic and Consular Staff in Tehran), 21, 36, 54–6
Hough *v.* P & O Containers (Bloem + Voss Holding AG, third parties), **342–5**
Hussain and Singh *v.* UK, 473

ICAO Council, Appeal relating to the Jurisdiction of the, 8, 13–14, 28–9, 30, 31–2, 57, 58–61, 67, 68, 79
Immunity from Legal Process of a Special Rapporteur of the Commission on Human Rights, Difference relating to, 489–90
Incal *v.* Turkey, **392–4**
Indiana Transportation Co., *Ex parte,* 350
Inessa Armand, The, 455, 484, 485, 487
Informationsverein Lentia *v.* Austria, 391
Interhandel Case (Preliminary Objections), 57, 62
International Status of South West Africa, 72, 88
Interpretation of Peace Treaties with Bulgaria, Hungary and Romania, 32, 57, 62
Interpretation of the Statute of the Memel Territory Case, 5
Ireland *v.* UK, 373, 383, 399
Iskandar Ishac (Elias) Case, 323

Jan Mayen Case (Maritime Delimitation in the Area between Greenland and Jan Mayen) (Denmark *v.* Norway), 303
Jersild *v.* Denmark, 399
Johnston *v.* Royal Ulster Constabulary, 408
Jurisdiction of the ICAO Council, Appeal relating to the, 8, 13–14, 28–9, 30, 31–2, 57, 58–61, 67, 68, 79

Kalfelis *v.* Bankhaus Schröder Münchmeyer Hengst & Co., 348, 428, 429
Kansas *v.* Colorado, 184
Kapitan Shvetsov, The, 341
Kaya *v.* Turkey, 375, **378–9**
Kirkpatrick *v.* Environmental Tectonics, 308
Klass and others *v.* Germany, 398
Kokkinakis *v.* Greece, 400
Kuck *v.* Germany, 399
Kuhnen *v.* Germany, 397
Kurt *v.* Turkey, 365, **380–2**, 384
Kuwait Airways Corp. *v.* Iraqi Airways Co. and another (1995), 305

Kuwait Airways Corp. *v.* Iraqi Airways Co. and another (1998), **305–14**

Lake Lanoux Arbitration, 131
Laker Airways Ltd. *v.* Sabena, Belgian World Airlines, 334
Land and Maritime Boundary between Cameroon and Nigeria (Preliminary Objections), 3, 8, 14, 54
Land Island and Maritime Frontier Dispute Case (El Salvador/Honduras) (Application for Permission to Intervene), 48
Larissis *v.* Greece, **400–1**
LCB *v.* UK, 362, 372, **374–5**
Legal Consequences for States of the Continued Presence of South Africa in Namibia (South West Africa), 89
Legality of the Threat or Use of Nuclear Weapons, 143–4, 280, 603
Letelier *v.* Chile, 309
Libyan Arab Foreign Bank *v.* Bankers Trust Co., 319
Libyan Arab Foreign Bank *v.* Manufacturers Hanover Trust Co., 319
Littrell *v.* USA (No. 2), 318
Lockerbie Case (Questions of Interpretation and Application of the 1971 Montreal Convention arising from the Aerial Incident at Lockerbie), 53
Lopez Ostra *v.* Spain, 367, 372
Lubbe *v.* Cape plc, 335, **336–40**
Ludi *v.* Switzerland, 406
Luther (A.M.) *v.* James Sagor & Co., 305, 308

McCallum *v.* UK, 473, 474
McCann and others *v.* UK, 376
McGinley and Egan *v.* UK, 362, **372–4**
Maciej Rataj, The (*Maciej Rataj, Tatry* (cargo owners) *v.* *Maciej Rataj* (owners)), 426
McMichael *v.* UK, 473, 474
Malaysian Industrial Development Authority *v.* Jeyasingham, 318
Malone *v.* UK, 472, 473
Marckx *v.* Belgium, 369
Marinari *v.* Lloyds Bank, 428
Maritime Delimitation and Territorial Questions between Qatar and Bahrain Case, 12, 16–17
Maritime Delimitation in the Area between Greenland and Jan Mayen (Denmark *v.* Norway), 303
Marks & Unman *v.* Iran, 67
Mathieu-Mohin and Clerfayt *v.* Belgium, 396
Mehemi *v.* France, **362–4**
Memel Case (Interpretation of the Statute of the Memel Territory), 5
Mentes *v.* Turkey, 362, **364–6**
Metall & Rohstoff AG *v.* Donaldson Lufkin & Jenrette Inc., 339, 353
Midland Bank plc *v.* Laker Airways Ltd., 335
Military and Paramilitary Activities in and against Nicaragua (Jurisdiction and Admissibility), 7, 8–10, 14, 15, 24–6, 30, 34, 36, 47, 49, 56–7, 68, 73, 80–3
Military and Paramilitary Activities in and against Nicaragua (Merits), 9, 20, 91
Military and Paramilitary Activities in and against Nicaragua (Order of 26 September 1991), 37
Ministero delle Finanze *v.* IN.CO.GE.'90 Srl and others, 420
Ministero delle Finanze *v.* Spac SpA, 420
Minority Schools Case (Rights of Minorities in Upper Silesia), 29
Mohammed *v.* Bank of Kuwait and the Middle East KSC, 335, 336, 337, 338
Monetary Gold Removed from Rome in 1943 Case, 18, 34, 37–9, 40, 47, 48, 49, 51, 52
Morguard Investments Ltd. *v.* De Savoye, 334
Mortished Case (Application for Review of Judgment No. 273 of the UN Administrative Tribunal), 57, 59–60
Moustaquim *v.* Belgium, 363
MS *v.* Sweden, **361–2**
Murthy *v.* Sivasjothi, **349–52**
Musisi, *In re,* 329

Namibia Case (Legal Consequences for States of the Continued Presence of South Africa in Namibia (South West Africa)), 89
Nasri *v.* France, 363
National and Provincial Building Society, Leeds Permanent Building Society and Yorkshire Building Society *v.* UK, **386–8**
Niemietz *v.* Germany, 367
Northern Cameroons Case, 12, 18, 19, 20, 32–3, 34, 39–42, 43, 44, 45, 52, 90
Nottebohm Case (Preliminary Objection), 10, 30, 32, 33, 34, 39
Nuclear Tests Case (Australia *v.* France) (Request for the Indication of Interim Measures of Protection), 22, 23
Nuclear Tests Cases (Australia *v.* France, New Zealand *v.* France), 12, 18, 19, 42–6: *see also* Request for an Examination of the Situation in accordance with Paragraph 63 of the Court's Judgment of 20 December 1974 in the Nuclear Tests (New Zealand *v.* France) Case
Nuclear Weapons Opinion (Legality of the Threat or Use of Nuclear Weapons), 143–4, 280, 603
Nuova Safim SpA *v.* The Sakura Bank Ltd., 316

O, H, W, B and R *v.* UK, 472, 473
Oberschlick *v.* Austria (No. 2), 388, 390
Observer and *Guardian* *v.* UK, 389
Oil Platforms Case (Iran *v.* USA), 19
Oliveira *v.* Switzerland, **408–9**

Open Door and Dublin Well Woman *v.* Ireland, 397
Oppenheimer *v.* Cattermole, 308, 309, 311
Ortenberg *v.* Austria, 387

P *v.* P, **316–18**
P *v.* S, 421
Paley Olga (Princess) *v.* Weisz, 305, 308
Palmisani *v.* INPS, 418
Papamichalopoulos *v.* Greece, 403
Parfitis *v.* Greece, 395, **402–3**
Pearce *v.* Ove Arup Partnership Ltd., 359
Peterbroeck *v.* Belgian State, 418
Petrovik *v.* Austria, 362, **366**
Phosphate Lands in Nauru Case (Nauru *v.* Australia), 34, 35, 48–50
Pigs Marketing Board *v.* Redmond, 415
Polly Peck International (in administration), *Re* (No. 2), **356–9**
Ponente Carni SpA and Cispadana Costruzioni SpA *v.* Amministrazione delle Finanze dello Stato, 418
Powell and Rayner *v.* UK, 371
Princess Paley Olga *v.* Weisz, 305, 308
Propend Finance Pty. Ltd. *v.* Sing, 318
Pullar *v.* UK, 393
Purcell *v.* Ireland, 399

Qatar *v.* Bahrain (Maritime Delimitation and Territorial Questions between Qatar and Bahrain), 12, 16–17
Questions of Interpretation and Application of the 1971 Montreal Convention arising from the Aerial Incident at Lockerbie, 53

R *v.* Bow Street Metropolitan Stipendiary Magistrate and others, *ex parte* Pinochet Ugarte, 305, 501, 503
R *v.* Foreign and Commonwealth Office, *ex parte* International Transport Workers Federation, 455–6, 461–2, 479, 482–6
R *v.* Inland Revenue Commissioners, *ex parte* Woolwich Equitable Building Society, 386
R *v.* Minister of Agriculture, Fisheries and Food, *ex parte* Compassion in World Farming Ltd., **414–16**
R *v.* Ministry of Agriculture, Fisheries and Food, *ex parte* Hedley Lomas, 416
R *v.* Ministry of Defence, *ex parte* Smith, and other appeals, 326, 331
R *v.* Secretary of State for Foreign and Commonwealth Affairs, *ex parte* The British Council of Turkish Cypriot Associations, **314–16**
R *v.* Secretary of State for the Home Department, *ex parte* Adan, **321–5**
R *v.* Secretary of State for the Home Department, *ex parte* Adan and Osman, 329
R *v.* Secretary of State for the Home Department, *ex parte* Ahmed and others, **330–1**
R *v.* Secretary of State for the Home Department, *ex parte* Brind, 283, 330
R *v.* Secretary of State for the Home Department, *ex parte* Bugdaycay, 283
R *v.* Secretary of State for the Home Department, *ex parte* Canbolat, 326, 329
R *v.* Secretary of State for the Home Department, *ex parte* Demiraj and Ethemi, 329
R *v.* Secretary of State for the Home Department, *ex parte* Elshani and Berisha, 329
R *v.* Secretary of State for the Home Department, *ex parte* Gangadeen and Jurawan, 330
R *v.* Secretary of State for the Home Department, *ex parte* Iyadurai, **325–30**
R *v.* Secretary of State for the Home Department, *ex parte* Kerrouche, 326–7, 328
R *v.* Secretary of State for the Home Department, *ex parte* Khan, 330
R *v.* Secretary of State for the Home Department, *ex parte* Robinson, 325
R *v.* Secretary of State for the Home Department, *ex parte* Sivakumaran, 327–8
R *v.* Secretary of State for Transport, *ex parte* Factortame Ltd. and others, 302
Racke (A.) GmbH & Co. *v.* Hauptzollamt Mainz, **412–14**
Radio ABC *v.* Austria, **391–2**
Raninen *v.* Finland, 365
Rees *v.* UK, 368, 369
Remer *v.* Germany, 397
Request for an Examination of the Situation in accordance with Paragraph 63 of the Court's Judgment of 20 December 1974 in the Nuclear Tests (New Zealand *v.* France) Case, 5, 12–13, 43
Réunion Européenne SA and others *v.* Spliethoff's Bevrachtingskantoor BV and Capitaine Commandant le Navire *Alblasgracht Voo2*, 344, 348, **427–9**
Rewe *v.* Landwirtschaftskammer Saarland, 418
Rich *v.* Società Italiana Impianti, 430
Right of Passage over Indian Territory Case (Preliminary Objections), 3
Rights of Minorities in Upper Silesia (Minority Schools Case), 29
Roque (Rui Alberto Pereira) *v.* His Excellency the Lieutenant Governor of Jersey, **423–5**

San Marco *v.* Commission of the EC, 417
Sarrio SA *v.* Kuwait Investment Authority, 347–8
Schöning-Kougebetopoulou (Kalliope) *v.* Freie und Hansestadt Hamburg, **422–3**
Schopfer *v.* Switzerland, **389–90**
Secession of Quebec, Reference *re*, 85
Selçuk and Asker *v.* Turkey, 365, **384–5**
Serbian Loans Case, 5
Sheffield and Horsham *v.* UK, 362, 366, **368–70**
Shevill and others *v.* Presse Alliance SA, 428

Sidiropoulos *v.* Greece, 400
Sierra Leone Telecommunications Co. Ltd. *v.* Barclays Bank plc, **319–21**, 477
Silver and others *v.* UK, 473, 474
Socialist Party *v.* Turkey, 400
Société Nationale Industrielle Aérospatiale *v.* Lee Kui Jak, 333
Somalia (Republic of) *v.* Woodhouse Drake & Carey (Suisse) SA, 312, 319, 320–1
South West Africa Cases (1962), 72–3, 293
South West Africa Cases (1966), 293
Spiliada Maritime Corp. *v.* Cansulex Ltd., 336, 337, 338, 340, 343
Stran Greek Refineries and Stratis Andreadis *v.* Greece, 388
Stubbings *v.* UK, 370
Sunday Times v. UK, 389, 472, 473
Sunday Times v. UK (No. 2), 389

T *v.* Belgium, 399
Tatry, The (*Maciej Rataj, Tatry* (cargo owners) *v. Maciej Rataj* (owners)), 426
Teixara de Castro *v.* Portugal, **406–7**
Tekin *v.* Turkey, 365, **379–80**
Temple of Preah Vihear Case (Preliminary Objection), 74, 76–7, 78
Thorgeir Thorgeirson *v.* Iceland, 392
Three Rivers District Council *v.* Bank of England, 302
Thynne, Wilson and Gunnell *v.* UK, 472, 473
Tinnelly and others *v.* UK, **407–8**
Toomen *v.* Australia Communication, 421
Trail Smelter Arbitration, 136–7
Treatment of US Aircraft and Crew in Hungary Cases (US *v.* Hungary, US *v.* USSR), 10, 11
Trial of Pakistani Prisoners of War Case, 21, 36
Twalib *v.* Greece, **405–6**

UN Administrative Tribunal, Application for Review of Judgment No. 158 of the (Fasla Case), 28, 57
UN Administrative Tribunal, Application for Review of Judgment No. 273 of the (Mortished Case), 57, 59–60
UN Administrative Tribunal, Application for Review of Judgment No. 333 of the (Yakimetz Case), 57
Underhill *v.* Hernandez, 308, 315
United Communist Party of Turkey *v.* Turkey, 392, **397–400**
US Diplomatic and Consular Staff in Tehran (Hostages Case), 21, 36, 54–6

Van Cant *v.* Rijksdienst voor Pensionen, 423
Van der Linden *v.* Berufsgenossenschaft der Feinmechanik und Elektronik, 339
Van Gend en Loos *v.* Nederlandse Administratie de Belastingen, 283
Van Uden Maritime BV, agissant sous le nom Van Uden Africa Line/Kommanditgesellschaft in Firma Deco-Line ea, **430–1**
Vereinigung demokratischer Soldaten Österreichs and Gubi *v.* Austria, 393
Vereniging Weekblad Bluf! *v.* Netherlands, 393
Vienna Convention on Consular Relations, Application of the (Paraguay *v.* US) (Request for the Indication of Provisional Measures), 21
Vishva Abha, The, 341
Vogt *v.* Germany, 398
von Colson *v.* Land Nordrhein-Westfalen, 283, 284

Webb *v.* EMO Air Cargo (UK) Ltd., 283
Western Sahara Case, 90
Williams & Humbert Ltd. *v.* W & H Trade Marks (Jersey) Ltd., 354
Winkworth *v.* Christie, Manson and Woods, 353–4
Worm *v.* Austria, **388–9**
Wyoming *v.* Colorado, 184, 185

X *v.* Austria, 399
X *v.* UK, 472, 473
X and Y *v.* Netherlands, 367
X, Y and Z *v.* UK, 368, 369

Yakimetz Case (Application for Review of Judgment No. 333 of the UN Administrative Tribunal), 57
Young, James and Webster *v.* UK, 398, 472, 473
Yugoslavia, Opinions of the EC Arbitration Commission on, 100–5, 106, 109

Z *v.* Finland, 362
Zabala Erasun *v.* Instituto Nacional de Empleo, 417
Zana *v.* Turkey, 393, **394–5**

INDEX

Abuse of rights, 129–30, 134
Acquiescence, 25, 26, 28–9, 571
Acquired rights, principle of, 134
Act of State, 305–16
Afghanistan, 573, 582, 583, 585, 606
  arms embargo on, 573, 582, 583, 585
  human rights in, 606
Aggression, 111, 513
Air space, definition of, 550–1
Aircraft, aviation, 13–14, 28, 31–2, 58, 60, 61, 67–8, 551
  Chicago Convention on International Civil Aviation (1944), 13–14, 28, 31–2, 58, 60, 61, 67–8, 551
  International Air Services Transit Agreement (1944), 13–14, 58
Albania, responsibility for mining of territorial sea of, 136
Aliens, responsibility for treatment of, 558
Angola, arms embargo and other UN measures concerning, 573, 578–9, 580, 581–2
Annexation: *see* Territory, title to
Arbitration, 18, 19, 30–1, 41, 57, 61–72, 445, 565–7, 570
  appointment of arbitrators, 18, 30, 62, 566
  compulsory arbitration, proposal for, 570
  effect of awards, 68–72, 566–7
  enforcement of awards, 67
  International Centre for the Settlement of Investment Disputes, by, 565–6
  International Court of Justice, review of awards by, 57, 61–72
  jurisdiction, power of tribunal to determine its own, 19, 41, 69
  Permanent Court of Arbitration, establishment of, 445
  procedure, 566–7
  termination of treaty providing for, 30–1
  validity of awards, 62–5, 68–72
Argentina, 536, 537–9, 550, 571–2, 573–4
  arms embargo on, 571–2, 573–4
  claim to Falkland Islands and South Georgia and South Sandwich Islands by, 536, 537–9, 550
  restoration of UK diplomatic relations with, 572
Armed conflict: *see* War and armed conflict
Armenia, arms embargo on, 573–4
Asylum, 321–30, 454: *see also* Refugees
  Asylum and Immigration Act 1996, 325–7
  Asylum and Immigration Appeals Act 1993, 322, 325

Asylum—*cont.*
  Dublin Convention determining the State Responsible for Examining Applications for Asylum (1990), 326, 329
  'safe third country', meaning of, 325–30
  'well-founded fear of being persecuted', meaning of, 321–3, 324, 327–30
Azerbaijan, arms embargo on, 573–4

Baltic States (Estonia, Latvia and Lithuania), 93, 96–7, 115, 457, 460, 534–5
  incorporation in Soviet Union of, 96
  independence of, 93, 96–7, 115, 457, 460
  Russian Federation, relations with, 534–5
Bangladesh, secession from Pakistan of, 92, 93, 95–6, 114–15
Belarus, EU Common Position on (1998), 525–6
Belligerent occupation: *see* War and armed conflict
Bosnia and Herzegovina, 11, 93, 99, 101–2, 103, 104, 105, 106, 109–10, 201–43, 573, 606: *see also* Yugoslavia, former
  admission to UN of, 102, 106
  arms embargo on, 11, 573
  constitutional structure of, 208–14
  Dayton-Paris Peace Agreement (1995), 99, 103, 110, 201–43 *passim*, 606
  electoral system in, 209, 220–4
  ethnic identity and conflict in, 201–43
  formation of State of, 93, 99, 101–2, 103, 105, 201, 202, 204, 208–26
  intervention in, 201, 202, 203–6, 209, 214–26, 227, 235, 240–3
    High Representative, role of, 205–6, 211, 212, 214–16, 217, 218, 219, 235, 240–1
    Implementation Force, role of, 205
    local politics, control of, 216–20, 241
    OSCE, role of, 214, 219, 220, 221, 222–5
    Peace Implementation Council, role of, 205–6, 212, 214, 217, 218, 219
    Stabilization Force, role of, 205, 218
  property rights in, 233–5, 238–9, 243
  recognition of, 102, 105, 206
  refugees and displaced persons, return of, 201, 202, 204–5, 208–9, 217, 223, 225, 226–39, 242–3
    UN High Commissioner for Refugees, role of, 217, 223, 227, 228, 230, 232, 233
  self-determination in, 104, 109–10
  succession to treaties and debts of former Yugoslavia by, 481

Bosnia and Herzegovina—*cont.*
Washington Agreement on the Establishment of the Federation of (1994), 204, 212
Boundaries, 103, 145–8, 150–5, 158, 535
delimitation of, 103, 535
pollution, prohibition in frontier agreements of, 145–8, 150–5, 158
uti possidetis juris, principle of, 103
British Indian Ocean Territory, 491, 537, 540, 549–50
fisheries conservation and management zone of, 549–50
Ilois, question of return of, 491, 540
status of, 537, 540
Burma, arms embargo on, 573

Cameroons, 33, 39, 90
administration of trust territory of, 39
termination of trusteeship for, 33, 39, 90
Canada, question of secession of Quebec from, 85–6
Cession: *see* Territory, title to
Channel Islands, 423–5, 471–2, 491–5
application of EC law to, 423–5
European Convention of Human Rights, proposed incorporation of, 471–2, 491–5
nationality in, 424
status of, 492–3, 494–5
Chechnya, status of, 108, 110–11
Children, abduction of, 316–18
China, 511–12, 573, 582–3
arms embargo on, 573, 582–3
Hong Kong Special Administrative Region, status of, 582
human rights in, 511–12
Citizenship: *see* Nationality and citizenship
Coercion, collective measures and countermeasures, 11, 321, 412–14, 513, 514, 530–1, 534, 552, 553–4, 569–85, 586–92: *see also* Intervention
arms embargoes, 11, 571–80, 581, 582–5
counter-measures, 552, 553–4, 569–71
EU measures, 412–14, 572–4, 580, 581, 582–5
OSCE measures, 572–4
UN measures, 11, 321, 467, 513, 514, 572–82, 586–92: *see also* United Nations, *subheading* peace-keeping by, *below*
unilateral measures, 530–1, 534, 569–74
Comity, 310, 311, 314–16, 333, 334
Comoros Archipelago, status of and self-determination in, 91
Conciliation, 565–6
Conflict of laws, 305–14, 319–20, 332–59, 426–31
Brussels Convention on Jurisdiction and the Enforcement of Judgments in Civil and Commercial Matters (1968), 333, 334, 336, 338, 339, 343–9, 357, 358–9, 426–31
arbitration exclusion from, 430–1
Conflict of laws—*cont.*
Brussels Convention on Jurisdiction and the Enforcement of Judgments in Civil and Commercial Matters (1968)—*cont.*
provisional measures under, 430–1
Civil Jurisdiction and Judgments Act 1982, 356–8
contract, 319–20, 342–9
choice of law, 319–20
Contracts (Applicable Law) Act 1990, 319
counterclaims by insurers, jurisdiction over, 345–9
exclusive jurisdiction clauses, limits on enforceability of, 342–5
jurisdiction, 342–9, 428, 430
Rome Convention on the Law Applicable to Contractual Obligations (1990), 319–20
corporations, law governing capacity of, 320
forum non conveniens, 359
immovable property, 307–8, 356–9
choice of law, 307–8
jurisdiction, 356–9
judgments, recognition and enforcement of foreign, 349–52, 427
jurisdiction, submission to, 349–52
law, recognition and enforcement of foreign, 305–14
lis alibi pendens, 426–7, 429: *see also subheadings* restraint of foreign proceedings *and* stay of proceedings in local court, *below*
Lugano Convention on Jurisdiction and the Enforcement of Judgments in Civil and Commercial Matters (1988), 333, 334, 336, 338, 343, 357
movable property, choice of law and, 307–8, 352–5
Private International Law (Miscellaneous Provisions) Act 1995, 353
public policy, 307–9, 311, 312, 313
restraint of foreign proceedings, 332–6, 342–3
stay of proceedings in local court, 336–41, 344–5, 359, 426–7, 429
tort, 306–7, 339, 353, 355, 428–9
choice of law, 353, 355
jurisdiction, 306–7, 428–9
place of commission of, 339, 428–9
Congo, Democratic Republic of, 475, 509, 573–4
arms embargo on, 573–4,
human rights in, 509
possibility of foreign intervention in, 475
Congo Brazzaville, UK relations with, 477
Consular relations, 21, 522–3, 524, 525, 527
privileges and immunities, consular, 522–3, 524, 525, 527
evidence, giving of, 524, 527
functional nature of, 522
inviolability of persons, 522–3

Consular relations—*cont.*
privileges and immunities, consular—*cont.*
inviolability of premises, 522–3
Vienna Convention on (1963), 21, 524, 527
Contiguous zone, delimitation of, 544–9
Continental shelf, 51, 182–3, 629
delimitation of, 51, 182–3
Petroleum Act 1998, 629
rights in, 182, 629
Contract: *see* Conflict of laws
Corsica, status of, 108, 112
Costa Rica, restrictions on passage through territorial sea of, 543
Counter-measures: *see* Coercion, collective measures and counter-measures
Court of Justice of the European Communities: *see* European Community and European Union
Criminal liability: *see* International Criminal Court; State responsibility; War and armed conflict, *subheading* war crimes
Croatia, 93, 99, 100–1, 102, 105, 106, 573, 584: *see also* Yugoslavia, former
admission to UN of, 102, 106
arms embargo on, 573, 584
independence of, 93, 99, 100–1, 105
Cuba, US measures against, 530–1, 534
Customary international law, 186, 191, 413, 443–4
creation of, 186, 191
source of law, as, 443–4
treaties, relationship to, 413
Cyprus, 314–16, 356–9, 498
accession to EU, question of, 314–16
independence of, 314–16
'Turkish Republic of Northern Cyprus', 356–9, 498
jurisdiction over claim of title to land in, 356–9
non-recognition of, 498
Czech Republic, independence of, 93, 106
Czechoslovakia, dissolution of, 92, 93, 106, 115

Decolonization, 85, 86, 87–92, 113, 114, 116
Denmark, sovereignty over Nicobar Islands of, 246–52, 255, 256–60, 263–5
Deportation, 330–1, 362–4, 423–5
Devolution, 86, 628, 629
Government of Wales Act 1998, 628
Scotland Act 1998, 629
secession, distinction from, 86
Diego Garcia: *see* British Indian Ocean Territory
Diplomatic relations, 306, 316–18, 499, 504, 522–3, 524–7, 572
privileges and immunities, diplomatic, 306, 316–18, 499, 504, 522–3, 524–7
cessation of, 317
civil and administrative jurisdiction, 525

Diplomatic relations—*cont.*
privileges and immunities, diplomatic—*cont.*
criminal jurisdiction, 524
Diplomatic Privileges Act 1964, 317
evidence, giving of, 524
functional nature of, 317, 522
inviolability of persons, 522–3, 526–7
inviolability of premises, 522–3, 525–6
nationals of receiving State, 524
preliminary issue, as, 306
special missions, members of, 504
State immunity, relationship to, 316–18
taxation, 525
protection, diplomatic: *see* State responsibility
restoration of, 572
Vienna Convention on (1961), 317, 524, 525–6
Discrimination, freedom from: *see* European Community and European Union; Human rights
Disputes, settlement of, 36–7, 45–6, 54–6, 189–91, 316, 445, 564–9
arbitration: *see* Arbitration
conciliation, 565–6
dispute, determination of existence of, 36
Investment Disputes between States and Nationals of Other States, Washington Convention on (1965), 565–6
judicial settlement: *see* International Court of Justice
negotiation, 36–7, 316, 564–5
Pacific Settlement of International Disputes, Convention on (1899), 445
Pacific Settlement of International Disputes, General Act for (1928), 45–6
Security Council, by, 54–6
World Trade Organization, by, 189–91, 569
Domestic jurisdiction, 114, 476

East Timor, 50–2, 89
delimitation of continental shelf of, 51
occupation by Indonesia of, 50–1, 52
self-determination in, 50
status of, 50–1, 89
Environment, protection of, 119–200, 370–2, 469, 541
Biological Diversity, Convention on (1992), 127, 175, 192, 193
Brundtland Commission (World Commission on Environment and Development), work of, 119, 123, 145
Climate Change, Convention on (1992), 127, 175, 187, 192, 193
Desertification, Convention to Combat (1994), 192, 193
Development, General Assembly Declaration on (1986), 125
Economic Rights and Duties of States, Charter of (1974), 124–5

Environment, protection of—*cont.*
Forest Principles, Statement of (1992), 127
Long-Range Transboundary Air Pollution, Convention on (1979), 141–2
Ozone Layer, Vienna Convention (1985) and Montreal Protocol (1987) on, 140–1
pollution, control of, 134, 139–200 *passim*, 370–2, 469, 541
Rio Declaration on Development and Environment (1992), 123–4, 127, 140, 187, 192, 193
Social Progress and Development, General Assembly Declaration on (1969), 124
State responsibility for environmental damage, 126, 128, 135–9, 164, 173, 185–6
Stockholm Declaration on the Human Environment (1972), 123, 135–6, 137, 140–3
Sulphur Emissions, Protocol on Further Reduction of (1994), 142
sustainable development, 119–200
criteria for attainment of, 125–9, 176–94
developing countries, special treatment of, 193–4, 200
elements of, 123–5
equitable utilization of international watercourses and, 119–200
intergenerational equity, 125, 177–9
polluter-pays principle, 128, 148, 195, 197
poverty, eradication of, 126, 192–3, 200
precautionary principle, 126, 128, 175, 186–92, 195, 197
Report of the Expert Group on (1995), 126–7, 177
Transfrontier Pollution, OECD Recommendation on (1974), 145
World Commission on Environment and Development (Brundtland Commission), work of, 119, 123, 145
Equity, equitable principles: *see* Watercourses, *subheading* equitable utilization, principle of
Erga omnes rights and obligations, 51, 570
Eritrea, 93, 106–7, 115, 116, 564–5, 567
border conflict between Ethiopia and, 564–5
independence of, 93, 106–7, 115, 116
territorial dispute between Yemen and, 567
Estonia: *see* Baltic States
Estoppel, 26
Ethiopia, border conflict between Eritrea and, 564–5
European Community and European Union, 100, 314–16, 323, 402–3, 411–31, 452–3, 466, 467, 469, 488, 525–6, 572–4, 580, 581, 582–5, 628, 629
Accession of UK, Act of (1972), 424
accession of Cyprus, question of, 314–16
Amsterdam, Treaty of (1997), 422, 453, 467, 469, 628
Belarus, Common Position on (1998), 525–6
collective measures by, 412–14, 572–4, 580, 581, 582–5
European Community and European Union—*cont.*
Court of Justice of the European Communities, 402–3, 411–31
appeals from Court of First Instance, jurisdiction and practice in relation to, 417–18
Brussels Convention on Jurisdiction and Judgments in Civil and Commercial Matters (1968), interpretation of, 426–31
jurisprudence in 1998 of, 411–31
practice and procedure of, 416–18
reference for preliminary ruling to, 402–3, 416–17
directives, 415, 418–20
implementation of, 418–20
validity of, 415
discrimination on grounds of nationality, freedom from, 422–5
discrimination on grounds of sex, freedom from, 420–2
EC/EEC Treaty (Treaty of Rome) (1957), 402, 414–17, 420–5
European Communities Act 1972, 316, 453, 466, 628
European Communities (Amendment) Act 1998, 466, 467, 628
European Parliamentary Elections Act 1978, 453, 628
European Union, Treaty on (Maastricht Treaty) (1992), 525
goods, free movement of, 414–16
persons, free movement of, 422–5
Privileges and Immunities of the European Communities, Protocol on (1965), 488
Recognition of New States in Eastern Europe and in the Soviet Union, Guidelines on (1991), 100
'Refugee', Joint Position on Definition of (1996), 323
Scottish Parliament, functions and powers in relation to Community law of, 629
scrutiny by UK Parliament of business of, 452–3
time limits under national law, validity of, 418–20
trade marks, protection of, 411–12
Welsh Assembly, functions and powers in relation to Community law of, 628
European Convention on Human Rights: *see* Human rights
European Court of Human Rights: *see* Human rights
European Union: *see* European Community and European Union
Exclusive economic zone, 138, 182–3, 544–9
delimitation of, 544–9
rights in, 138, 182
Exclusive fishery zone: *see* Fisheries

Expropriation and nationalization, 306–7, 313, 354, 558, 559, 560–1, 563–4: *see also* Human rights, *subheading* possessions, right to peaceful enjoyment of
Extradition, 498–506
  Criminal Justice (International Co-operation) Act 1990, 500
  European Convention for Mutual Assistance in Criminal Matters (1959), 500
  European Convention on (1957), 503, 505
  Extradition Act 1989, 501–6
  extradition crimes, definition of, 501, 503–4
  Pinochet, proceedings in relation to Senator, 498–506
  political offences, non-extradition for, 501, 504
  Secretary of State's discretion in relation to, 500, 501–6

Falkland Islands, 495–6, 536, 537–9, 550, 563, 571
  conflict in (1982), 563, 571
  self-determination in, 495–6, 536, 538–9
  sovereignty and jurisdiction over, 536, 537–9, 550
Falkland Islands Dependencies: *see* South Georgia and South Sandwich Islands
Faroe Islands, status of, 108, 109, 116
Federal Republic of Yugoslavia (Serbia and Montenegro), 93, 99, 102, 443–4, 467, 480–1, 573, 574, 580–1, 583–4: *see also* Kosovo; Yugoslavia, former
  arms embargo and other collective measures concerning, 467, 573, 574, 580–1, 583–4
  status of, 93, 99, 102, 443–4
  succession to treaties of former Yugoslavia by, 480–1
Fisheries, 138, 188, 544–50
  conservation and management of, 138, 188, 549–50
  fishery zones, delimitation of, 544–9
  Straddling Fish Stocks and Highly Migratory Fish Stocks, Agreement on Conservation and Management of (1995), 188
Force, limits on use of, 111, 312–13, 585–93: *see also* Self-defence
Frontiers: *see* Boundaries

Genocide, 6, 19, 21, 26, 29, 503, 508, 512, 513, 514–15, 517, 519–21
  Convention on the Prevention and Punishment of the Crime of (1948), 6, 19, 21, 26, 29, 512, 519–21
Georgia, succession to Soviet Union by, 455–62, 479–80, 482–7
Gibraltar, 476, 495, 496, 497, 537, 542, 543
  incidents in waters surrounding, 542, 543
  self-determination in, 495, 496, 497
  status of, 476, 495, 497, 537
Good faith, principle of, 129–30, 134
Good neighbourliness, principle of, 128, 129–30, 132, 134, 534–5
Greenland, status of, 109

High seas, freedoms of, 550
Hong Kong, transfer to China of sovereignty over, 582
Human rights, 102, 104, 112, 113, 114, 117, 209, 330–1, 359, 361–409, 420–2, 454, 462–7, 468–9, 471–4, 489–90, 491–5, 496, 506–12, 516, 519–21, 564, 570, 628, 629
  access to court, right of: *see subheading* fair and public hearing, right to, *below*
  appeal against conviction, right of, 509–10
  association, freedom of, 397–9, 497, 570
  Child, Convention on the Rights of the (1989), 330–1, 454
  Civil and Political Rights, International Covenant on (1966), 102, 112, 114, 421–2, 496, 508, 509–10, 511, 512
  defence, rights of, 394–5, 403–6
  development, right to: *see* Environment, protection of, *subheading* sustainable development
  discrimination, freedom from, 209, 366, 367–70, 386–8, 407–8, 420–2, 497, 510–11: *see also* European Community and European Union
    disability, on grounds of, 367–8
    Elimination of All Forms of Racial Discrimination, Convention on (1966), 510–11
    political opinion, on grounds of, 407–8
    race, on grounds of, 209, 510–11
    religion, on grounds of, 407–8
    sex, on grounds of, 366, 368–70, 420–2
  double jeopardy, freedom from, 408–9
  Economic, Social and Cultural Rights, International Covenant on (1966), 104, 496, 510, 512
  electoral rights, 395–6, 497
  equality of arms, principle of, 396
  European Convention on Human Rights (1950) and Protocols, 330–1, 359, 361–409, 462–7, 468–9, 471–4, 491–5, 507, 509, 510, 511, 628, 629
    Channel Islands, proposed incorporation into law of, 471–2, 491–5
    derogation from, 376
    domestic remedies, exhaustion of, 365, 376, 385, 401, 405
    effect in UK law of, 330–1: *see also subheading* Human Rights Act 1998, *below*
    effective remedy for violation, right to, 361–2, 364–6, 367, 377–85, 491–2
    individual petition, right of, 375, 376, 377–8, 380–2, 385, 395–6, 492
    Isle of Man, proposed incorporation into law of, 471–2, 491–5, 507

Human rights—*cont.*
European Convention on Human Rights (1950) and Protocols—*cont.*
just satisfaction, 364, 370, 378, 379, 380, 383, 384, 390, 391, 392, 394, 395, 397, 400, 403, 405, 406, 407
margin of appreciation, 366, 367, 369, 370, 387, 391, 395, 396, 399
'necessary in a democratic society', meaning of, 363, 376, 388–9, 390, 391–3, 394–5, 396, 398–9
obligation to secure rights and freedoms, 397–8, 491
proportionality, principle of, 362, 363, 369, 389, 393, 394–5, 396, 400–1, 408
Scottish Parliament, functions and powers in relation to Convention of, 629
Welsh Assembly, functions and powers in relation to Convention of, 628
European Court of Human Rights, 361–409, 469, 472–4, 509, 511, 628
implementation in UK of judgments of, 472–4
judges, election of, 469, 628
jurisdiction *ratione temporis* of, 375, 395
jurisprudence in 1998 of, 361–409
obligation to abide by judgments of, 472–4, 511
reform of, 509
expression, freedom of, 388–96, 398–9, 497
fair and public hearing, right to, 359, 361–2, 365, 367, 372–4, 375–6, 382–4, 386–8, 392–5, 402–8
family life, right to respect for, 362–6, 370–4, 384–5
home, right to respect for, 364–5, 384–5
Human Rights Act 1998, 359, 462–6, 468, 469, 628, 629
Human Rights Commission, privileges and immunities of Special Rapporteurs of, 489–90
indigenous peoples, rights of, 114, 497
information, freedom of, 370–2
inhuman and degrading treatment, freedom from, 364–5, 367, 379–85, 401, 564
legal assistance, right to, 403–6
liberty and security of person, right to, 367, 380–2
life, right to, 370–80, 570
marriage, right to, 368–70
minorities, rights, of, 114, 497, 510
possessions, right to peaceful enjoyment of, 384–8
private life, right to respect for, 361–2, 364–5, 367–74, 384–5
religion, freedom of, 400–1
retroactive law, freedom from, 390–1, 400
slavery, freedom from, 508, 570

Human rights—*cont.*
Torture and Other Cruel, Inhuman or Degrading Treatment or Punishment, Convention on (1984), 564
torture, freedom from, 382–4, 564, 570
trial within reasonable time, right to, 394–5, 402–3
Universal Declaration of Human Rights (1948), 475, 496, 506, 507, 510, 516, 519–21
Vienna Declaration on Human Rights (1993), 113, 117, 496, 506

Immigration, 321–31, 423, 454, 498
Asylum and Immigration Act 1996, 325–7
Asylum and Immigration Appeals Act 1993, 322, 325
Immigration Act 1971, 423
Immigration Act 1988, 423
Immunity of consular agents: *see* Consular relations
Immunity of diplomatic agents: *see* Diplomatic relations
Immunity of international organizations: *see* Organizations, international
Immunity of States, 305–6, 316–18, 455, 456, 458, 459, 479–80, 483, 485–7, 504
acts of sovereign authority, 318
diplomatic immunity, relationship to, 316–18
head of State, 504
preliminary issue, as, 306
ratione personae nature of, 305
separate entities, 306
ships, 455, 456, 458, 459, 479–80, 483, 485–7
State Immunity Act 1978, 306, 318, 458
waiver of, 318
Immunity of visiting forces: *see* Visiting forces, immunity of
Independence, 85–117, 314–16, 474: *see also* Secession
India, 245, 565
dispute concerning Kashmir between Pakistan and, 565
sovereignty over Andaman and Nicobar Islands of, 245
Individuals, liability for crimes under international law of, 512–21: *see also* War and armed conflict, *subheading* war crimes
Indonesia, occupation of East Timor by, 50–1, 52
Internal waters, definition of, 540–2
International Civil Aviation Organization, jurisdiction of Council of, 13–14, 58–61, 67
International Court of Justice, 1–83, 489, 567–9
effect of decisions of, 2–3, 10, 47, 52
enforcement of decisions of, 21, 67

International Court of Justice—*cont.*
intervention in proceedings of, 36, 38, 41, 47, 48, 49
joinder of applications, 10
jurisdiction of, 1–83, 568
burden of proof of, 15–17
competence, distinction from, 4–6
compétence de la compétence, 12–13, 18–19, 32, 35, 40, 41–2, 65
compulsory, 3, 4, 5, 8, 9, 16, 24, 25, 26, 30, 64–6, 76, 78–9, 82, 568: *see also subheading* Optional Clause, declarations under, *below*
conduct, giving of consent by, 24–6
consent as basis of, 4, 21, 22, 37–8, 44, 47, 51, 83
contentious cases, in, 1–83
counter-claims, over, 19, 41
decisions of other tribunals, in relation to, 57–72
definition of, 4–10
estoppel, by, 26
forum prorogatum, 11, 24, 27–30
incidental, 10–11, 17–23, 41–2
inherent, 41–5
merits, separation from, 6–10, 13–14
'mootness', 12, 33, 39, 46
PCIJ, succession to jurisdiction of, 24–7, 58, 72–83
preliminary, 10, 17–23, 41–2, 45
preliminary issue, as, 6–10, 13–14, 28
propriety of, 8, 19, 33, 34–57
provisional measures: *see subheading* provisional measures, *below*
seisin, distinction from 10–13, 39
sources of, 23–34
substantive, 17–23
third States, effect of interests of, 35–6, 37–8, 47, 48–52
treaties as basis of, 6, 24, 27, 30–4, 72–3, 77–80
UN organs, review of decisions of other, 52–3
non-appearance before, 8, 9, 10, 17, 44, 53, 54, 68
Optional Clause, declarations under, 3, 5, 8, 9, 16, 26, 30, 64–6
effect of, 3, 5
interpretation of, 16, 26
reservations to, 8, 9, 64–6
withdrawal of, 30
provisional measures, 11, 12, 18, 19–23, 29, 41, 53–4, 55
effect of, 20–1, 23, 41
jurisdiction to prescribe, 11, 12, 18, 19–23, 29, 41, 53–4, 55
reopening of cases, 12
role in settlement of disputes of, 567–9
Rules of Court (1946), Art. 67, 57–8, 61

International Court of Justice—*cont.*
Rules of Court (1978), 8, 9, 11–12, 28, 41, 45, 57–8, 61
Art. 38(5): 11–12
Arts. 73–8: 12
Art. 79(7): 8, 14
Art. 87: 58
seisin of, 10–13, 39
States, requirement that parties should be, 13
Statute of, 1–83 *passim*, 489, 568
Art. 36: 17, 23, 24, 27, 35, 76, 80–1
Art. 36(1): 6, 24, 31
Art. 36(2): 8, 9, 24–6, 51, 65, 66, 74, 76, 568
Art. 36(5): 8, 24–6, 72–83
Art. 36(6): 8, 18–19, 32, 35, 65
Art. 37: 17, 24, 27, 58, 72–3, 77–80
Art. 38: 35
Art. 41: 19, 20, 22, 41
Art. 53: 10, 17, 44
Art. 59: 3, 10, 20, 47, 52
Art. 60: 26
Art. 62: 36, 48
Art. 66(2): 489
UN organ, status as, 4, 567, 568
UN organs, litispendence between ICJ and, 37, 52, 53–7, 58
International Criminal Court, 446–7, 513–17, 518, 521
jurisdiction of, 513–17, 518, 521
Rome Statute of (1998), 446, 517, 518, 521
International law, 443–7
codification and progressive development of, 444–7: *see also* International Law Commission, work of
municipal law, relationship to: *see* Municipal law
private: *see* Conflict of laws
sources of, 443–4
International Law Association, work on watercourses of, 133, 163–5, 183–4
International Law Commission, work of, 35, 120–1, 135, 137, 165, 167, 168–9, 170, 171–3, 176, 194, 446, 520, 551–60, 561–3, 569–71
international criminal jurisdiction, 520
State responsibility, 35, 137, 170, 551–60, 561–3, 569–71
watercourses, 120–1, 135, 165, 167, 168–9, 171–3, 176, 194
Intervention, 87, 108, 201, 202, 203–6, 209, 214–26, 227, 235, 240–3, 475–6: *see also* Coercion, collective measures and counter-measures
Investments, treaties for the promotion and protection of, 560–1, 565–7
Iran, 475, 530–1, 540–1, 573–4
arms embargo on, 573–4
delimitation of territorial sea of, 540–1
fatwa against Mr Salman Rushdie, 475

Iran—*cont.*
US measures against, 530–1
Iraq, 88, 108–9, 305–14, 573, 575, 586–92
arms embargo on, 573
independence of, 88
Kurds, treatment of, 108–9
Kuwait, invasion and occupation of, 305–14
no-fly zones, 108
Turkish troops, stationing in Iraq of, 586
UN measures concerning, 108–9, 573, 575, 586–92
Isle of Man, 471–2, 491–5, 507
European Convention of Human Rights, proposed incorporation of, 471–2, 491–5, 507
status of, 492–3, 494–5
Israel, 88, 476, 594–8, 599–600
imprisonment of Mr Mordechai Vanunu in, 476
independence of, 88
occupation of territories by, 594–8, 599–600

Japan, claims for compensation by former British prisoners of war against, 561, 604
Jerusalem, status of and Israeli settlements in, 594–7, 599–600
Judicial settlement of disputes: *see* International Court of Justice
Jurisdiction, 114, 476, 530–4, 564, 628, 629: *see also* International Court of Justice, *subheading* jurisdiction
Criminal Justice Act 1988, 564
Criminal Justice (Terrorism and Conspiracy) Act 1998, 531–2, 628
domestic, 114, 476
extra-territorial, 530–4, 628, 629
torture, over, 564
war crimes, over: *see* War and armed conflict, *subheading* war crimes
Jus cogens, 19, 21, 55, 443, 555, 563

Kashmir, dispute between India and Pakistan concerning, 565
Korea, division of, 94
Kosovo, 103, 104, 110, 518–19, 579, 592–3, 604, 607
alleged atrocities in, 518–19, 604
jurisdiction of International Tribunal for the former Yugoslavia in relation to, 607
NATO intervention in, 592–3
self-determination in, 104, 110
status of, 103, 104, 110
terrorist activity in, 579
Kuwait, invasion and occupation by Iraq of, 305–14

Landmines, limits on possession and use of, 454–5, 469–71, 513, 600–1, 603–4, 628
Landmines Act 1998, 469–71, 601, 628
Landmines, limits on possession and use of—*cont.*
Ottawa Convention on the Prohibition of the Use, Stockpiling, Production and Transfer of Anti-Personnel Mines (1997), 454–5, 469–71, 600–1, 603–4, 628
Latvia: *see* Baltic States
Law of the Sea, UN Convention on (1982), 138, 142–3, 182, 540–2, 543, 549, 550
League of Nations, 72–3, 87–8, 449–50
Covenant of, 87, 88, 449–50
mandates, 72–3, 87–8
Liberia, arms embargo on, 573, 580
Libya, 488, 517–18, 530–1, 532–3, 573, 580
arms embargo on, 573, 580
arrest and trial of Lockerbie bombing suspects, question of, 488, 517–18, 531, 532–3
US measures against, 530–1
Lithuania: *see* Baltic States

Macedonia, Former Yugoslav Republic of, 93, 99, 101, 102, 105, 106
admission to UN of, 102, 106
independence of, 93, 99, 101, 105
Mali Federation, dissolution of, 94
Mandates, 72–3, 87–8
Maritime delimitation, 51, 125, 182–3, 540–2, 543–9
Mayotte, status of, 91, 112
Minorities, rights of, 114, 497, 510
Montenegro: *see* Federal Republic of Yugoslavia
Municipal law, 305–16, 330–1, 450, 451, 453–4, 458, 462–72, 479–80, 601, 628, 629
act of State, 305–16
non-justiciability, 305–16
treaties, effect of, 330–1, 453
treaties, implementation of, 450, 451, 453–4, 458, 462–72, 479–80, 601, 628, 629

Namibia, 72–3, 88
independence of, 88
mandate for, 72–3, 88
Nationality and citizenship, 308, 309, 311, 424, 454, 472, 557
Channel Islands, in, 424
deprivation of, 308, 309, 311
protection of nationals, responsibility for, 475, 557
right of nationals to enter and reside in a State's territory, 424, 472
Nationalization: *see* Expropriation and nationalization
Natural resources, sovereignty over, 126, 128, 135, 138, 141
Nauru, responsibility for administration of trust territory of, 48–50
Negotiation, 36–7, 316, 564–5

Netherlands, agreement on trial of Lockerbie bombing suspects between UK and, 517–18, 531, 532–3
Neutrality, 87
New Caledonia, status of, 89, 112
Nicobar Islands, sovereignty over, 245–65
Nigeria, arms embargo on, 573–4, 583, 584–5
Non-self-governing territories, 50, 88–92, 490–5: *see also* Mandates; Trust territories
North Atlantic Treaty Organization, intervention in Kosovo by, 592–3
Northern Ireland, status of, 536
Nuclear weapons, limits on possession, testing and use of, 42–3, 46, 372–5, 469, 513, 580, 601–2, 603, 629
  Nuclear Explosions (Prohibition and Inspections) Act 1998, 629
  Nuclear Test Ban Treaty (1996), 469, 629

Occupation: *see* Territory, title to
Occupation, belligerent, 594–600
Organization for Security and Co-operation in Europe, 100, 214, 219, 220, 221, 222–5, 443–4, 572–4
  collective measures by, 572–4
  Helsinki Final Act (1975), 100
  intervention in Bosnia and Herzegovina by, 214, 219, 220, 221, 222–5
  Paris, Charter of (1990), 100
  Politico-Military Aspects of Security, Code of Conduct on, 443–4
Organizations, international, 313, 488–90, 525, 572, 628, 629: *see also under names of particular organizations*
  International Organizations Act 1968, 490, 525
  legal effect of acts of, 313, 488, 572
  privileges and immunities of representatives of, 488–90, 525, 628, 629
Outer space, 550–1
  definition of deep space, interstellar space and outer space, 550–1
  Outer Space Act 1986, 551
  Principles governing the Activities of States in the Expoloration and Use of Outer Space, Treaty on (1967), 550

Pakistan, 92, 93, 95–6, 114–15, 565
  dispute concerning Kashmir between India and, 565
  secession of Bangladesh from, 92, 93, 95–6, 114–15
Palestine, mandate for, 88
Palestinians, right to self-determination of, 88, 498
Passage, innocent, 136, 541
Peace-keeping: *see* United Nations, *subheading* peace-keeping by
Permanent Court of International Justice, 5, 24–7, 58, 72–83
  Statute of, 5, 24, 26, 72–83
  succession by ICJ to jurisdiction of, 24–7, 58, 72–83
Piracy, prevention of and punishment for, 247, 250, 251, 252–9
Pollution, control of: *see* Environment, protection of
Prerogative, royal, 316, 330–1, 447, 448, 464, 482

Quebec, question of secession from Canada of, 85–6

Recognition, 50, 86, 92–110 *passim*, 115, 116, 206, 311–12, 319–21, 476–8, 482, 486, 487, 498
  EC Guidelines on Recognition of New States in Eastern Europe and in the Soviet Union (1991), 100
  governments, of, 311–12, 319–21, 477–8
  non-recognition, 311–12, 478, 498
  States, of, 86, 92–110 *passim*, 115, 116, 206, 476–7, 482, 486, 487
  territorial claims, of, 50
Refugees, 201, 202, 204–5, 208–9, 217, 223, 225, 226–39, 242–3, 321–30
  Bosnia and Herzegovina, return of refugees to, 201, 202, 204–5, 208–9, 217, 223, 225, 226–39, 242–3
  civil war and refugee status, 323–5
  EU Joint Position on Definition of 'Refugee' (1996), 323
  Geneva Convention (1951) and Protocol (1967) on Status of, 202, 321–9
  refugee status, definition of, 321–30
  'safe third country', meaning of, 325–30
  UN High Commissioner for Refugees, role of, 217, 223, 227, 228, 230, 232, 233
  'well-founded fear of being persecuted', meaning of, 321–3, 324, 327–30
Republika Srpska, 103, 104, 109–10, 209, 211, 221–2, 227, 228
  elections in, 209, 221–2
  provisions of Dayton-Paris Peace Agreement (1995) concerning, 103, 110, 209, 227
  return of refugees to, 228
  status of and claim to independence by, 103, 104, 109–10, 211
Res judicata, principle of, 66, 67, 68, 69
Rivers: *see* Watercourses
Russian Federation, 93, 98, 455–62, 479, 482–7, 534–5
  Baltic States, relations with, 534–5
  succession to Soviet Union by, 93, 98, 455–62, 479–80, 482–7
Rwanda, 512, 513, 515, 521, 573, 580
  arms embargo on, 573, 580

Rwanda—*cont.*
International Criminal Tribunal for, 512, 513, 515, 521

Scotland: *see* Devolution
Sea, UN Convention on the Law of the (1982), 138, 142–3, 182, 540–2, 543, 549, 550
Secession, 85–117
colonial territories, by, 85, 86, 87–92, 113, 114, 116
definition of, 85–6
devolution, distinction from, 86
dissolution, distinction from, 92–3, 117
non-colonial territories, by, 85–7, 92–117
post–1945 attempts at, 107–12, 115–16
self-determination and, 85, 86, 87–117
Self-defence, 143–4, 553, 569, 585–6, 588, 593, 604
Self-determination, 50, 85, 86, 87–117, 399, 495–8, 510, 602
colonial territories and, 50, 85, 86, 87–92, 116, 495–6, 497, 602
internal, 106, 114, 116, 117, 496–7
non-colonial territories and, 85, 86, 92–117, 399, 496, 497–8, 510
'people', definition of, 85, 91, 111, 112, 114
Senegal, status of, 93, 94, 115
Serbia: *see* Federal Republic of Yugoslavia
Ships, 455–62, 479–80, 482–7
immunity of State-owned, 455, 456, 458, 459, 479–80, 483, 485–7
Merchant Navigation, review and termination of UK/Soviet Union Treaty (1968), Protocol (1974) and Additional Protocol (1986) on, 455–62, 479–80, 482–7
Sierra Leone, 314–15, 319–21, 477–8, 509–10, 575–8, 606
arms embargo and other UN measures concerning, 321, 573, 575–8
human rights in, 509–10, 606
independence of, 314–15
recognition of and relations with government of, 319–21, 477–8
Singapore, status of, 93, 94–5, 115
Slovakia, independence of, 93, 106
Slovenia, 93, 99, 100, 102, 106, 481–2: *see also* Yugoslavia, former
admission to UN of, 102, 106
independence of, 93, 99, 100
succession to treaties of former Yugoslavia by, 481–2
Somalia, arms embargo on, 573, 580
South China Sea, claims to sovereignty in, 537
South Georgia and South Sandwich Islands, sovereignty over, 538
Southern Rhodesia, status of, 89, 91
Sovereignty, 4, 111, 126, 128, 130–1, 132, 134, 135, 138, 141, 245–65, 462, 466, 468, 474–5, 478, 536–40, 551, 582, 594, 595
Soviet Union, 93, 96, 98, 100, 115, 455–62, 479–80, 482–7
dissolution of and succession to, 93, 98, 115, 455–62, 479–80, 482–7
incorporation of Baltic States in, 96
Merchant Navigation, review and termination of Treaty (1968), Protocol (1974) and Additional Protocol (1986) with UK on, 455–62, 479–80, 482–7
Recognition of New States in Eastern Europe and in the Soviet Union, EC Guidelines on (1991), 100
Spain, 476, 495, 497, 498–506
Gibraltar, relations with UK concerning, 476, 495, 497
Pinochet, request for extradition of Senator, 498–506
State responsibility, 35, 37, 48–51, 126, 128, 135–9, 164, 170, 173, 185–6, 254, 365, 376, 385, 401, 405, 475, 551–64, 569–71, 604
aliens, treatment of, 558
circumstances precluding wrongfulness, 552, 553–7, 569–71
consent, 553–5
counter-measures, 552, 553–4, 569–71
distress, 554, 556
force majeure and fortuitous event, 554, 555–6
necessity, 554, 556–7
complicity, 35
criminal responsibility, 552, 561–3
environmental damage, for, 126, 128, 135–9, 164, 173, 185–6
expropriation, for, 558, 559, 560–1, 563–4
imputability, 35, 48–51, 552–3
International Law Commission work on, 35, 137, 551–60, 561–3, 569–71
local remedies, exhaustion of, 365, 376, 385, 401, 405, 557–9
mine-laying, for, 136
piracy, for, 254
protection, diplomatic, 475, 557
reparation, 37, 553, 554, 559–61, 563, 604
State succession, 85–117, 455–62, 479–88: *see also* Secession
debts, to, 93, 481, 488
treaties, to, 93, 455–62, 479–87
Vienna Convention on Succession of States in respect of State Property, Archives and Debts (1983), 93
Vienna Convention on Succession of States in respect of Treaties (1978), 93
Straits, innocent pasage through, 136
Sudan, arms embargo on, 573–4

Taiwan, status of, 86
Territorial sea, 136, 540–9
delimitation of, 540–2, 543–9
mining of, 136
passage through, 541, 543

Territory, title to, 50–1, 52, 85, 86–7, 92, 103, 107, 109, 111, 113–14, 117, 130, 131–2, 136, 197, 245–65, 312–13, 453, 474, 475, 536–40
abandonment, 245–65 *passim*
annexation, 251–62, 312–13: *see also subheading* occupation, *below*
cession, 245–65 *passim*, 453, 540
inchoate title, 263
occupation, 50–1, 52, 245, 246, 263: *see also subheading* annexation, *above*
territorial integrity, principle of, 85, 86–7, 92, 107, 109, 111, 113–14, 117, 130, 131–2, 136, 197, 474, 475
uti possidetis juris, principle of, 103
Terrorism, prevention of, 504, 531–2, 579, 602, 605–6, 628
Criminal Justice (Terrorism and Conspiracy) Act 1998, 531–2, 628
Suppression of Terrorism (Temporary Provisions) Act 1989, 504, 531
Thailand, delimitation of territorial sea of, 541–2
Tort: *see* Conflict of laws
Torture, freedom from: *see* Human rights
Treaties, 3, 13–14, 16–17, 25, 26, 30–4, 45–6, 70–2, 74–8, 79, 81–3, 93, 112, 191, 330–1, 412–14, 447–72, 479–87, 555, 569, 571, 601, 628, 629
breach, effect of, 455–6
capacity to conclude, 555
conclusion of, 447–54
customary law, relationship to, 413
definition of, 16–17, 448
effect in municipal law of, 330–1, 453
explanatory memoranda, 448, 449, 451–2
full powers, 447–8
implementation of, 450, 451, 453–4, 458, 462–72, 479–80, 601, 628, 629
interpretation of, 3, 25, 26, 32, 70–2, 74–8, 81–3, 191
Ponsonby Rule, 448–54
ratification of, 448–54
registration of, 449–50
reservations to, 112, 331, 454–5
signature of, 447–8
succession to, 455–62, 479–87
suspension of, 13–14, 30–4, 79, 412–14, 455–6
termination of, 30–4, 45–6, 413–14, 455–62, 484
breach, for, 455–6
denunciation, 45–6, 456–62, 484
fundamental change of circumstances, 413–14
ICJ jurisdiction, effect on, 30–4
Vienna Convention on Succession of States in respect of (1978), 93
Vienna Convention on the Law of (1969), 413, 447, 455, 555, 569, 571
Trust territories, 33, 39, 48–50, 87–8, 90
administration of, 33, 39, 48–50
establishment of, 87–8
termination of trusteeship, 33, 39, 90
Turkey, stationing of troops in Iraq by, 586
'Turkish Republic of Northern Cyprus', 356–9, 498
jurisdiction over claim of title to land in, 356–9
non-recognition of, 498

Ukraine, 455–62, 479–80, 482–7
recognition of, 482, 486, 487
succession to Soviet Union by, 455–62, 479–80, 482–7
Unilateral declarations, binding nature of, 42–3, 44, 45–6
United Kingdom, 245–65, 305–59, 433–629
Nicobar Islands, acquisition of sovereignty over, 245–65
practice in 1998 of, 305–59, 433–629
United Nations, 4, 11, 20, 21, 24, 37, 50, 52–7, 58, 59–60, 67, 73, 87, 88–9, 90–1, 92, 93, 94, 95, 96, 97, 98, 102, 106, 107, 108, 109, 113, 114, 115, 116, 117, 135, 141, 309, 312–13, 321, 444, 445–6, 450, 467, 475, 488, 489–90, 495, 496, 513, 514, 519, 522–3, 532, 537, 563, 567, 568, 570, 572–82, 586–93, 595, 596, 604
Administrative Tribunal, review by ICJ of decisions of, 57, 59–60
admission to, 90, 92, 94, 95, 97, 98, 102, 106, 107, 115, 116
Charter of, 20, 21, 24, 50, 53, 54, 55, 56, 59, 67, 73, 87, 88–9, 90–1, 92, 93, 95, 97, 108, 116, 135, 141, 309, 312–13, 444, 450, 475, 489, 490, 495, 496, 513, 514, 570, 572, 576, 586–7, 588, 589, 592–3
Art. 12: 55
Art. 24(1): 56
Art. 36: 55
Art. 41: 572
Art. 50: 570
Art. 51: 593
Art. 55: 490
Art. 56: 490
Art. 73: 88
Art. 74: 87
Art. 76: 89
Art. 77: 88
Art. 94: 20, 21, 67
Art. 96: 489
Chapter VII: 56, 108, 576, 593
Chapter XI: 50, 87, 88–9, 90–1, 92, 93
Chapter XII: 87, 90, 92, 93
collective measures by, 11, 321, 467, 513, 514, 572–82: *see also subheading* peace-keeping by, *below*
contributions, US liability for arrears of, 563

United Nations—*cont.*
General Assembly Resolutions, 88, 89, 91, 95, 96, 107, 113, 114, 116, 117, 125, 140, 444, 489, 522–3, 537, 567, 595, 596
89 (I) (Advisory Opinions), 489
1514 (XV) (Declaration on Independence), 89, 537
1541 (XV) (Implementation of Declaration on Independence), 89, 96
1542 (XV) (Portuguese and Spanish Territories), 89
1747 (XVI) (Southern Rhodesia), 89
2010 (XX) (Singapore), 95
2069 (XX) (New Hebrides), 89
2228 (XXI) (French Somaliland), 89
2625 (XXV) (Declaration on Principles of International Law), 91, 113, 116, 117, 444
2793 (XXV) (Bangladesh), 95, 96
2995 (XXVII) (Environmental Protection), 140
3161 (XXVIII) (Comoros Archipelago), 89, 91
3203 (XXIX) (Bangladesh), 95
41/41A (New Caledonia), 89
41/128 (Declaration on the Right to Development), 125
44/23 (UN Decade of International Law), 444
47/114 (Eritrea), 107
47/135 (Declaration on Rights of Minorities), 114
47/230 (Eritrea), 107
48/94 (Palestinians), 88
49/18 (Comoros Archipelago), 91
51/156 (Diplomatic and Consular Missions), 522–3
52/161 (International Court of Justice), 567
S–18/1 (Namibia), 88
ES–10/3 (Middle East), 595
ES–10/4 (Middle East), 596
High Commissioner for Refugees, role of: *see* Refugees
Human Rights Commission, privileges and immunities of Special Rapporteurs of, 489–90
International Court of Justice, 4, 37, 52–7, 58, 567, 568: *see also* International Court of Justice
judicial review of decisions of other UN organs by, 52–3
litispendence between other UN organs and, 37, 52, 53–7, 58
status as UN organ of, 4, 567, 568
peace-keeping by, 55, 56, 108, 586–92: *see also subheading* collective measures by, *above*
Privileges and Immunities of the UN, Convention on (1946), 489–90

United Nations—*cont.*
Rwanda, International Criminal Tribunal for: *see* Rwanda
Secretariat, work of, 445–6
Security Council, 54–6
peace-keeping, primary responsibility for, 55, 56
settlement of disputes by 54–6
Security Council Resolutions, 54, 56, 88, 95, 96, 97, 102, 107, 109, 313, 467, 488, 519, 532, 572, 574, 575, 576–9, 581, 586, 587, 588–92, 604
213 (1965) (Singapore), 95
307 (1971) (Bangladesh), 96
351 (1974) (Bangladesh), 95
457 (1979) (Iran), 54, 56
461 (1979) (Iran), 54, 56
678 (1990) (Iraq), 590, 591
682 (1990) (Namibia), 88
686 (1991) (Iraq), 109
687 (1991) (Iraq), 109, 575, 586, 587, 588, 590, 591
688 (1991) (Iraq), 109, 592
709–11 (1991) (Baltic States), 97
731 (1992) (Libya), 532
748 (1992) (Libya), 532
757 (1992) (Yugoslavia), 102
777 (1992) (Yugoslavia), 102
828 (1993) (Eritrea), 107
883 (1993) (Libya), 532
949 (1994) (Iraq), 109
1127 (1997) (Angola), 578
1132 (1997) (Sierra Leone), 575, 576–8
1153 (1998) (Iraq), 589
1154 (1998) (Iraq), 588–9, 590, 591
1160 (1998) (Federal Republic of Yugoslavia), 467, 519, 574, 579
1171 (1998) (Sierra Leone), 577–8
1173 (1998) (Angola), 578–9, 581
1199 (1998) (Federal Republic of Yugoslavia), 519, 604
1203 (1998) (Federal Republic of Yugoslavia), 519
1205 (1998) (Iraq), 590, 591
effect of, 313, 488, 572, 589–90
trusteeship: *see* Trust territories
Yugoslavia, International Criminal Tribunal for former: *see* Yugoslavia, former
United Nations Act 1946, 467, 572, 576, 578
United States of America, 530–1, 534, 563
Helms-Burton and D'Amato Acts, 530–1, 534
liability for arrears of contributions to UN of, 563

Vietnam, division of, 94

Visiting forces, immunity of, 466, 527–30
NATO Status of Forces Agreement (1951), 528
Visiting Forces Act 1952, 528, 529

Wales: *see* Devolution
War and armed conflict, 87, 111, 116, 217, 218, 235, 237–8, 242, 513, 515–16, 517, 519, 520, 561, 580, 594–607
anti-personnel mines: *see* Landmines, limits on possession and use of
Bacteriological and Toxin Weapons, Convention on (1972), 602–3
biological weapons, limits on possession and use of, 580, 602–3, 604
Chemical Weapons, Convention on (1993), 602–3
chemical weapons, limits on possession and use of, 580, 602–3, 604
Geneva Conventions Act 1957, 602
Geneva Conventions (Amendment) Act 1995, 601, 602
Geneva Conventions for the Protection of War Victims (1949), 595–7, 598–9, 605
Geneva Conventions for the Protection of War Victims, Additional Protocols to (1977), 116, 598–9, 601–2, 605
humanitarian law, 111, 116, 596, 598–9, 605–6
humanity, crimes against, 513, 515, 516, 517, 519, 520
landmines: *see* Landmines, limits on possession and use of
neutrality, 87
nuclear weapons: *see* Nuclear weapons, limits on possession, testing and use of
occupation, belligerent, 594–600
peace, crimes against, 520
prisoners of war, claims for compensation against Japan by former, 561, 604
reprisals, belligerent, 602
war crimes, 217, 218, 235, 237–8, 242, 513, 515–16, 517, 519, 520, 603–4, 606–7
Watercourses, 119–200
Boundary Waters Treaty (Canada/USA, 1909), 150–5
Colorado, Tijuana and Rio Grande, negotiations and Treaty (Mexico/USA, 1944) on, 130–1, 157
conservation of, 120, 122, 179–85
Danube, Convention on Co-operation for the Protection and Sustainable Use of (1994), 159, 196
equitable utilization, principle of, 119–200
frontier agreements, prohibition of pollution in, 145–8, 150–5, 158
Watercourses—*cont.*
Great Lakes Water Quality, Agreement on (Canada/USA, 1978), 155, 173
Helsinki Convention on the Protection and Use of Transboundary Watercourses and Lakes (1992), 160, 161, 188, 195–6
Helsinki Rules on the Use of International Rivers (1966) and supplementary instruments, 133, 163–5
Indian sub-continent, water disputes in, 132–3, 156–7, 180–2
Indus Waters Treaty (India/Pakistan, 1960), 156–7, 181–2
International Law Association work on, 133, 163–5, 183–4
International Law Commission work on, 120–1, 135, 165, 167, 168–9, 171–3, 176, 194
Mekong River Basin, Agreement on Co-operation for Sustainable Development in (1995), 197–8, 199
Meuse, Agreement on Protection of (1994), 159, 196–7
Non-Navigational Uses of International Watercourses, UN Convention on (1997), 119–22, 145, 162, 165–73, 176, 177, 179, 193–4, 198
pollution of, 134, 145–200 *passim*
Rhine, treaties relating to, 156–7
Scheldt, Agreement on Protection of (1994), 159, 196–7
Southern African Development Community, Protocol on Shared Watercourse Systems in (1995), 161–2, 198–9
sustainable development and, 119–200: *see also* Environment, protection of
territorial integrity and, 130, 131–2, 197
territorial sovereignty and, 130–1, 132, 134
US inter-State water disputes, 184–5
Western Sahara, 89, 478, 496, 497, 536
self-determination in, 496, 497
status of, 89, 478, 536
World Trade Organization, dispute settlement procedure of, 189–91, 569

Yemen, territorial dispute between Eritrea and, 567
Yugoslavia, former, 92, 93, 98–106, 115, 117, 201–43, 412–14, 480–2, 488, 515, 519, 521, 604, 606, 607: *see also* Bosnia and Herzegovina; Croatia; Federal Republic of Yugoslavia (Serbia and Montenegro); Macedonia, Former Yugoslav Republic of; Slovenia
Dayton-Paris Peace Agreement (1995), 99, 103, 110, 201–43 *passim*, 606
dissolution of, 92, 93, 98–106, 115, 117, 202, 206
International Criminal Tribunal for, 515, 518–19, 521, 604, 607

Yugoslavia, former—*cont.*
Recognition of New States in Eastern Europe and in the Soviet Union, EC Guidelines on (1991), 100
succession to assets and liabilities of, 488
succession to treaties of, 480–2
suspension of trade concessions under Co-operation Agreement between EEC and, 412–14

Zimbabwe, expropriation of land by, 559